Microsoft Excel 2013

Step by Step

Curtis D. Frye

The STANDING DEAD

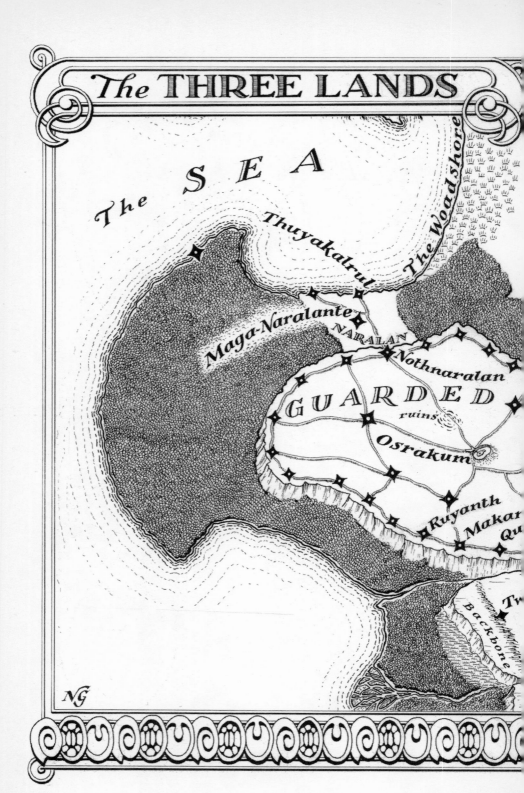

wheelmap

S.W.

LAND

The
EARTHSKY

Koppie

Upper Reach

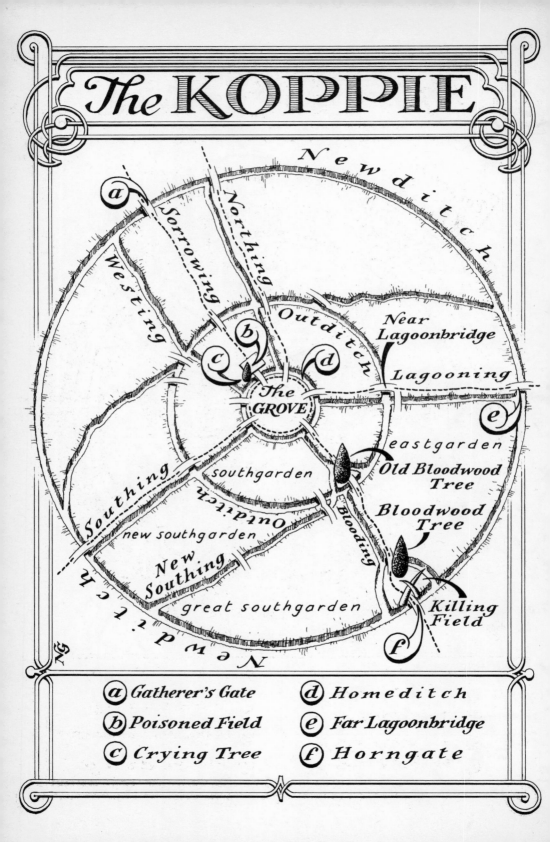

The KOPPIE

(a) Gatherer's Gate   (d) Homeditch

(b) Poisoned Field   (e) Far Lagoonbridge

(c) Crying Tree   (f) Horngate

The GROVE

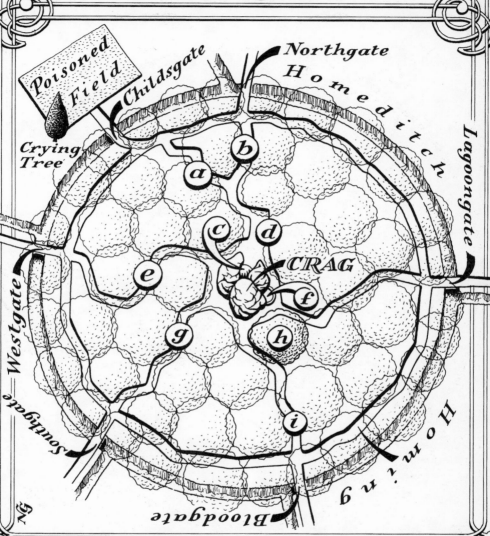

Poisoned Field

Crying Tree

Childsgate

Northgate

Homeditch

Lagoongate

CRAG

Westing

Westgate

Southgate

Homing

Bloodgate

Ⓝ

- ⓐ Sorrowing
- ⓑ Northing
- ⓒ Ancestor House
- ⓓ clearing
- ⓔ Westing
- ⓕ cistern
- ⓖ Southing
- ⓗ Akaisha's mother tree
- ⓘ Blooding

LOST

Father, do you remember me telling you I had found a lover? Then I believed he was a divided sybling: at the election I discovered him to be Osidian Nephron. I did not easily forgive him the deception. Can you understand our wish to have one last day together before we are parted for ever by his Apotheosis?
No search will find us. Expect us in the Labyrinth on the thirty-second day of Tuta; the thirty-third at the latest.
your son, Suth Carnelian

(a letter sent by Suth Carnelian to his father, the Ruling Lord Suth Sardian, at the time,
He-who-goes-before)

BENEATH THE IMPERIOUS GAZE OF THE FUNERARY COLOSSI OF THE Chosen, the fires lit by a hundred thousand tributaries formed a trembling field of light on the Plain of Thrones. High above the colossi, on a balcony cut into the cliff enclosing the plain, stood the Ruling Lord of House Suth. He turned his head enough that the eyeslits of his mask shielded his eyes from the dying sun, then surveyed the scene below. Flanked by the immense, towered saurians the barbarians childishly called dragons, the crowd seemed numberless. More than a third were the children brought by tribes from beyond the Commonwealth to pay their flesh tithe. The rest were either their kin or the deputations the cities had sent with their taxes of coined bronze. All had cowered there for days awaiting the ceremony of the Rebirth which would occur as the Rains broke over the crater of Osrakum. This Rebirth would include the Apotheosis of a new God Emperor.

1

Suth withdrew into the gloom of his apartments in the cliff so that he might free his white, unpainted hands from his sleeves without danger of them being tainted by the sun. He unfolded a parchment under a lamp and reread the glyphs drawn on its panels. The profiles of the faces in the glyphs were unmistakably in his son's hand. Further, the letter had been sealed with Carnelian's blood-ring. The letter promised that he would return on the last day of the year, but that had dawned and passed and his son had not returned.

Suth put the letter down, removed his mask and set it on top, then rubbed his eyes. He stretched his hands out and watched their tremor. To cheat the weakness from his unhealed wound, he had had to revert to the drug the Wise had given him. The powder gave him only a febrile strength. It was the Empress Ykoriana's agents who had wounded him, trying to ensure he did not reach Osrakum in time for the election. Foolishly, the election won, he had thought her beaten. Cursing softly, he let his gaze wander through the columns to the far shadows of the hall. If only he had probed Carnelian at the time when he had confessed to finding a lover. Neither the relentless demands of the sacred election nor the brittle mind-state the drug induced should have made him so dangerously uncurious about his son's expedition. Three days had passed since Tain had been scared into yielding up the letter. He had been keeping faith with Carnelian's command that he should only deliver it at nightfall on the day Carnelian disappeared. Though a half-caste, a marumaga, Tain was still Suth's son, but even then, in wrath, he might have condemned the boy to crucifixion had it not been that he knew Carnelian would never have forgiven him.

Sinking on to a couch, Suth dropped his head into his hands. That Carnelian should choose to disappear at such a delicately balanced time was bad enough, but that he should do so in company with the God Emperor elect, that was a disaster. Suth had not yet recovered from that moment of sickening premonition when he had read the letter for the first time. With terrible threats he had wrung from Carnelian's household everything they knew about his forays before the election. The clothes he had taken, the time away, all suggested a journey of some distance. Since at the time Carnelian had been with the court in the Sky, a descent to the Yden had been the only plausible solution. Suth had recalled rumours that other routes existed down from the Pillar of Heaven other than the Rainbow Stair. That morning, when he could bear to wait no longer, he had dared to send a search party of his guardsmen into the Forbidden Garden of the Yden. Fear for his son had made him risk alerting the Great to the situation. Of course, the expedition had returned from the vast water meadows with nothing.

Time was running out.

One of his blinded slaves disturbed his misery. 'Master, the Ruling Lord Aurum is at your door craving audience.'

Regarding the man with his stitched-up eyes, Suth mused that even Aurum was a welcome distraction from his imminent meeting with the Wise. Suth sent the slave to let him in, then rising, put on his mask and composed himself. Aurum must have found out about the disappearance of Osidian Nephron. Soon all the Great would know. Suth felt his grip on hope weakening.

'My Lord, a rumour led me to seek an audience with the God Emperor elect but I was turned away by ammonites. Why do the Wise seclude Nephron?'

Suth unmasking forced Aurum to follow him; he wished to see the old Lord's eyes. Under their misty blue survey, Suth could see that his weakness was betrayed, his misery. Aurum's eyes narrowed.

'My Lord . . . ?'

Suth handed him Carnelian's letter. Aurum hesitated before taking it, then opened the panels and read. Suth watched as what little colour there was in Aurum's alabaster face drained away. The blue eyes lifted.

'Is there still hope they will return?'

Suth shrugged. 'Soon it will make little difference. The Wise have summoned me to appear before them.'

The implication was not lost on Aurum. Suth, as He-who-goes-before, could not easily be summoned even by the Wise. Aurum flourished the letter.

'They know about this?'

'Some of it.'

Aurum nodded. 'They will offer Molochite the Masks.'

'What else can they do? The Commonwealth must have a new God.'

As Aurum sagged, Suth saw how aged the Lord was. Aurum lifted a pale hand corded blue with veins and began to massage his temples.

'Without the protection of Nephron as God Emperor, both of us will be exposed to prosecution by the Wise.'

Suth knew well how many times they had transgressed the Law-that-must-be-obeyed so as to reach Osrakum in time for the election. 'It is Ykoriana and Molochite that you should fear. Neither mother nor son will forgive our opposition.'

Aurum bared his teeth. 'She must be behind this.'

'Imago Jaspar as well, no doubt.'

Aurum's eyes wandered. 'There is still time for the God Emperor elect to be found?'

Staring blindly, Suth shook his head. 'I do not believe even their bodies shall be found.'

'She would not dare.'

'She dared to slay her daughter in these very halls.' Suth felt as if he were made of ice. 'I have lost my son.' Even to voice those words made real the horror he had been denying for days. 'I should never have let you persuade me to return. In my blood I knew that I would lose him. I should have kept him on our island far from this nest of serpents.'

Suth allowed his gaze to wander over the pillars of jade, the pavement of pearls; to soar up into the vaulted vastnesses where rays of light revealed exquisite carvings. Such splendours were sour without his son to share them.

Aurum fixed him with a stare. 'Suth Sardian, this is not the time to grieve. We must fight together if we are to save ourselves. The least we face is that, with the compliance of the Wise, she will seek our impeachment before the Clave.' Aurum's eyes lost hold of Suth's face. 'The worst, exile?'

Suth's laughter echoed through the hall. 'Of all the world, Aurum, you should know that exile holds no terror for me. Let her do her worst. If she has truly murdered my son, what more can she do to me?'

'Depose you.'

Suth tossed his head back. 'What pain that? Without my son, my lineage will die with me.' With smouldering rage he contemplated the thought that Spinel and the rest of the disloyal Suth secondary lineage should rule his House.

'My Lord can get himself another son.'

'Do you imagine that when she is married to Molochite and once more empress, Ykoriana would allow me to make a high-blood marriage?'

Aurum regarded the perfect gold face of his mask lying in his hand. 'You may choose to consider deposure or exile with equanimity, my Lord. I will do anything to avoid it.'

Suth watched him put on the mask, then begin his journey to the door. Suth had no doubt that Aurum intended to throw himself upon the mercy of Molochite. Unless Carnelian returned to him alive, Suth would never pay homage to the new God Emperor nor to his mother and soon-to-be wife.

It seemed a bright clearing up ahead, but it was lamps that lit the trunks of the sepulchres. The sight brought hope to the guardsmen who had crept through the stone forest of the Labyrinth after Suth and the ammonite guide.

Pointing ahead, the ammonite turned its silver face. 'My masters await.'

Suth gave a nod, dread welling in him at the thought of confronting the Wise. The silver masks of other ammonites showed their cordon around the clearing. Their purple robes were turned black by the brooding night. Suth opened his hand to show them the Pomegranate Ring. It was the only proof he had that he was He-who-goes-before, for the Wise had insisted that he come in secret, without his Ichorians, without his lictors who the Law demanded should be always at his side carrying the standards of his twin legion. They had even demanded that he should not wear the mask with its sun-rayed eye. So it was that he had come shrouded, with his own people and wearing one of his own masks, because he knew that, for his son's sake, he had put himself in the power of the Wise.

An ammonite came forward, hand raised. 'Only you may pass, Seraph.'

Suth turned. 'Wait for me here, Tain.'

His son bowed. Suth had brought the boy to let him know that he had forgiven him.

Passing through the ammonites, he walked towards the braziers around which stood four of the Wise, each with a childlike creature wearing a dead face of silver. Suth saw by the staves these homunculi were holding that their masters were none other than the Grand Sapients of the Domains Tribute, Rain, Labyrinth and Law. This last made his heart quail.

'My Lords.'

At his words they turned, each with his fingers meshed about the throat of his homunculus. Tribute's creature spoke.

'Where then, My-Lord-who-goes-before, is the God Emperor elect?' Its voice was beautiful but unhuman.

Crowned with crescent moons, the long, eyeless masks of the Sapients each had moonstone tears dribbling down the left cheek. Suth knew the Sapients were sightless but felt they could see him through the eyes of their homunculi.

'I know not.'

The homunculi echoed him so that from the vibration in their throats their masters might be able to feel what Suth was saying.

'When his disappearance was discovered, you assured us that he would return to us today,' said Rain.

'I myself had received such assurance.'

'From whom?' said Law.

Suth was still reluctant to reveal Carnelian's part in the disaster.

'We intend to apply to the Clave for access to your House, Seraph,' said Labyrinth.

'Your household shall be brought before our inquisition,' said Tribute.

'Your defiance now, Seraph, shall only make our interrogations more intrusive,' said Law.

Suth knew they had him snared. He began explaining to them the contents of Carnelian's letter.

'I believe they went together into the Yden.'

After the homunculi had finished their muttering they began speaking all at once, streaming sounds that made no sense, their shrillness betraying their masters' agitation.

Silence fell.

'If you had told us this before, we might have searched for them,' said Labyrinth.

Suth's fear burned to anger. 'Do not, my Lords, foist the responsibility of your indecision on to me. You chose to accept what I told you because you feared to act in case the Great should discover the disappearance.'

'Now the Seraphim must be told,' said Rain.

'When the God Emperor elect disappeared, the Regency should have passed to the Dowager Empress,' said Law. 'You have led the Wise into transgressing the Law-that-must-be-obeyed and so put us in her power. Now we discover that we must overturn the result of Holy Election. Without proof, not only the Seraphim but the House of the Masks will suspect impropriety.'

Suth could not let that go. 'I do not believe that my Lords can be wholly unaware that there are two in the House of the Masks and several others of the Great who will have no need of suspicion, knowing better than we what they have had done to Osidian Nephron and my son.'

'Be silent,' the homunculi chanted in unison.

Suth stared at the Sapients, startled that they should address him thus.

'Alive or dead, we shall find Osidian Nephron,' said Tribute. 'If you had not delayed us we might have found him in time. Now, it is he that will be sacrificed in place of his brother. The Jade Lord Molochite shall assume the Masks and we will transform him into the Twin Gods when the Rains begin the renewal of the earth in two days' time.'

'A propitious date mirroring the elevation of his grandfather, Nuhuron, on the same intercalating day at the beginning of the last forty-eight-year cycle,' said Rain.

Law leaned forward and made his homunculus speak. 'As for you, Seraph Suth, for the part you have played in this both you and your House shall be punished.'

Suth was chilled by the certainty of that statement. The Wise were speaking as if the Great were directly subject to their will. It was his heart that urged him to speak to them about Carnelian. He considered whether it would serve only to draw down on him their wrath, but in the end, he had to know.

'And my son?'

'If he is found, we shall examine his part in this affair so that he may receive punishment according to the Law.'

Suth commanded the ammonite guide not to take him back to his halls in the wall of the Plain of Thrones, but instead south-west towards the Forbidden Garden. Soon they were lost among the winding ways. Though the faces of the sepulchres were hidden in the darkness of the ceiling, Suth could feel their gaze on him. A paleness far away showed that the world outside was feeling the dawn. As they neared the edge of the Labyrinth, he could see some rays of sun catching on the Sacred Wall. The sky was clotted with angry cloud. The Wise had declared that the downpour would begin in two days' time. The Skymere was still in dusk. The brilliance of the terraces was still subdued, but he could see how they cascaded down the slope towards the sombre lagoons of the Yden. He searched them, hoping for some quick, pale movement that might have been Carnelian. Suth could not remember when his life had not been dominated by his passion to save his son. Now, at the very brink of victory, he had lost him and with him, everything.

FALLEN ANGELS

I have only tears
To water my face
Until the black sky comes

(Quyan fragment)

MUFFLED CROWS FLUTTERING ROUND MADE HIM WONDER VAGUELY IF IT was their beaks he could feel stabbing all the way up his back. His mind cleared enough for him to know he was curled up in the dark. Not crows but men were speaking beyond the wall that was coiling him tighter. Elbows were thrusting their blades into his ribs. Thighs were squeezing his belly. His knees were coated with a moist itchy and stinking skin of vomit. He could feel every tremor in the wall through his wedged-back toes. They were rubbing raw but his ankles would not bend enough to allow his heels to take the strain. Trying to drag his skull free from the jaw-clamp of his knees only grated the knobs of his spine down the wall like gear teeth. The scuffing burn forced him to groan out all the breath he had in his chest. His flesh crowded in to smother him. He managed to inflate his lungs a little before his legs closed like the handles of bellows. His heart pumped him against the wall as he choked on a soundless scream.

Suddenly, light flooded from above. A breeze coated his scalp with chill sweat. Jerking breaths, Carnelian worked his head free from between his knees, then hinged it back against the cramp in his neck, slitting his eyes against the dazzle. He was slow to realize someone was looking down at him. When he did, it was hard to focus. A grey bearded face, one half blacked by tattoos.

'Ichorian,' he breathed.

The man's halved face had the roundest eyes and gape, the most ashen pallor. That it was the right hand side that was tattooed proclaimed him to be one of the Red Ichorians that guarded the canyon entry into Osrakum. Carnelian let out a sigh of relief that he had been rescued, only remotely aware that his face was naked to the man's stare. The effort of holding his head up became too great, so that he had to drop it back into the cradle of his knees.

'Please,' he mumbled, 'help me . . . out of this . . . thing.' Silence made him find the strength to lift his head again. 'Release me.'

Still staring, the man shook his head.

'Now!' barked Carnelian, the eruption disrupting his breathing into a gulping cough.

The Ichorian's clammy hands trembled towards him. 'Master . . . can I . . . ? What can I . . . ?' The man made several attempts to touch him, but each time pulled back as if Carnelian were simmering plague.

Carnelian could see the tear trail bright on the man's tattooed cheek. 'But you . . . are sworn . . . to our service,' he hacked out between breaths.

The man's unmarked hand strayed to his throat where the collar he had worn had left its ghost. The hand fell and splayed itself before Carnelian's eyes so that he was able to read the tattoos of the man's service record: the number thirty-nine; a pomegranate and a curved diagonal cross above a zero ring beneath two bars.

'You see, Master, I achieved the rank of Righthand in a tower of the pomegranate dragons.' The old soldier looked worn out, used up.

Carnelian was confused. Each snatch of breath squeezed a tear stinging from his bruised eye. 'Please . . .'

'How did . . . ? Who has dared put you in this urn, Master?'

The man glanced away, focusing on something else nearby. Guilt stabbed Carnelian in the guts. Osidian. He had forgotten his beloved. 'Another urn . . . is there another urn?'

The Ichorian looked down, startled, dipped a nod before gazing away again. '. . . Another Master?' he whispered.

'Open it . . .' Carnelian hissed. 'He might be . . . smothering.'

The Ichorian's head moving away revealed rafters sagging under yellow, mouldering plaster. Where were they? Desperation to see Osidian convulsed Carnelian. He became an animal in a trap and would have gnawed away half his body to break free.

Shadow fell across him. 'Calm yourself . . . Master. He's dead.'

Despair clamped Carnelian's body still, making his urn shudder audibly. His breathing stopped and it was a fight to regain its rhythm. Ringing in his ears. 'Drugged . . .' he said, as forcefully as he could.

'Drugged? Oh, I see . . .' The Ichorian disappeared again.

To keep the panic at bay, the grief, Carnelian forced himself to count his breaths. Eleven had passed before the Ichorian spoke again.

'You're right, Master, it's deep sleep, not death.'

Relief flooded through Carnelian.

The light dimmed again. 'You were to be buried alive then?'

'Alive . . . ?'

'The Masters send me their servants dead in urns. I bury them.' The man's eyes opaqued. 'They don't know I open them.'

Under its tattoos, his face greyed. 'I'm dead.'

'Release me,' hissed Carnelian, 'and I'll protect you.'

The man's eyes came back into focus. 'But I've seen your face.'

'I'll . . . deny it.' Carnelian drew hope from the Ichorian's confused expression.

'Master, who dared strike you; dared put you in these urns?'

Carnelian was loath to name the Dowager Empress lest the Ichorian become terrorized. 'My enemies.'

'Masters, no doubt and more powerful than you or else you wouldn't be here.'

'They . . . trapped us.'

'And me with you, Master.' With a fixed grimace the Ichorian looked round as if he were searching for somewhere to hide. His head shook.

'Even not knowing I've seen you, they're bound to have me killed.'

'Trust me . . . I'm the son of . . . He-who-goes-before.'

The Ichorian gave him an idiot stare. He licked his half-black lips. 'If that's true, Master, that only makes it worse for me.' His eyes were twitching. 'I must run . . . find a hole to hide in.'

'Where could . . . you go? Your face betrays you.'

The Ichorian's face went blank. 'True . . . true . . . I must go far . . . bury myself away from prying eyes . . . maybe in a house in one of the more remote Ringwall cities . . . never go out . . . keep a servant to do for me . . . perhaps a blind slave . . . might need more than one . . . wealth . . . much wealth to buy this new life. Much, much wealth. A chest overflowing with bronze coins wouldn't be enough.' The Ichorian's greedy eyes made Carnelian flinch. 'Yes, a vast sum is needed . . . vast.'

'Sum?'

The Ichorian smiled uncertainly, but when he spoke, his voice had calmed. 'There's a man, in the south, in the city of Makar. I sell him relics.'

Carnelian went cold.

'Why else do you think I'd force open a funerary urn?'

Carnelian did not want to hear any more.

'In the cities of the Guarded Land, there are rich merchants to whom nothing's more precious than things that have belonged to a Master. By such charms they keep at bay their fear of you. Before today, all I've had to sell were flays of pale skin, some sky-coloured eyes; all from marumaga, naturally, but from those choice marumaga in the Mountain close to you whose whiteness the barbarians have no way of knowing is mere amber to your snow. Don't flinch. Now that I have you, I'd be a fool to cut, to deface a *living* Master . . . such a trophy must be worth at least a wagonload of bronze. If only I can find a way to take you south . . .'

As the Ichorian walked away, Carnelian concentrated on his breathing.

'Here, drink . . . I might be gone some time.'

Carnelian turned his face up as the Ichorian tipped water. Most of it found his mouth, though some trickled into the hot crevices of his flesh. It was Carnelian's choking that made the Ichorian stop and look down with fear.

'You mustn't die.'

'The other . . .' Carnelian managed to say.

'Why wake him from his drugged sleep?' He leaned closer, scrunched up his nose. 'You're only awake because you threw up.'

'Please . . . bind us . . . with ropes if you have to . . . free from these . . .'

The Ichorian frowned then shook his head. 'I prefer to keep my angels safe in their bottles.'

'But . . .' blurted Carnelian, choking on his anger, but the Ichorian was already eclipsing the light with the lid. Its weight squeezed Carnelian's head back between his knees.

In the outer world he heard the Ichorian say: 'Bide your time, Master, I'll be back as soon as I can.'

His thighs compressing his lungs denied Carnelian a roar of rage. A part of him knew that he must calm himself, lest he should shut off the narrow passage of his breathing, but panic made him lose control. Pressure roared in his ears; his muscles strained against the earthenware wall. Even through his convulsions, he felt the urn rock. Suffocating, he clutched at this tiny power over his world and he made his prison tip. The urn, lifting a little off the ground, punched his whole body as it settled back. He tried this repeatedly. At last, the toppling continued, seemingly forever. He tensed hungry for the smash of freedom, but there was only an earthquake then blackness.

He came to in darkness. His aching flesh was still packed into the urn but the pressure its wall exerted was now greater down his left side. Air cooled his shaved scalp. He unhooked his neck. That freedom told him that the lid must have been knocked out. Craning, he saw faint cracks of light; a vague uneven floor. Remotely, he was sure he could hear a murmuring of crowds. It came as a shock to realize he must be in the City at the Gates and so out of Osrakum. He listened to the city, remembering his journey through it. A yearning to be among its people made his heart pound. He hinged his head back against the rough earthenware lip as if that might pull his windpipe out of the urn and after it his lungs. He craved just one, deep chestful of air. It was no good. He calmed himself, concentrating on the quick throbbing of his blood. It occurred to him rescuers might be within earshot. He lifted his thighs with his expanding chest, then collapsing, let out a long, ragged wailing. With short, fast snatches of breath, he raced to another cry, then subsided, exhausted, hungry for some response. None came.

A thunderclap shook the room. The first gustings of a gale were catching in the angles of the walls and roofs outside. Carnelian rolled his eyes up to search for the black massing of Osidian's urn, but no shadow had a belly curve. With a cold flush, he began to fear that his cries might have woken him into the same suffering. Surely if Osidian were awake he would have made some response. The rattlings and whistling of the gathering storm were merging into a single voice.

Osidian hears you but is keeping silent.

Why does he keep silent? He's not dead! Carnelian sounded the words over and over again in his mind. Angry then? Yes, better that he should be angry. But not with me, not angry with me. Why should he be angry with me?

Why not? the storm said, wasn't it you who put him in the urn, who cheated him of his life, his destiny?

The venom of what the sybling Hanuses had said to him infused into his heart. Their two faces swayed sneering down at him from their single head. He tried to squeeze the poison out by blaming the Dowager Empress, Ykoriana, whose creatures the syblings were; by blaming the Lord Jaspar who had conspired with her, but it did not appease the nagging of the storm. You persuaded Osidian against his judgement down into the wilds of the Yden far from all protection. Ykoriana's henchmen only had to follow you to capture him. You have betrayed not only your beloved, but your father and all your people. It was always thus. All whom you have loved, you have betrayed.

As the storm tore the world apart, Carnelian could not wedge his head deeply enough between his knees to shut it out.

A tremor of footfalls jerked Carnelian free of a gnawing half-slumber. Some rays of light, a cry of surprise, the wind of something rushing up. He caught a glimpse of the Ichorian's tattoo-shadowed face, then felt the judder of the man's fists clamping to the rim of the urn. As Carnelian was lifted upright, it seemed to him the plaster ceiling was falling.

'You shouldn't have done that,' the Ichorian said.

Carnelian was grateful for the human tones that stripped the storm of its voice.

The Ichorian moved away, then Carnelian heard the grinding as a lid was slid off another urn.

'M-Master . . .' the Ichorian's voice trembled. His face returned to hover above Carnelian. The man seemed shaken. His gaze fell on Carnelian.

'I've arranged passage for us. It was hard, dangerous, but what's to come will be more dangerous still. I'm going to have to bind the lid closed.'

He stood back.

'Don't either of you even think of making a sound,' he said, shrilly. 'I've hired deaf mutes as porters. Be certain of this: if I hear even a sigh, I'll tip you both from the boat. You'll drop to the lake bottom and be drowned.'

He grunted as he hoisted the lid and perched it on the lip of Carnelian's urn.

'I'll be going with you all the way.'

The lid forced Carnelian's head down. As the Ichorian secured the lid with ropes, he kept up a chatter, his voice muffled: 'I've nothing to lose now. I'm leaving everything behind, even my slave. That way, no one will think I'm going away, not if I leave everything behind. It's the best thing to do. It's the only thing to do.'

A kick on the urn wall caused Carnelian's back to spasm.

'I only need one of you to sell, so don't imagine that I won't drown the other if I have to.'

Curled in the stinking dark, Carnelian felt the poles rasp by his head as they slid through the carrying handles. As he was swung into the air, the earthenware ground the raw meat of his back and feet. Bouncing on the flex of the carrying poles, he chewed his tongue until his mouth filled with the iron taste of blood.

At last, the urn was put down. When the agony had abated, he became aware of the swaying of a boat. With a judder, they set off. He tried to ignore the itch, the aching, his skinned flesh squelching in his own filth. Cries skimmed over him like gulls. Sometimes there would be a clamorous buzzing and his mind's eye would be assaulted by a vision of people climbing steps from the water up into the tenements of the city. Hubbubs vibrated past. When the boat clunked into others there were singing curses, or threats, once, a greeting.

Even through the earthenware, he began to feel the dawn. As they slipped in and out of shadow, the sun warmed and cooled the urn wall. Gradually, his world grew so hot that he began to hope he might die cooked in its oven. He was cheated even of that. With a rustling something covered the urn and the heat soon ebbed away.

Carnelian's world shattered, tumbling him into dust. The air was screaming. Men were quarrelling. It took time for him to realize he was free. He sucked at the wind with a gasp that relaxed every joint in his body. His spine uncoiling sent a knife filleting all the way up his back. His eyes tore open. Even as he saw the roiling sky, he was dazzled blind.

A voice shrieked: 'You didn't tell us what they were.'

Caught between gulping at the air and the rub of grit into his raw back, Carnelian flopped on to his belly. After the urn wall, the ground was kind.

'Masters! You've killed us all! They're Masters!'

Carnelian lifted his head and it became a keel in the flowing air. The world was rolling blackness. Dust pelted him. A lightning flash fixed a scene of more than a dozen men standing round him and, against the sky's torment, a broken youth glowing white.

'Osidian.' The word had hardly vibrated Carnelian's throat before the wind snatched it away. The dark fence of men recoiled as he rolled on to his knees. He sensed their cowering but it was Osidian who was the heart of his gaze. Carnelian rose, tottered unused to his legs, stumbled a few steps, then fell kneeling at Osidian's side. He reached up to touch an icy shoulder. More lightning showed him the wounds up his lover's back.

'Osidian,' he moaned and reached out to lift him. 'Beloved.' He pulled at his shoulders but Osidian refused even to lift his head.

'We must tie them up,' said a voice Carnelian knew to be the Ichorian's. He sensed the men circling and stood to face them. Their eyes caught the glare of lightning his skin cast over them as if from a mirror. As they shambled closer, he could smell their animal fear, could hear it in their voices as they incited each other on.

One braver than the rest reached out to touch him. Carnelian struck the hand away. More came up and he spun round striking out. Their terror ignited into rage and they threw themselves upon him. As their nails dug into his wounds he bayed at the stormy sky and threw them off with such fury that they backed away.

One produced a trembling flint knife. 'Let's butcher them.'

His companion gave him a sidelong look. 'Are you sure they can be killed?'

'Th-they're Masters . . .' said another.

'Angels.' The word taut with awe.

The brave one showed his hand. 'I've got this angel's blood here beneath my nails. If they bleed, they'll die.'

Erupting through them, the Ichorian slapped the man's hand down. 'There'll be no killing,' he bellowed. 'Where's the profit in that?'

He turned his back on Carnelian and scanned their faces. 'You've seen them unmasked. Now you're all in this as deep as me. Do you really believe you can kill two Masters and get away with it? Spill their blood and it'll stain your hands so red the Masters will hunt you like lice.' He glanced back at Carnelian. 'Our only hope is to take them south and sell them there for enough bronze to make us all rich.'

The slavers were wavering.

'Bind them,' barked the Ichorian.

As they moved to obey him, Carnelian backed away until his heels touched Osidian. He fought fiercely but the slavers' assaults wore him down until, at last, he was forced to the ground, powerless to stop them putting ropes around his neck.

Carnelian's arms were lashed together from wrists to elbows. The ropes strangling him were each bound to an ankle to bend him like a bow. The Ichorian had made the slavers do this to disguise Carnelian's height. Bitumen had been painted on his skin to hide its whiteness.

Sartlar crowding round Carnelian stank. Lightning revealed glimpses of their distorted shapes. Overcome with loathing and horror, Carnelian tried to back away, shamed at even being touched by the half-men slaves. Their inertness calmed him. He crouched, trying to get his fingers to the knots around his neck, but could not find an angle that would allow his joined arms to reach them. A knifing flash. For an instant, he saw the tarred wood of Osidian's wretched face. Carnelian became possessed by rage. He struggled frantically to unbend, to snap the ropes. Tightening, they tamed him, choking off his cries.

He let his head drop, centred himself. When the world lit again, he found a space beside Osidian's body and, kneeling, rolled into it. Enduring the pain, he shuffled round on to his side and managed to get his hands to Osidian's face. He rubbed at the bitumen, trying to reveal the beautiful face beneath. It was futile. Osidian's skin was canvas. Even through the tar on lips and teeth Carnelian could taste the salt of his tears. He rolled Osidian's head into his lap and rocked him back and forth, mumbling one of his nurse Ebeny's lullabies.

All through that shuddering night, Carnelian cradled Osidian, while the bitumen pulled his skin so taut he believed it must tear. The coarse, twisted bodies of the sartlar shoved against them. Each time the sky roared, Carnelian felt their trembling. The silence in-between was hissing earache.

As the lightning became intermittent, he began to feel the weight of the sky. Growling rumbled out from its black heart. A cooler wind was blowing. The waiting between thunderclaps left him raw. Osidian slept in his crooked embrace. Carnelian worked his mouth to ease the itching at the corners. The air was thickening, throbbing. Suddenly, with a final bellow, the sky opened. The air sighed relief. The earth spattered, pocked then pooled. The pools swelled to sheets foaming in all directions. Carnelian was blinded. Air had turned to water and he was drowning. Curled into each other, they were pebbles in a stream.

RUNNING CRUCIFIED

Characteristics required of a sartlar kraal are:
Firstly, that it shall be located south-west of two intersecting field tracks.
Secondly, that it shall be capable of stabling twice four hundred sartlar.
Thirdly, that the enclosure shall be circular and circumvallated with a
fence of hri wicker which shall be not less than an aquar in height and
nine hand spans thick at the base; said fence to have but a single point of
egress, this being at the north-east of the enclosure and under the tower
which must be constructed for the overseers. This tower shall abut on to
the outer face of the fence and be not less than two aquar in height.
Fourthly, the enclosure with its tower shall in turn be circumvallated by a
ditch which shall not be less than an aquar in depth and crossed by a
single, removable bridge. This ditch shall serve not only to reinforce the
incarceration of the sartlar but will also function as a fire-break in the
event that the stubble-burn from the adjoining fields should become
uncontrolled.

(from an agricultural codicil compiled in beadcord by the Wise of the Domain of Lands)

BLEATING, THE SARTLAR EDGED AWAY. THIN LIGHT WAS SEEPING INTO THE
world. Carnelian had to bring his knees up to his chest to put
enough slack in the ropes to allow him to lift his head and look
around. Men were pushing through the sartlar towards him. Among
them, only the Ichorian made no attempt to shelter from the rain.
Water varnished his half-black skin. Carnelian bore the cutting of
the ropes into his neck as he squinted up at the man's face. He could
see the doubt in the man's eyes.

'Please stand up,' the Ichorian said. Carnelian watched the

half-black lips hesitate over but not say the word 'Master'.

Leaning on his elbows, Carnelian managed to get his knees under him. He gathered his strength then jerked upright, but the tug of the ropes unbalanced him, making him fall back on to his knees.

Feet splashed approaching him.

'Stay back!' cried the Ichorian. 'Let him do it by himself.'

Carnelian tried again, this time bringing first one foot then the other under him, then he straightened his knees as much as he could and dug his elbows into his thighs for support. Two slavers brushed past him, barking orders. He twisted his head round enough to see Osidian still lying on the ground with the slavers over him.

'Get up,' one growled.

Carnelian watched the man jab a foot into Osidian's belly then draw back when he lifted his head to glare at them through his bitumen mask. When the slavers goaded him with their feet, Osidian closed his eyes and refused to budge. When they began kicking him, the Ichorian stopped them with a bellow. He made them hoist the Master on to his feet.

Osidian stood hunched, his head hanging. It agonized Carnelian. Then he became aware of the brooding mass framing Osidian, and his heart died. For he knew, within that mountain wall, the Wise and all the gathered Chosen were turning Molochite into the Gods while his brother, Osidian, whose place he had usurped, was trussed in the mud, an abject slave.

The slavers gagged the Masters and covered them with rags. The Ichorian ordered that the ropes securing their ankles to their throats should be loosened enough for them to walk. Each had a leash looped through between the wrists which a slaver could use to pull them.

Strain as he might, Carnelian could not break the ropes. His leash tugged and he had to trot after it or else fall over. He soon found he had to bend even lower so as to put enough slack in the ropes to allow his legs to move freely. Sartlar jostled him on either side, their thick heels kicking mud up into his face. He was forced to look down, to watch his bitumened feet slipping and squelching through the mud. The sucking churn of sartlar feet drowned out the hiss of the rain. Soon, Carnelian's breath was rasping past the gag wedged into the corners of his mouth like a bit.

He lost his footing, plunged knees first into the ground, was kicked hard in the back, then crushed by a sartlar falling on top of him. The creature rolled to one side and Carnelian used his joined-up arms as a shield against the flailing spades of its feet. The leash jerked him up, forcing him to stumble back into a run. Sartlar closed around him.

Concentrating on maintaining a steady, sure-footed rhythm, Carnelian feared for Osidian. He managed to turn enough to look at him. He was there, running mechanically, his head down so that Carnelian was unable to see anything of his face. Peering through the loping mass of sartlar, Carnelian glimpsed the surface of the lake, its glass scratched to granite by the rain. He let his head drop, rested, then lifted it again searching for the City at the Gates, hoping to discover where they were. Boats and figures crowding the shore were shrouded in tarpaulins. Strain forced Carnelian to sink his head.

For a long while he thought of nothing but making his running smooth and sure. Then he found he was kicking through ridges wheels had left in the mud. Smoky charcoal cut through the dull odour of his bitumened skin, through the sartlar stench. Voices and the lowing of beasts carried through the storm. Glancing up, Carnelian saw carts and people dragging their way through the puddle-rutted quagmire of a stopping place. If he made a run for it surely he would be spotted, the alarm given and then he and Osidian would be freed. Feeling the ground hardening beneath his feet, he saw stone surfacing through the red earth. It was hard climbing the incline of a ramp. When the stone flattened out, they came to a halt. He propped his bound arms on one thigh and slowly released the tension in his back. He sensed something giant looming over him. Panting through his gag, he twisted his head round, screwing his eyes up against the rain. A watch-tower. The sight of it forking the clouds brought memories of those he had stayed in with his father on their journey to Osrakum. Hope flared as he scanned the tower heights, but no lookouts were spreadeagled in the hoops of its dead-man's chairs.

The slavers were barking commands. The sartlar began to grumble. Even as the leash attached to Carnelian's wrists was drawing taut, he decided he would take his chance. Bracing himself, he pulled hard. Snarling, the slaver lost hold. Carnelian fell into a sart-lar, rocked back on to his feet, lowered his head and rammed his way out through the herd. Bursting free, he lifted his eyes to get his bear-ings. Dimly, through the rain, he saw the road all crusted with more sartlar. Their milling confused him and he hesitated. This hesitation gave the slavers time to surround him. As one pulled him up by the leash, another tugged on one of his leg ropes. He tumbled, falling so heavily on his shoulder that his head swam. Hands raised him to his feet. The leash pulled and, reeling, he stumbled after it.

The smooth road made it possible for Carnelian to trot along without fear of falling. He let his head hang bobbing and soothed his dizziness by keeping time with the slapping rhythm of sartlar feet. His shoulder ached. He brought his mind back into focus. He could feel the cold touch of the road and the jostle of the sartlar. His next attempt to escape would be successful, but first he must husband his strength. He dreamed of freedom, saw the rescuers, frowned at their staring terror as he and Osidian were revealed. It was probable the Law would slay them for looking on the naked faces of Masters. Carnelian tried to convince himself the bitumen was its own mask and that, in seeking help from others, he would not bring down disaster on them.

It was a change in the pace that brought him fully awake. Sartlar bodies were knocking erratically against his. As they slowed, he was forced into a shamble. The rain grew louder than their footfalls as it hammered on his aching back and shoulder. He remembered his plan. Before he could marshal his courage, the stone under his feet was sloping down another ramp. He cranked his head round and glimpsed another watch-tower and then he was sliding in mud again as his leash pulled him away from the road and into the vastness of the Guarded Land.

Gulping breath, Carnelian collapsed to his knees and cooled his forehead in a puddle. Along his spine it felt as if he were coming apart like a clam. His thighs and calves were juddering. He anchored his fingers into the mud to convince himself he was not still running. It seemed he had been ploughing his feet through the Guarded Land's red earth for days.

Lifting his face into the rain, he saw a high wicker wall encircling him, its circuit broken only where a slit gave into a passage that passed under a tower and through a wooden gate into the hri fields outside. The tower was just a skeleton of wood skinned here and there with more woven wicker. Some of the slavers were up there, the fire they had lit a curl of brightness against the black sky.

Carnelian saw Osidian crouched alone at one end of the crescent the sartlar made as they sought shelter against the kraal wall. Groaning, Carnelian got to his feet and plodded towards him. It was not more than a dozen steps but his muscles were already stiffening. As he approached, the sartlar mass recoiled as if he were a leper. He found a space near Osidian, backed into it, knelt and, gingerly, leaned his back against the wicker wall as his buttocks squelched into the mud.

Looking round, he saw Osidian had his head sunk into the crook of his elbows. His trussed forearms rose above him in unconscious mimicry of the kraal tower. Rain poured over his bitumened head. Carnelian thought of touching him but remembered they were gagged. He was reluctant to face Osidian's eyes without the defence of words.

Stretching away from them, the sartlar mass could have been a colony of birds miserable in the rain. Carnelian only realized he had been counting their bowed heads when he came across some that were grey. It had never occurred to him that sartlar might grow old. He peered at the creatures nearest him. Clinging, filthy hair betrayed their grotesque, distorted skulls. Immense hands and feet, swollen-jointed, clawed. Crooked backs shaped their rags. Carnelian found his gaze met by a pair of tiny dark eyes. A child that quickly hid its face. Though he knew that all animals had young, he had never imagined that sartlar might have children.

Carnelian's reverie was disturbed by a shudder of excitement passing through the creatures. As they lifted their faces, his eyes flitted from one to another, appalled by their fearful ugliness. Some slavers were approaching. They carried baskets into which they dug their hands and, coming out with hunks of something, they sowed these among the sartlar. One fell nearby and, straining, Carnelian managed to get his hands to it.

At first he thought it wood, but it was too soft, one edge sodden and muddy where it had touched the ground. He brought it to his face and smelled hri. 'Bread,' he murmured, his lips curling with distaste as he saw the weevils crawling through it.

'You will eat.'

Carnelian looked up and discovered that the Ichorian was standing over him. The man slapped the bread out of his hand.

'Here, I've kept the best for you.' He shoved a hunk of the black bread into Carnelian's lap. Carnelian worked it up his legs with his elbows and managed to get it into his hands. It looked much the same as the discarded piece.

The Ichorian leaned in close. 'Let's take this off.'

Carnelian held still as the man fumbled with the knots of his gag.

'From now on,' the man mumbled almost in his ear, 'you'll not be needing these. This far from the road, be certain no one will hear your cries.'

Carnelian endured the gag pulling tighter, his eyes following the black tattoo spirals on the Ichorian's face as he held on to the thought of escape. Scabs tore from the corners of his mouth as the gag came free. As the Ichorian moved over to Osidian, Carnelian practised gingerly opening and closing his mouth.

'Now look what you've done. Soiled or not, you'll eat it.'

The Ichorian was looking down at Osidian. He leaned to scoop a piece of bread from the mud and then rubbed it on his jerkin before forcing it on Osidian. The Ichorian removed his gag, then stood back.

'Eat. You'll both need your strength tomorrow.'

Carnelian peered at the bread. Rubbing away as many weevils as he could, he took a bite, gave it a chew, then swallowed as quickly as he could.

'Eat!'

Carnelian saw the Ichorian flinch as Osidian looked up at him. The untattoed half of his face darkened.

'You'll have that bread even if I have to force it down your throat.' It was costing the Ichorian dear to hold Osidian's glare.

'I'll see he eats it,' Carnelian said, quickly.

Relieved to have an excuse to disengage from the contest, the Ichorian turned to Carnelian. 'Make sure he does.'

As the man walked away, Carnelian leaned forward to look into Osidian's face. His eyes were windows giving into an empty house. Carnelian tried to formulate questions. He had so many, wanted to know so much, but Osidian seemed so far away that all Carnelian managed to say was: 'You must eat.'

Osidian made no sign he had heard. The bread lay in his lap ignored. Carnelian took his own piece and tried to manoeuvre it into Osidian's hands. Carnelian had to close the lifeless fingers round the bread. He stroked them. 'Please . . . please eat.'

The rain running down Osidian's face could have been tears. Carnelian frowned back his own.

'Eat.'

The word seemed spoken by another's tongue. Osidian became aware he had something in his hand. He seemed a puppet moving his mouth to it. Carnelian watched him take a bite and chew, his lips stroking the bread, the weevils running down his fingers. Carnelian watched him, waiting until Osidian had finished before he reached to take the other piece that was wedged between Osidian's stomach and his thigh.

As he ate, Carnelian licked rain from his lips to lubricate the stale mass.

'I almost escaped today,' he said in a low voice. He looked for a sign of recognition in Osidian's eye, but there was nothing. 'This time I failed but not the next. We'll be free soon, I promise.'

Osidian turned to him, vaguely frowning, his lips making shapes. Carnelian was forced to lean his ear close enough to hear Osidian's words.

'Go if you can. Leave me. I am already dead.'

At first Carnelian thought Osidian delirious, fevered, but then he understood and pulled away. He leaned the ache of his back against the wicker fence, exposing his face to the needling rain. The words ran round and round in his head. Osidian could not return. The moment his brother Molochite had been made God Emperor, Osidian's life was forfeit. Osrakum held only death for him. Carnelian tried to imagine a life for them in the outer world. It would have to be somewhere beyond the Commonwealth. A vision of his island home blossomed warm and inviting in his mind. It withered as he remembered the snow falling into the ruins Aurum and the other Masters had made of it when they had come to summon his father back from exile. Besides, there would be the sea to cross, not to mention the vast journey to reach its shore. Where else was there in the world in which the Masters were not hated? Even if he and Osidian found a haven, how could they live without wealth, without servants? The Ichorian needed to take the terrible risk of selling Masters so as to buy himself another life, though he could more easily hide his tattoos than Carnelian and Osidian could their height and pallid skin.

Lightning brought Carnelian a blinding realization. He could return alone to Osrakum. He saw his father's and his people's joy on the day of his return. He clung to the warmth of that vision but then, quietly, let it grow cold and dark. He opened his eyes to look at Osidian. It was hard to see in this battered creature the boy in the Yden. His love for that boy had been so fierce. Though it still burned, it had become as small in him as the slavers' fire was in the rumbling night.

'Then it is hopeless,' he said, aloud. He would rather tear his heart out than abandon Osidian. Whatever might come, he was determined to share his lover's fate.

Carnelian lost count of the days as he ran obedient to the rain's relentless rhythm. It drove his heart, his rasping breath, even the blinking of his eyes that saw nothing but two pale feet churning mud the colour of old blood. When he fell, he was up again before the leash pulling his wrists tugged taut. Once he saw stone and, for a moment, recalled the feet were his from the cold, and the impact shuddering up into his head.

Night would return him to a kraal. As the numbness of the running faded, he would be delivered to the torture of his ropes. Worse was the sight of Osidian suffering. The crusted weal around his neck drew Carnelian's eyes however hard he tried to look away. Even swollen by blood and rain, the rope had worn so deep it had become flush with the ruptured flesh. Waking feverish with agony, Carnelian would find Osidian twitching as he ran on in nightmare.

But it was Osidian's eyes Carnelian dreaded most. Once he saw a stirring in their depths and fear possessed him that some darkness had climbed down into Osidian's soul and was peering out.

When something crept across his flesh, Carnelian awoke. He saw the glimmer of the sartlar's eyes and jerked back from the hand it was extending. The rope biting into his flesh squeezed out a moan that closed his eyes. When he opened them again he saw the sartlar open a maw rimmed by rotten teeth.

'Blood?'

The word grated from nowhere. Carnelian wondered if he had spoken without knowing it. His eyes fixed on the sartlar, he tried the word but his tongue was leather in his mouth. The creature lifted its hand again, a gnarled wooden thing straying up, extending a finger. He shuddered as it touched his wound, then watched the sartlar draw it back and taste the fingertip. The lips moved.

'Blood.'

Carnelian stared. The word had come from the sartlar. He was certain of it. He peered at the creature and saw the empty sags of skin hanging on the chest. Breasts. A female then. A woman even. He saw through her lank hair her eyes watching him.

'But dead,' she said.

Carnelian tried to soften his tongue by chewing some moisture into it. His first word was just a groan. The second worked. 'Dead?' Perhaps the woman was only parroting words she had heard from an overseer.

She regarded him for a while, fearful, perhaps a little puzzled. 'Painful?'

He touched the rope and smiled inquiringly.

She made a grimace that might have been a smile.

'Yes, it is painful,' he said.

The woman poked among her rags and fetched out a package that she laid on his stomach. As she leaned forward the hair fell away from her face. He looked with distaste on the twin holes where her nose should have been. A scar channel ran over the holes climbing to her brow, there dividing, cutting deep into the flesh over her eye ridges, round to catch the edges of her eyes, down through her cheeks to meet again on her chin. He winced, imagining the agony of such a branding.

The bone of her wrist was moving against his thigh. Her crippled hands were opening the package on his stomach. The odour rising from it almost made Carnelian wriggle away. It was fear of the rope that kept him where he was. She poked a finger into the package and, raising it, showed him the tip swollen with pungent fat.

''ll sting.'

He realized the brand on her face was the womb glyph for earth. She opened her eyes wider, asking for permission. He gave her the merest nod and she reached out to touch her finger to his wound. He trembled with agony as she rubbed it round under the rope. As she returned for more ointment, his flesh, where she had touched it, ignited. His clenched teeth chattered with the burning while she smeared more on. As the fire died, he realized he could no longer feel the rope. He allowed her to treat his ankle wounds. When she was done, she rewrapped the salve and took it back.

'Bless you,' he sighed, euphoric from a lack of pain.

Her hair once more hid her eyes, but he could still feel her stare. She hobbled off into the night, releasing snorts among the sartlar as she pushed into their doughy mass. It was only then Carnelian groaned, cursing that he had not thought to have her treat Osidian's wounds.

Carnelian came suddenly awake, staring blindly. The air had died. It took him a while before he realized what had happened. The rain had stopped. It was as if he had spent all his life dancing to a drum and then, without warning, it had fallen silent. He held his breath, yearning for the next beat. The silence stretched, swelling louder, unbearable. Silence so deafening he tried to shout to fill it, but nothing came but a rattling cough far away in his lungs.

When the slavers came, Carnelian found he had forgotten how to move his body. As the sartlar funnelled through the kraal gate, he struggled to make his legs obey him. He lifted his head as much as he could bear, grating his eyes up in their sockets to be able to look further. Hunched, Osidian was already stumbling after the last few sartlar through the gate. That sight blinded Carnelian with tears. Grimacing, putting one foot before the other, he followed.

The gate gave out on to a narrow bridge that crossed a ditch to where four tracks met in the mud. Every kraal had its ditch and crossroads. Before the slavers beat him into the midst of the sartlar herd he craned round. The reflection of the kraal wall was twisting in the moat. Towards the horizon stood the prong of a watch-tower.

It was a struggle to stay on his feet as they ambled away. Without the rain, he had to make his own rhythm. Bowed beneath the tyranny of the brooding sky, he prayed for the dullness his mind had lost. The pace was merciless; his back, an arch of pain. The rope threatened to prune his feet off at the ankles and his head off at the neck. He was a running crucifixion.

His misery seemed to have already stretched for days when they came suddenly to a halt. Carnelian felt his heart give a flutter and almost go out. The mud and his feet were melting together. He crumpled to his knees thirsting for death. The hunger for it had set like concrete in his stomach. He could feel the sartlar settling to the ground. He was seeing the world through a window of water. A flicker of green caught at the centre of his vision. The colour was a salve for his eyes. He blinked his vision clear. A shoot was pulling its curled leaves out from the rusty earth. Fresh, reborn, it sought the sky. Its freedom mocked him. He dribbled as he cursed it for giving him just enough hope not to let him die.

They came to the edge of a lake of curdled blood. Carnelian caught glimpses of it as they were herded along its shore and up on to a road. He ran with the sartlar upon its stone.

When they began slowing, he stumbled, but was immediately pulled back on to his feet. The groan his lungs expelled brought a blow crashing into his head.

'Shut up!'

Through surging pain, he became aware of a commotion up ahead. His leash went slack and a long, dirty flint was shoved before his eyes.

'If you make as much as a whisper,' a voice hissed in his ear, 'I'll gut you with this.'

Eyeing the flint, Carnelian began building the strength to cry out. He longed for the relief of having that knife in his body.

A clamour of young voices, followed by the sound of the Ichorian answering them, made Carnelian listen.

'You're a half-black, a Bloodguard of the Masters.' A young voice speaking in thick-tongued Vulgate.

'Nothing . . .' Carnelian heard the Ichorian say.

'Not even a bronze blade?' This time the accented voice was a man's.

The paving brightened around Carnelian's feet as the sartlar shuffled away. He was gathering the courage to lift his head against the rope, when a huge, taloned foot settled on to the stone.

He watched it spread as it took the weight of its leg. Another came down in front of it as the aquar came walking towards him.

'What've we here?'

The Vulgate fell from the sky. Carnelian tried to see the aquar's rider. He felt as much as heard the impact of the man's weight as he vaulted down. Carnelian could smell his sweat. Two, dark, thick-toed feet came into sight.

'But . . .' The man gasped and began rubbing at Carnelian's ear. 'You're white under the black. A marumaga? A M-Master?'

Before Carnelian could find his voice, the man slashed with a blade. Carnelian felt it as a stabbing in his back. He heard the screams and the cries of battle as if he were coming up out of water. It confused him that the blade he could feel was filleting him up his back and yet the man was in front of him. He waited for oblivion, his heart pounding eagerly as if death were a lover. He wondered at the screams and anger. He saw without seeing the two ends of his ropes dangling under his chin. His eyes focused on them. They had been cut. The realization took hold. He erupted a roar, unfolding upwards to reach and breathe free air. Too late. Fire leapt from his white-hot spine to consume him. Aflame, he fell into blackness; a torch dropped down a well.

THE RAIDERS

A smooth bead is earned for each complete season of service. More may be threaded on to an auxiliary's service cord for any action deemed by a superior to go beyond those stipulated in the Legionary Code; such awards subject to ratification by a quaestor who shall index the action against the Categories of Valour.

Rough beads are threaded on to a service cord according to statute infringements as listed in the Categories of Offence.

The Protocol of Remission states that smooth beads may be given up to redeem rough beads subject to the Laws of Remission.

The Laws of Remission are: first, that a rough bead may be redeemed by the loss of a smooth bead; second, rough beads may be redeemed by mandatory or voluntary chastisement as determined by the Laws of Punishment; third, three rough beads can only be redeemed by the concurrent loss of three smooth beads.

The Laws of Punishment are: first, that a rough bead may be redeemed by a standard flogging; second, that three rough beads may be redeemed by progressive mutilation as described in the Schedule of Removals and according to the corresponding protocols; third, that at any time a service cord should have on it five rough beads, the auxiliary to whom it belongs shall, without recourse to appeal, be put to death by crucifixion.

The Schedule of Removals is applied as follows: on the first occasion, the middle fingers of both hands with associated knuckles; on the second, the ears; on the third, the nose; on the fourth, the right eye; on the fifth, the left eye.

(Extract from the Law of Legionary Service compiled in beadcord by the Wise of the Domain Legions)

IT WAS THE SUDDEN STILLNESS THAT PULLED CARNELIAN UP FROM HIS nightmare. He could no longer feel the sway of the black water. Confused, he wondered if the boat had brought him at last to the opposite shore? Opening his eyes, he found he was wedged in, buttocks pressing against a crossbeam, his knees almost in his face.

Somewhere, a man was speaking. Though his voice was harsh and nasal, its pouring of almost-words had a familiar sound that made Carnelian smile even as he strove to pluck out meaning.

'. . . the lads are scared enough already,' another voice was saying with a strange accent.

Dream still clouding his mind, Carnelian became convinced it was one of his marumaga brothers speaking. Grane perhaps, though Carnelian had a notion it was his Uncle Crail he had been expecting, who Aurum had had killed. Carnelian wanted to see Grane's face, but was unable to clear his head enough to call out.

'Do you imagine I'm any less afraid than they are, Father Cloud?' asked the nasal voice, speaking as if to the deaf. 'Through no choice of mine, I'm now as much involved in this sacrilege as the rest of you. If that weren't bad enough, what possessed you two to bring the Standing Dead with us?'

Carnelian did not recognize the voice, nor the strange term.

'Leave them be, Ranegale,' growled a weary voice Carnelian had not heard before. 'Can't you see their uncle and their brother lying there dead?'

Carnelian grew uneasy. All this talk of death and the strange names; worse, there was something peculiar about their speech that was making it hard to follow.

'Leave them be?' said Ranegale, the man with the nasal voice. 'You may be an Elder, Stormrane, but I don't believe even that gives you or your sons the right to let the dead ride.'

Realization came to Carnelian as a shock. The voices were speaking neither Vulgate nor the tongue of the Masters, Quya, yet he understood them. Incredibly, they were speaking the same barbarian language his nurse Ebeny had used with him and his brothers when they were children.

'. . . my doing, not theirs,' Stormrane was saying.

To hear the cadence of Ebeny's speech in a man's voice was startling.

'And was it you, my father, who ordered some of the lads to double up so as to free saddle-chairs in which to put the Standing Dead? I see by your silence it wasn't. Will you deny it was Ravan who first saw the Bloodguard and Fern who then found the Standing

Dead? No? Then it seems we all agree it was your sons who drew us into that bloodbath, so don't ask me to leave things be. If they'd let things be, your brother and your eldest son would still be alive; you yourself and the rest of us unwounded and, even now, we'd all be safely on the road to Makar. Instead of which we're out here tainted by this sacrilege, the Mother forgive us and, if that weren't enough of a curse, we now have these white scorpions to deal with.'

White scorpions? Was Ranegale talking about him? More than one Master. Guilt at having again forgotten Osidian gouged Carnelian's mind clear. As Ranegale continued droning accusations, Carnelian became desperate to see his beloved. His knees were blocking the view and he found that his head was wedged too tight against his chest for him to turn it. Out of the corner of his eye, he spied two youths squeezed one behind the other into a wicker saddle-chair.

'I won't allow you to accuse Ravan,' Stormrane was saying.

Forcing life into his hands, Carnelian swivelled them until they caught the edges of the saddle-chair. Gripping as hard as he could, he strained to pull himself up. The resulting spasm caused him to roll his eyes up into his head. Nausea surged in waves. Everything from neck to thighs was aching pulp.

'I don't recall you warning us of danger when my son spotted the Bloodguard among the slavers nor any complaints when we went in to rob them.'

The words pulsed with the blood hammering at Carnelian's temples.

'Sky and Earth! What's that got to do with anything?' Ranegale replied. 'It was only when Fern found the Standing Dead among the sartlar that the Bloodguard began to kill us.'

Sartlar? That word made the memory of his suffering seep in like rain through a cloak. He fumbled his hand up to his neck and trembled as it touched the raw crusty edges of his wound. He endured the agony as his fingers probed for and did not find the rope. That he felt naked without it made him weep bitter tears.

A voice carried from the distance and Carnelian heard creakings as the barbarians turned to look. He tried peering down the tunnel between his knees and saw that his saddle-chair curved up into a basketwork prow. Beyond stood his aquar's neck, past which he could make out, against the brooding sky, a giant from which the voice appeared to be coming.

'Thank the Skyfather that at least we're not pursued,' said Cloud, the man with Grane's voice.

'What need have they to chase us,' said Ranegale, 'when they know the dragons will do their work for them?'

'We must get back on to the road then?' A youthful voice taut with fear.

'There we'd have no chance at all, thanks to you, boy.'

'Ravan . . .' said Cloud, gently. 'The fight was sure to have been seen from the watch-tower. Our descriptions will have been sent all the way down the road. Patrols will already be on their way up from Makar as part of the scouring. On the road they'd trap us as easily as if we were on an earthbridge.'

'Then we must hide deeper in the fields,' said the youth.

'Without the watch-towers to steer by we'd soon be lost.' Cloud gazed out, sadly. 'This enslaved earth has no trees, no hills, no land-marks at all save only kraals, each identical to every other.'

'How far are we from the road?' bellowed Ranegale in the direction of the giant.

'We'll still see the tower flares,' a reply came back.

The voice seemed to Carnelian ludicrously thin for such a giant. He was still dazed. He focused on thoughts of Osidian, desperate to know if he still lived. Fearing another spasm, he gingerly applied pressure with his thighs and, gritting his teeth, slid himself back and up his saddle-chair.

Squinting against the pounding in his head, Carnelian saw there were perhaps twenty aquar ranged around him. A few were riderless, the others bore men and youths enveloped in black hri-cloth, their legs hooked over the peculiar transverse crossbars that formed the front of their saddle-chairs. Most of the raiders had their heads turbaned by more of the cloth so that only their faces were exposed. Save that these were free of the chameleon tattoo, the raiders could have been from his own household. Searching among them, he found a saddle-chair into which a patchy black body had been folded. Carnelian's heart leapt. He did not need to see the face to know it was Osidian.

The raiders were looking into the distance and, when he followed their gaze, he saw a man riding towards them behind whom rose the giant that Carnelian now realized was nothing more than the over-seer tower of a kraal.

'You saw no one in any direction, Loskai?' Ravan again. Carnelian located the youth standing on the ground, a slash of dried blood across his forehead and cheek, his face sweat-glazed, bruised.

Loskai shook his head. Ravan turned to look round at another rider who was hunched forward gripping his ankles, his loosely-turbaned head almost resting on his knees. Ravan sank his chin.

'You're right, Ranegale, this is all my fault. I was the one who noticed the Bloodguard.'

'Don't speak like that, son.' It was Stormrane reaching out to

31

grasp Ravan's shoulder. The man had a grey mane worked through with feathers, peppered with pale beads. Deep grooves around his mouth and eyes made him seem an old man, but if so, a strong one, though his sickly pallor showed how serious was the wound he bore. Stormrane had so much the look of one of Carnelian's people he was lost for a moment trying to work out which one he might be.

Ravan, looking up at his father with adoration, forced from him a grim smile. 'Son, you fought bravely. You made me proud. You'll have a good scar to show your hearthmates.'

Ravan tried a grin, but the corners of his mouth dragged it down. His eyes strayed to where two bodies were stretched out on blankets on the ground.

'Your brother and your uncle were warriors who brought the Tribe much salt,' said Stormrane, misery dulling his eyes.

Ravan was no longer seeing the dead but rather something in his mind. 'How was the Bloodguard able to kill them both?'

'They were overmatched,' said Cloud. Next to Stormrane, he seemed to be the oldest there. Wisps of greying hair framing his cowled face threaded beads similar to Stormrane's that Carnelian judged to be some of their precious salt.

The youth turned to look at Cloud. Standing over the corpses, he shook his head and frowned. 'I'd heard but not believed how fast the Bloodguard are, how skilled.'

One of the other youths stuttered something and, suddenly, Carnelian found the barbarians jerking round to gape at him. He watched the colour drain from their faces. Some were trembling.

Ravan made some comment about Carnelian's eyes.

'Angels or not, I say we kill them now,' shrilled Loskai. He darted looks at the other men, making sure to always keep Carnelian in view as he might a serpent. 'Kill them both, before they get their power back, before they bring the dragons down on us.'

Carnelian cared for nothing but the use of plurals, the pronouns that proved Osidian must be alive.

'What makes you so sure they *can* be killed?' asked Stormrane.

Carnelian's awareness of their fear, their hatred, was washed away by the warm relief of knowing Osidian lived.

Cloud lifted his hands and quietened the youths.

'Well, Fern,' said Ranegale, 'I'll ask you in the hope you'll stop hiding behind your father.' He let go of his ankles and straightened up to point at Carnelian. 'Why've you landed us with the poison of these Standing Dead?'

Carnelian wondered why they referred to Masters thus. He noticed Ranegale had only a single eye, the other being concealed by a leather band. Hidden beneath the windings of his head cloth, the lower half of his face seemed unnaturally flat.

Another man stepped into view. Young, slender, he was taller than Stormrane, much darker skinned. He looked quite unlike the other barbarians.

'I'm not hiding behind my father.'

Fern's voice was husky. He turned dark eyes on Carnelian, who was forced to bear their sharp hatred. Fern frowned and his stare lost its intensity.

'I don't know,' he said, sounding surprised. He seemed to be examining Carnelian for a sign who, in turn, registered the livid welt cutting along Fern's jaw line.

'Because of them my brother and my uncle are dead; my father's wounded; my little brother.' Fern glanced at Stormrane and Ravan and then back at Carnelian, his eyes slitting. Looking at Ranegale, his face becoming haunted with uncertainty.

'How can I answer you when I don't know myself. Finding them has brought death to my kin. Perhaps I just couldn't ride away with nothing to show for so much loss.'

Ranegale, who had cupped his hands to the sides of his shrouded face to listen, dropped them. 'You mean the way you ran away from the legions?'

Snarling, the young man sprang forward but Cloud caught him in a hug. Carnelian's aquar threw back its head crowned with startled plumes, rocking spasms of agony up his back and neck.

'You know perfectly well, Ranegale, why he left the service.'

In Cloud's arms, Fern glared. He glanced at his father for support, but Stormrane turned away and Fern's face fell.

'Because they hurt him,' whined Ranegale in a pantomime voice, rolling his head as he spoke. He froze. 'Service in the legions hurts everyone. I should know.'

His hand straying up to his face lacked a middle finger. Carnelian stared because, in spite of the swarthy skin, the hand resembled those of the Wise. A token of the four-horned Lord of Mirrors, war-like avatar of the Black God.

Stormrane threw back his maned head, making the beads tinkle. 'You're always parading your mutilations as if they were marks of honour. I and many of my line managed a longer service than you with only a few stripes on our backs and, when we returned, we each brought the Tribe many times more salt.'

Loskai edged his aquar closer to Ranegale, whose shrouded head was looking down at Stormrane.

'You'd better look around you, old man. The days when you and your kin could oppress us with your service records have passed.'

He stabbed a finger at the dead. 'Your brother and your eldest are corpses. Though you hide it, you yourself have taken a wound that's as like as not going to finish you. Then all that will be left of your line will be a few boys barely of age and, for a while, the half-breed.'

He cast a dismissive glance at Fern. 'Do you believe the brass still at his throat is going to command much awe in the Tribe?'

Carnelian searched for and found the plain legionary collar forged around Fern's neck which only the Masters had the knowledge to remove. Cloud let him go as Stormrane squared his shoulders to face down Ranegale and Loskai. Clearly, he intimidated them.

'When the time comes, Fern will pay for his desertion.' Stormrane glanced at Fern who hung his head.

The raised voices were making the aquar nervous. The youths on their backs were looking upset; several close to tears. Cloud forced his way between the two parties.

'Stop this! We're not going to help ourselves or our tribes by fighting each other.'

Cloud went among the aquar, smiling, addressing each youth in turn, putting straightness into their backs. Some dabbed their eyes, sneaking looks at each other to see if their unmanliness had been witnessed.

'Will the Elders do us the favour of letting us hear their plan,' growled Ranegale.

'Nothing's changed,' said Stormrane. 'We go on to Makar.'

'Through the scouring line? With the dead?'

Now at his father's side, Fern lifted a fist. 'Do you want to leave them here to rot and so deny them their place in the sky?'

'If it will save the rest of us from joining them. Besides,' he pointed towards the kraal tower, 'that will form a perfectly good burial platform.'

Stormrane shook his head with anger. 'Even if this sky were our sky, you deliberately forget this accursed land is shunned by all but the most unclean birds. Had you been in his place, my brother would never have left you behind.'

Cloud had returned. 'We'll just have to find some way to take them with us through the line.'

Stormrane did not seem to hear him.

'What about the Standing Dead?' asked Ranegale.

Stiff-faced, Stormrane and Fern both looked sidelong at Carnelian.

34

Cloud shrugged, grimacing apologetically. 'You did make us bring them, Fern. Surely you must've had some notion what to do with them?'

Carnelian was relieved when Fern looked away, running a hand up his forehead, pushing back the cloth and revealing some of his thick curling hair. 'Revenge . . . ? Some recompense . . . ?'

'Torture?' asked Loskai. 'Murder?'

Fern let his hand fall. 'What good would that do?'

Cloud was looking at them horrified. 'Torture? Murder? Are you all possessed? These are Standing Dead; angels? Can you imagine with what fury the rest of their kind would hunt us if we harm them in any way?' His eyes widened. 'For such a sin they'd torch the Earthsky from end to end.'

Ranegale gave a snort. 'They're rather shabby for angels.' Despite his bravado, Carnelian felt the man's unease as he turned his single eye towards him. 'Just being here they make a bad situation hopeless. Let's finish them. What more do we have to lose? If we bury them deep enough, they'll never be found.'

Stormrane shook his head. 'I agree with Cloud. The risk's too great. Besides, now we have them we may as well try and put them to some use.'

Ranegale sneered at him. 'And how do my fathers suggest we take them along with us? We've no spare aquar.'

Cloud looked at him tentatively. 'Some of the lads could double up.'

'Am I the only one who can see that the Standing Dead are too weak to ride? We barely got them this far,' said Ranegale.

'We're going to have to make drag-cradles to carry our dead,' said Fern. 'Making a couple more wouldn't delay us much.'

'Drag-cradles will slow us down.'

Loskai spoke up: 'My brother's right, whichever way we go, we'll run into dragons. Pulling drag-cradles, we couldn't hope to outrun them.'

Stormrane looked murderous. 'I'll not leave my son nor my brother behind.'

Fern clasped his father's arm but Stormrane tore himself free.

'I won't have to,' he said, oblivious of the hurt he had just caused his son. 'I'll work out some other way to get us through the line.'

'It becomes clear how the renowned Elder, Stormrane, achieved the rank of a three-squadron commander,' drawled Ranegale.

Stormrane's face hardened and he looked away to the horizon as if he had noticed something moving on it. 'Between the South Road and the Ringwall, the land narrows all the way to Makar. It would be preferable if we were to hold back: the longer we wait the more the line will stretch, pulling open the gaps between the dragons.'

He held up a knotted cord for all to see. 'This only holds fifteen days. Pulling the drag-cradles through mud we'll need every one of those to reach the meeting in time.'

'Do you think we'll make it, father?' asked Ravan, hope in his face.

Stormrane smiled. 'Of course we will, son.'

Cloud had become sombre. 'Let's hope so. Our tribes sent us to protect our tributaries. Only a few days remain before we're supposed to meet them in Makar. If we're late, they might try crossing the Leper Valleys without us.'

Ranegale fixed them with a baleful eye. 'And will you, Father Stormrane, and what's left of your line take it upon yourselves to look after the Standing Dead?'

Grimly, Stormrane glanced at Fern, then gave a nod.

As he leaned against the neck of Carnelian's kneeling aquar, the youth stared at him without a blink. It was easier to ignore that stare than the constant throbbing ache of his body. Sleep with its grinding, bitter nightmares was a poor refuge. Carnelian tried instead to distract himself by concentrating his attention on the demolition of the kraal tower. More of the barbarian youths were swarming its upper storeys, tearing off the woven matting to get at the scaffolding beneath. Poles that had been worked free were being fed down to the kraal bridge, where the men were splitting them with axes.

When his aquar stirred and seemed about to rise, Carnelian gritted his teeth, anticipating agony. Through his lidded eyes he watched the youth reach up and caress the creature's eye-plume fans closed. Carnelian looked for what had disturbed the aquar and saw Stormrane and Fern approaching. The older man had the same slow pained walk Carnelian's wounded father had had as they journeyed along the leftway to Osrakum. Snatches of that other life formed and melted before his mind's eye. He glimpsed but would not allow to fully surface the thought of his father exposed to Ykoriana's malice. For a moment it was better to relive what had been. Back on the leftway. It was strange that dark time should now appear so bright. At least then, a few pieces of his world had still remained unscattered.

Feeling someone beside him, he looked up. Grief sat over Fern's face like a mask. Carnelian saw the brown eyes registering surprise, perhaps at detecting his compassion, but then they flicked away.

'This one's conscious,' Fern said to his father, in their tongue.

36

Carnelian considered the man who had saved him from the slavers. His eyes were drawn to the brass bright against Fern's dark throat. The boss bore no legionary cypher and the band appeared to be free of rank and service sliders.

Carnelian became aware Fern was watching him. As their eyes meshed the barbarian erupted into anger.

'You have to get out of the saddle-chair,' he said in thickly accented Vulgate.

'I don't have the strength,' Carnelian said.

'We'll lift you.'

Carnelian saw the opportunity. 'Did you have to lift the other Master?'

'We don't have time for debate.' Stormrane grabbed Carnelian's arm and pulled on it.

Carnelian cried out as his spine twisted.

Fern's voice came through the ringing pain. 'You're hurting him.'

Carnelian opened his eyes and saw Stormrane throwing off his son's restraining hand. Carnelian could not help noticing it lacked a middle finger.

'If you're so concerned about this one, you sort him out,' snapped Stormrane. He snatched the shoulder of the staring youth and led him away. Fern watched them go with the look of one who had just been slapped. He became aware of Carnelian.

'Though he is an angel, your friend burns with fever.'

Carnelian looked from the barbarian's four-fingered hand into his face, fear for Osidian freezing everything else out. 'Can you let me see him?'

The barbarian crossed his arms, hiding his mutilated hands in his armpits.

'I can hardly tell you apart. Are you brothers?'

Carnelian was touched by the man's vulnerability.

'Well?'

Carnelian regarded the frowning mahogany face and wondered what answer to give. A nod was safer than the truth. 'Please show me where he is?'

Fern shook his head. 'We don't want you near each other.'

Carnelian considered befriending this barbarian by confessing that he understood their tongue, but decided this was an advantage he could ill afford to give away.

'You mean, the older man that was here doesn't.'

Fern's face darkened. 'That *older man* is my father, who with good reason blames you for the killing of our kin.'

'Do you?'

'What do you think!'

Carnelian caught a look in Fern's face that belied his words. 'Can you do anything for . . . my brother's fever?'

Fern looked surprised. 'You believe it possible he might die?'

Carnelian worried about what power his answer might lose him.

Fern frowned. 'If he were like other men there would be a chance he might wake from it. Until then, all that can be done for him is to give him water and what food he will swallow.'

Carnelian saw he had to speak. 'He *is* a man.'

Clearly, Fern had difficulty believing this.

'Will you see to feeding him yourself?'

When Fern gave a ragged nod, Carnelian decided that would have to be enough. The man made motions indicating that Carnelian should climb out of the saddle-chair. Twisting sent a deepening stab into his back.

'Perhaps it'd be better if I stay here.'

Fern set his jaw. 'No.'

'Are you afraid I'll escape?'

'Why wouldn't you?'

Carnelian was reluctant to attempt an explanation. 'How far could I get without reins?'

Fern's mouth curved with contempt. 'Real riders don't need them.'

Carnelian was too weak to argue.

It took them a while to manoeuvre him out on to the ground. He stood, swaying a little, stooping to relieve the agony which was squeezing a cold sweat from his skin.

Looking at Fern's feet, Carnelian began chuckling. The dark mirth bubbled out until over it he could hear the man, puzzled, asking him what was happening.

Carnelian managed to speak. 'I was just thinking . . .' Chuckling took over again. 'I might . . . might be more comfortable if you gave me back my ropes.'

Rain ran down Carnelian's face. It was the only part of him exposed. The rest sloped down to where, just beyond his feet, the two poles of the drag-cradle were gouging the earth. He could see their double track scratching off over the wake of chopped-up mud left by the aquar. Beyond, the land stretched featureless, greyed by the down-pour. Above him the tail of Fern's aquar swung like a tiller, narrowing to a whip that sometimes stroked his feet. Blankets and leather bands swaddled him to the drag-cradle frame. It quivered with each step the aquar took. Dozing, Carnelian thought he was back on the accursed ship that had brought him with his father and his brothers from their island to the shore of the Three Lands and the Commonwealth of the Masters.

When day began fading to night, the barbarians called a halt. The stillness of the drag-cradle came as a blessed relief. Fern walked out in front of Carnelian, his face haggard, his legs and cloak splattered with mud. He was motioning instructions. Carnelian felt a tremor in the frame. Turning his head, he saw brown hands holding on to the wood.

'What're they doing?' he asked.

Fern glanced down at him. 'Unhitching your drag-cradle from my aquar.'

His dark eyes flicked away. The frame gave a shudder that awoke Carnelian's pain. With a rasping, he felt the poles come free even as the aquar's tail started feeding away over him, its tip dragging up the blankets towards his face. He closed his eyes, anticipating its touch, but then he felt the frame being lowered to the ground.

He opened his eyes and blinked away the rain. 'What news of the dragons?' he said to no one in particular.

Fern loomed over him, issuing instructions in their barbarian tongue. Carnelian could hear the suck and splash of footfalls as the youths moved away.

Fern's face came close enough to Carnelian's that it sheltered him from the rain. He examined Fern's brown eyes. He could smell him and feel the heat of his anger.

Fern bared his teeth. 'Don't imagine they'll rescue you. I'd kill you myself before I let that happen.'

He disappeared. When the constant patter of rain on Carnelian's face had cooled his own anger, he began to wonder if he was going to be left all night in the rain. When Fern returned, it was to force some strips of leather into Carnelian's mouth which he had to chew or else choke. It was only as his mouth began to fill with musty flavour that he realized it was dried meat.

For days, Carnelian was dragged through a constant pelting rain. His blankets clung heavy and sodden. Often the mud grew so deep the poles stuck fast. As Fern's aquar struggled to break loose, Carnelian would suffer with each shudder. Though the barbarians were always hidden from him, he could hear the desperation in their voices as they urged their aquar on. Their march was a monotonous slap and suck amidst the downpour. Carnelian knew they were sending lookouts ahead. A voice would shout something down from the sky. The raiders would not pause but would continue on until the kraal tower would slide into Carnelian's view and he would watch it shrink and fade.

Each evening as the day was squeezed black by the rumbling sky, Fern fed him more strips of dried meat. Carnelian lubricated his chewing by opening his mouth and letting it fill with rain. When asked, Fern would confirm Osidian's condition unchanged. His moroseness discouraged conversation. Ravan was often there, resentful as he helped his brother with the feeding, with the unhitching, with the hitching that every morning freed Carnelian from the blinding rain. As he was angled up he was able to blink his eyes open and peer blearily at the infinite, drear monotony of the Guarded Land.

Against that landscape, Fern and his brother were often the only living things Carnelian could see. He became intuitive in reading their moods, seeing past the masks of fear they wore. Their grief was deepening and he felt he knew the cause: he could not recall the last time he had heard their father's voice.

The raiders pressed on towards Makar. Each day that passed put another twist of dread into their stomachs as they searched the horizon for the scouring line and its dragons.

The drag-cradle came suddenly to a halt. Carnelian heard Ravan cry out, then Fern. Young voices were making a commotion. Carnelian shook himself out of his stupor, anxious to know what was going on. Facing away from the barbarians, all he could do was strain to pick out their voices.

'Does he live?' asked Ranegale. There were some words Carnelian could not catch, then: 'Put him back in his saddle-chair.'

'We must make another cradle.' Fern's voice, sounding frightened.

'We've no time for that,' said Ranegale.

'We'll make time.' Cloud's voice. 'Do you really believe he'd be lying there in the mud, if he had the strength to ride?'

'He gave you the cord, Cloud. How many knots does it hold now?'

For a while Carnelian could hear only the whispering of the youths.

'Seven.'

'Our best hope is that whatever's delaying the scouring line will keep it in Makar for five days more. That's already bleak enough don't you think, Father Cloud? And now you've decided to back Fern in what will cause us at least half a day's delay.'

'Let's dump one of the Standing Dead,' said Ravan. 'My one's fever is going to get him anyway so we might as well use his cradle for my father.'

Ranegale's nasal voice rose to a bellow: 'No. We need them both alive.'

'Why?' demanded Cloud.

There was a silence during which Carnelian struggled but the leather bands were too tight.

'Why doesn't my father let us all in on his plan to get through the scouring line should we run into it.'

'My plan is that which Stormrane trusted me with. We fire some kraals and when the auxiliaries come to see what's happening we slip through the gap they leave in the line.'

There were murmurs of support.

'So you all feel this is a good plan, eh? I'd like to see you set fire to rain-sodden wood.'

Voices rose in protest.

'Listen. Listen! That's not really important. If you'll listen, I'll tell you what is. Have you any idea how close the roads have come on either side of us?'

They all fell silent.

'I can see you do. Well, imagine now how close together the aquar twenties will be in the line. It will be a city wall with dragons as its towers. Most of us have seen how fast dragons can move and we all know perfectly well how swift unburdened aquar run. The Standing Dead in the dragons' towers will spot us the moment we make a break for it. They'll close the gap like this.'

A slap like whiplash.

'Then we'll just have to creep through at night,' said Fern.

'If you'd stayed in the legions more than a few days you wouldn't be saying anything so stupid. They'll set their fires close enough for their light to overlap. Even if they didn't we'd never be able to time it. No. If we run into them there's only one way we'll get through. We'll have to move one of the dragons out of line.'

Everyone began shouting at once. Carnelian strained to hear Ranegale's voice among the others. He caught the phrase, 'Standing Dead'. The hubbub quietened.

'We'll leave them both, or maybe just one of them, in a kraal to be found by the auxiliaries.'

'Rather than suffer death for having looked on them, they'd murder them,' said Fern. 'How would their commanders ever find out?'

'We'll tie them up to the kraal's outer wall so they can be seen from the dragon towers. Of course the poor bastards will all die for seeing our Standing Dead, but it'll bring a dragon. With luck, more than one.'

'And you think this would make a breach in their line big enough for us to race through?' asked Cloud. From the tone of his voice Carnelian could tell the Elder was already half convinced.

'You're going to hand them over alive?' asked Fern, incredulous.

'If we give them corpses, the auxiliaries will leave them guarded in a kraal and then hunt us down,' said Ranegale.

'And alive, our Standing Dead will bring them down on us like lightning,' said Fern.

'Can you imagine the confusion when they find two living Standing Dead out here? Dead they'll bring down swift vengeance: alive, perhaps they'll open us a door in the scouring line. We'll flee towards Makar. Once we reach the pass we'll lose any pursuit. They'll never find us in the Earthsky.'

'They'll close the pass against us,' said Fern.

'Their laws forbid it for at least another twenty days.'

'Don't you think they'll overturn their laws to avenge two of their own?'

'Cloud, give me the reckoning cord.'

Carnelian could hear the movement of an aquar.

'Look at how few knots lie between us and Makar. If this cloud cover holds they won't be able to use the speaking mirrors. Their couriers, we might outrun.'

'With drag-cradles?' asked Cloud.

'We'll have to ditch those,' said Ranegale. 'Glare all you like, Fern. You know as well as I do there's no other way.'

'Fern,' Cloud said. 'You can cut their hearts out, take them home and, in your koppie, give them to the sky.'

'What about my father?' Fern demanded.

'Ranegale, are you sure we need both the Standing Dead?' Loskai interrupted.

'They're our only hope and one of them already looks like he might die,' said Ranegale. 'Besides, we might be able to use the trick twice to widen the opening in the line. We daren't throw away any chance.'

'What . . . about . . . my . . . father?' Ravan squeezed the words out one at a time through his rage.

As the barbarians fell to arguing Carnelian closed his eyes. The pain in Ravan's voice had awoken in him a memory of the anguish he had known on the road when his own wounded father had been close to death. He forced himself to work out what he should do. When he had it, to make sure they would listen, he hardened his heart and became a Master. When he spoke, his voice had the characteristic resonance of power.

'What is all that noise about?'

The arguing died. Carnelian felt the judder as Fern jumped down from his saddle-chair. He heard the sucking footfalls of aquar approaching. The ground trembled as they began moving round into sight. Barbarian faces frowned down at him, then Fern appeared at his side. Seeing the pain in his face, Carnelian faltered, dropping the attempt at imperiousness.

'Tell me what all the arguing is about. Please.'

Ranegale's eye flashed. 'Why should we tell you anything?'

Fern looked to Cloud, who shrugged. 'What harm can it do?'

Once he had Fern's gaze again, Carnelian held it as the man began recounting the arguments.

'Well then,' Carnelian said, when Fern was done. 'The solution is simple. Your father must lie here and I'll take his place in the saddle-chair.'

Ravan stared. Ranegale sneered through the cloth wrapped around his face, 'We might not be angels, Master, but that doesn't make us fools.'

Without disengaging his eyes, from Carnelian's, Fern said: 'He wouldn't try to escape as long as we hold the other Master. They're brothers.'

'Will he be any more able to ride than Stormrane?' asked Cloud.

Carnelian had seen the hope that had come into Fern's eyes. Though he had understood Cloud's words, he made Fern translate them for him.

'Do you believe I'm as enfeebled as your father?' he asked him.

Fern's pain and grief turned to anger. 'Why are you doing this?'

Carnelian wanted to tell him that he understood; that once his own father had been wounded. The word 'compassion' was on his lips, but he swallowed it. It was not a word they would believe coming from a Master's mouth.

'I wish to ensure you use Ranegale's plan. I know you'll not leave your father behind.' He glanced at Ranegale. 'In the end I don't think even he would leave him behind . . . not alive anyway. If they found your father alive, the legion would get from him the name of your tribe. You're wise to fear the Masters. If they can, they will exterminate you and all your people for what you've seen and done. Other options will cause a delay. Any delay makes it more likely you'll be forced to try Stormrane's plan. If you managed to elude the line, what would you do with us? I fear you would kill us, hide us in the earth, hope the vengeance of the Masters would be blinded and not find you.'

Ranegale's eye glared down at Carnelian. 'Have you considered, Master, that speed might bring us to Makar before the legion sets out?'

The blankets suppressed Carnelian's shrug. 'I'd consider it if your voice weren't telling me you don't believe it yourself.'

Ranegale frowned and Carnelian saw he had the knotted cord pulled tight between his fists. 'Free him and we'll see if he can ride.'

Fern released the bands that bound Carnelian to the drag-cradle, then peeled off the sodden blankets. The eyes of the barbarians on him, Carnelian turned with a groan to clutch one of the drag-cradle's poles. He allowed Fern to help him up. Ravan hung around in the background, uncertain whether to help. Tottering, Carnelian forced his spine straight. He took some steps towards the kneeling aquar swimming at the centre of his vision. He leaned on Fern, who, somehow, managed to help him into the saddle-chair.

'Her name's Blur,' Fern whispered in Carnelian's ear.

At his touch the aquar rose, thrusting Carnelian up towards the stormy sky. He clawed hold of the chair.

'Are you all right?' Fern asked.

Carnelian nodded. Ravan and the others were lifting Stormrane into the drag-cradle. Fern was freeing something from the side of the saddle-chair. Glancing down, Carnelian saw it was a spear. His eyes followed the haft to the head. He stared.

'Sky-metal,' he said, in Quya.

'What?' said Fern.

Carnelian pointed at the rusty iron spearhead that was the length of his hand.

Fern frowned at the spear. 'It is my father's, passed down through his line from father to son.' His frown deepened as he hefted it. Carnelian wondered if Fern was considering that it might soon pass to him.

'It's a precious heirloom.'

Fern regarded him. 'I shall not claim it.'

'You know its worth?'

'I'm not my father's true son,' he said, bitterly.

Carnelian realized Fern and the other barbarians could have no idea they had in their possession fabulous wealth. Though, when he considered it, it was wealth that could not easily be realized. Who but the Masters could afford such a treasure? To offer iron for sale was more likely to bring death than riches.

Fern was speaking. 'Can you move further up the chair?' He tapped the spear on the crossbeam of bundled rods that ran transversely across the aquar's back and stuck out on either side. 'Grip this with the back of your knees.'

Carnelian's buttocks were hard against it. As he pushed himself up the chair he felt as if his back were tearing apart. He was hardly aware of Fern's hand helping him.

'The chair's too small for you but we don't have the time to adjust it now.'

He helped Carnelian angle his shins so he could get his feet to the aquar's back.

'She's used to my father and will not respond well to kicking. If you lift your feet from her back, she'll kneel. To move right or left, apply more pressure on that side. To make her pick up speed, rock your feet from heel to toe.' He took hold of one of Blur's three-fingered hands to keep her steady. 'Try it.'

Carnelian found it was harder than it sounded. Feeling his foot being gripped, he leaned forward to watch Fern moving it in the way he had described. Sensing Carnelian's eyes on him, Fern let the foot go.

'To stop her, dig your heels in.'

Carnelian made some ineffectual attempts to follow the instructions. Fern twitched a smile at him.

'You'll pick it up. For the moment, just make sure you keep your feet flat on her back and she'll shoal with the others.'

As Fern had said, Blur maintained her position in the midst of the other aquar with no need of Carnelian's directing. But he failed to find a posture in which her every footfall did not jar his spine.

Carnelian was trying to doze when it occurred to him there was nothing stopping him from seeing Osidian. Recalling Fern's instructions, he dug his heels gently into his aquar's back. Blur slowed and the other aquar began passing by on either side. As she came to a halt, Carnelian searched the drag-cradles. There were four. Two carried Fern's uncle and brother, their corpse faces slimy with rain. In another he recognized Stormrane's grey tousled head. Furthest away, the fourth held nothing that looked like Osidian. Carnelian heard Ranegale's cry and looked up to see him stopped and looking round. Carnelian hardly noticed Fern coming up to Ranegale and paid no attention to their quarrelling. The whole group were beginning to pull away from him.

He focused his attention on the fourth drag-cradle and tried to apply Fern's lessons. Rocking both his feet from heel to toe, he made Blur begin walking. He tried putting more pressure on his left foot. Sweat running down his back, he held to his purpose and, to his delight, Blur veered towards the cradle. When they were near it, he sagged back and left it to her to match her stride smoothly to the rest.

The drag-cradle looked like the pupae of some monstrous butterfly. He managed to find a face, but did not immediately recognize it as Osidian's. Faded to brown, the bitumen made the white skin showing through appear to be leprosy. He could see nothing of the familiar beauty, nor any sign of life. There seemed not enough of the man he loved even to make Carnelian grieve. Osidian's life had reversed the order of things. He was a butterfly who had returned to melt his beauty into the filthy casing of a chrysalis. Carnelian could not bear to imagine what of Osidian might survive. It was better he should die. How could there be a life for him worth having in this outer world? Should Ranegale's plan work they might be found and then, no doubt, be returned to Osrakum. Even if Osidian were to reach there alive, he would suffer the death the Law decreed for those who were brothers to a new God Emperor. Over his corpse, Carnelian would accuse those responsible for the kidnapping, the defilement. He would unmask Ykoriana and Jaspar's schemes. He would liberate his father from whatever punishment they had inflicted on him. He, Suth Carnelian, would have his revenge on all of them. He closed his eyes, savouring it.

Laughter rattled his chest like a fit of coughing. It seemed the greatest irony that it was only now he had become a slave and captive that he should have finally acquired the taste for vengeance of a true Master.

Slow lightning was playing over the bellies of the clouds.

A word was passing among the raiders like a rumour. 'Dragonfire.'

Carnelian watched the next burst flicker for a while, then die. Looking round at the barbarians, he could see their fear. Voices made bleak requests about stopping, but Ranegale insisted they must push on until they reach the next kraal.

They headed towards the silent, flickering dragonfire until, at last, they reached a kraal. Ranegale scaled its tower accompanied by Loskai and Cloud. Carnelian waited with the others, his heart fluttering between hope and a bleak desire that the coming crisis should be delayed.

When the men came down it was obvious they had seen nothing but the dragonfire. Everyone was glad when Ranegale declared they would camp there for the night. Carnelian lifted his feet from Blur's back and she sank to the ground. He bowed his head as he mustered the endurance to climb out.

'Fern sent me to help,' a voice said in a thick Vulgate.

Carnelian lifted his head and saw it was a youth he did not know.

'I'm . . .' The youth hesitated, then smiled. 'Krow, from Father Cloud's tribe.'

In the uncertainty of that smile Carnelian could see the fears that had been haunting everyone for days. He let the youth take his weight and slowly they managed to get him standing. Carnelian lent back against the saddle-chair fearing he might faint.

'She's a good one,' said Krow.

Carnelian looked at him not understanding.

'This aquar . . .' said the youth, patting the creature's neck.

'Yes,' said Carnelian.

'I could try and adjust her chair for you, if you'd like.'

'You're kind but I'll not have much further need of it.' He indicated the flickering sky.

When Krow turned to look, Carnelian saw fear peeping through. 'You've never seen it before?'

The youth turned to look at him, then shook his head.

'Neither have I,' Carnelian admitted. Krow looked incredulous.

'No, really.'

They waited for the sky to light up again and then watched it until Carnelian noticed Fern approaching. He looked so morose Carnelian felt compelled to say something. Pointing he called out: 'No doubt you've seen dragonfire often before.'

As Fern blushed, Carnelian remembered his legionary collar had no sliders and he regretted his clumsiness.

Fern locked eyes with him. 'We're going to have to remove the bitumen from your skins. Krow here will help.'

'And Ravan?'

Fern sent Krow away to fetch some water. 'My brother and his father are very close.'

'He blames me,' said Carnelian, sadly.

'Does that surprise you?'

Carnelian held Fern's gaze. 'I can't regret that you saved our lives but I do regret at what cost.'

Fern looked down at his hands. 'Do you need help walking?'

'I'll manage, thank you.' They moved off, Carnelian enduring the awkwardness of each step.

'How far away are the dragons?' he asked to distract himself from the prospect that he was soon going to look upon Osidian.

'We'll meet the line tomorrow. That's why we've got to wash you now.'

'Of course.'

As they had reached the drag-cradles, Osidian's bitumen-mottled face came into view all glazed with sweat. Carnelian helped Fern undo the bands. Though a faded black, the blanket covering Osidian was woven with blue patterns that reminded Carnelian uncannily of those Ebeny had woven. He stared at it for a moment, remembering her. It strengthened his belief she had come originally from the same stock as the raiders. He reached out to touch the blanket but it was too damp for him to be able to tell if it had the same texture as Ebeny's. What he did feel were the tremors coursing through the body beneath.

'Fever,' said Fern.

'Yes,' said Carnelian.

'Soon you'll both be free.'

Carnelian glanced at Osidian's face.

'You don't seem overjoyed,' said Fern.

Carnelian looked up. 'He'll die.'

'You can't know that.' Fern frowned as he saw the certainty in Carnelian's face. 'How did you come to be among sartlar?'

'That's too long a tale for now,' said Carnelian. He busied himself peeling the blankets from Osidian's body. The rags the slavers had put on him could not conceal the shivering in his limbs and chest.

Fern put his hand on Carnelian's arm. 'At least tell me why you gave up your drag-cradle for my father?'

Carnelian looked into the barbarian's dark eyes. 'I remembered my own father who once was wounded and near to death.'

'Compassion?' Fern said with such disbelief that it made Carnelian ashamed to be a Master.

They crouched on either side of the drag-cradle. It was Krow appearing with a leather bowl that rescued Carnelian's composure. The bowl regained its shape as the youth put it down and Carnelian saw it was filled with brackish water. They removed Osidian's rags and all three began to wash him.

Carnelian could not help but contrast this with the time he had cleaned him in the Yden. To do for him what only slaves did had been a proof of love. Carnelian tried to hide his tears by leaning over Osidian, rubbing at the brown-edged bitumen patching his face.

'He's so bright,' said Krow in wonder.

'Angelic beauty,' breathed Fern.

Carnelian wiped his eyes and muttered, 'You've not seen the green fire of his eyes.'

'Can they differ much from yours?' Fern asked.

Uncomfortable, Carnelian busied himself with cleaning one of Osidian's stained eyepits. He could not help feeling he was preparing him for the tomb. Carnelian imagined Osidian and himself naked, gleaming bait for the dragons. Of course they would be taken back to Osrakum. No doubt the Wise would come themselves to the Three Gates to oversee a special purification before they should be let in. They would bleed Osidian; embalm him with myrrh. Carnelian leaned to kiss the cold stone lips. He could not bear that the Chosen should see him thus. Osidian's pride would have baulked at appearing so dishonoured; a piece of meat. Carnelian grew angry wishing to keep him from their eyes, their sneers. What delight they would take in witnessing one who had been almost the Gods, brought so low. Come what may, Carnelian determined he would find a way to bury Osidian in the Guarded Land's red earth where they would never find him.

Slowly, carefully, he straightened his back. He watched Fern rubbing away at Osidian's birthmark and he put his hand on his arm.

'He was born with that.'

The barbarian looked at Osidian with a strange intensity of which Carnelian was hardly aware. His life was a bitter taste in his mouth. Could he deny Osidian the second waking of the tomb, however high the price? What else then could he do but take him back to be slain in Osrakum?

He became aware Fern and Krow were staring at him.

'Couldn't you make two masks of leather to hide our faces?' he asked and saw they did not understand. 'The auxiliaries who look on us tomorrow will be killed.'

Fern's eyebrows rose but then he shook his head. 'It's your white faces Ranegale is hoping to use as bait.'

Carnelian stood naked in the midst of the barbarians, who were getting their aquar ready to make the dash through the scouring line. Ranegale and Cloud were up in the kraal tower trying to spy the dragons. Carnelian's gaze fell on Osidian. The bruised marble of his body had been laid out on a blanket. His legs stretched beyond it into the mud. Carnelian had covered him with another to shield him from any rain, though there had been none since dawn. His gaze lingered on this second blanket. Its indigo-patterned russet was so like Ebeny's it was hard to believe she had not woven it. Beside Osidian lay the corpses of Fern's uncle and brother, weighing the air with the sickening stench of their decay. Stormrane lay beyond them. He had died some time in the night. Fern was crouched over him, mourning, the misery of the decisions that would soon come upon him clear on his face. His back turned, Ravan was gouging a channel in the mud with his heel. Several times Carnelian had seen him glancing at his father, his face sick with sorrow. Around them, already in their saddle-chairs the youths sat, some staring at nothing, others intensely checking knots, testing the tension of ropes or, absentmindedly, caressing the necks of their aquar with their feet. Sometimes one would sneak a glance up at the tower.

Carnelian knew that when Ranegale came down it would be time to help them carry Osidian round to the other side of the kraal; the side exposed to the dragon line. Carnelian and Osidian would be bound to the two posts the barbarians had worked into the ground. From there, Carnelian would watch the scouring line draw nearer. He would have a good view of the consternation of the auxiliaries, their terror when they discovered the two Masters. A dragon would approach and one of the Chosen would descend from the tower on its back. The auxiliaries would be slain for having looked upon a Master's face. Perhaps Carnelian might even see them lit like torches by dragonfire. The Chosen commander would find masks for him and Osidian and they would ascend into the dragon's tower. He imagined the commander's reaction. Pity perhaps. A confusion of emotions when he, being of the Lesser Chosen, discovered they were of the Great. The questions, the endless questions all of which Carnelian would refuse to answer. Perhaps the legion would halt the scouring while a message was sent to the nearest watch-tower. From there, if Ranegale had been right, the watch-tower's ammonites might have to wait for nightfall before they could use flares to jump their messages from tower to tower all the way to Osrakum. No later than the next morning the Wise would know that two of the Great had been found naked in the midst of the Guarded Land. How would they react?

'Master?'

Carnelian turned to see Krow, his head bowed.

'Will you send the dragons after us down into the Earthsky?'

Carnelian considered it for a moment. He realized he was already beginning to feel like a Master again. It was almost as if he were towering before the youth in a court robe. He knew that should he demand it, Krow would kneel in the mud and worship him. He shook himself free from that mood and saw standing before him not a slave but a human youth. This could be his brother Tain or many others of his people. He felt ashamed. Krow had shown him kindness even though Carnelian was of the race who oppressed his people.

He reached out to touch Krow's shoulder. 'I'll do everything in my power to make them forget you.'

The youth gave him a trembling smile, a nod, then walked away.

Carnelian's gaze fell upon the miserable figure of Ravan regarding his kin lying dead in the mud. Carnelian could not help contrasting this with his own certain hope that soon he would be rejoining his own father and brothers. Compassion made him approach the grieving youth. As he neared the corpses, his disgust at their decay was overcome by pity. In a way these dead were his fault too. He noticed the tattoos Stormrane held in his hand and, crouching down, turned his head to read them. One gave the reign year, Ten Nuhuron appended to which, for some reason, was the number nine. Presumably the first two components showed the year in which Stormrane had enlisted in the legions. Carnelian mused that this was a couple of years after Ebeny had been sent to Osrakum to pay her people's flesh tithe. Below the date glyph was another larger and more complicated one that he was surprised to find he was unable to read. He peered closer, trying to decipher it by reading its syllabic components. Still a reading eluded him. He allowed his eye to wander here and there allowing combinations to release their sounds in his mind. Snatches of almost words but nothing that made any sense. What might the glyph be for? As he considered this, his eye found, scattered through the glyph, the three syllables making up the Quyan word ten; the same as the reign year. He concentrated on the components left and found, similarly scattered, the name Makar. He read the three remaining components aloud.

Ravan spun round eyes and mouth agape. 'How . . . how do you know?'

'Know? Know what?'

'The name of our tribe.'

'Your . . . ?' Carnelian stopped. He pronounced his utterance in the language of the barbarians. 'Ochre,' he said.

Ravan looked as if he were just about to be sick.

Carnelian reached over to lift Stormrane's left hand.

'Don't touch him,' cried Ravan. Before the youth snatched the hand from his grasp, Carnelian saw that it too held glyphs; mostly numbers.

Fern came running up. 'What're you doing to my father?'

Carnelian stood up to face him. 'When you cut out their hearts you must also take their hands.'

Fern looked incredulous. 'Hands?'

Carnelian reached out and took Fern's hand. The barbarian allowed him to splay the palm and read the tattoos there. Fourteen Kumatuya Nine, with, below it, another large glyph which contained 'fourteen' and also 'Makar'. The components remaining once again spelled out the name of Fern's tribe rendered into Quyan sounds.

Carnelian looked into Fern's eyes. 'All those of you who've been auxiliaries carry the name of your tribes tattooed on your hands. If the Masters find these bodies as they are, they'll know they're Ochre and will visit their vengeance on your people.'

Fern paled. 'But you know it and you're a Master.'

'But I won't –'

Carnelian was interrupted by Cloud rushing out from the kraal. 'They've found us,' he cried. 'Up, up, all of you. We must flee.'

Everything erupted into motion. Aquar squealed and flared their plumes as they lurched up, their riders clinging to their chairs.

Cloud strode forward. 'Auxiliaries riding fast in our direction,' he said quickly. 'A dragon's coming up behind them.'

Fern looked wildly at the dead. He drew a flint knife.

'Don't hurt father,' sobbed Ravan.

Carnelian grabbed Fern's shoulder. 'There's no time.'

Fern looked around desperately. 'But you've just told me we can't leave them.'

Carnelian grimaced.

Ranegale rode up. 'We'll have to kill the Standing Dead now,' he said in the barbarian language.

Carnelian looked deep into his single eye. 'You're welcome to try,' he said in Vulgate.

Fern gave him a startled glance before turning to Ranegale. 'Would you stay to bury them?'

'They're your problem.' Ranegale forced his aquar towards them so that Carnelian and Fern had to throw themselves from its path, then coursed away, followed by the majority of the others.

Carnelian saw the remaining aquar still crouching with empty chairs. 'Fern. Quickly. I'll help you tie their bodies into the saddle-chairs.'

Fern gaped and Carnelian could see the agony of indecision in his face, but then the barbarian gave a violent nod.

'Ravan,' he cried and the youth rushed up to help.

They lugged Stormrane's corpse, then hoisted it into Fern's saddle-chair. The pain in Carnelian's back made him more of a hindrance than an aid. He cast around for some way to help. He saw the blankets lying on the mud. He stooped to take one and was soon tearing it into strips.

Once all the corpses were stowed, Carnelian gave the two brothers some strips and helped them tie the corpses into the chairs.

Krow rode up. 'Hurry!'

Carnelian glanced round. Osidian lay under the russet blanket as if asleep. He frowned, seeing their return to Osrakum; seeing

Osidian being bled for ritual. Panic rose in him. He tried to fight it with thoughts of seeing his father, his people. He tried to imagine the meeting with them, but the vision would not come. There was no joy. He told himself they needed him. His return with Osidian would damage Ykoriana's power, perhaps bring her down. He would save his father from her.

Carnelian tried not to look at Osidian, but his eyes would not obey him. He gazed at the face of his beloved. 'You cannot save him,' he muttered.

This reverie was interrupted by Fern grasping his shoulder. 'Well here we part, Master. Thanks.'

Carnelian looked at his friend. The sincerity in his face gave rise to an impossible hope.

'Take us with you,' Carnelian blurted before doubt could make a coward of him.

Fern gaped. 'What?'

The man's honest puzzlement set the decision steady in Carnelian's heart. He pointed at Osidian. 'If the Masters take us, they'll kill him.'

Fern took a step back. 'But . . . but *you* in the Earthsky . . . it makes no sense.'

'We've nowhere else to go.'

Fern's eyes took in his kin sitting tied to their chairs, then returned to linger on Carnelian. He spun round. 'Ravan, I'll ride with you.'

Carnelian's panic returned. This was madness. Then he felt as if he was choking. What about his father?

Ravan was protesting but Fern cut through with a bellow: 'You'll do as you're told.' He turned and looked at Carnelian. 'Well, don't just stand there!'

Carnelian began moving towards Osidian. He tried to reassure himself that the Great would protect his father, if only to defend their ancient privileges from encroachment by the new God Emperor.

Fern was pointing at Osidian. 'Krow, will you give your aquar up for that one?'

Krow stared down, paralysed by fear.

'We can't leave the Standing Dead here,' cried Fern.

Krow turned in his saddle-chair searching, crying out: 'Father Cloud, Father Cloud.'

Fern rushed up and grabbed the youth's foot. 'That one,' he pointed at Carnelian, 'read the name of my tribe from the picture on my father's hand. By warning us, he saved my people. We owe him. Please, give up your seat and ride with him; Blur's stronger than your aquar and will more easily carry you both.'

Krow glanced over at Carnelian, then made his aquar kneel. Fern lurched over to Osidian, stooped, threw the blanket off him and, with a grunt, tried to lift him. He grimaced under the strain.

Carnelian rushed to help and together they dragged Osidian to Krow's saddle-chair, crammed him in and secured him as they had the dead.

'Come on,' shrieked Ravan. Carnelian turned to see Krow holding Blur for him. The drizzle that had begun to fall made Carnelian aware of his nakedness. He scooped the russet blanket from the ground and wrapped it around his waist.

'We must go *now*,' roared Fern as he vaulted into Ravan's saddle-chair. Carnelian ran over to where Krow was still holding Blur. He climbed into her chair and hooked his legs over the crossbeam.

Krow clambered in on top of him. 'Make her rise.'

Carnelian pressed his feet into her back and Blur swayed them into the air.

'Follow us,' Fern cried. Over Krow's head, Carnelian saw Ravan's aquar lurch into a run, then Blur was loping after her.

INTIMATIONS

What choice has a river in running down to the sea?
(from the 'Ilkaya', part of the holy scriptures of the Chosen)

EASTWARDS, BENEATH A GLOWERING SKY, CARNELIAN COULD SEE nothing moving but Ranegale and the other raiders until he noticed, obscured by distant rainfall, a mass of riders scudding towards them.

Fern and Ravan's aquar fell back to ride alongside Blur. Fern squinted round his brother. 'You lead the undirected aquar deep in among the others, we'll stay behind to make sure none stray.'

Krow jerked a nod and Carnelian rocked his feet to make Blur pick up pace. Krow shifted his weight as he looked behind them.

'They're following.'

Soon Blur was moving up among the other raiders whose aquar were maintaining a steady pace.

'We must go deeper in,' said Krow.

Carnelian urged Blur forward until they had almost caught up with Ranegale and Loskai. They scowled when they saw Carnelian, but it was when they saw the dead tied into their chairs that their eyes widened with disbelief. Ranegale began haranguing Krow, speaking too fast for Carnelian to follow. He squinted into the faces of the riders around him to see if he could read in them what was being said. Brittle with fear, the youths were gazing past Ranegale oblivious to the quarrel. Carnelian saw that the auxiliaries were still pouring towards them, but it was something beyond that was the focus of the youths' gaze. A shape was interrupting the regular pattern of kraal towers. Carnelian turned to stone as he realized he was seeing a dragon.

Ranegale fell silent as he became aware of the fear stiffening every face. More dragon silhouettes were appearing among the kraal towers, dwarfing them. Squadrons of riders welled over the ground before them. The auxiliaries they had seen before were beginning to veer away, northwards. The gap between them and the scouring line was occupied by a single dragon.

'His pipes are lit,' cried Cloud in Vulgate and Carnelian looked for and found, rising from the dragon, a tiny scratch of smoke that reminded him of plague sign.

'We can swing round to the left of him,' said Ranegale, pointing his mutilated hand north-east. 'You see where the auxiliaries have left a gap?'

'He must see us,' said Cloud, his voice tight.

'Let's make a dash for it,' cried Loskai.

'No,' roared Ranegale, 'we mustn't commit our aquar until we're sure the gap is real.'

Tension grew as more and more of the scouring line came into sight. The dragon from which smoke was rising was well ahead of the others. Behind it, the line stretched north and south as far as Carnelian could see. He kept glancing off to his left, expecting to see the auxiliaries there charging towards them.

'That lot won't catch us,' muttered Krow, as if he were trying to convince himself. Carnelian could see that, to get that far in front of the line, the auxiliaries must have been running their aquar for some time.

Cloud was craning over the back of his saddle-chair speaking to the youths. The tone of his voice was reassuring but his eyes were starting from his head.

'Let's go now,' shrilled Loskai.

Carnelian tried to ignore the trembling in Krow's body as he watched the squadrons of aquar positioned between the dragons becoming more distinct.

'Soon it'll be too late,' pleaded Loskai.

Ranegale gave out a wailing cry and the raiders sent their aquar into a run. Carnelian saw Osidian's creature slipping after them and the dead jiggling in their chairs.

Krow's voice exploded. 'Come on. Come on!'

Through his toes Carnelian could feel Blur's heart racing. He rocked his feet and she leapt forward. The clamp of his knees over the crossbeam kept his legs safe from Blur's thighs as they pistoned higher and higher with her lengthening strides. Krow pushed back into him as if he feared he might be thrown on to the ground. Carnelian blinked away the tears the wind put in his eyes. They were heading straight for the smoking dragon. He could make no sense of its size except that it rose mountainous above the riders running before it. Its four curving horns seemed even larger than his uncle Crail had claimed, so too the pyramid tower upon its back from which smoke was rising in two threads.

Krow gave a start. Cries broke from the raider youths. Carnelian saw a mass of riders had appeared from nowhere to block their path.

'A trap!' The word blown past him in the wind.

Overcome by panic, Carnelian let his feet leave Blur's back. As her running faltered, he quickly pressed them back. Ranegale was wheeling them southwards. Carnelian felt Blur's desire to follow and let her go by putting pressure on his right foot.

'High Father,' moaned Krow.

Carnelian shared his dismay as more squadrons of auxiliaries sprang into view. The dragon was looming in the corner of his eye. Blur straightened up and increased speed.

Krow groaned: 'Where's he taking us?'

Ranegale was not fleeing back the way they had come but, instead, running them along the front of the dragon line from whose towers more smoke was beginning to rise.

'How far can they breathe their fire?' Carnelian cried.

Unable to take his eyes off the advancing monsters, Krow answered him with a vague shaking of his head, over which Carnelian saw the watch-tower Ranegale was heading for. Squinting, Carnelian could make out the road into which it was embedded. The Ringwall, a fortification that enclosed the Guarded Land. Ranegale must be trying to take them through one of its gates. Carnelian prayed the barbarian knew what he was doing.

Following Krow, Carnelian craned round and saw auxiliaries racing to hit them in the flank. Even though he could already feel the first muscle tremors of Blur's fatigue, he rocked his feet to try and coax more speed. Krow sang encouragements, but still they were slowing and the watch-tower seemed no nearer. They clung to each other, willing the tower closer, despairing that they would make it in time. A glance showed the auxiliaries resolving into single riders. Their swelling battle-cries seemed separate from their gaping mouths. It became an agony anticipating their crashing impact.

Krow pushed back into Carnelian, who, gazing up, saw watch-tower ribs stark against the grey sky. Relief turned to despair. These towers rarely slept. For its lookouts suspended high on the ribs in their deadman's chairs, to sleep was to lose hold; losing hold, the mechanisms would drop them to their deaths. The tower would have had plenty of time to bar the gate it guarded in the wall.

Then Blur was striding up the ramp on to the road. Carnelian saw the wall and tower caught in a net of scaffolding awrithe with sartlar. A few strides more carried them across the width of the road. Astoundingly the gate beside the tower was open. Through its gape red mud stretched off as far as he could see. Then they were through and, fighting fatigue, Blur sped them away from the Ringwall and their pursuers.

'Great Father above! Why have you brought us here?' Leaning past Ravan, Fern was glaring at Ranegale.

'You've the gall to challenge me,' bellowed Ranegale. He pointed at the corpses in the saddle-chairs. 'Did you learn nothing from the last time?'

The raiders were staring at the corpse riders. Cloud grimaced as he looked from them to Fern.

'You really oughtn't to have done it again. And as for you . . .' Cloud looked straight at Krow and Carnelian felt the youth flinch then attempt a shrug.

Ravan sat up, his face fierce. 'We couldn't just leave them there.'

Ranegale turned on him. 'Why are you and your kin so determined to bring a curse down on us? Wasn't the death of your father warning enough?'

'Don't you *dare* say that,' bellowed Fern, and his aquar lurched forward carrying the brothers towards Ranegale, whose beast raised its plumes in alarm. Ranegale brought it under control with his feet and fixed Fern with his single eye.

'I can understand the boy might be too stupid to know better, but you?' he said. 'And why did you bring the Standing Dead?' He shook his shrouded head. 'If the auxiliaries didn't see them, the tower lookouts certainly did. What do you imagine will happen now?'

Cloud forced his aquar between Fern and Ranegale. 'We're alive and free, that's a lot more than any of us had a right to expect.'

'They'll hunt us down,' cried Ranegale.

'You know as well as I do that when the Ringwall gates are open, the laws of the Standing Dead forbid the legions to pass through.'

'Perhaps that would be so,' growled Ranegale, 'if we didn't have two of them here captive.'

Fern glanced at Carnelian. 'We had to bring them. They know we are Ochre.'

Loskai and Cloud gaped at him in horror.

'Which one of you told them?' Ranegale said in a dangerous voice.

Fern splayed his four-fingered hand and touched the palm. 'That one,' he indicated Carnelian with a nod of his head, 'saw it in my father's recruitment tattoo.'

Carnelian watched as the men looked at their hands as if for the first time. Ranegale squeezed his into a fist.

'Even if that's true, it's all the more reason why we should kill them now.'

Carnelian withstood the menace of Loskai's stare. Even Cloud was nodding as he looked at him. Carnelian considered whether he would be able to eject Krow without hurting him. He felt bitter that his decision had so quickly brought him and Osidian death. He had abandoned his father for nothing.

Fern moved his aquar to shield Carnelian. 'I'll not let you harm them.'

'You'll *not let us*?' cried Ranegale, widening his shoulders.

Carnelian saw Loskai's hand straying to the spear hitched to his saddle-chair.

'Look, we can argue this out later,' cried Cloud. 'For now what's done is done and arguing here in sight of the Ringwall is just asking for trouble. What we must decide now is where we go from here.'

Ranegale allowed his head to fall. He pointed eastwards. 'Out of sight of the Ringwall, we'll ride all the way to Makar.'

'How will we get into the city?' demanded Ravan.

Ranegale gave the youth a withering look but, when Ravan withstood it, he answered him: 'Since we're postponing decisions, we might as well leave that for later too.'

Ranegale raked them with a baleful eye and then, turning his aquar, he walked her off across the red mud.

They rode away from the Ringwall down muddy gullies. When they had lost sight of the wall, they turned east only to find their route slashed across by more gullies. Over and over again the aquar were forced to clamber down, then scrabble out the other side. Carrying two riders, Blur often needed more than one attempt. Sometimes they would climb on to a bony escarpment scored into slabs as if by some god's knife. There, the aquar had to pick their way carefully for fear of breaking their legs. To add to the misery, the sky opened and released a deluge. Soon the gullies were filling with water the colour of blood. One pool came up almost to the saddle-chairs. Fearing some might be even deeper, Ranegale began to go around them.

Every diversion took them further south. The gullies deepened, the ridges between them slicing up as sharp as shoulder blades. Soon they were being forced to follow the streams for long periods before they would find a gap through which to climb over into the next gully. When Blur was perched on one of these, Carnelian glimpsed the land stretching away to the north as far as he could see, all bony runnels thinly skinned with soil.

They sank into the land, her rock rising around them in leprous walls. Among the towers and pinnacles, Carnelian could almost believe he had returned to the Valley of the Gate that opened into Osrakum except here the pillars were pale and faceless. The gully they were following was swollen by others into a valley along one edge of which they filed, trying to avoid its torrent.

Suddenly, with a foaming roar, this tumbled in cascades into a ravine which, far below, framed in its narrow jaws a misty infinite world roofed by a stormy sky.

Ranegale held up the reckoning cord dripping in the rain. All could see it now only had two knots.

'If we return,' he said, indicating the way they had come, 'we're not likely to find a way to Makar. At least, not in the two days we have before our people give up waiting for us.'

In their saddle-chairs, the raiders sagged as miserably as did the corpses.

'So what do we do?' asked Loskai.

The cloth clinging to Ranegale's face was so drenched Carnelian saw with horrid fascination that the barbarian had a hole where he should have had a nose.

'We camp here,' said Cloud.

Storm clouds were conspiring with the approaching night to blacken the sky. Everyone peered through the gloom at the bare rocky valley.

'This'll have to do,' said Cloud.

There were a few unhappy nods. One of the youths found some shelter under a shelf of rock that projected out from the valley wall. Carnelian urged Blur to follow the other aquar towards it. It was a relief when he and Krow were able to climb free of her saddle-chair. They were stretching their limbs when Cloud approached. He stood over Krow.

'Why did you involve yourself in sacrilege?'

Hanging his head, the youth indicated Carnelian. 'My father, this one claimed he had read the name of our kin tribe in Father Stormrane's hand.'

Cloud regarded Carnelian for a while before offering him his hand. Carnelian bent over the palm. He used the method that had worked before to decipher the recruitment tattoos. Having teased out the appropriate sounds, he converted them in his head into the barbarian tongue.

'Twostone,' he said.

Cloud went pale. He placed his hand on Krow's head. 'You were right to help him.'

'My father,' the youth said with a nod and managed to slip Carnelian a smile of thanks as the Elder led him away.

Carnelian saw Fern and Ravan had untied the corpses and went to help lift them out of their saddle-chairs. Struggling with the noisome burdens, they laid them against the rock at some distance from the camp.

As Fern stood over his father's body, Carnelian could not tell if there were tears mixing with the rain running down his face. He took hold of Fern's shoulder.

'You have my gratitude for defending us back there.'

Fern looked into Carnelian's eyes. 'You know our speech, don't you?' he said using the barbarian tongue.

Carnelian's first instinct was to pretend not to understand, but he saw no threat in Fern's eyes. 'How did you find out?'

'At the kraal, you answered Ranegale when he threatened you in our tongue,' said Fern, shifting to Vulgate.

Carnelian thought back, then nodded, remembering it.

'Is this something all Masters can do?'

'No.' Carnelian saw Fern was waiting for more. 'Many in my household were chosen from the flesh tithe your people give . . . are forced to send to the Mountain.'

Fern frowned. 'How many Plainsman tongues do you know?'

'Plainsman?' said Carnelian, echoing the unfamiliar word.

Fern touched his chest then indicated the other raiders. 'It is what we all are.' He spread his hands as if smoothing a cloth over a table. 'Our tribes cover the Earthsky. How many of our tongues do you know?'

Carnelian shrugged. 'The one you speak. What others are there?'

Fern regarded him with frowning disbelief. 'Our tongue is peculiar to our tribe.'

'Surely the languages spoken by other tribes will be similar to your own.'

Fern frowned. 'We have such difficulty understanding one another we often resort to the Vulgate which the veterans bring back with them from the legions.'

Carnelian stared at him. Could Ebeny have come from the Ochre tribe?

'It's a strange coincidence,' he said.

'Very strange,' said Fern, clearly troubled.

Carnelian ran his hand down the blanket covering his leg. It was hard to believe it was not Ebeny's work.

'That is a woman's weave,' said Fern.

Carnelian looked up. 'The colour?'

Fern nodded. 'Women wear the earth's hues: men, the colour of the angry sky.'

'Still, I will wear it. It reminds me of my . . . Plainsman mother.'

'Why have you been pretending not to understand our tongue?'

'It was a weapon I might have need of.'

They stood for some moments regarding each other.

It was Carnelian who spoke first. 'Will you tell the others?'

Fern chewed his lip. 'I don't know yet.'

Carnelian could see he would just have to trust him. 'If you'll help me, we can move my brother away from the others. I'll stay with him and not bother you.'

Fern shook his head. 'I want you to sit with us. The decisions we'll be making will concern you.' He must have sensed Carnelian's reluctance. 'If Cloud and Ranegale decide you are to die, I'll stand with you against them.'

Carnelian stared in disbelief, but the fierce determination in the Plainsman's face did not invite discussion and so he nodded his assent.

They carried Osidian between them. Carnelian was certain he had been much heavier. Ranegale and Loskai made angry protests as Fern urged the youths away from the rock to allow Osidian to be laid out in what shelter the overhang provided. Ignoring the stares, Carnelian took a sodden blanket, crouched and smoothed it over him. He looked for life in the discoloured face but it might as well have been wax. Sick at heart, he rose and turned to face the Plainsmen. Though only the men looked directly at him, he could feel the general resentment. Carnelian could not imagine what had possessed him. Even if Osidian were to live, would he thank him for having brought them into the wilderness among barbarians?

Fern indicated a place beside him. Carnelian hesitated, but then sat beside the Plainsman, hunching to alleviate the ache in his back. A nudge made him lift his head to find Fern offering him what appeared to be a bale of rope and a flint knife. Carnelian took one in each hand. The rope was heavier than he had expected. He brought it closer and curled his nose up at its odour.

'Djada,' Fern whispered into his ear.

Carnelian saw the youth beside him waiting expectantly. He

pulled a length of the slimy rope through his fingers and cut off a piece then offered the rope and knife. The youth showed him he had his own blade, but took the rope. Carnelian turned to return the flint to Fern, but the Plainsman was staring at the ground, chewing. Carnelian put the knife down in front of him and, overcoming his disgust, he bit off a chunk from his djada. As he began to chew, he found it was, as he expected, the same dried meat he had been eating for days. It did not taste as bad as it smelled.

Continuing to soften the meat in his mouth, he watched the coil being handed round. Ranegale, his eye fixed balefully on Fern, lifted his finger in accusation but Cloud, looking at Carnelian, spoke first.

'This one here read the name of my tribe from my hand.'

Ranegale turned his anger on Cloud. 'The hands of the corpses could've been cut off.'

Fern glowered. 'They're my kin.'

Ranegale flung his head back in exasperation.

'There was no time to cut anything,' said Cloud.

'But the sacrilege –'

'Whatever harm might come to us from that, perhaps we've suffered it already.' The Elder glanced sadly in the direction where he knew the three corpses lay.

'And the Standing Dead?' asked Ranegale, forming ears with his hands.

'Remember it was this one,' Fern indicated Carnelian with his chin, 'who warned me of the tattoos.'

Ranegale began a protest, but Fern waved him down, speaking quickly. 'Do none of you see any significance in the way they came to us?'

Carnelian shared the general incomprehension.

Fern looked each of the men in the eyes. 'We've never asked how it came about that we should find two of the Standing Dead as slaves among sartlar and painted black.'

'I don't follow you,' said Cloud.

'When are men's bodies made wholly black, my father?'

Cloud shrugged. 'When they are dead.'

Fern's eyes caught a reflection of faraway lightning. 'Exactly.'

'But they weren't dead,' said Ravan.

'What are you trying to tell us, Fern?' Cloud asked softly.

Fern ran his hand down over his curls plastered flat by the rain. His eyebrows rose. 'I'm not really sure.'

Ranegale let his hands fall and gave a snort. 'I think he's trying to tell us he believes it was the Skyfather who sent the Standing Dead to us.'

A shiver ran up Carnelian's spine. Though the Masters used red for mourning and green for resurrection, their Black God in his many aspects was lord of the sky, but also, death.

'Is that what you mean?' Cloud asked Fern.

Fern seemed an uncertain child as he looked at Cloud. 'I suppose so, my father.'

'Because of the bitumen on their bodies?'

'And one of them bears a mark.' Fern stood up and walked through the youths to where Osidian was lying. As Cloud and then Ranegale and Loskai followed him, Carnelian resisted the temptation to join them. Instead, he craned round to watch them leaning over Osidian. Ravan had taken a few steps towards them.

'Look at his forehead,' Fern was saying.

Cloud straightened and looked at Fern. 'The mark is in his skin?'

'However hard I rubbed, it wouldn't come off.'

'It looks like an eye,' said Loskai.

'More like the mark that might have been left by lips,' said Fern.

'So you're claiming he was kissed by a black man?' sneered Ranegale. 'Did you kiss him yourself, Fern?' His voice seemed very thin in Carnelian's ears as they recovered from a thunderclap. He was remembering that Osidian had once told him the Wise believed his birthmark a sign put there by the Black God.

Fern's stiff posture betrayed his anger. 'If I had kissed him, do you think it likely my lips would've left a permanent mark?'

Cloud spoke gazing down at Osidian. 'You think he's been chosen by the Skyfather?'

'Chosen for what?' exploded Ranegale. 'Has the rain soaked into everyone's head? Can't you tell this is his grief talking? He's desperate to find a reason why his kin's all dead and so he fixes on this business; this possessed notion that the Skyfather descended from on high to plant a kiss on the forehead of this one.'

'What about the bitumen?' offered Loskai.

Ranegale turned on him. 'High Father, not you too!'

Loskai retreated behind a blank expression.

Carnelian noticed how the youths huddled together; how they trembled with each thunderclap. Ravan returned, deep in thought. Carnelian gave him a smile and was pleased when it was returned. He looked down at the knife. Was the Black God behind the disaster that had befallen them both? It seemed inconceivable the God should have delivered Osidian into the hands of barbarians and yet, there were the signs. It gave Carnelian hope he had made the right decision in seeking refuge among the Ochre but he could not rid himself of foreboding. The Black God was also the Lord of Strife and War.

As the men filed back, lightning flashed the valley into jagged relief. Ranegale as he sat down looked round him gauging the general mood.

'A great blessing this gift from the Skyfather's been so far.'

'I believe the decision whether or not to kill them should be left to the Elders,' said Fern.

Ranegale looked at Cloud. 'Even though you're no longer Ochre, you are an Elder, my father. If you chose to make the decision now we could rid ourselves of the burden of these Standing Dead.'

Ravan, Krow and many of the others were clearly anxious to see what Cloud would decide.

The Elder shook his head apologetically. 'I won't make this decision on behalf of your tribe. Besides, should we be considering anything that might turn the Skyfather even more against us?'

The sky rumbled as if in agreement and Carnelian saw everyone but Ranegale nodding. He gave a snort. 'Well, everyone here will stand witness to my counsel. Let's hope, Father Cloud, we don't have cause to regret your inability to make a decision.'

Lightning flared revealing stark shadows in the raiders' faces. The thunder that followed shook the very rocks upon which they sat and the rain redoubled its downpour.

'How are we going to get home?' Ravan asked over the hiss.

Only the storm answered him, but in the next flash, all could clearly see Ranegale was peering in the direction where the ravine cut down out of sight.

'Down there?' cried Ravan.

'The swamps?' said Loskai, aghast.

Carnelian listened to the stream gurgling into the throat of the ravine.

'If we go down there,' said Ravan, 'we might as well give up any hope of seeing our hearths again.'

The fear in his voice spread to Carnelian, who sensed a general unease.

'How do we know there's even a way down?' asked Loskai.

'The gate in the Ringwall proves there must be,' said Ranegale. 'Besides, the gradient of the ravine and the distance we seem to be from the land edge makes me certain it'll take us all the way down.'

'If you're right we've got to wonder what kind of people use it,' said Cloud.

'Marula?' Ravan asked, his shadow head turning as he tried to make out faces.

Carnelian felt Fern readjusting his position. Peering at his face, Carnelian saw the resemblance he had not placed before. Though paler than they; though not as tall, Carnelian saw Fern bore a decided resemblance to the black men who had escorted him and his father on the road to Osrakum. He should have seen it at once in his tightly curling hair.

'Their lands lie somewhere south of the Earthsky,' said Cloud.

'The swamp's a haunt of nightmares,' moaned Ravan.

'Demons,' muttered Krow.

'Hush,' said Fern. 'Those are just stories used to scare children.'

'There must be another way, Ranegale,' said Loskai.

'Makar will be hard to enter unseen. I've been worrying about that all day. Even if that weren't so . . .' He made a sound of disgust. 'We're burdened with the corpses and, thanks to Father Cloud, the Standing Dead. Besides there's no way we're going to make the meeting and that's the only reason we're heading for the city.'

'Except to spend our bronze,' said Loskai.

'However thick the swamp is below, we'll make better progress through it than we will up here. We can skirt its edge on higher ground until we reach the Leper Valleys. Who knows, we might even get there in time to meet up with our people.'

Night was robbing them of sight. They scattered to find what shelter they could but there was no escaping fear. Bent almost double, Carnelian fumbled his way to Osidian's side. He waited until lightning lit his face. When it did, Carnelian's heart faltered, certain he had glimpsed Osidian awake. He reached out. His fingers almost recoiled when they found Osidian's face smoother than marble but just as cold. His touch found the corner of a lidded eye. Turning, he settled back against Osidian's shivering body to give him what warmth he could.

The movements of the Plainsmen woke him. Blearily, through the rain, Carnelian watched them getting ready. No one spoke nor looked each other in the eye. He noticed Ravan steal a look down into the ravine. The gleam of Osidian's body caught in the corner of Carnelian's vision. His head, his back, his neck ached as he turned round. It was as if he had grown aged overnight. He burrowed under Osidian's blankets to reach the damp, cold flesh and pressed his lips against it until he could feel the tremor of a heartbeat.

'So slow,' he muttered. He covered him up. Looking at him, Carnelian reviewed again the decision he had made for them both. In the daylight, it was harder to believe the Black God was guiding him.

Sensing someone approaching, he looked up and saw it was Fern.

'Today we leave the Land of the Standing Dead,' Fern said, using Ochre in a low voice and trying a smile.

'Why do you call us that?'

Fern crouched down beside him. 'My mother told me it was because of the giants who stand around the place in the Mountain where we give our children to you.'

Carnelian knew he spoke of the colossi of the Plain of Thrones who stood astride the entrances to the tombs in which the Masters were laid to await their resurrection. He recalled how he had felt when he had walked beneath their gaze. It was not an unfitting name.

'We must move my kin,' said Fern, rising.

Carnelian looked to where the corpses lay grey in the morning light. After they had taken only a few steps towards them, the stench of their decay caught at his throat; beside them, it was over-powering. Fern crouched and dug his arms under one. Carnelian could see the creases in the Plainsman's forehead; the horror blanking his face. He waited for him to hoist the saggy mess that had been his father and then watched him stagger away with it to the aquar Ravan was holding ready. Averting his face, Carnelian squatted and worked his hand under the back of another corpse. He took the strain and lifted. The corpse's weight forced him to carry it clasped to his chest.

Carnelian was taking care with each step. They had tried riding, but the foaming water and scree made the ground treacherous. He paced beside Blur in whose chair Osidian lay. The creature's huge taloned feet gouged a grip on the slope, but sometimes he would watch with horror as one slipped. All startled plumes, the aquar would flail and scrabble to maintain her footing while Carnelian danced around her trying to be in a position to catch Osidian should he be flung out. Several times he jumped back sure Blur was about to topple over on to him like a hammer. He would tense up, anticipating her body punching the ground, smashing the saddle-chair, breaking Osidian across the boulders. Each time Blur righted herself and, panting, he would rush in to stroke her neck, or her clutching hands, clucking to reassure her and when her plume fans had closed, urge her a little further down the slope.

As the sky darkened, Osidian began babbling. Carnelian greeted this sign of life with joy. Wary of the movement of her knee and thigh, he clung to the crossbeam of Blur's chair and watched Osidian's rain-glazed face contorting, but it was impossible to pick out words from the rush and chew of sound.

A cry from up ahead made Carnelian release the crossbeam and stand away from Blur to look down the slope. The Plainsmen were dotted here and there below him, but a group had gathered on a promontory that pushed out into a gulf of air. Carnelian made sure there was no peril in Blur's path then scrambled down to join them.

He did not have to reach them before he saw that the floor of the ravine fell away from wall to towering wall. He pushed in among the youths and came to stand beside Ranegale and Fern, who were gazing into the depths of an abyss. Carnelian let his eyes follow the cliff down through the veiling rainfall, down and further down to where, remotely, a black river ran.

They retreated from that precipitous fall and found a cave mouth in the side of the ravine between two cascades. While the others coaxed the aquar into the darkness, Carnelian helped Fern and Ravan lean the corpses against the rock.

Ravan looked morose. 'Do we have to leave them out here?'

Fern put his arm around his brother then led him away. Carnelian followed them, his hand on Blur's neck, the dead men's aquar plodding heavily behind.

The walls of the cave were varnished with running water. As Carnelian crept deeper in, Osidian's ravings seemed to grow louder. Carnelian's eyes adjusted to the gloom allowing him to see a floor strewn with the boulders of crouching aquar, their glassy eyes catching the light.

'Here will do,' Fern said, at last.

They asked Blur to kneel and then carefully lifted Osidian from her chair and laid him out. Carnelian turned Osidian's head so his face might catch what little light there was. His eyes were closed and twitching; sounds were dribbling from his lips.

'What's he saying?' Fern asked.

Carnelian shrugged. 'It's his fever speaking.'

'Or the Skyfather through him,' said Ravan.

Carnelian became uneasy when he saw with what awe the youth was gazing upon Osidian. Frowning, Fern saw it too. He turned away and saw some of the other youths filing back to the entrance looking slight and vulnerable.

'They're the ones I pity,' said Fern.

Carnelian looked at him. 'Why did you bring them then?'

Fern grimaced. 'To let them see the world. They'd come of age and the Tribe's tributaries had need of an escort on their way to the Mountain.'

Carnelian turned back to look at the youths. 'I would've thought you could come up with a better escort than a posse of children.'

Ravan glared at Carnelian. 'We are men.'

Fern smiled and looked at his brother approvingly. 'It is a venerable tradition of our people.'

Carnelian sensed in them both a nobility that did not sit well with what he knew of their mission. 'Is it also a venerable tradition of your people to prey upon travellers?'

Fern's face became wooden. 'As much as it is a tradition of your people to take our children from us.'

Carnelian despised himself for having assumed so easily the haughty judging stance of his kind. Still he was enough the Master to be stung by the disapproval on the brothers' faces.

'The people on the road are innocent of the policies of the Masters.'

'How else can we strike at you?' said Fern.

Carnelian saw with his mind's eye Osrakum's soaring mountain wall, her gates, her turreted dragons. The vision melted. Fern's intense dark eyes were piercing through his defences and he regretted his insensitivity.

'We're here now and in your power.'

'But now we have you, you seem to me only men and not the angels we hate.'

Carnelian thought of Jaspar, Ykoriana and the other Masters he knew and felt he was misleading Fern. 'I'm untypical of my kind.'

Fern frowned and then glanced towards the mouth of the cave. Carnelian had more questions but could see Fern's impatience to join his people. 'You needn't wait for me.'

Fern gave him a curt nod and walked off, but to Carnelian's surprise, Ravan insisted on helping him make Osidian comfortable. This done, they threw damp blankets round their shoulders and walked to the entrance together. A couple of the youths shuffled aside to let Carnelian through. He found a place to sit between Fern and Cloud. He pulled his knees up to his chest and wrapped his arms around them with the blanket as he saw they had done and then he joined them gazing out at the cascades and the slanting rain.

'What do we do now?' asked Fern.

'Let's decide in the morning,' said Ranegale.

So near the cave mouth, Carnelian could feel the rain's spitting dance as cold pinpricks on his feet.

'What I wouldn't give for a fire,' said Loskai.

There were grunts of agreement as everyone huddled closer. The youths whispered to each other but the men were silent as they watched the world outside grow dark. Looking sidelong at their faces, Carnelian could not avoid seeing how much they resembled his brothers now far away in Osrakum. He was barely aware of the knot in his stomach beginning to work loose as he settled back into the warmth of their bodies.

THE ANOINTING

Ichor is the burning blood.
From blood comes life;
from ichor, Creation.
Blood sacrifice is the agent of this transformation.
Ichorous blood proofs the mortal vessel
to receive fire from the sky.
Every drop of blood within the vessel this fire ignites to purest ichor.

(from the 'Book of the Sorcerers')

LIGHT SEEPED WITH THUNDER DOWN THE CAVE TUNNEL TO WAKE Carnelian. He lifted his head and found his pillow was Blur's neck. Her eye plumes fluttered as he sat up. Plainsmen wrapped in blankets lay between the aquar.

Soon everyone was rising, yawning, stretching sleep from their limbs. After checking on Osidian, now as silent as the dead, Carnelian went to join the men gathering at the entrance of the cave to survey the colourless world outside.

Ranegale pulled a blanket over his head and went out. Loskai followed, then Cloud with Krow trailing after him. Fern raised his eyebrows at Carnelian and, when he gave him a nod, Fern crushed his curls under a blanket and ducked into the rain with Ravan. Cursing, Carnelian rubbed his lips over the blessed dryness of his own blanket before he cast it over him and followed.

Rain pattered on the blanket, which grew heavier until wetness began soaking through. Ignoring the discomfort, Carnelian had to peer to keep Fern in sight. Soon they had joined Ranegale and the others on the edge of the abyss. Around them water was spouting into space. Craning over, Carnelian could make out nothing in the vague and shifting greyness. Ranegale and Cloud were blinking away rain as they examined the walls of the abyss. Carnelian allowed his own gaze to wander over the pallid rock piled layer upon layer, everywhere pocked with holes. Countless ledges shelved the walls, in places seeming to form ladders that faded away into the trembling veils of rain.

'Up or down?' said Cloud, brushing a concerned glance over Krow and the other youths.

Heads turned to look back up the slope, which was a frothing cascade.

'We must descend,' said Ranegale grimly. 'What's the point of climbing that? If we reached the top, we'd still have the same problem we had two days ago except we'd have less djada.'

'There must be a better way,' said Fern.

Ranegale had cupped his hands to his ears to hear him. 'A better way? And how do you think we're going to find it? Shall we try every pass until we find one that takes us all the way down?' Gazing into the abyss, he shook his head. 'We must try here, while we still have the strength.'

'How're we going to get the aquar down?' asked Krow.

Carnelian tried to trace a plausible descent, but the ledges seemed as substantial as scribbles.

Ravan was looking at Ranegale for an answer. As the man's hands dropped to his sides and he turned away, the youth's mouth sagged open with horror and disbelief.

Loskai stared. 'Ranegale, you can't mean that you want us to walk all the way home?'

Fern glanced at him. 'For once I agree with your brother. We've no choice.'

Ravan looked from face to face. 'You can't do it. I've reared Runner since she was a hatchling.'

The men were all staring blindly into the abyss.

'We should leave them here in case we have to return?' tried Ravan.

Cloud took his shoulder. 'That would be more cruel. Would you want them to slowly starve?'

'We could set them loose; let them return the way we came.'

Cloud shook his head. 'You saw how barren it is up there.'

Ravan and Krow were struggling not to cry.

'What about our dead?' Cloud asked Fern.

Carnelian looked to where the rain was melting the corpses into the ravine wall, then to the cave in whose depths Osidian lay a fallen statue.

Fern was ashen. 'We leave them here.'

Ravan broke down and Cloud embraced him with one arm, reaching out with the other to Krow.

'Cut their hearts out to take with us,' said Ranegale.

Fern stared blankly while Cloud grew angry. 'There'll be no need for that. Birds from the Earthsky will reach them here.'

Morosely, Carnelian knew he must stay behind with Osidian.

'What about the Standing Dead?' asked Loskai.

Fern's eyes came back into focus. He indicated Carnelian with his chin. 'I'll help this one carry the other.'

As Carnelian gazed startled at the Plainsman, Ranegale shrugged, scowling. 'If you must.'

Carnelian stood against the cave wall keeping out of their way. He was still reeling from Fern's offer. He had tried to help with un-harnessing the aquar, but had quickly found he was only a hindrance. Grim-faced, the Plainsmen were soon working at tearing their saddle-chairs apart. The transverse poles they released from behind the chairs were being piled at the cave mouth. On to either end of each was wound a bale of djada rope the size of a man's head. To one side a parcel had been laid, carefully wrapped in oiled skins the length and girth of a boy's forearm. Beside it were some pouches that had clinked as they were put down.

Smiling crookedly, Cloud regarded the pile of saddle-chair wicker. 'If we'd known we could've had quite a blaze last night.'

Fern asked Carnelian to help him lash together several of the saddle-chair poles into a beam to which he added his father's spear with its iron head. As they worked, Carnelian thanked Fern, who merely gave a curt nod. When they were finished they laid the structure on the floor beside Osidian and Carnelian saw that it stretched longer than his body. They bound Osidian to it with leather bands, blankets and whatever else they could find among the debris of the saddle-chairs.

Each taking one end, Carnelian and Fern tried lifting him. At Fern's urging, they rotated the stretcher like a spit until Osidian hung from it facing the ground. The bindings creaked under his weight, but held. They turned him on to his side and laid the stretcher gently on the floor.

The aquar were standing naked towards the back of the cave, blinking the mirrors of their eyes, their plumes rustling behind their heads.

'They know,' broke Ravan's voice as everyone moved in among the creatures.

One of the youths began a wail that Fern cut short with a reprimand. He handed Carnelian a flint knife. 'You must do Blur.'

When Carnelian hesitated, Fern grabbed his hand and pressed the knife into it. Carnelian could see the tears in Fern's eyes as he made Blur kneel and showed him how she would allow him to bring her long head under his arm.

'You cut here.'

Carnelian watched Fern run his finger round the softly-scaled skin where the creature's jaw met her neck. He looked into Fern's face questioningly. His friend was fighting rage. 'We must do them all at once or else they'll panic.'

Carnelian watched him walk away before turning to Blur. He saw his own reflection in her eyes. She was returning his gaze. He felt a bond with her. Like him she had a beating heart; she saw the same sky. She had yearnings, knew strength and weariness; pain and fear. He reached up to caress his hand down the warm column of her neck, crooning, stroking her plume fans closed.

'Ready yourselves.' The words echoed round the cave.

Carnelian reached up and drew Blur's scaly heron head to his side and slipped his arm over her warm skull. As he hooked her head close he could feel the hot humid breeze of her breath and the tickle of her blink against his skin. It made him ache that she should be so trusting while all the time he was sneaking the flint blade down to her throat.

'Now!' the word harsh and ragged.

Carnelian took too long. The cave was suddenly deafening with aquar squealing their distress. Blur's fans burst open in his face and he almost lost hold of her head. He clung to her grinding his teeth as she tried to lift her head and clumsily, sawed her throat open. Then he had to ride the jerk and shudder of her head. Her warm blood licked his toes. As her plumes sank, he was able to see the raiders. They were crying, man and youth, as they knelt in blood and loved their dying aquar and he found he too was crying as he cradled Blur's now leaden head.

As they were getting ready to leave, Carnelian noticed Fern watching him from the mouth of the cave and turned away to wipe his eyes. When he looked back, Fern was gone. Carnelian needed to keep busy. He saw Ravan rubbing fat over the surface of a djada bale. When the whole ball was gleaming, the youth fed it on to the handle of Osidian's stretcher. Carnelian found a bale of his own. It was fleshy, reeking, the size and, he imagined, the weight of a severed head. Once he had greased it, he impaled it on the other end of the stretcher pole. Its smell clung to his hands.

Fern reappeared carrying two dark bundles. One of these he tucked away under the blanket binding Osidian's legs to the carrying pole. The other he held out to Carnelian.

'You must wear these.'

Fern pushed the black cloth into Carnelian's arms. It was sodden and gave off an odour Carnelian recognized. He repressed a desire to throw it away.

'Where did you get this?' he asked, though he already knew the answer.

'They were my father's. I washed them in a puddle.'

Ravan looked up. Carnelian expected anger, but the youth dropped his gaze and went on with his work.

Carnelian looked down at the shrouds and then offered them to Fern. 'You're kind but there's really no need.'

Fern scowled and looked down at the ochre blanket Carnelian had around his waist. 'You believe you can get down the cliff dressed like that?'

Carnelian saw Fern was right. He put the bundle down, then, reluctantly, he removed the blanket, found two corners and began to fold it.

'You can't take it with you,' said Fern.

Carnelian hugged the blanket. He could almost imagine it had Ebeny's scent.

'I'll get you another when we get home.'

Fern helped him pull on the dead man's robe. It was a tight fit and short. Carnelian tried to keep the disgust from his face as it clung wet to his skin. Fern handed him a long strip of cloth.

'This is an uba. It is wrapped around the head.'

Carnelian was mustering the courage to put it on when Fern suggested that, for the moment, he could use it for a belt. Relieved, he was further heartened when he found the cloak hardly smelled at all. Throwing it around his shoulders, Carnelian sensed Ravan was avoiding looking at him.

Cloud announced it was time to leave. Dressed as a Plainsman, Carnelian lifted his end of the stretcher, Fern the other, and together they carried Osidian out from the cave. The rain had soon washed the colour of slaughter from their feet.

Soaked and miserable, Carnelian stood among the youths peering through the rain, as Ravan and Fern with the other men climbed up to hang the dead on a crag, naked save for the charcoal that had been made and rubbed on their skin. Carnelian wondered at this strange custom.

When they came down, everyone sang a ragged lament. When they were done, Fern would not look at Carnelian as he bent to pick up his end of the stretcher. They lifted Osidian between them and set off. Ravan walked beside them embracing a djada bale, his head hanging so that his drenched uba hid his face. The other youths trudged up ahead, each with his burden, following Ranegale and Loskai while Cloud walked among them encouraging them to sing. All they knew were riding songs whose rhythms only served to remind them of the aquar they had left bleeding in the cave, so they soon fell silent.

At the edge of the abyss, where its pavement merged into the ravine wall, Ranegale found for them a ledge. He tested it then edged off along it, leaning into the cliff, followed by Loskai and then the youths in single file.

When it was their turn, Carnelian went first. He kept his eyes on his feet making sure not to slip. It was difficult not to let his gaze stray down into the abyss.

So they toiled, stopping sometimes to rub life into their arms. The ledge soon gave out and they had to clamber down to another. This was the first test. Ravan was ready to help and Krow too when he saw Cloud join in. As they lowered Osidian, he looked so serene as he hung suspended over the abyss Carnelian could believe him embalmed.

As they progressed, Carnelian found the limestone was inlaid with the spirals of ammonites and other sea creatures. His wonder was short-lived. As they grew tired, the desperate struggle to hold on put everything else out of his mind.

The day waxed and waned. The sky growled and sometimes a shock of lightning would blind them. To relieve the ache in their muscles, Fern and he took turns at being in the lead. Cloud said nothing but his hands were often there to help. When the ledges widened, they would sometimes turn their backs on the harrowing fall and stop for breath. As they chattered away their fear, they made sure only to watch each other's mouths so as not to see the staring terror in every eye.

Encroaching darkness made them fear they might lose their footing. They had passed many caves and, finding another one, they decided to stop there for the night.

Little was said as they had their djada. Carnelian chewed some for Osidian and gave him water. Then he lay beside him to warm him with his body. Cloud told a story but Carnelian was too tired to catch hold of the words and, giving up, he fell asleep.

For days they clung to the limestone with trembling fingers, the abyss echoing at their backs. Sometimes the terror clamped a youth so desperately to the cliff they had to resort to prising his fingers free. The rain leached their strength so that they were forced to rest more often. Mostly it was Carnelian and Fern who struggled alone with Osidian on his pole, though Ravan, Cloud and Krow helped when they could. Carnelian rarely had enough strength left to thank them.

Whenever Ranegale let them stop, they collapsed. Though care was taken to make sure the youths ate their ration, most were growing thinner. The inevitable happened: one of them fell and took another with him spinning down into the abyss. After that Carnelian's dreams, awake and sleeping, were all of flight.

Under Carnelian's fingers, Osidian seemed made of tainted alabaster. Was this the same vessel he had once touched with wonder, imagining it brimming with the ichor of the Gods? The light that once had been in him had gone out. The rounded beauty had sunk into his bones. Carnelian frowned back the tears as he struggled to remember how glorious his beloved had been. He glanced over to where Fern slept like the dead and wondered why each morning his friend chose to suffer another day carrying a fevered stranger down a cliff. How could Carnelian not wonder when he himself who loved him dreamed of letting the stretcher go; longing to watch this torture to sinew and spirit drop away from him into the depths.

A rattle and gasping drew him back. Osidian was muttering, his feet hinging spasmodically on his ankles. Carnelian crept through the raiders, placing his feet carefully among their bodies. At the entrance to the cave he crouched to lift one of the leather bowls they had left out to catch rain. He was deaf now to the downpour but heard behind it the dull roaring of the river and the waterfalls feeding it with their arches. Tomorrow, if the Gods willed it, they would camp upon its bank. Even on the black ship, hiding in drugged dreams from the storms, he had not desired to reach the Three Lands as much as he craved to reach the ground below.

He made his way back cradling the bowl, not wanting to spill it in case he should wake one of the youths. He set it down beside Osidian and knelt. Dipping the corner of a blanket into the water, he took it dripping to Osidian's mouth, touching a finger to Osidian's throat to make sure he was swallowing.

They spread themselves out on the moss, gazing up at the white rampart it seemed they had spent their whole lives descending. Cloud made jokes and poked the youths in the ribs. He would not stop even though they made no reaction but moaning. At first he only lit a smile here, another there, but somehow, he put light back in their eyes and choking laughter in their throats. They promised each other what they would do together once they got home. Some of the youths grinned, imagining their mothers' joy at their return.

Ranegale rose, fixing them all with his grim eye, and told them they were not home yet. Grumbling, everyone chewed djada and then, picking up what appeared to be much lighter burdens, they set off along the river bank.

Ravan and Krow took turns with Carnelian and Fern at carrying Osidian. There was time to admire the vast white columns buttressing the cliff and the boulders the size of hills they had to walk around.

All day they had been getting closer to where the walls of the abyss framed a vast expanse of storm-grey sky. They heard the rapids before they saw them. From the mouth of the abyss, the river spilled roaring down into what at first seemed the ruins of a city. Clambering over this masonry, they soon found it was nothing more than blocks that had crumbled from the white cliff of the Guarded Land. Among this jumble they laboured and as night fell they managed to find a dry place to make a camp. A greater delight was the fire they were able to coax from some damp wood, over which they roasted three small saurians Cloud and Loskai managed to catch.

Sitting with the raiders round the flame, Carnelian took pleasure in seeing them, ruddy-faced, lying back holding their stomachs. It was Osidian starting up his babbling that brought the return of unease. Later, when night fell, his body burned and cooled in quick succession.

'He wrestles the fever,' said Fern frowning.

Ravan looked anxious. 'Will he die?'

Fern looked his brother in the eye. 'Pray to the Mother for his recovery.'

In the morning they set off eager to put the abyss behind them. It was not long before the rain had worn them down. Sodden they clambered among mossy boulders, always making sure to keep the limestone cliffs on their left.

The going was so arduous they had to make frequent rest stops. The talk then was all about the Leper Valleys.

When they had set off again, Carnelian asked Fern discreetly, 'Is there danger in those valleys?'

Fern shrugged. 'We still have salt to pay their tolls.'

'Will having two Masters with you not cause you problems?'

Fern chewed his lip and looked round to make sure his brother was not in earshot. 'I'm more worried that, seeing us arriving on foot, they might try to rob us. I don't like the idea of getting into a fight with them. There's the youngsters to think of.'

'Surely if we give them the salt there'll be no further reason for them to attack us.'

Fern looked at him in horror. 'The salt we carry was intended to pay tolls and make purchases for the Tribe in the market of Makar. Every grain was bought with our men's blood.'

Though the sun was hidden behind the stormy ceiling of the sky, they could feel the day was waning when they came to a river; a fierce white roar of water whose further bank seemed impossible to reach. They stared at the torrent, allowing their eyes to follow it upstream, and saw halfway up the cliff wall the tall and narrow funnel of a ravine from which the river was tumbling.

Wearily they began the trek down its bank, but this was so littered with sharp rocks they were forced further and further away from the water. At last Ranegale declared he would go no further and slumped to the ground.

He looked round at them with his single eye. 'How can we hope to find a ford when we can't even get close to the river?'

He pointed westwards to where they could all still see the mouth of the abyss. 'Look how far we've come. At this rate it'll take us a moon to reach the Valleys.'

'Do you really believe this kind of talk is helping anyone?' said Ravan.

Cloud put his hand on the youth's shoulder to calm him. 'Ranegale has a plan.' He turned to him. 'You do have a plan, don't you?'

Ranegale looked down the rock-strewn slope that plunged into an ocean of fronds fading away into the stormy margins of the sky.

'No, no,' stuttered Ravan as every face went ashen.

Next morning, though rainless, they felt the weight of the black sky as they struggled down from the boulder-strewn foot of the cliffs. The ground began softening into a treacle that sucked at their feet.

Fronds began choking their path. Dense stands of horsetail rose as islands. The mud oozed brackish pools that bubbled up decay. The sky clattered and shook, then released a downpour. Dank and miserable, they pressed on into the thickening thickets and, though the ferns wove themselves into a roof above their heads, they provided no shelter at all.

They chose a mud mound to camp on. It was too wet to make fire. Hunched, they chewed djada, peering anxiously at the leaf wall they could almost reach out to touch and which shivered and trembled as if something were coming through it. It barely screened the rasp and trill of hidden creatures or the more distant wails and trumpetings. Once, some faraway high pinnacles of leaves shook in succession, showing where some monster was pushing through. With the rest, Carnelian pulled down fern fronds to hide his body and snatched what little sleep he could.

Morning found them pushing deeper into the swamp, winding their way along ridges, hacking their way through stems and creepers, catching glimpses of loathsome striped bodies sliding sinuous among the trunks. Every pool was certain to conceal horrors. Every stretch of mud had been printed by huge clawed teeth and the drag of undulating tails. They struggled, sinking into this soft world. The ferns grew monstrous, meshing their leaves above them until they could no longer see the sky and wandered lost among their trunks in a twilight where everything was a noisome, mouldering paste.

After two days of this they came into a region where the air stank of putrefaction. They could find no way around it. Uneasy, they pushed further into the gloom under the treeferns expecting some scene of carnage, but all they found were lurid red blooms, petalled with tongues whose throats exhaled a rotting breath. Flies swarming these carrion lilies clogged Carnelian's nostrils and eyes. Whenever he opened his mouth they crowded in, forcing him to swallow those he could not spit out. The pillars of this sombre world were hung with pitcher plants, their mottled bellies plump with such a gluttony of insects and birds that some had burst open, disgorging the half-digested mess all over the bone-carpeted ground.

Night approaching, they made camp. They managed to get a smoulder going, the smoke from which at least drove away the flies. Here, Osidian came suddenly awake with a gulping gasp.

'He seeks me out!'

The cry, in Quya, made the raiders jump up staring. Carnelian peered into a thin face lit by immense eyes.

'Who seeks you out?' he asked gently.

'The Black God,' Osidian whispered. His eyes closed as his body convulsed in its pupae of mouldy blankets. The pale lips released a hiss. 'Our Father of Darkness.'

Carnelian waited for more; tried talking in both Quya and Vulgate but received no response. He became aware that the Plainsmen had gathered round.

'The fever's broken,' said Fern.

Carnelian saw the fear lurking in the tunnels of his eyes. It was in all their eyes.

Hesitantly, Fern and Ravan helped him prise open the bindings cocooning Osidian to the pole while Krow looked on. The body they revealed had wasted to bones and skin. Carnelian remembered how glorious Osidian had been, how strong, when they swam in the dazzling lagoons of the Yden. He leaned close to whisper love names into his ear and, by this means, he roused him from sleep.

Pain and puzzlement played over Osidian's face.

'Where . . . ?'

Carnelian could think of no easy answer. Osidian's emaciation was so overwhelming Carnelian became obsessed with feeding him. He chewed djada and squeezed it in softened pellets into Osidian's mouth. To avoid seeing his stare of horror, Carnelian cradled him. He slept close. Sometimes, waking in absolute blackness, he would find Osidian's lips with his fingers and give him water to drink.

It was near dawn that Carnelian felt the tremor in the ground. He believed it to be thunder until he realized he was hearing it only with his body. The earth was shaking with a slow rhythm, as if some giant were walking by. The undergrowth rustled and sighed as something squeezed through it. Osidian must have heard it too, for Carnelian felt him stirring. He slipped his arms over the rack of Osidian's ribs and hugged him still. Holding on to him, Carnelian could feel Osidian's heart racing and knew he was listening. The presence circled them. Carnelian only released Osidian when he felt it move away.

In the morning twilight, Carnelian woke from a terrible, grinding nightmare to find Osidian deathly still. Carnelian touched him, then shook him, but Osidian would not wake.

'We'll have to bind him up again,' said Fern. 'It was stupid to imagine he'd have the strength to walk.'

Carnelian thought his friend had a haunted look. Many of the youths were peering among the trunks as if they were expecting to see something in the gloom.

He leaned close to Fern. 'Did you hear it?'

Fern bent over Osidian, making no sign he had even heard the question. He looked up. 'Are you just going to watch?'

Carnelian helped him lay Osidian's long bony body along the pole. They secured him, then hoisted him and followed after the others.

As the weary struggle of the day wore its way to night, Osidian woke again. He stared into the darkness pleading, negotiating with something that was not there. The pure consonants of his Quya were obscured by the protests of the Plainsmen.

'He draws the demon to us,' said Loskai.

'It's a ravener,' said Cloud.

'Without fire to drive it away, that's terrifying enough,' said Ranegale. His eye fell on Osidian, whom Carnelian was trying unsuccessfully to quieten. 'We should've killed him.'

Carnelian sensed most of them agreed with Ranegale. Osidian's voice continued its rambling. In the end, Carnelian only managed to silence him by plugging his mouth with djada.

The raiders struggled to gather leaves and twigs to make a fire but everything was too damp. As the last light faded, they gave up trying, huddled together and tried to sleep.

Rising at first light, Carnelian could not help seeing how haggard everyone looked. The presence had visited them again, but if in truth or only in their nightmares, he could not tell. Fern helped him lug Osidian on the next stage of their journey. Feeling eyes on him, Carnelian kept turning. At first he thought it must be one of the Plainsmen and put it down to their fearful fascination with Osidian's ravings, but every eye was busy finding a way for their feet. The sensation persisted and in the pit of his stomach the feeling grew that whatever it was looking at him was not human.

That night, Carnelian tried to pick words from Osidian's deranged incantations. The Plainsmen would only look at Osidian from the corners of their eyes. Only Ravan was brave enough to speak the common fear.

'He's drawing the soul of this accursed place down on us.'

Carnelian opened his mouth to protest but found no words. He looked at the Plainsmen expecting violence but only Ranegale and Fern would hold his gaze; all the rest were striving to hide in sleep.

Nightmare lumbered towards them tearing through the fabric of the enfolding treeferns. Screams like a scattering of birds followed by an agonizing silence. Blind, Carnelian could sense an immense presence. Above his head bellows were breathing a fetor that clung clammy to his face. A mass swung away, his face cooled and he dared to gulp a mouthful of rotten air. A whimpering. The immensity adjusting caused the earth to shudder. The victim's trembling was betrayed by the vibrating wail he began pumping out. Air was displaced by something massive falling through it. The wailing, snuffed out, was replaced by a grinding moistened by tearing and the iron smell of blood. Urine oozed warm down Carnelian's thigh.

'A spear,' shrilled Cloud's voice. 'For the sky's sake . . . a spear.'

Fumbling, terrified mumblings as the mass rose.

Carnelian forced his hand to creep over the mud feeling for a weapon. A wavering battle-cry Carnelian recognized with horror was Osidian's. A stinking breeze. Thunder in the ground. A scream, then slicing. The world detonated in a roaring frenzy. A wall slammed him flying into the night.

UNDER THE TREES

The poisons of decay can open the doors to other worlds.
(extract from a beadcord manual of the Domain Immortality)

DIRTY LIGHT WAS FILTERING THROUGH CRACKS BETWEEN THE LEAVES.
Carnelian's cheek was lying in mud. A corner of his mouth blew
bubbles as he breathed. He adjusted his body gingerly to feel if any
bones were broken. Groaning, he rolled over, pushed himself up,
then stood. He was crusty with blood, aching all over, but
apparently, whole.

A blush of panic threatened to overcome him when he peered into
the glooms and saw no sign of the Plainsmen. He set off to search
for them. Spying through the shadows some vague man shapes, he
stumbled towards them.

Eerily still, they were standing on the edge of a clearing recently
gouged from the forest. Ploughed-up mud was strewn with chunks
and ribbons of flesh. Carnelian wanted to look away. Cloud's left
shoulder was missing; from black-bruised neck to hip, his flesh
frayed into purple threads and splintered bone. His head was
thrown back on the broken hinge of his neck; his lips drawn thin
and tight, exposed his teeth in a manic grin. One of the youths
Cloud had been trying to protect had been crushed into the mud.
The other lay broken, skin mottled indigo edged with yellow. Brown
with blood, Osidian lay curled at the heart of this slaughter, his face
hidden by his knees.

In shock, Carnelian pushed through the Plainsmen and began the
crossing to Osidian's side. Gore slicked and cracked under his feet.

When he reached him, he crouched into the sweet rotting reek to touch his leg. He had expected it to be corpse-hard, but though cold, the skin gave under his touch. Hope made Carnelian's hand tremble as he reached above Osidian's rope scar to search for a pulse. He found one.

Seeing Fern sickly and staring with the rest, he breathed: 'He lives.'

Fern gave a slow nod and then, grinning with horror and disgust, he came through the carnage. Carnelian turned back to Osidian. Carefully grasping his head with both hands, he pulled the pale face free of the knees. Osidian seemed asleep. Carnelian slid his hands over him, searching for the wound that had bled enough to stain the ground.

'I'll help you turn him,' Fern said.

As they rolled him over, Ravan cried out, pointing: 'Father's spear.'

Carnelian and Fern saw the shattered spear upon which Osidian had been lying. The iron blade was caked with the same gore that had spurted down his arm and splattered his stomach and legs.

'The demon's blood,' breathed Ravan, his wide-eyed stare tracing the edge of the stain it had soaked into the earth.

Carnelian watched Fern lift the iron spearhead from under Osidian's hand and examine it with a frown.

'It belongs to me now,' said Ravan.

Carnelian and Fern both turned together to see Ravan with his hand outstretched.

Fern walked towards his brother. 'I had never intended to claim it.'

The pain in Fern's voice made Ravan blush. The youth became aware everyone was staring at them. 'You never had any right to it.'

Carnelian felt Fern's humiliation as if it was his own. His friend extended his hand with the spearhead lying on the palm. Ravan regarded the gory thing for some moments before snatching it, his uncertain smile twisting to a grimace as his fingers stuck to the blood.

Carnelian soaked a rag in the leather bowl, squeezed out most of the blood and used it to rub away some more clotted matter from Osidian's body. He needed to touch him, to feel the living warmth in his skin. The Plainsmen were arguing whether or not it was a demon he had driven off. Carnelian glanced round. Displaying the iron spearhead, Ravan was shouting at Ranegale. Loskai was siding with his brother. Beside them stood Krow, staring at the ground. The others formed an unhappy audience. Fern had disappeared.

Carnelian was about to resume the cleaning when he found Osidian watching him.

'Where are we?'

Overcome, Carnelian bent to hug him, but Osidian stopped him with a frown. 'Where are we?'

'The Lower Lands.'

Osidian's eyes widened. He stared up into the canopy and Carnelian watched memory returning: 'The slavers . . .' Osidian breathed.

His brows knitted together. 'And after? I remember emerald flashes, barbarian faces . . .' He went deathly pale.

Carnelian knew what Osidian was seeing in his mind's eye. 'The monster that attacked us had been stalking us for days.'

'He came for me.'

Carnelian smiled, loving him. 'It was a predator driven by hunger.'

Osidian fixed him with huge, green eyes. 'He came for me.'

The conviction in his voice was chilling.

'How is he?' said Fern standing over them.

Carnelian looked up and saw the awe lighting his friend's face.

'He's gaining strength,' said Osidian in Vulgate.

Carnelian sensed his acute discomfort at having the Plainsman look at his naked face. Osidian's eyes fell on Fern's brass collar. Realizing what the Master was looking at, Fern allowed his gaze to move down Osidian's neck to where the still tender scar of the rope formed its collar of dried blood. Osidian's hand strayed up to his throat. His mouth twitched as he felt along the rusty wound. His hand dropped away, his eyes closed, his face smoothed to wax. Thereafter, he would respond neither to Carnelian's voice nor to his touch.

Unhappy, Carnelian helped gather up the slaughtered bodies then stood with others watching as Fern sheared the hair from Cloud's head. Once he had removed it all, Fern put the salt-beaded tresses into Krow's trembling hands. Now that Cloud was dead, Krow was the only remaining representative of the Twostone tribe.

The men scaled the treeferns to hoist the corpses up as high as they could into their crowns while those below sang a hymn to the sky. Carnelian had watched them black the skin of the dead with mud. His instinct had been to wash the bodies first but Fern had told him the smell of blood would bring winged scavengers more quickly.

When Osidian came alive again, he declared he would walk. Carnelian saw that nothing he might say would change his mind. Fern received the news without surprise. From the wreckage of the stretcher, he salvaged the bundle he had put there the day of the aquar slaughter. As he unfolded the cloth it gave off a stale odour of decay. Inside was a mass of grey hair beaded with salt that Carnelian recognized as being Stormrane's. Fern surveyed it for a while before lifting it with both hands and, reverently, rolling it into an uba which he then bound around his waist.

At first Osidian refused to wear the dead man's clothes, but Carnelian pleaded with him that without protection, the flies would eat him alive and Osidian relented. His face twisted with disgust as Carnelian helped him into the robe and cloak, then wound the dead man's uba round his head.

Ravens and sky saurians had already descended to feast upon the corpses when at last they all set off. Carnelian was only too glad to be leaving the bloody clearing behind.

'Where are we exactly?' asked Osidian, his Quya ringing round another makeshift camp.

Carnelian was not sure what answer to give. The encroaching night was bringing with it a fear Osidian alone did not seem to share. He looked frail, but his eyes revealed the fire that had driven his body to keep the pace all day.

'Where did we leave the Guarded Land?'

'Somewhere west of a city called Makar,' Carnelian replied, in Vulgate.

Speak in Quya, Osidian signed using the hand speech of the Masters. 'I had seen the sky but not believed.'

'The sky?'

'The movement of the clouds suggested the deep south; their speed and opacity, that we are nearing the end of the second month of the Rains.'

Carnelian nodded. For a moment he was puzzled by this act of divination until he remembered how familiar Osidian was with the beadcord records of the Wise. It was in their Library that Carnelian, exploring, had come across him. Their first days together had been spent there as Osidian, secretly, taught him to read the strung beads, as the Wise did, by touch.

Osidian was frowning. 'What I have been wholly unable to unravel is what part me being here could possibly play in my mother's schemes.'

'It is likely she knows nothing of where we are,' said Carnelian.

Osidian fixed him with a stare. 'How so?'

Carnelian explained what the Ichorian had intended to do with them.

Osidian looked incredulous. 'Trophies?' His eyebrows rose. 'I would not have believed a minion would dare such sacrilege.'

'The Ichorian did not know *who* you were.'

'You did not tell him?'

'It did not seem to me he would have believed me.'

Osidian nodded, but his mind was already lost in calculation. To Carnelian, he seemed to have aged a dozen years. His skin had dulled, his carriage no longer seemed to hold his head among the clouds; even his neck had lost its graceful line. Seeing this, guilt churned Carnelian's stomach and a question formed in his mind which was an agony to utter.

'Do you blame me?'

Osidian's gaze came back into focus, emotion softening his face. For a moment Carnelian recognized the boy in the Yden and almost let out a mingled cry of joy and grief, but as suddenly as it had come, the vision passed away, leaving a coldness in Osidian's eyes as he smiled.

'How like you, Carnelian, to crave absolution. Tell me, have your recent experiences not hardened your heart even a little?'

Osidian reached out and Carnelian allowed himself to be taken by the chin. Osidian shook his head indulgently. 'Your beauty has weathered our adversity well.'

His hand fell. 'Tell me how we came to be here. Leave nothing out.'

Carnelian would have clung to that discussion, but Osidian had become limestone and so Carnelian saw no other path but to tell the story from the beginning. He had barely taken them in their urns through the City at the Gates, when Osidian began to look morose and Carnelian fell silent. Osidian's hand strayed up to the angry scar the rope had left around his neck. His voice was flat when he spoke.

'Of what follows I have memories enough.' He looked around in the gloom to where the Plainsmen sat away from them. 'Recommence from the time when we were captured by these barbarians?'

Carnelian poured the story out and as he did, lived in that time again. When he reached the morning when the raiders were intending to let them be found by the legion, he ran dry.

'I had to choose,' he said.

Osidian seemed startled. 'And you *chose* to come here?'

Carnelian gazed at him. 'I could not bear that you should die.'

Osidian's laughter wounded Carnelian.

'One has to keep reminding oneself that you really are everything you appear to be. It is inconceivable any other of the Chosen could have made such a decision: to willingly consign oneself to this life of savagery for another . . . Incredible.'

Now Carnelian wanted to hurt him. 'Perhaps, in truth, I was intent on saving myself. I cannot imagine your mother would welcome my return.'

'You would have no call to fear her. It is beyond doubt that if I had returned, my blood would have anointed my brother's Masks, but be sure I would have dragged my mother into the tomb after me.'

'And your brother?'

'Once a God Emperor is made, They cannot be unmade, but the revealing of Their plot would unite the Great against Them. Even They could not have harmed you then.'

Carnelian's anger ebbed away.

Osidian reached out to touch him. 'It was a kindness, Carnelian, I will do my best to repay.'

Carnelian burned up. 'It was no kindness, but an act of love.'

It had grown so dark they could no longer see each other, but Carnelian sensed Osidian had become as ensnared as he in uncomfortable emotion.

'And I had feared you would hate me for bringing you here,' he said almost to himself.

'I might have if it had not been revealed to be my manifest destiny.'

Carnelian felt the swamp smothering him.

'But tell me, why did the barbarians accede to your request? Surely even they must be aware of how dangerous we are.'

Though it felt selfish, Carnelian did not wish to dwell on what danger his choice might have brought upon the Plainsmen.

'I appealed to one of them. Fern.'

'Fern,' said Osidian.

'I had shown consideration for his father when he was close to death.'

'I can see how such condescension might be impressive to such as they.'

Osidian's hauteur irritated Carnelian. 'They have seen us as we are, my Lord. Do you really believe we still appear to them as angels?'

'What we appear to be matters less than what we are,' Osidian said in ominous tones. 'But I sense there is something else that caused this Fern to take us with him.'

Something deep inside urged Carnelian to hide the truth, but he was certain Osidian would see through any lie.

'You watched them blacken the bodies of their dead? Well, we appeared to them thus, clothed in bitumen.'

'And my birthmark?' Osidian asked in a strange voice Carnelian felt compelled to answer.

'That played a part.'

'If I read it right, then it must have been this Fern who found us among the sartlar.'

'It was his brother who noticed the Ichorian,' Carnelian said, feeling as if he were trying to deflect some attack.

'An older brother?'

'A younger, Ravan.'

'I see.'

Carnelian had a feeling that the night was taking possession of Osidian. 'The Empress must be aware we still live.'

'Why should she?' the darkness said.

Carnelian explained their ride past the watch-tower. 'So you see –'

'Most likely, the Wise will have seen us but as to whether they shall reveal this to my mother or my holy brother, that is another matter altogether; and one which will be determined by the balance of power in Osrakum.'

A harrowing thought occurred to Carnelian. 'Will they search for us?'

'The thought of the Wise is unfathomable,' said Osidian in a tone which was intended to terminate any further speculation.

'Please finish your account of how we came here.'

Carnelian did, sensing throughout how interested Osidian had become in Fern and Ravan. Carnelian concluded the tale with Osidian coming awake. He was reluctant to touch on the horror of the previous night.

'Tell me what you have learned about these barbarians.'

Carnelian relayed what he knew, but after a while, Osidian interrupted.

'You seem strangely privy to much which passes between them.'

Carnelian hesitated a moment before answering. 'The tongue they speak is one I have known since I was a child.'

'You are telling me you comprehend their barbarian speech?'

Carnelian could hear Osidian's amazement. 'It was the tongue my wet nurse, Ebeny, spoke.'

'That any wide assemblage of barbarians should speak a single tongue stands in vivid contrast to the belief the Wise hold that their languages are legion.'

'The Wise are not in error. These people have told me their language is only one of many.'

'Which you just happen to have been taught by one of your household slaves?'

'I have told you before she was much more than a slave.'

'How can you explain such a singular coincidence?'

It was something Carnelian had been unable to resolve. He could see how this development only served to harden Osidian's belief that some force was guiding their destiny. Dread welled up in him.

'Do they know you speak their tongue?'

'Please, Osidian. No more questions. I am tired. I cannot –'

'Do they know?'

'Fern does.'

'And has not revealed this to any other or else they would all know.'

Carnelian thought this a rather patronizing assumption. He hoped Osidian would say nothing more.

'Who leads them?'

Osidian's voice seemed one with the night. Carnelian did not want to answer, but to seek the escape of sleep. Anticipation of Osidian repeating the question became almost painful until Carnelian felt compelled to say: 'Look for the man who has suffered almost as many mutilations as a Sapient.'

In the long, weary days that followed, they struggled through the swamp following Ranegale and Krow who had become his shadow. They tried to keep to the mounds and runs of higher ground but these were often so overgrown they were forced down into the quagmire where they sank up to their knees in the stinking mud. A leg had to be dragged out, swung forward, then allowed to be sucked back in again. Fatigue made each step seem their last. They had to make innumerable rest stops. If they were fortunate, they would find a knoll to climb: if they were not, they might have to clamber up into the branches of a tree. Talk was rare. People chewed djada and licked at a saltstone, staring with unfocused eyes. Osidian's emaciated body was sheened with sweat as he struggled to breathe. His gaunt face betrayed his exhaustion but his eyes were green embers. Miserable, Carnelian tried to peer into his heart through those eyes, without success. Osidian seemed focused on some problem. Sometimes his lips moved as if he were holding a conversation.

As the darkness thickened round them, Ranegale would call a halt. Sometimes, Carnelian would be so grateful that tears would squeeze from his eyes even as his muscles went into their usual spasm. In the camps, only Osidian would not jump when an un-human cry came filtering through the dusk. When they heard crashings near them, they would wait almost without breathing until they had passed. Osidian would sit as calmly as if he were reposing in a garden. More and more, Ravan was to be seen beside him. Once, coming awake, Carnelian heard two voices rustling in the dark. Though he could make out no words he knew it was Osidian whispering to Ravan. Something made him fear for the youth. He felt something else which, eventually, he was unable to deny. He was jealous of the one person Osidian did not treat as a stranger.

Rain began to fall incessantly day and night. Nothing ever got a chance to dry. The djada became slimy. Before they ate, they had to scrape off a fur of purple-black mould. Disgust and the bitter taste made it hard to keep down. The blankets were transformed into a sodden burden which at last they had to reluctantly discard. The leather of the Plainsmen's shoes swelled up and chafed their feet so that they were forced to take them off and walk barefoot with the two Standing Dead. Each morning brought an aching rise from unrestful sleep with nothing before them but another slogging, punishing day. As night approached they would drop into the mud not knowing whether they were closer to the Earthsky or even if they had been plodding around in circles.

'We're lost,' said Ravan.
    Ranegale lifted his head and cupped a hand to listen.
    'Lost,' shouted Ravan.
    Ranegale shrugged.
    Osidian rose. Carnelian thought that, though still painfully thin, there was something in the way Osidian moved that made him look more like himself. As he watched him look round at the Plainsmen slumped here and there against the fern trunks, Carnelian wondered what he was up to.
    'I know the way if you'll follow me.'
    Carnelian came fully awake as Ravan translated Osidian's words for those youths who did not have Vulgate.
    Ranegale sneered at him. 'Why are you bothering to spread his nonsense, boy?'
    'Which of you wish to get home alive?' asked Osidian.
    'How could you possibly know the way?' said Fern.

Osidian looked at him. 'The sorcery of the Masters is beyond your understanding, barbarian.'

Irritated, Fern glanced at Carnelian. Osidian saw their exchange of looks and frowned. He addressed the youths.

'Which of you will follow me?'

As Ravan relayed what Osidian had said, Carnelian saw hope perking them up.

Ranegale surged to his feet. 'How do you believe one of the Standing Dead could possibly know a way through this swamp when even we do not?'

The youths looked crestfallen. Ravan stood to face Ranegale. Fern, now also on his feet, made to move to his brother's side, but Loskai signed aggressively for him to stay where he was.

'Why don't you just face it, Ranegale,' said Ravan. 'Every decision you've made has been bad, and have you forgotten it was the Master who drove away the demon and not you? I say that's worth respecting. If he now says he can get us home, I for one would like to let him try.'

Ranegale drew close enough to Ravan that his threats sprayed spittle on his face. The youth pulled back saying something. Ranegale put a hand up to hear. When the youth mocked the gesture Ranegale knocked him to the ground.

Fern leapt forward but Osidian stood in his way. For a moment it seemed the Plainsman would throw himself on the Master. In conflict, Carnelian hesitated to take Osidian's part. Fern, unable to hold the Master's gaze, looked away. Osidian turned, taking in Ravan who was nursing his shoulder; Loskai getting ready for violence and then the staring youths.

'Does anyone here believe Ranegale will get you out of this mess?'

Fern looked uncertain and Carnelian could see even Loskai wavering.

Roaring, Ranegale flung himself on Osidian who fell backwards with the Plainsman on top of him. As Carnelian lunged forward to pull the man off, Fern grabbed hold of him. Carnelian struggled loose, snarling, and would have attacked his friend if it had not been for the expression of shock on his face.

'We've no quarrel,' said Fern.

Carnelian turned to see Osidian struggling to push Ranegale off him. The Plainsman butted him in the face and Osidian's nose turned red.

'His blood,' Carnelian cried out, in outrage.

Fern grimaced apologetically. 'You mustn't interfere.'

'But he's still weak,' moaned Carnelian.

Loskai leered. 'If the Master wins, we'll follow him wherever he leads.'

He lost his leer when at that moment Osidian managed to roll Ranegale off him.

Ravan bared his teeth. 'Hurt him, Master, hurt him.'

Carnelian formed part of the ring of bodies shifting around the fight. He could not bear to see Osidian hurt more than he had been already. He looked round at Fern pleading with his eyes, but his friend shook his head.

'They'll have to sort this out some time.'

Carnelian saw the truth in that. A cry from Ravan made Carnelian turn back to the fight. Ranegale was holding a knife. Carnelian stared at its feint and stab. Another blade landed in the mud beside Osidian's foot. He saw it, but ignored it. Lunging ferociously, he caught Ranegale, then with appalling strength lifted him clear of the ground, then hurled him down.

Carnelian saw Ranegale had lost his knife, then his uba was torn away to reveal the pit above his mouth; the crusted eye socket, the earless holes in the side of his head. The man's hands trembled up to hide his disfigurements. Osidian stood over him. The Plainsman made to snatch the second blade but Osidian's foot struck like a snake, crushing his wrist. Hanging his hand, whining, Ranegale stared, tearful panic in his eye. He shrieked as Osidian took hold of him. The Plainsman struggled but could not break free.

'Let him go,' wailed Loskai.

Osidian knelt, bending the man backwards over his knee.

Carnelian shuffled forward. 'Osidian, you are victorious. Let him go.'

Loskai fell to his knees. 'Please, Master . . .'

Osidian gave no response and like a machine continued inexorably to bend Ranegale's back.

Carnelian threw himself on Osidian, trying to release his hold on Ranegale. Clawing blood from Osidian's thigh, the Plainsman flung his head back, his disfigured face shaping a silent cry of agony. The crack as his back snapped made everyone jump. Carnelian let go of Osidian's arms and stood back. Osidian rolled the man off his knee into the mud and rose. Gaping, Carnelian glanced at Ranegale splayed at his feet. Osidian was staring at the broken man as if he had come across him by surprise.

Ranegale begged his brother to kill him, but Loskai, staring, backed away. They all stood as if forced to watch the man's agonized attempts to stand. He scrabbled with his arms but his legs seemed to have been turned to stone. Loskai helped prop him up, but each time his brother collapsed back into the mud so that he began to look nothing like a man at all but rather some loathsome worm crawled up from the swamp.

'Kill me, Loskai,' shrilled Ranegale.

Loskai was doubled up, reaching out, stamping. 'We can carry you home, Ranegale. Perhaps the Elders can fix you.'

'I'm broken,' Ranegale squealed.

'Do it,' Ravan screamed at Loskai.

Among the sobbing youths, Krow stood silently watching.

Fern turned snarling in the direction which Osidian had taken when he had disappeared into the gloom. 'Were you possessed to do this?'

Though in shock, Carnelian knew it was guilt that made him speak. 'Have you forgotten it was Ranegale who wanted to leave your kin to rot?'

Fern lowered his head and looked at Carnelian from under his brows. 'And you believe that justifies this?'

Rage rose in Carnelian. Fearing he might unleash it on his friend, he turned and ran, hunting Osidian along the trail he had left in the mud. Slipping, he fell. The impact cleared his mind. Mercifully, he had come far enough that he could barely hear Ranegale's cries. Should he have stopped the fight? What Osidian had done disgusted him, but would any other Master have acted differently? This Osidian was not the boy that he had loved in the Yden. What Carnelian feared most was that it was he who was responsible for the transformation.

The first thing Carnelian noticed when Osidian came into view was his bony spine pushing through the soaked cloth on his back. Coming closer, he could see the brown scar he wore around his neck. Pity mixed with dread as Carnelian moved round to try and look into his face.

'It was necessary he should die,' Osidian said, looking at his hands as if they were not his own.

'He is not dead yet.'

'They will kill him.'

Carnelian hoped this was true. 'And now you will lead them?'

The face Osidian turned to him was one Carnelian recognized. Relief washed over him.

They embraced, clinging to each other.

'Where have you been?' he muttered into Osidian's shoulder.

'Where I would never wish to have you go, my blood.'

Carnelian pushed Osidian away to search his face. 'I know you now, but Fern was right, you have been possessed.'

Osidian raised his brows and, wearily, he laughed. The sound warmed Carnelian like the sun in winter.

'Would my Lord deny me a modicum of bitterness considering the way our lives have gone recently?'

'It is good and natural you should feel remorse.'

The change that came over Osidian was like sudden cloud shadow. 'You believe I could do wrong by hurting a savage?'

Carnelian backed away from the fire in his eyes.

'I have been touched,' he said in an ominous tone.

'Forget that now,' said Carnelian, trying to bring the brightness back.

'I am consumed by an inner night.' Osidian looked away and peered into the glooms between the trunks as if he were seeing something there.

'Just nightmares. You have had nightmares and as you said, how could you not? But you have woken now and left them behind.'

Osidian looked a little like a child, so that Carnelian wanted to embrace him again but he did not dare.

Osidian shook his head. 'There is no waking.' He pierced Carnelian with his eyes. 'You yourself have seen the signs.'

'They guide us to sanctuary among the Ochre where we can live together free from the oppression that would have been ours in Osrakum even if we had not been taken.'

Osidian's eyes widened. 'Do you really imagine the God cast me half-divine from my throne so that I might keep house with you among filthy savages? Is that really the full measure of your heart?'

Carnelian withered beneath his glare.

Osidian looked away. 'He prepares me for some great purpose.' His gaze fell again upon Carnelian. 'Did he not come Himself to me?'

Carnelian frowned at the divine pronoun. 'Do you mean the monster who attacked us?'

'A form He put on when He descended from the sky.'

Carnelian drew back. 'Why? Why would He come to you in such a form?'

'Why? To anoint me with His blood, as my brother was anointed when the Wise made him God.'

Fern and Loskai were hoisting Ranegale's mud-smeared body up into a treefern when Carnelian and Osidian returned. Several heads turned. Most ducked back afraid, but Ravan and Krow lingered, watching Osidian with a fascination that made Carnelian uneasy.

As the Plainsmen sang their laments, Carnelian felt Osidian move from his side. He was peering up through a gap in the canopy. Carnelian went to stand beside him and looked up too. All he could see was a low, charcoal sky. His gaze fell to Osidian's face. The madness seemed to have passed.

'What are you doing?'

Osidian replied without looking down. 'Gauging the movement of the clouds.'

The Plainsmen had fallen silent. Osidian walked towards them, so cutting off any more questions. Loskai regarded the Master with a look that mingled fear with hatred. Oblivious, Osidian looked like a signpost standing in among them as he pointed out a direction.

'We go that way.'

Fern looked a question towards Carnelian, who could only shrug. Soon he was joining the Plainsmen as they picked up the djada poles. When they were ready, it was Krow who was the first to follow Osidian as he led them into the gloom beneath the trees.

In the days that followed, everyone became ill. It was Osidian who made them force down the mouldy djada, to keep up their strength. Carnelian watched the Plainsmen cling more and more to Osidian's certainty as he led them through the swamp. Sometimes they would be forced to wait while he watched the sky. At those times, Carnelian would see adoration light up the faces of Ravan and Krow as they gazed upon the Master. Their faith in him was rubbing off on the others. Loskai had become nothing more than a shadow hanging around the edges of their group. Only Fern ever showed resistance to the Master's commands. Carnelian came to depend on his friend's frown to keep his own mind in balance.

Carnelian was concentrating on putting one foot in front of the other when he realized it had grown darker. He lifted his head and at first thought they had wandered dazed into the dusk. Then he saw the pillars rising on every side. In his stupor he imagined he was walking in the Labyrinth in Osrakum. He looked up expecting to see the faces of the Gods but the pillars ran smooth right up to the shadow ceiling. Scratches of light showed how far away the sky was. He stumbled towards a pillar and felt its ragged, yielding skin.

'What're you doing?' Fern's face was a part of the darkness.

'Trees?' Carnelian asked.

Fern looked around as if he were trying to avoid being seen by eyes hovering above him in the gloom.

'Come on,' he whispered, 'We daren't fall behind.'

They crawled tiny beneath the pillar trees. Thunder came echoing down to them from another world. Even the lightning played remotely beyond the shrouding canopy.

'This is the heart of darkness,' said Osidian, so close to Carnelian's ear it made him jump. He became aware they had stopped. Osidian's pale face was searching the lofty gloom. 'Can you feel it beating?'

Sensing a tremor in the air, Carnelian gave a solemn nod. His body was a bell resonating to a sound beyond hearing. The gloom between the pillars was pulsing. They were huddled together. Carnelian struggled to understand how he had got there. The Plainsmen stared, deaf, demented as they chewed rotting djada.

'This is the true Labyrinth.'

Carnelian turned to look at Osidian, whose eyes were misted over.

'Do you not feel that time itself has slowed? The Wise told me of this but I did not believe.'

Osidian's whispering seemed brutally loud.

'His madness was in the blood. I felt it clothe me with His grace. I am become His vessel.'

Osidian's hand touched his forehead. 'Have I not always borne His seal here?'

Carnelian saw Osidian had his finger on his birthmark.

'He stirs within me. I feel His wrath warming in my blood. He draws me.'

Osidian let his head flop back as his finger slipped down to his throat and ran along the rope scar.

'He guides me. He leads me. He fills me with dark purpose.'

They were smoke drifting among the pillars. Head and stomach aching, Carnelian wondered if he had died or had become ensnared in a dream from which he could not wake. Osidian was the white flame they followed; the only beacon in the darkness. Constantly, he drew strange portents from the gloom and, alone, was possessed of clarity when all about him were prey to murky terror. His voice became the core and centre of their being. The darkness rang with his Quya. The Plainsmen, who could not understand his words, believed he was intoning purest incantation: Carnelian, who could, feared for his soul.

THE EARTHSKY

For our Father so loved his children
that he plucked out his eyes
and hung them in the sky
to light the world.

(Plainsmen hymn)

CARNELIAN BECAME GRADUALLY AWARE, BLIND IN THE SUN. A HOT
breeze was blowing a strange perfume in his face. Drinking in the
pure air, he found himself wondering where he was. When his sight
returned, he saw stretching away beneath a vast and cobalt sky a sea
of swaying jade-green ferns.

The Plainsmen bounded through the fresh ferns as if through water.
In their midst strode Osidian, as sombre as a thundercloud. At his
side, Carnelian smiled, enraptured by the clear sunlight and the
infinite blue sky.

'Are you forgetting your skin?' asked Osidian.

Carnelian struggled to focus, but Osidian was lost among the
vibrant greens. Suddenly he appeared in Carnelian's vision as a
flash. A hard grip pulled Carnelian into the shade of some trees. He
sighed, leaning his back against the bark watching the youths
chasing each other, smiling, luxuriating in the shade.

'It's rather beautiful this Earthsky of theirs, don't you think?'

Getting no answer, Carnelian turned and saw Osidian was looking off across the plain. Following his gaze, he at first could make
nothing out but the fernland fading away to blue, but then he was

arrested by a bright band gleaming along the horizon. For a moment he wondered if it might be the sea and that thought caused him to drift into a dream of his island home. Sadness made him pull back. The tree shadows stretching away from him were pointing towards the bright horizon which, he realized, being in the north, could be nothing other than the cliff of the Guarded Land.

Trailing Krow, Ravan came bounding towards them grinning. 'You said you'd get us here, Master. I believed you and it's come true.' Wrinkling up his nose he displayed the mouldy, stinking bale of djada he had been carrying for days. He looked up into Osidian's face. 'We're thinking we could get fresh meat. Would you like that, Master?'

Osidian continued to scan the far horizons as if he had not heard the youth. The sight of the oozing djada made Carnelian retch. He was feeling dizzy. The faces of the youths were swimming in his vision. Had the rotten meat been poisoning them?

Krow screwed his face up in concentration, licked his lips. 'Though we're on foot that doesn't mean we can't hunt at all. Would you like us to, Master?'

Osidian suspended his survey and looked down at the youths frowning as if they were not what he expected to see. When he gave a nod, Ravan and Krow unhitched their bales and, making faces, flung them away into the ferns. They wiped their hands down their thighs, Ravan gave Osidian a grin, then he and Krow ran off through the ferns, whooping.

Carnelian watched Osidian's gaze return to the horizon, but refused to allow his eyes to follow. Sadness found him nevertheless. His heart ached for his father and his people in faraway Osrakum. He ground his teeth. 'We *cannot* return.'

Osidian's eyes were a fathomless green. 'You are already so sure?'

The menace in Osidian's voice froze Carnelian's response. He turned away, looking back the way they had come. In that direction the greens of the plain were muted by the encroaching forest. Carnelian's head began to ache again as he was drawn back into the nightmare they had endured under the trees.

Carnelian was glad when he saw Fern approaching. 'Aren't you going with the others?' he called out.

'I'd better stay here. This land is strange to you and dangerous.'

'We can look after ourselves, barbarian,' said Osidian, coldly.

Fern could not withstand the pressure of the Master's gaze. His eyes fell. Suddenly his face grew fearful. 'Sit. Sit quickly.'

'What?' said Carnelian.

'Your feet . . .' said Fern.

Carnelian looked down and saw his feet and legs caked in dust to the knees.

'Please, Masters,' Fern pleaded, 'remove your feet from the earth.'

Carnelian remembered the ranga shoes the Law had demanded a Master wear so as not to touch any earth outside Osrakum.

'You believe the earth will taint us?'

Fern looked up wide-eyed, confused. 'The Mother, taint you? How could . . . ? Not that . . .'

Osidian's eyebrows raised and he smiled. 'Surely you don't believe our feet will taint the earth?'

'The Mother only suffers women to walk unshod upon her. Please. You do yourselves great harm and you endanger all of us besides.'

Carnelian turned to Osidian. 'We should do as he asks,' he said, adding, in Quya: 'Whatever he believes, we would be taking the same precaution the Wise themselves recommend.'

The smile froze on Osidian's face. 'Do you imagine, Carnelian, we have come this far in our captivity unsullied?'

Carnelian could not answer him but searched Osidian's eyes to see if there lay in them accusation.

Oblivious to his probing, Osidian turned to Fern who had been looking from one to the other with pained impatience. 'Are we then to walk across this land upon our hands, barbarian?'

'I shall make you shoes, just please, please sit down.'

Osidian looked suddenly weary. 'Oh very well, we shall indulge your superstition.' He sank to the ground and laid his back against the tree and Carnelian sat down beside him. With furious speed, Fern cut some ferns upon which to put their feet. Then, after seeming to pray before a nearby tree, he peeled from it a sheet of bark from which he cut the soles of four shoes and, pleating rope from fern stalks, he bound them to the feet of the Standing Dead.

It was nearing dusk when the hunters returned to lay their catches at Osidian's feet: two saurians, the size of children but more slender; long of tail and neck, with narrow hands and bird-claw feet. Carnelian's gaze lingered on these for a moment but he was more interested in the faces of the hunters.

'Did you rub charcoal on your faces as a sign of mourning?'

Their eyes seemed very bright as they stared at him.

'In a manner of speaking, Master,' said Ravan. 'By wearing the Skyfather's colour we declare ourselves his children so that our saurian brothers might give themselves to us.' He indicated the dead creatures.

Osidian sat as impassive as an idol. Ravan and Krow regarded him as if they might at any time kneel in adoration.

'Night is fast approaching,' said Loskai, sending a ripple of unease through the youths. Carnelian saw that several of them were scouring the fernland with narrowed eyes. He rose to his feet.

'What is it they fear?' Osidian asked Carnelian in Quya.

'The darkness, apparently,' replied Carnelian.

Osidian gave him an unpleasant smile. 'And so they should.'

Ravan's black face was regarding them with a frown of incomprehension.

'Are we in some danger?' Carnelian asked, reverting to Vulgate.

'It is often at the beginning and the end of each day that the great raveners stir themselves to hunt.'

Carnelian's heart jumped inside him as he remembered the monster's attack. For a moment he and Fern locked eyes, mutually understanding each other's fear, then the Plainsman turned to his brother.

'Ravan, take some of the others. Go, find some dry dung. Gather enough to make a fire that'll burn all night and make sure you keep your eyes sharp.'

As Ravan reluctantly obeyed him, Fern crouched and scooped one of the saurians into his arms tenderly, as if he feared he might wake it. He rose cradling the creature whose head hung wilted over his arm.

'Where are you taking it?' Carnelian asked Fern.

'To prepare her for eating.'

'Can I help?'

'If you want.'

Carnelian lifted the other saurian. Unnervingly, it was like holding a baby.

As they walked off side by side, Carnelian glanced over at Osidian who was sitting eyes closed, his back against a tree.

'How is he?' asked Fern.

'As worn out as the rest of us.'

Carnelian was relieved when Fern accepted that. His friend was peering into the gathering night. He shook his head. 'I prayed we'd left the madness behind in the forest, but now the sun is going down, I feel the dread creeping back.'

Carnelian shuddered, feeling the same growing despair. 'Do you think we've been affected by the rotten djada?'

Fern's eyebrows raised. 'Perhaps.'

'At least you're home,' Carnelian said, affecting cheerfulness.

Fern stared at him.

'This . . . is the Earthsky, isn't it . . . ?'

'A part of it, but far away from any we know.' Worry welled in his eyes. 'And we are flightless without our aquar.'

Carnelian decided not to push for more. Carefully, Fern laid his burden on the ground and Carnelian put his down beside it. Fern brought out a flint from his ragged robe, then began to cut the newest growth from the fern croziers round about. Carnelian offered to hold the cuttings. The green smell rising from the tight spirals seemed a kind of hope. When Carnelian's arms could hold no more, Fern indicated a spot beside the saurians and Carnelian crouched there and spilled the spirals out on to the ground. Fern knelt beside him and began sorting them.

'What're they for?' asked Carnelian.

Fern looked up and grinned. 'You'll see.'

Carnelian watched as Fern used their desire to curl to skilfully weave them into a mat. He rolled the saurians on to it, then began to sing a lament. Carnelian could not understand more than one word in twenty. His friend's eyes were focused devoutly on the saurians. Carnelian waited puzzled until he had finished.

'Why . . . ?'

Fern looked at him. 'Why do I sing?'

Carnelian nodded.

'Don't you sing farewell to your dead?'

Carnelian looked down at the saurians, trying to imagine them as kindred creatures. Fern stroked his hand up the neck of one and, when he reached its throat, carefully straightened its head. He picked up a clawed hand using only finger and thumb and slowly flexed the tiny wrist. He looked up.

'Aren't they as much the children of this sky and this earth as are we?'

'But you killed them nevertheless?'

'We have to eat, but we give our little sisters here thanks for sustaining our lives through their sacrifice.'

Carnelian considered this as he watched with what tenderness his friend sliced the bellies of the saurians open. He scraped out their entrails and, articulating each limb in turn, began to joint them. The head, hands and feet he put into a hole he dug in the ground and then covered them up.

'Returning them to the Mother,' Fern murmured. He took hold of the mat by two corners and lifted it carefully so the blood that had pooled around the jointed saurians poured out over the ground.

'Having no women here it's up to us to make sure the Mother gets her due,' he said as the redness soaked into the earth.

Ravan, Krow and the others were returning at a trot, their arms bulging with soft boulders which Carnelian realized must be dung. Dumping their burdens, they turned to look back the way they had come, searching. Fern distracted them by making demands. One of the youths gave him some herbs. Carnelian watched them dig a pit, line it with fern fronds, lay the saurian joints over these, sprinkle the herbs on top, and cover it all with more leaves and a thin scattering of earth. It was on top of this that they arranged the dung and some kindling. Fingers clumsy with anxiety spun the fire-drill. At last, a teasing of smoke rose from the kindling, which when it was fed with crumbled dung, was soon followed by tongues of flame.

Chattering with relief, the Plainsmen squatted around the fire. Without trying to understand what they said, Carnelian enjoyed the murmur of their talk as he too drew comfort from the flames.

'It'll be ready soon,' said Fern to Ravan. 'Go and ask the Master if he wishes to eat with us.'

A while later, Ravan appeared with Osidian. Seeing him standing deathly white at the edge of the fire, Carnelian realized he had been deliberately putting him out of his mind. Carnelian tried a smile but it felt dishonest. As Osidian sat down beside him, Carnelian noticed the Plainsmen fell silent.

The night grew pitchy black. A bellow swelling from the far distance chilled Carnelian to the marrow. After that, only the fire spoke, its crackling enlivened by pops that shot sparks up into the air. Following these pinpricks of gold up in the smoke, Carnelian became lost in the Plainsman sky. It seemed to him a bleak god who lay behind such chill white stars. With a shudder, he pulled his gaze back down to earth and the comfort of their fire.

'They must be done,' said Ravan.

It took some moments for his words to break their huddling circle. Carnelian felt he was coming slowly awake. With a broom they had improvised, the Plainsmen brushed the embers aside and then the smouldering earth. With much yelping and a jerking back of hands to lick burnt fingers, they plucked off the blackened fronds, releasing delicious steam. The youths produced a stack of little mats they had woven and with these to protect their hands, they fished out pieces of meat and passed them round. Ravan made certain it was he and not Krow who offered Osidian a portion.

Carnelian began eating with the others. Silence fell, interspersed with grunts of pleasure. Carnelian closed his eyes to savour better every mouthful.

'This must be the most delicious food I have ever tasted,' he said, the juices running down his chin.

When Fern translated what he said, Carnelian was rewarded with grins and looks of pride. He looked round and saw Osidian's food lying untouched in his hand and that he was squinting into the heart of the fire. When he spoke, everyone jumped.

'How do you plan to get to your homes?'

'We must go east until eventually –'

'On *foot*?' said Loskai.

Fern looked grim. 'Have you a better idea?'

Loskai glared at Fern, who Carnelian could see was unhappy about the effect the confrontation was having on the others. He decided he would try to break the impasse.

'Fern, you were saying that if we go east we would eventually end up . . . where?'

His friend gave him a look of gratitude. 'At the Backbone, which we can follow to the Twostone.'

Krow looked up eagerly and Fern smiled at him. 'Once there, our kin tribe will lend us aquar to get us home.'

Krow smiled as he nodded, but then his smile fell away and Carnelian guessed the youth was imagining the day when he would have to tell his tribe about Cloud's death.

'. . . and, besides, they'll have news of our tributaries,' Ravan was saying and glanced over at Osidian.

'Describe this "Backbone",' he said.

'It is the Mother's own that rises out from her earth.'

'Do you mean a basalt ridge running deep into the south?'

'Basalt?' Fern frowned at the strange word.

'Black stone,' said Osidian.

Fern broke into a nod. 'Yes, it runs straight and true further south even than our koppie.'

Carnelian saw the calculation in Osidian's eyes. 'You knew of this already?'

Barely glancing at him, Osidian momentarily dipped his chin, then turned his fiery eyes upon Fern. 'Your destination lies near this Backbone?' He waited just enough time for Fern to nod before continuing his interrogation. He wanted to know how long the Plainsmen took, once they had descended from Makar, to cross the Leper Valleys to the Earthsky and, from there, how long a ride it was to the koppie of the Twostone. The other questions Osidian asked, Carnelian deduced, must be designed to determine the pace at which these journeys were carried out.

Osidian smiled. 'Why then not go directly to the Twostone koppie?'

'Because, Master, we have no idea how far south we are,' said Loskai, triumphantly.

'Can you not judge by looking at the cliff of the Guarded Land?' asked Carnelian.

Fern shook his head. 'This part of the Earthsky is foreign to both the Ochre and the Twostone.'

'I shall need two spears,' said Osidian.

They stared at him, recognizing the tone as that of their guide through the madness of the forest. They had grown used to obeying it.

When Osidian had his spears he laid them across his knees and, taking a blade from Ravan, began to gouge regularly spaced notches along their lengths. Carnelian could only stare with the rest. No better than they could he imagine what Osidian had in mind.

When Osidian walked off into the darkness carrying the two notched spears, Carnelian followed him. Hearing footfalls, he turned to see Ravan silhouetted against the fire.

'I'll go with him. There's no need for you to come.'

'You don't understand the dangers, Master,' said Ravan.

The youth had a point. Glancing round, Carnelian saw Osidian was already far enough away to be almost invisible in the night.

He turned back to Ravan. 'We'll be all right. You stay here.'

Sensing that the youth was on the verge of rebellion, Carnelian considered explaining to him that Osidian was in a dangerous mood. A stubbornness in the set of Ravan's shoulders suggested he would not be amenable to argument.

'Do what you're told,' Carnelian said, more harshly than he intended, causing the youth to shrink back. Carnelian would have apologized except he feared he would end up trapped in a discussion. Instead, he turned his back on Ravan and set off after Osidian.

When he caught up with him, Osidian was working one of the spears into the ground.

'What are you doing?' Carnelian asked.

Osidian looked up. 'Good. You can help me.' He walked around the spear adjusting it slightly. He looked at Carnelian.

'Is it vertical?'

Carnelian moved round it. 'Seems to be.'

Osidian pointed to a point halfway up the spear. 'Hold it here.'

When Carnelian hesitated, Osidian, stooping, took hold of his right wrist. Carnelian allowed his hand to be positioned on the spear.

'Make a fist about it.'

Carnelian complied. Osidian took some steps away, lifted the other spear, rested its haft on Carnelian's fist and asked him to hold it in place. Osidian held the other end and raised it until it was level.

'There should be a gouge near your fist.'

Carnelian searched for it and found it; one larger than the others. Osidian slid the spear towards Carnelian until the gouge lay above his fist.

'Is it a perfect cross?' Osidian asked.

The spears intersected at Carnelian's fist. After some adjustment, Carnelian declared they met at right angles. Being careful not to move the spear out of alignment, Osidian crouched and looked along it.

'What are you doing?' asked Carnelian, increasingly exasperated.

'Sighting the horizon.'

Carnelian turned and looked to the north where the starry sky ended in blackness. 'Why?'

'Let your fist slide down a little.'

Carnelian complied.

Osidian nodded. 'That's good. Now with your other hand, hold the top of the spear.'

As Carnelian did this, Osidian continued to speak. 'I am trying to determine the height of the axis stars.'

Carnelian stared up at the sky. 'The axis stars?'

Osidian loosed one hand to point. 'That pair, just above the horizon.'

Carnelian followed the pointing finger and, with some more help from Osidian, found the stars.

'Of course, this instrument is laughably primitive . . . Let your right fist slide a little down the spear.'

Carnelian did so.

'Not so far.'

Carnelian moved his fist up a little.

'A little more.'

Carnelian obliged.

'The Wise use finely calibrated cross-staves.' He whistled softly. 'Their books do not lie: this far south the stars do sit very low.'

'What does it matter?'

'Their height will tell us how far south we are.'

Carnelian frowned. 'Sorcery?'

Osidian chuckled. 'Of a sort. The sky turns around the axis stars. The Wise say it is the suspension point of the carapace. The earth is formed on the dome of the lower half of the shell of the Turtle. The further south one is, the shallower the angle at which one views the axis stars.'

Osidian had Carnelian check the cross was perfect and then Carnelian had to adjust his right fist a little.

'Now, stay perfectly still.'

Osidian carefully lifted the horizontal spear off Carnelian's lower hand and came to peer at the vertical one. Carnelian flinched when Osidian produced a blade. He lifted it so that it touched Carnelian's upper hand and there cut a mark into the spear shaft. He did the same just above Carnelian's lower hand.

'You can let go now.'

Carnelian did so and stepped back as Osidian plucked the spear free. He lifted it up and peered at it. Carnelian could see his lips were moving.

'You're counting?'

'The notches.'

'And?'

'There were almost exactly five between your fists.'

'Which means?'

'The angle is five twentieths.'

Carnelian made a noise of exasperation that caused Osidian to look up from the spear.

'The Labyrinth in Osrakum is eight twentieths, nine four-hundredths and fifteen eight-thousandths.'

'Blood fractions?'

'Quyan fractions which are used for describing the blood taint but which here indicate the inclination of the axis stars.'

'Did we not already know we were far to the south of Osrakum?'

'We did, but now we also know exactly how far south we are. If my memory serves, Makar is close to the most southerly point of the Guarded Land, which I recall to be five twentieths and eighteen four-hundredths. Estimating distances from what the barbarian told me, the reading we have just taken suggests we are north of our destination.'

'Which means?'

'Which means, my Lord, we shall proceed across this plain a little south of east.'

'What if we miss the Twostone koppie?'

'No matter. We cannot miss the basalt ridge. Once we reach that, the barbarians should be able to lead us the rest of the way.'

Carnelian looked back where the fire was glowing in among the Plainsmen like a candle in a lamp. Osidian gathered up the spears.

'Let us go and inform the barbarians of the good news.'

'How can you *possibly* know where we are when we do not know ourselves?' asked Loskai.

Osidian smiled coldly. 'I know many things you don't.'

Fern grimaced as he saw Krow and others nodding. 'With respect, Master, you've never been here before.'

'Nevertheless, barbarian, I know the direction in which the koppie of the Twostone lies.'

Loskai scowled at the fire. 'This is ridiculous,' he grumbled in the Ochre tongue.

Ravan turned his glare from Carnelian to Loskai. 'The Master did find a way across the swamp.'

Loskai scowled, his mouth opening to say something. He closed it, shook his head and turned back to the flames.

Ravan allowed himself a tiny smile of triumph and then made it his business to interpret for the others. Carnelian could see how eagerly they listened. Fern sunk his head in thought. When he next looked up he could not be blind to the hope shining from the face of every youth. He fixed Osidian with doleful eyes.

'It seems that again we are to follow you, Master.'

Enough rain fell during the night to wash the world away. The struggle to keep the fire going was quickly lost and, with it, any pretence they had of being protected from raveners. Shivering, Carnelian huddled with the Plainsmen, his nostrils filled with the reek of wet charcoal; water running down his back. Through the downpour the cries of monsters kept making him lift his head to search the blackness, imagining their shapes coalescing, lumbering towards them with malicious gluttony in their eyes.

When first light came they were cheated of far sight by a vapour rising from the earth. It was Osidian who made them set off. They grumbled, but were soon glad of the movement for it drove the chill from their bodies.

Ravan and Krow at his side, Osidian led them into the south-east where the sun peered at them blindly through the drifting mist. They swam through ferns laden with dew. Each swishing frond lashed water over them until the angles of elbows and knees could be seen pushing through the sodden cling of their robes and cloaks. They came into a region where the spiral heads of the ferns swung menacingly above their heads. Roots tangled their feet. Their curses sounded as if they were being uttered in the confines of a room.

When Carnelian saw shapes looming out of the mist, hovering above him as large as houses, his pace faltered and he leaned back to stare. The trees looked like the watch-towers of the Guarded Land.

Someone collided with him. It was Fern. They both gazed up at one immense candelabrum of branches.

'A cone tree,' said Fern and took Carnelian by the shoulder. 'Let's not lag behind.'

'Isn't this blindness dangerous?' Carnelian asked as they pushed through the wet thrash of more ferns.

'The sun will soon burn this mist away,' Fern said. His words were hurried, tense, and Carnelian could see the way the Plainsman's eyes were peering over his shoulder searching for danger.

A rumbling in the ground froze the Plainsmen in a staring panic. Shocked, Carnelian felt each tremor in his bones and saw the way everyone was searching the mist in all directions. It seemed to be ships that came hoving into view. He fell back gaping at these saurian leviathans. Cries. Confusion. He was grabbed and yanked around. He stumbled, regained his balance, then was fleeing with the others. A root snared his foot. He fell. The shaking of the ground entered him through his palms and knees. Leaping up, he was coursing after the human cries. A cone tree solidified suddenly before him. Around its trunk Fern was marshalling the Plainsmen. Unable to check his headlong speed, Carnelian careened into them. Hands pulled him closer to the tree.

He turned, feeling their elbows against his back, and stared out in the direction he had come. Where the mist was dissolving, a jade plain was revealed, teeming with saurians wading languidly through the ferns. Some were horned, some flecked or crested with scarlet. Rich golden hides baroqued with dusky reds like old wounds. Many, no bigger than aquar, ran in spurts, but others lumbered thunderously, their necks pushing their heads deep into the sky's blue.

At first Carnelian thought the Plainsmen were shrieking with terror, but glancing to either side he saw their faces were lit with joy.

Bright passion gushed from them in ragged song, their eyes brimming with love as they gaped up at the monsters. Among them, Osidian seemed more interested in their reactions than in the saurians.

Carnelian reached over Krow to grab at Fern's shoulder. 'Aren't we in danger?' he cried.

His friend turned, blinking tears from his eyes, struggling to focus on something as tiny as Carnelian. He nodded but quickly turned back, unwilling to forgo the sight of the leviathans.

Carnelian dared to gaze out again. One of the monsters was approaching. Carnelian pushed back against the tree in terror. The reek the creature gave off became the only air there was to breathe. A leg as large as a crag lifted from the ground, hung impossibly in the air, then came down again, punching a tremor into the earth that rattled his teeth. The bows of the creature's chest forged closer, its hide keel rising up to a neck which was leaning a faraway head into the branch-nest of their tree. Carnelian felt the wood shudder as the monster fed.

Fern was laughing with the rest, tears of joy running down his cheeks. Trusting the people round him, Carnelian allowed his fear to abate and began to share in their wonder. His eyes were unable to measure the immensity of the being before him. He became convinced he could feel its massive heart beating the air.

There was a tugging on his shoulder. It was Fern looking sidelong at him.

'A heavener,' the Plainsman breathed. 'Connecting earth and sky. Sacred. I've never seen one so close.' He shook his head in disbelief as he looked back at it. 'Isn't she just *the* most beautiful thing you've ever seen?'

Mesmerized, Carnelian could only nod.

The sun grew stifling hot, forcing Carnelian and Osidian to swathe their heads with their ubas for fear of their skin burning. A breeze stirred a swell in the fern meadows, spreading infinite ripples towards the horizon. Across their path there lay the dazzle of a lagoon. The vast blue dome of the sky was marred only by a teasing of cloud. The euphoria of their encounter with the heavener sustained them for a while. Carnelian shared in their laughter and delight but this mood withered as the sun rose ever higher. Flies plagued him. He grew too weary to consistently lift his feet over the snares of the root-ridged earth and he tripped often. His view of the fernland contracted down to his feet; to his burning throat until at last he caught Fern by the shoulder and demanded some water. Frowning, his friend passed him a skin.

'One mouthful only,' he growled huskily, and when Carnelian protested and pointed out, indignantly, the flashing water that lay in front of them, Fern narrowed his eyes and shook his head.

'We dare not approach open water. The herds cluster along their margins and where they are, raveners will be too. If we are to reach the Twostone alive, we must avoid taking such risks.'

Carnelian looked at him aghast as he lifted the skin, which was less than half full. 'Do you really believe there's enough here to see us through?'

'We'll find caches at which we may refill it.'

Carnelian pushed the waterskin back into Fern's hands and resumed his march through the ferns. However unjustly, he could not help being angry with his friend.

As they made a wide detour around the lagoon, its mirror trembled in the corner of their vision as a throbbing headache. Narrowing his eyes against its glare, Carnelian saw the creeping shimmer at its edge that spoke of the leviathans drinking there. Envy consumed him. Distracted, he caught his foot and crashed to the ground. Carnelian growled at the youths who rushed to help him up, rose by himself nursing another bruise, stumbled on, head bent, grumbling against the heat, the flies, the whole, accursed Earthsky.

As their shadows narrowed away from them, Fern called to Osidian that he thought it better they should make a camp for the night. When Osidian agreed, everyone flopped down. Groaning with relief, Carnelian lay back against the rough fern leaves, feeling the thick stalks bend and snap under his weight. He lay with his eyes closed, listening to his breathing. As this grew more shallow he was able to hear the trilling, the snagging textures of insect flight, the gentle susurration of the breeze among the ferns and a delicate knock, knocking that made him open his eyes and see above him two curling crosier fernheads butting against each other. Then he saw the sky's smooth fathomless blue depths and he smiled, contented.

When the Plainsmen began to stir he lifted himself on to one elbow, grunting as his bruises crushed and stretched. He saw how wearily the youths stood and, finding Fern still bent, grinned at him. His friend straightened, grimacing at the pain, and, catching each other's eyes, they both burst into laughter.

112

'Shall I hunt with you?' Carnelian asked him.

Fern shook his head. 'The Master wouldn't want us to starve, now would he?'

Carnelian ignited more laughter. 'Then the Master shall take it upon himself to gather dung to make a fire.'

'That would be kind of him,' said Fern with a grin. He gathered up some youths and they slipped in among the fern stalks, their spear blades the last part of them to vanish.

Carnelian felt Osidian's gaze and, turning, saw in his eyes a green anger. Carnelian felt as if Osidian were accusing him of something but was reluctant to imagine what. When Osidian's fingers strayed up to his rope scar it caused Carnelian to suffer an ache of guilt. He noticed Ravan watching them both with silent fascination. Carnelian turned his back, then chose Krow and a few others to go with him to gather dung.

Carnelian, Krow and the others flattened a clearing among the ferns and with their hands combed the dried matter in towards the centre upon which they built a dung fire. The hunters returned with a single, scrawny saurian.

'We'll just have to make do,' snapped Fern when one of the youths complained.

In the deepening dusk, weariness was turning to bad temper. As the heat of the day faded into a brooding night some quarrelling broke out among the youths, which Fern resolved with surprising patience. Even before they were finished eating, some of the youths had succumbed to sleep.

Each day was the same as the one before. Carnelian lost count of how many had passed since they had come up on to the Earthsky. The success of their evening hunts diminished with their strength. They drank whenever they found a brackish pool trapped between some roots or nestling in the crevice of a tree. Carnelian grew accustomed to his thirst sweetening even the filthiest water. His muscles hardened like drying fruit while weariness seemed to be softening his bones. The faces around him became cadaverous. With the others, he lost the will to speech so that the groans, the mumbling complaints, became the only human sounds he heard.

Each morning Osidian, Ravan and Krow would lead the way and, grumbling, everyone would stumble after them. Carnelian knew well with what growing resentment they followed Osidian because he felt it himself.

'How long shall we have to follow the Master before we accept that he leads us to our deaths?' said Loskai.

Night after night Loskai's complaints had become bolder, but this time there was a rebellious edge to his voice that made Carnelian sit up. All eyes were on Osidian, who sat as he always did, a marble idol, his sight tangled in the brilliance of the fire.

Loskai leapt to his feet and indicated Osidian with his head. 'Can't you see he's already a ravener?' he said in Ochre. 'When we can go no further, who will find us? Who will give us to the sky?'

When Osidian lifted his head to look at Loskai, the Plainsman grew pale. 'What're you babbling about?'

Loskai stared at him slack-mouthed.

Osidian smiled coldly. 'Do you want to lead, barbarian? Well then, I give them to you.' His gaze returned to the fire.

Loskai looked round for support.

Ravan leapt to his feet. 'I'll follow none but the Master.'

Krow joined him.

Fern frowned. 'Would you deny, Loskai, that the Backbone runs unbroken the length of the Earthsky?'

The Plainsman looked blank. Fern sighed. 'Going east we'll come across it eventually.'

'Eventually?' said Loskai snatching at the word as if it might bring him victory.

'If you've a better plan, let's hear it,' Ravan said.

Loskai said nothing.

'Well then, sit down, before you end up sharing Ranegale's fate.'

Loskai's face hardened. Carnelian watched him glance sidelong at Osidian. For some moments the Plainsman stood trapped in the fascinated stares of the youths, before he seated himself clumsily, a murderous light in his eyes.

Carnelian's head bobbed with each step he took. His eyes could see nothing but the endless weave of fernroot across which he was struggling to pick his way. The sun beat down upon his back so that he was breathing the moisture of his own sweat. His whole skin itched. His scar had become so tender he had to keep pulling the uba off it. He was aware of the sour taste in his mouth, his gummed-up eyes, the weakness he had to overcome for each step.

When shouting broke out around him, he looked up blearily, expecting to see a ravener or some other monster wading towards them through the ferns. He could see nothing. He narrowed his eyes to allow himself to concentrate on the shouting. It was fading and had the vibration of running. He looked for and found the disturbance in the ferns that betrayed the youths running headlong. It was then he noticed a ridge of rock rising from the fernland like a tumbled wall. North and south it ran as far as the horizons.

'Praise the Mother,' said Fern near him, in a ragged voice.

Carnelian turned to see his friend fallen to his knees. Tears were glistening down his cheeks as he stared unblinking. Carnelian looked back at the ridge and understood what it was.

Clambering up on to the Backbone, Carnelian took delight in the views it gave into the blue distance; in the cooling breeze, but most of all, in the tearful joy of the Plainsmen.

Fern came scrambling over the rocks towards him. 'We've talked amongst ourselves and even Loskai's had to admit we're not much more than a day's walk from the Twostone.'

Fern gazed over to where Osidian was standing with Ravan and Krow. 'The Master's sorcery is powerful.'

Carnelian wondered if now Osidian would lose his hold over them. 'Shall we get there today?'

Fern shook his head. 'Night would overtake us if we tried. It'll be better if we make camp here and complete the last leg rested.'

They built their fire up among the smooth black rocks of the Backbone. The Plainsmen were transformed. They moved their thin limbs with vigour. They smiled and laughed. Even their hunting was more successful than it had been for days. The moon rising full and bright seemed an omen of salvation. All the talk was of the delights, the comforts they expected to enjoy the following day once they arrived at the koppie of the Twostone. It was only when they saw Krow, grimly silent, that a shadow passed over their hearts.

Fern sat himself beside the youth. 'I'll talk to your Elders myself. No one'll blame you for Cloud's death.'

Krow gave him a thin smile and Fern put his arm around his shoulders. Loskai was scowling.

'What about our tributaries?' asked Ravan.

'I warrant that we'll find they passed through more than forty days ago,' said Fern and there were grins and nods of agreement.

'The Tribe will have given us up for lost,' said one youth.

Frowns all round, uneasy muttering.

'That's why we'll not linger more than one night with the Twostone,' said Fern. 'They'll lend us aquar and, in no more than six days, we'll be home.'

Eyes brightened as the Plainsmen turned again to discussing the festivities the Twostone would be sure to throw to welcome them back from their adventures. Carnelian watched the youths' eyes widening as they realized for the first time that they were now not only just one short day from safety, but in addition they would be returning as heroes.

'And what about us?' Carnelian asked Fern, quietly.

His friend looked at him, frowning. He angled his head to one side. 'I don't know,' he said at last.

Carnelian thanked him for his honesty. He did not hear the words after that but only the happiness in their voices. Ravan's face was not as bright as the other youths'. Beside him, Osidian looked morose. Carnelian saw how, apart from Ravan, the other Plainsmen were paying Osidian no more attention than they would have a rock. Carnelian could not recall anyone having thanked Osidian for getting them there. After the long nightmare in the wilderness, the Plainsmen had returned to a world they knew. In that world it was the Standing Dead who were powerless.

RAVENER GRIN

And the Skyfather made birds
That they might be everywhere his eyes
(Plainsman lore)

THE PLAIN LAY UNDER AN IMMENSE BLUE WEIGHT OF SKY. A DISTANT herd appeared to be foothills. Stands of horsetail, groves of ginkgos, a few vast spreading acacias were all that alleviated the blank horizon. Trudging along the spine of black rock, it took Carnelian a while to notice the mound rising green from the plain.

He fell back until he was walking beside Fern. 'That is the first hill I've seen since we came up into the Earthsky.'

'It certainly is a hill of sorts,' said Fern.

'Of what sort?'

Amusement raised the corners of the Plainsman's mouth. 'A tumbling of stones among trees.'

'It's a koppie isn't it, and the one we seek?'

Fern beamed. 'Yes, the koppie of the Twostone.'

Clearly, they were not the only ones that had seen it. Murmurs of excitement were passing among the youths, putting new strength into their legs.

Krow ran up grinning. 'They'll have been watching us for ages and no doubt will soon ride out to see who we are.'

Some of the youths broke into song. One cracked a joke that made his companions fall about laughing. For a moment their gaiety lifted Carnelian's foreboding, but then his stomach began churning as he imagined the reception the Twostone were likely to give him and Osidian.

Fern led them down from the Backbone, making directly for the koppie. This island in a fern sea made Carnelian remember the stories Ebeny had told of the hills on which her people lived. If these koppies were not as grand as his childish imaginings had made them, neither were they the paltry things his Masterly cynicism had later reduced them to.

Carnelian became aware of the deathly silence and saw how serious the faces round him had become.

'What's the matter?' he asked Krow.

'We should've seen riders by now.'

'Perhaps they're in no hurry. After all, we're approaching on foot.'

'If it were only that,' said Fern, grimly and pointed. 'Look.'

Carnelian looked. 'I can't see anything.'

'Exactly.' Fern turned. 'Smoke should be rising. Even this far out we should be able to see a stubble of lookouts on the koppie's brow.'

They walked on in an uneasy silence until they came close enough for Carnelian to discern that the hill was clothed with cedars. From their midst, two stone towers rose, uneven crags of boulders piled one upon the other, the whole mass bright in the sun. The hill lay within a swathe of land enclosed by a circuit of magnolias. With unblinking stares, his companions were searching for any sign of the Twostone Plainsmen.

Krow cupped his hands together and blew a note that echoed among the trees, but the koppie remained stubbornly still. The cedars on the hill seemed the only living beings as, languidly, they slipped sunlight over their flat canopies.

Krow took them in closer. The ground began sloping down to a ditch the other side of which rose steeply as an earthen rampart along which the magnolias formed towers. The youth led them alongside the ditch, until they were moving through the shadows the trees spilled out over the plain. At last they came to where a bridge of packed earth crossed the ditch to a narrow cutting in the rampart framed by two magnolias. They lingered for a while peering across at the cutting, which was barred by a spiked gate.

'Shouldn't this be guarded?' Carnelian whispered to Fern.

His friend dismissed the question with an angry flick of his hand. They watched as Krow crept across the earthbridge then leant forward, avoiding the horns studding the gate, to peer through the chinks in its wicker. Krow pushed against it and it opened and he was left standing black against the green beyond, beckoning them to follow.

Carnelian crossed with the others. On either side a ditch held mirrors of dark water. Passing through the gate, he beheld a path shaded by cone trees running in the direction of the hill. They carefully closed the gate behind them before setting off along the avenue. Another wall of trees lay ahead. When they reached them, these turned out to form a double circuit between which there lay a ditch deeper than the first. An earthbridge led to a second gate and, once through this, Carnelian found they had entered another fern swathe, not as wide as the first, at the heart of which lay the hill with its cedars. His gaze was fixed on those giants as he approached. Their wide-spreading branches each held a flat roof of needled leaves; the whole mass shifting in the breeze made a creaking that seemed almost speech.

At the margin of the hill lay a final ditch deeper and wider than the previous two. Immense cedars grew on either bank, their roots so densely reinforcing the ditch its walls seemed made of wood. The further rampart rose to a parapet of skulls from which horns curved the length of scythes. Krow led them over a bridge towards the rampart. Between two sentinel cedars a more substantial gate barred their way, before which stood the ghostly figure of a man.

'They can't have returned yet,' whispered Ravan.

Krow regarded him with a fixed, pale expression. 'This late in the year?'

Ravan shrugged and looked unhappy.

'What manner of creature is that?' Osidian demanded, pointing at the ghost.

'A huskman, Master,' answered Ravan. Though he turned towards Osidian, he made sure to keep one eye firmly on the ghostly man. The youth saw Osidian wanted more. 'For his sins against the Twostone he's been denied skyburial. They set him here as a sentinel to protect their koppie while they were away in the mountains.'

'Why is this considered a punishment?' asked Osidian.

Fern glanced round. 'His soul's trapped in his sun-dried corpse like a flame in a lantern.'

Carnelian looked at the mummy with unease. 'For ever?'

'Until those he sinned against consider he's suffered enough.'

'Or until he fails in his duty . . .' said Ravan.

Krow, who had been examining the huskman, gave the youth a look that silenced him. 'Help me.'

As Ravan's face grew pale, Krow frowned. 'Though we're not Elders, he'll recognize I'm Twostone.'

Ravan looked unconvinced as together they advanced upon the mummy. When they drew close, Krow began mumbling some charm. Gingerly they reached out and touched the mummy. Ravan shuddered visibly, as if he had felt the huskman move. Then, carefully, they lifted it and carried it to one side, leaning it upon its face against the tree. As they backed away, Fern pushed against the wicker of the gate. When it did not open, he shook it.

He turned to Krow. 'It is secured on the other side.'

The youth was soon scaling the thickly woven gate. He struggled for a moment to climb over its spiky top before dropping down on the other side. Soon the gate was swinging open. Careful not to touch the huskman, the other Plainsmen filed past into the gloom beyond. Carnelian could not help peering at the mummy as he passed it. A man shrivelled like a fruit. Feeling it might turn to look at him, Carnelian hurried on.

Through the gate, he found himself within the cedar grove. The towering trees not only cooled the air but sweetened it with their resinous perfume. The rafters of their branches and their spiny leaves made a ceiling delicately pierced by the sky's blue. A yielding carpet of russet needles muffled his footfalls as he began to follow the others up the hill. Shade spread off between the column trunks. Clearings shone like courtyards, in many of which Carnelian could see ashen hearths ringed with stones. Here and there boulders crouched all scabbed with moss.

Krow sprang away ignoring Fern's call that he should wait for them and was soon lost. As they climbed after him, Carnelian caught glimpses of the twin crags crowning the hill. When they reached them, he saw their flanks rising blue-grey splashed with lichen roundels. He craned his head back to see the jagged summits.

'Fan out and look for any sign they've been here,' said Fern.

Carnelian dropped his gaze to find the youths already slipping off among the trees.

'Can we help?' Carnelian asked.

Fern frowned, shook his head. 'You'd better stay here.' He looked over at Ravan. 'Stay with them.' With that, he was loping off down the hill and had soon disappeared.

'What do you think might have happened?' Carnelian asked Ravan.

Peering among the trees nervously, the youth shrugged.

Carnelian could see between the branches the plain of the Earthsky laid out as a shimmering sea. The twin shadows of the crags were spilling down over the forest and out on to the plain. The sweet air could not lull his feeling of foreboding. His gaze strayed down to a nearby cedar, among whose roots some shards were nestling. He went to pick up a piece. By its curvature, the crude earthenware had come from a large jar. He could tell from the different hues that several vessels had been shattered. Something stirring above him made him start. Looking up, he saw that the shoulders of the branches were hung about with bags and bundles, many of which had been torn open. Wrapped around one bough he saw what appeared to be a rope-ladder dangling crookedly, its rungs here and there torn or missing. Looking at it more closely, he discovered that the stumps still hanging in the twine were the ends of wizened roots. Stowed in the angles of the branches were more bundles in disarray.

Voices behind him made him turn. Seeing it was Fern returned, he ran back.

'Isn't it possible the Twostone are simply delayed in their return from migration?' Osidian was asking him.

Fern shook his head. 'No tribe would dare cross the Earthsky once the raveners have returned.'

Carnelian was about to tell Fern of the signs of looting he had found when a cry shrilled, so thin with panic it might almost have been the calling of a bird. Fern careered down the hill in the direction of the sound. Carnelian's urge to run after him made his heart race. Standing in the shade of an immense branch with Ravan, Osidian looked fearfully pale.

'Had you not better run after him?' he said.

There was a menacing coolness in his tone which Carnelian was in no mood to engage with. He looked down the hill and saw Fern dappling in shadows as he sped under the trees.

'Yes, I want to, but will you not come?'

'Masters do not run.'

Carnelian heard the shrilling cry again, uttered some excuse and sprang down the hill. Osidian's disapproval only served to spur him to greater speed. Resined air blew in his face as he rushed through the flickering shades. Hurtling round a rock, he saw Fern with one of the youths, whose tears showed how dirty his face was. He was sobbing words. Fern's grimace showed he could not understand.

'Show me,' he bellowed. The youth gaped at him, stunned, so that Fern had to shove him into motion. The youth ran off as if a ravener were after him. Carnelian and Fern gave chase.

The youth took them through another gate in the skull wall in the mouth of which another huskman lay, discarded. They crossed the two inner ditches and were tiring when they approached the outer ring of magnolias. Reaching the gate that led out on to the plain, the youth came to a halt. He stood transfixed, staring. Carnelian saw in the glare that the plain seemed to have been ploughed up.

'You had better stay here,' Fern said to the youth, before, setting his face into a grim mask, he walked out across the bridge. A premonition made Carnelian hesitate, but then, cursing, he left the shade and followed his friend.

Drag-cradles and saddle-chairs were scattered everywhere under a smashed littering of bones. Stained brown, crushed for their marrow; skulls cracked open for their meat: the inedible remains of people and aquar.

Carnelian heard footsteps. Glancing round, he saw the youth had trailed after them. His eyes were weeping like wounds, his lips glistening with mucus as he gaped at the carnage.

'You,' roared Fern, 'go back to the koppie, find Loskai and send him down here.' He made sure the youth was moving away before he turned back.

'A battle?' Carnelian asked, as his eyes flickered over the corpses.

Fern rounded on him. 'Can't you see this was a massacre?'

Carnelian lifted his hands. 'I didn't mean . . .'

'No,' said Fern and wandered a little deeper into the carnage.

Carnelian followed. 'Who could've done this?'

Fern shook his head slowly. The shock had frozen his mouth open. As they walked in among the dead, they had to pull their ubas over their faces as a filter against the charnel stench. Carnelian concentrated on putting his feet down without treading on splintered bone. A skull tumbled alongside a twisted drag-cradle still had grey wisps of hair. Another was too small to belong to an adult.

'These are the Twostone,' he breathed.

Fern's eyes twitched as he scanned them. 'The whole tribe as near as I can tell,' he said, speaking through the cloth pulled across his mouth and nose. 'Men and women. Young and old.'

Carnelian could not judge how many people were lying there but their bones were like shingle on a beach. An arrow projecting from a ribcage caught his eye. He stooped and withdrew it. It was as long as his arm, with a stump of obsidian where its arrowhead had broken off. It was fletched with black feathers.

He held the thing up for Fern to see. 'Is this a Plainsman arrow?'

Lunging towards him with burning eyes, Fern snatched it. He had to allow his uba to fall away from his face so that he could examine the arrow in both hands. He looked up to say something, then was distracted by something he saw behind Carnelian, causing him to turn.

Osidian and Ravan were coming towards them across the plain, keeping in the narrow shadow cast by one of the crags. A ghost walking upon a path of darkness accompanying a child. Carnelian's sweat went cold. He shook himself free of the illusion; told himself the horror was playing tricks with his mind. 'He's got you seeing omens everywhere,' he muttered. It was just Osidian seeking to protect his skin from the sun.

Osidian's Quya carried towards them on the rising fetor. 'Who is responsible for this?'

'We have found an arrow,' Carnelian said.

'Plainsman?'

'Apparently not.' Carnelian saw with what gaping horror Ravan was surveying the scene.

'Who did this?' Osidian asked Fern in Vulgate, but the Plainsman had noticed Loskai crossing the koppie bridge and was deaf to the Master.

'Plainsmen?' Osidian asked, more insistently.

Fern's face darkened as he seemed to see Osidian for the first time. 'Don't be stupid. Do you really believe one tribe would do this to another?'

Osidian pierced him with his green eyes. 'If not the Plainsmen, who?'

Carnelian had been watching Loskai. With a strange fascination he watched the man grow sickly as his eyes gathered in the enormity of the destruction.

'This must be all of them, poor bastards.'

Fern gave him the arrow. Loskai took it and frowned as he turned it in his hands. He looked up and shrugged.

'Whoever did this, might they not still be here?' Carnelian said.

Loskai grew even paler. 'He's right.'

Fern was looking in horror to where Krow was coming over the bridge from the koppie.

'We can't let him see this.'

Fern was clearly about to dash back to intercept the youth when Ravan caught hold of his arm. 'What about our people?'

Fern tore free. 'What are you talking about? I don't have time for this.'

'Our tributaries.'

'They would've been here well after this happened,' snapped Fern, but Carnelian could see with what intensified horror his friend regarded the carnage.

123

Bleakly, Ravan looked out across the bone-strewn earth. 'They might be here . . .'

Fern advanced on him. 'They're not here,' he bellowed. 'They couldn't be. They weren't meant to arrive here until at least twenty days after the Twostone returned.'

Ravan's face brightened with hope. 'And we delayed them . . .'

Loskai groaned. He pointed at the massacre. 'We don't even know if the murdering bastards are gone. Even if they are, they might well have been here when the tributaries came through.' He looked back at the koppie. 'We might find our people up there.'

Carnelian felt their misery as if it were his own. 'I'll go with you.'

Fern turned blind eyes on him. 'You wouldn't know what to look for; where to go. Do one thing for me.'

Carnelian saw his friend focus on him. 'Anything.'

'You and Ravan look after the Twostone lad. We'll send the others down to you. Build a fire somewhere within the outer ditch. Keep them safe.'

Carnelian gave a hard nod.

Fern thanked him with his eyes, grabbed Loskai's shoulder and together they ran back towards the koppie bridge. Carnelian, watching them, only after a while became aware of Osidian looking at him with cold eyes.

When darkness fell, Carnelian could no longer deny his fear that something had happened to Fern. He had sat with Krow while Ravan went to marshal the others to build a fire in the ferngarden, beside the earthbridge. Thankfully, dusk now hid the massacre.

Carnelian sneaked a look at Krow's face and saw it was still blank with misery. He had tried to comfort him but even to Carnelian his words had sounded empty.

He gripped the spear he was leaning against his shoulder more tightly and ground its haft into the earth. He glanced round and peered among the dark masses of the surrounding trees longing for Fern and Loskai to return, while all the time, fearing the sudden rush of a murderous attack.

The moon had risen when something came towards them through the ferns. Carnelian leapt to his feet, gripping his spear with both hands as he levelled it at the darkness. Some of the youths were asking questions in shaky voices. He was reassured to see in the corner of his vision Osidian alongside him ready with another spear.

'It's us,' Fern's voice called out as he and Loskai solidified from the darkness.

Carnelian raised the spear with relief. The youths released their tension in laughter and questions as they mobbed the returning men.

'Let us near the fire first,' said Loskai.

The youths quietened and let Fern and Loskai through. Carnelian watched the two men crouch and stretch their hands out seeking the comfort of the flames. Their foreheads moulded into frowns, their squinting eyes sought the burning heart of the fire. Uneasy, everyone settled down to wait until the two men were ready to speak.

At last, Loskai tore his gaze free of the flames and looked round the circle of faces, his burning eyes settled on Krow. 'They came in from the west across the Bloodbridge. The huskman there failed in his duty and allowed himself to be cast aside. They desecrated many hearths.'

'Why?' Krow demanded with a chilling voice.

Loskai shrugged. 'Searching for food; water perhaps, many of the jars were broken.'

'What else?'

Loskai dropped his gaze as if ashamed. 'They lit fires . . .' He paused. 'On the floor of your Ancestor House.'

Wide-eyed horror greeted his words.

'Some of them must've lived in there,' said Fern. He braved Krow's stare. 'The place was filthy.'

Fern's eyes followed a billow of smoke up into the black air. 'There's more.'

He closed his eyes and took a deep breath. He opened his eyes, lowered them, quickly glanced at Loskai, then looked at Krow.

'They felled three mother trees.'

Carnelian could see Krow's lip trembling.

'Then the Mother has abandoned this koppie,' said Ravan.

Krow jumped to his feet. 'You don't know that!'

Fern flared his palms. 'He didn't mean –'

'Why? Why did they need to cut down our mother trees?'

'To burn their dead,' said Loskai. 'We found a pyre in an outer ferngarden. Charred bones on charcoaled ground. The wind must've blown the ash away.' He opened his hand upon which there lay something like fragments of shell. 'They were raveners in human shape. Look at these teeth we found.'

Krow took them, his eyes falling on them with burning hatred.

'May I have one?' Carnelian said.

The look Krow turned on Carnelian struck like a blow.

'I might be able to tell you something about them.'

The youth extended his hand and Carnelian took one of the teeth and peered at it. Its human roots tapered to an animal point.

He turned the tooth in the flickering light.

'Filed,' he announced, remembering the teeth of the men who had escorted them from the sea to Osrakum. He looked over at Fern. 'Was there anything strange about these bones you found?'

Fern looked exasperated. 'In what way strange?'

'Were they long?'

'Long?' Fern's eyebrows raised. 'Now you mention it, I suppose they were, but what –?'

'Marula. Is it possible the remains were Marula?'

Krow's mouth fell open.

'How could they be?' said Loskai angrily. 'When have Marula ever attacked a koppie? Besides, we're far away from where their lands are supposed to lie.'

'They're very tall,' said Fern looking into the darkness as if he were seeing one of the black men standing there. 'I saw one in Makar on our way to the Mountain. I'd forgotten his ravener grin.'

'I'm sure your mother's not forgotten,' sneered Loskai.

Fern tensed and fixed him with a look that made the smile fall from Loskai's lips.

'What about our people?' said Ravan, scowling at Loskai.

Fern turned to his brother with anger still glinting in his eyes. 'We searched the whole koppie, but found no sign of them. It's likely when they arrived it was as it is now and they went quickly home.'

'They left no sign for us? They must've known we'd be through here.'

'None we could find,' said Fern.

'It's likely they believe us dead,' said Loskai.

Ravan looked unhappy. 'Then we must get back as soon as we can.'

'What are they babbling about now?' Osidian asked in haughty Quyan tones.

Carnelian could see how much the sound of that language oppressed the Plainsmen. 'How they might get home as swiftly as they can.'

Osidian turned to Fern. 'How shall we get to your koppie now?'

'Without aquar . . .' Fern shook his head.

'Couldn't you obtain aquar from a neighbouring tribe?'

Loskai gave a sneer. 'Do you believe, Master, they would just give them to us?'

'You have enough salt to buy the aquar several times over.'

Loskai patted the shape slung across his back. 'This was bought with the blood of the Tribe and must not be squandered lightly.'

'Besides, Master,' said Fern, 'we know the nearest tribes are on feuding terms with the Twostone and, thus, with us too. They're more likely to take our salt than accept it in exchange for aquar.' He shook his head and looked round sadly. 'We might as well face it, we're going to have to walk.'

The youths raised a chorus of protest.

'What if these Marula moved south to attack the Koppie?' demanded Ravan.

Fern smiled wanly. 'The cistern here was drained dry. Loskai and I believe from what we've seen the Marula were here throughout the Withering. We all saw how little water the cistern held when we set off from here with the tributaries. For such a length of time it wouldn't have sustained a large number of them.'

'They might've brought water with them,' Ravan threw back at him.

Fern shook his head. 'We saw no evidence they had aquar. Without drag-cradles, they could've carried only a few days' supply.'

Ravan looked childlike. 'Can you promise me the Koppie is safe?'

'The pyre we found here contained the bones of many men. However many of them came here, when they left, their numbers were severely reduced by the prowess of the Twostone.' He twitched a smile at Krow.

'Promise me,' Ravan demanded.

Fern frowned. 'How can I do that?'

Ravan opened his mouth to say something more but Loskai spoke over him. 'Your brother's right. Tomorrow we'll gather what supplies we can and begin the journey home on foot.'

Krow demanded Carnelian return the tooth and, when he had it, he put it away with the rest somewhere in his robe.

Fern woke them from disturbed dreams into the first grey of morning. Carnelian could barely make out the faces round him but could hear in their groans how low their spirits were. Several of the youths, glancing in the direction of the massacre, drew his eyes there too. Though he could see nothing, he was glad to turn his back on it and follow Fern across the ferngarden towards the cedars.

Even as they searched for unbroken jars in the glooms beneath the fragrant trees, Carnelian felt the redness oozing up into the sky as if its hem were steeping in the blood of the massacred. He moved quickly into the dusk beneath another tree.

Eventually, homing in on Fern's call, Carnelian converged with the others on a gate in the skull wall at the western edge of the cedar grove.

127

'This was where the bastards came in,' said Ravan, scowling.

Krow lifted his head but said nothing. Carnelian was glad of the koppie crags that stood grimly black between the youth and the massacre. As they sorted through the fernroot they had salvaged, Carnelian noticed with unease the guardian huskman lying discarded to one side staring at him. However much he moved around he could not rid himself of the mummy's attention.

At last they were ready to set off. He had volunteered to carry a waterskin. Each time he took a step he could feel the wobble in its belly of precious water. He had allowed them to tie a bale of fernroot to his back. Winding the uba over his face, he followed them out across the bridge and down an avenue of cone trees.

When he became aware of the grating sound following him, he turned and saw Krow dragging the huskman along the path by a rope. Seeing the tight mask of the youth's face, Carnelian bit back his questions.

When they reached the outmost ditch, they paused a while to prepare themselves for the brightening plain, then Fern led them out of the koppie. The scraping sound the huskman made set Carnelian to grinding his teeth. Then the sound stopped. Turning, he saw Krow standing over the huskman. He kicked it. Again. Again. Soon the huskman was bucking under a general assault as, one by one, the Ochre joined in until, at last, only Carnelian and Osidian remained aloof as they watched the Plainsmen vent their rage on the mummy. Fern it was who called a stop to the punishment. He had to drag Krow off. The youth swung at him, snarling and Fern took some blows before he managed to calm him down. Krow spat upon the huskman, turned away and began walking towards the Backbone ridge. Osidian went after him and, with his huge strides, had soon overtaken him and then they walked together, talking. As he followed with everyone else, Carnelian wondered, uneasily, what Osidian might have to say to Krow. Glancing back he saw the shrivelled, broken man, now food for scavengers.

The Backbone ran straight and true into the south. The Earthsky spread eastwards, spangled with lagoons, creeping with herds, to a vague purple fading. In the west, scarred with gullies, the land lay thralled by thorny scrub. In places the rocky road they walked lifted them high into the shimmering air, its stone sweeping up to jagged ridges on either side often too high to look over. In the morning and the afternoon, these often provided blessed shade. When the sun rose high, they would seek to clamber down to the plain or else suffer walking the black rock that would melt the air and scorch their feet even through their shoes. Sometimes the Backbone sank into the red earth, as if it were some immense, burrowing worm. Carnelian took his turn in leading expeditions from the safety of the rocks whenever a nearby source of water was spotted. Even the most brackish tasted like nectar. In the cool of the later afternoon either Fern or Loskai would brave the open plain to hunt with a party of youths. Under Carnelian's command, those who were left behind would build a fire up in the heights and wait anxiously for the hunters. Mostly they would return before nightfall. When they came empty-handed, it would be necessary to consume some of the meagre supplies.

Osidian sank into a morose silence from which Carnelian was unable to raise him. Often he chose to sit alone. Most of the youths seemed to have forgotten him, but Ravan and Krow brought him food or walked at his side during the day. Sometimes, Carnelian would find Fern regarding Osidian as if he were a puzzle to be solved. When Loskai looked in his direction at all, it was with barely concealed hatred.

The vastness of the Earthsky crushed whatever was left of Carnelian's belief that he was an angel. Osrakum and its splendours seemed faint and far away. These small, dark people toiling at his side were real. Krow's grief like an ache in Carnelian's own heart helped him at last accept he had lost his father and his other kin for ever.

Whenever he spied a koppie hill, Carnelian would long to go there, seeing it as a beguiling island adrift in the ferny ocean. Those of their party that were Ochre would force the rest to redouble their pace. Carnelian would see in their faces the desire to reach their own koppie mix with fear; the fear they talked of was that their kin must believe them dead; the fear they would not admit to was that their tribe might have suffered the same fate as the Twostone.

The Koppie had been wavering in the heat towards the south-east for a while. Carnelian was oppressed by the general anticipation of disaster. Suddenly everyone was shouting, waving, crying. Alarmed, he looked around and saw Fern frowning amidst the tumult, with Ravan dejected at his side.

'What's the matter?'

Fern answered by pointing. Carnelian looked and saw a thread of smoke rising from the Koppie's summit. At first it appeared to be a dark omen, for it seemed much like the smoke he had seen rising on the road to Osrakum that had been a harbinger of plague. Then he remembered what it must be.

'They've seen us.'

Fern gave a heavy nod. 'Thank the Mother, the Tribe is safe.'

Carnelian was unsettled that his friend was not greeting this discovery with joy but then remembered what news it was Fern was bringing home, not to mention that he had with him two of the loathed and fearful Standing Dead.

Ravan looked through his tears towards his home and was slowing his pace.

'She'll not blame you,' Fern said, looking round, 'neither will the Elders.'

Ravan came to a halt and glared at his brother. 'Who will take the blame then, you?'

Fern grew morose. Ravan resumed his stride, but this time kicking through the ferns. Their exchange had dulled the general celebration. Most of the youths now walked in silence, stealing anxious glances towards the brothers and the Standing Dead, which only served to increase Carnelian's dread of what was to come. He glanced over at Osidian pacing imperiously, but could tell nothing of what he felt as his face was hidden beneath the windings of his uba. Krow walked in his shadow, his gaze fixed unblinking on the Koppie.

'They're coming to check us out,' one youth cried in delight.

Riders were appearing from the line of tiny trees beneath the Koppie hill.

'Shall we go and meet them?' another youth asked everyone, his face lit by a childish grin.

Fern frowned. 'They'll be here soon enough.'

'You seem unhappy to be home, barbarian,' said Osidian, speaking from his shroud.

Fern looked sombre. 'We'll have to answer for our dead.'

'You mean *you* will,' cried Loskai and he sprinted away.

His action broke the discipline of the youths and, whooping, they coursed after him, leaving only Fern, Ravan and Krow with the Standing Dead.

Fern hung his head.

'We're a burden to you,' said Carnelian.

'Not as great as having to explain to my mother the death of her husband and eldest son.'

A peculiar ululating wafted on the breeze from the bullroarers some of the riders were whirling round their head. Their movement made Carnelian recall the weapons the Ichorians had used to decapitate the Marula escort on his entry into Osrakum. The riders were not coming any further and were returning to the Koppie, escorting Loskai and the youths. No doubt, at that distance, they had assumed it was Stormrane and his brother who were walking with Fern.

The trees had grown close enough for Carnelian to discern they were lining a wide ditch. Between their trunks, he could see some of the youths and the mounted Ochre already streaming through the ferns that stretched beyond to another wall of trees. People were still taking their turn to cross the ditch on a narrow earthbridge.

By the time Carnelian and the others reached the bridge it was empty. Carnelian followed Fern across, through a gate in the low earth rampart into a ferngarden where people were converging from all directions on their long-lost sons. As Carnelian watched them coalescing into a crowd, he yearned to slip away somewhere. He did not want to darken their joy, nor wish to intrude upon their grief.

They reached the mass of backs. All attention was focused on the youths already at its centre. So many people, hundreds of them, swarthy, reeking of sweat, many rusted with earth as if they had recently emerged from the ground. Several were turning puzzled faces on Carnelian, who sensed the beginnings of unease, annoyance even, as they registered Fern's miserable face and the height of his companions.

A keening broke out from the heart of the crowd that made the excited hubbub falter. More and more faces were turning to watch Fern and his companions. People were drawing back, unable to understand who they were walking with Fern that were so much taller than he. Looking down the corridor opening in the crowd, Carnelian saw the youths he knew so well being passed round and kissed.

Then, suddenly, the crowd hushed. A group of people were coming through, garbed in russet blankets worked with indigo designs, wrists and ankles loaded with rings and bangles of salt. Some of the group had grey hair matted with feathers and salt beads: the rest had their heads covered, as did every woman Carnelian could see. Loskai was guiding them, half turned towards them so that he was forced to shuffle sideways, nodding with deference and making sure to keep his distance.

As Fern came to a halt, Carnelian found a place at his side. A young woman pushed forward, her eyes accusing Fern. 'Where's my husband?'

'My son?' an older woman demanded of Loskai. She turned on Fern. 'You were supposed to protect them,' she cried, close to hysteria.

One of the covered figures lifted a bony arm and said something that caused Fern's accusers to move aside. The old woman came to stand before Fern, staring up into his face. She gave a harsh, commanding nod and, with head bowed, Fern fell on one knee before her.

'Where is your father, Akaisha's son?'

Carnelian saw that when the woman talked, everyone listened.

'Among the clouds, Mother Harth.'

Harth looked up at Carnelian and Osidian and as she did so, Carnelian felt the eyes of the whole crowd upon him.

She turned back to Fern. 'Your uncle and your brothers too?'

Confused, Fern looked round, searching, then returned his gaze to the old woman. 'Ravan is here somewhere, my mother. My other brother . . .' He locked eyes with one of the other old women. A shake of his head spilled tears down her cheeks.

'Who else?' demanded Harth, drawing Fern's attention back to her.

A moaning moved through the crowd as he called out the names of those who had not returned.

Harth hesitated, her hands trembling.

'And it grieves me, my mother, to tell you that Ranegale your son was also lost,' Fern said.

Harth backed into the other Elders. The woman Fern had looked at earlier came forward wiping at her eyes, setting her face.

'Who are these two strangers you've brought among the Tribe, Fern?'

Misery aged his face as he looked up at her. 'Mother, my father, my –'

'The time for mourning will come; first answer my question.'

The way Fern's head sank even further made Carnelian feel wretched for him. Through her grief, the woman's face showed the beginnings of fear as she witnessed Fern's dejection.

'What danger have you brought among us, my son?' she said almost in a whisper.

'Mother, they are . . . Standing Dead.'

Fern's mother's eyes grew round, her mouth gaped and it was with effort she turned her gaze up to the two shrouded shapes.

A murmur of hysteria was rippling outwards from where they stood.

Carnelian watched Harth as she shook her head slowly looking at them. 'I don't . . . I can't believe.'

Loskai stepped forward. 'Show them,' he cried in Vulgate. 'Show them what you are.'

Carnelian watched the mixture of pleasure and fear play over the

Plainsman's face. Then he became aware Osidian was advancing. Fern plucked Krow from the Master's side and pushed him away into the crowd. The old women cowered when the apparition came to stand in front of them, so tall they hardly reached his waist. Carnelian saw the contempt in Osidian's hands as they unwound the uba that concealed him.

Gasps gusted from mouths as the Ochre stared with gaping disbelief at the immense white man.

THE ELDERS

As youth has vigour
age has wisdom
so, is it not natural
the aged should rule the young?
(a precept of the Plainsmen)

LOSKAI STRODE BACK AND FORTH BEFORE THE CROWD SHOUTING repeatedly: 'Why do you fear these Standing Dead? They are two: we are many.'

Carnelian could feel their mood already turning to anger, when Loskai stabbed a finger at Osidian.

'That one murdered Ranegale. Because of them we lost Stormrane, Thunderskai, Talan, Thunderwing, Windcrow, Fether, Crowskai.'

The Plainsman kept jabbing his finger all the time as he spat out every accusation he could imagine to transform fear into murderous anger. Carnelian glanced at Osidian standing amidst the tumult as unconcerned as if he were alone on a seashore. Carnelian looked around desperately for some escape. Noting where the aquar were, he saw how he and Osidian might pull two riders down and take their place. He glanced back to the outer ditch, imagining riding out on to the plain. But then where? Could they eke out an existence in the wilderness?

A woman cried out, another. Men were roaring. The mob's voice was swelling to a pounding clamour. The veins beating at Carnelian's temples seemed to be making his head shudder with each pulse. He let his gaze range over them. Hatred reddened their faces. Mouths were slavering for blood. Their rabid stares fell on him like blows. He could feel how close their fury was to bursting free.

'You lie,' a familiar voice cried out, thin in the uproar. Fern was advancing on Loskai.

'You lie. You know they're blameless.'

Loskai retreated a few steps. 'Is the blame then yours?'

Fern turned on the baying crowd, his face distorted by rage as he bellowed. 'They're as much victims of the Standing Dead as are we.'

Loskai pulled on Fern's shoulder. 'You were never truly of the Tribe.'

Fern threw himself at Loskai and they crashed together to the ground. Soon they were rolling among the ferns, crushing them as they pounded each other.

Fern's mother strode forward barking commands. As if to listen, the crowd quietened until Carnelian could hear her voice carrying clearly over their storm.

'Stop this now!'

She thrust her hands between the brawlers. They separated, glaring at each other. Carnelian saw that her hands and arms were filthy as if she had just come from digging in the earth.

'Get up,' she cried.

Fern and Loskai staggered to their feet, heads bowed, sneaking glares at each other, growling challenges. Other women came forward to draw them apart. Fern's mother took her son from them, scolding him in a low voice. Trying to listen, the crowd fell silent. Fern was nodding, agreeing with what he was being told. Glancing across the distance, he locked eyes with Carnelian, who could see that his friend was still listening to his mother. He gave one more nod and limped towards Carnelian, wiping blood from his mouth with the back of his wrist.

'Follow me,' he said addressing the Standing Dead, then moved into the crowd. As Carnelian made to follow him, he became aware Osidian was stone still.

Fern turned back. 'Didn't you hear?'

Osidian looked at him as if the barbarian were far away.

'My Lord,' Carnelian said in Quya, 'we should do as he asks.'

Fern glanced anxiously at the people surrounding him. 'Come on,' he cried hooking his arm violently to beckon them. 'If you want to live, follow me.'

For some moments, Osidian regarded him before, impassive, he strode through the crowd towards the Plainsman. Sighing his relief, Carnelian followed him.

He kept his eyes fixed on Osidian's back. The glowering faces of the Ochre formed an avenue on either side. Carnelian could feel the heat of their hatred. He hardly breathed until he walked free and, even then, his neck was too stiff to allow him to turn his head to see their escort.

Fern maintained a furious pace that forced the other, smaller Ochre to jog to keep up. Carnelian saw how careful they were to keep their distance from him. Saddled aquar were ambling after them. Fern was leading them alongside another tree-lined ditch, inside whose curve there lay another swathe of ferns which washed its green to the edge of the darker massing of cedars upon their hill.

He leaned towards Fern. 'What's going on?'

Fern came to a sudden halt and turned on him. 'Couldn't you tell?'

Carnelian saw the blood in Fern's nostrils, the blue bruising round his eye. His friend was looking past him, back towards the crowd. Carnelian turned. Even at that distance he could hear the commotion.

Feeling Fern move off, Carnelian said nothing more, but followed him until they came to where the ditch forked. They walked along the edge of the left fork until they came to a crumbling earthbridge. As Fern took them across, Carnelian saw that here and there the walls of the ditch had collapsed, exposing cages of tree roots. Below, pools glinted among lush scrolling ferns. He saw their escort had remained on the other side of the bridge and were regarding him with unconcealed hatred. Fern opened another gate and Carnelian and Osidian filed through to find themselves at the corner of another expanse of fernland, all edged about with magnolias.

'Stay here until I return,' said Fern.

Carnelian felt an initial stab of panic at being abandoned, but fear for Fern quickly replaced this.

'What are they going to do to you?'

Fern was clearly taken aback by the question. 'Do to me?' He read Carnelian's eyes and then smiled grimly. 'Soon the Elders will sit in judgement over me, but now I'm returning at my mother's command to talk to her.'

His voice was still tight but he seemed more like the Fern Carnelian knew.

Fern indicated the gate they had come through. 'The men back there have been told to stop you crossing that bridge.'

'Weakened as I am, do you think they have the power to do that, barbarian?' said Osidian with a feral smile.

Fern sagged. 'Look, I've brought you here for your own protection. Didn't you see what almost happened to you back there? If my mother hadn't calmed the Tribe . . .'

'Your mother?' said Osidian growing pensive.

Fern glared at him. 'We've all lost loved ones to your child-gatherer. Don't expect anything but hate.'

Carnelian wanted to thank his friend for having saved them from the mob, but to his annoyance, Osidian was speaking again.

'Then why did you bring us?'

'I'm not sure any more.' He glared at Osidian. 'If you escape from here, where do you think there is to go? The nearest koppie is at least two days' walk from here. Even if you knew the direction you'd be sure to miss it.'

'I'd find it.'

Fern scowled. 'Perhaps you would, but do you really expect another koppie would give you a warmer welcome?'

Osidian turned his back on Fern and gazed out over the ferngarden.

'It's your choice,' said Fern, using his chin to indicate the curve of magnolias marching along the outmost ditch.

'There's another bridge over there at the opposite corner of this ferngarden. It leads out on to the plain. If the raveners don't get you, I'm sure another tribe will. Meanwhile, I'm off to do what I can for all of us. I hope for your sake and mine you'll still be here when I return.'

All the time the Plainsman had been speaking, Carnelian had been watching Osidian from the corner of his eye. There was something in his stance that belied his seeming passivity. Carnelian reached out and clasped Fern's shoulder, squeezed it and gave him a smile. 'Don't worry. We won't be going anywhere.'

Fern gave him a grim nod and had soon disappeared through the gate.

Carnelian and Osidian wandered deep into the ferns, here and there disturbing dragonflies into whirring flight. Carnelian searched Osidian's face for any clue as to what he might be feeling. The gulf between them seemed unbridgeable.

'You should have been kinder to Fern: his intercession saved our lives.'

Osidian grew stony. 'Those savages would not have dared to spill our blood.'

'Can you be so sure?'

'It would overturn the nature of things. We are Chosen: they are our vassals.'

'Did you not see how much they hated us?'

'All I saw was their animal fear.'

Carnelian stopped his hand going up to his throat to feel the scar the rope had left there. 'The Ichorian feared us and the slavers too.'

Osidian's imperiousness collapsed as he looked at Carnelian's scar.

'Could you not live here?' asked Carnelian gently.

Misery and horror passed across Osidian's face as he looked around him almost fearfully. 'This world is wholly alien to me.'

Seeing Osidian vulnerable, Carnelian felt his heart breaking. Guilt gnawed at him.

'It is all my fault.'

Osidian stared at him in surprise.

'I forced you down to the Yden and, then, it was my choice that brought us here from the Guarded Land.'

Carnelian was embarrassed by the intensity of love with which Osidian regarded him.

'You gave me a chance at life at the cost of your own return to Osrakum. All the rest was as much my choice as yours.'

Carnelian watched Osidian's eyes growing opaque as he was drawn away into some dark place.

'I was so sure,' he whispered. 'I felt Him around me in the shadows, I heard Him speak to me.'

The timbre of Osidian's voice took Carnelian back to the swamp and the gloomy forest. He pulled himself up before he became lost. He clung to the sight of Osidian suffering from dark memory and doubt. Carnelian took some comfort that at least they had slipped from Quya into Vulgate, the language of their intimacy that was free of the stark clarity of the Masters.

He reached out to touch him. 'We were none of us ourselves. Weak from fever, you had to bear more even than the rest of us.'

Osidian turned to him eyes over which cloud shadow seemed to be passing. 'I saw so clearly. I saw why this had all happened to us, why it all *had* to happen.' He looked skywards, mouth hanging open, breathing erratically.

Carnelian saw the boy he had loved in the Yden standing before him. How broken he had become; how bruised his once perfect confidence. The scar of the slave rope was around his throat. Suffering had stolen the divine gleam from his beauty. The unhealthy colours of long illness still lingered in his skin. Still, with time and love he could be healed. Joy at having regained him began to suffuse through Carnelian's pain.

A voice crying out arrested his mood in the midst of its transformation. 'Master.'

It was Ravan wading towards them through the ferns, coming from the direction in which Carnelian could see the Koppie hill rising like a pyramid above the trees. A glance showed him Osidian closing up, protecting himself.

Ravan nodded a bow to each of them as he came closer. 'I've come to wait with you.'

'You shouldn't be here,' said Carnelian sharply, causing the youth's nervous smile to fade.

Desperate to get rid of him before Osidian closed up completely, Carnelian was merciless. 'Does your mother know you're here?'

The youth blushed and made a face. 'Not exactly.'

'Have you even seen her yet?'

Touching Ravan's head, Osidian took away the youth's look of indecision. 'Leave him be.'

Carnelian's heart sank as he saw Osidian's hurt once more behind an impregnable façade of impassivity.

'But we need to talk,' Carnelian said, in Quya, hoping to prise him open again, even a little.

'There has been enough talking for now.'

Osidian looked down at Ravan, who had been looking from one to the other as they spoke in Quya.

'Is there any water nearby we could use to wash?'

Ravan, grinning, nodded vigorously and pointed in the direction from which he had come. Osidian strode off, the youth jogging at his side.

'Were you not frightened at all, Master?' Carnelian heard him say.

'Of what?' said Osidian as if he were looking down at the youth from the clouds.

Ravan continued his chatter. Following on behind, angry, despairing, Carnelian could only watch as the youth's expressions of admiration worked Osidian into an ever-increasing hauteur.

Ravan led them to a spot where the ferngarden crumbled into a ditch. A path wound down to a green pool that glimmered through the leaves. As they descended, Carnelian saw it was set about with ledges and ropes dangling from branches.

'The children come down here to play at this time of year, before the water all dries up.'

Ravan's comment lifted Carnelian a little from his sombre mood. The youth talked as if he himself had long been too adult for such pleasures, while all the time he eyed the ropes clearly itching to swing on them. It made Carnelian remember how young Ravan was, how much he had lost. It made it easier to let go of his anger.

'This water is likely to be as clean as any we will find here,' said Osidian in Quya.

Carnelian regarded the brackish pool with some distaste, but he could feel how thickly his arms and legs were caked with grime. He became aware Osidian was gazing at him with longing, his eyes catching the sinuous play of light on the pool. Carnelian recalled their bathing in the lagoons of the Yden.

'You mustn't do that, Master.'

They both turned to Ravan, having forgotten him.

'Mustn't do what?'

Wide-eyed, Ravan pointed. 'Touch your bare foot to the earth.'

Carnelian saw Osidian had been in the middle of taking off one of the crude shoes Fern had made for him.

'Ah, yes,' said Osidian with wry amusement, 'the barbarian superstition.' Suddenly his face turned to grim stone. 'I choose to disregard your beliefs, Ravan.'

Osidian stooped and quickly took off both shoes. His clothes fell to the ground and he strode into the water followed by Ravan's horrified stare.

Carnelian hesitated for a moment. If the Law-that-must-be-obeyed was truth, to touch the earth was to invite pollution, but then had he not run barefoot for days upon the Guarded Land itself? If the Plainsmen's belief were truth, then Osidian had already given insult to the earth and Carnelian would not have him suffer alone whatever punishment he might have incurred. He removed his shoes, closing his eyes as his naked foot touched the cool earth. He took a few steps towards the pool, enjoying digging his toes into the mud. Osidian came up out of the water gleaming and scattered sparks of water everywhere. At first Carnelian thought the smile Osidian wore was for him, but he soon realized it was being directed over his shoulder. Turning, he was puzzled by Ravan's look of shame. Moments passed before he noticed the youth was standing barefoot.

Fern materialized out of the night and approached the fire Ravan had lit for the Standing Dead among the ferns. Carnelian saw his friend standing for a moment watching them, the firelight animating the shadows in his face.

'So you've returned,' said Osidian, making both Carnelian and Ravan jump.

As Fern came closer, he scowled at his brother. 'I might have guessed this is where you've been hiding.'

Ravan scowled. 'I'm not hiding.'

'Do you even care how much mother's worried about you?'

'How did she take . . . ?' Ravan's voice tailed away as he frowned back tears.

Fern sunk his head, swung a leather sack down from his shoulder then, kneeling, opened it and thrust a hand inside. He pulled out a mat and spread it on the ground and began to lay over it the rest of the contents of the sack. There were cubes of meat wrapped in leaves, some floury cakes, bundles of delicate fresh fiddleheads. He produced some skewers.

'Well?' Ravan demanded.

'How do you think she took it?' said Fern, with the fire burning the tears in his eyes. Ravan lost his defiance and slumped down, his arms clasped about his body. Carnelian turned away, desiring to comfort the brothers but fearing to intrude upon their grief.

Fern speared the meat on to the skewers and propped them in the fire. He watched it dribble blood that hissed to steam. When it began charring he spoke.

'You may as well know that my mother told me the Elders will, most likely, want to have you killed.'

'Does she also wish our deaths?' said Carnelian.

Fern turned to look at Carnelian. 'I told her what I believe; what I know about you. She might even try to save you, but I can't see how . . . I'm sorry. I shouldn't have brought you here.' Squinting deep into the fire, he shook his head. 'I don't know what possessed me to let you come.'

'They're burning,' said Ravan. Fern plucked the skewers out from the fire. When he distributed the food, Osidian refused any.

'The Elders won't kill us.'

Ravan looked at him sharply. 'How can you be so certain, Master?'

Osidian ignored the youth's question and looked instead at Fern. 'They want to see us before they make their decision, don't they?'

The Plainsman narrowed his eyes and then dipped a nod.

Carnelian watched Osidian, who seemed to be looking through Fern, seeing something beyond him in the night. Carnelian worked out arguments that suggested it would be perilous for the Plainsmen to kill a Master, but nothing he could come up with was anything more than an argument.

'When?' Osidian asked at last.

'In the morning,' said Fern.

Carnelian disliked seeing the way in which his friend was obviously awed by Osidian's manner.

Carnelian was shaken awake by Fern. Fronds hung over him, black against a starry sky. He sat up. Ravan was rolling up the blankets he had slept in.

'It's still dark,' Carnelian said, in a low voice.

Crouched over the embers of their fire, carefully dabbing them out, Fern spoke without turning. 'The Elders wish to avoid us causing more unrest in the Tribe.'

Carnelian nodded and rolled his bedding. Soon the four of them were walking towards the corner of the ferngarden. They opened the gate and crossed the crumbling earthbridge. Their guards were lying on the ground asleep and grumbled as Fern roused them.

As they waited, Carnelian approached Osidian.

'Have you an idea what we shall do?' he whispered.

Osidian turned a shadow head. 'They are barbarians,' he said in Quya. 'They will not dare to raise their hands against us.'

Fern led them back along the path they had taken the day before. They reached the place where the crowd had stood and found a wider, more solid earthbridge which they crossed to a gate. Once through this, they were looking across a starlit meadow towards the mass of the koppie hill.

The path took them straight across the meadow. A faint blue was appearing in the east as they came under the first branches of the cedars. Carnelian peered into the blackness that hid their trunks. Looking up he saw stars winking through the canopy. Fern led them into the night the trees were still nursing and soon the bodies of two cedars emerged standing sentinel upon a high wicker gate. Carnelian breathed their resin perfume and felt more than saw the heavy rafters of their branches hanging above him. The gate rose on the other side of another earthbridge and was set into a rampart. A ditch curving away on either side moated the hill with darkness.

Fern was the first to cross. He approached the gate and Carnelian heard the murmur of his voice, which was quickly followed by the creaking of the gate opening. As he passed through, Carnelian saw the shapes of the gate wardens and, though he could not see their eyes, he could feel them watching him.

In the near darkness, Carnelian could just make out the hill rising before him pillared with the black trunks of trees. Fern made sure they were still following him and led them up an irregular stair that Carnelian discovered with much stumbling to be formed by tree roots clinging to the slope. The Plainsmen, who even in the twilight seemed to know each step, slowed to let the Standing Dead feel their way up with their feet.

At last they reached a narrow clearing which terminated at a pitchy rising mass of rock. Looking up Carnelian saw the head of the Crag glowering in the sky's starless indigo and discovered an ivory house nestling halfway up.

Hearing Fern and Ravan arguing in whispers, Carnelian drew closer.

'I want to stay,' Ravan was pleading.

'I said, go to the hearth and see mother before she comes up here,' said Fern.

The youth seemed to be waiting for some intervention from Osidian, but the Master seemed unaware of him and so he trudged off along a path that hugged the Crag. There were stirrings among the cedars on either side. Carnelian could hear a clink of earthenware, some voices, a lazy drawn-out yawn.

Fern urged them forward. The night still lingering at the foot of the Crag engulfed them. Carnelian felt the presence of others. A light came to life and showed them three Ochre standing guard at the bottom of steps cut into the rock.

'Are we to go straight up?' Fern asked.

Their eyes wholly on the Standing Dead, the guards nodded. Fern beckoned Carnelian to follow him. The steps were steep and uneven. Taking care not to lose his footing, Carnelian managed to catch glimpses, past Fern, of the pale house they were approaching. He followed him on to a porch on which guards stood to either side of a doorway. Peering, Carnelian realized with a shudder that the guards were huskmen. Fern was staring at the doorway, gathering his resolve. He pushed its leather curtain aside and led the Standing Dead into the blackness within.

Falling back into place, the curtain shut out the light so that Carnelian had to put a hand up to feel his way. His fingers found Fern motionless. Carnelian moved round to stand to his left. The floor felt strangely uneven under his makeshift shoes. The dullness of the scuffing echoes made him aware of how small the room was. His head brushed the ceiling. Reaching up, he touched cold, smooth ridging interlocking in some complex pattern. He let his fingers slide along one ridge and felt it swell into a double knob. His hand recoiled.

'Bones.'

'This is our Ancestor House,' said Fern's voice in a reverential tone.

Carnelian became convinced he could detect a faint mustiness of death. 'Your people?' he breathed.

'Under our feet, what remains of the Tribe's mothers, grand-mothers, aunts and sisters after the tree roots have eaten their flesh; drunk their blood. Between us and the sky, the ceiling is formed from what the ravens have left behind of our fathers and grand-fathers, our uncles, our brothers.'

'A tomb, then,' Osidian said, contemptuously.

'Not so,' said Fern, outraged. 'Our ancestors inhabit the earth and sky. These are nothing more than the bone cages that once held their souls.'

'A house of death,' whispered Carnelian.

'Rather, one where we, the living, commune with our dead. Their discarded bones make this place familiar to the souls of those who have gone before. They seep in here like the scent of the magnolias so that the Elders might breathe in their wisdom.'

'Wisdom, you say?' said Osidian. 'Then –'

'Hush, bow your heads, they're here.'

The curtain lifting let in enough light to spill the three men's shadows across the floor. Carnelian registered the tracery of the design before resolving one into the roundel of a woman's pelvis. Up through the opening the skull of a baby was squeezing, its bony face upturned, its eye-sockets welling red earth. More oozed every-where into the cracks of the mosaic so that it seemed to Carnelian he stood upon a raft afloat on blood. The floor swept up into a wainscot of ribs. Bony buttresses reinforced a wall that was an undulating gleaming mass of femurs jointed into each other. Halfway up, more tiny skulls patterned a band with their eye and nose holes. From this band a dense leg-bone arabesque rose to a ceiling of shoulder-blades and arm-bones knitted together in a swirling spiral. Carnelian imagined this must be what it would be like to be in the hold of one of the kharon bone boats that ferried the Masters across the lake in Osrakum. Darkness suddenly returned and he was left blinking a fading, ghostly impression of the scene.

Thin morning light entered again while, at the same time, some-thing was shuffling past so close Carnelian could feel its clothing brush against his leg. He became aware of the shape's odour of sweat and ferns; of the smell of hair. The light pulsed with each lift and drop of the curtain. The women rustling past were bent for-ward, swathed in blankets so that he could not glimpse even a sliver of their faces. Among them, uncovered, men revealed their matted hair all pebbled with salt and tangled with feathers. A clinking drew Carnelian's eyes down. Above their brown and calloused feet, the ankles of the women were swollen white by carcanets of salt.

Carnelian realized he was staring. Looking sideways he could make out that Fern had his head bowed. Carnelian turned enough the other way so that, the next time the room lit up, he was able to see Osidian, his chin up, striving to put imperiousness in his eyes. Seeing that struggle to deny humiliation, Carnelian chose from love to emulate Osidian's powerless defiance and, lifting his head, stared out fiercely.

More and more Elders were crowding in. Women were helping each other to sink to the floor. Their wrists were knobbed, their gnarled fingers ringed with more salt. In the niches sunk between the wall buttresses of bone, the men were seating themselves cross-legged on platforms and removing their shoes.

A nudge from Fern urged Carnelian to shuffle to the left. He reached his hand up to Osidian's arm and gently urged him to move. Leaning forward, Carnelian looked past Fern and saw Loskai had joined the end of their line.

The curtain behind them fell closed and did not lift again. Cradling fire, flickering-faced girls stepped carefully among the sitting women touching to life lamps that hung around the walls. When the girls flitted away, Carnelian was faced with the aged, perhaps thirty of them, the lamplight trembling shadows in the folds of their robes and skin, glinting their wealth of adorning salt, pricking points of light into their eyes. He itched under their silent scrutiny. Without releasing him, their heads drew together setting off a rustling of talk. Many pointed and there was much shaking of heads that set the salt discs in their ears tinkling.

Carnelian could feel the rage swelling up in Osidian and sought to release its pressure by turning to Fern for help.

'Please give us . . .' he began whispering to his friend.

The room fell silent.

'. . . their words,' said Carnelian, excruciatingly aware everyone was listening.

An old woman directed a mutter at Loskai, to which he replied before turning to Carnelian, barely concealing a smile. 'The Elders forbid you to speak to Fern for he stands before them accused.'

'I've no doubt who did the accusing,' said Carnelian, and was pleased to see the man's face sour.

A woman rattled out angry words Carnelian struggled to understand. Something about keeping silent.

Loskai gave a nod and looked first to one then the other of the Standing Dead. 'Here you'll speak only if you're spoken to.'

Carnelian tried to keep from his face any sign he had understood anything of what the woman had said. A glance reassured him Osidian was managing to contain his anger.

A woman Carnelian recognized as Harth fixed Fern with bird-bright eyes. 'Why have you endangered the Tribe by bringing us these Standing Dead?'

She spoke slowly, with emphasis, so that Carnelian found her words easier to decipher.

'Have you nothing to say, child? Have you no explanation for why you have betrayed us?'

Fern curved as if the woman were piling stones on his back.

'Why?' she barked, jerking her chin up when he hesitated.

Fern answered her in a low voice. 'I'm no longer sure, my mother.'

Carnelian knew that last word well enough for, as a child, it was what he had called Ebeny.

'You're no longer sure?' said Harth, mimicking his tone. She looked round at a woman, Fern's mother, head bowed, hands clasped in her lap. 'Do you hear, Akaisha, your son's not sure why he's brought the Tribe to the brink of disaster?'

Harth pointed here and there among the Elders. 'Ginkga and Mossie, Galewing and Kyte all waited for you in Makar until they could wait no longer. You realize they were forced to come through the Leper Valleys without protection?'

As many of the Elders pursed their lips with disapproval, Fern and Loskai hung their heads.

Ginkga spoke up. 'Tell us what happened, children, so that we might not judge you unfairly.' Her fierce eyes belied her gentle words.

The Elders cocked their heads to listen as, hesitantly, Fern and Loskai took it in turns, sometimes interrupting each other, to tell their tale of robbery all the way down the road from the City at the Gates.

'We were moving along the high road,' said Fern, sliding his hand through the air as if it were in a groove. 'We'd no reason to suppose there was any special danger.'

Loskai stabbed a finger at him. 'It was his brother, Ravan, who saw the Bloodguard and Fern himself who found the Standing Dead among the sartlar.'

Many of the Elders recoiled at those last few words.

'All the bloodshed stemmed from that,' said Loskai, looking eagerly into their faces.

'Among the sartlar, you say?' a woman asked, her eyes wide with disbelief.

Fern joined his nod to Loskai's. Carnelian could see as well as they that the Elders did not believe them.

146

Fern leaned close to hold a finger up to Carnelian's neck, asking him permission with his eyes.

Carnelian gave the slightest nod and bit his lip when he felt Fern's touch upon his scar. As his friend described how he had found them among the slaves bent by ropes and smeared with bitumen, the Elders shook their heads and began arguing among themselves. A couple of the old men, one of whom was the man Harth had said was named Galewing, fumbled on shoes and came to see for themselves. Osidian impaled them with a glare so that they did not dare approach him. One remained transfixed looking sidelong at Osidian but the other, Galewing, came to peer up at Carnelian's neck. Carnelian could smell the man and see the light catching the carving in the salt beads threaded on his hair. They clinked as he turned to the Assembly and confirmed Fern's claim to general amazement.

Harth rose and took a few steps towards the Standing Dead, her face moving in and out of shadow. Her bird eyes fixing on Osidian and, then, Carnelian.

She turned to Loskai. 'Ask the Standing Dead why they were among slaves.'

'My mother wants to know why you were hiding among slaves,' said Loskai.

His mother, Carnelian thought. He could tell by the way Loskai kept his eyes on Harth, how much he was in awe of her.

'We weren't hiding. We were being taken to be sold as trophies.'

Startled, Loskai translated this and as his mother understood, her mouth fell open.

'How could this happen?' Loskai asked for her.

Carnelian grimaced, fearing that at any time Osidian's apparent passivity might crack. 'It's complicated . . . politics . . . the Masters . . .'

Harth interrupted him. 'Ask them if it was others of the Standing Dead who did this to them?'

Loskai asked, Carnelian gave a nod and the Assembly burst into a fevered discussion which took a while to abate. Harth leaned close enough for Carnelian to see his own reflection in her eyes.

'We never imagined the Standing Dead might fight amongst themselves.'

Carnelian saw she was fascinated by his scar and so he leaned his head to stretch his neck for her. Her eyes narrowed as she reached up. He felt her dry touch. She pulled away frowning.

As she returned to her place, an old man encouraged Fern to continue. Resigned, he began describing what had happened on the

147

road. He persevered through all Loskai's interruptions. Carnelian watched the effect Fern's report was having on the Elders. At the end of each statement they would give a nod and when Fern made a gesture like a spear thrust, they flinched. They lived the skirmish through his words.

Whenever Loskai took over, Fern's anxious glances kept finding his mother, so that Carnelian began to wonder what his friend was expecting from her.

Loskai was describing how, after they had fled, they had found Fern's brother and uncle dead in their saddle-chairs.

'Sacrilege,' cried several of the Elders.

The old men clasped their hands over their heads in horror: the women traced circles over their bellies, their heads bowed.

Fern's mother, Akaisha, looked up. 'Tell me something, Loskai, when you were riding away were you yourself aware that my eldest son and my husband's brother were actually dead, not merely wounded?'

Loskai tried to find an answer that would deny her what she sought, but he could find none and scowled. Akaisha cut through her son's look of gratitude by urging him to continue his story. It took Fern some moments to regain his composure, but then he began to talk about the council the raiders had held.

An old man interrupted. 'So it was my son who took over the leadership?' He did not bother to hide his pride as he looked around at his peers.

'Yes, Father Crowrane, Ranegale took over,' said Fern, bitterly. 'Though only because my uncle and brother had died and my father had taken a mortal wound.'

'Cloud Twostone seems to have deferred to our son, child, even though he was an Elder,' grated Harth with a nod to her husband.

Fern shrugged and only resumed his story when voices cried out demanding he continue. He proceeded to describe the long trek with the drag-cradles and, as he spoke, Carnelian relived each weary day.

Suddenly, Fern was pointing at him. 'It was this one here who chose to give up his drag-cradle for my father.'

They looked at each other.

'You mean he'd recovered his strength?' Akaisha asked.

'No, my mother, he was still weak and in so much pain he could barely walk.'

Some of the Elders discussed this, others stared at Carnelian, but it was Akaisha's gaze that made him most uncomfortable. He was glad Fern drew all their eyes away, as he began relating the days that followed until he came to the night when they had seen dragonfire reflecting in the sky. A look of fierce attention leapt into the faces of those of the men whose missing ears or four-fingered hands proclaimed legionary veterans. They swelled up as they fired one question after another, wanting to know in excessive detail everything they could about the dragon line and its dispositions. Fern obliged them as best he could. With one hand he traced a wall into the air and pierced it with the other to show them Ranegale's plan. Crowrane looked around him, his pride returned.

Loskai drew angry looks when he said loudly, 'Let him tell you how once more the dead rode in saddle-chairs. This time he can't say he didn't know. They stank.'

Fern raised a fist. 'I knew well enough but believed the Mother would forgive me so that I might save their souls for her husband, the sky.'

There were gasps of outrage and more genuflections, but Carnelian was relieved to see some of the women looking with sympathy at Akaisha. For her part, if she was suffering, she hid it well.

'Did you do this by yourself, my son?' she asked.

Fern looked at Carnelian. 'Again, my mother, this one helped me. I couldn't have done it without him.'

Harth surged to her feet glaring first at the mother and then the son. Her face turned into shadow as she gazed over the Assembly. 'Whatever the mitigating circumstances, dare we allow sacrilege to go unpunished?'

Rising, Akaisha moved to her son's side and then set herself before him as a shield. She raked the Assembly with her eyes. 'Punish him? Don't you think he's been punished enough already? He's lost his brother, not to mention his father and his uncle, both of whom sat here among you.' Tears softened her glare.

Scowling, Harth sat down as women came to comfort Akaisha. As they mumbled kindnesses, her fierceness deserted her altogether and she let herself be guided back to her place. Harth, meanwhile, had become the heart of an angry conference. The men looked on, uncertain.

'Come, Fern,' said one of the veterans. 'You might as well show us how you escaped the dragons.'

Tearing his gaze from his mother, Fern shakily redrew in the air the dragon line and the raider's trajectory. As he showed the veterans what had happened, they nodded sagely and argued among themselves whether some better stratagem could not have been devised.

'And after that?' asked Galewing.

Fern described the struggle through the rugged land beyond the Ringwall.

'We decided then . . .' said Loskai.

'You and Ranegale decided,' interjected Fern and they scowled at each other.

Loskai fumbled in his robe and brought out a length of cord which he lifted up for all to see. Carnelian recognized it by its knots.

'My brother argued rightly we'd not make the meeting in time,' said Loskai triumphantly.

'He wasn't necessarily right,' said Galewing. 'We ourselves were delayed on the road and were late for the meeting by three days. It was because we thought you must've gone on without us that we hurried down to the Leper Valleys hoping to overtake you.'

Loskai lowered the cord, crestfallen.

'So what did you and Ranegale decide?' asked Galewing.

Loskai's hands hesitated on the verge of making some shape in the air.

'To take us down into the swamp,' said Fern.

This produced consternation. Questions were thrown at Loskai which he did his best to answer. Clearly, he was enjoying this less than he had expected. When Fern came to Loskai's rescue with answers of his own, the Plainsman regarded him with surprise.

It was Fern who described the descent to the edge of the abyss. He made his hands into the shape of the cave they had sheltered in for the night.

He stopped and looked at Loskai. 'Do you mind?'

The man's slow head shake allowed Fern to proceed. There was an audible sucking in of breath as he began describing the slaughter of the aquar. Many faces went pale, but Fern talked on and, when he faltered, Loskai began to add his own comments, until, whenever one was uncertain, he would look to the other for support.

Fern addressed his mother as his hands showed how they had hoisted the dead up on to the rock face. His mother nodded at him through her tears and much of the Assembly murmured their approval.

Then began the story of the descent into the abyss. Halfway down, Fern addressed himself to one of the women. His hands showed the fall of the youths and the woman asked him the details with a shaky voice.

The story continued and Loskai had to admit it had been his brother's decision that they should descend from the foothills into the swamp. Many of the Elders shook their heads, horrified. Carnelian watched them huddle together as they were told of the darkest part of the journey. Soon he was lost in it himself. Once more he felt the terror creeping round in the night. Some of the Elders were looking sidelong into the murky corners of the room. Carnelian brought his attention back to Fern's voice. He had to prepare himself for the full horror lying just a few sentences away. When it came, he saw many of the Elders, man and woman, hide behind their hands. Osidian, not understanding Fern's Ochre, was examining the Elders one at a time as if looking for a weakness in a city wall.

'My grandson torn . . . ?' wailed a woman, shattering the spell so that people blinked as if coming awake.

Bravely, Fern described to them the aftermath.

'How did my son die?' asked one old woman.

Fern left out the full horror of Cloud's fate, but told her he had died protecting the youths of both tribes.

She looked around her tearfully. 'Always he thought more of others than himself.' Others of the women took her hands and stroked them as they agreed with her. 'His heart was large. His adopted tribe would've joined with us in mourning him.'

'And this ravener took no one?' asked one of the veterans, incredulous.

'He was driven away before he could,' said Fern.

His words put a frown on every face.

'Driven away?' a voice asked for all of them. 'You told us you had no fire.'

Fern looked at Osidian and, as he described how they had found him painted with gore, holding Stormrane's broken spear, Carnelian saw with what renewed awe the Elders regarded this example of the Standing Dead.

Fern's voice wove on for a while and then he drew every eye once more to Osidian as he told of the fight in which Ranegale had been killed.

'Was it fair?' Harth barked, hungry for revenge.

'It was,' Fern answered.

'How can you say that,' cried Loskai. He stabbed a finger at Osidian. 'Look how massive he is.'

Fern glowered at Loskai. 'You know full well how wasted he was from the fever; from his struggle with the ravener.'

Loskai spluttered incoherently.

Fern gave a snort of disgust. 'You were happy enough with the fight when you thought your brother would win.'

'Was it as Fern says, son?' Crowrane pleaded. When Loskai looked at the floor, his father sank back scowling.

Akaisha gave Harth and Crowrane a glance of sympathy. 'Go on, my son.'

Fern spoke in a melancholy tone of their journey into the heart of darkness. Gloom settled over his listeners like the sudden night of an eclipse and, as Fern followed the Master through the nightmare, eyes strayed to Osidian who had been their beacon in that primeval dark. When Fern's story brought them out into the bright Earthsky there was a general relief. People lost their rigid postures and sat back. A gentler twilight settled on the Assembly as Fern and Loskai together described how Osidian had found a way for them across the uncharted vastness of the Earthsky. Carnelian could feel tension returning when the story began to draw them closer to the Twostone koppie. He could see everyone knew what was coming. It was now Ginkga who told the story.

'We found them hiding in a ditch, children mostly, a few women.'

'We tried to sprinkle at least a handful of earth over their dead mothers and to drive the wingless scavengers from their fathers, but you saw how vast the slaughter was, how hopeless a task it was to keep the raveners from their feasting.'

Silence fell as everyone, blind for the moment, contemplated the immensity of such loss.

'And the survivors?' asked Fern at last.

'We brought them home with us,' said Galewing.

'We've distributed them among the hearths,' said Kyte.

'But their wounds will take a long time healing,' a woman said and there were many slow nods.

'And it will be hard on the girls without a connection to –' said one man.

'Some wounds can never heal,' Ginkga said over him as if she was unaware he had been speaking. Carnelian noticed many of the women had hardened their faces.

'We brought a Twostone lad home with us,' Fern said.

'A hearth will be found for him,' his mother said, which pleased Carnelian.

'What of the salt you carried?' a voice demanded and, round the margins of the room, the men looked at Fern and Loskai with narrowed eyes.

'None was lost,' said Fern, and he stepped forward folding back the cloth from a bundle in his hand to reveal a long yellow cake. He placed it carefully at Harth's feet. She picked the salt up and it was passed back, through the women, to the man who had spoken. He examined it minutely, before, satisfied, he reverently rewrapped it.

A grumbling rose up, mainly from the men.

Galewing pointed a four-fingered hand. 'The lepers extracted from us more than twice the usual tolls. You're responsible for that loss.'

Fern flushed while Loskai began protesting his innocence.

'Not one, but both of you will bear the responsibility for this,' snapped Galewing. 'Unless you wish to blame the dead?'

Loskai seemed to consider it, but he saw, as quickly as Carnelian did, that the Elders would not stand for this.

A woman spoke out. 'Are you more concerned about salt than the safe return of our children?'

'This isn't a case of one or the other, it is –'

'I think you'll find, Galewing,' said Akaisha, 'the Tribe has lost no salt.'

'The leper tolls –'

'Perhaps the only advantage of not returning through the Valleys was that my son and his companions paid nothing to the lepers.'

'But . . . but their long detour caused more salt to be consumed,' blustered the Elder.

'We've seen with our own eyes the unbroken loaf they've brought back and there's a little more salt besides as well as twenty and eighteen bronze, double-headed coins.'

She looked at Loskai. 'Isn't that so, child?'

Loskai was forced to give a nod.

Akaisha turned back to Galewing. 'I recall you brought back two loaves and fifteen coins. If I'm not in error, this means that, of the twenty loaves this Assembly gave into your keeping, more have been returned than would've been expected from an uneventful journey to the Mountain.'

The veteran frowned, then ducked her an apology but still looked unhappy as he fingered one of the salt beads in his hair.

People were looking at Galewing, their raised eyebrows registering surprise. Akaisha twitched a smile at her son.

'What I still can't understand is how the Marula could come so early to the Twostone koppie,' said Kyte, looking haunted.

The Elders looked uneasy.

'We debated that enough when you returned,' said Harth. 'It's a mystery without solution. Now we must concentrate on the issue for which this Assembly was called.'

She moved out and turned to face the Elders. 'You've seen them and know why they came here. Think hard, my mothers and fathers, for the Tribe has never been in greater danger. What are we to do with these Standing Dead?'

'Could we not send them back to the Mountain?' said one man.

Harth turned to her son, her white eyebrows raised. 'Well?'

Loskai looked at Osidian with a cold smile broadening on his lips. Still smiling, he shook his head. 'I don't think so, my mother. If this one could find his way across the Earthsky to the Twostone, I'm sure he could as easily bring the dragons here.'

'They told me they wouldn't,' Fern blurted out.

Harth turned on him gaping. 'They knew where the Koppie lies?'

Fern grimaced. He glanced at Carnelian apologetically. 'They know *who* we are.'

Harth's eyes ignited. 'You *actually* told them?'

'They saw it in the pictures on my father's hand.'

Carnelian saw the veterans regard their palms as if they had suddenly snagged them on thorns.

'He looked at the pictures and spoke the name of the Tribe,' said Fern.

Akaisha rose and surveyed the Assembly. 'You see? If the bodies of our dead had been left behind they would've led the vengeance of the Mountain here.'

Ignoring her, Harth drew closer to Fern. 'Is that why you brought them, child?'

Fern looked at the ground, shook his head. 'No, my mother. I brought them because they asked me to.'

Voices rang out in anger.

Harth waited until the hubbub had subsided. 'They asked you to?' she said, quietly.

'They helped me save the souls of my nearest kin.'

'They led you into sacrilege,' said Harth, severely.

'They asked for sanctuary.' He opened his arms to the Assembly. 'My mothers, my fathers, you can all see how badly they've suffered at the hands of their own kind.'

'They are of the Standing Dead,' she shouted into his face.

Harth turned her fury on Carnelian, who flinched seeing the hatred in her eyes.

'They take our children. Fern . . .'

'Yes, my mother?'

'Give this one my words.'

'But, my mother, one of them –'

'Just do as you're told,' a man growled from off to one side.

Fern lowered his eyes, then looked round at Carnelian. 'Mother Harth wants me to translate for her,' he said, in Vulgate.

Carnelian gave a nod.

Harth was already speaking.

Fern translated. 'Do you know how much we hate you?'

With a glance to Osidian, Carnelian answered. 'I know you've every reason.'

When Fern translated the Master's words for her, Harth

laughed without humour. She said something in a sarcastic tone.

'Every reason?' As Fern was translating, Harth was already saying more.

'You take our children,' said Fern keeping her in the corner of his eye.

A man spoke.

'The best of us.'

A woman.

'I lost a daughter and a son,' translated Fern, his face gleaming with sweat. Others, mostly women, were calling things out and Fern was trying to relay as much as he could.

'Since I was born, my hearth's lost ten children.'

'Mine, twelve.'

'My grand-daughter just last year.'

Ginkga pushed past Harth and came to glare up into Carnelian's face. He could see the tears catching in her wrinkles. He could feel the drizzle of her spittle as she accused him. Fern's voice came from behind her.

'I've just returned from the Mountain where I had to give up my grand-daughter.'

Her face crunched tighter with her sorrow and Carnelian found he could no longer bear it and dropped his gaze in shame. He cringed as the woman went on, her words so violent Carnelian expected to feel her clawing at him. The tirade shifted to Fern.

Carnelian looked up and saw the Plainsman flinching.

'She was saying . . . her daughter's sorrow . . . the pain.' Fern was crying.

'We can hardly let them go if they know who we are,' she shouted at him.

'And where to find us,' someone else cried out.

'Do any of the other tribes know they're here?' Harth demanded.

'I can't see how . . . I can't see how they could,' said Fern.

Carnelian felt her eyes on him again, measuring him up.

'Their bodies must never be found. We must bury them so deep in the Mother that even a thousand Rains will not dig them out.'

Carnelian stared at the woman and saw Fern was sharing his horror.

'They came to us painted in the colours of the Skyfather,' he cried. He pointed at Osidian. 'That one bears a mark as if the Skyfather himself kissed his brow.'

The Assembly ignited into uproar. Several men pushed through the women to see for themselves. Withstanding Osidian's stare, they squinted up into his face and then fell to arguing.

Harth's voice carried above the din. 'How can we possibly let them live?'

She had the attention of the room.

'Just because the Gatherer's not due until the year after next doesn't mean the Mountain will not find out about these two.'

'Carnelian, do you understand all this hysteria?' Osidian's clear and ringing Quya chilled the room to silence.

The Elders stared at Osidian, who continued to focus on Carnelian as if they were alone.

'Well, do you, my Lord?'

Carnelian turned to Osidian. Just the sound of his voice seemed to have turned the Elders into the servants that were always present at the edges of a Master's vision.

'They were discussing by what means they shall dispose of our bodies.'

Osidian smiled and flipped a hand to point lazily at the Assembly. 'These filthy savages are *actually* discussing killing us?'

He inclined his head and masked his face with a pale long-fingered hand and while he stood thus, the Plainsmen gaped at him as if his gaze had turned them to stone.

Osidian revealed his exquisite face, his emerald eyes. 'Barbarians,' he said in Vulgate. 'Those of you who can understand this coarse tongue convey my words to the others.' Without pausing for their assent, he continued, regarding them from on high as if they were errant children.

'You presume to sit in judgement on us who are the Masters of Earth and Sky? You who live only because we allow it; whose children we have taken to be our slaves since the Creation?'

Carnelian saw his words being passed by those who understood to those who did not.

Osidian took a step forward and the Elders rose in alarm. He seemed to grow larger, brighter. 'Barbarians, you should take care.' His voice rang clear around the room of bones and a terrible fire seemed to spring from his eyes and teeth.

'The Masters have cast us out of Paradise and for that they have earned my hatred. They will forget us. But *you* – you can never forget them. And it seems you have already forgotten we too are Masters. If you kill us, our blood will be upon your hands. Do you think the servants of the God in the Mountain will not see its stain?'

As he scanned the Elders, Carnelian saw their staring terror of him.

'Do you think when the childgatherer comes he will fail to see the red reflection of our blood in your children's eyes? And what then?'

He paused looking for an answer. Where his gaze swept the Elders looked away.

'What do you think will happen then? Do you imagine for one moment, whatever enmity may lie between us, do you *really* imagine they would let such as *you* slay even the least of the Masters with impunity?

'There are those here who have taken the Gods' salt,' he said, stabbing his finger here and there at the Assembly. 'Others have knelt to kiss the dust in the Mountain. Of these I ask: are the Masters merciful? How many of you hide that mercy's stripes across your backs? I can see the mutilations of lost fingers and shorn ears. How many of you have wept in the night for your lost children? Do not delude yourselves. The Masters know less of mercy than you do of power. They will bring the dragons here.' He stamped his foot on the floor of their mothers' bones. 'They will exterminate you man and woman, young and old, until your tribe shall be nothing more than a whisper lost in the wind.'

Kyte stood bravely forth. 'What's to stop us . . . giving . . . giving you up to the Gatherer?'

Osidian smiled chillingly. 'Do you not recall, auxiliary, the penalty for having looked upon our faces?'

The Plainsman went pale, caught in the green ice of the Master's eyes.

With relief, Carnelian watched Osidian relapse back into a languid state. Long after the echoes of his voice had vibrated away the Elders continued to gape, transfixed. Though Osidian was no longer as white as he had been, still in that dark place, in contrast to Loskai dwarfed beside him, with his green eyes and the bright beauty of his face, Osidian seemed undeniably an angel.

'What did he say?' Harth asked Fern urgently in a half-whisper.

Desperate to undo whatever harm Osidian had done, Carnelian spoke before Fern had a chance to answer her. 'He threatens . . .' said Carnelian, crudely in their language, 'your destruction . . . if you touch us . . . or give us up to the Gatherer . . . but . . . Fern spoke truthfully. I promised . . . we wish no hurt on you.'

Harth joined her peers in turning her gape on him.

Galewing shambled towards Carnelian, stopping at a distance. 'You . . . you understand our speech?'

'Much of it,' Carnelian said, in Vulgate.

As Galewing relayed the answer to the Assembly, their unease turned to near hysteria.

Harth turned on Fern. 'You knew this?'

Fern made a grimace then nodded.

His mother rose. 'What of it? We've always known the Standing Dead have sorcery. Is a broken knowledge of our tongue so great a mystery?'

Galewing glanced at Carnelian. 'But that they should understand our tongue when even many unkith Plainsmen cannot . . .' He shook his head. 'Are we being fools? Perhaps Fern is right, perhaps they are a gift to us from the Skyfather.' He regarded the Assembly. 'Imagine what secrets they could teach us.'

As protests rose against Galewing, Akaisha approached Carnelian. When she was close she looked up and he saw a yearning in her eyes.

'How is it you come to speak Ochre?' she asked, quietly.

Harth grabbed her arm. 'What are you doing?'

Akaisha tore herself free. Many voices among the Elders cried out that she should be allowed to ask whatever she wanted. Akaisha gave them a nod of thanks and turned her eyes up again to look into Carnelian's.

He was moved by her need.

'Mother.' He stopped, seeing Ebeny there in her face. 'My servants . . . were taken . . . from the Earthsky tithe.'

Akaisha shook her head. 'The tongues of the Plainsmen are many, yet, when you speak, your words are Ochre.'

'A woman . . .' Carnelian knuckled his head trying to find the words. 'A servant woman . . . she was . . . not my mother . . . but she *was* my mother.'

Akaisha's eyes were very bright. 'Her name?'

'Ebeny.'

The Plainswoman shook her head, deeply disappointed. 'No. Not that.'

Carnelian looked around trying to find something. He reached out to catch Akaisha's blanket between finger and thumb. He tugged it. 'She made blankets like this.'

Hope relit Akaisha's eyes. 'The same pattern?'

Carnelian looked at it carefully. 'It seems very much like I remember.'

Akaisha grabbed hold of his arm. 'Did she tell you anything about us?'

Carnelian saw the tears in the woman's eyes and desperately wanted to give her what she desired, but was too emotional to think clearly. Other women had crept up and were whispering to her. She let go of him.

'You have to leave now,' she said gently. 'Leave with this other one of your kind. Please wait outside.'

158

He nodded, then moved to Osidian's side and gingerly put a hand on his arm. Carnelian expected anger but Osidian seemed content to be led out. They had reached the curtain before Carnelian realized Fern was not following him. He turned and saw his friend looking very alone encircled by the Elders.

With his eyes, Carnelian asked Fern why he was not leaving with him, but the only answer Fern could give him was an angry shake of the head.

Pushing out past the curtain, Osidian let in a flood of light in which Carnelian could see nothing but Fern's back. He was reluctant to leave him with the Assembly and his accuser, Loskai, but knew he could do nothing to help him.

As Carnelian stepped out from the house of bones, the glaring brilliance of the plain forced his eyes shut. His heart was racing, his mind dazzled by the certainty the Ochre really were Ebeny's people.

THE HEARTH

Fire is the heart of living.

(Plainsman proverb)

'WHERE ARE YOU GOING?' ASKED CARNELIAN AS HE SAW OSIDIAN BEGIN to move towards the steps that led down from the Ancestor House.

Osidian half turned. 'Away from this filthy hovel.'

'Fern's mother asked us to wait here.'

Osidian's face distorted with rage. 'Since when do the Chosen obey savages?'

Carnelian saw a guard coming up the steps, looking at them uncertainly, a spear ready in his hands. When Osidian swung round, the man flinched. The spear lowered to point at Osidian's chest in reaction to him moving towards the guard. Carnelian could see the man's narrow-eyed fear and the way he was adjusting and readjusting his grip on the spear.

'Let me pass,' Osidian growled in Vulgate.

'I must stop you descending,' the man said, in Ochre, and threw a nervous glance down to where one of his companions was mounting the steps to his aid.

Osidian looked back at Carnelian. 'What did the creature say?'

'He has been commanded to bar our descent.'

'Has he indeed,' Osidian said, turning the menace of his face on the guards, both of whose spears were now questing for his throat.

'Osidian!' cried Carnelian.

Behind him the muttering of the Assembly faltered. Osidian seemed intent on throwing himself upon the guards. Carnelian saw their flint blades and how narrow were the steps, how high the fall. He lunged forward and took hold of Osidian's upper arms and pulled him back.

'Release me,' Osidian hissed as he struggled.

Carnelian held on, cursing.

'Let me go,' bellowed Osidian.

Voices were speaking behind him but Carnelian ignored them. Osidian pulled and almost broke free. For a moment Carnelian believed Osidian was going to be dashed upon the ground below.

'Do you want to die?'

Osidian sagged back into Carnelian, who embraced him. Osidian turned within the circle of his arms and looked at him with infinite sadness.

'What is there left to live for?'

Carnelian looked deep into his eyes. 'You still have me.'

He became aware of the dark faces staring and felt naked under their gaze. He did not know what tongue he and Osidian had been speaking but was certain the two guards could see the way it was between them. Osidian looked as vulnerable as a child. Carnelian became aware Galewing was regarding them from the doorway of the Ancestor House.

'He's still weak . . . illness . . . I'll look after him,' he said, in the Ochre tongue.

The Elder ducked back behind the leather curtain. His hand still clasping Osidian's arm, Carnelian's attention returned to the guards. The smile he gave them caused them even more confusion. His gaze scaled to the heights. He looked for and found steps climbing from the porch to the summit of the Crag.

'Can we go up there?' Carnelian asked the guards in Ochre.

They looked startled, uncertain, so Carnelian made the decision for them. He coaxed Osidian towards the steps and gently urged him to climb. Careless of his own safety, he shadowed Osidian with his hands all the way up, terrified he might miss a step.

The summit was windblown and scorching in the sun. Even with the uba covering most of his face, Carnelian had to squint. The place was more extensive than he had expected: an uneven floor of blocks and cracks and shadows. Three men were sitting on a promontory. One of them rose, staring at him. Soon all were staring.

'Lookouts,' said Carnelian indicating them with a jutting of his chin. 'See the beacon ready to be lit.'

Osidian was gazing out over the plain, turning slowly as if searching for something. Carnelian allowed his sight to soar. A vast sky fell into a single encircling, melting horizon. Trees danced in the heat.

He saw the mirrors of lagoons, the ragged drifts of herds. The curves of the two outer ditches were betrayed by their borders of magnolias. At his feet, smoke was rising through chinks in the cedar canopy.

Carnelian turned to Osidian. 'They are better organized than one might have expected of barbarians,' he said, hoping to encourage a more sanguine outlook on their situation.

'They merely ape the Chosen,' said Osidian.

'How so?'

'Can you not see this place is marked out in the form of a wheelmap or a legionary camp?'

Carnelian looked again and saw the three concentric ditches: the outer two each containing a swathe of land divided by the crooked spokes of smaller ditches into ferngardens; the third the grove of cedars on the koppie hill. If the first were the Outer Lands and the second the Guarded Land, then the hill and stone upon which he stood would represent Osrakum. The sight of these fortifications forced through his hope the bleak awareness that he and Osidian were Masters powerless among people who had every reason to hate them. His eyes fell on the ivory roof of the Ancestor House, in which their fate was being decided by the Elders. What would they do to Fern? Surely his mother, Akaisha, would be able to protect him. Carnelian recalled the look of need in her eyes. Tiny figures were moving through the inner ferngardens. Faint voices drifted up from the cedar grove; bright laughter and the smells of cooking. Had this really been Ebeny's childhood home? Even the possibility warmed his heart a little.

He turned to Osidian. 'You know, Ebeny, my nurse, it seems certain to me she came from this tribe. Of all the koppies, that we should end up here . . .' Carnelian shook his head in wonder.

Osidian was looking at him as if he were listening to an echo.

Carnelian smiled remembering her. 'In my heart, she is my mother.'

Osidian's lips curved into a sneer. 'When will you realize, Carnelian, these sensibilities are an affectation. You are Chosen. Your persistent desire to hide from what you are is a delusion I find increasingly repulsive.'

Fear that Osidian might be right only made Carnelian despise his cold Master's face. 'Do you know, Imago Jaspar once said something very similar to me.'

At the sound of that name, Osidian's face became as rigid as a mask, but Carnelian did not care. He delved inside himself for the truth of what he felt and was sure his love for Ebeny was real.

'Besides,' he said, burning up in her defence, 'it is perhaps those very sensibilities that might secure sanctuary for us here.'

Osidian's face sagged. 'Here? How can you expect me to live *here*?'

Seeing the distress bleeding out of him, Carnelian could not sustain his anger. He remembered who Osidian had been. He remembered the pressure he had put on Osidian to go with him to the Yden one last time before the Wise made him God Emperor. Despair soaked through his confidence. He tried to rally.

'Even if we care nothing for ourselves, there are others we cannot abandon.'

'Your precious half-caste, for example?'

Carnelian was stunned. 'You mean Fern? That half-caste saved your life not once, but many times.'

'Do you hope to blind me by throwing that in my face? Do not play me for a fool, Carnelian, I have seen the way you two look at each other.'

Osidian's bitter words struck Carnelian like blows. 'I don't . . .' He shook his head. 'I really don't know what you are talking about.'

Osidian shrugged, then went seeking a shadow in which he might find refuge from the sun.

Carnelian was dozing in the shade when he heard a scuffle of feet approaching. Sitting up, he saw it was Fern with Akaisha, Harth and some other woman Elders. Carnelian nudged Osidian awake and rose to face them. He tried to read Fern's face. As their eyes meshed, Carnelian could not help considering what Osidian had said. Fern gave him a brave smile that was hiding some pain.

Harth stepped forward. 'You understand my words?'

Concerned for Fern, Carnelian gave her a nod even as he realized Osidian had not bothered to get up.

'We have decided to postpone our decision as to what we are going to do with you. In the meantime, Mother Akaisha has offered to keep you in her hearth. You will be under her authority. The first time you disobey her you will both be put to death. What do you say?'

Carnelian glanced at Fern, then at Akaisha, who was searching his face as if she were looking for a sign.

From the sour look on Harth's face, Carnelian deduced it was Akaisha who had bought them a reprieve. 'Will the Tribe accept this arrangement?'

Harth raised an eyebrow. 'The Elders have accepted it. We are the Tribe.'

Halfway round the Crag, Akaisha took a rootstair down into the mottled shade of the cedar grove. She was asking Fern for news of Ravan.

'He should have appeared at the hearth before you went to the Assembly?'

A shake of his mother's head made him scowl. She reached out to take his arm. 'Most likely he fears my grief.'

She half turned her head. 'We're nearly there.'

Carnelian nodded, but his attention was on a group of people under a nearby tree who had stopped everything to watch them pass.

'It is considered impolite to stare into another's hearth,' said Akaisha and looked surprised when he apologized.

Some children began following them, daring each other to run in close to the white giants. Osidian frowned, studiously ignoring their dash and screaming flight, until Akaisha turned on them. Her scolding sent them scuttling for cover. The gurgles of their furtive laughter made Carnelian smile and remember his own childhood.

'We're here,' said Fern gloomily, stepping from the stair on to the hillside.

A cedar spread its branches above them. Its trunk was the centre of the arc they walked, crossing the radiating ridges of its roots. Carnelian heard squeals of delight and saw some children chasing each other in and out of the shade. Ahead, Akaisha seemed to catch fire as she reached a space unroofed by the tree. Carnelian approached, narrowing his eyes against the dazzle. He stumbled over a root that ran across his path. He could smell the smoke but it was too bright to see the flames. As Carnelian's eyes adjusted, he saw a woman standing with two boys at the edge of the long, oval clearing.

'Whin, these Standing Dead are to be our guests for a while,' Akaisha said.

She turned to Carnelian. 'This is Whin, a daughter of my hearth who, next to me, is the nearest to the roots of our mother tree.'

Whin was possibly forty, though her weathered skin looked older. She regarded the Standing Dead with a severe face. To avoid her eyes, Carnelian looked at the boys, who were also staring, their cheeks flushed from the heat of the fire. He smiled and they smiled back. Sharply, Whin told them to resume stirring the earthenware pots sitting upon the embers.

Fern moved round the fire towards the woman, who lifted her hand. He touched his palm to hers and their fingers meshed.

'May our roots grow together,' both said.

Their hands fell.

'You are to be punished, Fern?'

Fern winced. 'For my sin against the Mother, I am to labour as a woman, Aunt Whin.' He sneaked a look at her face.

'You deserve worse,' she said, but her eyes warmed a little.

They grew cold when her gaze fell on the Standing Dead. 'Go, Fern, give our guests some bedding and let them choose hollows. I wish to speak to your mother alone.'

Fern seemed to be waiting for her to look back at him.

'Whin, has Ravan been here?' said Akaisha, anxiously.

'Ravan, your mother wants to see you,' cried Whin.

From the gloom gathering round the trunk of the cedar, Ravan emerged using his arm to shield his eyes from the glare. He came to a halt, looking at the ground.

'Son.'

Ravan glanced up at his mother and then saw the Standing Dead.

'They're to stay with us a while,' she said.

Ravan's smile was dazzling as he gazed at Osidian. Carnelian noticed the momentary frown with which Akaisha observed this.

'It warms my heart to see you again, my son.'

Ravan disengaged his gaze from Osidian and looked at her.

Akaisha opened her arms. 'Will you not kiss me?'

Awkwardly, Ravan advanced into her embrace and planted a kiss on her cheek. Carnelian could see how unhappy they both were as they separated.

Whin looked over. 'Are you still here, Fern?'

Grunting something, Fern motioned for the Standing Dead to follow him. Ravan made to join them but Whin stopped him.

'You stay with us, dear.'

Uncomfortable, Carnelian followed Fern into the shadows, then up a hollow lying between two roots. Where the hollow narrowed into the trunk, it was packed with jars. Above their heads, ropes hugged packets and bundles to the bark. The shoulders of the branches were hung with coils of djada, with fernroot forming the rungs of ladders. Fern took hold of some loops of rope and pulled himself up into the tree. Carnelian watched him walk out along a branch and undo a bundle. He tugged two black blankets free, hesitated, tucked one back and pulled a russet one out instead.

'Catch,' he cried, then let them drop. Carnelian caught both. Fern landed on the ground beside them. Carnelian crushed the blankets with his chin so that he could look over them.

'Where do we sleep?'

Fern did not answer. Squinting, he was watching his mother and his Aunt Whin talking as they cooked. Ravan was sulking beside them. Fern looked at Carnelian.

'Eh?'

'Sleep. Where do we sleep?'

Fern looked puzzled and then brought Carnelian's face into focus. He took them round to the uphill side of the tree where the ends of the branches hung nearer to the ground. Fern swung his hand in an arc. 'Take whichever of the empty hollows you want.'

Carnelian watched him walk off towards the women. The Plainsman glanced back. 'Don't leave the shade of our mother tree.'

Carnelian nodded and turned to Osidian. 'What do you make of this?' he asked, in Quya.

Saying nothing, Osidian walked off up the slope. Hugging the blankets, Carnelian followed him. The roots faceting the ground defined hollows in many of which blankets and other bundles were neatly stowed. Of the empty hollows, most were too short for a Master to lie in. Higher up, they found a hollow large enough to accommodate them both.

Carnelian looked at Osidian. 'Will this do?'

Osidian gazed round with distaste. 'Their animal eyes will be on us wherever we go.'

Carnelian spotted the faces looking at them from the shade of the nearest tree. Turning slowly, he saw there were others staring. He thrust the black blanket on to Osidian and then pushed his nose into the russet one. He was disappointed. However much the blanket might look like one of Ebeny's, it did not have her smell. He shook the blanket open and let it settle on the cedar needle floor, then laid himself down along the hollow with his head up-slope. The perfume of the needles rose around him.

'It's surprisingly comfortable,' he said.

Morose, Osidian looked down at him. Behind his head the needle-brush canopy was aflicker with blue specks of sky. Carnelian could not bear another argument.

'They'll soon tire of staring.'

He closed his eyes and breathed deeply the warm, resinous air.

The air had cooled when Carnelian was woken by voices. He sat up in the hollow. Down the slope, among the deepening shadows, people were coming up the rootstair. Their trudging and the way many let their heads hang betrayed their weariness. For a moment Carnelian felt like lying back before they should see him, but he stayed where he was, knowing he would have to face them some time. A woman glancing up spotted him and was transfixed. Asked why she had stopped, she replied by pointing up at Carnelian and her companions found him with their stares. He imagined how ghostly and terrifying he must appear to them.

The discovery was passed by cries out through the Grove and

soon Carnelian was having to endure stares from other directions. He tried a smile, but this only seemed to intensify their horror. Elders among the hearths must have begun spreading the news of the decision they had made, for Carnelian could see and hear the reactions of disbelief. Reluctantly the Ochre tore themselves from their staring and continued up the hill to their hearths.

'What are you doing?' asked Osidian lying at his side.

Carnelian looked down. For a moment Osidian seemed as strange a creature to Carnelian as he himself must appear to the Ochre. He shook himself free of the illusion.

'Nothing. Well, just watching the people returning for the night. We must prepare ourselves to meet Fern's kin.'

Frowning, Osidian closed his eyes. Carnelian fought the desire to shake him. He forced himself to look out again. A group of women and men were approaching up the rootstair, some walking hand in hand, others carrying infants. Shrieking with excitement, the children that had been playing near the hearth ran down to them. Carnelian watched with a kind of envy their joyous meeting. A man caught a little girl and threw her up with a whoop and, catching her, hugged her as she squealed with delight. He slung her over his shoulder and continued climbing. A woman bent to embrace a boy, kissing him, nodding as he began to pour out his day for her. Several of the children were already pointing up at the strange white giant. Carnelian saw Akaisha approaching the group. The women handed the children to their men and gathered round her. Carnelian could hear the mutter of their talk and felt the sharp glances they cast up at him. Most of the men were frowning. Carnelian rose to his feet, wondering if he should go down and brave them himself.

The group resumed their climb behind Akaisha, who now had a baby in her arms. The children clung to their parents' hands. As the group left the stair, they fanned out towards the sleeping hollows. Akaisha caught Carnelian's eye and beckoned him. Obeying her, he was forced to pass through the others. They moved from his path as if he were a leper.

'I can't speak the soldier tongue,' Akaisha said as he approached.

'If you don't speak fast, I'll understand your Ochre . . . my mother,' he replied.

Her eyebrows raised. 'You really do speak our tongue.' She frowned. 'Walk with me.'

She led him towards the stair of roots and soon they were descending it side by side. Everywhere Carnelian glanced, he found eyes. He was glad it was necessary to fix his gaze on his feet, to find a way down the uneven steps.

'We call this stair the Blooding,' Akaisha said.

Carnelian could not help noticing some women undressing under a cedar, their skin smooth and brown in the deepening shade. There was a glint of water as they began to wash each other. A breeze from the east drifted a mist of cooking smoke across his path. Its smell reminded Carnelian's stomach of how hungry he was.

'We'll eat soon,' said Akaisha as if she had heard his thoughts.

'It was kind of you to . . .' Carnelian could not find the next word.

'You're not the way we imagine you to be,' she said.

'We must be . . . disappointing.'

She stopped to look up at him surprised. 'In what way?'

'You believe us angels . . . and now see we're only men.'

Her eyebrows rose again, causing Carnelian to feel he had been caught saying something childishly conceited. She reached up and he allowed her to touch his cheek.

'You really are just a man,' she said. 'And, though your beauty is unsettling, your face is not the lightning which we believed you hid behind your masks.'

She resumed their journey down the winding stair. 'But it was not that which I meant. It is your manner that is unexpected. The other, he is what we expect of your kind. But you . . . you are almost like one of us.'

'I speak your tongue . . . a little.'

'No, there is something else.'

'I grew up among Plainsmen.'

They had almost reached the foot of the slope so that they could gaze out from under the cedar canopy across the ferngardens, golden in the dying sun. The easterly caressing them was rich with the perfume of the magnolias. Carnelian felt an ache of joy that forced him to stop and close his eyes. It was as if he had come home after being a long time away.

He sighed. 'It is so peaceful here.'

'Tell me of this servant woman who spoke our tongue,' Akaisha said.

Carnelian opened his eyes to look at her. Her upturned face had a tightness around the eyes and mouth that made it clear this was the reason for their walk. Seeing how vulnerable she was, Carnelian considered his words carefully. He began to relate everything he knew about Ebeny and of his childhood with her across the sea.

'So far away,' Akaisha breathed, staring sightlessly as if she were seeing the island at the other side of the world.

She came back. 'This Ebeny spoke our tongue and she wove our patterns. Was there anything else she had from her people?'

Carnelian saw the yearning in Akaisha's eyes and, as desperately as she, he wanted to give her some proof. He closed his eyes and searched his memory. Suddenly, he grabbed her hand. 'She . . . she . . .' He calmed himself. 'Her mother . . .'

Akaisha gave an eager nod of encouragement while Carnelian tried to stitch the words together in his mind so that he could utter them in a piece. 'Her mother gave her a stone woman.' He showed the size of it in his hands. 'She called it her Little Mother.'

With her free hand Akaisha pulled something out from her robe. Carnelian made to take it but she snapped it into her fist and pulled away from him. Her eyes burned. 'You mustn't touch it. A man must never touch a sacred image of the Mother.'

Carnelian was glad he had not told her that Ebeny had given him her Little Mother to keep him safe on his journey to Osrakum.

'All Plainswomen have these from their mothers,' she said, slumping down on to a root.

Carnelian shared her bitter disappointment. 'I can think of nothing more.' He sat down beside her, resting his chin in his hand. Something occurred to him. 'This woman –'

'My sister.'

'Did you send other girls that year?'

Akaisha looked at him with hope. 'She was the only one. The other four were boys.'

Carnelian controlled his excitement. He showed her his palm. 'Do you remember her tattoo?' He almost groaned when he saw Akaisha's expression of strain.

'If I drew it for you?'

'Perhaps.'

Carnelian searched around for something to write on. 'Mud,' he said at last.

She understood and led him down to the path running alongside what she told him was the Homeditch.

'Wait here,' she said. She found a path down into the ditch and had soon disappeared into its gloomy depths. He waited and then she returned cradling a pool of muddy water in her hands. She found a piece of ground still bathed in the last red light of day. He cleared it of needles and she poured the water over it. Crouching, Carnelian smoothed the mud and carefully drew out the glyphs Ebeny had on her hand: Eight Nuhuron. He drew back to allow Akaisha to have a look. He chewed his lip as she peered at it.

At last she turned to him, nodding, a look of almost girlish wonder on her face.

'It is the same.'

She looked away towards the scarlet horizon. The east wind made her salt earrings clink. When she turned back she was frowning.

'When the Assembly voted, most of the men and some of the women voted for your deaths.'

'Mother Harth?'

'She will never forgive the killing of her son. I carried most of the women against her and we won, but we bought you only a momentary reprieve. Those who voted with me did so from fear of what might come from killing angels. It will not take them long to see you are flesh and blood.'

Carnelian's stomach clenched. His hopes had come to nothing. He felt a pang of regret that he had not after all returned to his father in Osrakum, but he dismissed this, knowing he could never have abandoned Osidian to die alone. There was nowhere else to go. He managed to find a smile for her. 'I only wish I could have told Ebeny that I met you; that I saw her people and her home.'

Akaisha was watching him. 'I can save you.'

Hope surged in Carnelian.

'I could adopt you into my hearth.'

'I don't understand.'

'Within our ditches, each hearthmother rules the children of her hearth.'

'Surely the Elders —'

She shook her head. 'The Assembly has no authority over a hearth nor over a hunt outside the Koppie.'

'But the Elders punished Fern.'

'It was I who set his punishment. He appeared before the Assembly merely to give an account of your journey.'

Carnelian considered everything she had said. 'Why would you do this, my mother? Surely this will bring you nothing but trouble.'

'You helped save the souls of my husband and my eldest son. Even if you had not, I would do this to keep the honour of my son who brought you here. Beyond all this, I will save you because my long-lost sister loves you.'

'You only have my word that that is so.'

Akaisha smiled. 'My sister wouldn't have taught you our tongue unless she loved you. As much as you say you consider her your mother, she must have considered you her son.'

'Will the rest of your hearth welcome me?'

She grew grave. 'They'll accept my decision because they must, but it might take a while before you are welcome.'

'And my friend?'

She gave him a sharp look. 'You mean your brother?'

'Fern told you that?'

She nodded, still wary. When he said nothing, she said, 'I've been wondering why if you are brothers he doesn't also speak our tongue.'

'He never knew Ebeny.' Carnelian saw in her eyes that her welcome for Osidian was conditional on his relationship with him. He could not risk the truth.

'We were separated at birth.'

Akaisha still looked unconvinced. 'I do not believe he will settle in among us easily.'

Carnelian took one of her hands. 'Don't judge him too harshly, my mother. His life has been very different from mine. Besides, he has been ill and is not yet fully recovered.'

Akaisha's face softened. 'My son Ravan seems fond of him.'

Carnelian bit his lip and let that pass without comment. 'If it had not been for him, none of us would have made it here.'

She paused some moments, examining him, so that he began to fear she did not believe him. 'For your sake, he may join us too.'

Carnelian looked at his feet, ashamed of his deceptions; overcome by her kindness.

'Will you enter my hearth?'

As he looked up at her, a feeling of dread rose in him as if something fearful lurked on the edges of this decision. He mastered himself. There was no other way.

'Gladly,' he said giving her hand a squeeze.

'What's your name?' Akaisha asked Carnelian as they climbed the rootstair back up towards her tree.

'Carnelian,' he said.

Her try at the Quya made him smile. 'Your accent is the same as Ebeny's.'

Her eyes sparkled. 'Is this strange name what my sister called you?'

'She called me many things.' He grinned. 'But the name she used for me; that the household used for me . . .' He winced at that reminder of what was the usual nature of the relationship between their two peoples. He felt she was trying hard not to judge him.

'My Plainsman hearthkin called me Carnie.'

'Well, that's what your new hearthkin shall call you too.'

When they reached her cedar, Akaisha stopped him. Carnelian watched her survey the branches with a loving gaze.

'Behold my mother tree,' she said. 'Incarnation of all my mothers. She's been here since the world was born, her roots reaching deep into Mother Earth. The women of my lineage have lived their lives out in her shade. In death, they've lain among her roots with which she has drawn their souls up into her so that, sometimes, you can hear their voices speaking from her leaves. Her shade defines our hearth's sacred rootearth. Only here may you walk barefoot as I may go uncovered.' She drew the russet blanket back from black hair veined with silver all worked through with salt beads. 'Take care you treat her well.'

Carnelian stooped to remove his shoes, glad of the distraction to hide the shame he felt from having already sinned against Akaisha's beliefs. Not only had he followed Osidian's lead to stand unshod upon the earth but he had done nothing when Osidian led Ravan into sacrilege. Should he warn her of the unhealthy influence Osidian had over her son?

Laughing, Akaisha snatched one of his makeshift shoes away. 'Where did you get this?'

Carnelian explained that Fern had made it for him.

'Well, we'll have to see if we can't do better than that, won't we?'

A mutter of talk and some laughter came from the direction of the hearth. Carnelian could see people gathered there and that Osidian was not among them.

Akaisha looked grim. 'And now you will meet your new hearthkin and share your first meal with us.'

'I should go and fetch my brother.'

'As you will. It is our custom to wash before we eat.' She must have seen his uncertainty, for she added, 'I shall send Ravan to show you where to wash.'

Half bowing to her, Carnelian made for his sleeping hollow. He found Osidian laid out in it as if in a tomb.

'Are you awake?'

Osidian's eyes when they opened seemed windows into a cave.

Carnelian explained Akaisha's offer and how it would save them from the Elders.

Osidian frowned. 'Have you not yet grown weary of fraternizing with savages?'

The haughty Quya stung Carnelian to anger. 'I have just had to lie to those *savages* to save your life.'

Footfalls approaching made him jump. Turning, he saw it was

Ravan. Thankfully, they had been speaking in Quya. The boy looked past Carnelian at Osidian.

'Master, my mother invites you to come and eat with us.'

'Will you show me, Ravan, where I may wash?' Carnelian said. Still waiting for Osidian to answer, the youth ignored him so that Carnelian took him by the arm. 'Show me.'

Pulling his arm free, Ravan scowled, but he led Carnelian towards the trunk of the cedar where a large earthenware jar was wedged between the roots. Ravan plucked one of the leather bowls lying flattened against the tree and, opening it, set it down by the jar. He grated the lid off, took a ladle that hung above it, dipped it in and began to fill the bowl. When this was half full he hung up the ladle and then turned to Carnelian his hands on his hips. 'Do you need help?'

Carnelian shook his head. 'Go join your kin.'

It irritated him when he saw Ravan ignore him again and go straight back to Osidian in the hollow. Carnelian scooped up some water from the bowl and rubbed it over his face and neck. His fingers touching his scar increased his irritation. He had betrayed Akaisha already by lying to her. Glancing back he saw Osidian sitting up talking to Ravan. He wondered if it could be jealousy that made him uneasy about their relationship. He dismissed the thought. There were more important things to worry about, chief amongst these finding a way to encourage Osidian to accept life among the Ochre.

Carnelian poured the remaining water over his feet, folded the bowl and leant it back against the trunk. He stood for a moment listening to the murmur of talk, to the laughter coming from the other side of the tree. He began the walk round. His stomach churned as the hearth came into sight. Perhaps thirty people of all ages were sat on the two barrelling roots that enclosed the hearth hollow: the men and boys with their backs to him on one root, facing the women and girls sitting in a row along the other. Smoke was rising from the uphill end of the hollow. As he approached boldly they all turned to look at him. Akaisha was sitting uphill where the two roots met in a fork. She motioned him round to enter their gathering at the downhill end of the hollow. He had to walk past the men's backs. The further down their line he went, the younger they became. At the end sat an infant whose legs did not reach the ground. Carnelian circled him, aware of the boy's gaping stare, stepped over the root and came to stand at the open end of the hollow under the full pressure of their scrutiny. They were ranged up the slope: men on his left; women on his right. On the other side of the fire, Akaisha gave him a nod of encouragement. As she rose he felt the release as all heads turned towards her.

'I have decided to adopt the two Standing Dead into our hearth.'

This news was greeted with shocked expressions, none more so than Fern's. Whin was glowering at Akaisha but the matriarch ignored her.

'Treat them with courtesy. They themselves have suffered grievously at the hands of their kind and we're in their debt for the kindness they showed our hearthkin.'

'This one is called "Carnie",' she said, causing them all to turn back to look at him. She proceeded to introduce them one by one. He nodded, making sure to look into the eyes of each; struggling to pronounce their names and follow the ways in which they were related to each other. On her left three sisters sat looking much alike, of whom one was Whin; opposite them and on Akaisha's right, their husbands. The introductions moved down the benches on either side, introducing the daughters of the three sisters, two of whom had children on their laps and, sitting across from them, their husbands. Akaisha turned her attention back to the woman's root to point out a daughter of her own who also had an infant, with her young husband sitting facing her. The last young woman, who was clutching a baby, Akaisha introduced as Sil, Whin's daughter.

'She holds our grand-daughter,' Akaisha said, gazing at Sil's child with adoration. She looked at Fern, who was beaming at her.

'My son, who is Sil's husband, of course you know already.'

The news that Fern had a wife and child came as a shock to Carnelian. As Akaisha continued pointing, rattling off the names of the dozen or so children, he tried to hide his confusion by giving his attention to each in turn. They gaped at him as if he were a talking aquar.

'Have I forgotten anyone?' Akaisha asked, smiling.

People shook their heads.

'Well, let's eat then.'

She pointed to a spot near Fern. 'Carnie, sit beside my son.'

Carnelian obeyed, walking up the centre of the hollow until he reached the space the men had opened beside Fern on the root. He sat down. Out of the corner of his eye, he was aware that the boy on his right was staring into the side of his head. Across from him the girls and women were pretending not to be looking at him.

His attention was drawn to Akaisha as she stamped her foot three times. 'Thanks be to the Mother from whom this food is born.'

'And to the Skyfather,' said Whin's husband, glancing up into the heavens, 'who makes her fruitful.'

Akaisha brought a small ivory box out of her robe. Still frowning, Whin leaned forward to take the lids off pots. Dipping into the box, Akaisha began to sprinkle salt over their food, a pinch at a time.

'Our men's sacrifice,' she said.

The hearth echoed her. Akaisha put the box away and sat down on the root fork. Whin stirred each pot and then she and her sisters began ladling their contents out into bowls which they sent down the two lines. Carnelian watched a bowl being passed hand to hand towards him. When Fern gave him it, Carnelian turned, taking care not to spill its contents, and offered it to the boy beside him. The boy gaped at Carnelian, who recognized him as one of the two who had been with Whin when he met her. He offered the bowl again but all the boy did was stare.

Akaisha's voice carried over to them. 'You know, Blue, dear, if you don't close your mouth you'll end up swallowing a fly.'

Blue disengaged his eyes from Carnelian and glanced at Akaisha.

'Yes, my mother,' he said with a nod and, careful not to touch Carnelian's hands, he took the bowl and passed it to a smaller boy sitting to his right.

At that moment, Ravan appeared. Blue and the other boys moved down the rootbench to make room for him beside Carnelian. Regarding the youth, Carnelian wondered what he and Osidian could have found to speak about for so long.

'I'll take food to the Master,' Ravan announced.

'No you won't,' said Akaisha. 'If he wants food, he'll have to come her and eat it with the rest of us.'

'Then I'll not eat either.'

'Oh yes you will. Sit down.'

Ravan scowled at his mother, but did as he was told.

Carnelian had to pass several bowls to Ravan before he could keep one himself. The earthenware held some kind of stew with what appeared to be dumplings floating in it. He felt a handle being pushed into his hand and, looking up, saw a little girl was offering him a spoon. Thinner than the other children, she did not seem to share their fascination in the stranger.

'Thank you,' he said, quietly.

The girl looked up at him through her lashes. There was a shadow of grief around her eyes. When he smiled at her, she looked away and moved on down the line distributing more spoons. Carnelian leaned close to Fern. 'I don't remember being introduced to her.'

Fern raised his eyebrows as he watched her. 'I've no idea who she is.'

'Fernie.' It was his wife, Sil, sitting across from them. 'Twostone,' she mouthed, slid her gaze over Carnelian's face and, balancing her baby, began to eat.

Carnelian dug his spoon into the bowl and scooped up a dumpling with some gravy. He put it in his mouth. Chewed it.

He nudged Fern. 'This is good.'

'I'm glad you think so,' said Fern. 'It's what we eat almost every night.'

Carnelian concentrated on the stew, trying to work through his earlier upset. Fern had a wife and child and that was it. Osidian had been right: he did have feelings for Fern. He would suppress them and they would fade.

Scraping the last spoonful, he looked up to find Sil staring at him. She turned her focus on the baby on her lap. Carnelian decided Sil was rather pretty. He watched her chew food to the front of her mouth, then stoop to transfer it into her baby's mouth. It seemed something an animal might do, but then he remembered that he had done the same for Osidian.

All around the hearth, people were discussing him. He tried to distract himself by listening to them but could only pick out a few words and even that grew tiring. Fern was giving all his attention to his bowl though Carnelian could see it was empty. His friend looked sad. Carnelian realized he had been so busy trying to adapt to his new world he had forgotten about Fern's punishment. Carnelian wanted to know what he had meant by labouring as a woman. Fern's look of dejection did not bode well.

Whin's voice carried across the chatter. 'Skai, fetch me Carnie's bowl. If his appetite is in keeping with his size, I'm sure he could do with some more.'

'Whin,' said Akaisha, a note of warning in her voice.

Carnelian lifted his gaze and found that, defying Akaisha, Whin was regarding him coldly. Without taking her eyes off him, she nudged a boy standing beside her. 'Do as you're told.'

As the boy came towards him Carnelian tried to decipher the expression on Whin's face. She seemed to be waiting for something to happen.

Skai, who was about eight, was the second boy Carnelian had seen before with Whin. The boy stood in front of him, looking at the ground, his hands extended for Carnelian's bowl. Carnelian could not avoid seeing the glyphs tattooed on the boy's right hand. 'Kumatuya Seventeen', he read, knowing instantly the boy had been selected for the following year's flesh tithe.

Carnelian raised his eyes. Whin was wearing an expression somewhere between triumph and anger. Everyone else was motionless, staring at him.

Fern snatched the bowl from Carnelian's hands and thrust it at the boy. 'Do as your grandmother told you.'

Carnelian was startled by his friend's anger. When the boy returned with the bowl refilled, Carnelian thanked him and began eating, even though he had lost his appetite. The eyes looking at him were loaded with reproach. He could see their pain at knowing they were going to lose Skai. Carnelian stared down, stirring the meat and dumplings in their gravy. How did the boy cope, knowing he would be taken from his kin for ever? He thought about the people of his household who had been taken from the Earthsky. In Osrakum, the marked boy might very well be chosen to serve House Suth.

'Don't show your feelings,' said Fern in Vulgate.

Carnelian looked up.

Fern's expression was severe. 'Guilty looks will only stir up the Tribe's lust for retribution.'

'I regret –'

'You might as well regret the rising of the sun.'

Carnelian followed his friend's gaze to the baby cradled in Sil's arms. Fern became aware Carnelian was looking at his child.

'Leaf was born after the last visit of the Gatherer. Next year, when he comes again, she'll have to be put forward with the other children. If we lose her, we lose her.'

Carnelian could hear the bitterness in Fern's voice but could think of no way to soothe him. He watched Sil kiss-feeding her baby.

'You want to hold her?'

Carnelian turned to find Fern glaring at him.

'Well . . . if you . . .' Carnelian blustered.

Fern jerked to his feet and, putting his hands out, asked for his child. Everyone fell silent. Uncertain, Sil glanced down the line of women to her mother, Whin. This enraged Fern.

'Give me my daughter,' he said in a dangerous tone.

Sil glared up at him, chewing vigorously. Bending, she put her lips to her child's and transferred the food. She wiped the baby's mouth and held her out to Fern, who took her, then offered her to Carnelian. He flared his palms in front of him.

'I'll not take her against her mother's wishes.'

'Hold her,' Fern commanded.

There was no denying the determination in his eyes. As Carnelian took the baby and cradled her, around the hearth there was a catching of breath. Sil protested. Whin said something in anger.

Fern turned on her. 'As much as she's your grand-daughter, she's my child.' He pointed at Carnelian. 'He's not like the rest of his kind. Look at the way he holds her. Is that the way you would hold a slave?'

Carnelian felt the little girl warm against his heart and, looking down, became trapped in her brown eyes. He could not help smiling at her.

'Does the way he holds a baby make him less of a danger to the Tribe?' Whin demanded.

'This hearth is in their debt,' said Fern. 'Isn't it our tradition to honour our debts?'

'That works for Plainsmen, not for the Standing Dead,' said Whin.

'He saved the souls of my husband and my son,' said Akaisha.

It made Carnelian miserable to be the reason for such conflict.

'By sacrilegious means,' said Whin.

'Do you doubt that I will make sure my son makes full recompense for his crime?' asked Akaisha. When Whin did not answer: 'As for the Standing Dead, here I am hearthmother and so I say that they are now as much a part of this hearth as are you.'

Whin looked outraged. 'And how will they earn their keep, my mother? Or does my mother intend we should slave for them as do the children they steal from us?'

Fern glanced at Carnelian holding his baby. 'They'll do as other men.'

'Work in the ditches with us; hunt?' one of the men said, startled.

'I can vouch for their strength and valour,' said Fern.

'So can I,' said Ravan.

Carnelian had forgotten he was there. He rose, the child safe in the crook of his arm, and reached out to clasp Fern's shoulder with his free hand. 'What's your punishment?'

Fern flushed. 'I'm to work beneath the Bloodwood Tree.'

Carnelian was none the wiser and felt he had only served to embarrass his friend in front of his kin. He made his decision even though he had no idea what he was committing himself to. 'Then I'll work with you there.'

Ravan leapt to his feet. 'The Master can't do that.'

'Sit down,' said Fern. 'Can't you see Carnie was only speaking for himself.' He turned to Carnelian. 'I appreciate the offer, but you don't understand. This is the Mother's work; something which men don't do, only women.'

'Nevertheless, I'll join you,' said Carnelian. He went over and gave Sil her baby. She looked from him to her husband, then back again. He sensed she had become aware of the feelings there were between them. Trying to hide his confusion, Carnelian pushed past

178

Ravan, stepped over the rootbench and walked away.

'Carnie.'

Carnelian turned to see Akaisha following him. He watched her approach. Her voice when she spoke was low and conspiratorial.

'If you're determined to work with the women, then tomorrow you should come with me down to the earthworks.'

He smiled. 'Where I can cause you trouble as I did just now?'

'Don't you worry about Whin, she'll come round. The day after tomorrow it will be the turn of our hearth to work under the Bloodwood Tree. Tomorrow, the women there will be under the authority of Ginkga.'

'She voted for my death?'

Akaisha nodded.

'Nevertheless, my mother, I'm determined to share your son's punishment.'

'Why?'

There was anger in Akaisha's voice. Carnelian stooped and took her hand. 'I'm at least as responsible for Fern's sacrilege as he is himself and owe him many debts of gratitude. How could I let him suffer the punishment alone?'

'Is that all it is?'

Carnelian was glad the twilight hid his embarrassment.

'Take care where your emotions will lead you.' She gave his hand a squeeze and then returned to her hearth.

The twilight was thicker under the branches than it had been at the hearth, so that Carnelian had to take care picking his way across the root-ribbed hillside. He could just make out Osidian in their sleeping hollow, his face and hands like patches of moonlight.

'The sky here is very deep,' a voice said.

'Are you not hungry?'

'Only to wake from this nightmare.'

Carnelian slipped into the hollow and stretched himself out beside Osidian.

'We can live here,' he asserted.

'I do not believe I can.'

Stars were coming alive in the darkening sky.

'We will have to work with them.'

'A Master shall not be seen to labour,' growled Osidian.

'What will you gain by quoting the Law at me? If we do not work, they will not give us food.'

'Then I shall starve.'

Carnelian sat up but found he could not make out Osidian's face.

Morning would be a better time for them to talk. He reached for a blanket and shook it open over them. He leaned across Osidian to make sure to cover him. His body seemed carved stone.

Carnelian lay back. Osidian would come round. He had to. Despair began catching at the edges of his mind. A burning vision of Osidian as he had been in Osrakum: a prince among books, music, palaces, slaves; all of such perfect beauty; the exquisite distillation of millennia. All wealth. All power. Osidian was to have been God. How could life among rude barbarians ever compare? There he lay beside him between the roots of a tree. What had he condemned him to?

Carnelian tried to find hope in the stars, but they seemed nothing but ice in a bleak sky. What had he thrown away for the sake of a love that must surely die? Never again to see his Ebeny. Never to see Tain nor any other of his brothers; not one of the people he had known all his life. For him, all were now dead. His yearning for them was an ache, but there was a deeper grief choking him. His father. The father he had abandoned to Ykoriana's web.

THE BLOODWOOD TREE

Wife, you are the earth
the giver of gifts
the blessed mother of blood
come, sate my hunger.
(from a marriage ritual of the Plainsmen)

CARNELIAN WAS WOKEN BY FERN. 'DO YOU STILL WANT TO COME WITH me?'

It was too dark for Carnelian to see his friend's face.

'Yes,' he whispered, his heart still aching, wondering how long it was until dawn. As he made to rise, a hand reached up to pull him back.

'Where are you going?' asked Osidian.

Carnelian was glad of the gloom that hid his face. He explained the decision he had made to share Fern's punishment. Osidian withdrew his hand and turned away. Carnelian stared at his back, trapped between his promise to Fern and his feeling that he was deserting Osidian.

'I brought you some breakfast,' said Fern, pushing something into Carnelian's hand. He peered at the two crumbly discs.

'Rootflour cakes,' Fern said as he gave Carnelian two more. 'Give those to your brother.'

Carnelian leaned over Osidian to put the cakes down on the ground in front of him. 'One of us at least must work,' he whispered.

When Osidian gave no response, Carnelian rose. At least he had been spared having to face Whin. 'Lead the way,' he said, to the shadow that was Fern.

As he followed him down the Blooding rootstair, Carnelian's thoughts remained behind with Osidian. He only became aware he was chewing the cake when it began to flood his mouth with its peculiar, bitter taste.

A breeze was blowing from the indigo east when they reached the foot of the rootstair. A group of shadows were gathered in front of a wicker gate speaking in low tones with women's voices. The gate creaking open let enough light in under the arching cedars to allow the women to notice Carnelian; as he could tell by the raised tempo of their talk. Fern pushed through their midst so that Carnelian was forced to follow. He sensed their wonder as he moved through them.

Crossing the earthbridge with Fern, he was glad the women remained behind. The easterly was ruffling a swell into the ferngarden. Soon they were walking alongside a drainage ditch beneath the dark, overhanging masses of the magnolias. Laughter carrying towards them over the sighing of the ferns seemed to be the cause of Fern redoubling their pace. Carnelian followed him across another, smaller earthbridge over a forking of the ditch, the prongs of which enclosed a meadow dominated by a huge tree with leaves the colour of old blood. As they crossed this meadow, Carnelian snatched glimpses of Fern's face. Its grim expression did not invite conversation.

The meadow ended at a double wall of soaring magnolias between which ran one of the concentric ditches Carnelian had seen from the summit of the Crag. Taking them through the first line of trees, Fern found yet another bridge. As he stepped on to it, Carnelian could see that the roots of the magnolias buttressed the sides of the ditch so thickly they had forced it into a jagged course. Gazing off towards the Koppie's outmost ditch, Carnelian was sure the trees defining its edges were not so ancient. It gave him something to ask Fern.

In response to his question, his friend came to a halt and turned. 'This is the Outditch which long ago defined the limits of the Koppie, before the Newditch was dug out there.'

Fern set off again, through the second line of magnolias into the wider expanse of the outer ferngardens. They were heading directly towards the Newditch, so that Carnelian began to believe they were making for the open plain. Again he wondered what it was he had agreed to.

Before they reached the Outditch, the drainage ditch they had been walking alongside split in two once again. The arms curved off to meet the Outditch, embracing another triangular fernmeadow, though larger than the first, but which had in it another russet tree. Something gigantic lay beneath its branches, from which wafted the sweet beginnings of decay. A wisp of laughter made Carnelian turn to see figures filtering across the earthbridge they had just crossed. Carnelian turned back and caught up with Fern, who had almost reached the tree. The morning had become bright enough for Carnelian to see that what lay beneath it was a saurian, which with its horns and sweeping crest was much like those he had seen pulling wagons along the roads of the Guarded Land.

'A huimur.'

'An earther,' corrected Fern, in Ochre.

One whole flank of the creature had been cut away, revealing the grimy architecture of its ribs. A stench was rising from the blood-soaked earth. Boulders as flat as tables were set about in an arc. Upon these, long flint knives lay in rows.

Fern was scowling. 'Well, here we are beneath the Bloodwood Tree.'

Carnelian stared at the tree and spoke his thought aloud. 'Bloodwood?'

For an answer, Fern lifted one of the flint knives, strode towards the trunk and swung a slash into it. The cut began to weep along its length. Drawing closer, Carnelian saw the tree appeared to be bleeding.

About three dozen women and a few girls gathered beneath the Bloodwood Tree. Under the pressure of their scrutiny, Carnelian did not know where to look. Fern hung his head. The girls chattered and pointed. The women laughed, nervously.

'Don't you all have work to do?'

Carnelian recognized the Elder, Ginkga. The crowd dispersed as she came through them. She clamped some bone pins in her lips. As she approached Carnelian and Fern, she twisted her hair into a tress, then wound it tightly around her head. She came to a halt in front of them and looked up into Carnelian's face. One at a time, she took the pins from her mouth and inserted them into her coil of salt-beaded hair. Carnelian tried to hold her gaze, but eventually he had to look away.

'You two will load the offal on to the drag-cradles,' she said, when her mouth was free. She pointed to where five cradles were laid out in a line well beyond the shade of the tree. It was Carnelian who led Fern off towards them. Carnelian could smell them before he was close enough to see they were caked with gore. Infants screaming drew his attention to the open ground where he saw them chasing

183

each other among rows of frames, many of which were hung with ribbons of flesh adjusting heavily in the breeze.

Carnelian grimaced at the filthy drag-cradles. 'What're we supposed to do?' he asked Fern. His friend gave a shrug for an answer.

The women were painting each other's faces red. Those that were done went to stand around the boulder tables testing the edges of the flints. Some had to be knapped sharp. Blood-faced, two women were appraising the saurian corpse as if it were a house they were about to demolish. Soon they were in among its bones, hacking away with their knives. The hunks of meat they released were caught by other women who lugged them over to the boulders, where they were sheared into slices and then ribbons. Carnelian watched as the girls began knotting these into ropes which they wound around their arms like yarn. Bloody to the armpits, the girls carried the meat away from the tree and draped it over the frames as if it were washing being hung out to dry.

Ginkga's voice carried over to Carnelian and Fern. 'You two.'

They exchanged a look of resignation and went towards her. She confronted them arms red to the elbows; face the colour of fresh blood.

'You should take off as much as you can.'

Fern pulled off his robe and, reluctantly, Carnelian followed his lead. They both endured the ribald comments the women made about their bodies.

Ginkga offered them a bowl that appeared to be filled with blood. 'You're here to do penance for your insult to the Mother. You must wear her colour as we do.'

Fern scowled, but took the bowl. He kneeled and put it on the ground and motioned Carnelian to join him. Facing each other, they dipped their fingers in the bowl and smeared the redness over their faces under Ginkga's grim supervision. When they were done, she led them to their work. Shouldering the slimy sag of a lung between them, they struggled to heave it back to the drag-cradles.

Sweltering, they laboured, their torsos and their heads itching with gore. Carnelian had tried to make a joke about their red faces but Fern was not much inclined to humour. The sun had brought with it a plague of flies that swarmed the growing mounds of offal. A constant procession of people came to stare. Worst of all for Carnelian was the mob of jeering children that had collected, who hung around him as he worked, coming as close as they dared. Already weary, past nausea from the stench, their baiting was almost more than he could bear.

Fern gave him a look of sympathy. 'At least their antics are driving away the flies.'

Carnelian frowned. 'I'd prefer the flies.'

Fern chuckled.

'I'm glad at least it amuses you.'

Fern looked concerned. 'I didn't mean –'

Carnelian cut off the apology with his hand. 'I know you didn't.'

'If I asked her, perhaps Mother Ginkga would send them away.'

Carnelian began to shake his head, then winced as it adhered to the bundle of tendons he was carrying over his shoulder. The children laughed, delighted, and he growled, scattering them.

'The Standing Dead haunt their nightmares. To see one of them here, doing this work . . .' Fern shook his head, frowning, himself overcome by the wonder of it.

'It's not that I'm blaming them,' said Carnelian. 'I just wish they'd leave me alone.'

'They'll tire of it.'

For some time after that Carnelian despaired they ever would, but gradually the gang began to thin until the last few children were wandering back across the earthbridge, making for the shade of their mother trees.

The blaze of the sun managed to enter through Carnelian's slitted eyes to give him a beating headache. The air scorched his lungs. The sun was nearing its greatest height when Ginkga called for a break. Panting, brushing away flies, Carnelian and Fern scrambled for the shade of the Bloodwood Tree as if it were a river in which they might swim. As shadow slipped over them, Carnelian put his head back and groaned with pleasure. A delicious breeze cooled his skin. He saw two girls ladling water out from a jar that lay against the trunk of the tree. Fern called over to them and they came with slow, reluctant steps. They stood uncertain, staring at Carnelian.

Fern grew angry. 'Come on, fetch us some water.'

The girls ran back to the jar.

'They shun me,' said Carnelian.

'Both of us. Do you blame them?' Fern opened his arms to display his grimy torso.

Carnelian chuckled. 'I suppose not. You look as if you've been peeled.' He laughed when Fern raised an eyebrow.

'Red's not your colour, Carnie.'

The girls returned with a bowl of water and some roasted fern-root which they carefully put on the ground in front of them. Fern insisted Carnelian drink first. When they had quenched their thirst, they went to sit with their backs against the tree. As they munched away at the fernroot, they gazed across the sun-bleached fern-meadow to the Newditch and into the wavering mirage of the plain beyond.

Carnelian looked round. Fern's red face was crusted black with blood. He was scratching his head, where the curls were stiff with brown matter. Glancing round, he saw Carnelian looking at him. Carnelian thought his friend's eyes very bright.

'Where did you get that hair?'

Fern frowned.

Carnelian looked away, narrowing his eyes against the glare of the world beyond the shade. 'Perhaps I shouldn't have asked.'

'My mother was travelling through the Leper Valleys on her way back from the Mountain when she became separated from the other tributaries. She was raped.'

The murmur of the women's talk was a buzzing of bees. Carnelian turned his head to look at Fern, whose chin was resting on his chest. His eyes were focusing on the fernroot in his hands that he was snapping into little pieces.

'A Maruli?' asked Carnelian.

Fern's chin dug into his chest. 'Smeared all over with ash, yellow-eyed with a ravener grin.'

'It must have been hard for you growing up here.'

'My mother protected me.'

'And, surely, so did the rest of your hearth?'

Fern turned to look at him. 'When I was born, Whin sided with those who urged my mother to expose me on the summit of the Crag.'

'But you're married to her daughter.'

'My mother claims Whin agreed to that because she shared her passion for reuniting their two matriarchal lines, but I don't believe it. As is our custom, I had tried to find a wife in another hearth. Because of the way I was fathered none would have me. My mother must have begged Whin.'

Seeing the anguish in those dark eyes, Carnelian fought a desire to embrace him.

'What's the matter with you?' Fern asked.

Carnelian did not know what to say. He could hear the women on the other side of the tree returning to work and used it as an excuse to rise.

'We'd better get on with it,' he said and, without even glancing at Fern, he strode off towards the drag-cradles with their heaped, rotting entrails; their clouds of flies.

*

186

'The Skyfather be praised,' Fern sighed, as Ginkga announced an end to the day's work.

With a grunt, Carnelian dislodged a quivering mass of membranes from his shoulder. They tumbled with a wet thud on to a drag-cradle, splashing him with mucus. He was past caring. Lifting his gaze to the west, he saw the sun was drowning in its own blood. At least the air had cooled.

'You worked well enough,' said a woman's voice. Turning, Carnelian saw it was Ginkga. He could see how hard it had been for the woman to make that admission.

'Thank you, my mother,' he said in Ochre, and Fern echoed him.

The Elder came close. 'You may have bewitched Akaisha but don't imagine the rest of us will leave this as it is.'

Carnelian withered. Her eyes lingered on him a while longer before she went off to join the other women who were washing themselves beyond the margin of blood-stained earth.

Fern's eyes shone bright in his filthy face. 'My mother will protect you.'

'You're a mess,' Carnelian said, trying to make light of it all.

Fern grinned at him.

Carnelian suddenly itched everywhere. 'I'm desperate to get clean.'

'We'll have to wait our turn,' Fern said, indicating the women with his chin.

'I suppose it's forbidden for us to go up there,' he said, looking with longing at the cedars on the hill.

Fern gave him a heavy nod. 'The mother trees may only drink their daughters' blood.'

They waited, tormented by itching, until they saw the women plodding back towards the Grove. He and Fern ran to take their place. His friend indicated a patch of dry, clean earth on which he wanted Carnelian to stand, then he rushed to fetch water and pluck some leaves from the Bloodwood Tree.

When Fern returned, Carnelian scrunched the leaves into a ball as he saw his friend do, dipped them in the bucket and then used them to scrub away at his skin. When they had done as much as they could unaided, Fern began doing Carnelian's back. Carnelian submitted to this and, when his friend asked, tried to explain how the scars running down either side of his spine showed the blood-taints of his father and mother.

When Fern was finished he gave Carnelian the leaf-ball. Fern took Carnelian's hesitation for pride. Unwilling to explain his feelings, Carnelian turned Fern and began rubbing at his back. The only other man he had ever done this for was Osidian.

187

They said nothing to each other as they made the weary climb up through the Grove. Carnelian's heart warmed as his eyes fell on the spreading beauty of what he allowed himself, for the first time, to consider his mother tree. When they reached the edge of her earth, they removed their shoes which they had done their best to clean. Both groaned with pleasure as they sank their feet into the fragrant carpet of needles. Side by side they made towards the hearth, where they could see people already gathering for the evening meal.

When Carnelian came to a halt, Fern stopped too. 'What's the matter?'

'Osidian,' Carnelian said bleak with the realization that he had almost forgotten him. He peered up towards the sleeping hollows. Shapes were moving there, but none that could have been Osidian. He remembered Fern and squeezed his shoulder. 'You go on ahead, I'll join you as soon as I can.'

Without waiting for an answer, he began climbing the slope. His steps faltered as he neared their hollow. He recalled the day spent with Fern, the intimacy of their washing, and felt he had already betrayed Osidian. He took the final steps and looked down into the hollow.

Osidian was lying in it asleep. For several heartbeats, Carnelian regarded him, moaning as his mind touched on a yearning that Osidian should not be there at all. The sound made Osidian stir. As he opened his eyes, Carnelian fought the desire to hide.

'Are you well?' he said with a voice that did not seem his own.

Osidian turned his head to look at him. Carnelian was transfixed by the green-eyed stare. He managed to find his tongue. 'Have you eaten?'

'You eat their filthy food, I will not.'

Carnelian saw the two cakes he had left there that morning were still untouched. The confusion of his emotions fused to anger. 'If you will not eat, my Lord, then you shall die.'

'So be it,' Osidian answered in an eerie voice. His eyes narrowed, seeing something behind Carnelian, then they closed.

Turning, Carnelian saw it was Fern.

'My mother sent me to fetch you.'

Carnelian turned back to Osidian. How much did his behaviour stem from jealousy? Carnelian felt wretched. 'Please come with us?'

Osidian seemed asleep. Carnelian tried to find an argument that might bring him back, but Fern's presence was making that impossible.

'What's the matter with your brother?' the Plainsman asked.

Carnelian turned on him. 'Nothing!'

Fern's shock at his tone upset Carnelian. Knowing Osidian was listening made Carnelian reluctant to apologize. He felt trapped between them. Unable to speak, he pushed past Fern and made off in the direction of the hearth.

Ignoring the stares, Carnelian marched up between the rootbenches towards the fire. There was a gap in the line of men and boys where he and Fern had sat the night before. Reaching it, he sat down and focused his gaze on his hands. Grime still clung to the fine cracks in his skin. He felt Fern brushing against him as he sat down. Carnelian busied himself prising rinds of dried blood from under his nails. The smell of iron evoked Osrakum; spilling into his mind the usual horror and yearning.

'Fern. Carnie.' His name was charming in Akaisha's accent. Carnelian raised his eyes and looked past Fern to the head of the hearth where she was smiling at them.

'We were told you worked hard today.'

Carnelian gave her a smile. Whin at her side was stony-faced.

'It's only the first day of many,' said Fern, gruffly.

Carnelian glanced round at him. A blush of ochre lingered on Fern's face. Their eyes locked. Carnelian was the first to disengage. He knew he could not explain his anger to him. A bad end to an otherwise promising day.

Across from him, Sil was regarding them both with a fixed concentration. Carnelian feared she was seeing how he felt towards her man. She looked weary. Traceries of red earth incised her arms and hands.

He tried a smile. 'You seem to have been working hard yourself.'

Sil stared for a moment, but her face softened to a lovely smile that made Carnelian warm to her. She gave a nod, then looked shyly down at her hands and then up at him. 'No doubt you'll find out yourself in time . . . Carnie.' She flashed a bright row of teeth. 'The repair of the ditches is a task the men share with us.'

Sil's friendliness smoothed some of the tension out of Carnelian's shoulders. He sank back into the domestic comfort of the hearth chatter as food was passed down the line. He saw again the thin Twostone girl and smiled at her.

When the girl had passed on, Carnelian leaned towards Sil. 'What's her name?'

Sil shrugged. 'She's not said a word since we found her living wild in her koppie.'

Fern interrupted them by putting the first bowl in Carnelian's hands. Turning, Carnelian offered it to Ravan. The youth scowled at him.

'The Master's not eating?'

This was the last thing Carnelian wished to discuss. 'He's still recovering from his fever.'

'How's he going to get better if he doesn't eat?'

Carnelian offered the bowl again. 'Go on, take it.'

Ravan continued to scowl at him. Fern leaned out to look at his brother. 'Take the cursed thing. What's wrong with you?'

The youth turned his scowl on Fern.

'Ravan, do as your brother says,' Akaisha said, loudly. In response, her son snatched the bowl so violently it spilled half its contents over Carnelian. He jumped up, scalded. Fern leapt up.

'You stupid, little –'

'Sit down, all of you,' cried Akaisha.

Carnelian sat down and, glowering at each other, Ravan and Fern did so too. The passing of the bowls resumed. When Carnelian got his, he ate, wondering how long he could conceal Osidian's utter rejection of the Plainsmen.

Carnelian awoke gripped by fear. He struggled to order his thoughts. He had been dreaming he was with Fern watching Osidian die. Carnelian's hand found Osidian's body warm beside him. He listened for his breathing, but could hear only the sighing as the mother tree sifted the breeze through her needled canopy. Her voice was comforting. Through her roof there was a hint of dawn in the colour of the sky. He became aware of the sounds of the Tribe waking. He slipped out from under the blanket, being careful not to disturb Osidian. Carnelian sat for a moment with his arms crossed, rubbing his shoulders, peering at him lying in the hollow. He denied the memory of his dream. He assured himself Osidian would soon give up his fast. As he blew warmth into his hands, he smelled yesterday's blood. He had to go to work. He rose, his body aching all over, dressed, then padded towards the huddle of shapes around the hearth to share their warmth and to have breakfast.

It was Akaisha who led them down towards the Bloodwood Tree with Whin at her side, with Sil and the others of their daughters and grand-daughters following on behind. Carnelian was further back with Fern. Three girls walked behind them, one of them carrying a baby. The little Twostone girl brought up the rear.

The earther lay beneath the tree, most of its bones now exposed.

Akaisha wrinkled her nose up at the stench. 'We'll have to finish her today.'

'We'd have to anyway,' said Whin. 'Crowrane's hunt is supposed to be bringing in another earther today.'

After everyone's face was painted, Akaisha asked Whin to marshal them to the boulder tables and to make sure the knives were sharp, then she turned to Fern and Carnelian. 'You two know what you have to do.'

Carnelian removed the new shoes Akaisha had given him before they set off and put on the makeshift ones already stained with gore.

Sil was standing nearby rocking her baby in her arms. She looked up. 'I'll help them, my mother.'

Akaisha put a hand on her arm. She shook her head. 'No, Sil. Fern must see this through to the end, alone.'

She registered Sil's glance at Carnelian and smiled at him. 'I never imagined that any man would choose to share Fern's punishment.'

Both women smiling at him made Carnelian embarrassed. 'I owe him.'

'I don't need your gratitude,' said Fern.

Those were the first words they had spoken to each other that morning.

'Nevertheless, I will work at your side until you are released.'

Fern shrugged. Carnelian yearned to re-establish the easy friendship of the previous day, but remembering his dream, he decided it might be better to leave matters as they were.

Just before midday, it was Sil who brought Fern and Carnelian food and water as they took their rest with everyone else. Carnelian saw she had the thin Twostone girl to help her. The waif walked behind Sil taking small steps, her whole being focused on the bowl of water she was carrying.

Fern made a lunge at his wife. 'Come here, let me kiss you.'

Sil eluded him, grinning. 'Look at the state you're in. I'm not letting you anywhere near me until you wash.'

Suddenly, water exploded everywhere. Carnelian, who had been watching the play between Fern and Sil with mixed feelings, saw the little girl staring appalled, the bowl lying empty on the earth near her feet. Carnelian went cold. The last time he had seen the expression the girl had on her face was on his brother Tain's face, when Jaspar had deliberately unmasked in front of him so as to ensnare him in a threat of blinding. He followed the girl's unblinking stare to Fern, his dark skin marbled with gore.

'What's the matter with her?' Fern demanded, clearly unsettled.

Sil crouched beside the girl. 'Why did you drop the bowl?'

The girl did not seem to be aware the woman was even there. Carnelian thought he understood. He looked Fern in the eye. 'Most likely she witnessed her people being butchered by Marula.'

Fern's face blanked with understanding. Sil had turned to look at him and now turned back pale to the little girl. She gently stroked some hair from the girl's temples. 'It's all right, little one,' she said gently, but the girl just kept on staring.

'Make her stop,' Fern said.

Carnelian approached the girl and knelt in front of her. She looked right through him. He moved aside to let her see Fern again. 'He's a friend. He's your friend. The blood comes from there.' He pointed at the earther corpse stretching out from behind the tree, and she turned to look at it, then back at Fern.

Her eyes, so unnaturally large in her thin face, put a lump in Carnelian's throat. He smiled at her. 'What's your name?'

The second time he asked the question he was rewarded by her focusing on him. He indicated himself. 'You see, I'm just as filthy as he is. You're safe.' He would have hugged her if he had not been covered in blood.

To everyone's surprise, the little girl said something. Carnelian did not understand and glanced urgently at Sil, who shrugged.

'I believe she's telling you her name. Poppy.'

Carnelian turned his attention back to the girl. 'Is that right? Is your name Poppy?'

The girl stared so deep into his eyes, Carnelian felt she was looking at his soul. When she surfaced, she gave him the tiniest of nods.

When they returned to their labours, Poppy sat beneath the Bloodwood Tree and did not once take her eyes off Carnelian. Any time he paused to glance back, he would find her there, gazing at him. At first he found it unsettling, but as the day wore on, he realized, with surprise, that if he had found her interest in him gone, he would have been disappointed.

He and Fern had, over the day, disassembled the remains of the earther; dragging the bones like logs. All that was left was the immense beaked head with its flaring crest and horns which was clearly too heavy for them to move.

'What do we do with that?' asked Carnelian.

Fern frowned at him. 'We wait until they bring in the next one.' With that, he turned to walk towards the shade of the tree. Carnelian caught up and walked at his side. Glancing at Fern's gory, resolute face, Carnelian knew he would get nothing more out of him.

Sil came to the edge of the tree shade to meet them. 'Mother Akaisha says you might as well wash while we wait for the new earther to come in.'

Her husband acknowledged what she said with a gruff nod and walked on past her. Carnelian saw with what concern she watched him move away.

'Why's he so morose?' he asked her.

'He can't be brave all the time,' she snapped and looked at him as if had said something callous.

Carnelian was taken aback. He had sensed that Fern had reconciled himself to his punishment. Seeing the pain that lay behind her anger, Carnelian did not feel he could ask and, instead, went off to wash with Fern. Poppy eyed him as he walked sighing with pleasure at the cool relief from the sun. He smiled when he heard her creeping after him. When he turned, she froze.

'Could you please fetch us water to wash with, Poppy?'

When the girl nodded, he jogged to catch Fern. They walked together in silence.

'Poppy's bringing us water,' Carnelian said.

Fern turned, frowning. 'You mustn't get too attached to her. She has the kind of prettiness the Gatherer likes.'

When Poppy brought them water, Carnelian's thanks made her look at her feet as she handed it to him. She stood and watched him and Fern washing each other. When they were clean, they went to sit with their backs against the tree, surveying the dazzling plain beyond the Outditch. Poppy followed them and sat herself near Carnelian. Remembering Fern's warning, he tried to take no pleasure in having her there.

Later, a dozen aquar appeared in the gate that was flanked by earther horns and that opened from the fernmeadow on to the plain. They approached, crushing the ferns in a wide arc. Ropes hitched to their crossbeams pulled taut radiuses from a common centre. The riders kept looking back over their shoulders. When they had come closer, Carnelian was able to see the boulder of flesh and hide with which they were ploughing up the meadow: another vast earther. Riders trotted up to the head of the butchered one and, slinging ropes over its horns, they made their aquar tow it away. The drag-cradles with their heaped rotting gore were hitched up and pulled away too. Soon the new earther was being tugged into position on the rusty earth under the Bloodwood Tree. The riders showed it off to the women, proudly. Among them he saw Krow and they exchanged smiles. Someone beside the youth scolded him. Startled, Krow looked round at two riders who Carnelian realized were Loskai and Crowrane. Father and son fixed Carnelian with a look of hatred that chilled him to the bone.

Poppy trailed after Carnelian as he returned with Fern, Akaisha, Whin and the others to their hearth. As he came within sight of the mother tree, anticipation of seeing Osidian filled him with dread. He put his hand on Fern's shoulder.

'I'm going to see my brother.'

Fern nodded and Carnelian glanced round at Poppy, who had stopped a few steps down the rootstair and was gazing up at them.

'Could you please take her with you?'

Fern shook his head disapprovingly, but smiled. Carnelian crouched and beckoned Poppy. The girl came slowly up the steps. Even crouching, Carnelian had to look down at her.

'Will you go with Fern, Poppy?'

The girl looked up at the Plainsman and then back at Carnelian, then gave a solemn nod. Fern offered her his hand. She would only take it when Carnelian gave her a nod of approval. He let them go ahead of him. He could not help smiling each time she glanced round to make sure he was following. He parted company with them when they reached the rootearth of their hearth. He gazed towards his sleeping hollow, hesitated and, then, reluctantly, began walking towards it.

Even though he had anticipated finding Osidian weakened, what Carnelian saw shocked him. The body lying long and pale in the hollow did not give the impression of someone sleeping, but rather seemed a corpse lying in a sarcophagus.

Leaping into the hollow, Carnelian bent over it. He sought a pulse on the neck; the bony wrist. Unsure he could detect any life, Carnelian began shaking Osidian with ever increasing violence, until, coughing, he came alive. His green eyes swam. Carnelian felt himself being examined. Osidian's forehead creased.

'It's you,' he sighed.

Carnelian was shocked by how quickly he had deteriorated. 'You must eat,' he said. He leaned close and looked into the glass of Osidian's eyes. 'You must eat.'

Carnelian stumbled to his feet and almost broke into a run so that he might not hear Osidian forbidding him. People were gathering for the evening meal. He saw Akaisha with Whin and others of the women talking among the steam and smoke rising from the pots.

'Akaisha,' he said as he approached, 'Mother.'

The women all looked at him. He could see his fear reflecting in their eyes. Akaisha reached up to touch his face. 'What is it, Carnie? Why do you stare so?'

Carnelian calmed himself. 'Osidian, my . . . my brother, he is dying.'

Whin's face became leather. 'He's been keeping to your sleeping place, lying between the roots like one already dead.'

Carnelian searched Akaisha's eyes. He did not want to believe she wanted him to die, though he understood how it would rid her of a burden.

'He's not eaten since we arrived and was already weakened by the fever. You will let me take some food for him?'

Whin spoke: 'No one has stopped him coming to eat with us.'

Carnelian did not want to explain why Osidian had not. 'He's not like me.'

Akaisha nodded slowly, her eyes seeming to search deep into him. 'Even though you are brothers.'

Carnelian looked away ashamed of his lie and saw Whin, her lips pressing tight with disapproval. He looked down at the pots.

'Take as much as you need,' Akaisha said.

'Those not prepared to work should not expect the Tribe to feed them,' said Whin.

Carnelian grimaced.

Akaisha patted Carnelian's shoulder. 'Carnie has been working hard enough for the both of them. Go on, take him some broth.'

Carnelian looked for a ladle, a bowl. It was Sil who found them for him. She began to take food from a pot.

'Not so much,' he said. 'He'll not eat much if he eats at all.'

She looked up, her face full of concern. She put some of the broth back, wiped the rim and then handed Carnelian the bowl. He looked her in the eyes, thanked her, glad they seemed to be friends again, then carried the bowl away as fast as he could, trying to avoid spilling it.

'Why does the Master refuse to eat?' pleaded Ravan, following him.

Carnelian kept his gaze fixed on the hollow. 'He doesn't want to live here.'

'I've promised him everything I could think of, but he won't even talk to me.'

Carnelian felt the youth was crowding him, threatening to jostle the precious broth on to the ground. 'He's one of the Standing Dead . . . being here . . . he can't . . . it's hard to explain.'

Ravan's face darkened. 'It's you, you're killing him. I've seen the way you've been working on my mother. How desperate you must be that you're prepared to humiliate yourself to impress her by working with Fern. The Master would never lower himself to that and so you're getting rid of him. If he dies I'll make sure you're thrown out of the Koppie.'

Stunned, Carnelian watched Ravan move away. The urgency of Osidian's need made him resume his journey to the hollow. When he reached it, he set the bowl carefully on the nearest root, climbed over and sank into a crouch beside Osidian, who looked no better. Carnelian dug an arm under him and struggled to make him sit. Osidian's eyes opened as Carnelian propped him against the root. Carnelian glanced at the bowl nervously, worried he might knock it over. He retrieved it, balanced it on his knee, dipped a spoon into the broth then held it up to Osidian's mouth.

'Eat,' Carnelian said.

Osidian's nostrils twitched as the steam rose from the broth. His eyes focused on the spoon. Slowly, wearily, he shook his head.

'You must eat,' Carnelian pleaded.

Osidian looked into Carnelian's eyes. 'Let me die. It's better that you should let me die.'

Carnelian was seeing him through tears. 'I won't let you.'

Osidian gazed at him.

'You are my heart,' Carnelian whispered, an echo of the vows of love they had made to each other on that terrible night they had been taken in the Yden. Again he offered Osidian the broth.

Osidian's lips smiled a little. 'I cannot be less than I am.'

Seeing the death rings around Osidian's eyes, Carnelian's fear for him heated to anger. 'And what is that? A Master? One of the Chosen? A Lord of the Earth, perhaps? Such claims sound splendid in Osrakum, but looking at you so easily defeated, they are revealed to be nothing more than empty boasts. Any man can be a god behind legions, behind mountain walls. Are you brave enough to be simply a man?'

Irritation sparked in Osidian's eyes. 'You bait me as if I were a child.'

'You have been behaving like one.'

'There is no life for me here.'

'Then make one.'

'Labouring like a slave; living as a savage?'

'These people have no slaves, and though they are poor, they have dignity. If you were to open your heart, you would see they are even possessed of a certain nobility.'

Osidian looked disgusted. 'They live in such ghastly squalor.'

'Are you so much more delicate than they? Or is it fear, Osidian? Are you afraid that you might be less capable of survival here than are these barbarians?'

Anger had brought Osidian fully back to life. 'What labour do you perform?'

196

Carnelian described the work he did.

'And this you do out of some sense of debt to your savage?'

'Fern saved our lives.'

Carnelian watched Osidian frown, then lose his gaze in the sky. He dared not breathe. Osidian's eyes fell on him.

'I shall work with you.'

Carnelian imagined Osidian, weak as he was, labouring among the flies and heat. His head shook of its own accord.

'Akaisha will find you something else until you have regained your strength.'

'Strength is not in the body but flows from the will. I shall share this penance with you.'

Carnelian did not care to argue. At that moment there was only one victory he sought. He pushed the spoon to Osidian's lips. 'Eat then.'

Osidian's trembling hands took the spoon and bowl from him and began to eat. As he did so, Carnelian hurried to fetch water from the jar against the tree. When Osidian had drunk enough, he refused any help and lay back in the hollow. He was instantly asleep. Carnelian watched him for a while. Osidian, sleeping, seemed whole again. Carnelian stooped to kiss his forehead, then crept away.

At the hearth, he sat down in his usual place. When Poppy brought him a bowl, he made sure to thank her. It was Ravan who asked him the question everyone wanted to ask.

'How is he?'

Carnelian knew that Ravan would find out some time. 'He's decided to come and join me beneath the Bloodwood Tree.'

Ravan gaped. 'No! You're lying.'

Sil looked startled at the violence of Ravan's reaction.

'Of course he can join us tomorrow, Carnie,' said Akaisha.

Ravan turned his gape on his mother. 'You must forbid it.'

Akaisha raised her eyebrows as a mutter of unease went around the hearth.

Whin stood up. 'Ravan, have you forgotten who you're speaking to?'

Ravan scowled and looked around him as if he were being assaulted from every side. Jumping to his feet, he stormed off, knocking over one of the children's bowls as he went.

Akaisha called after him but he seemed not to hear her. Concern mixed with anger as she looked at Fern. 'What's the matter with your brother?'

Fern looked bitter. 'The Master has turned out not to be such a good replacement for his father as he had hoped.'

THE CHALLENGE

Beware of forcing a locked door
unless you know what lies behind it.
(A Chosen proverb)

CARNELIAN WOKE TO FIND SOMEONE LYING AGAINST HIS CHEST. ONLY half awake, he assumed it must be Osidian, until he realized he could feel him lying against his back. He allowed the confusion to sit unresolved in his mind as he turned to regard the dark morning sky through the branches of the mother tree. At last, he found the will to sit up. Whatever it was curled up against him grunted as it adjusted its position. Gently he put his hand out and felt a small head. Peering, he saw it was a child. Poppy. He stroked her hair, drawing comfort from her warmth. He could just make out Osidian, his breathing fitful. Carnelian wondered whether Osidian would have the strength even to stand up, never mind to labour in the heat under the Bloodwood Tree.

Taking care not to wake either of them, he rose, dressed silently and then picked his way across the roots towards the hearth. Several of the women were already gathered in the pale light filtering down to the hearth. Sil saw him coming and smiled brightly.

'Breakfast?'

He nodded and watched her count out enough fernroot cakes for two people.

'My hollow seems to have acquired another mouth to feed.'

She looked at him surprised. When Carnelian explained, she looked thoughtful.

'It was obvious yesterday she'd taken to you, Carnie.'

'Will anyone mind?'

'I can't see why they should, do you?'

Carnelian shook his head.

She beamed. 'Well then.' She plucked up another cake and gave it to him.

He thanked her and returned to the hollow. In his absence, Poppy had snuggled into Osidian. Carnelian wondered how Osidian would react to the girl. He woke her gently. Poppy yawned, rubbed her eyes and then came suddenly awake in a stare. He thought of welcoming her, but then considered he should not do so until he was sure Osidian was not going to reject her. To reassure her he gave her a cake with a smile.

Osidian was next. Carnelian had to shake him. Osidian opened his eyes and for a while could do nothing more than gaze up into the branches of the cedar. When, at last, he sat up with a groan, Poppy looked at him as if he had suddenly come up out of the ground. Carnelian offered him a cake. Osidian's eyes fell on Poppy, who smiled winningly at him. As he turned away from her, Poppy's face fell and Carnelian reacted by cupping her cheek in his hand. She backed into his leg, making sure to keep an eye on Osidian. Carnelian offered him the cake again. To Carnelian's relief, Osidian took it and bit into it.

The cakes were finished by the time Fern appeared. Osidian greeted him with cold eyes. Fern addressed Carnelian as if Osidian were not there.

'Are you sure he's going to be strong enough?'

Carnelian was not sure, but was determined he would not allow him to remain in the hollow. When it came time for them to leave, Osidian refused any help. Grimacing, he rose and then stood looking none too steady.

'Where's Ravan?'

'He'll be on warding duty around the Koppie today with the rest of his hunt,' said Fern.

Carnelian saw in Osidian's raised eyebrows that he had expected Ravan to join them. Osidian caught Carnelian's look and smiled.

'So our little friend thinks it too humiliating to work with us.'

Carnelian was half pleased that this might lead to a break between the two.

They moved towards the rootstair, Osidian tottering after them. Poppy would not leave Carnelian's side. Together they descended the stair with Fern. Osidian followed them, taking each step as if it were his last.

*

His face wet rust, Osidian stood naked beneath the Bloodwood Tree. His pallid skin could have been soaked cloth wrapped around the frame of his bones. Carnelian and Fern looked at each other. Neither could imagine where Osidian was even finding the strength to stand, never mind for the day's work. Akaisha called out to them. Bloodied, she stood by the butchered corpse, the black boulder of its liver bleeding at her feet. Carnelian saw her look of concern as she watched Osidian advancing with them. Sil could not hide her distress. Even Whin's forehead was creased with something like pity.

Carnelian decided to act. He took Osidian's stick arm.

'You're too weak,' Carnelian said.

Osidian pulled his arm free and continued his advance upon the liver. Soon he was wrestling with it. Its blood smeared all across his chest. Carnelian saw Osidian was intent on lifting the whole mass of it himself and rushed in to help. Fern was soon there beside him. As they heaved the quivering mass to the drag-cradles, they had enough of a struggle coping with its weight themselves to have any energy left over to worry about Osidian.

They toiled in the withering heat. Carnelian had become accustomed to the itch of flies walking upon his sweating skin. The stench no longer seemed unbearable. It was different for Osidian. Carnelian's wonder at his strength dulled into an ache of fear. Osidian's limbs seemed so thin they might snap; his muscles so wasted he should have been unable to move. Yet he worked as hard as Carnelian did, as hard as Fern. Carnelian could not rid himself of the conviction that such miraculous strength was consuming what little life Osidian had left.

Carnelian almost cried with relief when Akaisha announced their midday rest. He threw down what he was carrying and made a show of moving from the drag-cradles to the welcoming shade of the Bloodwood Tree. As Fern and he headed for it, Carnelian kept turning just enough to make sure Osidian was following them. As soon as Carnelian reached the trunk he sat against it to encourage Osidian to do the same. Osidian slid down painfully. His eyes stared unblinking from his ochred face. Sil and Poppy brought them food and water. At Carnelian's urging, the girl made sure Osidian ate his share. Unable to look at him any more, Carnelian rested his head against the bark of the tree and closed his eyes. He allowed himself to drift away upon the waft of the women's chatter. The leaves of the Bloodwood Tree sighed a soothing air.

Half drowsing, he became aware of the women calling out a name. It took a moment for his mind to assemble the sound into a word. 'Ravan.'

Carnelian opened his eyes and searched among the shifting shades until he found the youth. Ravan was standing in the blaze just beyond the shadow of the tree. Carnelian followed his line of sight to Osidian. The glint of Osidian's eyes showed he was watching the youth. When Osidian closed his eyes, Carnelian saw the veneer of anger on his face. When he looked for Ravan, he was gone.

People grew used every morning to seeing the two Standing Dead accompanying Fern down to the Bloodwood Tree. Poppy did not like to leave Carnelian. When Akaisha and the other women of her hearth went away to work upon the ditches, Poppy remained behind. Akaisha was happy someone would be there to take care of her son and Carnie. Sil's gratitude towards the Twostone girl soon turned to friendship. Poppy lost her bony look. As he worked, Carnelian would send her down to help hang the djada ropes out to dry. It warmed his heart when he saw her begin to be welcomed by the other children. She helped them chase the ravens away from the racks back to their nests on the Crag. She made friends. She smiled. Carnelian knew joy the first day he heard her laugh. Poppy did not forget 'her men', as she called them. Every day, as the heat became unbearable, she insisted it was her privilege to bring them their meal. Fern, against his better judgement, grew fond of her. Even Osidian tolerated her, as if she were a pet Carnelian had adopted.

The fear Carnelian felt for Osidian had abated, as each morning found him stronger. He rarely spoke. Even when they lay together in their sleeping hollow, Osidian revealed nothing of what he was feeling. Exhausted from the work, Carnelian did not have the energy to prise him open. He told himself Osidian needed to make his own accommodation with their new life. In the evenings, around the hearth, he sat in his place on the rootbench between Fern and Carnelian. He ate everything he was given and never asked for more. Neither he nor Ravan acknowledged each other's existence. Mostly, Osidian looked deep into the fire as if he were watching some drama being played out there. At first his brooding presence had unsettled everyone, but after a few days he became as familiar a part of their world as the boulders that sat upon the hillside in the grasp of cedar roots.

Every three days or so, men would drag a new earther in from the plain. Many aquar were needed to drag the corpse into position under the Bloodwood Tree. The first time a set of hunters came they would look at the Standing Dead only from the corners of their eyes. Carnelian could see himself how terrible Osidian looked. Gigantic, clothed in gore, his blood-matted hair barely concealing the green fire of his eyes. With each succeeding visit, Carnelian began to notice that the men were losing their fear. Seeing the Standing Dead labouring where they themselves would not, they were beginning to feel contempt. For the time being, their disrespect was only in their eyes, but Carnelian knew this could not last and he feared for the effect any mockery would have upon Osidian.

It was Loskai who started it. He had returned from the hunt with other men, among whom Carnelian could see Ravan busying himself checking the knots on the tow-lines. Krow was gazing at Osidian. The hunters were filthy from days out on the plain. Fierce pride shone from their faces as they delivered the immense horned corpse to the women.

Loskai moved towards Osidian, pointing. 'There he is. There's the white bastard who murdered my brother.'

He turned to survey the faces of his companions. 'They neither of them look so impressive now, do they?'

He swung round and regarded Osidian and Carnelian, his lip riding up his teeth.

Carnelian bore the goading, his attention on Osidian, watching him, nervous of his reaction.

The women were gathering round. Mother Mossie appeared among them her hands half-raised, her face hesitant.

'Please stop this,' she said.

Suddenly Loskai shoved Carnelian, causing a hot surge of anger. 'You're not so scary now are you, Master?'

Before he had time to react, Carnelian felt someone at his side. 'You touch him again and you'll have me to deal with.'

Loskai stepped back, regarding Fern with an expression of mock fear, and then, spitting in contempt, he advanced on Osidian, taunting him in Vulgate.

'Loskai, where's your father?' said Mossie.

Osidian lifted his head and looked at Fern, then Carnelian, as if Loskai were not there. Carnelian felt the green eyes in the red-painted face were asking him a question. Enraged at being ignored, Loskai threw a punch into Osidian's ribs. Osidian hardly flinched, his gaze remaining fixed on Carnelian.

'Why's he not defending himself?' muttered Fern.

When Krow stepped forward, protesting, Loskai turned on him. 'Stay out of this, Twostone.'

Leering, Loskai threw a harder punch into Osidian that forced a groan out through his clenched teeth. Carnelian relived the slavers' tormenting of Osidian. In a blind fury, he fell on Loskai, punching him, hurling him to the ground. A pair of hands pulled him off. Still enraged, Carnelian fought loose of their grip and felt his elbow connect with bone.

'Carnie, it's me . . .' he heard. He saw it was Fern. With something like surprise, he gazed down at Loskai lying on the stained earth, his face bloody, his eyes unfocused with shock. The Plainsman rolled over, pushed himself up, facing Carnelian. He spat bloody teeth on to the ground.

'You've only yourself to blame, Loskai,' said Fern.

Mossie and the other women had their hands over their mouths.

'You at least are here at an Elder's command, but these two . . .' Loskai indicated the Standing Dead with his chin. 'Why are they here if it isn't because they fear to be men? Are they scared to leave the safety of our ditches?'

'What is the savage raving about?' Osidian asked, casually, in Quya. Carnelian translated Loskai's words.

As Osidian's gaze fell on Loskai, it caused the Plainsman to go pale. 'You should be careful what you ask for, barbarian. If it's really what you want, I'll come with you, tomorrow.'

Loskai tried a laugh. 'Tomorrow . . . ? Everyone knows tomorrow our hunt rests.'

Osidian gave Loskai a look of contempt that stung him into saying: 'Tomorrow it is then. I'll persuade my father.'

He turned and swaggered back to join his fellows, among whom Carnelian saw Ravan, a turmoil of emotion on his face.

'I'll be reporting this. I'll tell the Elders all about it,' said Mossie.

Carnelian felt a hand on his shoulder and turned to see Fern looking horrified.

'The Master doesn't know what he's doing.'

'He knows exactly what he's doing.'

'Loskai didn't do this by himself. Why do you imagine his father's chosen not to be here? He sent his son to bait you.'

Carnelian had already come to the same conclusion. Glancing at Osidian, Carnelian could tell his mind was made up. 'Nevertheless, I will have to go with him.'

Fern clasped his hands over his head. 'Can't you see they're just trying to get you away from my mother's protection so they can kill you?'

At that moment, Poppy appeared, all eyes and concern. Carnelian picked her up and reassured her. 'Everything's fine. Really.'

He regarded Fern over her shoulder. His friend looked miserable. Carnelian shrugged and put Poppy down. 'Look, I've gone and covered you in blood.'

He sent her off to wash herself. Carnelian saw the bruise already developing on Fern's jaw and indicated it with a grimace. 'Did I do that?'

'It doesn't matter,' said Fern, morose.

Osidian was already returning to the drag-cradles. Brooding, Carnelian followed him.

At the hearth that night, Carnelian was agonizing over whether he should go with Osidian or not when he felt a tugging on his robe and saw it was the boy, Blue, wide-eyed. 'Carnie, is it true you almost killed Loskai today?'

Fern leaned out past Osidian. 'All he did was make him lose a couple of teeth, Blue. Loskai had it coming, he started it.'

'Yes, he started it,' said Poppy fiercely, making Carnelian laugh.

Skai looked at Carnelian over his brother's head. 'But you *are* going out with Father Crowrane's hunt tomorrow?'

'I haven't decided yet,' said Carnelian.

Sil's eyebrows rose and she looked up and down the men's bench. 'Isn't Father Crowrane supposed to be warding tomorrow?'

'I heard he's swapped with Father Kyte,' said Whin's husband, Ravenseye. 'Tomorrow, his hunt is to fetch water with Father Galewing's.'

'Why the swap?' asked Sil.

'Apparently, Loskai persuaded him,' growled Fern.

His wife regarded him with puzzlement, thought a moment, then looked up to the head of the hearth. 'Mother Akaisha, if Carnie goes, I don't suppose there's any chance you'd allow Fern to go with him? It would be just one day away from his punishment.'

'Although I set the punishment, I acted on behalf of all the Elders and can't set it aside on whim.'

'Could you not ask the other Elders?'

Fern glanced at Carnelian. In his eyes Carnelian saw not only his friend's embarrassment, but also a yearning he could not read.

'I've said all I'm going to on this matter, child.' Akaisha's gaze fell on Carnelian. 'There are others, perhaps, you should be challenging, others who made commitments they now seem happy to set aside.'

Carnelian hung his head. It was true that to go with Osidian, he would be reneging on the promise he had made to Fern to share his punishment until its end. It did not matter if what she had said to Sil was true or not. Carnelian knew that Akaisha would do anything she could to stop her son becoming embroiled. Carnelian lifted his head. Ravan was looking past him to Osidian. The flicker of the fire showed the bones underlying the marble of Osidian's face. Carnelian remembered the question he had read in Osidian's eyes before the fight. A direct appeal to the love they had sworn to each other. There really was no choice. How could he let Osidian go into danger alone?

'Ravan dear,' said Whin. 'Do you think you could stay and help us tomorrow? We are going searching for herbs in the Eastgarden and need an escort.'

Angrily, Ravan shook his head. 'My place is with my hunt.'

Poppy approached Osidian, offering her bowl. 'I've left some for you.'

Osidian's gaze did not move from the heart of the fire and the little girl's face fell. Carnelian reached out, took her arm and drew her to him. He pushed the bowl gently towards her. 'That's kind of you, Poppy, but he's eaten his. That's yours.'

She gave Carnelian a piercing look and mouthed: 'But he's so thin.'

'So are you,' he mouthed back sparking several chuckles. It pleased Carnelian he could no longer so easily see Poppy's bones. Her eyes were bright and the bruising under them was now only the merest shadow. He had been avoiding considering the impact his decision would have on her. How hard would it be for her if he were not to return?

Poppy sat down with her back against his legs. Peering over her shoulder, he watched her dig her spoon into the bowl. When he lifted his eyes, they meshed with those of Sil, who was smiling warmly. He thought perhaps she might be prepared to adopt Poppy. He looked past Osidian at Fern. His friend liked the girl and might be prepared to be her guardian. Fern's jaw betrayed the anger he was suppressing. Carnelian decided it was too much to ask. He glanced up past the fire at Akaisha. He would ask her. Besides, he owed her an explanation as to why he felt he had no choice but to go with Osidian.

When he saw Akaisha leaving the hearth he waited a little while. Eyes watching him rise, quickly lost interest as he slipped into the darkness.

When Carnelian's vision adjusted to the dark, he saw Akaisha moving towards the rootstair. When he caught up, he reached out to touch her shoulder. She jumped.

'It's only Carnie, my mother.'

She pressed a hand to her chest. 'What're you doing stalking me in the dark?'

'I wanted to talk to you alone.'

'I'm going to relieve myself, child.'

Carnelian did not know what to say.

She sighed. 'I suppose you could walk some of the way with me.'

He remembered to put his shoes on before they left the rootearth. As they climbed the rootstair, he ordered his thoughts.

'Mother Akaisha, if I were to go tomorrow with Crowrane's hunt, would I go with your blessing?'

The night was very black so that, although Carnelian had made this journey many times himself, he still did not know the steps so well that he was free from the fear of stumbling.

Akaisha did not speak until they had reached the Crag. 'You must not go.'

The path round the Crag was lit by starlight.

'I know it is likely to be dangerous.'

'Well then.'

'My brother is determined to go.'

Their footfalls were no louder than the sighing of the cedars.

'The party of the Elders who wish you dead daily dwindles,' Akaisha whispered.

'If it was up to me, my mother . . . but my brother will not be swayed by me or any other. For him it's a matter of honour.'

Akaisha gave a snort. 'Honour? Why does honour so often serve only to turn men stupid?'

Carnelian could think of no reply.

'What if I forbade him?' asked Akaisha.

'You'd have to be prepared to restrain him with force.'

They had reached the top of the Westing rootstair. Without hesitation, Akaisha plunged into the blackness beneath the mother trees.

'Then I can only pray the Mother will protect you.'

Akaisha had to slow her pace to allow Carnelian to find his way safely down the stair. Though he had to concentrate his mind in his heels, he was still aware of the illuminated underside of the cedars that made it seem as if shadowy halls were laid out on either side.

At last they reached the flat ground before the Westgate, where he knew he must part from Akaisha. The stretch of the Homeditch the women used lay off to the left along the Homewalk: that which the men used, to the right, towards the Childsgate, overlooking the strangely barren rectangle which the Tribe called the Poisoned Field.

Akaisha brought them to a halt. 'It will be hard for my son to work under the Bloodwood Tree without your company.'

'I cannot abandon my brother.'

She clasped his arm. 'Harth may be behind this; Crowrane certainly is or he would have returned with his hunt. That he did not and that Loskai made his challenge when poor Mossie was on duty seems altogether too much of a coincidence. You have one narrow hope. Their plan was certainly to take you out hunting. That they agreed to the Master's counter-challenge has forced them to change the rota. It takes two hunts to fetch water and so you will be going out with not only Crowrane, but also Galewing. When the Assembly voted on your fate, Galewing was the only man who supported me.'

Carnelian pondered this.

Her hold tightened on his arm. 'Do what you can to keep Ravan from any trouble that may arise.'

Carnelian put his hand over hers. 'I will.'

They let go of each other.

'I'm relieved Fern isn't coming with us,' said Carnelian. 'I wouldn't have been able to stop him getting involved.'

'I'm glad some good has come to him from his punishment. When I imposed it on him, it seemed just, but now I can only see that it is wasting much of what little time he has left.'

Carnelian became confused. 'Time left?'

He could sense her surprise. 'Surely . . . surely you can't be unaware of the collar round his neck?'

'The collar . . . ?' Coldness flooded his stomach. Fern had deserted from the legions.

'When the Gatherer comes next year, Fern's life will be forfeit.'

'I hadn't imagined . . .' He remembered the anger Sil had shown him which he had not understood.

'You hadn't imagined the vengeance of the Standing Dead would seek him out?' she said with incredulous anger.

'That they could find him.'

'You yourself revealed to us our name pricked into the palms of our service men. How do you think it got there?'

'They give it over when they are recruited,' Carnelian said. He stared into the night. 'I just didn't . . . I'm so stupid.'

'It seems the Standing Dead are unaware of much of the suffering they inflict upon the world.'

Carnelian burned with shame. 'Couldn't we hide him?'

She gave a hollow laugh. 'If we did, they'd take a child in his place.'

How small was the mesh of the net the Masters had cast over these people. 'Will they . . . punish him here?'

'Most likely they'll take him to Makar where, as an example to others, they'll hang him, mutilated, upon a cross.'

The flat resigned tone of her voice was chilling.

'If that's all?' Akaisha said.

Carnelian saw her shape begin to turn away and reached out and fumbled in the darkness for her hand.

'Perhaps, my mother, while I'm away you might take care of Poppy for me.'

He felt some tensing in her hand and then it was gently pulled away. 'You shouldn't care for her so much, Carnie.'

'I don't share your prejudice against her,' he snapped.

Akaisha took him by the arm. 'It's not that . . . It is only that when the Gatherer comes she might be selected for the tithe.'

Carnelian felt he could bear no more pain. 'Fern told me the same thing. But surely she's Twostone.'

'She ceased to be that when I accepted her into my hearth.'

'Then why did you risk her by . . . ?' He paused remembering Ebeny. 'You don't want to lose more of your kin?'

'My grand-daughter is my heart.'

Carnelian knew it was cruel to say more but could not help himself. 'And Poppy has the kind of prettiness the Gatherer likes.'

She snatched her hand from his arm. 'I'll look after her for you,' she said and walked away.

When Carnelian returned, he did not want to go to the hearth where he would have to face Fern and made his way instead to his hollow. Osidian was there already asleep with Poppy. Carnelian lay down between them. Poppy moulded herself into his side. Her warmth stirred a panic in him that she might be taken away to Osrakum. Panic turned to anger. How could Akaisha be so selfish? She was no better than Harth and all those others who hated him and Osidian.

Carnelian's heart beat faster as he imagined the dangers the next day would bring. Above him stars twinkled in and out of existence as the breathing night stirred the branches of the cedar. He saw again Osidian breaking Ranegale over his knee. Loskai had had to witness that. How could he judge him; judge his father and mother's desire for revenge? Plainsmen had to endure, repeatedly, the rape of their people. It tore at him that, in spite of this, Akaisha had taken them both in. How could he think it was she who threatened Poppy? Was it she who forced countless barbarian tribes to pay a tithe of their children to become the playthings of the Masters in Osrakum? What right had he to blame any of them when it was his own kind who were the root of the world's evil?

Shame cooled to despair as an image of Fern crucified thrust into his mind. Struggle as he might, he could not dislodge it. He turned in to Osidian desperate for the comfort of their love. Feeling him coming awake, he mumbled into his neck: 'I'm afraid.'

'And you accuse *me* of cowardice?' Osidian said, his body unyielding.

Carnelian edged away, as chilled as if he had been embracing marble, and lay as far from the warm comforts of the world as any of the Wise.

BREAKING EGGS

Everything begins with an uncurling.
(a precept of the Plainsmen)

CARNELIAN WOKE FEELING RAGGED. HE LAY LISTENING TO THE GROVE coming awake, glad to lie in the hollow as long as he could. He was reluctant to face the day. He wished he could go back to not knowing about Fern's impending fate. A desire came over him to stay behind, to go down to work under the Bloodwood Tree as usual. But he knew that, even if it led them both to death, he could not allow Osidian to go alone, curse his pride.

It was Osidian rising that flushed Carnelian from his warm hiding place. As he drew himself out from under the blanket, he took care not to disturb Poppy. There lay another goodbye he was not looking forward to. He pulled on his robe and made for the hearth. As he approached its mutter, he found the smell of smoke and breakfast comforting. He took his place on the rootbench. Around him, people were scratching, yawning. Mothers were kissing the children that appeared tousle-headed, rubbing the sleep from their eyes, grinning at gentle teasings. Carnelian looked round at Osidian, whose gaze was already fixed on the fire. Fern appeared. As he came to sit down beside him, Carnelian watched the light run along his brass collar. Carnelian had never noticed how tightly it clutched his throat. Fern was aware of where he was looking.

'Forgive me for not working with you today,' Carnelian managed to say.

Fern leaned close. 'Just make sure you take care today.'

'What're you two whispering about?'

They pulled away from each other, guiltily, and looked across at Sil. The smile on her face faltered. Disturbed, she looked from one to the other.

'I'll tell you . . . later,' said Fern.

Sil put on a smile for him.

Carnelian became aware Osidian was watching him. The look in his eyes intensified Carnelian's feeling of guilt. He was glad Akaisha chose that moment to begin passing out the gruel.

'Carnie, you and your brother make sure you eat well.' Her face was smiling but her eyes were filled with concern. Even Whin seemed troubled as she looked at him. This only served to make his stomach churn with anxiety. He was not sure he was going to be able to keep anything down. He stirred the gruel in the bowl that was passed into his hand. Something cast a shadow over his feet. Glancing up he saw it was Poppy. She sidled up and was soon sitting on his knee cradling her own bowl. He watched each spoonful she put into her mouth as if it was the last time he would ever see her eat. He had to resist the desire to hug her hard. He put off speaking to her until she was finished. At last, he nudged her with his chin and she turned to look up at him.

'I'm going away today.'

Her eyes widened with alarm. 'I'm going too.'

He shook his head. 'You can't. I'm going to fetch water.'

'I can't see why I can't go with you.'

Someone stood over them making them both look up. It was Akaisha. 'You know well enough, girl, that fetching water is men's work.'

Poppy's lower lip began trembling.

Akaisha cracked a smile. 'Today, you can come with me instead.'

Poppy looked at Carnelian and he could see she was on the verge of tears.

'You want me to be proud of you, don't you?'

Poppy gave a slow nod.

'Well then, Poppy, thank Mother Akaisha.'

When the little girl did, Carnelian planted a kiss on the crown of her head and then rested his chin on her hair. He looked into Akaisha's eyes and smiled his gratitude.

'About last night. I'm sorry –'

Akaisha stopped his lips with her fingertips. Carnelian could see the warmth in her eyes. She crouched to look Poppy in the face.

'Do you want to come with me now and sit at the head of the hearth?'

Poppy lit up and wiggled her way off Carnelian's knee on to the ground. Akaisha offered a hand and Poppy took it. Carnelian glanced up at Akaisha to thank her and found she was looking down the length of the hollow. Ravan was there standing in the gloom. At first Carnelian thought the youth was looking at him but he quickly realized his attention was fixed on Osidian.

'Come and have your breakfast, my son,' Akaisha called to him.

Ravan shook his head. 'I've come to get the Standing Dead.' He stared even more intensely at Osidian. 'If they're still coming, that is . . .'

'But you should eat before you go.'

'Are you coming, Master?' Ravan said in Vulgate as if his mother had not spoken.

Osidian rose and passed in front of Carnelian, who had no choice but to join him. People grumbled as they looked from Akaisha to Ravan. Osidian loomed over the youth, both of them waiting.

Carnelian saw the upset on Akaisha's face but could think of nothing he could say. He glanced at Fern and they exchanged nods, then he left the hearth and did not look back once.

Every one of the men waiting with aquar at the earthbridge turned to watch the approach of the Standing Dead. A group came out to meet them, among whom Carnelian could see Loskai with his swollen lips. As they came closer, Carnelian recognized Crowrane and Galewing, both of whom he remembered from his appearance before the Elders. Galewing seemed much younger than the other Elder.

'My fathers,' Ravan said bowing his head and Carnelian did the same.

Galewing regarded both Standing Dead with a frown. Without taking his eyes off them he turned. 'You're sure you want to risk taking them with us?'

'Yes,' said Crowrane, his face wooden.

Loskai's eyes were burning with a malicious hunger. A fixed grin showed his missing teeth.

Galewing looked into Carnelian's eyes and then into Osidian's. 'You ride out of the Koppie under the authority of Father Crowrane,' he said, in Vulgate. 'If you disobey him, if you try to escape, you will be killed. You understand?'

Glancing at father and son, Carnelian was sickened at the thought of delivering himself into their hands.

'Do you accept?' demanded Galewing.

Osidian shrugged. He was gazing off towards the brightening

plain. Carnelian searched his eyes for any sign that he was aware of the danger they were putting themselves in.

'Answer Father Galewing,' barked Loskai, making Carnelian jump.

Carnelian saw there was going to be no backing out and so gave Galewing his nod.

The Elder turned away, bellowing. 'Mount up.'

As aquar sank to the ground, Carnelian's attention was attracted to one being walked towards him by Krow. They exchanged smiles.

'It's good to see you, Krow.'

'And you, Master.'

Carnelian would have liked to talk but it was not the time. He was soon preoccupied trying to get comfortable in the narrow saddle-chair. Its sides cut into his thighs. His legs, hooked awkwardly over the crossbeam, were forced almost against his chest as he angled his feet towards the aquar's back. Glancing over, he saw Osidian was having the same problem. He used his feet to make the creature rise and immediately had to turn her on to the path towards the bridge riders were already crossing.

Notwithstanding the discomfort, Carnelian managed to manoeuvre his aquar safely across the bridge and was soon being jogged down an avenue of magnolias to the outer ditch. He was shaken into a more natural position and was soon, in spite of his fears, enjoying the ride.

Crossing the final bridge, he looked down into the Newditch and saw it was filled with baskets and mattocks. Its inner wall was striped with the ropes that dangled down into it from the trees all along the edge. Craning round, he saw riders accompanying a group of women through the ferngarden towards the workings.

A judder in his saddle-chair forced him to look where he was going. Riders were milling in all directions.

'Master.'

It was Krow, pointing to where he should go. Carnelian thanked him and saw the riders had formed up around a solid centre of perhaps two dozen aquar yoked to drag-cradles stacked with empty waterskins. He took up position near Osidian and Ravan who were squinting into the far distance, to which only some acacias gave any scale. All around them were riders with unhitched javelins, with bull-roarers ready across their laps. Carnelian ran his hands along the outer surface of his saddle-chair, but could find no weapons. This discovery sunk him back into despondency.

A high warbling cry rose up and, as one, the aquar lurched forward. Carnelian attempted to settle into the rhythm of his aquar's pace, snuffling the musky breeze, trying to lull his unease by listening to the chatter of the riders, the hiss of ferns along his aquar's flanks. Every so often he had to adjust his position to alleviate the discomfort. He looked back to see how much the Koppie had receded. The air had grown hot enough to make it waver like a mirage. He thought of Fern already labouring among the flies under the Bloodwood Tree. When he lost sight of the Koppie altogether, a stab in his stomach was the realization he might never see it again.

Their shadows were short by the time the land ahead began to pool with fire. The incandescence of the lagoon twitched and flickered as herds slid before it. Soon Carnelian could see its full horizontal stretch and the creeping mass of saurians. The riders had fallen silent, their shoulders and arms tense as they made slow scanning turns with their heads.

As the hunt drew closer to the water, the herds resolved into the individual boulders of backs; into necks that stretched to the very tops of the acacias. Several times the hunt curved a detour round what appeared to be rocks nestling among the ferns. When one of these lifted a head larger than a man and grinned a mouth packed with dagger teeth, a trickle of sweat ran down Carnelian's spine. It made him understand why his aquar was holding her head so high, shifting it nervously from side to side, hardly blinking her huge eyes.

Entering a herd, Carnelian began to feel as much as hear their lumbering thunder. Horned heads were everywhere cropping the ferns. Sometimes one would lift dull eyes to watch them pass. On occasion, this lifting would cause so many heads to rise it was as if a host lying hidden in the ferns sprang up in ambush.

The herds crowded the lagoon margin. Out from the shore, the water was dulled by drifts of wading birds. Islands rose here and there that Carnelian might have imagined to be cities except their towers were shifting more than they should in the melting air.

Crowrane led them parallel to and at some distance from the shore. When they spotted a thinning in the herd, they slowed to a walk and began veering towards the water. Carnelian gaped at an assembly of mountainous heaveners, their heads reaching far out over the lagoon. He watched one rising, leaking water, climbing so high he had to crane to see it swaying black in the blinding sky.

As they neared the shore, Carnelian saw how nervously the riders were spreading out, javelins and bull-roarers hanging from their hands. Some dismounted and, looking round them all the time, led the aquar with the drag-cradles to the water.

No one seemed to be looking at him. Carnelian allowed himself to relax a little. It was hard to believe all these preparations were an elaborate attempt on his life and Osidian's.

Locating Krow, Carnelian rode towards him. 'What can we do to help?'

The youth pinched his lips together with his fingers, which gesture Carnelian read as meaning he should speak more quietly. Krow caused his mount to kneel and climbed out. Carnelian waited for Osidian and Ravan to dismount before doing the same. Standing on tremoring earth, he glanced at the heaveners. It seemed madness to walk so near such giants. One detonated a snort. Its hide rippled as the water made the journey down its throat. Its musk weighed the air as heavily as it appeared to do the earth.

Krow took Carnelian's arm and pulled. 'Come on,' he whispered.

Carnelian and the others followed Krow to a drag-cradle from which men were distributing waterskins. Carnelian was given one. Making sure Osidian was close, Carnelian returned with Krow to the lagoon. Earth began softening to mud. They waded out into the lapping water and Carnelian sank his waterskin as he saw Krow was doing. He narrowed his eyes against the swaying dazzle. Warm water licked up his body. He opened the mouth of the waterskin and it began to swallow. Shadow slipped over him as if from a cloud. A wave surging up his chest made him lose his footing for a moment. A glistening wall was rising from the lagoon as a heavener lifted its leg from the water. Wading deeper, the vast arch of its back eclipsed the sun. Fear mixed with wonder as, riding the surge, Carnelian watched the monster lead a procession of heaveners away from the shore.

His waterskin was drowning and so he drew it up, folded its neck, secured it, then hefted it round on to his shoulder. He plodded back to the drag-cradle where he swung it into the arms of a man who was stacking them. Carnelian took an empty waterskin. Other drag-cradles were being loaded nearby. A rising falling whistling made him whisk round, his heart hammering. Three riders were arcing bull-roarers round their heads, focusing on an earther which was ambling towards the cradles. The creature made Carnelian remember the Bloodwood Tree. The bull-roarers spinning faster opened the whistling to a moan. The bull swung away and they chased him from the drag-cradles.

Carnelian became aware Crowrane and Galewing, standing together, were watching him while speaking to each other. He was sure they would not make their move until they were far from the dangerous shore.

Osidian and Ravan were still in the lagoon filling waterskins.

Wading out towards them, Carnelian saw Osidian was gazing towards a nearby island crowded with crested saurians. 'Are they nesting?'

'Yes, Master,' Ravan replied.

'Their eggs would make good eating.'

'Such roosts are impregnable.'

Aware of Carnelian's presence, Osidian turned and acknowledged him with a frown. 'What's wrong?'

Still brooding over Fern, Carnelian did not answer quickly.

'My Lord seems distracted,' Osidian said. 'Is it that he fears the saurians, or perhaps, the savages?'

The shift into Quya was shocking. 'Both are unsettling,' Carnelian said in Vulgate.

'Is my Lord missing the blood and gore of his previous employment?' Osidian said, insisting on Quya. 'Is it then your savage *friend* you miss, Carnelian?'

Carnelian groaned. 'Why do you even now persist –?'

'That some matter is perturbing my Lord can easily be read from his face.'

'If you must know . . .' Carnelian was aware Ravan was there trying to glean what was being talked about. 'I discovered last night that when the childgatherer comes, his brother,' he indicated Ravan, 'will have be handed over for punishment.'

'You are being melodramatic, Carnelian.'

Carnelian flared into anger. 'He saved your life not once but several times.'

Osidian grew pale. 'How often do you intend to throw that back in my face? The savage broke the vows he swore of service to my father. Crucifixion is the price the Commonwealth demands for such sacrilege.'

Carnelian's anger cooled to ice. 'You knew this was going to happen?'

Osidian raised an eyebrow. 'You did not? One would have thought it common knowledge even among exiles.'

Carnelian's dislike of him at that moment must have showed in his face, for suddenly Osidian discarded his waterskin and began wading back towards the shore.

Ravan looked horrified. 'What did you say to him?'

Seeing Osidian already leaving the water and striding into the midst of the Plainsmen alone, Carnelian became frantic. He discarded his waterskin and bounded back to shore. Osidian was already mounted and guiding his aquar away through the perimeter of Plainsmen riding guard. Carnelian raced for his own beast, threw himself into her chair and made her rise. He aimed her along the shore in pursuit.

Perimeter guards rode to intercept them. 'Where in thunder are you going?'

Crowrane's voice came floating from somewhere near the drag-cradles. 'Let them go.'

The men scowled, shrugged and moved their aquar out of the way. Beyond their protection Carnelian felt exposed. The raised voices had disturbed the herds. Carnelian became aware another aquar was shadowing him and saw it was Ravan's.

The ground was being shaken by immense footfalls, the air was wafting thick with the stink of the saurians and rasped by their cries. He and Ravan skirted the denser clumps of them keeping as close as they could to the shore. When they caught up with Osidian, he did not acknowledge their presence. Carnelian feared the anger he had provoked was going to get them all killed.

'Let's ride back, Osidian. Out here, we're vulnerable.'

Osidian spoke without taking his gaze from the island roost. 'I have faith in my God.'

When the roost was perhaps only a javelin cast from the shore, he brought them to a halt. Flamingos were an undulating pink commotion obscuring the water. Beyond them rose the island upon which Carnelian could clearly see the saurians with their swept-back scarlet crests.

'Bellowers,' said Ravan, his eyes round.

Osidian turned. 'Are they noted for their ferocity?'

'They'll defend their nests against even the most malevolent raveners.'

'Excellent.'

Bewildered, Carnelian and Ravan followed Osidian back to the relative safety of the drag-cradles.

'What did he say?' Osidian asked Carnelian, all the while regarding Loskai with a look of amusement.

'Something along the lines of, you must be mad.'

'Ask him if he's afraid.'

Carnelian did, somewhat reluctantly.

'There's a difference between wanting to stay alive and being afraid,' said Loskai.

At that moment Crowrane approached demanding to know from his son what was going on. As Loskai explained, his father frowned, all the time keeping his eyes on Osidian.

'Well, I'm going to get myself an egg and anyone else who isn't afraid can come with me,' said Osidian in Vulgate to the younger men who were gathering round.

Osidian looked at Ravan. 'You at least aren't afraid to come with me, or are you, son of Stormrane?'

'I'll go . . . I'll go with you,' the youth answered, his face shiny with sweat. He took it upon himself to translate the Master's words for those who had no Vulgate. Krow, among others, moved to stand with Ravan at Osidian's side. The rest looked for guidance to Crowrane, who was surveying the roost as if he were calculating the odds. He brought the men of his hunt into focus.

'Shall we allow one of the Standing Dead to slur our manhood?'

The older among them shook their heads slowly, regarding the Elder in puzzlement. The youngsters declared their bravery noisily. Their commotion brought Galewing, accompanied by several of his hunt.

He cowed them into silence with a glare. 'Are you lot trying to get us trampled?'

Crowrane encouraged the Elder to move away with him. Carnelian could see Crowrane explaining. When Galewing grew angry, Crowrane calmed him. Carnelian did not like the glances they gave him as they talked and approached Osidian.

'You must not do this,' he said in Quya.

'It is no longer possible to turn back,' Osidian replied.

Carnelian glanced off to where the Elders were still in discussion. 'You are putting us in their trap.'

'On the contrary, I am turning their trap against them.' He smiled, fire in his eyes. 'Will you join me?'

Crowrane returned. 'Father Galewing will make sure the water gets back safely to the Koppie. Those of you who wish should return with him.'

No one moved.

'Well, then, let's go and get ourselves some eggs.'

Grinning, excited, the youngsters ran for their aquar. Crowrane followed them, frowning. At his side, Loskai was giving him an anxious look.

Carnelian became aware Osidian was still waiting for an answer. Carnelian's unease turned to irritation.

'Do I have any choice?'

As Osidian cantered into the lagoon, flamingos rose like a sudden dawn. Carnelian was mesmerized by their flashing wingbeats. The cloud cleared to reveal dazzling water stretching to the island upon which many of the bellowers were turning to watch them.

'What now, Master?' Loskai cried, hanging back with his father.

Osidian ignored the Plainsman. He swung his arm round, his hand tracing a bright arc in the air. At this signal, Ravan, to whom Carnelian had earlier seen Osidian giving instructions, waded his aquar off into the deeper water on their right leading some of the youngsters. Carnelian watched them curve round towards the shore of the island, wondering that they were so readily prepared to obey Osidian. As Ravan and his party drew nearer to the bellowers they rose up alarmed, rending the air with a trumpeting that set aquar plumes and Carnelian's heart to fluttering. The brazen cries rose and fell in angry fanfares as more and more of the bellowers came down to the water's edge. The riders continued wading parallel to the shore until they moved out of sight, drawing the bellowers away.

Without a backward glance, Osidian sent his aquar forward at a lope towards the island. Carnelian could feel the general hesitation and sent his aquar after Osidian, hoping to encourage others to follow. Even before he had caught up with Osidian, Carnelian could hear the water behind him being churned to foam by the feet of many aquar. Carnelian did not dare look to either side, lest he should break the spell that was drawing them.

At its deepest, the water came up to the high ankle of Osidian's aquar. Soon they were coming up out of it, riding along a ridge that swelled up to form the island. A few bellowers trumpeting madly defended the passage to the roost.

Osidian swung round and addressed Crowrane's hunt. 'Throw as quickly as you can.'

Leaning back with a weapon Ravan must have given him, Osidian hurled it whistling through the air. Soon others were being thrown from all around Carnelian. For a moment, Carnelian imagined Osidian might be their target, but the volley was falling among the saurians. Though the javelins scratched harmlessly off their hides, the bellowers dropped forward on to all fours and brought their narrow flaring crests down in front of them like shields. All the time they kept up a furious, deafening cacophony and lashed their tails. Spotting a gap in their line, Osidian crashed through. Carnelian swore under his breath, gritted his teeth and followed him. A bellower rose, falling back so heavily on to its haunches that the earth shook. Carnelian's aquar veered wildly and it was all he could do to keep her running. He rode into the shadow of the towering monster, into its musky stench. He felt it begin to avalanche towards him and threw himself forward even as it punched the ground with an impact that shuddered up through his chair and whiplashed his head against his knees. Then he was through and hurtling through a landscape of cratered mud.

Osidian's aquar slid and almost lost its footing as he forced it to a halt with his heels. Carnelian's veered just in time to avoid a collision. He swung in the saddle-chair for a moment, his heart pounding, his forehead aching from the impact with his knees. Then he became aware no one had followed them.

To one side, more bellowers were surging up out of the water lifting their long muzzles into the breeze. Others were mobbing the rookery's further shore, drowning the warcries of Ravan's diversionary force with their screeching.

Seeing Osidian staring back the way they had come, Carnelian incandesced with rage. 'Where's your God now? Are you happy?'

The line of saurians they had broken through was fragmenting as the creatures saw the tiny intruders among their nests. Suddenly, another volley of javelins fell among them and screeching, they turned aside. Riders came pouring up through the gaps, Krow at their head.

'Crowrane commanded us to retreat!'

Osidian knelt his aquar and vaulted out on to the mud.

Stunned, Carnelian was hardly aware of dismounting. Nests lay all around; craters gouged into the mud. Plainsmen were descending on every side. Osidian led some of them to face the trumpeting with their bull-roarers and javelins. Carnelian saw a volley glancing off a heaving wall of mottled hide and then saw the men around him gaping.

'Eggs,' he cried, overcoming his anger, remembering why they were there. He ran to the nearest nest and reached over its curving embankment. He burrowed his fingers into the warm rot of vegetation and touched a smooth hard shape. Quickly he scooped the stuff off to reveal a spiral of long narrow white eggs. He lifted one out. It slid in his green-slimed arms. It was three spans long and as heavy as if it were made of stone. He cradled it as he ran over to his saddle-chair.

'What do we do?' screamed Krow clutching an egg.

Carnelian looked over to where Osidian and some others had remounted. He could see they were running out of javelins. They were riding at the bellowers, bellowing, waving their arms. The creatures fell back, letting out a fearsome fanfare of outrage.

Carnelian saw Krow's panic-stricken face among others. 'Line some saddle-chairs with blankets to carry the eggs. The rest of us'll have to get out of here two to an aquar.'

They hurried to obey him. He helped them quickly ferry as many of the eggs as he could into the chairs separating each layer with the fold of a blanket.

Carnelian was not the only one to notice a change in the tone of the bellower calls. He whisked round. What he saw made him drop the egg he carried so that it smashed its yolk and foetus down his legs and feet. A deeper baying like warhorns. Fluted crests longer and more elaborate than the ones he had seen were visible above the bellowers.

Krow went white. 'The mothers are returning.'

A scramble began into empty saddle-chairs or clinging on to cross-poles.

A blast of screeches rolled over them as the bellower mothers saw the despoiled nests. Carnelian found himself gaping at their charge and Osidian and the others fleeing towards him.

'Master!' shrieked a voice.

The earth quaked as the bellowers lumbered closer. Carnelian saw Osidian's aquar, readied himself and caught hold of its cross-pole as it hurtled past. The impact threatened to tear his arms from their sockets, but he managed to hang on. He was half running: half carried. His weight was unbalancing Osidian's aquar. Its pistoning leg buffeted him. Its clawed foot would shred him if he were to swing in its path. He kicked his way through a nest before he pulled his legs up. He held on desperately as they careened down the slope towards the water. His legs trailed through it, the drag leeching the last strength from his arms. He squeezed his eyes closed against the pain. His hands unhooked and he smashed into the lagoon. He was drowning. His feet found the bottom and he came up coughing water, gulping for air, to see a wall of bellowers crashing towards him. He covered his head with his arms, waiting to be crushed. The wave the bellowers were driving before them washed him off his feet but he managed to regain his balance. He opened his eyes as something brushed past him. Osidian on his aquar screaming Quyan curses at the oncoming saurians. Carnelian gaped with wonder as the creatures dropped ponderously on to all fours. Their stench was overpowering. Their cries battered his ears. Then, miraculously, they began to turn away.

He remained frozen, staring until the water stopped eddying around his legs, until the flamingos had settled back down to the lagoon.

When Carnelian became undazed, the first thing he saw was the relief in Osidian's face. They gazed at each other, for a moment the lovers they had once been. Carnelian became aware of Ravan's excited voice. 'Did you see the way the bellowers obeyed the Master? Did you?'

Loskai was scowling. 'They were already pulling back before he rode at them.'

'What do we do now?' someone asked.

Crowrane seemed deaf, blind and it was to Osidian that faces were turned in awe.

The Master had them repack the eggs more carefully because some had been broken in their flight.

'Wash it all out,' barked Crowrane. 'We don't want the smell attracting raveners.'

Rage distorted his face as people, hesitating, glanced over at Osidian for instruction. Crowrane pointed out several of them.

'You and you . . . yes, you, Twostone, get water, now.'

Sullenly, Krow and the others did as they were told and soon came waddling back with bloated waterskins. Carnelian watched one Plainsman wash the mess out from his saddle-chair. The foetus the egg had cradled dropped its hook on to the ground. The man had not noticed the tiny creature lying there but Ravan had and moved to retrieve it. But before he reached it, Osidian, oblivious, trampled it into the mud.

Because of the saddle-chairs packed with eggs, the hunt had to return at walking pace. Krow offered Carnelian his aquar but he declined. Carnelian remembered it was Krow who had been the first to defy Crowrane.

'We owe you our lives.'

The youth sunk his head. 'I owe the Master much.'

'Father Crowrane and his son will not quickly forgive you.'

Krow shrugged.

'Why have you ended up in their hunt?'

Krow looked up. 'Because their hearth took me in.'

The youth's eyes betrayed something of the unhappy conditions in which he had to live. 'They know I am your friend.'

Carnelian became aware Loskai was observing them. He realized now it was Krow who was in danger.

Unable to ride, the hunt was in peril from raveners. The hunters kept fear at bay by describing to each other the Tribe's delight when they received the precious cargo the hunt were bringing home.

Galewing appeared with his men, saying that they had come to offer any help that might be needed. He told them the Tribe knew of their expedition and were worried for their safety. The amazement the Elder and his hunt showed over their haul of eggs lifted spirits. Still, many would be unable to flee a ravener attack and so the first sight of the Koppie rising out from the plain was greeted with audible sighs of relief. The closer it came, the wider grew the smiles anticipating a triumphant return.

Grim-faced, a large portion of the Tribe were waiting for them across the earthbridge. Carnelian saw among them Harth, Ginkga and others of the Elders. He was disappointed when he could not see Akaisha. He had hoped she would be there with Poppy.

The hunters rode over into the ferngarden and dismounted.

Hands on hips, Harth confronted her husband. 'What possessed you?'

Crowrane made a face, painfully aware of the people watching. His wife gave a snort of disgust and, seeking out her son among the press, withered him with her gaze.

Ginkga gazed out over the hunters. Where her eyes looked, their heads fell in shame. 'Have you any idea how much worry you brought your hearths?'

'But no one was hurt, my mother and –' Ravan began, before the Elder silenced him with a look.

'If we hadn't begged the Mother to shield you, who knows how many would've been killed?'

She stabbed a finger at Osidian and then Carnelian. 'They put you up to it, didn't they?'

'But it worked out exactly as the Master said it would,' cried Ravan, red-faced.

He reached over into a saddle-chair and lifted out an egg. Walking into the crowd, he handed it to a woman who received it like a baby. Ravan grinned as he heard the excitement rippling out through the crowd.

'There may be as many as two for each hearth,' he announced.

The crowd came alive as they began clamouring for theirs. The hunters beamed as they began unpacking and handing out the treasure they had brought back for their people. Bright with pride, Krow joined in. Carnelian did not feel he should, though he was fired by the general elation. Crowrane stood eyes downcast behind his wife, so that it was Galewing who oversaw the distribution.

'Losing so many young will hurt the bellowers,' cried Ginkga over the commotion. 'You don't understand what you've done.'

Carnelian was sobered by the woman's dismay. The rest of her cries were drowned out by the sounds of celebration.

Ravan basked in the approval of his hearthkin as he told for the second time the tale of the expedition against the bellowers. Osidian strode heroic through that tale and as the Plainsmen savoured the delicacies that had been made with the eggs, eyes kept flicking to the Master, sitting as he always did watching something only he could see in the dancing of the flames.

Not Whin, not even Akaisha were falling under the spell of Ravan's story. They witnessed his swagger, his naked adoration of the Master, with unhappy eyes. Earlier, returning red-stained from the earthworks, they had uncurled the foetuses from the two eggs the hearth had been given and went to bury them among the roots of their mother tree.

As Carnelian watched Ravan, he fondled Poppy's head as she sat against his knee. He glanced at Fern. When he had returned to find Carnelian alive he had run to him and, taking hold of his arms, had regarded him with undisguised delight. This had made Sil unhappy even though she had kissed Carnelian as she did the others, glad to see them safely returned. Aware of her reaction, confused by Fern's intensity, Carnelian had disengaged from him. When Fern became aware of Sil, the three of them had been left isolated, prey to confused emotions.

A movement at the edge of Carnelian's vision drew his gaze down to Osidian's pale hand signing: *It seems we are heroes.*

Carnelian turned to look at him.

Use handspeech.

Carnelian obliged him. *The boy speaks only of you.*

Osidian made a sign connoting amusement, then: *This popularity will, I judge, keep our lives safe outside the ditches.*

I intend to return to work with – Carnelian indicated Fern.

No. I need you with me.

From petty jealousy, you endangered our lives and many others.

Osidian made a contemptuous gesture of dismissal. *I made a bid for power.*

You make my decision firmer. I will take no further part in your machinations.

Osidian's hand fell still. Then, slowly, he turned to watch Ravan who was enacting the arrival of the bellower mothers. Without turning back, his hand began to shape signs again. *He will not now leave my side.*

Carnelian frowned, staring at the pale hand. The fingers curled.

The outer world is perilous.

Carnelian grew inflamed and pulled at Osidian's shoulder to make him look at him. 'Do you stoop, my Lord, like Jaspar did with my brother, to use threats against another as a means of controlling me?'

Carnelian's Quya made Ravan fall silent. The whole hearth were staring at the Standing Dead.

Osidian's eyes burned furiously. 'You should remember why we have ended up here, Carnelian.'

Carnelian was painfully aware of the people round about.

Osidian smiled at Ravan, who smiled back. 'Do not imagine when the time comes I will have mercy on the boy.'

IRON SPEAR

Husband, you are the sky
the angry one
the winged sower of rain
come, quench my thirst.
(from a marriage ritual of the Plainsmen)

THE GROVE WAS WAKING WHEN CARNELIAN PICKED HIS WAY AMONG THE sleeping hollows towards Fern and Sil's. He knew where it lay even though he had never been there. It was Sil who first noticed him approaching and raised her husband. Little Leaf began to cry and Sil put her to a breast to quieten her.

Carnelian felt he was intruding. 'Can I speak to you, Fern?'

Seeing that Carnelian wanted to talk to him alone, Fern rose. Both men made an apology to Sil, who looked concerned.

They moved up the slope a little to where the branches of the cedar forced Carnelian to bow his head.

'I won't be returning to the Bloodwood Tree,' Carnelian said.

Fern frowned. 'You've decided to stay with the hunt?'

As Carnelian nodded, he could see Fern was waiting for some explanation, but how could Carnelian tell him what Osidian had threatened to do; how could he tell Fern that he had made Osidian swear on his blood that, if Carnelian went with him, Osidian would not deliberately harm any of the Tribe?

'Well, you've told me,' Fern said at last and returned, still frowning, to his wife.

*

That day Crowrane's hunt was warding so Carnelian, Osidian, Ravan and several others accompanied Akaisha and her women down into the ferngardens. Akaisha had watched Fern go off to work alone and Carnelian had to endure the pressure of her scrutiny. She was clearly unhappy not only with his decision but with the way in which he had made it without giving her an explanation.

In the perfumed shadow of a magnolia, he spent that day, wretched, watching the women harvesting termites from mud towers and trying to ignore Ravan and Osidian. In the evening, he made himself blind to Sil's enquiring looks and, studiously, tried to behave towards Fern as if nothing had happened.

The following day, he helped keep watch over Akaisha and her women as they dug fernroot. He would have helped if Ravan had not insisted that it was tradition that men should rest on their warding days.

Next morning the women had to return to the earthworking. By coincidence, Crowrane's hunt were working in the ditches too, so that Carnelian went with Akaisha and was able to work with Poppy by his side all day.

Three days he laboured thus under the resentful gaze of Crowrane and Loskai. Carnelian saw the deference with which the other members of the hunt were treating Osidian. It was the youngsters, Krow among them, who were most in awe of him. Some dared to ask him questions through Ravan, but the Master remained aloof and worked as if he were alone, carrying the baskets filled with earth up the ladders to the ramparts, his strength fully returned. The women who worked alongside them outnumbered the men almost three to one. The men had to work hard to match them. The older people oversaw the repair of the ditch, or did the lighter work. Carnelian took turns at digging, carrying the dislodged earth up the ladders, or beating it into the ramparts with paddles. The sun was merciless. Carnelian was sheathed in the slime his sweat made of the red earth on his skin. During the hottest part of the day they hid in the depths of the ditch where its high walls, or one of the trees fringing it, cast delicious shadow. They ate, sipped water, napped. At the end of each day they returned to wash under their mother tree and slumped exhausted around the hearth, almost too tired to speak.

The way it worked out, the hunt and Akaisha's women completed their stint in the ditches on the same afternoon. In the morning, Carnelian had to leave Poppy in Akaisha's care when she took her hearth down to the Bloodwood Tree. For the next six days, it would be Crowrane's hunt in company with that of Ginkga's husband who would make the journey each day to fetch water for the Tribe.

It was a relief to ride out from the Koppie to the vast spreading lagoon. At first, Carnelian maintained a careful watch on Loskai and his father. In full view of both hunts, Crowrane made a point of telling the Master that more heroics would not be tolerated. The Elder might as well have directed his tirade against a statue. Osidian's impassivity drove Crowrane and Loskai into an anger which only served to reveal how powerless they were.

That first day, water was brought back to the Koppie without mishap. The aquar pulled the drag-cradles right up to the Homeditch. From there it was unloaded and everyone made at least two journeys up the Lagooning rootstair with a waterskin to pour the precious contents into the cistern that lay in a cleft in the Crag.

The second day they saw riders moving on the other side of the lagoon. Ravan claimed they were from a neighbouring tribe, the Woading.

It was on the fifth day that Carnelian learned why it was the Plainsmen considered fetching water perilous. They were returning from the lagoon when they found themselves in the path of a stampede. Burdened with their fully laden drag-cradles, the hunt could not evade the charge. The bleating earthers thundered through their line. Many of the monsters managed to swerve around the obstacles; others were skilfully deflected with bull-roarers, but one gored a man and another crashed headlong into a cradle, exploding its waterskins everywhere. The hitched aquar was hurled over on to its side. Screaming, it flailed its clawed feet. The earther, tossing its head to free its horns from the ruins of the drag-cradle, ripped open the belly of the aquar and was, in turn, gashed by the aquar's claws. One of the Plainsmen leapt in to end the aquar's agony, others dared to approach the earther to hack it loose. Erupting free, the monster trampled a man. It was clear nothing could be done for him. Crowrane put an end to the man's agony by slitting his throat. They carried the body back on a drag-cradle, for fear of raveners, using earth to cover the trail of blood they were painting across the plain.

That night the Tribe mourned their loss. Akaisha took Carnelian with her to watch the blackened body being carried up to the summit of the Crag. Osidian came too, with Ravan. At one point, Carnelian overheard them discussing the next day, which was to be his first hunt. He forced the anxiety from his mind by trying to pick meaning from the song of lamentation rising up with smoke into the sky. The dead man's soul would soon be carried up into that blueness by the birds that fed on him.

Akaisha and Poppy came down to the Southgate to see them off. In the predawn twilight many other women had gathered to bid their men farewell. Everyone spoke quietly.

Carnelian was holding his shoulder where Fern had touched it when he had wished him a safe hunt.

'You'll be careful, Carnie, promise me you'll be careful?'

Crouching, Carnelian looked into Poppy's dark eyes and nodded solemnly. Kissing her, he rose and saw Osidian standing apart from them, aloof and remote as he examined a huge spear he was hefting in his hand.

'I'm not a child any more,' said Ravan, looking aggrieved, as he confronted his mother. 'Fern had no right to it. It came to me from my father. It is mine to give away.'

Carnelian looked back at the spear in Osidian's hand and realized it had been fitted with Stormrane's iron blade.

As Akaisha watched her son join the Master, she had the look of someone who had just been slapped. Carnelian looked away so she would not become embarrassed. Harth, who had come down to see her son and husband off, was regarding Osidian with baleful eyes. Krow stood behind them, forgotten, sullen.

A hand on his arm made Carnelian look round into Akaisha's face. She made a point of glancing at Harth, who was hugging Loskai while her husband, Crowrane, stood by. Akaisha looked at Carnelian and raised her eyebrows to see if he understood her warning.

'I'll be careful, my mother.'

As her gaze moved to Ravan, she seemed suddenly old and frail.

'I'll keep an eye on him too,' he whispered and was rewarded by a squeeze of thanks.

'Come, child,' she said, offering her hand to Poppy. 'Today's our last day in the ditches for quite a while. The sooner we start, the sooner the day's work will be done.'

'And tomorrow we'll weave, my mother?'

Akaisha shook her head. 'The day after.'

As Akaisha led her off chattering along the Homewalk, Carnelian waited for Poppy to sneak a glance back at him. He grinned when she did, waved and then he turned grimly to the business of the day.

Once the hunt crossed the Newditch, they rode south-west with the morning breeze streaming their shadows like pennants. At first curious, Carnelian looked around him at the land they were riding through, but he soon grew weary of the infinite fernland where only the acacias showed they were making steady progress. They had brought drag-cradles with them piled high with fernwood. He whiled away some time trying to imagine what they were going to do with it. He played with the javelins Ravan had given him. Though crude, they were nicely made. The tops of the horsetail shafts had been split to take a blade of sharpened flint. Many windings of gut held the blade in place. Though sharp enough, he was sure the blade would prove brittle and he was envious of Osidian's iron spear.

It had grown torrid when the first glimmer appeared on the horizon. He knew it must be water and for a moment wondered if they had been riding in an arc towards the bellower lagoon. A glance at his shadow was enough to convince him otherwise. Squinting, he saw that to the east of this lagoon there lay another smaller one he had never seen before.

When he spotted the specks of a saurian herd, his heart began hammering. No doubt the hunt would soon be upon him. A thousand fears took possession of him; chief among these that his inexperience was going to make a fool of him. To quell these anxieties, he busied himself moving his grip up and down a javelin to find its balance. When he found it, he realized it was marked with notches. All his weapons were.

Eventually, there was nothing left to do but watch the steady approach of the herds, motes barely visible against the quivering dazzle of the lagoon. Soon they would be close enough to hunt. He wondered how it would be done. Who would choose their victim? What part would he be expected to play? Most likely, he and Osidian would be assigned positions of danger. There was nothing he could do about it. He would have to see the business through to the end.

Crowrane veered their march towards a stately acacia. As each rider entered its shade, he dismounted. Relief at the reprieve flooded through Carnelian, but was soon replaced by an ache anticipating the coming ordeal.

As he rode in, the shade slipped its cool delight over him. He dismounted, taking care to keep his hand on his aquar's neck so that he would not lose her. He was puzzled to see that people were unhitching waterskins, food bags and all manner of other baggage from their saddle-chairs. He found Krow.

'Are we stopping here long?'

The youth looked startled. 'All night, Master.'

'All night?'

'We must make many preparations.'

'Preparations,' said Carnelian.

Krow smiled and reached up to pat Carnelian's aquar. 'Come on, I'll show you where to put her.'

The Plainsmen cleared ferns from ground that lay just beyond the roof of branches and in the direction of the lagoon. They scraped a shallow crescent in the red earth and filled it with some of the fernwood they had brought. Hobbled, the aquar were near the trunk of the acacia. The hunters settled between the aquar and the fernwood crescent which they lit, taking care to keep the fire from spreading from the centre into either horn of the arc. Cooking pots were produced, bundles of fernroot, fernbread, some fresh meat wrapped in fronds. Ravan, Krow and the other young men began to prepare a meal while the older men busied themselves checking what appeared to be brooms whose twigs were matted with yellow fat. Leaning on his spear, Osidian stood gazing off towards the lagoon, now only a smoulder in the dying afternoon. Carnelian sat quietly, seeking release from the general tension by watching the men cooking

Dusk creeping over the land was curdled by a screaming roar. Carnelian huddled closer to the fire with everyone else. The heat of the day had not lingered long and he clasped his hands to his bowl of broth to warm them. They ate in silence. When they were done, Crowrane sent Loskai to one of the drag-cradles that had been propped up against the tree. He returned, carrying a piece of an earther's horn which might have been a carving of the moon and which he laid, reverently, in his father's hands. The old man muttered something before plunging the fragment deep into the embers.

A sequence of ravener bellows set everyone trembling. They tried to drown it out with their talk. Mostly they lingered on the glories of the next day's hunt. Solemnly, Crowrane put a choice piece of meat in the flames and, as they watched the smoke it made spiral up into the sky, they mumbled prayers to the Skyfather.

'Success and coming home safe,' said Crowrane and the Plainsmen echoed him.

The talk then turned to their wives, their children, to their sweet mothers. It was as if they already half believed they would never see them again. The gloom soaked into Carnelian, until the Koppie seemed faraway in another, brighter world.

Crowrane began telling them a story. Not following the old man's mutter, Carnelian watched the light catching the faces round him.

The Plainsmen seemed so like children, blind to the world as the tale played out before their mind's eye. There stirred in him a love for these people. A cry rent the night, breaking the spell; causing eyes to search the blackness fearfully. Only Osidian seemed unconcerned, his attention rooted in the flames. Crowrane gathered them back into the story with the warm rumbling of his voice. Carnelian could feel how much the courage of the hunters was anchored in the old man and was glad, for he needed it too.

In his dreams, Carnelian was being hunted by a ravener who saw him through Osidian's emerald eyes. He awoke and saw above him glowing, gilded rafters and, for a moment, he was back in his room in the Hold. The rafters resolved into branches. He sat up. Crowrane was sitting hunched before the fire. Beyond, a winter world stretched moonlit all the way to the camphor-white lagoon. Malice was stalking the land. Carnelian jerked his gaze back to the fire. The old man leaned forward and stirred life into the embers. Seeing that he was keeping watch over them, Carnelian lay back, comforted.

At first light, the horror of the night began to lose its hold. Carnelian rose with the others, groaning as he stretched the stiffness from his back. The fire, burning merrily, drew him. Crowrane was making breakfast. He looked so weary Carnelian felt concern the old man might have kept guard all night. Excitement in the youngsters soon had Carnelian as eager for the hunt to begin as they.

After eating, he helped as much as he could packing up, among other things, returning the unburned fernwood from the two ends of the fireditch to a drag-cradle. Carnelian fed djada to his aquar by hand as he saw the others doing and gave it water to drink. Krow helped him knap his javelin blades to a finer sharpness, whistling over them as a charm.

When everything was ready for them to leave, he saw the Plainsmen gathering at the fire and went to see what was going on. Crouched, Crowrane was poking among the embers with a stick. He uncovered something which he drew out gingerly. It seemed nothing more than a piece of charcoal until Carnelian recognized, from its curve, that it was the piece of horn Crowrane had inserted into the fire the night before. A bowl was brought and the charred horn crumbled into it. Several of the older men took turns in pounding it with a mortar. Fat was added and the grinding resumed. At last the bowl was handed to Crowrane who, sampling it, pronounced himself satisfied.

The bowl was passed round. When it came to him, Carnelian took a little of the paste on to the ends of his fingers as he had seen the others do. He saw Osidian frowning but then sitting on the ground to allow Ravan to reach and apply the black stuff to his face. Carnelian was distracted from this strange spectacle by Krow appearing before him.

'Would you like me to do you?' he asked.

Carnelian gave the youth a nod. As the warm stuff was smeared upon his skin, Carnelian wrinkled his nose against its acidic tang. When his face was done, Carnelian painted Krow's. The hunt were eerily transformed, each with his black face. More unsettling was Osidian, who Carnelian felt bore too close a resemblance to the monster in his dream.

As Crowrane led them into the herd, the earthers lifted the horned boulders of their heads. Carnelian held the lazy stare of an ancient bull, smelling his earthy musk, measuring the dangerous curves of his horns with nervous glances. Carnelian had been warned that any sudden sound or movement might alarm the earthers. He felt the tremor as the monster slid forward to reach his beak into a nest of ferns. The sinews holding his battering-ram head ran like hawsers under his scaly hide. Carnelian could not believe flint blades would dent such armour.

At last, Crowrane chose an old cow, wise from many years, rich with folds and creases. One of her horns had broken close to the slope of the crest that flared behind her head. Carnelian could see the bulge in her neck where the muscles had swelled to take the unbalancing strain of her other major horn. His companions gave the Elder their agreement with nods as slow as the saurians' as they lumbered across the plain.

They fixed their gazes on the cow as they kept pace with her. With somnolent signals, Crowrane divided them into groups. Carnelian found himself with two youths and an older man. The man gave Carnelian a nod and motioned for him to follow, smiling with relief when Carnelian did so.

They rode away. The further they were from the saurians, the faster they went until they had left them behind and were moving parallel to the lagoons into the path of the sun. Squinting against the glare, Carnelian saw, far off, other groups keeping up with them.

'Aren't we going to hunt?' Carnelian asked.

The leader craned round in his chair. 'The hunt'll be brought to us.'

Carnelian did not understand, but said nothing more. A while later, they came to a halt facing north. Carnelian was thankful of the eastern breeze: it cooled him and kept down the flies. The herd of earthers crept slowly towards them. Sweat was trickling down his back, his chest. A groaning was adding to the lowing wafting on the breeze. Squinting, Carnelian saw parties of the hunters sweeping down on the herd, whirling bull-roarers as they came in, scattering the earthers like a storm. Their horned wave rolled its rumble across the plain. Carnelian stared as he felt the thunder swell, the dark front getting ever closer. Looking round, he saw fear in the faces of his companions, but also grim determination. He set his teeth. He would trust in their knowledge. Come what may, he would not flee unless they did.

As the front came on, he saw its stampede was being led by one creature more massive than the rest. This maintained their flight, narrow. Carnelian's aquar began shifting nervously with the rest, her hands clasping and unclasping, her fan-plumes trembling on the verge of being fully open.

'She comes!' bellowed his leader.

The cry woke Carnelian rudely into action as he felt the aquar round him lurching into motion. Soon he was coursing with the others, riding parallel to the charging herd. Bull-roarers were singing above the tumult. Leaning towards the piston of one of his aquar's legs, he craned round the back of his saddle-chair and saw the cow with the broken horn close behind him. Separated from her herd, she was being swarmed by hunters screaming battle-cries, spinning bull-roarers, striking at her with the flat of their spears. Maddened, in terror, she lumbered on, bucking like a ship in a swell. Then she was abreast of him and Carnelian added his shouts to the clamour and, clumsily at first, but then with fierce strokes, added his attacks to theirs. He could feel her exhaustion and saw how heavily she lumbered on and how her heavy head was hanging lower and lower, until, at last, she stumbled and fell, rolling into golden ruin and they closed on her and, baying, started feasting their spears on her blood.

The Plainsmen's fury ended when they knew she was dead. A sadness spreading from them cooled Carnelian's bloodlust. Through its pulsating heat, he watched them dismounting, approaching the hill of hide now all striped with blood. He descended too and, stepping out from his saddle-chair, found it strange to walk among the ferns. He stared with wonder at the creature he had helped to kill and felt no joy, so that, when the Plainsmen began to sing her a lament, his heart joined his voice to theirs even though he did not know the words. When they fell silent, they grew wary again, scanning the plain as if they feared some thief might come to steal her. Carnelian helped them unbale the ropes and lash them to her horns, her neck, around the collapsed pillars of her legs. When she was hitched up to the crossbeams of their saddle-chairs, he did as he saw them do, leading his aquar until she had pulled her crossbeam ropes taut, then, at a cry from Crowrane, all the aquar were made to lean into the ropes. With a shudder, the mass of the saurian began slowly to crush a bloody road across the fernland.

They towed the earther to the nearest acacia and drew her into its shade. They dug a crescent ditch as they had done the night before. The aquar were unsaddled and some of the younger men went to protect them as they grazed. Some leaf-wrapped bundles were produced which, when opened, gave off an odour of cedar that made Carnelian homesick for his hearth. Under Crowrane's supervision, they scooped some of the cedar-impregnated fat and began to rub it into the hide of the saurian corpse. Carnelian asked Krow about it.

'It helps disguise the rot which otherwise might draw raveners here.'

When they were done, they laid their fire but did not light it and then they sat down to await the night.

The blackness suddenly came at them, causing them to leap to their feet. Clutching a javelin, Carnelian backed away with the rest of the hunt as tall shapes emerged into the flicker of their fire. Riders, their aquar coming on at a slow walk. A sound of laughter.

'Look how afraid they are,' one of them said, his accent so strange Carnelian could barely understand him.

Plainsmen from another tribe. Swathed in their ubas, only their eyes caught the fire. Carnelian drew himself further back into the shadows where, to his relief, he found Osidian. He sensed it would be a disaster should they be discovered.

'You're on our land, Ochre,' one of the strangers said, a touch of laughter still lingering in his voice.

Crowrane stood forward to confront them. 'The earth belongs to no man, besides, here we are nearer our koppie than yours, Bluedancing.'

Their leader made his aquar take a step towards the Elder. 'Perhaps, but even so, we're the great Bluedancing and we go where we want. Do you wish to fight us, old man?' The tone of mockery stung even Carnelian.

Crowrane stared fiercely up at the invader. 'We've no quarrel with you.'

His eyes followed the riders that were moving around the camp. The gaze of their leader fell upon the slope of hide rising behind them.

'Perhaps we should take your earther from you.'

Carnelian saw the way the men of his hunt moved to shield the saurian with their bodies. He felt possessive of her too. He set his teeth. If it came to a fight, he would stand with the Tribe.

'At least we should take the best cuts,' drawled another of the riders.

A mutter of amusement passed among the Bluedancing. Their leader made a gesture of contempt. 'Let's leave her to them. Look how scrawny she is. I doubt they had the strength even to take such a clapped out old cow themselves. Probably found her collapsed from age. Look,' he pointed, 'she doesn't even have both her great horns.'

This was greeted by a chorus of snorts and derisive laughter. Their leader caused his mount to spin round and then leap forward, kicking through the fire, scattering its embers into the darkness then, whooping, the riders rushed headlong back into the night.

As Carnelian helped the hunt gather up the burning fernwood, he was as angry as they were.

'Why don't we mount up and pay them a return visit?' cried Ravan.

'Riding across the plain in the middle of the night?' said Crowrane. 'Are you possessed, child? Have you forgotten there are raveners out there?'

'If they can do it why can't we?'

'You know perfectly well, son of Stormrane,' said Crowrane. 'The Bluedancing have at least twice our numbers. Do you want to bring a war down upon the Tribe we couldn't hope to win?'

'They grow more arrogant with each passing year,' Ravan gave back.

'They've always been arrogant,' said Crowrane.

Ravan confronted the Elder with a stare.

'Do you doubt, child, that I can remember further back than you?'

It took a while before the fire went out of Ravan's eyes. 'No, my father.'

For some moments the old man glared at him, but then he too swallowed his anger.

'Consider yourselves lucky they didn't spot the Standing Dead.' Face sweaty with anxiety, he looked round at Osidian and Carnelian.

Gloving his hand with fern fronds, the old man stooped to scoop some embers. 'Come on, let's get this mess sorted out before we find ourselves having to fend off a ravener without a proper fire.'

Crowrane woke them before dawn and made them breakfast as they sat ready with their javelins and spears. Raveners were still abroad. Crouching by the fire, Carnelian flinched at their every cry. He savoured his meal as if it were his last. Then they waited until the edge of the world began to show. His heart lifted as the aquar sang their welcome to the dawn.

'The raveners fear our fire too much to attack,' said Krow.

'We're not home yet, child,' said Crowrane severely and set them to hitch their aquar up to the earther.

When it had grown bright enough for them to see the Koppie tiny on the horizon, they set off towards it. When the sun rose, it found them moving laboriously northwards. It was slow work and they had to stop often to allow the aquar to rest. At midday, they stopped within the flickering shade of a copse of ginkgos. Carnelian, who had hoped they would soon be home, saw through the trembling air that the Koppie seemed as far away as when they had set off. Gloomily, he realized they would be spending another night out on the plain. The sickly odour of death was already penetrating the saurian's cedar aura and floating away on the air.

Dusk robbed them of the guiding hope of the Koppie. Crowrane set them to rubbing more of the cedar balm on the earther, but this did not stop a mist of decay hanging around their camp. When a breeze picked up, they built a barrier of ferns on the saurian's windward side, hoping thus to stop the wind from carrying her odour out across the plain. Having done what they could, they huddled around their fire, eating, talking, while all the time sneaking glances out into the night.

Carnelian drowned slowly in nightmares and, when he managed to come up for air, his half-waking was haunted by the shrieks in the blackness. Eventually he forced himself fully awake. He rose and stood until his legs would no longer support him. Then he tried squeezing pain into his thighs. He was not the only one watching the night.

They were yearning for dawn when the raveners came. They felt their approach in the trembling ground. Crowrane slapped a youth's arm that held a flare questing for the flames.

'It could be anything,' he hissed.

236

A waft of carrion breath soon changed his mind. Foolishly, Carnelian did not think to look away when he lit his flare. Blind, he heard the Plainsmen's fear and, blinking for sight, he could just make out vast shapes coalescing from the darkness. Flares danced around him amidst a tumult of shrill battle-cries. Roars carried on a foul breeze of breath. The vast presence of their smell. A clashing of jaws. The fire describing their hideous shapes in monstrous movement. Then they left as quickly as they had come and the yelling raggedly abated until all Carnelian could hear was the guttering of the flares.

'Put them out,' came Crowrane's command. 'Mustn't waste them.'

'I've never seen them so unafraid of fire,' one man said.

Loskai pointed his flare at Osidian. 'The Standing Dead bring the raveners down on us as they did in the swamp.'

Ravan stood forward. 'Remember it was the Master that saved us then.'

Krow was nodding, his face pale as he relived that time. Crowrane shoved him so that the youth dropped his flare.

'I said, put them out.'

As the flares went out one by one, Carnelian glared at the Elder, disliking the way he had treated Krow, but also reluctant to lose the sorcerous protection of his flare. He ground its flames out in the earth. Then he stood with the others waiting, hardly drawing breath through his dry throat until the first light seeping showed the land free of the monsters.

The drudgery of another day pushing through the ferns, encouraging the aquar, dragging the saurian after them as if she were a slab they were bringing back from a quarry. The heat, the plagues of flies, the beacon of the Koppie staying obstinately the same size. Carnelian plodded on, drifting into a walking sleep haunted by black terror, squinting up at the cruel sun, watching with despair its slow fall to earth with its promise of another night.

Deepening dusk found them sullen behind their fire, fingering their flares nervously. It was then their fear was taken by surprise. The raveners came before the sun was fully down. Three black shapes loping against the bloody edge of the sky, heads slung low, their bobbing accenting each heavy stride.

A hand grabbed Carnelian's robe and clung to him. He steadied himself on the edge of flight. He stooped to put flames upon his flare. Wielding it gave meagre comfort. The last snuffing out of day stole away their view of the raveners' final charge. Thunder in the ground. Then the death grins slavering in the firelight.

Crowrane wailed: 'Light the wings, sweet Mother, light the wings.'

On their right, the horn of their crescent ditch grew a plumage of flames which lit the underside of a jaw connecting back and up to a dark mass which swung away gurgling, revealing for a moment an eye bright with malice. Gaping, Carnelian became aware the fire glow was missing on his left. The earth groaned as a ravener stepped across the unlit ditch. Firelight showed the wall of its flank; the grinning length of its head. It was among them and the Plainsmen were shrieking. Without thought, Carnelian tore himself loose of their hands and joined the two or three men keeping the monster at bay with wild swings of their flares. The sound of Quya froze him: the clear voice intoning an incantation. Osidian, haloed by his flare, was advancing on the monster with his iron spear.

The ravener's head turned to look at him with one of its tiny eyes. Osidian thrust fire up at it, so that it drew back screeching. Pouring Quyan syllables he rushed at it, driving it back. He cast his flare away and grasped his spear with both hands. As the monster lunged, Osidian shoved his spear up into its jaws. The monster impaled itself, driving the blade up through its mouth, snapping its jaws closed in a froth of blood, roaring, splintering the shaft. Carnelian cried out as the monster recoiled. Its legs knocked one into the other and it toppled, twisting, its tail lashing up and round, its mass punching thunder into the ground.

Osidian froze before it. Rage possessed Carnelian. Hardly knowing what he was doing, he leapt through their fire and charged the other two raveners. The hunt running after him lit the fernland erratically as they ran. The monsters fell back under the bright onslaught, turned and were soon thundering off into the night.

Carnelian chased them screaming, until a stumble brought him back to his senses. Flares dotted the darkness. Looking back the way he had come, the glow of their campfire seemed far away. Fear returned like a deluge of cold water. The other flares were converging on their camp. Quickly, he started making his own way back.

'He felled the ravener like a tree,' said Ravan.

They had watched all night, stunned, at any time expecting the monster to lift itself from where it lay just beyond the firelight. Now, with dawn breaking, they stood watching Osidian as he crouched within the angle of the monster's jaws and dug the iron spear blade from its head. When he had it free, he walked towards them displaying the bloody iron on his palm.

'May I cut a tooth, Master?' asked Ravan and, when he received a nod, the youth unsheathed a flint and ran towards the ravener and was soon busy gouging a tooth from its jaw. When he held aloft the pale sickle longer than his dagger, the Plainsmen gave out a cry of triumph and soon Osidian was giving permission to everyone else in the hunt to take one. Even though he disdained to take one for himself, Loskai tried to appear to be sharing the general elation but a scowl was never far away. Crowrane was behaving as if nothing had happened, but Carnelian saw the old man sneak an awed glance at the Master. As for Osidian, he seemed as unaffected as if he killed raveners every day.

All the younger men wished to get as close as they could to the Master, but it was Ravan whom Osidian let walk at his side and carry what was left of his iron spear. Though the going was as hard as it had been the day before, their trek seemed to have turned into a jaunt. Their home seemed to respond to their high spirits by growing steadily larger on the horizon. A breeze blowing from the east cooled the torrid plain. Carnelian felt sufficiently at ease to take pleasure in the beauty of the waves chasing each other through the ferns so that the plain seemed to be a green and smiling sea.

They had hardly finished dragging their earther into position under the Bloodwood Tree before Ravan and the others were telling the women the story of the ravener slaying. Laughter broke out among them, swelling to a general cry of disbelief, but this was quickly silenced when the hunters produced the fangs they had gouged from the monster's jaws. Passing the blood-crusted trophies among them, one by one the women lifted their eyes up to the Master. Carnelian watched Osidian receive their awe with indifference while Loskai and his father tried to hide their hatred behind smiles.

Carnelian's gaze returned to Fern, whom he had been watching. He had the appearance of a peeled man and was the only one still working. As Carnelian approached him, he became aware of the stench coming off him and his halo of flies, but he forced himself to move closer.

'Fern.'

As the Plainsman looked up, his eyes were the only things that seemed alive behind his mask of gore. He resumed his work. After some moments, Carnelian turned to walk away, not wishing to increase Fern's humiliation.

Girls and women brought them water to wash under the Old Bloodwood Tree. If Crowrane had not insisted that they clean themselves carefully, many of the hunt would have rushed through it so as to get to their hearths more quickly. Leaves were kneaded into balls. A youth hurled one at a friend, soon involving everyone in a battle.

At first Carnelian remained as aloof as Osidian and Crowrane, but it only took the sting of missile to release the boy in him and he joined in. Before Crowrane managed to calm them, Osidian's disapproving gaze had already taken all the fun out of it for Carnelian. When Krow offered to clean him, he chose to return the favour just to irritate Osidian, however childish that might be. It was only when he noticed the way Loskai was looking at Krow that Carnelian realized he had got the youth in trouble.

'Perhaps you should do someone else.'

Krow must have seen where he had been looking, for he glanced at Loskai and shrugged. 'I've given up caring what they think.'

The pleasure of being clean and in the shade made Carnelian remember Fern's situation and he pitied him. Ravan was working at cleaning Osidian as carefully as a slave might. Much as he wished to, Carnelian knew he must not return to share Fern's work.

Their hearthmates were waiting on the edge of the rootearth for the return of the hunters. None dared speak to the Master as he walked towards the sleeping hollows. By the way they looked at him, Carnelian knew the news of the ravener slaying must have already spread through the Tribe. Poppy ran into his arms. He laughed, lifting and nuzzling her as she clung to him.

'I've looked for you every day, Carnie.'

Whin nodded in their direction and Carnelian returned the gesture. Akaisha released Ravan from a hug and advanced on Carnelian. Still holding Poppy, he stooped to receive a kiss and an embrace.

'Welcome home, sister's son,' she whispered in his ear, then stood back, the joy in her face as she regarded her hunters making them grin like boys.

'You must all be hungry,' she announced.

'Ravenous,' growled Ravan and everyone laughed.

Holding Leaf, Sil was standing watching Carnelian. She twitched a smile as he approached her and kissed both her and the baby. People were moving back towards the hearth, their arms weaving them into couples around which the children chattered. Carnelian hung back. Akaisha glanced round.

'Aren't you coming, Carnie?'

'I'll wait for Fern.'

Akaisha frowned as she saw Sil's face. As they all moved away, Carnelian felt that he had handled the situation badly, but convinced himself that it would only make it worse for him now to back down.

Sitting on a root of the mother tree, Carnelian watched the twilight thicken in the Grove. He wriggled his toes in the prickly needle loam. The feeling of being safe and at home swelled up in him. The interplay of voices coming from the hearth made his heart surge with a wish to join them. He grew sombre, considering what Sil might be feeling.

It was almost night before he saw a lonely figure coming up the rootstair. He rose.

'I waited for you, Fern.'

'You needn't have.'

'I wanted to.'

Fern's face was a vague shadow. 'It's good you and the others have returned safe.'

Carnelian reached out to take his shoulder, wanting to say something. Working out words, confused, he just said the first thing that came into his head. 'I'm missing you.'

Fern shrugged his shoulder free. 'That's nice.' He pushed past, leaving Carnelian feeling a fool.

Yet again Carnelian considered proving how he felt by returning to work with Fern, but fear of what Osidian might do made him stay with the hunt. He took his turn on the brow of the Crag: a long languid day observing the headache dazzle of the land through narrowed eyes. He escorted the women gathering fernroot from the Tribe's ferngardens. When the hunt collected together in the Newditch, he took his place with them earthworking in the dust and stifle. Then it was out once more on to the plain to fetch water from the bellower lagoon.

That day, on their way back, the air began to haze from the east as if it were swarming with flies.

'Sporewind,' cried many voices and Crowrane had them redouble their pace.

By the time they reached the Koppie, the air was so thick with fern spores it seemed like dusk. Even through their ubas, it was hard to breathe. Lumbering blind over an earthbridge, one of the drag-cradles slid off, so that they had to cut it loose for fear it might pull its aquar down into the ditch.

For days the Tribe hid in their sleeping hollows while the sporewind choked the world. People moaned that it was the worst they had ever endured. Shrouded in his blanket, Carnelian ventured out only for water and to relieve himself as others did. For food there was a coil of djada in their hollow which he shared with Osidian and Poppy.

On the first morning when the air was clear, Carnelian unwrapped the uba from his head and pumped great, clean lungfuls. The world seemed much as it had been. As he resumed his tasks with the rest of his hunt, he might have considered the sporewind a dream if it had not been for the dust blanketing the plain.

It was on his third hunt that Carnelian witnessed his first earther hornwall. It was Osidian's impetuosity that startled the herd. Defended by the older cows, the saurians fell back into a closed ring facing out, their horns and armoured heads forming a fearsome rampart within which their calves were safely corralled.

'Fascinating,' said Osidian in Quya. 'This behaviour may well have been the model for the shieldwalls favoured by the levies of the Quyan cities.'

He glanced over at Carnelian and pointed. 'Behold the horns like spears, their crests like interlocking shields.'

Loskai rode forward and let his uba fall from his mouth. 'For all his legendary prowess, the Master has ruined this day's hunting with his babble.'

Krow's aquar moved towards Loskai's. 'Did you never cause a hornwall when you first started hunting?'

'Shut your mouth, Twostone.'

Krow advanced on him scowling.

Crowrane closed on the two of them. 'Back down, Twostone.'

Carnelian tried to redirect Krow's rising defiance. 'Surely they'll move apart if we ride away.'

His comment was greeted with disdainful looks but it did have the effect of breaking up the confrontation.

When Carnelian returned to the hearth, he discovered a stranger about his age sitting next to Fern on the rootbench. Akaisha introduced him as being Father Galewing's son, Hirane, who had married Whin's sister's daughter, Koney, while Carnelian had been away hunting. Carnelian kissed the young man and called him hearth-brother and received a look of thanks from his wife, who was sitting beside Sil.

Later, Poppy, wide-eyed as she relived the wedding, insisted on telling Carnelian everything. How they had spent the day washing Koney with cedar water and decked her out in a new robe the women of the hearth had been embroidering since before the Rains. How they had rouged her face and woven magnolia buds and petals into her hair. How when Hirane had come with his father and the rest of his people, wearing the black face of a hunter, he had found her waiting for him concealed beneath a wedding blanket of the richest ochre. How both his hearth and theirs had danced around the couple. When the moon rose high enough to make bright the root fork of their mother tree, he had poured water on Koney's blanket and she had come out of it as beautiful as the stars. Sitting in the fork they had spoken their vows, broken salt together, and then Akaisha had removed his shoes so that he might stand barefoot upon his new rootearth and all his new hearthkin had given him the kiss of welcome.

As the girl spoke, Carnelian saw the light filling her face and he would have kissed her but did not want to break her vision, but as she described the newly-weds being led to the sleeping hollow where they would make and bear children, he saw trouble come into her eyes.

'What's the matter, Poppy?' he said stroking her cheek.

She looked through tears at him. 'When I'm old enough, will you marry me, Carnie?'

Carnelian was taken aback.

She sank her head. 'None other will,' she whispered.

He raised her chin and looked into her eyes. 'You'll be beautiful, many will seek your hand.'

She shook her head. 'I'm not rooted in this earth.'

Carnelian glanced up at the boughs and branching roof of Akaisha's cedar.

'This mother tree is yours now too.'

'She shelters me but knows nothing of my mothers.'

Carnelian was becoming upset when he saw a glimmer appear in her eye. He watched her reach inside her robe and fish something out from an inner pocket. She placed a tiny bundle on her knee and lovingly unwrapped it.

'A winged seed,' Carnelian said.

She looked up at him. 'I brought it from the koppie of my people. Within there sleeps a daughter to my mother tree.'

'Then you must plant it,' he said, elated.

'Will the Elders allow it?' she asked.

Carnelian's excitement died. He could not give Poppy the answer she craved.

'Will you ask them for me?'

'When the time is right.'

Accepting this, Poppy rewrapped her seed with infinite care, then returned it to its place next to her heart.

On the last morning of Carnelian's fourth hunt, while he and the others were preparing for the final day's journey with the earther they had killed, Ravan cried out, pointing. Smoke was rising from the Crag up into the dawn sky. As one they converged on Crowrane begging permission to return. The Elder stood some moments in the midst of their tumult, narrowing his eyes towards the signal, before he turned grimly to them nodding his head.

Carnelian did not need to be told something was wrong. As he worked the tow ropes loose from the crossbar of his saddle-chair, he grew sick imagining what might be happening at home.

He was soon mounted. The eyes of the riders around him betrayed that they too were listing dangers. Those who were still worrying at knots were cursed by those already mounted. With a cry of frustration, one of them produced a blade, hacked through a rope, then flung himself into his saddle-chair.

When everyone was up, Crowrane, without a word, turned his aquar towards the Koppie and sent her into a jog. They all followed him in a great raising of dust.

Their aquar reached the Newditch in a lather from the run. Smoke was eddying up from the brow of the Crag.

'The Mother be praised,' a voice cried, and several women ran across the earthbridge to meet them.

'What is it?' Crowrane demanded, speaking for everyone.

'The Gatherer's here,' one of the women panted, eyes darting from one black face to the next.

The men who had young children rode past her, their saddle-chairs clacking against each other as they scrambled across the bridge. Carnelian stared stunned, then remembered Poppy.

'This can't be,' said Crowrane, aghast. 'He's not due until next year.'

Carnelian was gripped by another sickening realization: Fern's doom had come.

The woman seemed to be swallowing a stone getting her breath back. 'He came in the night as he always does. The Tribe woke to find his tents already set up in the Poisoned Field.'

More of the hunt were streaming into the ferngarden while the women rushed around trying to stand in their way. 'We must hide the Standing Dead. They must be hidden.'

'Hide them where?' Ravan demanded.

Verging on hysteria, the women looked to Crowrane for help. 'The Elders, my father . . . they've told everyone . . .' They looked at Carnelian, at Osidian. 'They mustn't be seen.'

Carnelian felt nauseous. His world had come to pieces and now so would that of all these people he loved. If he or Osidian were found there, the Masters would destroy the Tribe. He saw desperate indecision in Crowrane's eyes.

'What are the creatures babbling about?' a voice asked in Quya.

Carnelian turned to see Osidian calm amidst the storm. His hand commanded Carnelian to answer. Finding his voice, he explained the disaster. Of all the emotions he had been expecting Osidian to feel, rage was the most unexpected.

Crowrane was arguing with the women.

Osidian looked away to the northern horizon. 'They seek us. I had expected that they would, but not so soon. I am not yet ready.'

'Ready for what? Who is it that seeks . . . ?' Carnelian remembered whose creatures the childgatherers were. 'How could the Wise know we are here?'

'I did not say that they know where we are precisely, but you yourself told me they saw where we left the Guarded Land; saw our captors were from this plain.' Osidian smiled a dark smile. 'Of course, down here, without their watch-towers, they can only fumble blindly hoping to find. The fact they have set their childgatherers to the search implies much.'

Carnelian thought about it. 'Otherwise it would be the legions that sought us out.'

Osidian's smile grew colder still. 'My mother would see to that.'

'Then they do this without her knowledge. Why?'

Osidian frowned. 'Who knows what has come to pass in Osrakum since we left.' He smiled again. 'Still, this development is suggestive.'

He leered at Carnelian. 'Tell me, my Lord, shall we allow ourselves to be found?'

Carnelian regarded him with horror. 'Why would the Wise seek to know where we are, other than to destroy us?'

'Or by finding us, pull down my beloved mother.'

Cold rage infused into Carnelian. 'If we are found here these people will be punished.'

'Exterminated,' said Osidian, taking pleasure in the word.

'You two Standing Dead, dismount,' commanded Crowrane, but Carnelian ignored him and addressed Osidian.

'I will not allow you to endanger the Ochre.'

Osidian sneered. 'Will not allow? I do not yet choose to reveal myself to the Wise, but you can be certain my decision pays little heed to your threats, Carnelian; even less to what might happen to these.' He indicated the people round them with a dismissive gesture of his hand. 'I have other plans.' Osidian turned his aquar with his feet. 'Come.'

'Dismount, I say,' bellowed Crowrane. 'Surround them.'

Carnelian saw Ravan, Krow, others of the young men of the hunt hanging back, looking from their Elder to the Master.

'Where?' Carnelian asked Osidian.

'We shall return to our quarry.'

Carnelian glanced at Crowrane, who was pouring threats on the youths. 'The two of us, Osidian? Alone?'

'And why not. Do you fear the predators?' He snorted. 'You are transparent, Carnelian. You hope to save your barbarian boy.'

Carnelian glared at Osidian, hating him. 'We both know he cannot be saved.'

'What then?'

'Poppy.'

Osidian frowned hearing the name.

'Akaisha means to give her up to the childgatherer.'

Osidian dropped his head in exasperation. He looked up. 'And?'

'I will not let her do it.'

Osidian let his head flop back closing his eyes and groaned. 'And if you go back in there and the ammonites see you? I thought my Lord expressed the wish to save his precious barbarians?'

'I will be careful.'

Osidian fixed him with the terrible green intensity of his eyes. 'I forbid it. This course of action imperils your life.'

'Nevertheless, I will attempt to save the girl,' said Carnelian and coaxed his aquar forward towards the bridge.

Ravan began pleading with Osidian who turned on him. 'Choose to follow me or remain.'

He glared at Krow. 'You too.'

The youth moved his aquar to Osidian's side.

'My mother will expel you from our hearth,' cried Loskai.

'So be it,' said Krow.

This exchange seemed to make Ravan decide. 'I'm yours, Master.'

Crowrane raged. 'I'm your huntfather. You will obey me.'

Carnelian could not bear to watch any longer and directed his aquar towards the bridge.

'You mustn't,' the women cried trying to grab hold of his saddle-chair. 'The Elders . . .'

'Hang the Elders,' Carnelian cried, making his aquar advance through them, then, when he was sure they would not be hurt, he spurred his aquar into a run across the bridge. He was through the gate before they could bar it against him. Once in the ferngarden he glanced back and saw Osidian already riding away with Krow, Ravan and some others.

THE CHILDGATHERER

The flesh tithe is a core instrument of the Policy of Domination.

Ammonites of the appropriate lores and levels (feel the appendices attached to this reel) are despatched annually to perform a demographic audit and evaluation of the tributary populations.

It is the core of the Policy of Domination that the tributary populations shall enforce the strictures of the auditing procedure upon themselves. In seeking to protect their own offspring from the tithe, kin can be expected to betray any infringement by others in the group. The greatest benefit accruing from this technique is not that it compels obedience without expense to the Commonwealth, but rather that it foments internecine conflict in the tributary populations precisely at the points where its individuals are most closely bonded.

(extracts from a codicil compiled in beadcord by the Wise of the Domain Tribute)

MORBID SILENCE REIGNED BENEATH THE MOTHER TREES AS CARNELIAN crept up rootstairs and along paths fearing that, at any moment, he might be spotted. It seemed that the brooding menace of the faraway swamp had come to lair in the Grove. Peering through the branches of a cedar he spied people engaged in furtive rituals around its trunk.

When he reached Akaisha's tree he did not approach it by its open, downhill side, but instead ducked under the uphill branches. Hearing voices, he remained crouched, peering across the sleeping hollows to where he could see many of his hearthmates. Sil's lilt carrying through the silence was answered by her mother's heavier tones. Imagining Whin's reaction to seeing him there, Carnelian's courage slipped away. The danger he was putting them in froze his feet to the ground. This is my home, he told himself, but did not believe it. Not today. Today you are a Master; one of the Standing Dead. One of the monsters who have sent their servants to rape the Tribe of its children. He despised the arrogance that had made him imagine that he could save Poppy. In the gloom beneath the cedar, a boy was being prepared by his mother. Who was there to take care of Poppy, to give her comfort? It was her need that melted Carnelian into motion. The cedar bristled against his shoulders, then he was able to straighten up and, shaken by his heart, he began to wind his way through the hollows.

'Great Mother!' cried Sil.

Grief drained the blood from his head as Carnelian saw Fern standing beside her.

'You're not welcome here,' shrieked Sil. 'You brought the Gatherer.'

Carnelian could do nothing but stare at the accursed legionary collar gleaming darkly at Fern's throat.

'Why are you here?' his friend asked.

Akaisha appeared with Whin. 'Are you trying to get us all killed?'

'Where's the other one of your kind?' asked Whin.

'Out on the plain,' Carnelian answered.

Akaisha grasped Carnelian's arm. 'Didn't they catch you at the Newditch? Did no one warn you? We sent messengers to every gate in case you should return.'

'Yes, but . . . Poppy,' he said.

Akaisha's face sagged and she let go of him as Whin flamed to anger.

'You risk the Tribe for the sake of one child?'

Carnelian saw the pain in Fern's eyes and wanted to tell him he had come for him too.

'One child?' barked Sil.

Her anger ignited Carnelian's own. 'Do you find that so hard to believe?' He scanned their faces. Whin's eyes glazed as she looked into herself. The same expression came over the other faces. Only Akaisha's eyes were seeing him and, in her face, there was something of shame.

She turned to her hearthsisters. 'I'll deal with this.'

Wild-eyed, Sil was led away by her mother.

'Where's Ravan?' asked Fern.

'Out on the plain . . . he remained with the Master out on the plain,' Carnelian replied.

Fern hung his head. Akaisha looked at her son, already grieving for him. She put on a smile.

'If your brother hasn't come it's because he can't bear to see you torn from us.'

Her certainty was only a veneer. She peered out through the leaves and branches towards the plain as if she might hope to see Ravan in the far distance. 'Otherwise, he would most certainly be here.'

Carnelian wished he could confirm her hope. Her eyes lensed with tears, she took his hand and led him away from Fern. Carnelian saw as if for the first time the children of the hearth, shivering naked, the hair being scraped from their heads. Fathers and mothers, faces coloured by anger and pale fear, stiffened to masks by the tears they refused to shed that would break their children's courage.

Carnelian searched for Poppy and saw her, alone, kneeling over a leather bowl, water dripping from her face and hair. She began rising, ready to come running, but he shook his head and she understood and fell once more to her knees.

Akaisha squeezed his hand. 'She's not as abandoned as she looks, Carnie. Before you appeared, I was helping her get ready.'

'I've never believed you to be uncaring.'

Akaisha flushed. 'I pray the Gatherer will take her in place of my granddaughter.'

'I know,' he said, letting her see in his eyes he was not judging her.

Carnelian glanced round looking for Fern. Holding his daughter in one arm, he was stooped over a bowl with Sil. As he concentrated on shaving the tiny head, his wife was examining his face as if she were engraving every curve and line in her memory. Carnelian envied her closeness to him.

'Don't mind his manner, Carnie, he's beside himself with fear,' said Akaisha in a low voice.

He looked round at her. 'His daughter?'

'My granddaughter will not be chosen,' she said fiercely. 'Of course he fears for her but today he has more reason to fear for himself.' She looked over at her son, sorrow ageing her. 'He's lived bravely with what must happen but he didn't expect it to come so soon. He's not had time to prepare himself for what will be done to him today.'

'Today?' Carnelian said, his stomach knotting.

Misery was welling in her eyes. 'They're sure to want to make an example of him before the Tribe . . .'

Tears began to spill down her cheeks. Instinctively, Carnelian embraced her, but she pushed him away, running the back of her arm across her eyes, holding on to him tightly so he would not think she was angry with him.

'It was as much for him as for Poppy that I risked –'

'You think I don't know that?' she said, finding a smile.

At that moment one of the children began to whimper. Carnelian looked furtively round, feeling his gaze was an intrusion.

'Don't expect kindness today,' said Akaisha.

'Fern made it clear I'm not welcome here.'

She raised an eyebrow. 'Men see so little,' she said, and when Carnelian frowned, not understanding, she shook her head. 'He told you he's worried what disaster you being here might bring down on the Tribe, but perhaps even more strongly, he fears for you.'

That warming jolt was not enough to free Carnelian from the burden of what he was. 'I don't blame the Tribe for hating me.'

'It's not you they hate, but all the Standing Dead,' she said severely. 'The arrival of the Gatherer, unexpected as it is, has come as a bitter shock to everyone.'

She looked at Carnelian, waiting for him to answer the implied question.

'The Master believes they seek us. If they find us here . . .'

Akaisha nodded. 'I know well enough what will happen.'

He saw in her eyes that once the childgatherer had gone, there would be a reckoning.

'I'll hide, my mother, but first, please, will you allow me to tend to Poppy?'

She looked uncertain.

'Surely today every child is entitled to love.'

Screwing her face up to hold back more tears, Akaisha gave in with a nod.

Poppy looked up at him with enormous eyes. 'I just *knew* you'd come, Carnie.'

He smiled. 'How could I not?' He knelt beside her and got her to bend forward and then, lifting water in his hands, he let it flow down over her head. She spluttered and, rising, made to part her bedraggled hair. Carnelian caught her hands. How smooth and unmarked they were. He let them go and wrapped her in a blanket to keep her warm. He plucked the flint razor from where Akaisha had left it and then gave his attention to hacking Poppy's hair off as close as he could to the roots. Tresses fell like black ribbons to the earth. Her tufted scalp seemed a desecration. Sensing she was reading his thoughts, he ran his hand over the soft bristles and gently teased her about them until she twitched a smile. In that watery counterfeit he saw the depths of her terror. Blinking away his own tears, he concentrated on finding the sharpest edge of the flint. He sniffed, then glanced up.

'We wouldn't want . . . At least I know from experience . . .' His voice tailed off. It was hardly the time for reminiscences about the head-shaving habits of the Masters.

He set himself to scraping the stubble from her scalp. In spite of his care, he drew blood. He snatched his hand back expecting Poppy to cry out and was made even more miserable when she did not.

When they were done, he washed her head clean and patted it dry with an edge of the blanket. Her head seemed as fragile as eggshell. He saw she was watching one of the older boys who was clearly afraid, his father kneeling face to face with him, loving him, telling him to be strong. The boy stood stiffly, lower lip quivering.

Carnelian snatched her up into a hug. She clung to him. 'You won't let him take me, will you?' she whispered urgently.

He did not know what to say and ran his hand over her tiny naked head, rocking her, making sure she could not see the bleakness in his face.

From somewhere on the other side of the hill, the alien voices of trumpets blared setting Poppy violently trembling. She turned her face up.

'You'll be there, won't you, Carnie?'

He gave no answer, not only because he had none he wanted to give, but also because he saw their hearthmates were beginning to gather around the mother tree. Over their heads he could see Fern standing with his mother. Turning to the cedar, he embraced her bark, kissed her. A warm murmuring rose from his family.

Carnelian felt a familiar hand slip into his and glanced down.

'What's happening, Carnie?' Poppy asked.

For answer Carnelian lifted her up and swung her on to his shoulders. Together they watched as one by one the hearth filed in to kiss and embrace Fern. Their grief at losing him was a pressure in the air. Soon Carnelian was joining his tears to theirs. This parting was an ache in him and yet he felt shut out. Though Fern looked in his direction several times, he did not beckon Carnelian and, without a sign, Carnelian was unwilling to breach the ring of his family.

When Fern had said goodbye even to the smallest child, he rose and, for a moment, they stood silent with him and Akaisha in the heart of their gathering. Sil joined them, handing her baby to her husband. Then Akaisha broke the circle as she made towards Carnelian. Behind her came Fern holding his baby, Sil at his side.

Carnelian lifted Poppy down and crouched to say goodbye to her. He had forgotten the power her eyes had over him.

252

'You'll have to be going now, Poppy,' he said, his voice breaking. Crying, she shook her head. 'You must come. You must.'

For a moment he contemplated running down to the aquar carrying her off into safety.

He glanced up to find Akaisha standing over them. Reading his eyes, she edged closer.

'If the girl doesn't take her chance with the rest, those who will find out today they're to lose their children *will* kill her.'

Akaisha's face seemed carved from her mother tree. Carnelian fought panic as she reached out for Poppy. He could feel her trembling against his chest. Her eyes looking up into his were those of an animal in a trap.

He kissed her, wanting to, needing to give her some comfort. 'I'll be watching you,' he whispered in her ear. It was an impulse he instantly regretted. He cursed himself silently. Turned to stone, he let Akaisha pull Poppy off him. He watched the little girl glancing round, catching the fear stiffening every face. When her gaze returned to him, he saw her hunger for confirmation of his promise and he could not deny her the nod she wanted. His stomach clenched as he saw the courage it gave her. She nodded back as he watched Akaisha walk away with her. Carnelian became aware Fern was looking at him with a strange burning in his eyes. Carnelian felt suddenly overwhelmed by the enormity of what was about to happen. He felt queasy imagining the pain, the humiliations Fern would suffer before his execution in faraway Makar.

Fern handed his child to his wife. 'I'll join you in a moment.'

Sil burst into tears and he embraced her, muttering into her neck. When he released her she glanced round at her mother, as if Whin might forbid Fern. Instead, her mother gathered her and Leaf into her arm and, leaning against each other, they made off after Akaisha who had turned to wait, Poppy hanging miserably from her arm. Whin's sisters followed, with their husbands, their daughters, their grandchildren coming after them.

Carnelian forgot them, seeing Fern's face. It had a pallor which appalled him. Such bloodless lips, but his eyes were burning.

'Please forgive my wife.'

'She has reason to hate me.'

'She doesn't hate you.' Fern examined Carnelian's face. 'Will you take care of her for me?'

'Gladly,' Carnelian replied.

'And Ravan?'

Carnelian felt sick. He wanted so much to confess the choice he had made to return to see Fern and Poppy and which had freed Osidian from his oath.

Fern misunderstood his hesitation. 'I know that recently he's been unbearable, but he has a good heart.'

'I'll do what I can.'

Fern nodded slowly, pondering. 'The Tribe might well turn against you and your brother.'

Carnelian could not bear hearing that lie. 'He's not my brother.'

Unaccountably, Fern smiled.

'You knew?'

'I'm not a fool.'

'You must know that I did it to –'

Fern stopped him by putting his fingers to Carnelian's lips. 'I know.'

Carnelian bit his tongue against the further questions he wanted to ask.

'My mother will stand by you, but even she might not be able to save you.'

'I'll not allow her to stand alone against the Elders. She's done enough for us already.'

Fern's eyes flashed. 'You will accept every scrap of help offered you.'

Carnelian's heart was stilled by Fern's intensity.

Fern glanced round and Carnelian saw Akaisha and the others were already ascending the rootstair towards the Crag. Fern turned back.

'In the last hope, you must cling to our mother tree and beg for sanctuary. None then may touch you unless my mother allows it.'

Carnelian grew exasperated. 'Forget me, what about you?'

Fern took hold of Carnelian's arm and held it hard enough that it hurt. 'Did you hear what I told you?'

Angrily, Carnelian twisted his arm free. 'I heard, but today, I'm more concerned about you.'

Fern grew paler. 'Don't be, I'm already dead.'

'Run. What's to stop you taking an aquar, riding far away from here?'

Fern managed to find some laughter which, for a moment, made him seem carefree.

'I'd go with you,' Carnelian said, surprising himself.

Fern frowned and shook his head, looking at Carnelian hungrily. 'You're a strange man, Carnie. You know I can't go. If I did, they'd punish the Tribe instead of me.'

'We could ride out after you, after the Gatherer has taken you away from here. We could take you from him.'

Fern scowled. 'You're being stupid now. You must know that only when the Gatherer reaches his next koppie in safety will he give the Tribe the warrant which we'd need to protect us from the Standing Dead should anything happen to him.'

His brow smoothed. 'Stop fighting this, Carnie. I'm a dead man. I've been one since I deserted the legions. I've lived with this doom for more than a year until it's like a stench in my nostrils.'

His eyebrows raised. 'You know, it's almost a relief.' He grew sombre again. 'I'm only glad you at least won't have to witness what they'll do to me today. Let's say goodbye now.'

The terror Fern was repressing was squeezing tears out of the corners of his eyes however much he clenched his teeth to stop them. Carnelian took a step forward and enveloped Fern in his arms. He felt Fern's arms slipping round him. Carnelian squeezed the solid body, digging his chin into the shoulder. He felt Fern's lips against his neck; felt his warm tears and turned into them; found Fern's neck and kissed it. They clung together thus and Carnelian felt an intensity of desire which made him cling all the harder, not knowing how to express it.

It was the metal screeching of trumpets that broke their embrace. It gave a voice to their pain. They could not look at each other.

'Stay here . . .' growled Fern. 'For my sake.' He turned away and Carnelian watched him move to the rootstair, then climb it until he had disappeared behind the traceries of the branches of the mother tree.

As Carnelian sat morose with his back against the mother tree, the trumpets sounded again. Their sinister screams forced on him thoughts and feelings about the Masters, about Osrakum. Even after the fanfare had fallen silent, the memory of the sound lingered like a smell, making the shadows under the mother tree strange and menacing.

He could not help thinking about the way he and Osidian had parted. A conviction was rising within him that their destinies had separated. He had chosen the Tribe over Osidian. A time would come when he would have to pay for making that choice. He feared that others might also have to pay.

He clamped his head between his fists and made himself remember why he had defied Osidian. 'Fern and Poppy,' he said through clenched teeth and saw again that last look she had given him. Why had he made her that promise?

He rose, and stumbled among the many bowls still standing with their water to find the one he had used to wash Poppy. Her hair formed a sad pattern around the bowl. He hesitated, then spilled some of its water on a clear patch of earth and rubbed it in with his palms. The mud he made looked like blood. He cursed. It seemed an omen of death. He gouged some of the red stuff on to his fingers and smeared it over his face, round his neck, his lower legs and feet, the backs of his hands. He searched around for the largest blanket he could find and wrapped it round him.

Another fanfare made his heart jump up into his throat. How much would he be endangering the Tribe? Though he told himself he was doing this for Poppy, perhaps he was only desiring to satisfy his curiosity to see the childgatherer that had haunted his childhood. Was it a craving for one last glimpse of the exquisite wonders of Osrakum? He could feel his mind tainting with self-loathing. He was a Master. He held his hands up. Nothing could hide the brightness that lay beneath the brown. Nothing could change that he was a Master. Osidian was right; his kind had all been right. What were his sensibilities but a thin garment he wore to conceal his true nature from others; from himself. A sickening fear oozed into him that his revulsion of what was happening to the Tribe down at the Poisoned Field might be nothing more than an attempt at denying the appetite in his blood at this rare chance to fully experience, to soak in the misery of the Plainsmen; to savour the torture of these barbarians he chose to fool himself he loved.

Wild with the torment of these thoughts, he ran to clutch the mother tree. He laid his cheek upon her soft bark. He could feel the power in her coming up from the good earth. She cleansed him. She gave him the courage to believe it was not wholly a Master's heart that beat within him. Salvation came from the love he bore Poppy, Fern, Akaisha and the Tribe. A love he had to believe in or else be lost, not knowing who nor what he was.

Tentatively, he released the tree and folded his arms over his chest, trying to catch any vestige of the warmth Poppy had left when her body had trembled against his. He could not abandon her. Whatever Fern had said, or Akaisha, his place today of all days was with these people who had given him love in spite of what he was. He must share their suffering. He began to mutter to himself, listing arguments why he would not really be putting the Tribe in danger.

'No one could see me. No one would expect to. Least of all the childgatherer. How would he guess that one of the Seraphim would choose to conceal himself painted in mud among barbarians.'

He shook himself free of this mood. He had to do this now or not at all. Before self-hatred could weaken his resolve any further, he made off in the direction he had seen Fern go; a direction which he knew led over the hill and eventually down to the Poisoned Field.

The air was deathly still as Carnelian crept around the Crag. He could hear nothing but the sound his feet made on the path. Peering down the slope into the Grove, he saw the branches of the mother trees were mute. It was as if they were listening out for their lost children. In that frozen world, he alone seemed to be capable of movement.

The clearing that lay below the Ancestor House was filled with amber heat. He groaned at the shock of passing into it from the shadows. He ran down the clearing to its further end, panting relief as he regained the cool, concealing shade.

On the edge of the rootstair he could see meandering down between the cedars, he paused to peer in the direction where he knew the Poisoned Field lay, but could see nothing through the meshing canopy. He descended the stair until he reached a fork. The right hand one led to the Northgate; the left one, to the childgatherer. Today, he could feel in his stomach why the Tribe called it the Sorrowing. He forced himself down it lest his doubts should make a coward of him.

The Sorrowing brought him within sight of the Childsgate. Wary of the light pouring through on to the stair, Carnelian left it, slipping under the cedars, aware he was trespassing on the rootearth of another hearth. Picking his way over roots, he made his way down the slope, approaching the Homeditch with stealth.

When he reached one of the cedars bordering the ditch, he crushed his back against it and closed his eyes. It was a while before he could hear anything over the beating of his heart. Then eerie silence. Carefully he turned and, clamping his chest to the trunk, he edged round. Every crack and channel in the tree's russet skin was starkly visible. Every tendril of moss, each molten glowing drip of resin. At last one eye was able to look out over the Poisoned Field.

The Tribe were formed up on the other side of the Homeditch, with their backs to it. Looking out over them were creatures from another world, with faces of pure sunlight from behind whom rose a billowing cloud of purple speared through with poles that were shafts of light topped with spiralling fire. Carnelian tried to still the beating heart of his terror. Ammonites, they were only ammonites catching the sun on their silver masks. His eye was drawn squinting to the centre of their glaring line. Some giant stood there, an alarming monster with two heads, masks; no, it was just the green and the black face standards of the God Emperor, rising up behind a chair that seemed to be made of shimmering water.

It was his heart that made him search for Poppy. He was forced to move around the tree and peer out the other side. She must be there beneath the Crying Tree, in among the massing of rosy brown skin that was the naked children of the Tribe. When Carnelian glimpsed the face of a mother or father, he saw it wore a strange passivity. Even the youngest looked old. Only their eyes moved, furtively, as if they feared they were being watched.

A throaty fanfare broke out, so harsh, so terrifying, Carnelian clapped his hands to his ears. He located the source of the sound: three ammonites, the lips of their fiery masks fixed to the mouthpieces of curving trumpets whose bellies were sunk into the dead and ashen earth. His attention was arrested by an apparition rising up from behind the platform like a sun, its perfect face, of metal, flashing. Dragging its purple brocades, accompanied by a staff of ammonites, the Gatherer came to the edge of the platform and looked out over the assembled Tribe. Wherever he looked, light moved over the crowd of covered heads, as if sunrays were leaping from his eyes.

'We are come from the paradise that lies within the Mountain at the centre of the world.' The clear Vulgate rang the silver of the Gatherer's face. 'Come as the emissary of the God and their angels to speak to you their commands. Obey them as you have always done. The tribute you give to them of your flesh should be a thing of joy to you. Those of your children chosen here today will at the proper time be given to them. They are to be considered fortunate indeed whom the God and his angels consider worthy to be their slaves. Shall you obey them?'

Carnelian broke free of the compulsion to gape and glanced at the sullen faces of the Tribe, knowing that few of them could have understood. But then, as one, the crowd rumbled: 'As they command so shall it be done.' A response in Vulgate many could only have learned as sounds.

The Gatherer waited for them to fall silent and then sat himself down upon the silver chair. At a lifting of his hand, one of the ammonites nearby let drop a length of glimmering string Carnelian knew must be a beadcord record.

'At the last audit, how many of the male-gender?' the Gatherer asked.

The ammonite felt a portion of the cord. 'Eighteen twenties, and eleven, my master.'

'How many of the female-gender?'

'One four-hundred and three, my master.'

'How many creatures in this tribe?'

'One four-hundred, eighteen twenties and fourteen, my master.'

'How many live offspring are projected by the Wise for this octad?'

'Eighteen twenties and twelve.'

'How many were not delivered to the Mountain?'

'Six, my master.'

'The number to be chosen is therefore . . . ?'

'A twenty and eighteen.'

'Ignoring the fractional part?'

'Precisely so, my master.'

The Gatherer turned his polished face towards the Plainsmen and cocked it slightly to one side. 'Are we not generous then in this calculation of your flesh tithe?'

The Tribe seemed to have been turned to stone. Mouths were lines. Eyes shadowed by hatred did not move their narrow stare from the mirror of the Gatherer's face.

As he threw up his hands, their honey-gold betrayed him to be a marumaga in whose veins some tiny portion of the blood of the Masters ran.

'You may petition us now.'

The Elders of the Tribe were let through, each accompanied by a youngster. Carnelian looked for but could not discern which of them was Akaisha. The Elders seemed suddenly very old as they leant on the youngsters and climbed the few steps to a shelf that lay below the Gatherer's feet. Slowly, painfully, they slid down to sitting. The wealth of salt in their hair seemed dull and mean in comparison with the flashing silver of the Gatherer's face.

'Petition me,' he said again, impatiently.

For an age the Gatherer and the Elders negotiated, the process made necessarily slow by those among the Elders who spoke Vulgate having to translate for those who did not. At last, one of the Elders stood to face the Tribe. Carnelian saw it was Harth.

'They asked for thirty-eight, which takes into account the marked children who died before they were taken to the Mountain.' She paused. Her posture spoke of defeat. 'We've managed to reduce their demand by three.'

It was a small victory but Carnelian could see how much hope it gave the Tribe.

'Begin,' said the Gatherer.

Everyone craned to see the children creep forwards towards the ammonites. Those who could not yet walk were carried by those who could. Carnelian watched the first few being clasped in the hands of the ammonites, shrinking from their instruments and the reflections of themselves they could see distorted in their masks.

In ones and twos, the rejected were forced to plunge their hands into jars of black paint and then were released, coming tottering back into the arms of their families. Others, however, were driven up the steps to the Gatherer. One at a time they were given to him. He took their heads and squeezed, felt their bones, his fingers controlling their squirming as if they were nothing more than fish. He forced their mouths to gape by putting pressure on the hinges of their jaws and peered inside. He prised their eyelids open. Watching this, the faces of those waiting in line creased with terror. One little boy looked out across the Tribe screaming for his mother. Breaking, a woman's voice answered him. At the sound the children on the platform began whimpering. More women shrilled names, encouragements. The Tribe began to lose their sullen composure as their agony began bleeding out of them in a wailing. Carnelian felt himself being unmanned by the sound. He lived again the day he was forced to abandon his people on the island to famine. It was only the hard faces of some of the men that helped him retain control. He chewed his tongue like them and ground his teeth and clenched his fists against the lust for violence.

And so it continued as the sun rose high and scorched them and then began sinking. Carnelian's legs ached from standing too long, but he would not even allow himself to seek the relief of crouching when he saw how the Tribe were bearing their pain.

The Gatherer examined one child after another, sending some down to the tattooists with their needles, releasing the rest to have their hands blackened. The mothers of these rejected children would push through the press and grab them, shrieking with joy. The other mothers looked on these scenes with a kind of hatred, before resuming their bleak vigil.

Carnelian could not see the selected children among the tattooists, but could hear their moaning, their cries for their fathers and mothers as the glyphs were pricked into their palms. These too would find release at last into their mother's arms. Many stumbled as they ran, dropping the small pieces of cloth they had been given to staunch the bleeding. The bloody palms would be stared at in the vain attempt to read there how much time they had before they must be sent away.

Wearied by the heartache, nevertheless, Carnelian kept searching the snivelling line of children being fed up the steps for examination. At last he saw what he had feared to see. Poppy, her tiny face looking for him. He willed her to see him though he knew that if she did, so might others and that would bring disaster down upon the Tribe. As she drew closer and closer to the silver chair, he wrung his hands until they hurt. The moment came that Carnelian had been dreading: Poppy was pushed into the Gatherer's hands. He forgot to breathe as her little shaved head was turned this way and that. The

Gatherer pressed it with his fingers as if he were determining the ripeness of a melon. Carnelian gulped air again when the Gatherer seemed to have detected some fault. He clamped the girl as his face of silver leant close to one of the scribes. The mask flashed as he nodded and then Carnelian fought nausea as he watched Poppy being shoved off to be tattooed. She was crying as she looked back, hopeless, distraught at not seeing him among the crowd. As he imagined his little girl gritting her teeth against the needle's pain, Carnelian cursed himself bitterly he had not thought to disfigure her.

DEADLOCK

The deadlock common to all two player games is rarely found in Three.

(from 'The Three Coloured Game' by the Ruling Lord, Kirinya Prase)

UNDER AKAISHA'S CEDAR, CARNELIAN WAS PACING BACK AND FORTH, every so often looking towards the rootstair for any sign of the Tribe returning. Unable to be among the crowd as a comfort to Poppy, fearing he might witness Fern's punishment, Carnelian had fled in misery. All his life, he had known about the childgatherer. Once, when he had pushed Ebeny until her reticence broke, she had described the miserable day she had been selected for the Mountain. He had had nightmares for a long time afterwards. Now he had seen it for himself, he was soaked through with such heartache and shame that he wanted to creep away and hide. He glanced back up the slope, desperate to see Poppy. An irrational fear possessed him that the childgatherer might have already taken her away. Then he became filled with dread at the thought of seeing her and, for a moment, seriously considered fleeing the Koppie. He allowed his gaze to be burned by the incandescence of the plain. Out there was an unwelcoming world and Osidian; a Master who would have nothing but shrivelling contempt for such feelings.

The sound of footfalls was coming from the direction of the Crag. He resisted the temptation to hide, though he backed towards the comfort of the mother tree. As the first people appeared upon the stair, Carnelian held on to her bark as if it were a hand. It was not long before they noticed him. Their descent faltered as they stared with red eyes that seemed to have sunk into their faces. Their scrutiny soon forced him to lower his gaze. A woman's voice urged them on. More and more of the Tribe were coming into sight. Carnelian stood where he was, enduring their terrible, silent hatred. He would gladly have set aside his height, his white skin, his burning blood to become one of them. As it was he would not allow himself to deny it was his kind who had just raped them.

When he sensed someone approaching, he lifted his gaze, holding his arms stiffly by his sides ready to take whatever was said, whatever pain inflicted, even death, but when he saw it was Fern, his knees threatened to buckle. His friend simply stared and Carnelian fought panic. Fern's face was unreadable, though his red eyes showed he had been crying.

Carnelian searched his friend's body for any sign of mutilation. 'You are unhurt?'

Fern looked as if he did not know the answer to that. After a while, he said: 'They did not call for me.'

'Then you are saved,' Carnelian said, clutching at the hope there was in that; some joy on such a joyless day. Instinct urged Carnelian to keep his pain to himself, but he was weak enough to want to share it.

'I should have disfigured her. That's what I've been thinking.'

Fern looked at Carnelian as if he were seeing him for the first time. 'What?'

'I should have disfigured Poppy. The Gatherer wouldn't have chosen an imperfect child for the Standing Dead.'

Carnelian recoiled from the rage that sprang into Fern's face.

'You were there? You knew the danger to the Tribe and, still, you were there?'

Carnelian wanted to back away but the mother tree was a wall against his back.

'I promised Poppy . . .'

Fern gaped at him. Even to Carnelian's ears, his words sounded absurd.

Fern grew suddenly tired and his curly head fell against the cedar.

'Disfigure her. Don't you think we might have thought of that? She'd grow up carrying on her face the proof that another child had been sent to the Mountain in her place.' His voice was unsteady. 'All the hearths who had lost a child would hate her.'

Fern lifted his head and Carnelian saw he was crying.

'Perhaps it's the best thing for her. What kind of life would she have had here.' Fern became distraught. 'He's taken my baby.'

Carnelian stared dumbfounded. At the examination he had been so focused on Poppy he had not even remembered to look for Leaf. He saw his friend's anguish and could think of nothing to say.

As they approached, hearthmates gazed at Carnelian as if he were a ghost of the children the Tribe had lost. Sil's eyes accused him, her mother's were trying not to. Whin was pulling Poppy by the hand. The little girl was looking at her feet, the fist of her left hand wedged into her armpit. Carnelian forgot everyone else, praying that when she would look up at him it would not be with hatred. Whin brought her up close.

'Look at Carnie, child. You mustn't blame him.'

Carnelian gave Whin a smile of gratitude, muttered something of his regret about her own loss, then squatted down and reached out for Poppy's face. He almost pulled away when he felt the skin wet with tears. Gently he lifted the little face, waiting for her eyes to see him. He stopped breathing when he felt her stare, then gave out a sigh of relief when he did not see hatred in her eyes but only pain and fear. He folded her into his arms, put his lips to her neck, lifted her from the ground. He rocked her, humming, feeling her sobbing, her fist a stone against his heart.

'Carnie.' It was Fern's voice.

Carnelian turned with Poppy still wrapped in his embrace and looked round. Fern was tearful, looking at him, leaning close to Sil, their baby nestled between them. Carnelian saw the tears in Sil's eyes, everyone's eyes and almost let out a wail. He wanted to make it better, to take away their pain.

Fern released his daughter's tiny hand from her swaddling, peeled the pad from her palm and let it fall red to the ground.

'I can't wait until the Gatherer gives the Elders a picture of the tithe. Tell us how long we'll have her.'

Carnelian feared Sil's eyes, but felt that beyond Fern's need to know, he was trying to make things right between the three of them. Carnelian drew close enough to see. He adjusted Poppy and, gingerly, took the baby's bloody hand and peered at it.

The green patterns of the date tattoo were smeared red and swollen in the tiny palm but he could still read the number eight and the hated name of Osidian's brother, Molochite.

He looked up at Fern and Sil, waiting in dreadful suspense. 'Not counting this year, seven more.' They would have her for the longest possible time allowed a marked child.

When Fern thanked him, Sil held Carnelian's eyes, searching them. She must have found there what she sought, for she reached out and took his hand. 'We have all lost today.'

Relief brought more tears. He lifted her hand in his and kissed it.

Carnelian became aware of Poppy's stony fist wedged between

them. A part of him did not want to read what was written there. He realized he had not seen Akaisha. He searched for her.

'She's with the other Elders talking to the childgatherer,' said Sil.

'Does that always happen?'

Sil grew pale as she glanced at Fern and then looked back up the slope the way they had come. Carnelian realized with a jolt his friend was still in danger.

Poppy shifted against him and when Carnelian looked down it was directly into her eyes. He took his leave of Sil and Fern and carried Poppy to their hollow. He laid her down upon a blanket. They sat looking at each other while she clutched her left fist in her other hand. She released it and opened it for him. He stared at the cloth blushing blood. It was obvious what she wanted. He took her hand in his and carefully peeled off the cloth. He used it to wipe away the blood. He saw the two tattooed spots and his heart stopped.

She saw the colour leave his face and drew back terrified. 'This year?'

'No,' he cried, shaking his head.

'The next then?'

It was unnecessary for him to nod; she saw her fate in his eyes.

Akaisha's face was gaunt when she appeared beside Carnelian's hollow. He disengaged from Poppy who had been sleeping in his arms and rose to face Akaisha.

'I don't know what to say, my mother, about your loss.'

She glanced at Poppy. 'All have suffered loss.'

Carnelian was withered by shame.

'Come with me,' she said.

He followed her. When they reached the deepest shade of the mother tree, she fixed wild eyes on him. 'Where is the Master?'

'On the plain.'

'But where?'

He half shook his head. 'Perhaps returned to the earther we were bringing here when we saw the signal.'

She frowned, looking at the ground, her eyes moving in thought, her hand gently stroking the bark. She looked up.

'The Master was right. The Gatherers are looking for you.'

Carnelian swallowed hard. 'They asked about us specifically?'

'The Gatherer claimed to be seeking two white marumaga renegades. He told us that any tribe handing them over or giving information resulting in their successful live capture will have their tithe rescinded for a full eight years.'

265

Carnelian could see the desire for such a prize was a passion in her which she was having difficulty suppressing. It promised the salvation of her granddaughter.

'They're trying to trick you,' he said.

Akaisha's eyes flamed. 'Do you believe, Master, that we are fools?'

His contrition calmed her. 'The Tribe's survival depends on you not being found. We're sure we didn't give anything away. Our terror is of the Master out there . . .' She glanced away towards the plain. 'If he should be seen by another tribe . . .'

'I could go out and try to bring him in.'

She looked back narrow-eyed. 'So Crowrane was right. The Master fled knowing what might happen to him here.'

Carnelian felt almost relieved that it had come at last. 'We are to die, then.'

Her eyebrows raised. 'I won't deny there are many now who wish it and I can no longer protect you. Not now.' She frowned and examined his face. 'Was I wrong to take you in?'

The pain of doubt in her eyes forced Carnelian to speak. 'I deluded myself with the hope the Master would settle here. I lied to you, Akaisha, to protect him. He is not my brother.'

She gave a snort. 'You only tell me what I knew already. No mother could produce two such different sons.'

Considering Fern and Ravan, Carnelian found that a strange statement.

'You are lovers?'

Carnelian was embarrassed by her directness. 'We have grown apart.'

She nodded as if she had known that too. 'Go on with what you were saying.'

'I believe he may never settle here. He's unable to let go of his old life. Dark passions move him.'

'To what end?'

Carnelian frowned. 'I'm not sure, but before the Gatherer came, I was already fearing that his growing influence among the young men might harm the Tribe.'

Akaisha looked deep into his eyes. 'You tell me this even though you love him?'

'I love the Tribe too.'

She examined him for some moments, then smiled. 'Everything you say, Carnie, I already knew in my heart, but you renew my faith that you are indeed my sister's son.'

She grew grim. 'We still have to deal with the danger the Master poses to us.'

'I could go out,' Carnelian offered again.

Akaisha shook her head. 'The other Elders would not allow it.'

Carnelian bowed his head, questioning his desire to tell her everything. He raised his eyes to mesh with hers. 'He threatens Ravan.'

The colour drained from her face. 'Is this why you abandoned Fern?'

Carnelian nodded. He saw her fighting temptation. 'No,' she said firmly. 'The decision must be left to the Assembly. We'll meet tomorrow night when Galewing, Crowrane and the others return from escorting the Gatherer.'

She looked at him. 'What will we do with you until then?'

'Might I be permitted to return to the Bloodwood Tree?'

She smiled wanly. 'My son's reprieve is the only joy that has come from this dreadful day. I know they'll come for him. At worst, next year when we had expected it, but who knows, perhaps we mightn't see a Gatherer for a full eight years. There's much living that can be done in such a span of time.'

Carnelian's heart grew heavy. It had been foolish to hope that any system administered by the Wise would be fallible enough to overlook the punishment of a deserter.

'No doubt Harth and others will be horrified, but I trust you, Carnie. Go spend tomorrow with my son. Today, both you and he, each in his own way, have had to face death and suffered the certain loss of a daughter.'

Something woke Carnelian. He sat up. Though it was still dark, he could feel morning was near. Akaisha's voice spoke and was then answered by a man's. Footfalls faded into the creaking of the cedars. He waited listening for a while but there was nothing more. In the darkness it was harder to be brave. He was scared for those he loved and for himself. Death was close enough to suffocate him. To cheat the terror, he drank deep of the perfumed exhalations of his mother tree. Her branches embraced the air he breathed. She soothed him with her sighs. He lay down again, nuzzling into Poppy.

When the hearth awoke, Akaisha was nowhere to be seen and the older men were absent too. People breakfasted in silence, stealing glances at Carnelian and Poppy, at Fern and Sil and her mother. The horror of the previous day lingered like a chill in the air.

They were getting ready to disperse to their various tasks when Akaisha appeared. Though weary, her face was not so haunted with fear. She saw the question in their eyes.

'He's gone.'

'The Mother be praised,' said Whin with a sigh and everyone echoed her. Carnelian could see the tension leaving their shoulders. Some even smiled. The sun had risen high enough to slip its rays down into the hearth. It seemed a kind of hope.

'Carnie?'

Carnelian looked at Sil. Their eyes met.

'Your hunt are warding today,' she said.

'I thought today I might work with Fern.'

A sadness came into her eyes, but then she smiled. 'He'd like that.'

Carnelian returned her smile, then leaned back trying to see round to the sleeping hollows.

'He's gone already,' said Sil. 'He's taken to missing breakfast.'

'I'll go down now, then,' he said, rising.

Poppy clutched his hand. He saw how anxious she was to go with him. They might only have a few days left. He looked at Akaisha, who cleared it with a nod. Carnelian put his hand on Poppy's head. 'Come on then.'

Together they ran down through the sun dapple among the cedar shades and out into the ferngardens. They caught up with Fern on one of the stretches of the Blooding path.

He turned and frowned. 'Did I forget something?'

'Us,' said Carnelian with a grin.

Fern glanced at Poppy then into Carnelian's eyes. It was clear to both of them that Fern was going to argue, so Poppy took his hand and began pulling him in the direction of the Bloodwood Tree.

Beneath the angry eyes of the butcher women, Carnelian laboured with Fern heaving offal on to the drag-cradles. They did not talk as they worked; to open their mouths was to swallow flies.

As they waited for the next pile of entrails, Carnelian's eyes were drawn to Poppy, sitting in the shade nursing her tattooed hand.

'She's young,' said Fern. 'Her hand will soon heal and then she'll forget.'

Carnelian turned to look at his friend. 'She only has a year.'

'A year can seem a lifetime to a child.'

They both knew Fern might only have the same time to live. Carnelian gazed at his friend, loving him. He fought the desire to tell him. Why burden Fern even more? How could it ever come to something?

'Hey,' said a woman to get their attention. They returned to their work.

'The hatred some in the Tribe feel towards you will fade,' said Fern.

Carnelian frowned, thinking of his own death, then remembered to nod.

Later, in the shade of the Bloodwood Tree, Fern confessed the dreams he had had of seeing his daughter growing up. Carnelian nodded, but was not listening as he watched Poppy returning with their food and water. His mind filled with visions of the woman she would become labouring in some palace on the shores of the Skymere in Osrakum. If she were to fulfil her promise of beauty, she would most likely be taken to bed by a Master and then, perhaps, like Ebeny, become mother to a brood of marumaga. She was destined to have much the same memories of the Earthsky Ebeny had had and told him of. He prayed then that somehow Poppy would be chosen from the flesh tithe for House Suth and become a part of his father's household, where she might find Ebeny. Carnelian determined that that evening, while he still could, he must tell Poppy about Ebeny; he must empty as much knowledge as he could into the girl in the hope that, when the time came, it might help her adapt to her new life among the Standing Dead.

The sun was a gouged eye when one of the women called out: 'Hunt returning.'

Carnelian's head jerked up. Coming through the Horngate was a front of aquar from behind which rose the hump of the earther they were dragging. A single rider rode before them who, by his size, could only be Osidian. Carnelian's heart jumped up into his throat. He scanned the riders behind Osidian for Ravan, but because all were shrouded, he could not tell if the youth was there. Why was Osidian putting himself in danger? Looking round, Carnelian saw the agitation among the women standing round the Elder in charge. Two girls were already running back up to the Grove, no doubt to fetch men to attempt Osidian's capture. A warning was in Carnelian's mouth, but he swallowed it. He would not save Osidian at the cost of the Tribe.

Osidian came on so that Carnelian and Fern were forced to back away from his aquar. Nothing could be seen of him but the slit of black skin holding the emeralds of his eyes. Carnelian was pinned by their scrutiny and felt they were reading his heart.

'You missed the party,' he said.

'My Lord is being uncharacteristically flippant,' said Osidian in Quya.

Carnelian looked past him towards the approaching riders, trying to count them.

'All are there, my Lord.'

'Their hearths will be glad to see them returned safely.'

'Their hearths will not see them. They are mine, now.'

Carnelian recoiled from the cold Quyan verb that was used to denote the owning of slaves.

'Come with me now, Carnelian.'

'I cannot. Akaisha has my promise that I will not leave the Koppie.'

'Perhaps you should fear the consequences that might come from keeping promises to savages.'

'You threaten Ravan?'

'Why would I hurt the boy when he has proved himself such a willing catamite.'

Carnelian felt as horrified as when he had discovered that Jaspar had similarly used his brother Tain. Osidian was not describing love.

'You did this to wound me?'

Osidian laughed. 'I merely take my pleasure where I can find it.'

Carnelian almost leapt forward to pull Osidian down. He calmed himself. 'Let's not fight.'

The black of Osidian's robe and uba were crusted with blood. 'You must be weary. Surely you desire to wash. Come up to our hollow, rest in the shade and we can sort things out.'

'Would recent events not make such a course of action rather perilous?'

'Perilous?'

Osidian watched the women creeping closer. 'I do not see a warm welcome in their eyes.'

Carnelian felt he had no choice but to put everything into one final appeal. 'Osidian, if you value our lives, our only chance lies in throwing ourselves on the mercy of the Elders.'

Osidian laughed without humour. 'Your counsel then, my Lord, is that I who was to have been God Emperor should grovel at the feet of savages?'

At a motion of his hand, two riders came up to flank him. Carnelian saw behind them, the earther looming near. A woman Elder approached the corpse and made a show of examining it. 'How did so few of you manage to keep her safe from raveners?'

One of the riders turned in his chair. 'One who dared attack left much of his blood soaking into the ground before he fled the Master's spear.'

Carnelian recognized Krow's voice.

'Reconsider, my Lord,' Osidian commanded.

Carnelian shook his head.

'Very well. You know what to do, Ravan?'

The second of the two riders bowed his head.

Osidian turned his aquar and rode away. Carnelian addressed the youths and cried out: 'You betray the Tribe.'

'Where the Master leads, we follow,' said Krow, then swung his aquar round and sent her chasing after Osidian. The half a dozen riders who had been pulling the earther dismounted, unhitched the ropes from their crossbars and were soon up and heading after him.

Only Ravan remained.

'Why're you still here, Ravan?' growled Fern. 'Can't you see your master riding away?'

Ravan pulled his uba down, tucked it under his chin and looked down at his brother with his black hunter's face. 'I come with his message for the Elders.'

Fern grew angry, grabbed his brother's foot and yanked it. Ravan bared his teeth as he kicked free of Fern's grip. 'His words are for the ears of the Elders alone . . . brother.'

Seeing the violence threatening to erupt between them, Carnelian took hold of his friend's shoulder. 'Come on, Fern, let him be.'

Fern threw his hand off. 'Let him be?' He turned on his brother. 'Did you even care that the Gatherer might have taken me; that we might never again have seen each other?'

Ravan regarded his brother with a blank expression but his eyes were uncertain.

'They marked Leaf, but I don't suppose that will concern you much.'

Frowning, Ravan rocked his feet on his aquar's back and she carried him off towards the Grove at a bouncing lope.

In deepening dusk, Carnelian hand in hand with Poppy was following Fern as they all returned wearily to the hearth. Osidian's appearance had spoiled what might be their last day together. The men who had gone to escort the Gatherer to the next koppie would most likely have returned. The moment they did, the Elders would assemble. With Osidian abroad, what choice had they but to kill the Standing Dead. Akaisha might manage to save Carnelian but he would not, even now, allow Osidian to die alone. Everything was ruined. Carnelian could not even smell the perfume of the cedars because of the odour of butchery clinging to him.

When they reached their rootearth, they saw a single silhouette sitting on the men's bench.

'My faithful brother,' growled Fern.

Carnelian knew his friend was unaware of how much Ravan was in Osidian's power. 'Don't be too unforgiving; the Master has possessed him.'

'Today, I saw altogether too much in my brother of the boy my father spoilt.'

It was sensing Fern's intention forming to go and have it out with Ravan that made Carnelian speak. 'We'll find out soon enough what he's come to say when your mother returns from the diggings.'

Without another word, Fern made off towards the sleeping hollows. Left gazing at Ravan, Carnelian was remembering the cruel way Jaspar had used his half-brother Tain to blackmail him, reliving all the atrocities he had witnessed the Masters commit on their own households. Poppy was destined to enter one of these and he must do what he could to prepare her for it. His fingers were still in her grip. He pulled her after him saying softly: 'I want to tell you a story, Poppy.'

Sitting in their hollow, Carnelian began to tell Poppy about Ebeny. At first she was sullen but she perked up when he told her that she had come from Mother Akaisha's hearth.

'Did she miss the Tribe?'

Carnelian told her she did but that she grew happy in her new life. As he did so thoughts of Jaspar haunted him. His talk had put the first smile he had seen on Poppy's face since the arrival of the childgatherer, but he realized he was misleading her. For all he knew the kindness of his father's household was unique. It was true House Suth preferred to choose Plainsmen from the flesh tithe, but there were many Plainsman tribes, so most of their children would end up in the households of other Masters.

He sought balance by telling Poppy of Ebeny's harrowing experiences in the Plain of Thrones, taking care to explain that though the Masters might seem like angels, they were men; that the dragons, though fearsome, were only giant earthers with houses on their backs.

He stopped, seeing how frightened she looked.

'Are the Standing Dead then very cruel?' she asked in a little voice.

How could he answer that? He tried to hide the truth behind visions of the wonders she would see, but he had lost her, made it worse.

She looked at him from under her lashes. 'I had hoped . . .'

'What?' he asked her, dreading to know.

'That you might save me,' she said almost in a whisper. She saw the answer in his face.

'Will you take me to the Mountain?'

Carnelian was shocked when he realized that he could. He could return with her, perhaps take her into Osrakum with him to his father's house. He crushed the hope. Most likely he would be dead by then. He had not thought this out, and had been avoiding facing the terrible blow his death would be for the girl.

Poppy reached into her robe and brought out her seed. 'We must bury her.'

'Do you mean plant her?'

She looked at the seed across her palm. 'No. I wouldn't want her to wake to find none of her daughters to look after her.'

Carnelian tried to argue, but only managed to make Poppy cry. Morose, he gave in, and they dug a hole at the foot of their hollow deep enough to kill the seed, placed it in the hole and buried it.

When Carnelian heard the women coming back, he and Poppy walked round to the hearth to meet them.

The women looked stooped from their earthworking. Poppy nudged Carnelian.

'Mother Akaisha won't blame me for going with you, will she, Carnie?'

Carnelian made reassuring noises, though his mind was entirely focused on finding out what Osidian had sent Ravan to say. Akaisha's seat in the root fork was empty and, when he looked for her, he saw she was a little way apart talking conspiratorially with Ravan. Fern was watching them with unconcealed impatience. Others kept glancing, curious to find out what was happening.

Akaisha terminated the discussion suddenly with some comment that left Ravan red-faced. As she moved to her place, everyone could see how angry she was. Whin raised her eyebrows enquiringly but received nothing but a curt shake of the head.

As he came up to sit beside Carnelian, Ravan drew some disapproving looks. Everyone could see how troubled Akaisha was. When she glanced up at Carnelian, his heart jumped and he knew he must be deeply involved. He tried a smile but she seemed blind to it.

They had not finished their meal when a voice came carrying from the edge of their hearth.

'May we step on to your rootearth, Akaisha?'

'You may,' the matriarch answered and five shapes approached which the firelight revealed to be Elder women, Ginkga among them.

'The men have returned.'

Akaisha gave her bowl to Whin, pulled a blanket up over her head and made her way round the fire to join the visitors. When Akaisha glanced back at Carnelian, the other Elders did so too and then, they moved into the darkness.

Unable to sleep, Carnelian whispered her name in Poppy's ear. Certain she was asleep, he crept from his hollow round to the hearth. Fumbling around, he found a stick lying in Akaisha's root fork and used it to stir some light from the embers. In the soft glow he huddled on the men's bench, slowly edging round to get nearer the heat until he found the warmest place was in the fork itself. He sat there listening to the susurration of the cedars, drawing what contentment he could from knowing the Tribe were sleeping peacefully all around him. He fell asleep waiting for Akaisha to return.

Shaken awake, Carnelian let out a cry that was snuffed out by a hand closing over his mouth.

'Hush,' a voice hissed, in his ear. 'Do you want to wake the whole Tribe?'

Carnelian knew it was Akaisha by her scent. 'Move round from there,' she whispered, giving him a nudge in the ribs. Still only half awake, he slid round on to the men's bench. She groaned as she fell to her knees facing the elbow of the fork. He heard the mutter of some prayer she was addressing to the mother tree, then she sat herself in her usual place.

'Only on his wedding day is a man permitted to sit here.'

'I'm sorry, my mother, I didn't know.'

'Nevertheless, you should be punished.'

They sat side by side for a while until her breathing slowed enough to weave into the sighing of the mother tree.

At last Carnelian could bear to be silent no longer. 'My mother –'

'What did you tell the Master?'

'Tell?'

Akaisha peered at his face as if searching for something. 'He sent us word that, should we attempt to harm either of you in any way, he'd reveal your presence among us to the Bluedancing.'

That Osidian was fighting for his life, even that he might have done this for his sake, did not leave Carnelian feeling anything but shame. Like any other Master, Osidian had resorted to extortion. Akaisha was still watching him, waiting for his answer. Had she not confided in him that this was what the Elders most feared? He spoke not in his own defence, but to reassure her.

'I told him nothing.'

'How then did he guess?'

'The Master was once intimate with those who sent the Gatherer.'

She frowned. 'Who else but the Standing Dead sent the Gatherer?'

Carnelian realized that even if he should manage to make her believe in the existence of the Wise, he would find it impossible to explain Osidian's access to their world without revealing who he had been. 'Did the Master not guess the Gatherer had come searching for us?'

'You told us that much.'

'My mother, did I not tell you this before it was confirmed by the Gatherer himself?'

She nodded.

'Is it then too hard to believe the Master guessed the rest?'

'Would he really betray us to the Bluedancing?'

'It is not difficult to deduce that, given the immediate danger we pose to the Tribe, the Elders would wish to have us killed.'

'If the Master had wanted you to be found, he could have revealed himself to the Gatherer. His threat is empty.'

Carnelian grimaced. 'Don't underestimate the appetite the Standing Dead have for vengeance.'

Akaisha bowed her head in thought.

Carnelian could see no way out of the dilemma that would allow the Tribe to escape harm. The whole, long, weary journey from his northern isle to Osrakum had been slaked in the blood of massacres; the wounding of his father; the intrigues of the election; the escape from slavery and his decision to go with Fern, all had led finally to this moment. He could see no other way.

'You must kill us both.'

Akaisha lifted her head. 'How might we do that safely? Earlier, you told me he had influence among the young. I'd go further, since he slew the ravener, there're many in the Tribe who idolize him.'

She peered into the night. 'Even now he has them with him out there somewhere. We daren't risk making the attempt.'

Carnelian's heart raced. He could see the path of hope she was showing him. 'I could go out and convince him we are in no danger.'

'I might let you go, but the other Elders wouldn't. By threatening you they hope to bring him in.'

Hopelessness returned. 'He'll not come.'

She nodded. 'He will have to when the Withering forces us to go to the mountains. Until then, as long as we have you, he'll not put us in the hands of the Bluedancing.'

'How can you be so sure of that, my mother?'

'I've seen the way he looks at you.'

'And will the Tribe be able to live with this?'

'If they found out about the Master's threat, there are those who might act and so bring disaster.' She fixed him with a glare. 'You understand?'

Carnelian nodded, not blaming them.

'Harth demanded that you should be bound but I argued that might give the Master enough of a pretext to betray us. I told the Assembly you could be bound by an oath. Promise me you'll make no attempt to join him.'

'Is my word guarantee enough?'

She took his hand and placed it firmly down on the root he was sitting on. 'Swear on my mother tree who is a part of the Mother.'

'I swear on her and also on my blood that I'll remain within the Koppie as your hostage.'

She gave his hand a squeeze. 'Well then, it seems that, for the moment at least, we have ourselves a deadlock.'

'You'll send Ravan to tell him this?'

'My treacherous son,' she said, bitterly. 'Yes, we'll send him back to his master in the morning.' She kissed him upon the cheek. 'At this moment, Carnie, you seem more Ochre to me than does my own son.'

'Don't blame him too much.' Carnelian remembered how, when he had thought his father dead from his wound, he had become involved in the intrigues of House Suth and so brought about the crucifixion of Fey, one of his father's marumaga half-sisters. Grief could blind those it struck.

He smiled at Akaisha. 'For the moment your son is in the Master's thrall, but I believe, in time, he will see what the Master is and then he'll return to his people.'

THE WITHERING

Death is the mother of life.
(a precept of the Plainsmen)

THE NEXT MORNING AT BREAKFAST, PEOPLE ASKED WHERE RAVAN WAS
and Akaisha informed them he had returned to join the Master.
They looked at each other, knowing that Ravan and the others were
meant to be warding with Father Crowrane.

'Why do you tolerate this affront to our ways?' asked Fern.

'It is every man's right to choose with whom he hunts,' retorted
Akaisha, and no one dared to ask her anything more.

Carnelian listened to Sil and others whispering to each other the
story going around about how the Master, with only a handful of
their men, had not only managed to bring their earther home but
had, besides, protected it all night from ravener attacks.

A few days later when they did not return to take their place in
the ditches, their hearths began to worry. Father Crowrane and the
few older men who were all that remained of his hunt worked as
best they could, but when three days later they were supposed to go
and fetch water, there was not enough of them and the rotas had to
be readjusted, which caused a general anger.

During the day, Carnelian could suppress his fretting in
his toil under the Bloodwood Tree, but in the evenings, by the
hearth, he could not avoid seeing Akaisha's thinning face.

When Ravan appeared at the Horngate with Krow and others, the
women at their butchery dropped everything and rushed to meet

277

them. Carnelian and Fern lifted their heads and saw the hunters, their aquar hitched to a construction upon which there lay an earther so immense that for a moment it seemed they would not be able to get it across the earthbridge. With a glance at each other they hurried after the women.

As the aquar came towards them through the ferngarden dragging the earther, children ran out from the drying racks to swarm the hunters and their catch. Carnelian watched one tiny pair clamber up on to its head, run along it, then scale the slope of its crest to reach the hill of its back. Carnelian did not like the childish shrieks of excitement nor the swagger of the hunters. Osidian did not seem to be among them.

Carnelian slowed to a walk as he overtook the women. As the procession drew nearer he grimaced, recognizing one of the children sitting astride the monster's back as Poppy. Ginkga, the Elder in charge, gave him a glare, warning him not to try to escape. The youths were boasting of the hunt, running their hands up the great sweep of the bull's horns, pointing out the hawser tendons beneath his smooth young hide, while all the time, the children frolicked, or drank in the glory of the hunt, wide-eyed.

Ravan called a halt and strutted out accompanied by Krow, who was beaming. At the head of the women, Ginkga confronted the youths.

'Where've you lot been? Do you know your hearths are half mad with worry?'

Smiles were fading all around her. Krow held on to his, but looked uneasy.

Ginkga pointed at the earther. 'What do you expect us to do with that monstrosity?'

Ravan frowned as if he was finding himself unexpectedly among strangers. He peered past the women to where a smaller earther lay half dismembered under the branches of the Bloodwood Tree. 'Get rid of that scrawny carcass. It's clear ours has far more and better meat.'

Ginkga scowled. She walked past Ravan and several of the women followed her. She pointed at the sled of roughly hewn wood upon which the bull lay.

'Where did that come from?'

'We made it,' said Ravan.

The Elder raised an eyebrow. 'It's made of wood.'

Ravan frowned more deeply. 'So, we cut down two or three acacias. There's plenty more where they came from.'

His comment produced a catching of breath among the women. Ginkga addressed her words to the youths standing behind Ravan. 'Are any of you here unaware that every tree is holy to the Mother?'

Many of the hunters blushed; looked away; let their eyes fall.

The Elder approached the saurian, nodding as she appraised him. 'I can't deny that he's magnificent.'

The youths lifted their heads desperate for her approval.

'But you've cut him down in the full flowering of his strength. He should be out there fathering more of his kind. Didn't that occur to any of you? Did you also forget his herd will need him to defend them against raveners?'

The hunters withered under her disapproval.

'We've brought meat for the Tribe,' said Krow, aggrieved.

'Meat?' Ginkga demanded. 'Can't you see that even if we were ready for him, he's got more on him than we could possibly process before he begins to rot? Not to mention that we're expecting Kyte's hunt in tomorrow.'

'So some'll be wasted.'

Ginkga regarded Ravan as if he were speaking a foreign tongue. 'All flesh is a gift from the Mother.'

Ravan gave her a sneer as he pointed at the young bull. 'We weren't given that. We took it,' he said, snatching a handful of air.

People gaped in shock. Fern strode forward, his skin and hair stiff with blood.

'Have you lost every last bit of sense you had? How can you say such things?'

Ravan's smile chilled Carnelian. 'The Master has taught me to be a man.'

Ignoring Ginkga's glare, Ravan turned on his heel and, accompanied reluctantly by Krow, strode towards his aquar.

'You come back here,' she bellowed, but Ravan was deaf to her as he unhitched his aquar from the sled.

'Child, I command you to return with me to the Ancestor House.'

Ravan vaulted into his saddle-chair, made his aquar rise and sent it striding away towards the Horngate. The other youths looked, some apologetic, some angry, but they too were unhitching their aquar. They ignored Ginkga, who was in their midst pulling at them; berating them. Carnelian moved forward with Fern, but neither was sure what to do.

Raising a choking cloud of red dust, the hunters flew after Ravan. The women pulled their ubas over their noses and mouths, all the time staring at the Elder. She was coughing, squinting at the veiled shapes of the riders as they rode out on to the plain. A movement above her drew her eye. Poppy and a boy were still astride the bull.

'Have you no respect? Get down from there!'

The children slithered to the ground and fled with the others back to the racks.

Ginkga turned on Carnelian. 'Are you satisfied, Master?' Then she rounded on the women.

'Well? Don't you think we'd better get on with it or shall we just stand here all day watching the poor bastard rot?'

News of Ravan's defiance spread quickly through the Koppie. Carnelian saw how keenly Akaisha and Fern felt the hearth's shame. At first rumours abounded of the punishment that would certainly be meted out upon the errant youths, but as time passed it became clear the Elders were not going to act. People looked at their old people and wondered at their powerlessness.

Ravan did not return, but the youths who returned periodically with their kills upon other sleds confirmed he was hunting with the Master.

One time, Krow came with others boasting of a brawl in which they had triumphed over some Bluedancing. Around the hearths it was difficult not to greet this news with approval. For as long as anyone could remember, the Bluedancing had been provoking the Ochre. It was high time those bullies were shown there were men prepared to stand up to them. Whin was clearly unimpressed by the assurances that the Master had remained concealed throughout the brawl. Carnelian and Akaisha exchanged glances, both wondering if Osidian was sending them a warning.

The increasing glamour of hunting with the Master made more and more of the Tribe's young men desert their hunts for his. Forced to defend them, their kin declared that all they were doing was risking their lives daily beyond the safety of the ditches for the good of the Tribe, for its pride. Others were not so forgiving. They were resentful so many of the young men should refuse to fetch water or to work in the ditches, but they did not feel they could protest too much in case people should believe they spoke out of envy at the evident success of the Master's hunt. These malcontents carried their anger to the Elders, who once more showed themselves unwilling or unable to act.

There were other concerns. The mother trees declared the beginning of the Withering by producing cones while, beneath a high pearlescent sky, the sun was burning the world to dust.

One day, struggling against smothering heat, Carnelian became aware that every fern frond he could see was brown. Gazing out past the Newditch, he saw the world beyond was sepia to the horizon.

'How can anyone possibly survive out there in that shadeless world?' he rasped through his parched throat.

Fern had a sombre look. 'The lagoons will soon dry up and then the herds will begin their migration to the mountains. We must follow them or else die.'

Carnelian smiled. 'At least we'll be free of this,' he said, lifting up his brown, blood-stained arms. He watched Fern return to his work miserable, frowning, and only then remembered it would also be time to send children to Osrakum.

'Smoke,' Carnelian cried, pointing at a mass of it rising well above the crowns of the magnolias, bending its back as it leaned towards the west.

Not hearing other cries joining to his own, he turned and saw that only a few people had even bothered to lift their heads. He pulled at Fern.

'Fire.'

His friend seemed infuriatingly unconcerned.

'There's fire spreading within the Newditch,' said Carnelian.

Fern gave a nod. 'We must burn the ferngardens now while they still have the memory of green life in them.'

Carnelian watched the edge of the pall fraying in the breeze and understood. Soon the ferngardens would be tinder-dry.

Fern spoke again. 'If we burn them now, any fire that comes across the plain will find nothing here to consume and so turn aside.'

Carnelian gazed out over the plain and his breathing stilled as he contemplated how easily it could all turn to flame.

Every day after that, a ferngarden was set alight, beginning with the westernmost and moving progressively closer to the Grove. Soon, while at his work, Carnelian was able to watch the neighbouring field being sown with fire. Starting at its western margin, gradually retreating with the breeze at their backs, people wrapped in soaked blankets beat smoke from the flames as they steered the smoulder over the land.

The day that they burned the Eastgarden, Carnelian and Fern were spared their labours. From the safety of the Homeditch they stood and watched the Bloodwood Tree sifting clots of smoke through its branches. That evening and for many after, they had to quit the Grove, for the breeze carried the smoke in among the mother trees. Carnelian took his turn at moving along the eastern run of the Homewalk, his mouth and nose smothered beneath his soaked uba, his eyes stinging, making sure that, though serpents of blue smoke might be curling among their trunks, no spark would live long enough to harm the mother trees.

At last, men returning from the lagoon announced it had shrunk to brackish pools. What water they had managed to bring back they distributed directly among the hearths. Standing round with Akaisha, Whin and the others, Carnelian saw their allowance was not even enough to fill their water jar halfway.

Akaisha tasted it and, grimacing, spat it out. 'This isn't good enough to drink.' She smiled grimly round at her hearthkin, then pointed at the jar. 'Wash yourselves as best you can with that. There'll be no more washing until we reach the mountains. I'm going to meet with the other Elders.'

Sil touched her emaciated arm. 'My mother, can we take water from the cistern to drink?'

'A little,' Akaisha said and walked away.

Carnelian caught her up and fell in step. 'Migration?'

'A few days at most.'

'Why do we delay?'

'We daren't expose the Tribe to the plain until we are certain the raveners are gone.'

They walked on some more in silence. The charcoal reek of burning still persisted disturbingly in the Grove.

'I'm worried about Ravan, the others,' said Carnelian.

She stopped and looked him in the eye. 'Don't you think their mothers are too? Thirst *will* bring them in.'

She took leave of him and he watched her go. Peering out through the cedar canopy, he hoped she was right. He imagined Osidian and the others out there alone in what had become a desert. If he came in, it was certain the Elders would have him killed. They had waited long; had suffered enough humiliation. A turmoil of emotions churned Carnelian's stomach. It was a while before he remembered that Osidian's death might be closely followed by his own.

Next day, half the Tribe came down to the djada field to bale the dried meat and load it on to the drag-cradles that had been laid flat on the ground in neat rows. Night was falling when the job was done.

With Poppy, Carnelian proudly surveyed his stack of djada coils. 'It took longer than I thought.'

'It always does,' said Fern. 'Come on or we'll be late for the feast.'

'Feast?' Carnelian asked seeing how sad Fern had become.

His friend glanced at Poppy. 'Tonight is Skai's Tithing Feast. Tomorrow, he leaves for the Mountain.'

The girl took his hand and clung to it. Sharing the pain, Carnelian was relieved his friend's eyes held no blame.

Together they wandered up past the rows of drag-cradles.

'There's a lot of djada, isn't there, Poppy?' Carnelian said. The girl gave the merest nod.

'It'll have to feed us all until we return, as well as the aquar on the journey,' said Fern.

'How long will we be away?'

Fern shrugged. 'Until the Rains come: between four and five moons.'

Carnelian squeezed Poppy's hand. 'It'll be quite an adventure, won't it?' She gave him a watery smile.

He and Fern continued making conversation about the migration as they passed under the Old Bloodwood Tree. The ferngarden on the other side of the Outditch was black and barren.

'I can't get used to the stench of burning.'

'The Rains will wash it away,' said Fern.

His friend's blank expression made Carnelian certain Fern was thinking about his daughter. Carnelian walked the rest of the way brooding about whether he would survive to suffer the day of Poppy's Tithing Feast.

They did not hear the usual talk and laughter as they approached the hearth. Instead there was a murmur, as if people were afraid of making echoes. They formed two rows of shadows enclosing the fire glow. One rose; it was Akaisha coming to meet them.

'We've been waiting for you,' she whispered, then led them back towards the hearth.

As Carnelian came fully into the firelight, he made a smile for all the sad faces ruddy in its glow. There was one among them he had not expected to see.

'Ravan,' he gasped. 'Have the others returned with you . . . ?'

Vestiges of hunting paint deepened the shadows around the youth's eyes. 'They choose to remain with the Master.'

'Then why are you here?' said Fern.

'I've come as the Master's emissary.'

Fern snorted a laugh. ' "Emissary?" Do you really believe you're going to impress anyone with those airs?'

Ravan reddened. 'I suppose you consider yourself fit to speak for the Tribe. I would've thought the past season hardly prepared you for anything better than carrying offal.'

Fern's murderous advance on Ravan was stopped by Akaisha's voice. 'Shut up, both of you! You shame me even more than you shame yourselves. Have you forgotten whose night this is?'

Fern paled and returned to his place. Ravan remained standing, not even looking at his mother, still glaring at his brother.

'Sit down,' Akaisha hissed through her teeth.

Ravan glanced at her, then shrugged before dropping insolently on to the bench. Separating from Poppy, Carnelian waited to see her in her place, then he walked round Ravan to sit beside Fern. Sil was watching her husband with concern. Akaisha was looking down at her lap. When she lifted her head sorrow was softening her face.

'Whin, dear, will you be first?'

As Whin rose, Carnelian saw Skai sitting where the rootbenches met; Akaisha's traditional place. Leaning over the pot, Whin ladled some of its contents into a bowl. She held it up to Skai and looked at him through her tears.

'My heart will ache for you for ever, my little one.'

Carnelian watched as one by one his hearthkin took the bowl, put a little more broth into it and pledged him their love. Then Akaisha told Carnelian it was his turn. He glanced at Whin, at the boy's parents. He was overcome that they should show no hatred for him on such a terrible day. It was all he could do to manage the ritual without spilling the bowl along with his tears.

Beneath the Crying Tree, the Tribe formed a ring around the five tithe children and the men and women who were to accompany them to the Mountain. Appraising the gathering with a Master's eye, Carnelian saw a crowd of unkempt savages standing around a brown-leafed tree among the ashes of a dying land. In their midst the tithe children seemed a beggarly tribute to pay the Lords of the Three Lands in Osrakum. Carnelian looked around him at the dark faces and saw their human pain. Shame crushed his false aloofness. It was in his blood, his bones, that he felt the value of what was being given up. These children were flesh torn living from the body of the Tribe. It only took the thought that the following year Poppy would be standing there for him to be suffering with them. He drew her closer to his side.

'Why is he here?' cried a woman's voice.

Harth, pointing at Carnelian, drew the eyes of the Tribe to him. He broke into a sweat and horror. Akaisha clasped his shoulder.

'As a member of my hearth, Carnie has as much right as any to be here.'

Fern and Sil, holding each other and their baby, both gave him a solemn nod. Whin's bleak eyes saw nothing but her grandson.

Scowling, Harth looked away. Beside her Crowrane kept his glare fixed on Carnelian but people were turning back to the tithe children.

'We go, fathers and mothers,' said the men and women standing beside them. 'We go, brothers and sisters.'

Those going looked at those remaining and they in turn looked back. Ash floated in the air like infernal snow.

'Son,' a father cried and ran in to embrace one of the children. His action released many others. People streamed across the divide; the sound of their grief a winter wind.

Ginkga, her voice none too steady, commanded that they must all face this bravely. The ring re-formed slowly. The sobbing died to a groaning, then to a rocking of heads. Aquar were brought laden with djada, fernroot as well as cone-nuts and the other few luxuries the Tribe had managed to hoard for this day. Solemn-faced, Harth held aloft a loaf of salt which she showed to the Tribe.

'The blood of our men,' she said, then wrapped the loaf lovingly in an oiled cloth before handing it to one of the tribute-bearers. A gap appeared in the further curve of the ring and the tributaries moved out through it. The whole Tribe walked with them across the Poisoned Field and down to the Outditch, where the tributaries had to wait for them all to cross. They followed them across the blackened ferngarden to the Newditch and out on to the gold of the plain.

The whole Tribe stood watching as the aquar carrying their tribute took the first steps of their long journey to the distant Mountain. Looking back with tear-striped dusty faces, the children were soon lost beyond a veil of dust.

The Tribe buried their grief in the feverish final preparations for leaving. Carnelian went down with Fern and others to the djada field to fetch the packs their hearthmates would be carrying on the migration. Poppy aside, the children did not seem haunted by the hearth's loss and ran around in shrill excitement. Whin and her sisters frowned, but most looked on indulgently, glad these at least they had kept. Carnelian felt people were trying not to look at him.

Most of the cooking pots had been stowed and so that night they had the first meal of what promised to be many of djada washed down with a mouthful of water. The taste brought back to Carnelian memories of his journey from the Guarded Land. These forced Carnelian to confront his feelings for Osidian and what he was doing. Ravan had returned to him that morning. Carnelian shared the Tribe's desperation to see their young men return safely. All day he had been finding it difficult to stay silent when he saw the accusing looks the Elders were getting from everyone. Time was running out. Osidian must return. It was inconceivable he had not planned for this. There was hope in Ravan's visit. Surely he had come to bring the Elders some proposal from the Master, but if they had come to any arrangement, they were keeping it to themselves.

He looked for Akaisha in the root fork and found it was empty. He leaned close to Fern.

'Where's your mother gone?'

'Preparing the guardians for the Grove gates.'

'Guardians?' Carnelian said, wondering who was being left behind.

'Huskmen.'

Carnelian rose. 'Where will I find her?'

Fern pulled him back. 'Waking the huskmen is a ritual tinged with death and thus dangerous to all but the Elders.'

Carnelian nodded and sat down again. The hearth felt dead without its fire. He was cold and unhappy. Glancing at the packs all lying neatly stowed against the trunk of the mother tree, he realized he was already feeling homesick. He looked up into her branches and smiled. He would miss her and her perfume. Looking down, his eyes met Poppy's. She looked away sadly, glancing in the direction of the sleeping hollows. Where, Carnelian thought, her own tree lies buried.

The Tribe rose with the sun. Poppy's face was beautiful in its melancholy. 'Today we go to the mountains.'

'To the mountains,' said Carnelian, searching for Akaisha. He spotted her by the rootstair marshalling the men. He set Poppy to stowing their blankets to keep her out of his way. As he approached Akaisha, the men began filing down the hill. She regarded him with a frown.

'Where are they going, my mother?'

'To hitch the aquar to the drag-cradles. You should go and help them.'

'May I first speak with you?'

Akaisha thought about it. 'Wait here a moment.'

He watched her go and give some final instructions to the women, then she beckoned him. As he neared her, Sil walked past him avoiding his gaze.

Akaisha watched her move away, then glanced at Carnelian. 'You two should be better friends.'

Carnelian would have asked Akaisha what she meant but saw she had more important matters to attend to. He accompanied her as she toured the hearth. They checked each sleeping hollow to see nothing had been left behind. Then they moved towards the mother tree and made sure everything had been properly stowed among its trunks. As she strummed ropes and tucked in the corner of a blanket Akaisha mumbled at him. 'We don't want to come home and find this stuff all rotted by the rain.'

'The Master . . . ?' he began, but the stare she gave him struck him mute.

'My care is more for the lads he has with him.'

He thought of protesting but saw her mind was only half with him and could not bring himself to speak. Instead, he waited while she busied herself checking what she had already checked before.

She turned to look at him. 'Will he bring them in?'

Carnelian grew excited. 'Did he say he would?'

'My son . . .' Her brows creased. 'Ravan said the Master would on the condition that we should vow not to raise a hand against him. We swore on our mothers' and our fathers' bones.'

'When will they come in?'

Akaisha shrugged.

'Will we wait for them?'

Akaisha flared to anger. 'We cannot. We dare not consume another day's water here.'

Carnelian caught her eyes and saw how powerless she felt. So Osidian had won. He saw Akaisha's need for reassurance.

'He will come. Even he cannot survive here without water.' Then, as an afterthought, 'You have all the water there is.'

She put a warm hand upon his arm. 'Stay with me.'

They came round the tree and found the women already gone. All that was left was Carnelian's djada pack with their blankets that Poppy was trying to pick up.

'What are you doing?' Carnelian said, walking up to her.

'I just thought I'd carry it for a bit.'

He laughed. 'It's nearly as big as you are.' He kissed her and hoisted the pack up on to his shoulder; then, giving her his hand, the three of them began walking off towards the rootstair.

Carnelian touched Akaisha's shoulder. 'I've forgotten something, my mother.'

She raised an eyebrow. 'We'll wait.'

'You may as well go on, I'll soon catch you up.'

Akaisha shrugged, took Poppy's hand and they set off. Carnelian ran back to his sleeping hollow. Certain they were now well out of sight, he began digging where he and Poppy had buried her mother tree seed. He was despairing of finding it when he felt it in the earth. He lifted it carefully. Though its wing was black and tattered, the seed was still whole. Perhaps one day Poppy might be allowed to grow her mother tree in some garden in Osrakum. He slipped the seed carefully into an inner pocket and then ran towards the rootstair.

Carnelian and Poppy stood with Akaisha by the Lagoongate, watching the aquar go by pulling drag-cradles that sagged under their loads of swollen waterskins.

'You two can go ahead,' Akaisha told them. 'I'm just waiting to seal this gate.'

'We'll wait with you if we may, my mother,' said Carnelian.

He had already counted sixty drag-cradles and he could see an apparently endless line of them stretching off round the Homing under the cedar trees. It was strange to see aquar allowed into the Grove. Even though the morning was still cool, he savoured the comfort of having the canopy over his head.

Carnelian gazed out over the golden plain. 'No doubt we'll soon miss this shade.'

'Be sure of it,' said Akaisha.

Eventually the last drag-cradle scraped past and they were followed by a party of Elders led by Harth. She gave Carnelian a look of disapproval before addressing Akaisha. 'What's he doing here?'

'Keeping me company.'

Harth looked up at Carnelian. 'So you believe you've beaten us?'

Carnelian did not know what to say.

'How many times have I told you, Harth: Carnie is on our side.'

Harth gave a snort and moved away. Carnelian saw the other Elders were carrying two jars and, on a drag-cradle, something covered with a blanket. They came through the gate and put everything on the ground. Akaisha closed the gate and then one of the old men dipped his hand in one of the jars and brought it out black and reeking of charcoal. Reaching up, he drew his hand across the gate leaving shiny black daubs on its wicker. Harth did the same with red chalky ochre.

When they were done, the Elders all stood back and began a grumbling incantation. The blanket was pulled back to reveal a bony cadaver of a man, leathery brown, with holes for eyes, his papery lips pulled back from a yellow grin. Carnelian was reminded of nothing as much as one of the Wise he had seen unmasked, which made him shudder. He felt Poppy clutch his arm and slip her body round behind his leg.

'He can't harm you,' he said, gently.

Harth whisked round. 'He has more power than you might imagine against our enemies.'

Between them, the Elders raised the huskman and propped him up against the gate. Drawing back they began shouting at him, arraigning him with the crimes he had committed against the Tribe, promising him that if he should fulfil his duty well and protect their home, one day they would expose him on the summit of the Crag tower and allow his soul to be carried up to Father Sky.

Leaving that wizened sentinel, they wandered under the trees along the Lagooning, walking in the ruts the laden drag-cradles had gouged in the rusty earth. Fern and Sil, with Leaf strapped to her back, were waiting for them by the final gate. All together, they walked across the earthbridge into a world drenched by the gold of the sun. The Tribe and the aquar with their drag-cradles were dark motes beneath a copper sky.

Akaisha and the other Elders moved in among the people dictating the order of their march. Slowly, the aquar were formed up around the people with their burdens. Riders floated in dust clouds further out. With thin warbling cries the Tribe stirred into movement, fading Carnelian's view of the world behind their dust.

A weaving of withered ferns held the parched earth in thrall. Trees waved flags of scorched leaves at the Ochre as they passed. The herds were gone. Dust spat at them on the torrid breath of the wind. The heat was terrible. With a leaden heart, Carnelian had given up looking for Osidian. Making sure Poppy was well protected, he wrapped the cloth of his uba around his face and bowed his head to protect his eyes from the grit and glare. Blind, he trusted to the feeling in his feet, using the burn of the sun upon his forehead to tell him in which direction their path lay.

'The lagoon,' said Fern.

Carnelian looked at the handful of cloudy water-holes. Pointing, Fern undulated his hand and Carnelian saw the faint curves printed on the earth that were the ghosts of the vanished water. He lifted his eyes up to the featureless heat-grey sky and could not believe it would ever rain again. Around him the Tribe were marching across the cracked lagoon bed. Carnelian watched with curiosity as some women brushed the ground with their feet. Youths hung around them keenly waiting.

'What are they doing?' he asked Sil.

'We'll show you.'

Sil felt the earth with her calloused foot, she smiled and tapped the sand with her heel. Fern fell on his knees and dug where she indicated. Carnelian joined him. The earth had been baked so hard that at first it was like clawing stone. Then it began to soften, grow moist. Fern sat back to watch him.

'Go on,' he encouraged.

Carnelian felt something cold and slimy and yanked his hands out of the hole.

'I'll do it then,' said Fern, pushing him out of the way. He slipped his hands in and fetched something out that glinted in the sun. A fish. Carnelian was too astounded to say anything.

'Dreaming,' said Fern, giving it to Sil, then turned his back so she could tuck it into his pack.

'Even in the Withering, Carnie, the Mother provides for us,' she said, grinning.

The dark mass of the march had crested a ridge ahead.

'Come on,' said Sil, breaking into a lope. Carnelian scooped Poppy into his arms and ran to catch up. On the way they passed some boys dancing around a murky puddle jiggling their spears. One after another they plunged them in then, together, drew out a struggling dwarf-crocodile. They held it up as a trophy and Sil touched it to bless it for them.

'Kill it mercifully,' she said.

'And quickly,' said Fern. 'Or else you'll be left behind.'

Carnelian put Poppy down as they came over the crest of the slope and saw the soft circular outlines and egg-shells scattered everywhere half filled with sand.

'The remains of the bellower rookery,' Carnelian muttered. For some reason, the site reminded him of the ruins of the Quyan city he had seen from the leftway on his way to Osrakum.

The Tribe plodded on until the sun fell behind them, spindling their shadows off in the direction of their march. As the women of each hearth made a ring of blankets, the men cleared a great space among the brown and brittle ferns. They piled great armfuls of the stuff in the centre of the blanket rings and lit fierce fires. Carnelian saw

Akaisha and others gazing off back the way they had come until it became too dark to see anything. It grew quickly cold. Carnelian huddled round their fire with the rest of his hearthmates as they all tried to recapture something of the comfort of their home. He sensed that much of the sombre mood was due to worry about the missing youths. As a djada rope was passed around, Fern produced the fish he had dug from the ground and buried it in a cooler corner of the fire. When it was cooked, he distributed pieces of its charred flesh, which were delicious. A waterskin came round from which sips were taken to help lubricate the chewing of the djada. Whin was telling a story about animals who spoke with human speech, in which her sisters and Akaisha had roles and the children joined in gleefully with the choruses.

As the sky frosted with stars, they quietened so that Carnelian began to notice the muttering, a rare laugh drifting from the other hearths. People grew drowsy in the warm flicker of their fires.

'We are so naked here,' Carnelian whispered to Fern.

'Our mother trees are already far away,' said Sil.

'And the tribute bearers and the children too,' said Whin.

In the firelight Carnelian saw Fern looking over to Leaf, sleeping in her mother's arms, and drew Poppy to him and stroked her head encouraging her to sleep.

Commotion broke suddenly around them. Carnelian leapt to his feet even as the whole Tribe did so, obscuring the light of their fires with their bodies, everyone jabbering.

'Is it raveners?' he asked.

'Silence,' cried Akaisha. Other Elders all across the camp could be heard echoing her cry. The people quietened, calmed. Carnelian could see vague shapes moving in the dark.

'Riders,' Fern breathed.

'We are returned,' said a voice in the night.

Carnelian knew it was Ravan. Those who hoped their sons were returning to them began to call out the names of their hearths. It was a while before Akaisha began to speak her name into the darkness. The calls subsided and still she called: 'Akaisha, Akaisha.'

A black mass looming up out of the night silenced her. It divided into the shapes of two riders. Their aquar knelt and two men dismounted. One was vast beside the other. Silence.

'Make them welcome,' Akaisha hissed.

At her command, Carnelian and the others moved round the fire so that its light poured out to illumine the figures. They strode in to close the ring and then sat down. They were offered djada and water.

'It's good to have you back, son,' Akaisha said.

When Ravan did not even turn to look at her, Fern grew incensed. 'Didn't you hear your mother?'

The younger people were sneaking glances at each other. Whin was regarding the Master with unconcealed loathing. Akaisha was struggling for composure.

It was Poppy who pointed out the shape standing watching them in the night.

'Come forward,' said Whin.

Moving into the light the shape revealed itself to be Krow.

'Well?' Whin demanded.

Krow's black hunter's face glanced at the Master for guidance but he seemed unaware of him.

'Krow has nowhere else to go,' said Carnelian, at last.

Akaisha found a smile for the youth. She beckoned. 'Join us.'

Krow muttered his thanks to Akaisha and shot Carnelian a grateful look. After that, people spoke in whispers, giving the Master anxious glances, while he sat, a massive shadow gazing unblinking into the fire. Once he did look at Carnelian, who saw in his eyes fierce triumph.

In the morning the Tribe flung the embers of their hearths into the wind. Where fire caught, smoke leapt quickly westwards. They turned their backs on the flames and trudged into the sepia east. The Master walked in their midst as if he were alone. Observing him, Carnelian feared what he might be feeling. He needed to probe him, but Osidian never spoke. What little he ate he passed through the folds of his uba so that only the pale mouth in the blackened face was revealed. His eyes seemed to have no more sight in them than glass. Poppy shunned him as if he were a stranger. Ravan served him like a slave so that his own people turned away, not wishing to see his humiliation. Krow might have been the Master's shadow.

As the days passed, Carnelian gave up waiting for Osidian to speak. He strove to bear the weariness of the march as well as he saw the Elders and the children do. Still, each day was like a fever to which only the cool repose of night brought some relief.

One day, feeling a tremor of thunder coming from the west, Carnelian asked Fern with eager delight whether it might be some rain.

Fern's eyes peered out between the folds of his uba. 'There'll be no rain for several rebirths of the moon. Until then, the Withering will tighten its grasp on the land, relentlessly.'

Carnelian waited for more, but Fern only said, 'I fear we may soon enough see what is following us with thunder.'

Carnelian did not have the energy to pursue it. The sun was turning the world to molten gold. Their store of water was the very heart of their march. Over the first few days they had come across waterholes, puddles, which they drained down to the mud and even that they did not waste, but plastered it on the aquar to cool the burning in their hides. Eventually the land had nothing to offer them but dust.

The thunder following them became a shuddering in the ground. Looking back, Carnelian saw a sandstorm bearing down on them. The Elders began shouting orders. The arc the Tribe made across the plain began coalescing around groups of Elders. The children huddling in beside them were walled in by the kneeling aquar. On the outside men swung their bull-roarers while women gathered stones.

Carnelian stood with Osidian, Ravan and Krow on one side, Fern on the other whirling the blade of a bull-roarer around his head, dizzying Carnelian with its strobing, moaning cry. The women had built a cairn of stones in front of them. Sil pushed herself between Carnelian and Fern. She glanced anxiously back to see Leaf in Akaisha's arms. Poppy was there too. Carnelian gave her a smile and she returned it nervously. He turned back to watch the storm roll mountainously towards them.

'Their heads,' a voice screamed and many arms pointed up into the clouds that were billowing up and obscuring the sun.

Carnelian looked and saw dark shapes floating high among the veils of dust; the necks that held them there, then emerging through the murk, their chests and the column legs that were churning the earth.

Carnelian fell back against Sil. 'Heaveners,' he gasped in fear and awe, as every eye was locked to the oncoming giants.

'Such power,' exclaimed a voice in Quya. Looking out of the corner of his eyes Carnelian saw Osidian's, fierce and staring. But the shaking of the ground forced him to think about himself. He ignored the stones tumbling at his feet. He caught one glimpse of the nearest Ochre clump before all vision was blasted away by a tidal wave of grit.

Madness took them all. Carnelian shouted and screamed with the rest as he cast stones up at the lumbering, sky-filling shapes. Cliffs of hide slid past on either side. Each footfall shook the ground. Grey with dust, the mouths of the Tribe choked and bellowed. Coughing mixed with screams and the rattle of stones glancing off hide. Then the heaveners were gone, rumbling away into the east. Carnelian sagged exhausted among the ashen crowd, feeling the thunder slowly recede even as the sand stopped hailing.

People burst into song and laughter, with wonder at witnessing such sacred power and majesty; hugging and kissing each other in delight at their survival. Carnelian was pulled into a dance by Sil and Fern, tears smudging the dust around their eyes. It took Carnelian a while to notice Osidian emotionless, gazing off after the cloud-shrouded giants.

They tramped eastwards along the wide roads driven through the dead fernland by the herds. Carnelian was grateful the load of djada he carried had been reduced by consumption, to match the depletion in his strength.

One morning he saw, rising with the sun, mountains liquid blue in the dawn.

'Drink deep of that sight, Carnie,' Fern said. 'Though we've still more than half our journey before us, it's a promise of cool air and crystal water.'

Until the sun rose to its full fiery strength, the sight of the mountains was enough to put smiles back on to the dust-bleached faces of the Tribe. Soon the glare had turned the sky opaque so that it appeared the mountains had been nothing but a mirage.

Often in the morning and in the quick dusk of evening, they could gaze with longing at the mountains that grew day by day more solid. At last the morning came when Akaisha promised her hearth they would soon be climbing up out of the burning plain. They chewed knotted djada, their eyes grit-reddened and weeping, but they made better speed drawn on by the sight of journey's end.

The land began to fold, and here and there a leaf missed by the passing herds, or a still green fern crozier, gave them hope. They wound up into the hills along ever-steepening paths. The mountains formed a distant turquoise wall across the lower sky from which noisy rivers poured their colour down into the valleys.

As the day was waning they reached a land of verdant valleys curled with delicious mist. They kept to the paths that wound around the slopes. In the valley bottoms, the ferny pastures were filled with the creatures of the plain.

By a narrow defile, they entered the valley which, Fern told Carnelian, the Tribe considered its own. Men that had been sent ahead waved down from the craggy heights to indicate the place was free of danger. Once through that gateway, the aquar fanned out and

Carnelian found he was walking into a long and narrow valley, green-walled and watered by a stream.

People all around him sighed their relief, kicking their hot feet through the coolness of the ferns lining its banks. Eastwards, the mountains rose dipped in the cool blue of the fading afternoon. For Carnelian it was a sacrament to kneel before the glimmering stream. He bent to scoop a tiny pool into his cupped hands and, blinded by its dazzle, drank. He winced as the water drove its iciness through his teeth and deep into the bones of his face, then laughed with the sheer pleasure of it. When he had drunk his fill, with Poppy holding his hand, they went to luxuriate in the shadow of a tree.

IN THE MOUNTAINS

Height sees further
further sight brings knowing
so, is it not fitting
that our Father should choose to live in the sky?

(a precept of the Plainsmen)

THE BLUE OF THE MOUNTAINS SUFFUSED THE STREAM. AIR SO FRESH IT
almost hurt to breathe it; so clear it seemed to Carnelian that should
he stretch out his hand he might cut his fingers on the peaks.

'Up there, each breath must be as pure as light,' he said to Fern.

'It's where we believe the Skyfather rests after the effort of making
rain.'

As they walked back to the camp, Carnelian delighted in the wash
of emerald ferns against his legs. The people were ranged along the
margin of the stream, watching the children scattering diamond
spray as they gambolled in the shallows. Mothers were pleating their
daughters' hair. Fathers were showing their sons how to knap flint
into blades. Here and there Carnelian saw billows of steam rising
from pots stewing djada and fiddleheads. Under the water near the
bank, bowls were filled with dried berries swelling. The Elders lay
under the still-flowering trees talking, smiling as they watched the
children play. Lovers lay together, playing with each other's hair,
smiling, nuzzling each other with whispers.

Fear clutched Carnelian that such peace should be threatened by
Osidian's discontent. Taking his leave of Fern, he went searching for
him, determined to force whatever plans he had out into the open.

He found him standing away from the Tribe, alone save for Ravan. Carnelian saw how much they resembled a Sapient with his homunculus and shuddered. He decided he would try to talk to Osidian later, when he might hope to find him alone, but just then Osidian turned and looked his way. He still had not washed the hornblack from his face. Carnelian suspected he wore the colour as a mask. It made his eyes so bright and compelling. Carnelian approached and was relieved when Osidian dismissed Ravan. Carnelian glimpsed the youth's envy before, with a nod that was almost a bow, he moved away. Carnelian watched him go, not ready to confront Osidian. He marshalled his arguments, then faced him.

'His obsession with you eats at him like a canker.'

Osidian shrugged as if at some pleasantry. He lifted his perfect eyes to survey the mountains.

'They are wondrous tall . . .' Carnelian said.

Osidian gave a slow nod. 'They remind me of the Sacred Wall.'

For a moment he seemed again the boy in the Yden, and Carnelian discovered from the hammering of his heart that he still felt love for him. Shocked, he reached out but stopped short of touching, afraid he might cause the moment to vanish like a reflection in water. Osidian noticed the movement. Carnelian could see the mask of indifference slipping back over Osidian's face and blurted out the first thing that came into his mind.

'We . . . we could climb them together.'

Seeing Osidian poised between who he had been and who he had become, Carnelian added, quickly: 'The two of us . . . alone . . . in air untainted by mortal breathing. They claim their sky god lives there.'

Osidian frowned, considering it. For a moment Carnelian was certain he had pushed him too hard, but then the boy in Osidian looked him in the eyes and nodded.

Carnelian was rolling some djada to take with them. 'Are you sure I won't need to ask your mother for permission?'

Fern shook his head. 'There's no escape up there.'

Carnelian packed the djada. 'Will you tell Poppy and keep her with you? If I tell her she'll hate it; perhaps even follow me.'

Fern nodded, frowning. 'Are you sure you want to go, alone, with him?'

'We need to talk and down here he'll not open up.'

Carnelian saw the depths of Fern's feelings. 'He'd never harm me.'

The answer seemed to confuse Fern. He reached for a waterskin. 'I'll fetch you some water.'

'That would weigh us down too much,' said Carnelian. He looked at Fern, trying to work him out. Could it be jealousy? 'We'll take what we need from the stream. We'll not be away more than a day or two.'

He hoisted the pack and went off to meet Osidian. When he glanced back, he saw Fern watching him. There was a part of Carnelian that took pleasure at seeing Fern annoyed.

Carnelian ignored the look of indolence on Osidian's painted face. Part of him was already regretting the expedition. 'Come, my Lord,' he said in Quya and made off along the bank.

The stream filled the air with its babble. Birds screamed as they knifed through the air. The valley funnelled up into a twilit gorge where the stream quickened, its deeper voice vibrating the air. Their path narrowed so that they had to go one behind the other, their skin dampened by the spray. Light began filtering brighter through the ferns and soon they were coming up into cool, open land. They drew the pure wind into their lungs. Seeing how alive Osidian's eyes had become, how lustily he climbed, Carnelian allowed himself to believe he was seeing the boy he had loved.

'There is something in this of the climb we made back up to the Halls of Thunder.'

Carnelian knew immediately he had made a mistake. Osidian grew morose. 'My dear mother and her son will be up there now ruling in my place.'

It was nearing the middle of the day when, already high up a shoulder of the mountains, they came to where the stream foamed in steps into a deep, clear pool. Small trees grew around it, and arching ferns. Carnelian unrolled a blanket he had brought upon a narrow shelf of rock and they sat on it, lowering their feet into the spray, listening to the gurgle of the stream.

Carnelian saw Osidian was blind to the place; deaf to it. He followed the drop of his forehead, the jutting of his nose, the paler lips set in the black face.

'Here I might even forget Osrakum,' he tried, tentatively.

'Never,' said Osidian without turning.

His bitterness made Carnelian angry. 'Can you not even here allow yourself some peace?'

Osidian turned to look at him. 'Have you truly found peace?'

Carnelian gazed up at the mountains and then back into Osidian's eyes, greener than the sun through the ferns. 'It is beautiful and we are alone together as we have not been since the Yden.'

'An abyss has opened between us.'

'Ravan?'

Osidian laughed. 'You believe I could love such a creature?'

Carnelian looked away to hide his vexation.

'I used him to meet my needs; to wound you.'

Carnelian met his gaze. 'Fern, then?'

The pupils of Osidian's eyes contracted. 'Your tastes afflict me but deeper betrayals have dug the ground from under my feet.'

When the sybling Hanuses had told Carnelian that without him they would have been unable to capture Osidian, that accusation had lodged its barb in Carnelian's heart. Now it gave a twist that brought tears to his eyes.

Osidian reached up and stole a tear. 'Things can never again be as once they were.' He tasted the wetness on his finger. 'I have no more tears.'

Carnelian took hold of him by his shoulders. 'Where are you?'

Osidian broke his grip and turned back to watch the flow. 'Alone, standing on a pinnacle from which there leads only a single, precarious path.'

Carnelian saw the pain on Osidian's face and yearned to kiss it but had lost his way to him.

'Would you not feel better if you washed the blackness from your face?'

'Would it wash the blackness from my heart?'

Carnelian remembered the razors he had thought to bring. 'Surely you would enjoy once more to have your head smooth?'

Osidian looked at him, then shrugged, but Carnelian could see he was intrigued. He opened the pack and on a corner of the blanket laid out the things he had packed. There was a small pot and a handful of flint razors. He was pleased when he saw Osidian showing interest in these preparations. Osidian allowed him to unwind the uba from his head. Carnelian saw the rope scar. Osidian's hair was thick and Carnelian liked the feel of it, but he began to shear it off. He sensed Osidian examining him as he worked. The flints yanked at the hair but Osidian did not seem to feel any pain. After a while, Carnelian sat back. Osidian's head was covered with a thick uneven stubble. Carnelian smiled. 'You look somewhat bizarre.'

He went to scoop some water from the pool. It was ice in his hands but Osidian did not flinch when Carnelian trickled it over his head. He thumbed some of the paste from the pot and rubbed it between the palms of his hands. Seeing Osidian's raised eyebrows, he said: 'It is a kind of soap they make from ochre, ashes and fat which the women use. It will make the blades glide.'

He lathered the red stuff over Osidian's head, disliking its look of blood. With care he began to scrape the stubble off with a flint, making sure he turned to a new edge before the previous one became blunt.

When he was done, he urged Osidian to go and wash. Osidian surprised him. He threw off his robe and slid naked into the pool. Carnelian cried out with joy as he watched him submerge.

When Osidian broke the surface, his face was white. He clambered out, dripping, and Carnelian got up and welcomed him into the blanket, wrapping it round him, kissing his reddened scalp.

Osidian embraced him hard through the blanket. 'Surely you don't imagine I'm prepared to suffer all this alone?'

Carnelian melted into the comfort of his arms, his Vulgate, his boyish smile. He shivered with delight as he allowed Osidian to shave him. His black hair fell around him on to the rock as Osidian's arms crossed and recrossed his line of sight. Carnelian had plenty of time to decide he liked the new honeyed tones of Osidian's skin.

When it was done, Osidian stood up and with mock imperiousness pointed at the pool. 'In there.'

Carnelian did as he was told, disrobing and leaping into the pool before Osidian could push him. He gasped as the iciness engulfed him. But then Osidian was there beside him and the smallness of the pool forced their bodies close. The touching of their skin led to passion. Lust took Carnelian by surprise. Its heat was almost violence. The release when it came left them both gasping. They enjoyed each other again, at first fiercely but then with increasing tenderness until they were left with hardly enough energy to creep into the blanket. They huddled together, getting warm. They grew quiet as a melancholy settled over the glade. The water rushed and foamed. The goose-pimples stood out on their skin as they used its sound to send shivers up and down their backs; ripple upon ripple sheathing them in the ecstasy that was the Chosen sacrament of the feeling from the sound of rain.

Carnelian felt tension returning to Osidian's body. He needed to talk to him before he retreated back into remoteness. He forced Osidian to turn his head and held it while he looked deep into his eyes.

'We've enough here for happiness.'

Osidian tried to shake his head from side to side.

'Let Osrakum go,' Carnelian pleaded. 'Let it all go. Only when you do will your heart begin to heal.'

Tears welled into Osidian's eyes and with them, anger. Carnelian was thrown away as Osidian surged to his feet, glaring.

'I will not let it go,' he bellowed in Quya.

He threw his head back and let the madness brighten in his eyes. 'I shall return to where I belong. I shall bring down vengeance on my enemies.' He bent to pick up his robe and threw it on.

Shocked, Carnelian rose to face him.

Osidian's eyes were haunted fire. 'You can come with me or remain behind with the savages if that is your desire.'

Naked to his heart, Carnelian shrugged. He stooped to pick up his robe and put it on, fighting back tears that came from the rage of defeat. He wound his uba round his head. He punched the blanket back into the pack. Saw Osidian waiting for his answer, shrugged again, turned away and, careless of the boulders, strode up the slope.

They climbed into the heights in angry silence. Carnelian maintained a furious pace until all he could hear was his own harsh breathing. The sun was setting the mountains aflame when they agreed to stop for the night. Carnelian gathered branches with which he made a fire. They sat with the flames between them, nibbling djada. As darkness brought with it bitter cold, the flames dwindled and there was no more fuel. Eventually they were driven into huddling together. Neither said anything. Pride would not allow Carnelian to speak first. Osidian's warm body awakened passion which Carnelian smothered with sleep.

The sky woke them with its flawless blue. Carnelian sat up and saw the sun had not yet risen above the mountains. He longed for its heat.

'Shall we go up or down?' Osidian asked.

Carnelian was sure if they climbed higher another night would kill them, but what was there to return to? Besides, he was not going to admit any fear to Osidian and so he shrugged.

Osidian's face turned to stone. 'Then we shall climb.'

Carnelian was thankful the effort of the ascent put life back into his aching limbs. When the first sun-rays fell on him, Carnelian called for a halt. Both basked like lizards on the rocks while they chewed djada. Then Osidian led them, climbing ever higher until the valley below had become merely a green wedge and the rest of the world spread turquoise and umber into the endless distance.

That night they made sure to gather enough wood to keep the fire going well into the night. Still, when he woke the next morning, Carnelian's body was ice and it was with difficulty he managed to move at all. He searched for signs of the Tribe but the land below was still in twilight and he could see nothing moving save for an eagle curving its flight.

Osidian asked him the same question he had asked the day before and, again, though it cost him, Carnelian gave another shrug. So it was they climbed even higher until Carnelian was rasping breath, the path welling in his vision. They had to stop often to get their breath back; to slow the hammering of their hearts.

One time Carnelian caught Osidian looking longingly down to the valley, but when he saw he was being observed, Osidian forced them on. That night neither of them could keep anything in their stomachs. They sipped the little water they could find. Even supposing they had had the strength to gather firewood, they had climbed above the trees and there was none to be had. Under a frost of stars, they clung to each other all night and hardly slept.

In the morning Carnelian could not move. He lay squinting at the sky feeling strangely elated, until a ray of sunlight found his face and woke thought in him.

'Sky-sickness,' he croaked. He knew it, having suffered from it on his first, over-rapid ascent of the Pillar of Heaven in Osrakum.

He marshalled his strength and, at last, groaning, managed to roll over. He stared for a long time at the deathly face peering from the blanket before he remembered who it was. Grief came like lightning. Carnelian fell on to Osidian and managed to scrape away the cloth so that his lips found the icy neck beneath. A pounding in his head made him blind. His lips could feel only the merest tremor of life in Osidian's body. Carnelian rolled back and saw nothing but blue. Osidian had not regained his former strength. It would be so easy to fall asleep, to die. Osidian would die with him and the Tribe would finally be rid of them both.

Carnelian made one last effort and turned his head. He saw Osidian's livid scar. The red mark of the rope. That colour made him dream his life again. Every scene was there. He wept for all the suffering but no tears came. He could not move his head and so was forced to watch Osidian die. Carnelian had taken his life from him once, he could not bear to do it again. He tried to sit up. He panicked when he found he had turned to stone. Anger swelled in him until he could hear it roaring in his ears. He pushed and pushed and forced himself to sit up. He shook back and forth, rocking, groaning with each folding of his belly until he felt life returning. Then he concentrated on Osidian; reaching under the blanket to rub his chest, his back, his arms, his legs until, slowly, he brought Osidian back from death.

They stumbled down towards the valley a few steps at a time, each half carrying the other. Reaching the first trees before nightfall, they collected twigs with trembling fingers. Carnelian almost cried when after much fumbling with their fire-drill he was unable to produce a single spark. Osidian tried. A spark lit hope and they fed this until there was a flame and then a fire.

That night was milder and, with the morning, they found enough strength to continue the descent. The sun was still low when Carnelian saw smoke rising.

'We'll be home soon,' he said, pointing.

Osidian did not turn to look at him but only gave a nod.

Drums were beating like hearts when Carnelian awoke. The air was warm and fragrant. Branches slipped the blue of the sky between their leaves. He made an effort to sit up and saw he was safe in the heart of the Tribe. He could see children winding a dance through a commotion of preparation. Their young joy gladdened him.

'Carnie,' a little voice cried, and before he knew it, Poppy had flung herself at him. He hugged her hard, kissed the nape of her neck and muttered: 'I'm glad to see you too.'

She pulled away from him and stared. 'You're better now?'

Carnelian was going to ask her what she meant, but then remembered and turned to look round to where the mountains rose purple to the clear sky. It came as a shock when he realized he could not remember reaching the camp.

Poppy saw his puzzlement. 'We spotted you wandering dazed with the Master.'

'We?'

'Fern, Sil, many others.'

'How long have I lain . . . ?'

'Two days,' she said.

'And the Master?'

'Ravan is tending him.'

Carnelian's attention was drawn to the rhythm of the drums. 'What's happening?'

'The Tribe are getting ready for the gatherings.'

'Gatherings?'

'All the tribes are up here in the mountains.'

Carnelian started. 'Coming here.'

Poppy calmed him with a shake of her head. 'It's not our turn. We're sending people to other valleys.'

He reached out and took her hand. 'Have you been looking after me?'

Poppy grew fierce. 'Fern wanted to but I wouldn't let him.'

He laughed and kissed her again, then threw back the blankets.

'Are you sure you're strong enough, Carnie?'

'Let's see,' he said and, rising, found he felt weak, but otherwise well enough. Poppy looked unconvinced as she brought him his robe and helped him wind on his uba.

'Are you going to see the Master?'

Carnelian felt he should but did not really want to. 'You said Ravan is looking after him?'

Poppy nodded. 'He and the other from my . . . from the Twostone.'

'Krow.'

She gave a nod.

'Well, in that case, I think it better we should let him rest. Shall we go and see what's going on?'

Poppy beamed and grabbed his hand.

As they walked together, the excitement of the drums transferred itself to their hearts. Soon they were among the women who were singing as they worked. They watched them grind red earth in the hollows of saurian shoulder-blades. One girl poured the resulting powder into a jar which another was stirring. It looked like blood. Carnelian could see other jars holding the rich pigment and wondered what it was for.

'You're up,' a voice cried, and Carnelian saw it was Fern bounding towards him. He looked closely at Carnelian.

'You seem well enough.'

'I don't think he is,' Poppy piped up.

Fern gave her a look of concern. 'Do you think he should rest longer?'

Carnelian interrupted Poppy's reply. 'Would you like to be alone to discuss me?'

They all grinned. He made sure to hold each of their gazes. 'I'm fine. Really.'

He laughed when he saw Poppy and Fern exchange glances. 'Now will someone please tell me what's going on here?'

'What happened up there?' asked Fern.

Carnelian saw by the serious way they were both looking at him that he would have to give them some kind of answer. 'We got lost.'

Fern frowned. Poppy glanced up at him and then she frowned too.

For a moment, Carnelian was overwhelmed by the love he felt for them both. The easy flow of his feelings for Fern surprised him. With a shock, Carnelian realized he felt free of Osidian. He no longer felt that Osidian's darkness was a burden he had to share. Sadness at the love they had lost threatened to overwhelm him.

Poppy and Fern were watching him. Carnelian took his friend's arm and pointed. 'What're they doing there?'

Fern looked uncertain. Poppy shook her head, then shrugged. 'They're making ochre, Carnie.'

'For the women?'

'For everyone that's going,' said Fern. 'The gatherings are held under the protection of the Mother.'

He pointed to a pole set upright in the ground from which there hung a flag woven from scarlet feathers. 'A trucestaff inviting us to the valley of the Smallochre.'

'A kin tribe?' asked Carnelian.

Fern shook his head. 'One of those neighbouring the Koppie. All our neighbours will be there: the Woading, the Tallgreen, the Darkcloud, the Bluedancing.'

'The Bluedancing?'

'The trucestaff will ensure there'll be no trouble.'

Carnelian gave Poppy his hand and then put his other arm about Fern's shoulders. 'Come on, give me a tour.'

They watched mud gouged from the bank of the stream being piled upon a sled. They helped some boys drag it back to where the women threw handfuls of it into leather bowls. Fires were burning smokily where cubes of fat were being melted into oil. One bowl, brimming over, was lifted with a pole by two men. Children were scolded out of the way as it was carried to where women were kneading mud into balls. The women punched depressions into the balls into which the oil was carefully poured. They watched it cool. When it was just beginning to set, they began to fold the edges of the depression into it and then resumed their kneading.

Mud balls that were ready were rolled in ochre earths. The red dough produced was being worked into men's hair, which was then lifted up and moulded into crests. Several women worked on each, helped and pestered by children, using their palms to shape and smooth them up until each man had a curving fluted crest like a bellower's rising from his head.

Next the ochre dyes were brought. With these, patterns of concentric circles were painted on their skins using flexible lengths of cartilage or dabbed on with fingers. The men grinned and the women laughed and scolded them as they tried to evade the tickle of the painting.

A little further on, under an awning, Fern showed Carnelian the women that were to go on the embassy. Akaisha was there, grimacing as Whin worked wax and fat into her hair.

'Is he all right?' she asked Poppy.

Carnelian tapped his chest grinning. 'I'm here, my mother.'

She grinned. 'I know you are, dear.' She looked at her son. 'You should be getting ready, Fern.'

Fern looked embarrassed, but proud. 'I'm going too.'

'It's a great honour,' said Whin, pleased for him.

They hung around just long enough to watch as a cone of basket-weave was placed on Akaisha's head, around which her salt-beaded hair was wrapped to make a glossy horn. Whin gave them a nod as they took leave of her.

In the stream, aquar were being scoured clean. On the bank, others were having their hides layered with fine mud. On this smooth ground rings and spiral designs were being daubed. Feather-wreaths were being clasped around their necks. Their saddle-chairs were being prepared with bright standards and banners of tattered, scarlet saurian-leather.

Fern took Carnelian's shoulders. 'I really should go and get ready. Are you sure you're fine?'

'Yes, now get going.'

They grinned at each other and then Fern moved off into the crowd. Carnelian allowed Poppy to draw him into the children's dances and their games. Still not wholly recovered from the sky-sickness, he grew quickly weary and, seeing this, Poppy led him away from the hubbub. It was a sense of duty that made him ask her to take him to see the Master.

Osidian had chosen an acacia away from the Tribe under which to make his camp. As Carnelian and Poppy approached, two shrouded figures came out to meet them.

'He will not see you, Master,' said one, who turned out to be Krow.

Carnelian looked beyond him but could see nothing in the brooding shadow beneath the tree.

'He mentioned me specifically?'

'Yes, you,' said the other figure, Ravan. He drew his uba from his face, revealing a sneer.

Carnelian considered his next words carefully. 'You should take care, Ravan; his feelings for you might not be what you believe them to be.'

Ravan smiled unpleasantly. 'You're just bitter you've lost him to me.'

The youth was distracted by the hubbub floating towards them on the breeze. His eyes, gazing off towards the Tribe, were filled with longing.

'Why don't you all come and see what's happening?' offered Poppy, brightly.

Ravan gave her a filthy look, turned on his heel and strode back towards the acacia. Ducking an apologetic smile, Krow followed him. As Carnelian walked away he was haunted by a feeling that he should have left Osidian on the mountain to die.

Carnelian stood among the Tribe watching the embassies set off. Around him bull-roarers were producing a slow, undulating moan. Bone struck on bone: stone on stone. Everyone was jigging up and down in an oceanic surge. Through their midst, with barbaric pomp, rode the embassy of the Tribe, the truce staff carried before them. He saw Fern beside Akaisha and waved. Harth was there with Crowrane and Loskai. Carnelian spotted Ginkga, Galewing, Kyte. The Elders' saddle-chairs were the gaudiest; hung with feathers, tinkling trinkets, pieces of stolen brass that caught the light like mirrors. These wizened men and women with nodding crests, hung with their jewellery of salt, sat enthroned in their saddle-chairs, to the backs of which had been lashed feather-pennoned poles. Behind them came the riot of their warrior escort, dark skins agleam with sweat and vermilion designs.

When Sil announced she was going to gather herbs in the foothills, Poppy asked if she and Carnelian might go with her. Sil and Carnelian glanced at each other, embarrassed.
'I don't –' Carnelian began, but was interrupted by Whin.
'You should go, Carnie. Poppy will enjoy it and, though there's unlikely to be any danger, I would feel happier if my daughter had an escort that I trust.'
Carnelian and Sil both stared at Whin, surprised by her endorsement. The rest of the hearth reacted as if the matter had been decided and helped bundle them off, so that soon, Sil and Carnelian with Poppy on his lap were riding towards a far edge of the valley.
At first Carnelian and Sil could think of nothing to say to each other. It was Poppy who decided she and Sil should teach Carnelian songs. At first reluctant, Carnelian began to enjoy himself, even their teasing of his accent. They found a rash of berries the birds had overlooked and dismounted to pick them, putting as many in their mouths as in the baskets. When Sil caught her robe on some thorns, Carnelian helped her loose. They watched Poppy plucking berries, her mouth stained with their juice.
'She's a lovely girl,' said Sil.
Her eyes met Carnelian's and they saw each other's grief at what they were to lose to the tithe.
'You know Fern loves you?' Sil said, quietly.
Carnelian looked into her eyes again and nodded. 'I love him too.'
She smiled a little and looked at her berry-red fingers.

He reached out and took her hand. 'He may love us both, but you are his wife.'

She looked up solemn, beautiful. Poppy chose that moment to return. She beamed when she saw them holding hands.

On the day Carnelian noticed that the valley was losing its green vibrancy, the embassy returned. Children's shrieks of excitement pierced the lazy afternoon and soon people were streaming across the meadow to welcome back the riders. Carnelian was among them with Poppy and Sil, laughing as the noise deafened him, adding to it himself with a bellow or two.

The riders came to a halt, Akaisha at their head, unable to make any progress against the throng. From every throat came calls for news. Akaisha signalled the riders to make their aquar kneel. Seeing her lowered to the ground, Carnelian and Sil pushed through to help her out of her saddle-chair. They could feel in the tremble of her arms how tired she was. She was hiding some pain behind her smile. Fern appeared beside them. He waved people away while Akaisha leaned on Carnelian as he walked her towards the encampment.

'What news, my mother?' Sil asked.

She made a face. 'The usual. Marriages, talk of hunts, of fernroot yields.'

'What about the Gatherers, my mother?' Carnelian asked.

Akaisha's face sank. 'It's as we'd guessed; they came this year to every tribe.' She looked with concern at Carnelian, trying to read his expression.

'So what if they search for you? No one knows where you are.'

He leaned down and gave her wrinkled cheek a kiss. Sil put her hand on his arm. 'Leave her with me, Carnie, I'm sure you and Fern will want to talk.' She leaned close and kissed him on the lips and then she and Akaisha moved away.

Fern was looking at him with eyebrows raised.

'We've become friends,' said Carnelian, embarrassed.

Fern grinned. 'I knew you would.'

Carnelian noticed a nasty bruise on the side of his friend's head. 'How did that happen?'

'Trucestaff, or no trucestaff, we had a run in with the Bluedancing.'

'A fight?'

'A brawl with some young hotheads wanting revenge for the beating we gave them earlier this year.' He grinned. 'We gave them another good hiding.'

HAND OF DARKNESS

And when, for her bride-price, she gouged out his eyes
she held the thorn in her left hand.

(from the 'Ruáya', the first book of the 'Ilkaya', part of the holy scriptures of the Chosen)

THE BREEZE COULD NOT DISPERSE THE PALLS OF SMOKE THAT HID THE dawn. The Tribe had fired the further reaches of the valley. The Withering had at last stretched up to find them; parching the blue out of the sky; scorching the green from the earth. Their stream had dwindled, choking dry. The fern meadow turned amber, dying.

Harth and others of the Elders had sniffed hope floating on the air. Several had gone out beyond the entrance to the valley to confirm it. When they returned they went among the Tribe claiming they had smelled the rain in the breeze blowing from the west. When the young looked sceptical, they were reassured it was not a matter of having a keen nose but of being blessed with the experience to recognize the subtle perfume of the Skyfather's approach. After that it had been all hurried packing.

'We must rush to meet the rain,' said Fern. 'Even now it rolls towards us across the Earthsky.'

Carnelian wondered at the certainty in his friend's voice. Carnelian could smell nothing in the air but burning. 'To reach it we'll have to cross a desert.'

'We still have water,' said Sil, Leaf strapped to her back.

Carnelian had seen how lightly loaded the drag-cradles were with waterskins.

Fern craned round. 'Would you have us stay here?'

309

Carnelian looked back at the wall of smoke clogging the sky. Aquar ambled on every side as the Tribe made gentle progress towards the valley entrance.

Osidian approached, attended by Ravan, Krow and other youths. Carnelian felt Poppy, Fern and Sil close around him like a faction. He greeted Osidian in Vulgate and he gave a nod but would not meet Carnelian's eyes.

Osidian turned to watch the smoke rising. 'It hides the sky.'

'The fire will renew the earth,' said Fern. 'When we return next year this valley will be as green as it was when we arrived.'

Osidian was not listening. His eyes were grey, reflecting smoke as he spoke. 'Even the sun cannot see through that curtain darkness.'

Thirst drove them west with ever greater speed. They had been struggling across the torrid land for days. Dawn found them plodding and so, too, the dusk. They had redistributed the djada and what little water was left so as to free drag-cradles for the pregnant, the younger children, the old and those who had to take turns resting. It was being whispered that the wind-blown promise of rain had been false. People gazed accusingly at the Elders, so many of whom were not having to walk. Carnelian understood there was a need to blame someone. It was difficult not to despair. The land was beaten gold. The furnace air driving into their faces snatched all moisture from throat and eye. The sun glared relentlessly down. Carnelian choked on the ashen dust rolling hissing across a desert desolation. Whenever he lifted his itching eyes, the charcoaled plain stretched before him limitless and droughty to an umber horizon.

The water they carried dwindled day by day, as had the stream in the valley, and still the rain did not come. Every day, in the calm before the dawn, Carnelian saw Akaisha lift her head and dilate her nostrils like dark eyes. She shook her head and, when asked, she swore by the Mother that the Skyfather's rain was hiding unseen in the hem of the sky. With the others, Carnelian wanted to believe her but as each day withered into a chill night, they had to camp again in an unwatered land.

Aquar began dying. The Elders had ordered they should be given less water to save what was left for the people. Carnelian and Poppy saw one creature reel, stumble and fall, tumbling its rider into the dust. The woman rose, wearily, now the colour of the ground. They watched her urge the aquar to rise; she stroked it, talked to it, begged and even struck the creature in desperate rage. It would not budge and, forlorn, she joined the column of people toiling on foot.

When rain came it came unseen. People were leaning forward, straining for each step, eyes closed, despairing faces hidden in the coils of their ubas. The scorching west wind flung a hail of sand against them. It was a distant flash that woke eyes all along the march. Carnelian squinted blearily and saw a darkening horizon. Thunder rumbled. Even as he stopped to stare, the separation between earth and sky was inking black.

'A sandstorm?' he gasped, but the only answer he received was Poppy grabbing hold of his hand.

'Can you feel the Father in the air?' Akaisha shrilled.

Then Carnelian heard the rushing. The front struck them screaming, tearing the uba from his face. Veils of darkness were flowing towards them, hissing. The sand before him pocked as if a thousand tiny feet were sprinting towards them. Then he smelled the water and it was upon them, running down his face, drowning the air.

The march of the Tribe dissolved into a riot. Carnelian danced with Poppy. People slipping down from aquar were throwing themselves on each other. Many ran about shouting, their faces turned up into the rain, their arms outstretched seeking to embrace the Skyfather's gift of life.

The sky poured its water into the thirsty earth, washing the air clean of dust. Those next few days were a carnival. The rain raised the wilting necks of the aquar and the spirits of the people. Everyone seemed younger, renewed along with the world. Laughter was everywhere and singing. When they camped, children ran laughing, playing muddy games under thunderous skies.

Calm interspersed the storms: the clouds would open and allow the sun in to dazzle them. Now they smiled to feel its warmth upon their faces. Too soon the clouds would close and the rain resume its downpour. So much rain that the plain began softening into a marsh, in the midst of which lagoons were spreading. Soon every day had become a plodding, sodden slog through sucking mud.

Carnelian collapsed beside Fern. Akaisha had chosen a ginkgo for her hearth and had made them hang blankets in the branches, though these gave scant protection. They hung sodden, collecting the rain which spilled over in rivulets, splashing them, besieging them with puddles. All around them in the rumbling gloom the Tribe sheltered as best they could, but even the aquar drooped drenched.

Whin and Sil had nestled a fire between the roots of the tree.

When the wind gusted, it forced the smoke towards them in choking, eye-stinging drifts. The lurid flicker sporadically lit Osidian's face.

'Will this curse never cease?' he moaned.

'It'll not stop until after we reach the Koppie, Master,' said Ravan.

'As much as once I loved the rain, I loathe it now,' Osidian said in Quya, addressing Carnelian as if the youth had not spoken.

Embarrassed by the sound of that tongue, Carnelian looked round apologetically.

'It makes me remember,' Osidian continued, relentlessly, his hand straying up to his neck scar. Fire flashed under the ceiling clouds some distance away. Carnelian waited for the thunder. It came rolling, heavy, stuttering, sonorous.

'Hark, He speaks,' said Osidian in an ominous tone and the rain fell with increasing ferocity.

Carnelian's eyes snapped open. A scream. Questions cutting across each other. He sat up. The smouldering fires revealed black shapes scudding through the camp. For a moment one fire was blotted out by a vast hurtling shadow trailing a wild whoop. A battle-cry choked to gurgling by an arcing shape. Everywhere mounds of darkness were rising uttering fearful cries.

Someone pushed by him, crying in Quya, 'The Two. The Two.'

Osidian was too fast for Carnelian. He saw with dismay Osidian's bright naked body leaping towards their attackers. He was too visible. Cursing, Carnelian overthrew his immobility, rummaging violently among the piles of baggage. When the haft of an axe slipped into his hand, he flung himself round wielding it, crashing after the cold flicker of Osidian's body. Kicking his way through obstructions, his foot caught and he was flung to the ground. He rose, groaning. Something whistled past his ear even as he was thrust back into the mud.

'He almost had you,' cried Fern in anger.

Carnelian could make out the mounted shape as it scooped up a piece of darkness that shrieked with a child's voice, then it was coursing away. Fern helped him up as the cries receded into the darkness. Only a few fires still burned.

'Are you hurt?' said Fern, running his hands over Carnelian, searching for wounds.

Carnelian slipped away from him and stumbled through the dark, steering by the faint beacon of Osidian's body. Everywhere, shapes were stirring, moaning. Some voices wailed while others rang out begging for light.

Carnelian approached Osidian's long white back, glowing in the gloom. Ravan and Krow were already there, reluctant to touch him. Carnelian crept round to peer into Osidian's face. Motionless marble. He gingerly reached out to touch the stone. Cold. Sticky. He jerked his hand back. Osidian seemed to be a corpse, standing. Carnelian licked his fingers and tasted salt.

'Is he wounded?' asked Ravan.

Nothing.

'Well, are you?' Carnelian demanded.

'It is the other that is slain.'

Carnelian could not help drawing away from the eerie voice. He stumbled backwards over the body lying on the ground and fell. Dazed, he lay there feeling the rain falling on his face in a steady rhythm.

Poppy clung to Carnelian. Through the rain, he saw the camp, now a battlefield. All their makeshift shelters were leaning at crazy angles with their blankets trampled into the mud. Bales disembowelled their contents into puddles. People, moaning, were bending among the wreckage, searching. Some were pulling things together as if they had been merely blown down by a freak gust. Many just stood sightlessly staring out over the featureless land.

The Elders began moving among them, ordering things. Some were so weak they had to lean on the arms of their grandchildren, but, even so, they were listened to with the rest.

Akaisha pulled at Carnelian's shoulder. 'Carnie, don't just stand there, dear. Help me clear up this mess.' She noticed Poppy and they exchanged a glance. Both could see in the girl's face that she was seeing the massacre of her people.

'I'll look after her,' Akaisha said, softly.

Carnelian nodded and carefully transferred Poppy's grip to Akaisha's robe; then, kneeling, he kissed her before going off to help Sil tug a blanket from the clutches of the mud. When it came free, they scraped it as clean as they could and put it on a drag-cradle that was propped up against a ginkgo. They were returning for another when a cry of anguish made them stop and turn. Osidian was standing among women shouting at him in anger.

Carnelian touched Sil's hand. 'I'd better . . .'

'I'll come too,' she said.

Osidian saw them. 'Carnelian, tell these savages I slew him and so he is mine.'

The women caught Carnelian in their crazed stares. Ginkga came to his rescue, ordering the women all back to work, growing angry when they resisted her. 'First let's get things back to normal. After that there'll be plenty of time for retribution.'

As the women moved off they revealed the corpse lying at Osidian's feet. He was not Ochre. He wore a black hunter face and his hands were painted blue.

There was a slap on Carnelian's arm. He whisked round, angry. Seeing it was Ginkga who had struck him, Carnelian let go of his rage and went back to pulling blankets from the mud.

The Tribe assembled at the centre of the camp around the frame Osidian had made from two drag-cradles and from which the corpse hung, naked, dangling its blue hands. A livid cut across its shoulder was pulled open by the weight of its head. The sight of one of their attackers had awoken snarling hatred among the crowd.

Akaisha came to stand beside Osidian and called for silence. Grimly, she counted out for them their losses. Five mothers had had young children carried off. Two women had miscarried. One man had lost his wife; another had spilled his brains into the mud; five had sustained cruel gashes.

A young, pregnant woman spat out a chilling description of what she wanted to do to the body.

Akaisha shook her head. 'Mutilating this dead man will not bring your son back, Ceda.'

'What will then?' the woman cried. She looked around her with narrowed eyes and every man she looked at averted his gaze. She gave a snort as she placed her hands on her swollen belly. 'You're all such men when it comes to making babies, but you'll not bleed to keep them.'

Ravan pushed past Krow to stand beside the corpse. He reached down to lift its hand, then turned the painted palm in all directions. 'Can everyone see the colour?' He dropped the hand with disgust and wiped his fingers down his robe. 'We know his Tribe.'

'The Bluedancing,' cried the crowd.

'Let's take our revenge on them. Let's go and bring our children back.'

Several of the younger men cried out their support.

Ginkga shoved Ravan out of the way and glowered at the Tribe. 'Yes, this bastard is Bluedancing.' She turned to Ravan, contempt on her face. 'Do you know how many men the Bluedancing have, boy?'

Ravan gave a shrug as if he could not care less.

'Well, if you don't know . . .' She pointed at each of the youths who had shouted out support for Ravan. 'Can any of you young fools tell us? No? Well let me tell you. For every one of us, they have two. Heed my words; even were the numbers on our side, fighting would be risky: against such odds, it would be madness.'

Harth came to stand beside her. 'Ginkga speaks the truth. We've lost enough already. We'd lose more in attempting revenge.'

'That's easy for you to say,' a woman cried out. Others joined their voices to hers.

Harth raised her arms, then waited until they fell silent. 'Why is it, you think, the Bluedancing attacked us at all?'

Carnelian felt the blood draining from his face. He put his arm over Poppy to stop her trembling.

'I'm sure it's well known to you by now that, recently, the Master . . .' she looked round at Osidian, 'put some of our lads up to starting a brawl with the Bluedancing in which several of their people were badly hurt and –'

'We didn't start it!' Ravan bellowed as he advanced on the woman.

Harth and the other Elders regarded him with horror.

Akaisha interposed herself between Harth and her son. 'Who do you think you're speaking to?'

Harth stepped out from behind Akaisha. 'If the Bluedancing had seen the Master, they could've betrayed us to the Gatherers, bringing disaster down on the Tribe.'

Ravan grimaced, dropped his head, shaking it as if he was being confronted by an exasperating child. He lifted pleading eyes to his mother. 'It wasn't like that. The Master made certain they could not see him.'

When his mother's frown deepened, he pointed at Harth. 'Can't you see she's lying? It wasn't like that, it –'

Akaisha's slap across his face brought Ravan to a halt, gaping, accompanied by the crowd's catching of breath. Akaisha's voice carried clear and harsh. 'Never again will you *dare* address an Elder in that insolent way.'

Ravan bared his teeth in cold rage. 'Every man here knows the arrogance of the Bluedancing's been swelling with every passing year. Are we to accept that any number of brawls, whoever started them, is justification for killing us and carrying away our children?'

'This was the action of some hotheads,' cried Crowrane. 'It couldn't possibly have been sanctioned by their Elders.'

'What does that matter?' a woman cried out and was answered by a surge of approval.

Carnelian was sharing the general feeling when he felt Osidian speak something in his ear. He turned and looked into his eyes.

'Tell them,' said Osidian in Quya.

Carnelian shook his head. 'I will play no part in your games, Osidian.'

'Then I will use another.'

'What are you saying?' demanded Harth.

Carnelian shook his head. 'I will take no part in this.'

Osidian began to speak in Vulgate. Harth asked her husband to translate. He frowned.

'He said that, even though their numbers are greater than ours, they still feared us enough to attack at night like cowards.'

Harth smiled slyly. 'Does the Master counsel us to make war upon the Bluedancing?'

Osidian narrowed his green eyes as Crowrane told him what his wife had said.

'And who would we put in command of this expedition?' Harth continued as if she were reeling in a fish. She raised her eyebrows waiting for an answer. Osidian seemed not to hear her.

'The Master himself, no doubt?' she said and smiled.

Osidian spoke and Crowrane, scowling, refused to translate. Harth began to look uncertain.

Ravan turned to face the people. 'The Master says that perhaps under his command we might find the manhood we lack.'

The Tribe erupted in outrage. The men, who had been feeling the humiliation, cried out that they had no need of the Master to find courage. They boasted of their bravery in the hunt.

Carnelian saw Harth's horror as she realized she had lost control. The mothers who had lost children and husbands; the men who had lost wives, fired up the anger of the Tribe until there was a universal baying for war. Harth, Akaisha and other women Elders tried to calm them with commands, then appeals, but the crowd's mood overwhelmed their opposition. Shouting against the tumult, Galewing, Crowrane and other Elder men gave their leave for war. Watching in horror, Carnelian froze when he saw the smile Osidian was making no attempt to conceal.

As the Tribe scattered to their preparations, Carnelian approached Osidian.

'Why did you smile?'

The eyes Osidian turned on him were those of a stranger. 'Matters have come to pass according to my will.'

Carnelian went cold. He considered asking Osidian how he had brought this disaster down on them, but knew he would get no answer. 'Why?'

'It is the God's will.'

The cool, indifferent Quya made Carnelian boil. He would tell Akaisha and she would put a stop to Osidian's madness. He looked around him and saw the hollow-eyed determination on every face. Even if Akaisha believed him, would she be able to tell the mothers to forget their lost children?

He felt empty as he regarded Osidian. 'You will at least fight with them?'

'I will lead them to victory.'

'Lead them? Did Ravan not tell you that they rejected you?'

Osidian smiled again. 'They will follow me.'

Carnelian felt tired, not understanding what he meant, not wanting to understand.

'And you, my Lord,' Osidian said. 'Who will you fight with?'

Carnelian clasped his head in exasperation. 'How many sides are there?'

'Either you will choose to stand with me or else number yourself among the savages. Which will it be?'

Carnelian considered whether he might refuse to fight at all. But could he watch Fern and the others march out and remain behind? The waiting would be unbearable. He searched Osidian's eyes for any glimmer of the boy he had loved, but all he saw was a Master.

He shook his head. 'Not with you.'

Osidian turned away.

Carnelian stood there for some moments, considering all the arguments he might make, the appeals, but he knew the Master would never listen and, desolate, he went off to find Fern.

Carnelian wandered sick at heart through the encampment. Fresh edges were being struck on to the flint blades of their spears and javelins. Aquar were having their saddle-chairs adjusted. Unnecessary equipment was being removed. Men were taking turns hornblacking each other's faces.

Carnelian's heart sank when he saw Fern approach with Sil and Poppy. The girl looked like she wanted to run to him, but Sil was holding her hand. Fern offered Carnelian a freshly honed spear.

'Will you fight with us?'

'Do you really want this?' Carnelian said.

Fern looking unhappy, shrugged. 'It's happening. To try to match the Bluedancing's numbers everyone's going: from the eldest to the youngest. We need every warrior we can get. Will you fight with us?'

'Warriors?' Carnelian snorted and when he saw Fern's dismay, he

317

reached out to take the spear. 'Of course I'll fight with you.'

Poppy ran into him. 'You mustn't go, Carnelian. You mustn't.'

He crouched, holding her away from him so he could look into her eyes. 'You wouldn't want Fern to go by himself, would you?'

Poppy looked at Fern and then back at Carnelian. Sil put a hand on Poppy's head. 'They'll take care of each other.'

The girl looked up at Fern. 'You promise?'

'I promise,' said Fern.

As Carnelian rose, Sil looked at him with a question in her eyes. He gave her a nod in answer, then put his hand on Fern's shoulder.

'Come, paint me for war.'

The Ochre warband had a ferocious aspect. Swarthy sinews, midnight faces and, already, something like the joy of battles had come upon them. Seeing them round him laughing, even Carnelian began to believe in the possibility of victory.

'Who can stand against such prowess?' one man cried, and was greeted with much punching of the air.

As they mounted up, Carnelian looked among the women searching for Osidian and was puzzled when he could not see him anywhere. Searching among the warriors, he saw Ravan and Krow. He frowned. It was strange to see them separated from Osidian.

'Our prayers go with you all,' Ginkga cried, making the best of a bad situation.

'Take your strength from the Earth and your courage from the Sky,' cried Harth, looking morose.

Akaisha was trying to conceal her worry. 'May the Mother and the Skyfather bring you back safely.'

Cacophony broke out as women called out their men's love names; mothers the names of their sons; daughters their fathers'. Catching Akaisha's eye, Carnelian gave her a salute and she replied with a curt nod. Sil was there beside her and Poppy. He waved at them and they waved back.

The warband rode out on this swell of anxious love, perhaps two hundred of them, following the trail their enemies had left churned into the mud.

The pace dropped as the camp fell out of sight. Word was passed round that they must conserve the strength of their aquar for the coming battle. Their ardour seemed harder to keep alight once they were all alone cantering across grey desolation. Even the sky seemed to be against them, dashing its downpour mercilessly against their faces as they rode along the muddy trail.

Sharing the increasing feeling of unease, Carnelian looked to the Elders who were riding up ahead. For a while now they had been in discussion amongst themselves, often looking back with anxious faces. At last they broke apart and began falling back, calling a halt. It was Galewing, frowning, who announced that they had chosen Crowrane to be their leader. Loskai looked smug as his father surveyed the warband.

'Organize yourselves according to your hunts.'

As everyone moved their aquar in the direction of their hunt leader, a mêlée ensued in which unease flared to anger and loud recriminations. Shouting commands, the Elders rode round the edges trying to untangle the situation.

Eventually, Carnelian found himself with Fern, Ravan, Krow and the others of his old hunt in a clump in front of Crowrane. Loskai regarded them with satisfaction. One of the youngsters asked if their raid was going to be like hunting and Crowrane slapped him down in a way that only served to betray how thin was his composure.

'What do we do next?' asked Ravan, loudly.

Crowrane fixed him with a scowl. 'We send scouts to locate the enemy.'

All the Elders who had been auxiliaries wanted to go. Confusion reigned once more, until Galewing's hunt was nominated to go scouting. The rest remained behind under Crowrane's authority. With Loskai as his lieutenant, the Elder busied himself making all manner of elaborate arrangements that seemed to serve no purpose but to make them acknowledge he was their commander.

As they waited, they dismounted and walked about. Carnelian surveyed the people round him with foreboding. Even through their warpaint, the youngsters seemed pale and sick. Most of the men were convincing as warriors only when they were conscious they were being looked at. There was nothing to do; nothing to think about except the coming battle.

Carnelian noticed Krow kept scanning the blank horizon. What was Osidian up to? He was amused to see the youngsters drawn to Fern, whose brass collar perhaps lent him a military aura.

When the scouting party was sighted returning, Crowrane gave in to the pleas of the youngsters that the warband should ride to meet them. As they closed on the scouts, whose faces were swathed, Carnelian could tell by the cast of their shoulders that they were not bringing good news.

Galewing pointed over his shoulder. 'They're there,' he said, trying to sound calm. 'They march across the Plain. We can be fairly certain they didn't see us.'

'Let's attack them now,' Ravan declared, causing everyone to look at him.

Crowrane fixed him with baleful eyes. 'You don't know what you're talking about. If we come at them across the open plain they'll have all the time they need to receive our charge. For any chance at victory, we need surprise.'

'This is madness,' cried Kyte. Carnelian could see the way his gaze shifted here and there among the warband as if he were already counting casualties.

'I have to agree with Father Kyte,' said Galewing. 'We don't have the numbers nor the training. We have nothing. We must forget this and return to our people while we still can.'

Ravan rode forward, regarding the Elders with a contemptuous gaze. 'All my life you've claimed to be soldiers, but now I can see you never did anything more than catch thieves in the marketplace or stand guard upon a gate.'

The voices of the Elders rose in protest but Ravan's young voice could still be heard above them. 'We're no less brave, nor less skilled with weapons than the Bluedancing and don't you remember this morning, Father Crowrane, when you declared their raid the work of a few hotheads? If they could do it, so can we.'

'Ravan's right,' a man cried. 'I say we get the bastards. They took my son. How could I face my wife if I don't bring him back?'

Many agreed.

'Could any of us live with the shame of returning without even having tried?' someone said.

'Is this how you all feel?' cried Galewing and was answered by a swell of affirmation. As the hubbub died away, the Elders looked at each other grimly.

'If we go in, it must be at night,' said Crowrane. 'To hide how few we are.'

'How will I find my son in the darkness?'

'We can't hope to find him or any of the captives whether we attack by day or by night. We snatch some of their children and then make a trade,' said Crowrane.

There was a lot of nodding. Carnelian felt a wash of relief that at least they had postponed the terrible moment.

For the rest of that day they rode parallel to the march of the Bluedancing. With each step their aquar took, Carnelian saw their spirits fail a little more. Despair was growing in his stomach. Their proud demeanour had faded. Bedraggled, their warpaint now made them look like the jugglers Carnelian had seen in the marketplace before the gates of Osrakum.

When next they stopped Carnelian approached Fern. 'This delay has turned into a fatal error.'

His friend turned bloodshot eyes on him, grimaced, but said nothing.

Crowrane looked resolute, but his son betrayed him with every doubtful glance he gave him.

The rain continued to lash them. Carnelian felt more than saw the approach of night. As it closed about them it seemed to be their dread. He saw the queasy looks everyone was trying to hide. He yearned then for Osidian's certainty as he tried to dismiss the fear that he and many others might well not live to see another morning.

Carnelian was thankful of the darkness that hid his fear. The night was filled with furtive whispering. The old were remembering their hunts, the good, long years of their lives: the young their sweet-hearts, their mothers, their dreams for the future. When a voice spoke, it seemed very loud. Carnelian felt everyone turning to listen with desperate hope.

'We'd better go now . . . while we still dare.' It was Fern.

'This is a mistake,' said Galewing.

'We go,' rumbled Crowrane.

'Perhaps we should listen to Father Galewing,' said Ravan.

'We must go or return to the Tribe as cowards,' said Fern.

Affecting strength, voices added their agreement and the Elders tried as best they could to marshal the warband. They rode out under a black sky dead of moon or stars. Carnelian let his aquar follow the others as they crept towards where they thought the camp of the Bluedancing lay. Stone spearheads clinked against each other. Leather sighed against aquar hide. The tiny sparks of their enemy's fires came alive in the night and drew them on. Moths to a flame, thought Carnelian.

When they had come close enough to hear the voices of their enemy, it was Fern who stopped them turning back. He gave a battle-cry and sent his aquar careening in a charge. As his voice rode away from them, fear was swept away by shame. They would not allow one of their own to die alone. Carnelian sat startled as he heard their shrieks sweep by on either side. With his heels, he held his aquar where it was and heard their voices thin as they sped away. He was almost unmanned imagining the mayhem lying there waiting for him. Fern's battle-cry sounded again and, cursing, Carnelian coaxed his beast to furious speed desperate to catch him up.

They huddled in the black heart of the night. A gash ached in Carnelian's forearm. A whimpering, wounded boy was trembling against his thigh. The darkness was filled with shaky breathing and moaning. Many must have been wounded. Some had been lost. Voices were whispering names insistently. Someone pushed in beside him.

'Carnie?'

'Fern,' he replied, dazed, glad to his core to have him near.

'Are you bleeding?'

Carnelian fumbled and grabbed his friend's trembling arm. The solid feel of it opened a way for his voice. 'The whirling.'

'It was my first battle too.'

'It's like the darkest dream. I felt the soft give of flesh, the screaming . . . Oh, dear mother, the screaming.'

They crushed into each other. A shadow loomed beside them.

'It will pass,' said Galewing in a strange remote voice. 'It's always hard to kill a man, even if he's your enemy.'

'Were we victorious?' a childish voice asked suddenly.

It was Galewing who answered: 'We were routed. They were ready for us. They were too many.'

'Even the Skyfather fought against us,' someone said, his tone incredulous, recalling the rain that had flung its needles at their faces.

'Are we safe now?' pleaded a boy.

Over Fern's shoulder Carnelian scanned the darkness for their enemy.

'They'll begin their hunt for us with the morning light,' said Galewing.

'We must flee,' said Loskai.

'We can't.' It was Ravan. 'Too many of us are wounded. We've lost too many aquar. Even if some of us escaped, do you think they'd be enough to defend the Tribe against the revenge of the Bluedancing? We must wait here until dawn.'

Groans were the only answer.

'No, it's best we wait,' said Ravan, insistently. 'If we can get some sleep then at least we might be able to sell our lives dearly.'

'They might spare us,' said Crowrane.

'Would you beg them for mercy? Would we have given any if our situations were reversed?'

Fern disengaged himself gently from Carnelian. 'They'll show mercy, Ravan. We're all Plainsmen. No tribe has ever destroyed another.'

'Go and tell that to the hearthkin of those we killed and maimed,' said Ravan. 'They'll show no mercy. We must make an end of it here. At least the sons and daughters of the Tribe might live. The Bluedancing might adopt them to swell their strength. The most we can do is to make sure our people don't remember us with shame.'

Sobbing broke out here and there. Carnelian despaired for Poppy. She had lost so much already. At that moment something like the moon came out from the clouds and, drifting towards them, resolved into a ghostly face.

Carnelian felt a violent shudder against his leg.

'The Master,' gasped several voices.

Carnelian saw it was Osidian who stood before them, personifying the darkness. He spoke.

'In my right hand I hold defeat: in my left, victory. Which will you have me open?'

As Ravan translated Osidian's words, even through his relief, Carnelian was overwhelmed by a sickening foreboding, for the Wise taught that the left was the hand of darkness.

THE BLUEDANCING

The most elegant system of domination is one in which the dominated are unaware of their state: they believe the world has always been and always will be as they know it; that the order under which they toil is as immutable, as unassailable as the sky.

War is a clumsy means of enforcing such dominion. Not only is it costly and wasteful of resources, but it is difficult to control and subject to catastrophic and unforeseeable changes of fortune.

Famine is a surer tool of statecraft, with the crucial proviso that it must be seen to arise naturally from the land. Hunger will keep not only the body, but the mind in chains.

(from a treatise on statecraft compiled in beadcord by the Wise of the Domain Lands)

AT FIRST LIGHT, OSIDIAN LED THEM TO THE EDGE OF A LAGOON. HE spent time surveying the ground and eventually settled them on a ridge on the shore. After a brief conference with Carnelian, he rode out across the dried-up bed with the better half of the warband: he had chosen only the unwounded and, of those, predominantly the young. Ravan went as interpreter. Galewing had volunteered to go to represent the Elders. Krow had chosen to stay behind. That Osidian had not objected to this made Carnelian suspicious that the youth had been left as a spy.

Standing on the shore with the rain flying in his face, Carnelian watched the riders fade into the grey south among gentle hills that would soon become islands. He had been left with clear instructions, delivered by Osidian as if they were strangers. By using Quya,

Osidian had ensured that only Carnelian could be aware of his plan. Carnelian had had to obey him. If he had refused to command the men left behind, Osidian had said he would abandon them all to the revenge of the Bluedancing.

Carnelian could feel his men staring at his back. He leaned close to Fern. 'Will you be my second?'

Fern grimaced. 'The Elders will like taking orders from me even less than from you.'

Carnelian yearned to rid himself of the burden of command. He forced himself to look round. The Ochre remaining were massed on the ridge, sunk into their saddle-chairs, miserable in the downpour, many wounded, all disheartened, every one of them older than him. Their eyes accused him.

Carnelian turned back. 'If that's how they feel, then they shouldn't have agreed to follow the Master in the first place.'

'What options did we have?' said Fern.

'Do you believe I'm less trapped than you?'

'Have you more experience of war than the veterans?'

'You know perfectly well I don't, though I'd question how much experience they have of fighting on foot.'

Fern had no answer to that. He smiled winningly. 'Things are as they are, Carnie, but you know you can count on me.'

Carnelian had them all dismount. The kneeling aquar were hobbled to ensure they could not wander away. He oversaw the removal of their saddle-chairs. The Plainsmen looked at him as if he were mad when he asked them to pile the chairs in a heap. Discontent turned to outrage when he told them to set the heap alight.

'Do you want to bring the Bluedancing down on us?' said Crowrane.

'That's exactly what I want.'

Carnelian's answer produced incredulous consternation.

'All of them?' said Loskai, scowling.

'If we're on foot, they'll ride us down,' said Crowrane.

'That's what the Master hopes they'll think. You saw how carefully he chose this site? He knows what he's doing.'

Krow was nodding.

'How do you imagine we're going to be able to ride home without our saddle-chairs?' demanded Kyte.

'Let's worry about that when we're victorious,' said Carnelian.

The Plainsmen fell silent as the desperate reality of the situation soaked into them.

'The moment they see us, the Bluedancing will know only half of us are here,' said Fern.

Carnelian was relieved that they were beginning to move along the path of argument Osidian had predicted. 'Knowing that, what do you think the Bluedancing will imagine is the reason we're making all this smoke?'

He was answered with many frowns.

Understanding came over Fern's face. 'A signal. They can't know how many of us attacked them last night. They'll assume we're signalling the Tribe to send the rest of our men.'

Fern looked out across the lagoon bed in the direction Osidian had ridden. 'The Master will come at them from an unexpected direction.'

As Carnelian gave a nod, he saw a tinge of confidence dawning in the faces around him.

Loskai, alone, retained his scowl. 'How can we hope to stand for long enough against four times our strength?'

Carnelian had been primed to answer that too. 'How do the earthers fend off raveners?'

Carnelian formed them up in ranks along the ridge in a dense formation they all understood was an imitation of an earther hornwall. He distributed the veterans along the front and put himself at the extreme right with Fern at his side. Each man was armed with a spear and a shield improvised from the wicker backs of the saddle-chairs. Looking down the line, Carnelian almost winced at how flimsy their hornwall looked. He caught one of the men looking at him, eyes red from fear and lack of sleep, and forced fierce resolve into his face.

He squatted down on his haunches, calling out, 'We might as well relax while we wait.' The movement rippled all the way down the line.

'Does anyone know a good song?' Carnelian asked. It was Krow who began a ballad which told of the love between the Earth and Sky. Raggedly others began joining in. The smoke from the saddle-chair pyre was being driven back over the aquar that lay like a field of boulders protecting their backs. Carnelian felt the flanks of the hornwall were too exposed and curved them back a little. He went over and over in his mind how Osidian had said the battle would go. His wounded forearm itched. He gazed out over the lagoon, squinting through another volley of rain, his heart racing every time he thought he saw the Bluedancing.

Carnelian was the first to spot them marching across the lagoon bed. He rose on to shaky legs and the rest of his men followed his lead. The Bluedancing were advancing towards them in a rabble.

'They can't have seen us yet,' Fern said in a low voice, as if he feared they might hear him.

Carnelian nodded, wishing the rain was not slanting into his eyes. He turned to survey his men and his heart faltered, seeing how few they were. He forced a grin.

'The Tribe will sing with pride of this day.'

Some answered him with watery smiles, others stared unblinking at the approaching enemy.

Faint cries confirmed the Bluedancing had seen them. Their front widened, then broke into a charge.

'Make ready!' Carnelian cried.

They locked their makeshift shields together as best they could and thrust their spears over the top, holding them in their fists, leaning their hafts on their shoulders as Carnelian had shown them. The spear points made their front a hedge of thorns, but Carnelian still felt desperately exposed on his unshielded right.

As the Bluedancing crashed towards them, Carnelian scoured the vast grey spaces of the plain but Osidian was nowhere to be seen. Fear of abandonment and death rose up into his throat. He slowed his breath, focused his mind on the play of rain on his skin. His was the command; his the heart that must strengthen them. He denied his fear its hold on him, then reached round to take Fern's shoulder.

'The Master will not fail us,' he said. 'Pass it on.'

Fern smiled grimly and sent the message along the hornwall. Carnelian saw how they gripped their spears more tightly. He locked eyes with Fern and they smiled fiercely at each other. When Carnelian looked out across the lagoon bed he saw rolling towards them a storm of threshing mud that far out-flanked their hornwall on either side. The blackened faces of the Bluedancing were holed by the red of their screaming mouths. Their hair flickered black haloes round their heads. Their ululating warcries were swelling louder. The percussion of clawed aquar feet set the ground trembling, flinging earth up in all directions.

Around Carnelian the spear hedge bristled. The odour of their attackers washed over him. He felt more than saw the hornwall around him softening. He felt the Ochre on the verge of running from the screaming tidal wave rushing at them.

'Steady,' cried Carnelian in a long-drawn-out tone. Then, almost as if he had commanded it, the charge broke before them. Osidian had seen that there marshy ground formed a trough along the shore. Aquar screamed as their legs buckled and they tumbled forward. The whole front shivered and broke and his vision was filled with the twisting necks of aquar, eye-quills flaring like hands to stop their fall, the looks of dismay as their riders were sucked down into the collapse. In front of Carnelian, an aquar twisted, falling before the feet of another who tried to leap it, failed, and the two became entangled, rolling in a turmoil of thrashing legs, saurian screeching and then the death cries of their riders as they were folded into the mangling, threshing mass.

Some of the riders made it through the soft ground to crash their aquar into the Ochre's wavering front. The spears of the hornwall impaled one beast: others waded in, snake necks writhing with splayed plumes. The air was filled with a splintering of spears. In a nest of these a blue-painted man fallen from his saddle-chair was thrashing around him with a stone axe, but was quickly cut down by a dozen, fevered blows. Another man was hurled forward as his aquar fell. He struck the shieldwall like a boulder, rolling right through their ranks where he was set upon and butchered.

Carnelian bellowed at his men that they must heal the breaches in the hornwall. In the corner of his eye he was aware of Bluedancing rising from the wreckage of their charge. They threw back their hair and snarled. Still they far out-numbered the Ochre. Avoiding the death-kicks of the aquar, they came on at a lope in twos and threes. Some who had lost their weapons tore shards of splintered wood from the saddle-chairs that were sinking into the soft mud. Those who had to clamber over the debris to get at the Ochre hissed curdling promises of what they would do when they reached them. They fell upon the hornwall clawing, shrieking, tearing at the wicker with bladed stone, with their hands. One man came at Carnelian from his exposed side so that he was forced to abandon his spear. The man swung a blade that Carnelian heard singing through the air. Though he ducked, it still scraped along his skull. He swung his own axe up and buried it beneath the man's ribs. Frantic, he worked it free, aware more Bluedancing were pushing into the hedge, heaving against the wicker shieldwall seemingly oblivious to the spears snapping off in their flesh. Blood arced through the air. Enraged Bluedancing chopped at them like demons.

Pulling the encumbrance of his torn uba from his head, Carnelian tried to order his men back, to reform their line, but the hornwall had dissolved into a confused mêlée. Two blackened faces close enough for him to see the veins in their eyes that gaped at him in frozen disbelief. He swung his axe. Blood seemed to be thickening the air so that, as hard as he pushed, his blade took time to reach them. He watched its scalloped edge puncturing blacked skin scarlet. Teeth and foaming gore. Carnelian poured his strength into the killing, ploughing through the thicket of their flesh. Each impact sent a slow judder up his arms. He felt a cut opening his face; a remote bruising impact to his shoulder. He clubbed a man from his path and saw more of them leaping towards him through the carnage of their beasts. Counting them, Carnelian began turning his head, despair rising in him like vomit. His voice erupted even as his people slid into sight. He saw them set upon, harried, too far away for him to help. Other cries were rising above the din of chopping. He could not understand the expression of surprise in the faces he knew. Slow, drawn-out battle-cries were rising from behind their enemies. They faltered. Recognizing the voices as Ochre, new vigour shot from Carnelian's heart down his arms. He could sense the enemy tide turning. Aquar were coming up behind them. He glimpsed the fierce black faces of their rescuers. The Bluedancing were turning away, their faces flaccid with dismay. He saw several collapse under a succession of blows. Some were in full flight. Their backs drew Carnelian on with a lust for slaughter. He surged forward snarling in pursuit. He was in a forest of wounded aquar and shattered saddle-chairs. The earth was trying to suck him down. Through a red haze a man fleeing drew him on. He ducked under a swinging huge clawed foot. First his victim, then Carnelian, reached more solid ground. Carnelian careened in pursuit. Judged the distance. Raked his axe blade down the length of the man's back. The body fell forward vomiting blood. Carnelian slipped on gore. Regaining his footing, he came to a halt, swaying, his mind seeping free of fury. Panting rasped his throat. The axe felt suddenly unbearably heavy in his hand so he let it go.

'They . . . will . . . escape . . . us,' he said, between breaths as he watched the Bluedancing streaming away.

'No they won't,' said a voice nearby.

Carnelian turned, beginning to feel the pain of his wounds. It was Fern, heavily lifting his arm to point. Carnelian followed the finger. At first he could not understand what he saw. A rushing, dark, many-legged mass. Then he saw the huge figure at its apex and heard a cold voice raised in a Quyan paean. It was Osidian, bearing down upon the luckless, routing Bluedancing.

Carnelian and Fern approached the mob of Ochre cavorting around Galewing and Osidian. Ravan detached himself from the others and threw himself on Fern, hugging him hard. Fern pushed his brother away, holding him at arm's length to see his face; a laughing mask of sweat and gore.

'It's unbelievable,' the youth said. He spun round, hanging on his brother's arm. 'Just look at what we've done . . .'

Seeing the carnage, Carnelian was back on the ship that had brought him to the Three Lands, reliving the massacre he had caused when its crew had seen his face unmasked. Nausea gripped him, forcing him to double up while, all the time, Ravan kept pouring out his gloating chatter. Amid the universal glowing mood of celebration, others interjected details of the fighting, laughter, jests.

Coming up for air, Carnelian saw Fern surveying the field upon which the Bluedancing had been turned into so much butchered meat and was relieved to see his friend sickened by what he saw. Krow crouched, vomiting. Carnelian realized how similar this looked to the massacre of the Twostone.

Osidian towered severe among the youths, each vying with the others for the privilege of his attention, but he seemed unaware of them. His gaze was gliding across the dead as if he could not believe they were real.

Carnelian walked towards him and the youths made way as they might have done for Osidian himself.

'You knew this would happen,' Carnelian said in Quya.

Osidian's eyes had lost their over-bright look. He shook his head slowly, narrowing his eyes as he gazed out.

'You are in error, Carnelian, I did not know.'

Carnelian became aware Ravan and others were as keenly watching their exchange. Carnelian sensed Ravan's resentment, but chose to ignore it. He felt compelled to address Osidian in Quya, even though it was turning all those around them into barbarians.

'But you promised it when you left us there.'

As Carnelian lifted his arm to point he became aware of the blood staining it to the elbow. His mind was drawn back to the slow dance of the battle. He saw past the vision to the marshy ground littered with the broken remnants of men and aquar; spears and saddlechairs. The men of the hornwall were slogging towards them. With some effort, Carnelian wrenched his gaze back to Osidian's serene face.

'You promised us this . . . this victory,' he said, spitting out that last word because it felt filthy in his mouth.

Osidian turned his green eyes on him. 'I would have promised anything, anything at all for this chance. The dead would not have reproached me in defeat.'

'Chance? What do you *mean*, chance?'

Osidian turned away, seemingly distracted by the moaning of the dying. An aquar that had been felled lay intermittently screeching, its tail lifting then subsiding, its taloned foot feebly gouging the bloody mud. The youths' excited chatter seemed to be mocking the poor creature's attempts to rise. Then they quietened. Following their gaze, he saw the Elders approaching, faces sagging with age.

Ravan stepped up to welcome them. 'My fathers, is this not a vast victory the Master has given us?'

Kyte surveyed the carnage. 'Yes, vast.'

Fern's eyes were welling tears. He grew suddenly enraged. 'What are you all doing behaving as if this were a wedding?'

Then everyone saw Crowrane, bowed, the body of his son in his arms. A silence fell which allowed them to hear the dying.

'Are you all deaf?' Kyte demanded. He seemed to have become ancient since the morning. His hand shook out. 'Go finish what you've begun.'

Sullenly, in ones and twos, taking their flint axes, the Plainsmen wound off across the battlefield.

Tears were rewetting the blood on Kyte's face as he watched them. 'This is an abomination.'

'What?' shouted Ravan. 'Haven't we been delivered from destruction? Wouldn't this have been our own fate if the Master hadn't saved us?'

Fern regarded his brother with horror. Kyte wiped away tears and regarded Ravan with unconcealed wrath. 'Can't you see, boy, all the men of the Bluedancing lying as carrion at your feet?'

'What of it?' said Ravan, face reddening.

' "What of it?" ' echoed Kyte. He looked up blinking at the sky. His bloodshot eyes fell on Ravan. 'Who'll protect the hearths of the Bluedancing? Who'll hunt for their mothers and their children now their strength lies here rotting on this ground?'

Ravan's mouth hung open but he did not seem to have anything to say.

'Well, thank the Skyfather you've run dry at last,' said Fern and was rewarded with a look of hatred.

'What did the old man say?' Osidian asked Ravan.

The youth regained something of his composure as he translated Kyte's words into Vulgate.

'I regret this but we clearly had no choice,' said Osidian. 'Is it certain the Bluedancing are finished?'

Galewing nodded. 'They are no more.'

'Then we must do what we can to save what is left.'

The old men focused narrowed eyes on Osidian.

'You could take their children into the Ochre to swell your strength.'

The old gave wary nods: the youths standing round looked uncertain.

'Their salt shall swell the wealth of the Ochre.'

This the Elders listened to more attentively.

'They'll have a good quantity of it, sure enough,' said Galewing. He looked over to where their men were moving, silencing the dying with blows.

Osidian addressed his next comment to everyone. 'We can send those of them already marked for the tithe to the Mountain in place of your own children.'

Carnelian watched the look of disbelief turn on many faces to hope. Shocked, he contemplated the joy of keeping Poppy from the Masters.

'But what about their women?' asked Galewing.

Osidian shrugged and then looked the Elder in the eye.

'Either we let them die or else you might welcome them into the Ochre . . . as servants.'

The old men considered this. 'As servants . . .' they muttered, uncertainly.

They fished the Ochre dead from the carnage on the ridge. They salvaged saddle-chairs to replace the ones they had burned and improvised drag-cradles to carry the casualties.

'We must do something about all these bodies,' said Galewing in Vulgate, watching his people move among the corpses despoiling them of salt.

'Look around you,' Osidian said, sweeping his arm round. Sitting in his saddle-chair, he towered over the Elder. 'How shall we give them to the sky? See how numerous they are. It's impossible to take them with us. Would you leave a contingent of our strength here to keep away the scavengers? Consider that the Ochre are wholly unprotected.'

Galewing looked up sad, fearful. 'Then we've not only destroyed their tribe but we also damned the souls of all their men to live as raveners.'

Krow looked ill. Ravan was gazing uneasily over the battlefield, but then burned doubt away with anger. 'It's what they deserve. Rather them than us.'

Binding up Carnelian's wounds, Fern made no attempt to hide his contempt for his brother. Unabashed, Ravan strode to his aquar and when he was mounted, said, 'Let's go and save their women and children.'

Riding over a ridge, they saw an encampment spread on the plain.

'So many,' someone exclaimed.

'Even without their men they would still outnumber the Tribe,' said Fern.

'How can we hope to feed them all?' said Galewing.

'If you set them to work in the ditches you will be free to hunt more,' said Osidian. 'In time you can use their labour to extend the Koppie.'

As they rode closer, Carnelian saw the Bluedancing had formed their drag-cradles into a barricade behind which they stood waiting. Osidian brought the warband to a halt when the women's faces could clearly be seen peering out from under their head-blankets.

A shrill voice cried out a challenge.

'What?' Carnelian asked Fern.

'I'm not sure,' his friend replied. 'Something about their men. By the tone of her voice, a warning.'

'They don't know what's happened.'

Fern looked morose. 'I think it more likely they're clinging to the hope we've got here by somehow eluding their men.'

'I wouldn't like to be the one who has to tell them,' said Krow. His statement was greeted by a murmur of agreement.

The Elders talked quickly among themselves. Kyte called over to Crowrane, who sat hunched in his saddle-chair, but the old man showed no sign of having heard. He had been like that since the battle and the death of his son.

Galewing forced a decision. 'We'll go down and talk to them.'

Osidian interrupted Ravan as he began to translate. 'I understood.'

They watched the Elders and the men who had lost children to the Bluedancing ride down towards the barricade. What if the women became violent? Carnelian did not doubt Osidian would be prepared to attack them.

The Elders were dismounting. They addressed the women over the meshed drag-cradles. Kyte made a speech. His head dropped before he was finished. A wave of consternation moved round the circle of the defenders. They began detaching themselves from their defensive ring and running towards where Kyte was speaking. His posture betrayed his shame, as he turned to point up the slope. Wailing wafted on the wind. The Elders fell into a long discussion with them.

'Father above, what can they be finding to talk about?' said Ravan.

Osidian made him fall silent with a look. 'Everything depends on how much they love their children.'

Carnelian's heart was down there with the Bluedancing women. He watched the Elders remount and ride back.

'They'll agree to come with us for the sake of their children,' Galewing cried out while he was still some distance away. 'But they demand that they be allowed to collect the bodies of their men for proper burial.'

Osidian waited until the Elders had reached him before he spoke. 'We can't allow this.'

'Why not?' Kyte asked.

Osidian raised an eyebrow. 'If you insist, I shall point out the obvious. Firstly, it would delay our return to the Tribe. They'll already be worrying about us and, besides, the longer we remain out here the greater the danger to us all from raveners. Secondly, this would mean we have to take those bodies back to the Koppie. Can you imagine the Ochre welcoming so many dead? Not to mention the sheer labour of it. Thirdly and, perhaps, most importantly, how do you think those women down there will feel towards the Ochre when they see all their men dead? You can see how numerous they are. How could we hope to control them in their grief?'

Kyte frowned and glanced back at the barricade in misery. He shook his head. 'Perhaps we should just let them die.'

'If that's your wish,' said Osidian.

The old men returned to the barricade, round-shouldered. When they gave out their decision, the wailing grew so that even at that distance, Carnelian felt harrowed. The children stolen from the Ochre were being given back. The women untangled their drag-cradles and began to load them up.

The Elders returned wan and tearful. 'We should help them.'

Osidian shook his head. 'In their midst we'd only give their grief a focus for revenge.'

So it was the Ochre sat and watched until at last a mass of the Bluedancing came up the slope towards them, a great march of aquar pulling drag-cradles. Looking among them Carnelian could see the dejected faces of the women, their snotty children, but it was to the people leading them that his eyes were drawn: old women, their grey hair jewelled with salt, their eyes brighter still with hatred and a staring disbelief.

Uncertain, the Tribe watched their men approach followed by the mass of the Bluedancing. The returning men and their women gazed at each other over the divide and Carnelian could feel the yearning drawing them together. The pull of it was stronger than their wariness at the crowd of strangers. The riders accelerated into a wild rush and the women came streaming out to meet them. Carnelian found himself left behind with Osidian and the Elders; the dead and wounded. The aquar slowed, then intermingled with the advancing women. Men were slipping down from their saddle-chairs into the continuous turmoiled mass in which everyone was shouting, hugging, kissing. It was through this the women Elders came riding with Harth and Akaisha at their head.

Carnelian smiled at Akaisha but her eyes were fixed on the people and drag-cradles coming up behind them.

'The Bluedancing,' announced Galewing.

'All their women. All their children,' said Kyte.

Harth frowned. 'What are they doing here?'

'It'll take some time to explain,' said Galewing.

Ravan's aquar advanced. He grinned. 'We won a great victory and killed all their men.'

'All?' Akaisha gasped, in horror.

'Did anyone tell you, child, that you could speak?' said Harth, severely.

Ravan recoiled as if she had slapped him. He opened his mouth to say something, but a sharp look from his mother made him shut it again. He focused on his knees, struggling to contain his anger.

Harth turned her glare on the Elder men. 'What is this you've allowed to happen?'

'The boy spoke out of turn, Harth, but he spoke truth,' said Kyte. 'We snatched victory from a dangerous defeat.'

'You mean the Master did!' erupted Ravan, before he rode off towards the Ochre crowd.

Harth gave Akaisha a glance of approbation and then her eyes fell on the Elder men. 'Did we suffer loss?'

Her face paled as she saw none were prepared to meet her gaze. She noticed Crowrane, head bowed. 'Husband?' She rode towards him, spoke again but still he did not respond. She noticed the drag-cradle hanging behind his aquar. She dismounted and, seeming infinitely old, walked round to find her son lying dead in it.

'How many dead?' asked Ginkga, tearful as she watched Harth collapse to her knees beside her son.

Nervously, Kyte gave a full account of their casualties.

Akaisha indicated the Bluedancing. 'And why are they here?'

'We couldn't very well leave them to die,' said Galewing.

'Which they would do without their men,' added Kyte.

Akaisha looked severe. 'We don't need lessons in husbandry from you, though perhaps you could tell us how we're going to manage to feed them all?'

'If you set them to work in the ditches we will be free to hunt more,' said Galewing.

'We can use their labour to extend the Koppie,' added Kyte and it seemed to Carnelian that Osidian was speaking through their mouths.

The Elder women greeted these suggestions with a thorny silence.

'We have back the children they stole from us,' said Kyte.

The women nodded. Ginkga shook her head. 'Was this worth the spilling of so much blood?'

Galewing glanced at Osidian. 'The Master has suggested we could send their tithe children to the Mountain in place of our own.'

The women started in amazement. Ginkga was the first to recover her composure.

'There is something shameful in this.'

Akaisha's face showed she believed she was speaking not only for herself but for many of the others when she said: 'But there is also hope.'

In the days that followed, the Tribe plodded on through the mud and storms drawn by the yearning to be home. The Bluedancing slogged on behind like the Tribe's grim shadow. Gradually, people were becoming accustomed to them being there. News had spread like fire of the plan to save their children. Carnelian sensed many could not help seeing this as a gift the Master had given them beyond even the victory that had brought most of their men back safely from the battle. Like him, others were drawing reassurance from glancing back at the treasure of these foreign children. Unease increased when the Tribe began to grow familiar with them. People told each other that the Bluedancing children were bound to suffer from the same fatal arrogance as their fathers. Ochre youngsters began to be forbidden to play with the Bluedancing. It was said that their marked children would have gone to the Mountain anyway; that they deserved to go. The list of claims and accusations grew until the rainy wind had washed away the stain of guilt from the faces and hearts of the Tribe.

In the lull before the dawn, Carnelian was woken by whimpering. He rose, knowing it was Poppy. Sil had told him that, since the night of the Bluedancing raid, the girl had been suffering from nightmares of which she would not speak. Carnelian rose and woke her. Poppy flung herself on him. He thought her shaking a result of her being cold and drew her into his blanket. There was light enough to see her staring blindly. When he asked her gently what she was seeing, it all came pouring out.

The black demons had attacked as her tribe returned, joyous to be home. Her mother had managed to reach the ditch carrying Poppy. They had tumbled into the outer ditch and managed to find a hiding place. Morning revealed her mother dead. Then Poppy's tale grew garbled. Carnelian gleaned that she had hidden in the ditches from the demons who were haunting her koppie. At night she would creep out to dig up fernroot which she ate raw. She drank from pools deep in the ditches. When she had heard the Ochre tributaries calling she had thought it a trap but had eventually come out. They had allowed her to return to her mother tree.

Poppy looked up into his eyes. 'Is it true I'm no longer going to the Mountain?'

Carnelian suppressed his foreboding at what the price might be for her salvation and nodded. She buried her face in his chest and began sobbing. Her grief did not open to anything he said. He grew desperate, not knowing what she was feeling. At last she calmed down enough to say: 'She's dead. I killed her.'

'Who?'

'My seed.'

Carnelian sagged with relief. She watched him fumble in his robe. When he pulled his hand out he opened it to reveal the seed and was rewarded by wide-eyed wonder and delight.

When the familiar shape of the Koppie was spied against the stormy sky, the Tribe wept tears of joy and, imagining themselves already sitting under their trees, felt suddenly exhausted. They struggled on, cursing every step, urging each other to ever greater speed with promises of the homely comforts of their hearths.

When they were close enough, their march dissolved into a furious dash to see who would be first to reach the outer Lagoonbridge. Carnelian's heart was pounding. He too was desperate to be safe within the rings of the Koppie's ditches. He almost gave way to the eagerness he could feel his aquar had to join the race, but then he saw sullen Ravan, nervous Krow, and between them Osidian, his ivory face indifferent to the Tribe's excitement. This Masterly serenity disturbed Carnelian and forced him to remember the Bluedancing. Craning round, he saw them stretching away so far behind they seemed to be a frayed hem to the stormclouds. They showed no joy but only a sad weariness. For them there would never again be a homecoming.

The Koppie's welcome was everything Carnelian had hoped for. That first night, the Tribe held a solemn feast of thanksgiving for their safe return; for the Father's rain that they prayed would renew the Earth and bring healthy children and easy births. Loskai and the other men who had fallen in the battle were given sky-burial. The Bluedancing killed by Osidian in the raid was to work out his debt to the Tribe as a huskman. Whin and her husband, Ravenseye, among others, were elevated to the Elders.

The hearth had returned to find every branch of Akaisha's mother tree edged with new jade growth and the rootearth beneath littered with her seeds, many of which had germinated. Both seeds and seedlings were lovingly plucked and buried deep among their mother's roots. Now that Poppy had been reprieved, Carnelian asked Akaisha if she might be allowed to plant her seed. Tenderly, Akaisha had told him it was already too late that year but that she would talk to the other Elders and see if it might be allowed before they set off on their next migration.

Rain continued to fall in heavy, but intermittent showers. Sometimes, the clouds would tease apart revealing sky that was the purest blue. The red earth responded by uncurling fresh fronds into the humid warming days and, as if this were a sign, the women of the Tribe seemed to give birth all at once. Soon the sun was reigning over a world so green it hurt Carnelian's eyes. Ambling, the saurian giants returned, their herds stretching along the horizon.

Carnelian slipped back naturally into the rhythms of koppie life. It was better this time, because Fern no longer had to work beneath the Bloodwood Tree. He became the companion Osidian had long ceased to be. The Elders and others muttered against the Master when he made himself a hearth under one of the unclaimed cedars that buttressed the Homeditch, though none opposed him openly. Ravan, Krow and many other youths joined him there and each day he would lead them to fetch water. To meet the needs of the Koppie, almost three times as many men and aquar were needed now. Ravan relayed Osidian's wishes to the men and they obeyed willingly. Since the battle, many would follow no other.

Each day when they set off they would ride down the leafy avenue past the encampment of the Bluedancing which lay between the Homeditch and the Outditch. The ferngarden had become a village from which smoke was always rising. The Bluedancing were brought water and what food the Tribe did not need. In return, the women and children replaced the men at the ditches, labouring in the mud to shore them up where the Rains had brought collapse. There were so many new workers that even the Ochre women began to free themselves from this heavy work. They told themselves it was necessary, because the men had to hunt more often and the women to gather more fernroot to maintain an adequate food supply.

Eventually, the only Ochre remaining at the earthworkings were those who acted as overseers.

One evening, as they sat around the hearth, the discussion turned, as it often did, to the subject of the Bluedancing.

'There're so many of them,' Sil complained.

'And their settlement has devastated a large part of the Southgarden,' said Whin, who still looked strange with salt beads in her hair.

'With all their extra aquar, I can see we won't make the end of the season before we'll be forced to take them out of the Koppie to graze.'

There was much grumbling at this suggestion.

'The Bluedancing eat so much.'

'And at the moment they're supplementing what we give them with the djada they've saved from their migration. What'll happen when that runs out? How much hunting will we have to do?'

People hung their heads, worrying about it.

Sil looked at Akaisha and Whin. 'If we don't feed them they might rise against us.'

Several of the men snorted their derision at this suggestion. 'What threat are women and children?'

'My daughter's right, they outnumber us,' said Whin.

'Even without their men,' Sil added.

'And you're not always here,' Whin said to the men.

Fern looked grave. 'And we're going to be out hunting, perhaps further afield than we're used to.'

'Couldn't we send them back to their own koppie?' said Koney.

Akaisha shook her head. 'Without men to hunt for them, we'd be condemning them to death. If our situations were reversed, would you want to be thrown out on to the plain with your children?'

Nursing her newborn, Koney shook her head. 'No, my mother.'

Whin frowned. 'Our compassion might yet bring us disaster.'

'Perhaps we should consider using their labour to extend the Koppie, as the Master has said.' Ravan had come visiting as he sometimes did. People no longer felt him part of their hearth.

'The Elders don't need the Master to work that out for them,' said Akaisha without looking at him. 'The area of new land we would have to enclose would have to be enormous to solve the problem of grazing the aquar as well as to bring enough fernroot into safe gathering to feed us all.'

'Then we must hunt more,' said Fern.

'We already hunt more,' said Akaisha. 'And though we're hunting enough to feed everyone, not enough's left over to make djada for the next migration.'

Everyone looked grimly into the fire. They looked up as Ravan stood to speak.

'The Master sent me to tell you he's devised a way in which more than enough food can be provided for everyone.'

Ravan stopped to take pleasure in their rapt attention.

'Tell us then,' snapped Whin.

Ravan shook his head. 'He's not yet sure, my mother; he's not fully worked it out, but it would necessitate all the Tribe working together under his direction.'

'Would it indeed,' said Whin angrily, but Carnelian could see, though she tried to hide it, how attentively Akaisha was listening to her son.

'When will he be ready to reveal to us this plan?'

'It'll be ready when the Elders give him the authority to put it into action.'

Though Akaisha and Whin frowned, Carnelian saw they were considering it and only then did he fully appreciate how desperate the situation had become.

One day, Carnelian and Fern were fetching water with Osidian and his hunt along the margin of the bellower lagoon. Flamingos in fiery clouds had just touched down and their chatter and busy sculling were rippling both air and water.

Carnelian was watching fish darting. 'It's a miracle,' he announced. 'They have sprung up from what was dust.'

'Mother Earth is bountiful,' said Fern, then smiled, 'just after the Skyfather's made love to her.'

Their musings were disturbed by a call from Krow. They saw an aquar speeding towards them.

'News from the Koppie?' said Fern and everyone frowned expecting the worst.

The aquar skidded to a halt. 'The Elders command that the two Standing Dead should appear before them.'

As Ravan translated, Carnelian glanced at Osidian, expecting defiance but saw only a mild, even contented, acquiescence.

'We'll ride back with you,' he said, then turned to Ravan. 'You will come with us.'

'I'll come too,' said Fern.

'You will remain here,' Osidian said, severely.

Fern looked to Carnelian, but he was seeing how much his friend's defiance had angered the other men. Fearing what might happen should he support him against the Master, Carnelian decided to say nothing and, angry, Fern backed down.

Osidian was smiling coldly as he gave Krow command of the hunt. The youth looked at Fern as if he were measuring him up. Riding away, Carnelian worried that he had made a mistake in leaving Fern behind at the mercy of Osidian's followers.

THE GREAT HUNT

Forgive our need, little sister
Receive the salt from our tears
Know that we are grateful for the gift you give us of yourself
Know that we have gloried in your beauty and your strength
Return to sleep in the earth, the mother of all
Until the Skyfather comes to make you rise again
In the uncurling of unending time

(Plainsmen hymn of thanks sung over creatures they have killed)

CARNELIAN FOLLOWED OSIDIAN AND RAVAN INTO THE ANCESTOR HOUSE. In the gloom, he could only just make out the Elders there waiting for them. It felt very different from the first time he had appeared before them: many were known to him now.

'We've brought you here so we might consider the freedoms which you currently enjoy within the Tribe,' said Kyte, in Vulgate.

Osidian smiled. 'I had imagined you were going to beg me to save you from famine.'

Ravan hesitated, then translated Osidian's words for the Assembly.

Harth rose to her feet, eyes flaming. 'The famine you've brought upon us.'

As some of the Elders berated her, Osidian bent to hear Ravan's translation of her words. He gave an elegant shrug. 'Can you deny the benefits the Bluedancing have brought you?'

Ravan translated. Harth ignored him and addressed the Assembly. 'We must sort this out amongst ourselves.'

'What would you have us do, Harth?' someone said.

'Let's be rid of the Bluedancing.'

Her words produced a murmur of protest. Akaisha rose. 'Would you have us send our own children to the Mountain?' She glanced round at the faces of those whom she knew had grandchildren marked for the tithe, then she looked back at Harth. 'Do you want your own son to have died for nothing?'

Harth scowled to hold back tears. Her husband, Crowrane, spoke up. 'We could keep the marked Bluedancing children, they wouldn't be too much to feed.'

'Shouldn't we also keep some of the unmarked ones so we might use them to replace any that might die?' said Mossie.

Harth turned on her. 'Why not keep some of their women? I'm sure some of our men could get them with child. That way we could breed children to present to the next Gatherer in place of our own.'

'It would be heartless to separate them from their mothers,' said Ginkga. 'Do we really want to keep them here as orphans for as long as seven years?'

'Besides, the labour of the Bluedancing frees us,' said several people at once.

Harth looked suddenly frail. 'Our ferngardens won't yield any more than they've always done: our men already hunt as much as they can and yet every earther they bring us is immediately consumed. We've been home for more than a moon and haven't managed to make a single rope of djada. Mothers and fathers of the Ochre, if you're determined we must keep all the Bluedancing, can one of you tell me where we'll get food for our migration?'

Carnelian considered her words. It was a choice between starving or else sending the Bluedancing out to die on the plain, with the consequence that Poppy and the other tithe children would, after all, have to be sent into the clutches of the Masters.

Carnelian became aware Akaisha was looking at him hoping for some other way. He shook his head and she looked disappointed. Frowning, she turned her gaze on Osidian. 'Ravan told me the Master knows a way out of this dilemma.'

She looked at her son. 'Ask him what it is he'd have us do.'

Ravan relayed the question to Osidian who whispered a reply.

'The Master says that he has in mind a great hunt; a new kind of hunt that will bring the Tribe an abundance of meat,' said Ravan.

'What's the bastard talking about?' demanded Crowrane.

Osidian muttered and Ravan spoke. 'It isn't something that can be described but only something he can do for you. If you –'

Whin cut in. 'Your price?'

Once he had her words, Osidian gave Whin an angelic smile. 'There's no price, merely a question of means.'

Carnelian watched resignation and defeat come over the faces of the Elders as Ravan began relaying conditions.

'The Master says that he must be given authority over the Bluedancing women. Additionally, for a period of up to two moons, he must be allowed to lead the men of the Tribe as he did in the battle against the Bluedancing.'

'But not into battle,' Akaisha said quickly, fear stiffening her face.

Osidian promised they would merely hunt.

'And how shall we be fed during these two moons?' asked Whin, clearly outraged.

'The Master will make sure the Koppie is kept supplied with meat,' said Ravan, failing to conceal his triumph.

Galewing rose and surveyed the Assembly. 'I for one say we should let him try.'

Many grumbled but none opposed him. Galewing offered to go with the Master to keep an eye on everything he did. With a heavy heart, Carnelian witnessed the Elders bowing their heads as a sign they were giving Osidian their mandate.

As they walked under the cedars, Ravan grinned as if he had helped the Master win a famous victory. Sick with foreboding, Carnelian saw Osidian was walking blind, his inner sight occupied with some vision.

'I will not go with you,' Carnelian said.

Osidian took a while coming back from wherever he was. 'That is fortuitous, since I had intended to leave you behind.'

Carnelian had not expected that and felt cheated.

'I need you here,' said Osidian.

'Why?'

'I shall show you.'

Unhappy, Carnelian followed Osidian round the Crag, down the Blooding Stair and out into the ferngardens. They reached the Bloodwood Tree, which seemed strange without its ochre-faced women, and walked on into the fernmeadow beyond. Osidian fixed Carnelian with his green eyes.

'All I ask of you is that you should supervise the work of the Bluedancing here.'

'It depends what kind of *work* you want them to do.'

'Digging, my Lord. Nothing more offensive to your sensibilities than that.'

'Show me where you want them to dig.'

Osidian traced a wide circuit through the air. 'The ditch all around this meadow must be cleared and cut to its full original depth. Its walls must be beaten hard and strong. All the earth you dig out should be piled up in a rampart on the outer edge.'

Carnelian surveyed the meadow. He saw that, apart from the earthbridge they had used to cross to it, the Horngate was the only other entrance. He looked at Osidian.

'You wish for me to make a bottle into which you are going to drive a herd?'

Osidian smiled. 'It was the way my forefathers provisioned their hosts when they campaigned down on this plain more than seven hundred years ago.'

Carnelian gave a nod, appreciating how it might work. He walked over to the ditch with Osidian and Ravan following him. Standing on the edge, he peered down. Where tree roots did not buttress the walls, they had crumbled. Mud and weeds clogged the ditch along its whole length.

'This is no trivial labour.'

'You shall have the use of all the Bluedancing. I will send messengers back to bring me news of your progress. If it be not fast enough we shall see if we cannot bend the Ochre to the task.'

Carnelian looked at him. 'And where will you be?'

Osidian looked away to where the plain could be seen shimmering green. 'Out there,' he said with a jutting of his chin, 'training the hunters.'

'If he chooses to help me, I'd like to use Fern as my assistant,' Carnelian said.

'Oh no, Carnelian,' said Osidian with a shake of his head and a feral grin. 'That one will come with me.'

Fear gripped Carnelian. 'Do you intend to hurt him?'

Osidian shrugged. 'Hunting involves an element of risk.'

'Do you forget that you owe him your life?'

Osidian controlled anger. 'He will risk the hazards with the rest.'

'I will not aid you unless you promise to keep him safe.'

Osidian chuckled. 'Do you imagine you are that essential to this project?'

'I shall reveal to the Elders the true goal of your schemes.'

Osidian smiled. 'A crude manipulation but one Chosen in mood. Do you believe those decrepit savages even have the imagination to see my plans are possible? They will laugh at you, my Lord.'

'I will make them believe me.'

Osidian threw up his hands. 'Enough. I shall not touch your precious savage. Is that enough?'

345

Carnelian considered trying to get Osidian to swear a blood oath, but he feared pushing him too far and so he gave a nod.

That night Akaisha's hearth were disturbed by a succession of women visitors saying they had come to see if it was true the Elders had given the Master command over all their menfolk. Over and over again, wearily, Akaisha had to confirm it, but Carnelian could see the visitors were hardly attending to what she said, but rather sneaking sidelong glimpses at Osidian, whose face the firelight was making brighter than the moon.

Later, men began to come in twos and threes to talk to the Master. Ravan at his side, Osidian received them away from the hearthlight near the rootstair.

When Fern and Sil left the hearth, Carnelian followed them. Both turned to face him.

'Be careful,' Carnelian said to Fern.

Sil frowned. 'You will be going with Fern tomorrow, won't you?'

Carnelian shook his head. 'He wants me here.'

Sil glanced at the Master. Fern was examining Carnelian's eyes and saw from where the danger might come.

Sil smiled at Carnelian and then led her husband away to their sleeping hollow. Unhappy, Carnelian watched them go. He felt someone near him and saw it was Akaisha.

'Has the Master told you his intentions, Carnie?'

As he told her what he knew, her forehead creased into an ever deeper frown. 'I don't like it. It has a smell of impiety.' She gripped his arm. 'Are we doing the right thing?'

'What choice do we have?'

She looked up at him, probing his face, then letting go, she looked away. Following her line of sight, Carnelian saw the black shapes of two men nodding as they received a mutter of instructions from Ravan, beside whom loomed Osidian's immensity.

Carnelian saw how much she was struggling with doubt. 'I must start tomorrow. Will you help me?'

She tore her gaze back to him. 'You'll need quite a few of us to oversee the work.'

The next morning Carnelian took Poppy down to the Newditch with the rest of the Tribe to watch the men ride away. Osidian rode at their head with Galewing and his son, Hirane. Ravan and Krow were close behind. Searching for Fern, Carnelian found him further back. He watched until Akaisha and a score of other women came for him and, together, they went down to the Bluedancing field.

Their camp had trampled all the ferns into the earth. He saw the attempts they had made at forming hearths. These were so close to each other that the scatter of sleeping bodies formed a single mat of grubby cloth and flesh which reminded Carnelian, uncomfortably, of the way their men had looked lying on the battlefield.

'Poor creatures,' Sil said in a low voice.

'They brought it upon themselves,' Akaisha snapped to a nervous nodding murmur of agreement.

Before they reached them, the Bluedancing began coming alive. Carnelian could see their dirty faces gaping. They stumbled to their feet, clutching their children to their hips. A deputation of their Elders came out to meet the Ochre. Akaisha brought her own people to a halt. The salt bangles of the Bluedancing hung loose with their skin on the sticks of their limbs. Most had made an attempt to brush back their hair, but their faces were grimy, and their robes and head blankets filthy. They stank. It was clear that however much water they were being given, it was not enough to wash with.

Their dark eyes were fixed on Akaisha.

'Today you work elsewhere,' she said. The uncharacteristically harsh tone in her voice caused Carnelian to look at her. Akaisha's narrowing eyes, her taut thinned lips seemed to show aloofness but he knew her well enough to see her pain.

The Bluedancing women bowed a little and made their way back to gather their people, and then, woman and child, carrying mattocks, they all followed Akaisha and the Ochre down to the Bloodwood Tree.

'How shall they dig?' Akaisha asked him.

Carnelian shrugged. 'You know more about this than I do, my mother.'

She peered over the edge. 'You want us to bring this up to the condition of the Newditch?'

'That would do to begin with.'

She looked up and down the length of the ditch. 'It's going to take a lot of work.'

Carnelian looked round to see the crowd of the Bluedancing. 'There's a lot of hands to do it.'

Akaisha frowned. 'But we've had them in the ditches since they came. Earth-moving is hard work even when a person is well fed. With what we've been giving them . . .' She grimaced.

Carnelian grew morose contemplating the trap Osidian had them in. 'The Master will keep his promise and then not only the Tribe, but the Bluedancing will have all the meat they need.'

They set the Bluedancing to working in the ditches. Carnelian wandered along the edge of the meadow, sometimes stopping to look down. Everywhere, women and children were labouring in the mud. He gazed out past the Horngate. The sun had risen high enough to melt the view and beat down on him like a migraine. An Ochre voice was barking instructions. Carnelian felt useless and worried that Osidian had only left him there to stop him interfering with whatever it was he was up to on the plain. He made for the Bloodwood Tree, seeking solitude in its shade. The rot of blood was in his nostrils even before he could see its stain in the earth. He walked round behind the tree, putting its trunk between him and the sun. Lying against its bark, he relived the times he had spent there talking with Fern. He cursed himself that he had not after all bound Osidian with an oath.

Hearing Akaisha calling his name, Carnelian walked back into the searing sun. Squinting, he could make her out, beckoning. He sighed, reluctant to leave the shade.

'We need you to check we're doing it right,' she said as he approached her.

He allowed her to lead him back to the ditch where he helped her down a crumbling slope. Soon they were among the workings. When Bluedancing turned to watch them pass, Whin forced them back to work with a shout. Carnelian's glance of surprise only served to make her angrier. He was feeling he did not know her, perhaps never had, when the anger slipped from her face like a mask and, looking ashamed, she ducked away.

'Down there,' said Akaisha pointing among the heaving backs. Carnelian saw her against the rise and fall of their mattocks, saw her distaste. His apparent detachment angered her.

'You're the one who asked for my help!'

Carnelian could find no way to explain how he was feeling. 'Please show me.'

Akaisha turned and he followed her as she wound her way through the Bluedancing. Carnelian saw it was their young women who were hacking at the muddy walls. The older women and the children were clawing the crumbled earth into baskets which, when full, they dragged one heave at a time away from the ditch wall.

'Look here,' said Akaisha and showed him with her hands where the earth on either side had been cut back. 'Is that enough?'

Carnelian's eyes were drawn back to the people slaving. He saw an old woman, an Elder by the salt beads in her hair, struggling, tugging at a basket filled with soil.

'They shouldn't wear their salt, it'll be lost,' grumbled Akaisha.

The old woman was still pulling but her basket had dug into the ground. She stopped, bowed, misery making her red eyes tear.

Carnelian ran forward and, taking hold of the wrinkled hands, peeled them off the basket handle. 'This is too much for you, my mother.' He turned from the confusion in her gaze and tore at the handle, yanking the basket free and then dragging it until he backed into another. He strode forward looking for another one to pull. He felt a touch on his arm.

'What're you doing, Carnie?'

He looked up into Akaisha's face. 'Helping them.'

'We're helping them already,' she said, her voice unnaturally sharp. 'If it wasn't for them we'd have no need to have the Master involve us in this.' He saw the tears she was fighting as she walked away.

By order of the Elders, the Bluedancing were stripped of their salt. Akaisha and Whin stopped coming to the fernmeadow and gradually, all but a few Ochre overseers began to stay away. Morose, Carnelian took to labouring in the ditch. He had the Bluedancing move their camp to the neighbouring ferngarden and made Akaisha force the Elders to send a demand to Osidian that more water must be brought to the Koppie daily for the earth-workers.

The men who brought water described the circular earthwork Osidian was making them dig near the lagoon. At night they had to light great fires to keep the raveners at bay. When asked what the earthwork was for, they would shrug and say they just did what the Master told them to. They seemed to Carnelian much grimmer than he remembered them.

These same men regularly brought with them not only water but a saurian carcass. The Tribe were beginning to feel hunger. Hearths sent people down to watch the butchering to make sure to get some of the fresh meat. It was Carnelian who insisted that the Bluedancing should at least be given the offal.

The day after the Tribe had celebrated the return of the tributaries, Carnelian was breakfasting when cries of alarm began sounding here and there in the Grove. Everyone leapt to their feet and some youngsters were sent to find out what was going on. When they returned they answered Akaisha's questions by drawing everyone to where a gap in the cedar canopy allowed them to see smoke rising in the south.

Whin exchanged an anxious look with Akaisha. 'It's too much smoke to be a beacon.'

'Their koppie burns,' said Sil.

Akaisha shook her head. 'Their ferngardens wouldn't be dry enough.'

Poppy was clinging to him. Carnelian knew what he must be seeing was a fire in the koppie of the Bluedancing. Akaisha and Whin stared bleakly out.

'What is it that is burning, my mothers?'

Both women turned wild-eyed. 'Their mother trees.'

Leaving Poppy with Sil, Carnelian followed Akaisha, Whin and others of the Elders down to the Eastgarden. He sensed they were expecting trouble. The camp of the Bluedancing seemed much the same as it always did except that the women were all standing gazing to where the pall of smoke was hanging over the southern horizon.

'Imagine how they must feel,' whispered Mossie, and Ginkga shut her up with a glare.

They crossed the earthbridge and went down the Blooding, turning often to observe the motionless ranks of the Bluedancing. Akaisha took the path of barren earth to the camp. As the Ochre approached, the Bluedancing seemed unaware of them, but then some children cried out and the women turned.

'What're we going to say to them?' asked Mossie.

'Hush, dear,' said Akaisha.

The eyes of the Bluedancing, red from weeping, regarded the visitors with hatred.

'We must order them to their work,' said Whin.

'The work will make them forget,' said Ginkga.

'Would you so easily forget your mother tree?' asked Akaisha, her eyes flitting among the Bluedancing.

Carnelian could see how that thought was being passed between them with glances.

Compassion and fear warred in their faces.

Harth glared at them. 'I warned you not to trust the Standing Dead.' She advanced towards the sullen Bluedancing.

'Get to your work,' she commanded.

The Bluedancing made no move and continued to stare. Behind them Carnelian could see the smoke from the burning of their mother trees swelling the horizon.

Harth repeated her command and still there was no response. Carnelian was becoming aware of how many there were of the

Bluedancing. So many eyes filled with grief and anger.

'We'd better go back,' said Akaisha, nervously.

'Shouldn't we try –?' began Mossie.

'Let's go now,' hissed Akaisha and, retrieving Harth, they retreated back over the bridge and made their way at speed for the beckoning safety of the Homeditch.

The Elders armed the Tribe as best they could and set them to guarding the two most easterly gates and the arc of the Homeditch which lay between. The Crag beacon was lit to summon back their men. Carnelian waited with Akaisha by the Bloodgate. All eyes were scanning the ferngarden, looking for the expected Bluedancing attack.

When he told Akaisha he thought they were overreacting, she flared to anger.

'What! You don't understand. How could you? If anything should happen to my tree, the grief . . .' She shook her head and resumed her look-out for the Bluedancing.

Carnelian felt like asking her if she imagined her grief could turn into murderous rage, but he said nothing more. Guilt at the way the Tribe had treated the Bluedancing was the true root of her fear.

Carnelian paced back and forth beneath the mother tree. When Galewing had appeared with many riders, Carnelian, fearing bloodshed, had spoken out in defence of the Bluedancing. He had declared them to be nothing more dangerous than frightened, dispossessed women and children. His words clearly had force for the Elder men though, unhappily, he sensed this was because he resembled the Master. Outraged, Harth had commanded him to be silent, saying the matter was for the Elders to decide. Akaisha had sent him to their hearth to wait for her.

His brooding was interrupted by a voice calling from the rootstair. Seeing it was Krow, Carnelian invited him into his hearth. Astride the men's rootbench, they faced each other. As Krow nibbled at his nails, he was smearing hornblack from his lips to his fingers.

Carnelian asked him how the men were, mentioning names, among which he included Fern so as not to draw attention to his concern for him. Without lifting his head, Krow told him everyone was fine.

Carnelian decided against asking more specifically. 'How goes the great hunt?'

Krow looked up at him. 'I know nothing of a great hunt.'

'Is his earthwork finished?'

Krow nodded grimly. His eyes unfocused as he saw it in his mind's eye. 'It parts the herds on their way to the lagoon. Even heaveners walk round it.'

Carnelian was surprised. 'Two moons and that's all you've done?'

Krow shook his head. 'He makes us ride against the herds in lines, in arrowheads. He divides us into groups and, with his spear, commands us to strike against earthers in waves.'

Carnelian narrowed his eyes. 'Why?'

Krow shrugged. 'Perhaps this great hunt you spoke of, Master.'

There was something in that shrug that suggested Krow was hiding something. It seemed to Carnelian obvious Osidian was training them for war.

'Why did the Master burn the Bluedancing's mother trees?'

Krow grew troubled. 'He told us that as long as their trees lived, the Bluedancing might hope for freedom and revenge.'

'It was cruel and impious.'

Krow sunk his head again and resumed his nibbling.

'You of all people should know how it feels.'

Krow's head jerked up. 'The Marula murdered my hearth and tribe.'

'As we did the Bluedancing men and, besides, made their mothers, wives, sisters and children slaves.'

'We showed them mercy.'

'The Master's mercy was meant to force the need for this hunt so as to give him power over the Tribe.'

Krow looked away haunted. 'What choice do I have but to follow him?'

'Akaisha might welcome you into her hearth.'

Krow turned back fiercely. 'To remind her that her son is possessed by the Master?'

Carnelian had no answer to that.

'I'm sorry, Carnie, but the only place I have left is at the Master's side.'

Carnelian could not deny the plea in the youth's eyes that he should stop. He smiled at him. 'Why have you come to see me, Krow?'

'The Master wants to know how much progress you've made here.'

Carnelian closed his eyes and tried to imagine how much of the ditch was still to be cut; how much they had already cut and how long it had taken.

He opened his eyes, feeling sick at heart. 'In the end it will come down to whether the Bluedancing will still work.'

Krow smiled coldly. 'They'll work all right.'

'You're returning to him today?'

Krow nodded.

'Tell him that in eight days the work here will be complete.'

Krow took leave of him with a kind of bow and then Carnelian was left alone to brood on what he had learned about Osidian's preparations. Sil and Poppy appeared and Carnelian helped them make the evening meal.

Night had fallen before Akaisha and Whin returned. Everyone could see they had been quarrelling. Akaisha said they had come up from the Homeditch gates, now guarded by the men of the Tribe. Though everyone was desperate to know what the Elders had decided, neither Akaisha nor Whin volunteered anything.

Later, Akaisha took an opportunity to talk to Carnelian alone. 'I suppose you'd better know.' She looked unhappy. 'We have had to take some of their children away from them. There's no other way we can be sure to be safe when our men are away.'

Carnelian was aware she would not look him directly in the eye.

'We have to send them away to ensure the good behaviour of their mothers.'

'Send them where?'

'Galewing will take them with him tomorrow when he returns to the Master.'

Carnelian could not believe this. 'If you must take their children, why not bring them up here where you can keep an eye on them?'

When Akaisha would not answer, he took her hands in his. She glanced up at him.

'Surely you understand, Carnie? How could we hurt them ourselves?'

Carnelian let go of her hands. 'But you're happy to let the men do it?'

'It won't come to that. Their mothers would do nothing to risk their children.'

'I can't believe you want to send any children out there, among the herds and the raveners. Who'll care for them?'

Akaisha grimaced. 'We can't have them here. We can't.'

'What do you fear, Akaisha?'

She shook her head in answer. He thought about it.

'Is it that having them among the hearths the women won't be able to distinguish the Bluedancing children from those of the Tribe?'

Akaisha looked up at him and there were tears in her eyes. 'What have we become?' she whispered. 'What have we become?'

Akaisha conspired with Carnelian to draw out breakfast as long as they could. It was the other overseers gathering waiting for them at the edge of their rootearth that eventually forced them to rise.

'We'll have to face it some time,' Carnelian said.

With the others, they marched in silence down to the camp of the Bluedancing. When it came in sight, Carnelian was as reluctant as everyone else to go any nearer, but he pushed forward nonetheless.

The Bluedancing seemed carved from wood. Carnelian tried not to catch glimpses of their eyes as they were ordered to their work. They shuffled along, their chins digging into their bony chests. They looked like sartlar.

He accompanied them to the ditch and, removing his robe, was determined to work among them as he had done for days. It made him feel better to be sharing their labour.

He clawed at the mud, but hard as he worked, he was aware of the space there was around him. Every time he glanced up he would catch glimpses of the hatred in their eyes. It sapped his strength. Their eyes made him question why he was sharing their work. Was it that he was doing penance for the guilt he felt? Was it that if he pretended to share their suffering no one would be able to blame him for his part in what was being done to them? It was Osidian who had brought all this about, but who was it had brought Osidian to the Koppie and at every turn protected him, nurtured him until he had grown into what he was today? Ultimately, Carnelian could not pretend his hands were clean of any of Osidian's crimes. He dropped his mattock and looked at his red, earthy hands. He left the ditch. It was about time he took responsibility for what he was and what he had done.

He ceased worked with the Bluedancing but tried instead to get as much food and water as he could for them. He made sure to keep an eye on their Ochre overseers. He understood what spurred these women to cruelty. Sometimes, when he saw the thin arms of the Bluedancing plucking at the red earth, he grew enraged, desiring to lash them, to heap abuse on them, but he had delved deep enough to see this was guilt taking possession of him; by bringing his victims low hoping to justify keeping them in their place.

He did not judge the Ochre. They had lived all their lives with the constant threat of having their children stolen from them. It was not easy for them to have become the very thing they most hated.

Days later Carnelian, worn down by another day working as an overseer, returned to the hearth desperate for its familial warmth. Sil and the other women were lining their bench. A smell of stew was drifting in the air. He went to wash first and smiled when one of the children greeted him, then jumped when something in the shadow under the mother tree moved.

'You,' he gasped, seeing it was Osidian.

'I have come to impart to you the role you will play in my great hunt.'

Osidian said no more and Carnelian was glad when he left him alone to his washing, for it gave him time to order his thoughts. When he joined the hearth he found Osidian was not there.

'Ravan?' Carnelian asked as Akaisha handed him a steaming bowl.

'The Master came without either of my sons,' she said, severely.

'Did he say –?'

'He said nothing.'

Akaisha must have seen his anger, for she put her hand on his arm. 'We need him, Carnie,' she said, quietly. 'If his plan fails, the Tribe will starve.'

He gave her a nod, smiling, and she released him.

Carnelian carried the bowl to his sleeping hollow. Osidian was there.

'I have brought you some food,' Carnelian said, in Quya.

'Leave it on the ground,' the shadow replied.

Carnelian put the bowl down. 'Are the hostage children well?'

'Well enough.'

'Was that your idea?'

Osidian smiled. 'Amusingly, the savages thought it up entirely on their own. It seems they have the capacity to learn something from their superiors.'

'Why are you training the Ochre for war?'

'Carnelian, you have known my intentions since the day we reached the Earthsky.'

Carnelian became exasperated. 'You really believe the Ochre can win you back your throne?'

'They shall be but the first tribe of my host.'

'Plainsmen against the legions?'

'My first move in the game that is to come.'

Carnelian felt he was talking to a madman.

Osidian took him by the shoulders. 'Believe me, Carnelian, we shall return to Osrakum and regain everything we have lost.'

Carnelian took a step back to break the hold Osidian had on him. 'Even if you were successful, you would be returning to Osrakum alone. I shall remain here with these people.'

'I will not allow that,' said Osidian, his voice ice.

' "You will not allow?" You may control events here, Osidian, but you do not control me. I know you could manipulate me, use force even, but my heart will no longer yield to you.'

Carnelian felt Osidian's anger in the stillness. 'In addition, I will play no further part in your schemes. If you continue on your path I will do anything I can to stop you.'

Osidian smiled. 'Anything?'

Carnelian restrained his lust to punch Osidian's white face. He thought of again threatening to betray his plans to the Elders, but he feared what Osidian might do to Fern. A murmur was coming from the hearth.

Osidian chuckled. 'Thinking up threats, Carnelian?' He grew serious. 'I will devise a way to change your mind, but take care; what I have set in motion here cannot easily be stopped. Whether or not you decide to oppose me, accept that your precious "Tribe" can never return to the life they had. Either they shall follow the path I have chosen for them or else they will be destroyed. However much I may feel the God working through me, a successful outcome is not assured, but be certain of one thing: I alone can hope to control the forces I have unleashed.'

Carnelian felt he was being possessed by Osidian's vision.

'Are you sulking, Carnelian?'

It seemed a different person saying that. Carnelian felt annoyed at being spoken to like a child and then, realizing how childish this was, he smiled.

Osidian glared. 'Do you mock me, my Lord?'

This made Carnelian burst into laughter, which he took some time suppressing. 'Not at you . . . at me,' he managed to say.

As the tremors of mirth subsided, the horror flooded back.

'You were going to tell me about this great hunt of yours.'

Osidian frowned. 'You will play your part?'

'Do I have a choice?'

'Knowing you, none at all.'

Carnelian could feel the faraway thunder through his saddle-chair. His aquar was very still as she blinked her enormous eyes at the horizon. Her eye quills twitched at every sound.

'Make ready,' he cried.

He was outside the Newditch on one side of the Horngate. Other riders formed a line with him stretching away into the lush fernland. On the other side of the gate under Sil's command was another line of aquar raked back, each hitched to one of the drag-cradles he had modified according to Osidian's instructions.

The thunder deepened under the clear sky. The ground was now shaking so that Carnelian, seeing the breeze ruffling the fernheads, could imagine the earth they concealed was undulating with the slow rhythm of deep water.

The riders, all women, coughed their tension. Carnelian joined them in gazing off to where they could see the horizon darkening with a mounding mass. He swallowed past a parched throat.

Closer and closer rolled the flood. The earth's shaking jostled him in his chair. His aquar's quills half-flared as she drew back her head and stared veiling her eyes with their inner lids. He rubbed his feet on her back to calm her.

Carnelian began to see details in the flood. Necks reaching up to the sky like tornadoes.

'Heaveners,' the cry of shock went up from the women round him.

Carnelian sagged, knowing they were right. Osidian had said nothing about the giants being the victims of his hunt. Carnelian felt he had been tricked. The women were arguing among themselves. Should he sabotage Osidian's hunt? Gripping his saddle-chair against the tremors, Carnelian looked round at the fernmeadow. He relived the grinding labour of the Bluedancing; the conflicts among the Ochre. Could he dismiss all those sacrifices? Could he deliver the Tribe into famine?

He surveyed the women, all pale indecision. He saw how they were having difficulty controlling their aquar. The heaveners were close enough for him to see the mountainous churning of their legs. It was now or never.

'Light up now!' he bellowed.

The women confronted him with stares. It was Sil who spoke for them. 'Carnie, they're sacred.'

'Do you want the Tribe to starve?'

That made up their minds. Craning round he saw more women flinging torches into the drag-cradles. The kindling piled on them ignited with a blast that caused Carnelian's aquar to take several steps forward. He let her go and saw at the edges of his sight the other riders lurching raggedly into movement. He urged his aquar into a run. Craning round, he saw his drag-cradle shaking and jumping, rolling fire into the ferns. Smoke the colour of old teeth was snaking in among their stems.

Looking forward, he gasped with horror as he saw the heaveners' tidal wave was almost upon them. The quakes were rattling his bones. The saurian stench struck him so that he could almost not breathe. His left foot trammelled the aquar's back, insisting she keep her headlong lope towards the onrushing stampede. Still she was veering slowly to the right as Osidian had predicted she would.

The hills of muscle were almost upon them. Their backs eclipsed the sky. Then the saurians were pouring their thunder past him and he heard the thin ululating and the human cries. He saw the tiny Plainsmen scurrying among the giant's legs, faces distorted in an ecstasy of fear. He glimpsed Osidian among them like a lightning flash and then they were past and for moments he gaped at the road they had crushed across the plain as he felt the thunder recede.

He turned his aquar and saw the heaveners narrowing their herd into the cone he had helped create. On either side of the giants a hedge of smoke was rising, rooted in flame. Clouds billowed and greyed his line of sight. A tiny darting of aquar pulling flames closed the gap.

Then the storm fell silent. The mass of smoke thinned slowly as it rose into the sky. The fire was spreading, rustling, as if it were some creature scratching its back through the ferns. Turning, he saw that the drag-cradle he had been pulling was threatening to become a ball of flames.

More and more of the Tribe were coming down to gape at the captive giants. Among the younger hunters, the excitement of the chase had not yet worn off. Beaming, red-faced, they were telling everyone everything they had seen and felt. The silent reception smothered their ardour until they too were watching the heaveners milling within the imprisoning circuit of the ditch and rampart. Pushing through the crowd searching for Fern, Carnelian and Sil found him standing staring at the heaveners through tears.

'Husband,' Sil said, and reached up to touch his face.

Fern turned and saw them. 'Seeing them there . . .' He blinked away his tears. 'We've robbed them of their thunder.'

The three of them looked at each other guiltily.

Sil began to cry. 'We had no choice. The Tribe . . .'

Fern looked at them wild-eyed. 'Galewing said the same to us as we discovered what it was we were to hunt. Many wanted to send word to the Elders, but Galewing said the women would oppose this on religious grounds and so they must not allow the Tribe to die for their beliefs.'

'Our beliefs,' said Sil.

His eyes on Fern, Carnelian began worrying if he had erred in setting his friend's safety above that of the Tribe. This was all part of Osidian's schemes. Searching, he found him towering among a group of youths. Carnelian began making his way towards them.

Krow was the first to see Carnelian approaching and, clearly troubled, he looked away.

Ravan grinned. 'Well, the Master's delivered as he said he would.'

Carnelian talked over the youth in Quya. 'My Lord, the Ochre loathe what you have made them do.'

Osidian turned, smiling. 'Have I not given them what they wanted?'

'These creatures are sacred to them.'

Osidian's smile broadened and Carnelian realized, sickened, that this was the very reason for the hunt. Carnelian felt people stirring and saw they were turning their backs on the rampart. Following their gaze, he saw the Elder women approaching. The horror in their faces was clear to see. They came close enough for Carnelian to reach out and touch Akaisha but she shook his hand off as she watched the heaveners' necks crossing and recrossing against the sky.

'This is unholy,' Whin cried from their midst, and many of the other Elders joined their voices to hers.

A stunned silence fell.

'But you sanctioned this,' said a voice.

'We did not sanction *this*,' cried Whin.

Ravan confronted her. 'The Master's brought us more meat in one day's hunt than our warriors could've managed in two whole seasons.'

'These aren't meat,' bellowed Akaisha.

Hand on hips, Ginkga was standing in front of Galewing greyed by the dust of the hunt. 'You allowed this . . . this sacrilege?'

When the man said nothing, she grew enraged. 'Have you forgotten that heaveners are sacred?'

'So is the survival of the Tribe,' Galewing said in a high clear voice which found many echoes in the crowd.

'Would the other Elders have us set them free?' cried Ravan.

Galewing turned regarding the people. 'If we do, we'll starve. Shall we choose life or death?'

The answer seemed to come hissing like a sandstorm. 'Life.'

'This is unholy,' Carnelian heard Akaisha cry, but the rest was drowned out by the rumble of the Tribe stamping on the earth and the chant: 'Life. Life. Life.'

BETRAYAL

Venerate your aged for in their memories the past finds its only refuge.

(*Plainsman proverb*)

WHEN POPPY FOUND CARNELIAN, SHE PREVAILED UPON HIM TO LIFT HER up on to his shoulders so she might be able to look over the rampart at the heaveners. Carnelian was hardly aware of her gurgles of childish delight. He had watched the Elder women fleeing back towards the Grove. Fern, Sil, the whole Tribe was being marshalled by Galewing. Osidian stood apart, his face swathed, his eyes lazily following the carnival of preparations. It was Poppy's cry and shudder that alerted Carnelian to the first volley of javelins. Perched on the rampart, the younger men cast another volley at their trapped victims. As these dropped from their hides without leaving even a wound, there was a swell of consternation among the watchers. Carnelian lifted Poppy from his shoulders and saw how frightened she was. He did not feel he could send her back to the Grove on her own, but neither did he feel he was free to take her. Finding Sil, he was relieved when she agreed to go with her.

'Look after Fern,' Sil said. 'There's something wrong with him.'

'The heaveners –'

'Something else. He won't tell me . . . perhaps you . . . ?'

Carnelian nodded solemnly, kissed Poppy, then waved them off and went looking for Fern.

When he found him, Fern was helping some women improvise a billhook: a long horsetail pole with a curved end tipped with flints. To get close to him, Carnelian became embroiled in its construction.

360

When it was finished, many bodies were required to counterbalance it as it swung, swivelling upon the earth rampart. Swarms of children ran about screaming and laughing as if it were a game. The women waited, poised, until one of the heaveners came to eat from one of the magnolias edging the meadow, then swinging the bill-hook, they slashed a cut into its throat. The screaming head lifted away, seeding the air with blood. As more of the giants fell prey to the billhook, cries of amazement became laughter at how stupid the heaveners were.

Carnelian tried to strike up a conversation with Fern but he was apparently deaf to anything he said. They ended up working together in silent anger making more billhooks.

Under constant attack, the heaveners raged and stamped and backed away, but hungry, they kept coming in to feed. Blood pour-ing from their countless wounds soaked into the earth and, when the earth could drink no more, blood began trickling into the ditch. The slaughter went on, until, even as the sun shed its own red light over the scene, it was outdone by that gory place where the dying heaveners rolled scarlet in their own blood.

The heaveners' booming death-cries followed Carnelian and Fern all the way back to the hearth. Seeing them, Sil questioned Carnelian with her eyes. He shook his head. Heads were hanging everywhere around the hearth.

Wearing a deep and seemingly permanent frown, Akaisha welcomed her son back to the hearth and everyone else murmured their welcomes.

'I don't suppose your brother's going to join us?'

Fern shrugged.

Akaisha went back to ladling stew into bowls. Carnelian watched her and saw how haunted she looked.

'At least we'll soon have plenty to eat,' said one of the youngsters, going pale as her mother glared at her.

As they ate the only sound was their slurping. The rest of the Grove was unnaturally silent, as if even the mother trees themselves were listening to the heaveners dying.

Poppy had to shake Carnelian to wake him. The first thing he saw was that she had been crying.

'Everyone's going down to butcher the heaveners.'

'Surely just the women,' Carnelian said, knowing it was a false hope.

Poppy shook her head. 'No, Carnie, Mother Whin said the men must help too.'

To give himself a chance to find courage to face the day, he sent her to fetch some water. He had slept badly. The sorry, plaintive heavener cries had haunted his dreams and his half-wakings.

When Poppy returned, he thanked her, drank the water and then rose. Akaisha, Fern and the others were there: men and women, the children too. The women were carrying the scythes the men had made for them the night before. The young were subdued. Fern looked miserable: Akaisha, aged.

'You didn't sleep, my mother?' Carnelian asked her as everyone began moving down the hill.

She looked up at him angrily. 'Did you?'

Fern put his arm about her shoulders and she leaned into him.

They were walking along the Blooding when the massacre came into sight: mountains of hide beneath swirling scavenger clouds.

'So much meat,' Sil said, sadly.

The Bloodwood Tree had been partially pushed over by a heavener that lay against it like a landslide. Its neck formed a dyke running for some distance on the other side of the earthbridge.

'Can we go over?' one child begged, her voice shrilly echoed by others.

'Over to the Killing Field.'

Other children took up the cry. 'Killing Field, over to the Killing Field.'

Gaping, people were clambering up the rampart to peer at the monsters. Ravan was there with Krow and many other youths. They began throwing stones and no one stopped them. Carnelian watched them bounce here and there off the carcasses, causing ravens to screech and hop into the air. He saw a stone roll down the back of a heavener, eventually being swallowed by a brown, blood pool.

'They must be dead,' cried Ravan, hurling another stone to prove it.

At last, gingerly, he led others across the narrow earth bridge, holding their scythes in front of them. They tapped the hide wall of the neck then stepped back, anticipating it lifting into the sky, but it might as well have been the trunk of a fallen cedar. Ravan lunged forward, swinging his scythe, tearing a red gash in the wall so deep it exposed white vertebrae. Soon he was joined by others, hacking at the flesh while up to their ankles in blood.

The Bluedancing were evicted from their camp in the Eastgarden. Huge fires were lit and trestles made and set above them. The rituals were to be maintained as best they could. There was not enough red ochre and so Ginkga commanded the Bluedancing to paint their

362

faces with blood. Hunks of meat were carried on bending poles and dumped on any spare piece of ground, then the Bluedancing were made to fall on them; slicing, hacking, tearing the flesh into chunks which were then packed on to the trestles. It was Osidian who had suggested they smoke the meat, declaring that sun-curing would be too slow. Soon, to feed the fires, they were forced to fell some of the magnolias running alongside the Outditch. As well as the Bluedancing, the whole Tribe had joined the race to harvest as much as they could before the heaveners began to rot.

Beneath palls of reeking smoke, taking a rest from the bloody work, Carnelian wandered with Poppy among the fires in a daze. Entrails were draped across the ferns like fishing nets. Expanses of hide were laid out; scarlet rugs dense with flies. In one corner of the ferngarden they were throwing everything they did not want. Much was being put on to that brown hill that usually they kept. With such an abundance of flesh, only the better cuts were being saved.

Telling Poppy to wait for him, Carnelian picked his way across the earthbridge which was slick and treacherous with mud. When he reached the Killing Field, it seemed he was standing on a sunset-reddened strand. Carcasses lay like so many beached ships, half stripped of their hulls of flesh, exposing their white ribbing. The ground was covered by a flotsam of entrails and membranes. Nearby a head as large as a man gave him a macabre grin, its lips pulled back and hanging loose. Carnelian reflected that that head had once woven among the clouds like a bird. The neck that had stretched a link between earth and sky was nailed by its vertebrae to the ground. Ruddy children scurried, laughing and shouting amidst that architecture of death, playing hide-and-seek in the caverns of the ruined heaveners.

'Enough is enough,' Carnelian said under his breath. He decided that that evening he would betray Osidian's scheme to Akaisha.

Night had already fallen when the Tribe returned exhausted to their hearths. In the face of so many people, the Elders had suspended the requirement to wash underneath the Old Bloodwood Tree. Carnelian's hearthmates' skin was caked with blood; their hair matted with gore.

Complaints rising from near the water jar drew everyone to go and see what was going on.

'It hasn't been refilled,' Akaisha said, peering into it, and then began to cry. Everyone stared open-mouthed as she stumbled off towards her hollow. Carnelian felt queasy. He must follow her and betray Osidian.

'Who was meant to fetch water today?' demanded Whin.

Everyone looked at each other but no one seemed to have an answer. Carnelian was not the only one to notice the guilty expressions on the men's faces.

'Do any of you know?'

'We were ordered not to go, my mother.'

'By whom?'

'Father Galewing.'

Whin looked weary, confused. Carnelian grew uneasy, suspecting Osidian was behind this. He realized he had not seen him for a long time. He looked towards the rootstair. Carnelian had imagined Fern was lagging behind him when he had returned with the others. A dark foreboding clutched him. His eyes met Sil's. He was sure they were sharing the same feeling.

'Did they tell you why?' asked Whin.

The men exchanged sidelong looks. It was obvious they were reluctant to speak.

Whin stepped towards them. 'Come on, out with it.'

'We were told to keep it to ourselves,' said one of them.

'So as not to worry anyone,' added another.

Whin looked exasperated. 'What're you talking about?'

The first man to have spoken looked to the others for permission. 'It's because of the Woading.'

Sil looked startled. 'Our neighbours, the Woading?'

'They've been threatening us for days.'

'Threatening you?' said Whin.

'Each day, the men they send to fetch water have grown in numbers.'

'And become more heavily armed,' added one of the others.

'Why have they suddenly chosen to interfere with us?'

The man shrugged. 'Our new earthwork's near where they traditionally come for water.'

'Didn't any of you think of telling the Master that that was likely to provoke them?'

Carnelian thought it unlikely Osidian had needed to be told.

The man shrugged. 'He had us dig it where the lagoon is narrowest and easy to cross.'

'What has this to do with our water supply?' demanded Whin.

The man looked at her anxiously. 'The Master feared the Woading might attack the hunts we send out to fetch water.'

'So we're to die of thirst instead?'

'It was to be only one day, my mother; so that we could all help making djada.'

364

'And tomorrow . . . ?'

'We'll go in force so that if they try anything, we'll be ready for them.'

'So you're all in on this?' said Whin looking round at the men.

'What do you mean, my mother?'

Whin dug the heel of her hand into her forehead. 'What I mean is, does this conspiracy spread to the other hearths?'

'Just the men.'

Whin smiled coldly at him. 'Just the men. Well, that's fine then. As long as it's just the men.'

Many of them lowered their heads. 'We assumed the Elders had approved this.'

Whin dismissed the comment with her hand and glanced at Carnelian. 'It's not you I'm angry with.'

Everyone stood in silence watching her brood. She glanced over to the sleeping hollows.

'I'm tired. We're all too tired. It'll keep until morning.'

Carnelian began moving towards the hollows.

'Where are you going?'

Carnelian faced Whin. 'To speak to Mother Akaisha, my mother.'

Whin shook her head. 'No you're not.'

'But there's something I want to tell her.'

'It'll keep until tomorrow.'

Carnelian saw how determined Whin was. He considered telling her, but was not sure she would believe him.

Whin looked round at her hearth, all of whom were staring at her. 'Well, are you all just going to stand there stinking of blood?'

'But the water,' said Sil.

'We'll take out what we need for drink and then we'll just have to manage with the little that is left.'

They did as she said and Carnelian joined them. There was only enough to soak into the strips they tore from a worn blanket. They used these to wipe off as much of the blood as they could, but it was impossible to get it out of their hair.

Woken by a commotion, Carnelian sat up. Shapes were moving among the hollows, where voices were loud with anger. Poppy appeared beside him.

'All the men have gone.'

He threw on his robe and went to find Akaisha. She was standing near the hearth with Whin, who had her hands on her hips.

'You don't know anything about this, do you?'

Carnelian's and Sil's eyes met.

'What do you two know?' demanded Whin.

'Yesterday, Fern was hiding something from me,' said Sil.

Carnelian began to feel afraid. Osidian was behind this.

'Look,' said Sil, pointing.

Through the canopy they could see a mass of smoke rising against the predawn sky. Carnelian judged it must be the curing fires in the Eastgarden.

Akaisha groaned. 'What're the Bluedancing up to? Who's overseeing them? They know they're supposed to wait for us. Sil, go down and see what's happening.'

'Can I go too?' asked Poppy.

Sil glanced at Carnelian, who nodded. He watched the two of them move off.

'Carnie, you're sure you don't know what's going on?' said Akaisha.

'I'm as baffled as you are, my mother,' he replied. Her sad, nervous look added to his worries.

Others of their hearthmates returned in ones and twos, shaking their heads, saying the same thing. All the men were gone and no one knew where.

Akaisha asked Whin to go up to the summit of the Crag and light the beacon. She went with some helpers. Akaisha and Carnelian's attention was drawn to the rootstair by a shouting coming up it. Sil appeared staring wildly. They both rushed to meet her. Akaisha had to take hold of her to calm her enough so they could understand what she was saying.

'Battle,' she gulped. She swung round and pointed. 'A battle down in the Eastgarden.'

'Our men?' demanded Akaisha, gripping her hard enough to make Sil yelp. The young woman nodded. Akaisha released her and looked up into the canopy of her mother tree, appalled. Cries of panic were breaking out all around them. Sil stared at Akaisha, waiting for her to say something.

'We must hold the Homeditch gates.'

Sil nodded again. Akaisha strode around, bellowing: 'Grab mattocks, sticks, whatever you can find. We must hold the Homeditch gates to make sure none of these attackers break into the Grove.'

Carnelian ran for his spear. On his way back, Poppy flew at him.

'Fighting, Carnie, fighting!'

He caught her. 'I know.'

Gripping the spear with one hand, he took her by the other and they began descending the rootstair. Sil, who was faster on the steps, overtook them. 'Come on,' she cried.

Carnelian remembered Akaisha and, looking back, found she was coming down after them. They waited for her. He reached out to take Akaisha's arm, to be her support, but she pulled herself free, glaring at him, and continued to take the steps as quickly as she could on her own. Carnelian and Poppy followed her, ready to catch her should she fall, every so often nervously trying to catch a view of the battle through the branches.

Even before they reached the bottom of the stair they saw the gate at its foot was swinging open. 'Earth and Sky!' Akaisha cursed. 'Didn't they hear what I said?'

When they reached the earthbridge they saw the women of the Tribe streaming down the Blooding towards the Eastgarden above which the air was slashed with smoke. Stare as hard as he might, Carnelian could see nothing of the battle. Akaisha bent forward, bracing herself on her knees.

'You know of course what this will be?'

'The Woading attacking.'

She closed her eyes and nodded slowly, gasping for air. 'War,' she gulped. 'The Master's brought war right into our home.'

'He'll beat them,' Carnelian said, desperate to believe it.

She caught him with one bright eye. 'More men killed: theirs and ours. For what? His vanity?'

Carnelian felt sick; the moment had come. 'Power. He's after power.'

She frowned.

Carnelian crouched and looked deep into her eyes. 'He dreams of returning to the Mountain.'

Akaisha's wrinkles bunched up as her eyes narrowed with incomprehension.

'For that he needs an army,' he continued.

Akaisha chuckled without humour. 'Our men against the dragons?'

'He'll conquer many tribes.'

'Conquer?'

'Even now his schemes are maturing. There's not much time.'

Akaisha clasped her head. 'But what can we do to stop him? If he wins this battle . . . ? If he doesn't . . . ?'

'We can do nothing here,' he said, rising. 'We must stop the women getting caught up in the fighting.'

As they crossed the earthbridge into the Eastgarden, Carnelian and Akaisha could see among the trampled ferns the dead forming a line running to the Newditch. The women were singing as they ran to meet their warrior men. The proud victors were pulled from their saddle-chairs into embraces. Several were acting out the fight while their women and the children gawped wide-eyed. Breath was sucked in and hands slapped over mouths in horror as one man ducked and then leaning his head showed where an enemy spear had grazed his neck. Another man was producing gales of laughter as he pantomimed the flight of the Woading and the desperate way they had had to leap their aquar over the Newditch to get away.

Carnelian and Akaisha had reached the edge of the crowd when cries broke out: 'The Master, the Master.' Carnelian pushed through, making a path for Akaisha. He could see Osidian towering above the crowd, whose tide was breaking round him in adulation. Joy blazed from every face.

Akaisha, shouting something, could not be heard above the tumult. Carnelian saw a man standing with a bull-roarer and tore it from his grasp. He whirled the thing above his head until it began to keen. The crowd fell silent.

'You must not worship him,' Akaisha cried. 'He uses us for his own ends.'

Voices answered her by listing the children the Master had saved, the abundance of meat and now, victory.

'Victory, victory, victory.'

Carnelian whirled the bull-roarer again to bring quiet.

'Why do you think he does these things for us?' Akaisha cried. 'What is it you think he wants?'

The rest of her speech was drowned out by whistling and stamping.

Galewing rose above the crowd in a saddle-chair and began speaking. The noise abated as people struggled to hear what he said. Hands reached up to stroke his aquar, whose eye-plumes were stiff with agitation.

'The Woading crept here last night so they might treacherously attack us when we were gathered making djada. They've received only what they deserve.'

Carnelian was sure the Elder noticed Akaisha attempting to get his attention but he chose to focus on the crowd's roar of approval.

Galewing pressed his hands against their noise. 'Should we let them off so lightly?'

'No!' the crowd bellowed.

'Shall we seek compensation and a promise they'll never attack us again?'

'Yes!'

Galewing swung around in his saddle-chair. 'Who'll ride with me to the koppie of the Woading?'

For answer men vaulted back into their saddle-chairs and soon they were all aloft, seeming to float on the fevered applause of their women.

Carnelian saw Fern was there, taking his leave of Sil. He cried out his name until he was hoarse.

'We'll return tonight,' cried Galewing. 'Prepare a feast of thanksgiving.'

Fern saw Carnelian and his mother and, colouring with shame, he turned away. Osidian was mounted in their midst, Ravan and Krow beside him, then with Galewing they led the Ochre in a thundering mass across the ferngarden. Akaisha was gazing up towards the brow of the Crag, from which smoke was rising. She turned to look at him and he could see the fear in her eyes. As the women saw their men disappearing into the plain, Akaisha moved among them, sending the Bluedancing back to tending the curing fires while she, with some others, set about gathering the bodies of the Woading dead.

Carnelian was hiding from his feelings by labouring among the Bluedancing when Akaisha found him. She indicated he should follow her. They walked off together.

'I've just received news that riders have been seen heading here,' she said.

'Ours?'

'Most likely.'

'All of them?'

She shook her head. 'Only a handful.'

They looked at each other. 'You think it might be the Master.'

She frowned, shrugging. 'An Assembly has been called.'

She looked up into his face. 'Carnie, you must tell them what you told me.'

Betray Osidian to the Elders. Angry as he was, it made him feel sick.

'I need you to do this,' Akaisha said.

He bowed his head nodding. There was no other way to stop Osidian.

Akaisha breathed her relief. 'Let's go then. We must hurry if we're going to make it before he gets here.'

369

Akaisha left Carnelian standing on the porch of the Ancestor House and went in. Shortly afterwards, Carnelian was told to enter.

It took a while for his eyes to adjust enough to see the Elders squatting round him. He looked for Akaisha and found her in her place. Their eyes met.

'Why're you here, Carnie?'

Carnelian could not back out now. 'To warn you of the Master's intentions.'

'Why would you betray your own kind?' asked Harth.

'To save the Tribe.'

Harth laughed coldly. 'You expect us to believe this?'

'Mother Harth, would you believe me if I told you there are people here I've grown to love?' He allowed himself a glance at Akaisha, then returned his gaze to Harth's face.

'A pretty speech,' she said through a sneer.

'I believe it to be a true one,' said Akaisha. 'Tell us what you told me, Carnie.'

Carnelian steeled himself; this was it. 'The Master manipulates you. He plots to change your world, to put himself at its centre.'

'Why would he do this?' demanded Kyte.

'The lust for power is in the blood of all the Standing Dead.'

'Though you, of course, are different,' said Harth.

Carnelian grimaced. 'I was brought up by one of your own.'

Harth raised her eyes up to the ceiling as if to say, "that again", but she made no sound.

'You don't answer,' grumbled Crowrane.

'The Master intends to conquer himself an empire in the Earthsky.'

'The Standing Dead would not permit it,' said Kyte.

'It is the Standing Dead he wishes to defeat.'

The old men were frowning. 'To what end?'

'To fight his way back into the Mountain.'

For a moment everyone looked startled, but then Crowrane burst into laughter and took with him most of the Assembly.

Carnelian endured the gale of derision.

Still chuckling, Crowrane spoke out. 'How many . . . how many Plainsmen do you think it would take to overcome a single dragon?'

'Have you ever seen one?' asked Kyte, grinning.

'From a distance.'

The man turned to either side. 'From a distance, he says.' There was more laughter.

'Have you seen the fortresses guarding the entrance into the Mountain?' asked Kyte.

Carnelian nodded.

'Well then. Do you believe that even if all the peoples who pay the flesh tithe rose up against the Standing Dead they could breach such defences?'

Carnelian had seen the Three Gates and knew them invulnerable.

Akaisha turned on the Assembly. 'Laugh away, but did you imagine our men could destroy one tribe or cow another?'

'Or produce as much meat in one day as we have never had in the best hunting season,' added Whin.

Carnelian watched the men lose their smiles as they considered this. 'Does it matter whether what the Master seeks is possible? Surely it is enough that he intends to try it and in so doing he will bring down disaster on the Tribe.'

Crowrane gave his wife a sly look. 'What then, Master, do you advise we do?'

'You must kill him.'

The Assembly stared at him. Harth cocked her head to one side.

'And what do you seek for this advice, your own survival?'

Carnelian looked at Akaisha sadly. 'You must kill me too. It was I who persuaded Fern to bring us here. In my heart I should have known the strife we would bring you. You showed us kindness and look how we repay you. The Master is like a ravener and must be destroyed, but still I have loved him and could not live on with my betrayal.'

The Assembly greeted his speech with silence. Akaisha had tears in her eyes. Harth rose, frowning. Her gaze lingered on Carnelian. She looked sidelong at Akaisha.

'I begin to see why you chose to give this one the protection of your hearth. Still, with his honeyed tongue he has condemned himself.'

Akaisha and Whin began speaking in Carnelian's defence but were interrupted by the curtain lifting to dazzle them all. A figure walked in which, once the gloom returned, they saw was Galewing. He had a rolled-up blanket in his arms.

'Has the Master come with you?' asked Akaisha.

'Tonight he will remain at the earthwork by the lagoon.'

The sighs of relief made him uneasy. He frowned, noticing Carnelian.

'Why did you come, Galewing?' asked Harth.

The Elder smiled looking round the Assembly. 'I've come directly here from the koppie of the Woading. They've accepted that from now on they shall be our children and have sent us a ransom in exchange for the bodies of their men.'

371

He kneeled, then laid the blanket on the bone floor and carefully rolled it out. When it was a flat rectangle like a hole, he leaned over to take the two corners furthest from him and, looking up expectantly, drew the cloth back. The Elders gasped. Laid out on the blanket were discs, pierced and whole, some rayed like suns; there were crescent moons, horned saurians in the round, lip plugs, a huge pectoral incised with figures. Every piece gleaming salt. Kyte crept close to lift a pendant from the hoard and turned it this way and that in his calloused hands. He licked it and turned, grinning.

When they questioned Galewing, he assured them the treasure was theirs.

'And our sons?' Akaisha asked.

'They're spending the night in the earthwork. The Woading need time to choose the children they're going to send us to keep as a surety of their alliance with us. Until we have them here, the Master thinks it best we should protect ourselves against any reprisals.'

'Alliance?' said Akaisha.

Galewing opened his hands and looked at the faces of the Assembly. 'Subject of course to our approval.'

'Alliance for what purpose?' said Harth.

'We've promised that if they accept our rule, we shall, in time, return their children and obtain replacements for those marked for the tithe, as well as treasure to compensate them for this loss.' He indicated the salt jewels on the blanket.

'Obtain how?' said Harth, her face screwed up.

Galewing shrugged. 'Our other neighbours. It isn't as if we can trust them. We've seen one tribe attack us out of jealousy. What do you imagine will happen if we allow the others to combine against us?'

Harth blinked her disbelief. Her head was slowly shaking. She licked her lips. 'Are you possessed, Galewing?'

'Look, Harth.' Kyte was pointing at the jewels still lying on their blanket. 'That represents more than a year of service. More than one year of a young man's life lost to us.'

The Assembly gave his words a murmur of approval.

'It is stolen!' said Harth.

'As our children used to be before the Bluedancing came to take their place. No one here likes the taste of these changes, but we swallow them down for the good of our daughters and our sons. For my part, while the Master still spares our children and' – he pointed at the blanket – 'the blood of our men, then I shall leave him be.'

'Carnie, tell him.'

Carnelian explained what he knew and watched Galewing's frown deepen as he spoke.

'You see how dangerous he is?' said Akaisha when Carnelian was finished.

'More than a ravener,' said Galewing, 'but we have him by the throat. While it's our men he uses to do his fighting, we can have him killed at any time.'

Akaisha stood up. 'You're too complacent, Galewing. Haven't you seen how popular he's become among the Tribe?'

'Sooner or later he'll lose that. One day he'll overstretch himself, and then we'll have him.'

Mossie looked aghast at Carnelian. 'Should we be saying these things in front of him?'

'One of them is here and the other out on the plain. Even if that weren't so, do you think for a moment they don't know how we must be feeling about all this?'

The woman sat down cowed.

Harth raised her eyes. 'And this overstretching, does it not occur to you that should it happen it might well bring disaster down on us all?'

Carnelian had to speak. 'Listen to Mother Harth. Time is running out for you. Daily he grows more powerful among the young.'

The Assembly rose in stormy protest. 'Do you suggest that our own children would turn against us?'

'Underestimate the Master at your peril,' Carnelian cried above the din.

'We know you bleed, white man. If you bleed, we can kill you,' Crowrane cried back.

'Leave us now,' Akaisha said to Carnelian, fear for him bright in her eyes.

He stood for some moments regarding her. She lifted her chin, urging him to go. Bending, he passed under the curtain and into the brilliance of the day. He descended to the Grove, then walked to his mother tree. He lay in his hollow waiting, watching through the branches wisps of clouds changing shape in the sky.

When Akaisha came he saw in her face what she had come to say.

'We shall light the signal fire. When our men return, we shall kill the Master.'

Carnelian's stomach clenched. So it was done. 'Who can you trust to do it?'

Akaisha's face set into a mask. 'We shall do it ourselves.'

He met her eyes. 'And what is to happen to me?'

Her eyes twitched as she regarded him. 'Carnie, you too are to die.'

*

Smoke rising from the Crag brought the Tribe running to see what was wrong. Standing on the summit near the fire, Carnelian was watching for Osidian's return. Crowrane and a couple of the other veterans armed with spears stood around him and he had been told that if he should cause any trouble, they would run him through. Narrowing his eyes, Carnelian could see nothing but a speckling of herds clinging to the horizon.

A shout made everyone rise to their feet. Carnelian watched riders dew from the herds: a dark rivulet trickling towards him. In the vanguard was the figure Carnelian sought; a giant among the rest.

Carnelian waited with the Elders in the Ancestor House. Outside, down the steps, the Tribe had gathered in the clearing, so many their crowd stretched off into the mottled shade. All eyes were turned up to the little house of bones.

Eyeing Crowrane, Kyte and the others waiting beside the doorway, Carnelian felt the depth of his betrayal. Looking round, he saw shame on every face. It reminded him how far these people had been pushed that they dared not trust their own children; that they should be prepared to defile their most sacred place with murder. His eyes locked with those of Akaisha, who twitched a smile.

They heard the footfalls on the porch outside. The assassins narrowed their eyes and readied their spears. Carnelian wanted to turn away but refused to allow himself the cowardice of not watching Osidian die. He had asked the Elders to allow him to deliver the fatal blow, but they had refused him, staring. Carnelian was filled with fear at how close his own death was, but his heart welcomed it.

The curtain lifted and a figure stood framed by the dazzle of the day. It walked in and was followed by another and another, and Crowrane and the others drew back, protesting that these people, whoever they were, had not been given permission to come in. The last figure to enter eclipsed all light. Carnelian struggled for his vision to return and saw it was Ravan and some other youths, with Osidian standing behind them a marble colossus against the bone traceries of the wall. Amidst the storm of protests, Carnelian had attention for nothing but Osidian's face. There was a stillness in his downcast eyes. Carnelian knew that manner, that stance: it was the imperial demeanour of a Master.

As Osidian lifted his gaze, Carnelian felt the Elders quail but it was Ravan who spoke.

'Why are you armed, my fathers?'

Crowrane and the others regarded the spears in their hands with a kind of surprise.

'Is it perhaps because of the emergency that made you light the signal fire?'

The Elders had fallen silent, their gaze focused on Ravan.

'What is that made you light the fire, my fathers and mothers?'

Kyte spoke up: 'The Master is a danger to the Tribe.'

Ravan affected surprise. 'A danger? Did he not save us from the Bluedancing and the Woading? From famine? Did he not free our children from the tithe?'

'But why has he done these things, my son?' said Akaisha.

'He seeks power,' said Harth.

'To make war first on the tribes and then the Standing Dead,' said Ginkga.

'He's ravener possessed,' cried Crowrane.

Ravan smiled. 'It seems to me it is you who are possessed.' He pointed at Crowrane's spear. 'You were going to spill his blood here, on the sacred floor of our mother's bones.'

Many of the Assembly cast down their eyes, ashamed.

Carnelian stepped forward. 'Listen to them, Ravan, everything they're saying is true.'

'You have already betrayed the Master once and now you try to do so again.'

Carnelian felt Osidian's gaze and was drawn to meet his eyes. Expecting hatred, he was shocked to see there nothing but an amusement that chilled him to the core.

Ravan stepped towards the Elders. 'You fear the Master because he does what you cannot do. You disgust me. Is there anything you would not do to keep your bony grip on power?'

Akaisha leapt to her feet in fury. 'Be silent.'

'I will not, mother.' He regarded the old with sad contempt. 'You are few and we, the young, are many. You cling to the old ways and cannot see the new world we are making. You are unfit to rule and so, reluctantly, we shall have to rule in your place.'

THE WORLD REMADE

Slaughter is the mother of new worlds.
(from the 'Book of the Sorcerers')

'THE TRIBE WILL NOT LET YOU RULE,' CRIED HARTH.

'The young men will,' replied Ravan. He smiled. 'Without us the Tribe will have no water and the Koppie will be exposed defenceless to our enemies.'

Ginkga looked aghast. 'You're prepared to threaten your own people?'

'It is the men who shall protect them from all want, as we have always done.'

Crowrane stood forward. 'We are the protectors of the Tribe.'

Mossie was crying. 'Our children will not turn away from us.'

Ravan opened his arms wide. 'Ask them.'

The Elders did, all at once, some petitioning, some threatening their grandsons. The youths standing behind Ravan went paler, but they held their place and nodded.

As they fell silent, Akaisha raised her voice. 'You, Ravan and this gang of boys might be prepared to betray your people, but we shall see how many of the rest will support you.'

Ravan glanced at Osidian then looked back at his mother. 'You should consider carefully before doing anything that might lead to bloodshed.'

Akaisha blinked and stared at her son as if she was seeing him for the first time. Around her, the other Elders seemed to sag and age before Carnelian's eyes.

'Go now,' Ravan said, harshly. 'Prepare the people for the new world.'

Some glared at him through their tears, but even they obeyed him. As they filed past, Carnelian felt ashamed. Akaisha looked at him, but he could not bear to see her face and turned away. He kept his gaze averted as they shuffled past him. Finally, the curtain fell and the gloom returned.

'Are you sure, Master, they will not raise the Tribe against us?' whispered Ravan.

'They will do nothing,' said Osidian. 'Now go and steady the men.'

Ravan gazed at him for some moments, before he too left.

Left alone, Carnelian looked at Osidian. Their eyes met.

'If they do nothing it is only because they love their people.'

Osidian smiled. 'That, of course, formed a part of my calculations. Come, Carnelian, are you not even a little relieved I have survived this attempt on my life?'

Carnelian was not sure what he felt. He himself had been given back his life, but at what price. There was triumph in Osidian's beautiful face. Carnelian became possessed by a need for light and air. He pushed past Osidian and out from the room of bones. The Tribe in turmoil at his feet was receiving the first of the Elders into their midst; panic already spreading.

Armed youths did not stop him reaching the steps. On the ground, the crowds parted before him and he moved swiftly into the shadow of a mother tree. He picked up speed, until he was almost running down a rootstair, his gaze fixed on the brightness of the ferngarden. He did not look to either side until he had left the cedars behind and was walking waist-high through rustling ferns, dizzy in the sun.

He went down to the Eastgarden where the Bluedancing were working among the fires and trestles. He allowed himself only a glance over to the Killing Field with its heaps of bones. When he neared the Blooding Ditch, his pace slowed. He crossed another bridge into the inner ferngardens and, from the shade of the Old Bloodwood Tree regarded the Grove where the Elders were spreading the news of their overthrow. His eyes ranged over the delicately shifting cedar canopy. There lay what he now called home and yet he had allowed it to be destroyed as he and his father had allowed the Hold to be pillaged by Aurum and Jaspar. Was he cursed to be involved in the destruction of everything he loved?

He imagined Akaisha's pain and wanted to go and beg forgiveness for what he had brought upon them. He looked up at the cedar hill and his stomach churned. He overcame shame, fear of the rejection that might await him, and forced himself to begin walking towards it.

People turned away from him as he climbed the hill; from fear or hatred, Carnelian could not tell. He did not allow himself to hesitate when he came within sight of Akaisha's mother tree. His hearth-mates were there, under her branches, gathered near the hearth. Approaching, his spirits lifted as he saw Poppy gazing at him and Fern alive and well.

'You can stop pretending now, Master,' Fern said.

The tone as much as the form of address wounded Carnelian.

Fern turned to his mother. 'It's clear now that this one's been working with the Master all along.'

Akaisha looked at her son with puffy eyes, confused. 'But he betrayed the Master's schemes to me.'

'Wasn't it that very betrayal that led the Assembly to make the decision which more than anything made the men give the Master their support?'

Fern turned on Carnelian with hatred in his eyes. 'Did you imagine us too stupid to work it out?'

Poppy pushed between them and glared at Fern. 'You leave Carnie alone.'

Carnelian vaguely tried to calm her, shook his head. 'I don't know what . . . it can't be . . .'

'How else could the Master know the Elders were going to try to kill him today?'

Appalled, Carnelian tried to imagine another explanation.

Sil's eyes widened. 'You're not denying it, Carnie.'

Carnelian felt Poppy's little hand slip into his and gripped it. 'If this is true then the Master used me. I swear on my blood I acted in good faith.'

Fern snorted. 'You Standing Dead are better at using people than keeping promises.'

Poppy cringed at every word.

'How could the Master persuade so many of our people to turn against us?' said Whin, still in shock from what had happened in the Ancestor House.

'For two moons he has filled our minds with the proofs of his invincibility,' said Fern. 'Many have come to believe he will make the Ochre feared and respected among the tribes. After all, did he not win the battle against the Bluedancing, against the Woading? Did he not bring us the meat he promised?'

Carnelian felt sick as Fern's words forced the pieces to form a mosaic in his mind. He saw it all. How easily he had allowed himself to be manipulated. He shook his head, trying to disbelieve it. 'I thought he did it from spite, but it was policy, calculated to break up the cohesion of the Tribe.'

Fern frowned then continued. 'He chose to site his earthwork camp near the lagoon at the best crossing into Woading territory. I believe he only burned the Bluedancing mother trees to frighten and provoke the Woading and our other neighbours. He judged that our absence during his heavener hunt would give the Woading a chance to explore the earthwork.' He regarded Carnelian through slitted eyes. 'The Master knew very well that every Woading who had done his service in the legions would recognize it to be a military camp. Frightened we meant to strike against them, they struck first and when they did, he was ready for them.'

He looked at Akaisha and Whin. 'When we saw your signal, he claimed the Skyfather had come in a dream to warn him; jealous of his successes, fearful their power would pass to the warriors, the Elders had determined to treacherously murder him.' Fern's face showed disgust. 'Ravan dutifully stirred up the men by listing all the Master had done for us; instilling fear of the revenge the Woading would take once they knew we no longer had him to lead us.'

Whin ignited. 'You knew all this yet didn't act.'

Fern confronted her. 'What could I do alone against the others? My great mistake was to have faith in the wisdom of the Elders.'

The people round about gasped. Poppy's second hand joined the first and held on to Carnelian's fingers. Fern ducked an apology to his mother, then to Whin who seemed to subside.

'I can't deny we acted foolishly.'

'Can it be true that the Skyfather spoke to him?' said Fern.

The glance he gave Carnelian was filled with misery.

Akaisha was gazing at her son, aghast. 'I no longer know what is true and what is not.'

Whin gave her a look of concern. 'Go and rest, dear. I'll handle this.'

Akaisha nodded and Whin sent one of her daughters with her. The hearth watched the two move away with dismay. Carnelian understood. Like them he had come to rely on Akaisha's strength.

Sil regarded Carnelian tearfully. 'If you have betrayed us, Carnie, then there is no hope, for you have seen how weak we have become.'

Reaching out with his free hand, Carnelian clasped Sil's hands and looked her in the eyes. 'If it is all as Fern says, then I have been a fool, an instrument in the Master's hand.' He let her go, freed himself from Poppy's grip and spun round looking at every face. 'He made *you* slaughter heaveners; can you not believe it possible *I* could be used without my knowledge?'

Carnelian saw with relief that even Fern was no longer certain of his guilt.

'Do you still believe the Master intends to attack the Standing Dead?' asked Whin.

'I'm sure of it, my mother.'

'You believe he cannot win?'

Carnelian considered the changes Osidian had wrought upon the Ochre. 'I have only one certainty; if he is not stopped, the Master will bring disaster on the Tribe.'

'How do we free ourselves from him?' said Sil expressing the general feeling. She caught a look in her husband's eyes and her face grew pale. She grabbed him.

'He'd kill you!'

Fern pulled himself free.

Carnelian understood. 'Listen to her, you'd never get close enough.'

Fern grew enraged. 'What do you suggest?'

Examining his friend's eyes, Carnelian knew there was only one way. 'I'll do it.'

Fern narrowed his eyes, judging him.

'What will you do, Master?' said another voice.

No one had noticed Ravan approaching. People looked at each other, fearing he had heard everything. Ravan frowned, sensing a conspiracy.

'Why've you come?' Whin asked, coldly.

'Because the Master wishes to see this one here.' He indicated Carnelian with his chin.

Fern gave his brother a look filled with contempt. 'I thought it was the young who now ruled the Tribe?'

Ravan found he was enringed by his scowling hearthmates. He blushed and walked away. 'The Master doesn't like to be kept waiting.'

Carnelian saw Poppy forgotten, crying. He pushed her towards Sil. Receiving nods of encouragement, he went after Ravan.

Carnelian quickly caught up with Ravan. As he fell in beside him, the youth moved his head to one side but did not look at him.

'Now we have the power, everything will be much better. The Tribe will soon come to see we were justified in what we've done.'

'Your mother doesn't see it that way.'

'She's an old woman and should be glad to be free of the burdens of rule.'

Carnelian watched Ravan from the corners of his eyes. 'Fern was right, it is not the young but the Master who now rules.'

'What if it were true? The Master will make the Ochre great among the tribes.'

'You fool yourself, Ravan. You must know by now he cares for nothing but himself. Plainsmen are nothing more to him than savages. If it suited his purposes, he would care no more about the Ochre than he did the heaveners.'

Ravan turned on him, eyes flaming. 'Though you look like him, you're nothing alike. You don't know what he cares about. Because you've betrayed him do you expect everyone to be as treacherous as you?'

That barb struck home. Carnelian found he was remembering the love he had had for Osidian; the part he had played in bringing him to the Earthsky. He suppressed all guilt. Now he had to steel himself to murder him.

Young men standing with spears at the foot of the Crag steps moved aside to let Ravan and Carnelian climb them. Reaching the summit, Carnelian pulled his uba up over his nose so that only his eyes were exposed to the withering sun. Ravan led him across the burning rock to where Osidian stood massive, shrouded black with Krow and some other guards.

'Go and make the preparations for immediate departure,' Osidian said.

Krow gave a nod. As he passed Carnelian on the way to the steps, they exchanged grim greetings.

Osidian gave the iron spear he was holding to Ravan and beckoned. 'Come, my Lord.'

Carnelian fell in beside him and they walked together in silence. He was aware Ravan and the others were following. He watched Osidian gaze out over the plain and saw how close he was to the edge of the Crag. A lunge, then a push and he would be over.

'Have you nothing to say, Carnelian?'

Carnelian looked up and was immediately transfixed by Osidian's jade eyes. Was there sadness there?

'I betrayed you.'

'Yes, you betrayed me.'

Carnelian had expected anger, dissimulation, but not this sadness which struck at his heart. 'Stop pretending. I know you manipulated me as you have everyone and everything since we came here.'

Osidian looked up into the sky. 'Did your barbarian friends help you work that out?'

The contempt stung, but it was fear for Akaisha, Fern and the others that possessed him. To protect them, he must kill Osidian.

As Osidian walked away, Carnelian followed.

'The overthrow of the Elders has been an exercise which the Wise would probably consider trivial. Still, I have never presumed to achieve their level of mastery, though I have gleaned many techniques from their treatises on statecraft.'

Carnelian's mind was fixed on getting Osidian between him and the edge. He spoke hoping to disguise his manoeuvring: 'The Elders have wisdom of their own.'

'Whatever wisdom the old may have pales before the beauty, the youth and vigour of the young. This fracture is present in all peoples but cuts deeper into the tribes of the Earthsky than most. It was not over difficult to hammer some wedges in and so cleave the young from the old.'

Carnelian clutched at one last hope to delay the act of murder. 'People? You concede then that they are people? They love each other, their children, as the Chosen do; suffer pain similarly, loss. Even they have pride and beauty and honour.'

Osidian turned fierce eyes on him. 'I have borne this predilection you have for these savages long enough! I cannot understand why you are unable to overcome the deficiencies of your upbringing.'

Anger rose in Carnelian. 'Do you still delude yourself they believe us angels? They have seen we become weary, that we sleep, that we bleed as they do.'

Wrath set Osidian's eyes alight. 'We do not bleed as they do. Forget your blood if you wish, but I will not allow you to forget mine. In my veins, blood runs infused with holy fire.'

Seeing him there unrepentant, Carnelian was about to run at him, not caring that they would tumble together from the Crag when, shocked, Osidian moved away from the edge. 'You would slay me?'

He pulled the uba from his face and stared, gaping. 'I cannot believe . . .' He motioned Ravan and the others away when they began voicing their alarm.

Osidian's desolation struck at Carnelian's heart. Osidian moved further from the edge, never taking his eyes off Carnelian.

'Have you forgotten when I said to you that my blood ran in your veins?'

Carnelian recalled the night when they had made their vows of love to each other. It was the same night they had been captured in the Yden, just before they were cast into the outer world.

He saw the long agony of time that had brought him to this rock where he wished only to see Osidian dead.

Osidian looked close to tears. 'Never once has my love for you wavered.'

Carnelian hardened his heart. 'Do you believe that excuses what you have done?'

He saw Ravan's shadow moving in the corner of his eye.

'I tested your love, you know?' said Osidian.

'You mean you baited a trap for me!' Carnelian spat back.

'It was your choice to take the bait.'

Carnelian was seeing him through tears. 'What else could I do?'

Osidian shook his head again as if he could not believe what he was hearing.

'What would you have done if I had said nothing to the Elders?'

Osidian shrugged. 'The truth is, I never for one moment doubted you would betray me.'

Tears were running down both their faces.

'I should kill you,' said Osidian.

'You should. I will not cease fighting you.'

Osidian nodded, considering it.

'But you will not kill me,' said Carnelian, wiping his eyes. 'Seeing any Chosen die would diminish your glamour in their eyes.' He indicated Ravan and the others gaping at them.

Osidian looked as vulnerable as a child. 'That may not always be so.'

They gazed at each other, feeling the depth of what they had lost. Carnelian was the first to speak. 'What now?'

'I go to conquer,' Osidian said, his face turning to stone. 'You will remain behind and conduct yourself with due care, my Lord, or else those you seek always to protect will suffer my displeasure.'

Saying this, he broke through Ravan and the other guards and, sweeping across the Crag summit, disappeared down the steps leaving Carnelian impotently to contemplate his failure and his betrayals.

No one at the hearth blamed Carnelian for failing to rid them of the Master, but Sil was not the friend she had been and Whin was colder. Akaisha had grown suddenly old. Bent almost double, she never seemed to leave her place in the root fork by the fire. Gradually, Whin took on more and more of the duties and powers of hearthmother.

Tortured by guilt, Carnelian threw himself into the continuing struggle to cure the heavener meat before it spoiled. Great hunks were smoked until they looked like wood. Fires burning day and night were fed with the magnolias cut down from the margins of the ferngarden. The Killing Field had long been abandoned to the ravens. Drifts of them turned the carcasses into ivory ruins. When, rarely, a breeze would blow from the west, a sickening stench wafted over the djada field. But it was the east wind everyone feared most, for then the hill of offal soaked the air with its miasmas and Carnelian and the Bluedancing would be forced to slave even in the hottest part of the day with their faces swathed in cloth.

The men whom the Master sent to bring them water brought also news. The warriors of the Tribe and their allies the Woading were digging another earthwork, to the north-east, at the crossing of the lagoon nearest to the koppie of the Smallochre. From this earthwork they daily harried them when they came to fetch water. Scuffles had already broken out. It was only a matter of time before the Smallochre would be stung into giving battle.

Carnelian was down in the Eastgarden watching the Bluedancing braid the heavener djada into rope when, pointing, Poppy let out a cry. Smoke was rising from the Crag. Fern and the others returning, thought Carnelian, and began running towards the Blooding. Poppy's shouts pulled him up short. Turning, he saw she was running after him. He returned, scooped her up and ran on.

They found the gate to the Grove unguarded. They met Sil and some others of his hearthmates halfway up the rootstair moving at Akaisha's pace. Anxious as he was to find out if the signal really meant their men were back, Carnelian walked the rest of the way with them. He glanced furtively at Akaisha. He could not bear to see how fragile she had become.

When they reached the clearing before the Ancestor House they found many of the womenfolk gathered there and, near the Crag steps, many of the Elders craning to listen to a woman up on the summit. Her words were passed back.

'The Master and Ravan.'

The woman on the summit was shouting something else. Her words came accompanied by a murmur of fear.

'They're bringing dead.'

People began to move to the opposite side of the clearing where a path led to the Lagooning, but Ginkga climbed the first few steps up the Crag and urged them to wait. Her face hardened when her words were ignored by many. Carnelian decided it would be better if he waited.

At last a massive figure appeared at the edge of the clearing repelling the crowd. It was the Master and, beside him, Ravan. Together they walked through the Elders to the steps and began to ascend them. Behind them came a procession carrying drag-cradles on which lay shrouded bodies. No one could tell who they were because their faces were hidden by ubas. As the crowd moved back to let the drag-cradles be set down, their murmuring began tearing into sounds of grief.

'Why do you mourn when you should be joyous and proud of your noble dead?' said Ravan from the porch of the Ancestor House. Behind him the Master was just a shadow.

'Fern?' said Carnelian beginning to move forward but Sil's hand stayed him.

'I'll go.'

'See here,' cried Ravan and from his hands hung tresses of grey hair loaded with salt beads. 'This is the tribute the Smallochre pay you as the Woading did before them.' He shook the tresses and they could hear the beads tinkling. 'This salt and more like it means our men will never again have to go and serve in the legions.' He pointed with his fists at the dead. 'These heroes died to bring this blessing to the Tribe. Honour them.'

Sil returned pale from the women swarming the dead. She shook her head. 'He's not there.'

Carnelian, Akaisha and Sil shared the relief. A pale movement made Carnelian look up to see Osidian's hand signing.

Come up and talk to me.

Still worrying about Fern, Carnelian began moving towards the steps.

'Where are you going?' asked Akaisha.

'The Master summoned me.'

Akaisha looked from him up to where Osidian was climbing up to the summit. 'What sorcery could let you know his thoughts?'

'None, my mother.' He lifted his hands meaning to explain, but Sil caught them.

'Find out about Fern.'

Carnelian looked into her eyes and nodded, before he began pushing his way through the mourning crowd.

Ravan was waiting for him at the Ancestor House. He had transferred all the beaded hair to one hand. Carnelian examined it distastefully, almost expecting to see bloody fragments of scalp attached to the roots.

'Where are the rest of the men?'

Ravan smiled. 'You mean my dear brother?'

Carnelian searched the youth's eyes for Fern's death.

'Oh, he lives. The Master left him commanding a joint force of Woading and Ochre in the Woading earthwork.'

Carnelian caught some resentment in the youth's voice. 'Not you?'

Ravan scowled. 'He needs me as his interpreter.'

The youth lifted his empty hand towards the steps leading up to the summit and Carnelian took the lead.

Climbing up on to the summit, Carnelian saw the signal fire was still smoking. Osidian was there with some guards. As Carnelian approached him, the guards put themselves between Osidian and the edge. Carnelian ground his teeth, angry at that reminder of his failed assassination.

'So you have absorbed another tribe into your empire, Osidian.'

'The first of many.'

They stood gazing at each other; only their eyes exposed. Carnelian felt Ravan standing behind him.

'How goes the curing of the heavener meat?' Osidian asked.

'Well enough.'

'If the slaves have been worked hard then the process should be nearly complete.'

'It is.'

'Good. I have other work for them.'

Carnelian waited, dreading it already.

'They will cut a new ditch to annex more of the plain. The fern-gardens must be greatly expanded if I am to pasture the multitude of aquar I intend to gather here.'

Osidian turned and swept his arm round, pointing out an arc as far from the Newditch as the Newditch was from the Grove.

'Surely you don't mean to take this ditch all around the Koppie.' Work on the margin of the Killing Field had taught Carnelian what a vast labour that would be.

Osidian nodded.

'But that would take for ever.'

'I have calculated it will take four years if they work without ceasing.'

'They are not to accompany us on the migration?'

'That would be impractical.' Osidian sketched some gestures in the air. *Aquar, the valley, many impediments . . .*

'How do you expect them to stay here without water? The cistern would not hold nearly enough to give drink to so many mouths.'

'We shall dig new cisterns.'

'There's not enough time.'

'You are in error.' He pointed out along the Lagooning. 'We shall dig them there where my men can most easily fill them. If we put them close to the path they will be in the shade of the magnolias.'

He looked back at Carnelian. 'The cisterns will hold enough for the Bluedancing but also for the warriors of the Ochre and the four other tribes I shall rule before the migration.'

Carnelian knew there must be reason behind this madness but he could not see it. 'The Tribe has to be escorted to the mountains. You must see that.'

'All my tribes will be escorted. Their warriors will take them as far as the mountains and then return here.'

'Why would you want . . .' He fixed Osidian with a stare. 'You fear that in the mountains their Elders and their women might work them free of your dominion.'

'There, you see, you can think like one of the Chosen when you want to.'

Carnelian knew what was to come and raised his hand. 'Please, Osidian, spare me your threats. I will do as you ask.'

'Thank you for being so understanding.'

Carnelian controlled his anger. Nothing would be gained at that moment from violence. He would bide his time.

The next day Carnelian began work on the cisterns. He had explained to Sil that the Bluedancing were going to stay in the Koppie during the withering. Once she had overcome her disbelief, then horror, she helped him find women to act as overseers.

By the end of the second day, the first cistern had been cut: a rectangular hole in the ground the bottom of which was bedrock. He had sent the men Osidian had given him to the lagoon and, when they returned, their drag-cradles were sagging under the weight of the clay they had gouged from its banks. This was tipped into the hole, where the Bluedancing used it to plaster the walls and floor. When it had dried, waterskins were carefully emptied into the cistern. All that day, drag-cradles arrived laden with more. Slowly the level of the pool rose brown and murky up the clay sides of the pit. When it had nearly reached the top, Carnelian laid over it covers of woven fernfrond strengthened with horsetail poles. The structure sagged a little but held. Days later, as the Bluedancing and the others were digging the next cistern, Carnelian had the covers lifted off the first. A sigh of relieved delight rose from his Ochre helpers as they saw the clay had settled, leaving the water clear.

When the mother trees announced the Withering with their cones, Poppy came to Carnelian eager to plant her seed. Though Akaisha had promised to ask permission from the other Elders, Carnelian was reluctant to ask her if she ever had. Besides, he suspected it was no longer their decision to make. He became anxious about what might happen to Poppy's precious seed once it germinated. In the end, he persuaded her it would be best to wait. A year was not, after all, such a long time in the life of a mother tree. Tearfully, she agreed.

Torrid days blazed in indistinguishable continuity. Each morning the men set off to fetch water to fill the cisterns. Each time they had to ride further as the lagoon shrank away.

'Most of its bed is cracked like old skin,' one of them coughed, resting his hand on the pole of a drag-cradle, trying to keep in his aquar's shadow. Their mouths and their eyes opened in faces caked with dust.

Carnelian reassured them they had enough water stored. He had himself surveyed the nearly forty cisterns that morning. The wall of one had crumbled. The levels in each had fallen, no doubt through seepage as well as evaporation. Still, after consulting Whin, he gauged that they had enough for those who were to remain behind, at least until the Rains came.

A morning after a full moon, the air began to haze with spores. Soon they so choked the day even the sun could not peep through. At night, hiding with Poppy beneath blankets, they could not sleep for the hissing. Seven days the storm lasted and on the eighth the whole world seemed to have rusted.

The weddings held during the next moon were not the joyous events they had once been. People were uncertain whether the old should preside over them as they had always done. Besides, the ceremonies were tainted by mourning.

When the Master came, he always brought dead with him. Never very many, he was a skilled commander, but enough to haunt the Grove with wailing. Ravan would talk to them of victories and show them the salt tribute they had forced their victims to pay. He and the Master would spend the night on the summit of the Crag and did not seem to mind sharing it with the corpses nor with the ravens that came to feed upon them. Carnelian shunned the Master, as did the rest of the Tribe, who had grown to dread his returns.

Even in the shade, each breath was toasting Carnelian's throat dry. He looked out past the Newditch to where the curve of Osidian's ditch was already cutting into the burning plain. He imagined the Bluedancing suffering there with only improvised hats to keep off the sun; ubas over nose and mouth to filter the air their digging kept always clouded with dust. They already knew their fate. They were to labour all through the Withering on the new ditch. Worse, Carnelian imagined, was the news that it was nearly time to fire the ferngardens. The Tribe would then leave for the mountains. The Bluedancing knew this was when their tithe-marked children were to be sent to the Standing Dead in place of the Ochre's own.

Carnelian wondered how the Wise would react once they discovered that the Bluedancing had not come to Osrakum to pay their tithe. Would this alert them to Osidian's presence? Perhaps the crime would be lost for a while in the ocean of their bureaucracy. This seemed a bleak hope. What was certain was that if Osidian continued to disrupt the Earthsky, one day there would be retribution. On that day, Osidian would have the war he craved.

In the cool of the night, the Grove was sometimes disturbed by the cry of some woman calling for her husband. In the day it was hard to believe any of their men would return from the torrid, shadeless plain. The heavener djada was packed on to the drag-cradles ready for the migration. The Tribe sipped water drawn from the cisterns. Even the men who had come to tell them the lagoons were dried up were long gone. So it was that when the messenger came to declare that all their men would be returning the next day, he was disbelieved. No one dared to challenge the Gods by feeling hope. The next day many dared the summit of the Crag, but nothing solidified from the wavering air. Despair saturated the shade beneath the mother trees.

Shouting raised Carnelian from fevered drowsiness. The greatest heat of the day had passed. When word reached them riders were approaching the Koppie, Carnelian joined the rest of his hearth running out along the Lagooning across the black deserts of the ferngarden to welcome them.

That Fern was there alive would have been cause of joy enough for Carnelian and the hearth, but that there were no dead at all stunned people to silence. Riding at the Master's side, Ravan announced that the Ochre were everywhere victorious. The Tribe burst into song, ecstatic that what they had dreaded had not come to pass.

The tension between Fern and Ravan had subdued the carnival atmosphere of the hearth. That and the demand the returning men had made that the Elders should give up their salt regalia so that the warriors could protect it along with the rest of the Tribe's wealth. Whin's and Akaisha's hair looked lank without its beads. Even Sil's joy at the return of her husband could not withstand his moroseness. Carnelian was desperate to talk to him but he felt it was Osidian watching them through Ravan's eyes.

Something woke Carnelian. Taking care not to disturb Poppy, Carnelian sat up. Someone was moving towards the rootstair. Instinct made Carnelian rise and follow. The cold night air made him glad he had thought to bring a blanket. The figure was climbing towards the Crag, its footfalls lost in the sighing of the mother trees. Carnelian went as fast as he could, but when he reached the path that hugged the Crag, he found he had lost the figure. He hurried on, guessing that whoever it was was going down the Westing to the latrines. Suddenly, a shape appeared before him.

'Why are you following me?' it whispered.

Carnelian realized with relief it was Fern. He had hoped it would be him.

'It's me.'

'Carnie? High father, you frightened me. Why are you stalking me?'

'I need to talk to you.'

Cursing softly, Fern pulled Carnelian after him. They said nothing as they descended the Westing. When they reached the Homing, they turned right and walked along it until they reached two cedars from between which a piece of rock extended out over the ditch. This was one of the men's latrines.

Fern turned to him. 'What do you want?'

Carnelian could not make out his face. He tried to find a question. 'Something needs to be done.'

'Why should I trust you?'

Carnelian grimaced. As well as he could, he explained what had happened on the summit the day he had intended to kill Osidian.

'Do you still love him?'

Carnelian bit back the easy denial he was about to make. 'A part of him, but the rest, I despise.'

Silence fell between them. The cedars on either side of the ditch creaked. Beyond, the burned ferngarden was a paler darkness.

'Don't worry. I'll do it.'

Carnelian was shocked by his friend's cold determination. 'You can't.'

Carnelian could feel Fern growing angry. 'Even now you try to protect him. Will you also betray me?'

Carnelian became angry too. 'If I'd wanted to do that don't you think I've had plenty of opportunities?'

He hesitated, then reached out and gripped Fern's hand, holding on to it when it made to pull away. 'He controls me by threatening you.'

Fern's hand relaxed in Carnelian's grip. 'You must see we need him now. Who else will stand between us and the revenge of the conquered tribes?'

'You.'

'What?'

'Take his place.'

'Would the men follow me?'

'Why not? One of the Standing Dead is very much like another.'

Carnelian considered it. He released Fern's hand. 'I couldn't do it.'

'The men would follow you. The other tribes too.'

'I'm not the Master. I don't have his stomach for violence.'

'I've seen you fight well enough when you have to. Besides, if we're careful, there shouldn't be any need.'

'What would we gain?'

'The end of this madness. I believe the Master is possessed. Somehow, the spirit of the swamp ravener passed into him when he spilled its blood.'

Carnelian was chilled by how close this was to what Osidian believed. 'I could slowly undo what he has done. Eventually restore the Elders.' The very thought warmed him, but then he was pulling his blanket round him. It was one thing to kill Osidian in the heat of anger: quite another to plan it coldly. There was no other way. 'When would we do it?'

'Not now. It's too close to the migration and, with the other tribes involved, only the Master knows how it is to be arranged. We can do it in the mountains.'

Carnelian felt Fern's hand seeking his own and clasped it to seal their agreement.

Poppy insisted on going with Carnelian to the Crying Tree. They walked down hand in hand as dawn was breaking. People were dowsing their fires in preparation for leaving the Koppie. The Tribe's palpable relief they were not losing any of their own children was soured by the shame that they were putting other people's in their place.

Glancing round, Carnelian saw Akaisha, helped by Sil, following him with Whin and Fern behind them.

'At least we'll be off to the mountains,' Sil had said, smiling nervously, for the moment it seemed, having forgotten that her husband and almost all the men would be returning across the desert to the parched Koppie. Still people had smiled back though their eyes avoided contact.

The five Bluedancing children were there with their mothers beneath the Crying Tree. A forbidding circle of Tribe warriors stood nearby with Ravan as their commander.

Fern indicated the men. 'Did you really need to bring these?'

'We wouldn't want any of them escaping,' said Ravan. 'Have you come to gloat, brother, or to give thanks that, through his mercy, the Master will one day spare your daughter?'

Fern scowled. 'I've come to show respect to those whose sacrifice saves our own.'

Ravan frowned. 'I don't know why you're all so grim.' He indicated the tithe children with his chin. 'They would've all been sent to the Mountain anyway.'

'Ravan, if you've nothing kind to say, say nothing at all,' said Whin.

Ravan flushed. 'Who do you think you are speaking to me like that?'

'What're you going to do, nephew, have me killed?'

Ravan was unable to hold his aunt's glare and ended up glowering at his fist gripping his spear.

The Bluedancing mothers were taking leave of their thin children. All were crying, the tears smearing their dirty faces into fearful masks. Akaisha hobbled towards them. Her hair snaked out from under her head blanket and clung to her face lifeless without its beads. She lifted her hands shakily and then let them flutter down to her side. 'It's better . . . but then you must know. It's better to let them go quickly.' She was crying.

One of the Bluedancing mothers began shrieking at her and all Akaisha could do was nod her head. Ravan bellowed at the woman and, instinctively, she grabbed her boy and put her body between him and Ravan's lowered spear.

Akaisha flew at her son, snatched the spear from his grip, then flung it down. She spluttered something angrily. He stooped to pick it up and backed away. Ashen, Sil was holding Fern back. Poppy was watching it all through tears.

Whin took some steps towards Ravan menacingly. 'Where's the salt the Master gave you for their journey?'

The youth fished a loaf from his robe and handed it to Whin, whose eyes were stony. She gave the salt to one of the tribute bearers. They made sure the children were secure in their saddle-chairs. Then, without ceremony, the tributaries rode away.

'They're the lucky ones,' said Ravan.

'What do you mean?' asked Carnelian.

'The rest of them are staying here with their mothers until the Rains come.'

Sil and her mother exchanged a look of misery. Akaisha was frowning while staring at nothing. Carnelian was imagining how terrible the coming heat would be.

'Where's the Master?' he asked Ravan, who shrugged, already busy bustling the Bluedancing mothers back to their digging.

That the steps leading up to the Ancestor House were unguarded made Carnelian certain Osidian was not on the Crag summit. He wandered around asking any men he saw, but none knew where the Master was. When he glimpsed through the cedar canopy men gathering by the cisterns, Carnelian went down there.

Osidian looked up as Carnelian approached. 'You have saved me having to send for you. Come walk with me.'

Osidian waved Krow and his other guards away and Carnelian fell in beside him as they sauntered up towards the Grove. Neither said anything until, with sighs of relief, they reached the cool relief of the cedar shade.

Carnelian found it strange Osidian felt safe to be with him unguarded. 'Are the cisterns what you wanted?'

'They are functional,' Osidian replied.

'Why are we not taking the Bluedancing children with us?'

'You are not coming.'

Carnelian stared at him.

'You will stay here to oversee the Bluedancing.'

Carnelian realized that he should have expected this.

'You seem surprised.'

'Who will you leave with me?'

'Krow and enough men to make sure you can control the slaves.'

'It will be hard here.'

Osidian searched the canopy as if he were looking for holes. 'These cedars will maintain their leaves and you will have water. Use it sparingly. Remember I shall be returning here with the men of all five tribes.'

Carnelian realized his plotting with Fern had come undone and became terrified his friend might act alone.

'You seem distracted, my Lord.'

'Take the Bluedancing children with you.'

Osidian shook his head. 'Their mothers will work better if they remain here.'

'In the mountains the children would act as a guarantee of their good behaviour.'

Silence deepened between them before Osidian fixed Carnelian with a cold smile. 'I will take the children, though it is transparent that you only seek to protect them.'

Carnelian would not look him in the eye.

'You will make sure the earthwork continues apace?'

Carnelian nodded. 'I had better go take my leave of Akaisha and the others.'

Osidian assumed the pose of a Master weary of the world. 'I suppose you had better.'

Carnelian walked away and only broke into a jog once he was sure Osidian was out of sight.

'Cisterns or no cisterns, anyone who stays here during the Withering will die.'

Carnelian was desperate to find Fern, but he could see Akaisha was getting upset and was reluctant to abandon her. She looked so wretched. Reaching up to stroke her hair, her hand hesitated when it did not find the familiar beads.

'Really, my mother, we've taken every precaution not to run out of water,' he said, reaching out to reassure her.

She threw his hand off angrily. 'You've no idea what it'll be like here.'

She turned away, wet-eyed, blind, her eyebrows raised. She gave a little shrug. 'Not that what I feel matters any more.'

Her dark eyes fixed on him. 'What about the huskmen?'

Carnelian knew nothing about that but supposed it unlikely the Grove gates would be sealed with so many people left behind.

'I'll be here to protect the Koppie.'

Akaisha made a face.

At that moment Poppy ran up. 'Carnie, it's time to go.'

Carnelian sagged. He had forgotten he would have to say good-bye to Poppy. 'Have you seen Fern?'

Poppy shook her head. Carnelian was in an agony of indecision. Akaisha hefted a sack. He disliked seeing her burdened like that.

'Is there no one coming to help you?'

'I can manage.'

Carnelian grimaced. He insisted on taking the sack, then,

motioning Poppy to go round to Akaisha's other side, they proceeded towards the Lagooning.

On every side, under the trees, people were moving, converging on the Lagoongate. Carnelian, Akaisha and Poppy reached the crowd and had to wait until it was their turn to cross the earthbridge into the ferngarden. As they walked along between the cisterns and the magnolias, Carnelian kept scanning the crowd looking for Fern.

'Carnie,' cried a woman's voice. They turned and saw Sil pushing her way towards them.

'Thank the Mother,' she said as she saw Akaisha. 'You were supposed to wait for us by the mother tree. My mother and I didn't know where you were.'

Akaisha scowled. 'I'm not a child, Sil.'

'No, my mother.' She and Carnelian exchanged glances.

'Do you know where Fern is?' he asked her.

She frowned. 'Ravan came for him. No doubt he's off with the Master.'

He must have shown his dismay because she said: 'What's wrong?'

'Will you tell him something from me?'

'Why can't you tell him yourself?'

'He's not coming with us,' Akaisha growled.

'Carnie?' cried Poppy, her eyes wide with panic.

He lifted her up and looked her in the face. 'I have to stay here, Poppy, to look after the Bluedancing.'

'You can't!'

'Don't waste your words, child,' said Akaisha. 'His mind's made up.'

Poppy's lower lip quivered. 'Then I'll stay with you.'

Carnelian shook his head. 'No.'

Poppy clung to him. 'I'm not going!'

'Oh yes you are,' he said with a voice that froze her. He forced a smile and kissed her. 'I'll be here when you return.'

'Sil will look after you.' He glanced round at Sil, who gave a nod.

Whin caught up with them and he stayed with them until they reached the Far Lagoonbridge and saw the Tribe gathering in the blaze of the open plain. Carnelian took his leave of them. He hugged Poppy, who had still not got over him shouting at her. He was thankful because he knew that if she began crying he might end up joining her. He put Poppy down and put her hand in Sil's.

Sil looked distraught. 'What did you want me to tell Fern?'

Carnelian thought. 'Tell him he must wait until he returns here with the Master.'

He kissed her lips to stop questions. She frowned, then turned to allow him to kiss Leaf. Akaisha took her bag back from him. He leaned in to kiss her but she turned her face away.

Krow had found him and together they watched the Tribe march away. Carnelian saw riders and was sure one of them was Fern. Dust rose in clouds to hide them but still he stood watching the dark shapes trembling behind the veils. Soon the plain had claimed them all. The few men who had come to watch began to slog back to the cedar shade. It was Krow's discomfort from the heat that made Carnelian leave. As they walked back, he glanced over to where he knew the Bluedancing were slaving in the sun. He was not feeling brave enough just then to go among them. At that moment, what he most wanted was to go and sit against his mother tree.

THE ORACLE

It is too late to avoid a scorpion once you have felt his sting.
(A Chosen proverb)

SMOKE FROM THE BURNING PLAIN TURNED THE DAYS TO DUSK; AT NIGHT
it stole the stars, leaving the blackness to come alive with furtive
smoulderings. It was hard not to believe they were witnessing the
end of the world.

Then the sun began to peer through the haze. The moon rose full
and flooded the cold dead plain. Through numberless molten-glass
days, Carnelian craved the shade of his mother tree but he chose
instead to stay with the Bluedancing. He spared the warriors exposure
to the terrible gaze of the sun and left them cowering in the shade of
the cedars. Krow chose to join him. With his help, Carnelian tried to
arrange the labour of the Bluedancing so that as many as possible
should work in the shade of the ditch wall. Still, many women were
forced out into the torrid air; on to earth so hot they had to wrap cloth
around their feet or else be blistered. Even in the ditch, the sun
threatened to sear tongue and eyes. Drinking, each gulp had to be held
in the mouth to cool it a little before swallowing. The more unbearable it became, the more Carnelian refused to abandon the women.
He could give them no promises, no reassurances. He hoped it was
enough they knew their children were safe in the mountains and that
each day they saw him suffering at their side.

On a day like any other, a warrior not of the Ochre came to find
Carnelian at the diggings. Carnelian ignored the man's stare. Skin

slimy with sweat and dust; mouth and throat choked dry, Carnelian's eyelashes gummed together every time he blinked. He closed his mouth and allowed it to fill with spittle. When his tongue came loose, he used it to scour his mouth. He gathered it all and spat it out, licked his lips, spat again, swallowed.

'What is it?' he croaked.

The man's eyes widened. 'Smoke.'

Carnelian peered at the man waiting for more. Krow appeared.

'What's happening?'

The man pointed back the way he had come. 'Smoke rising. In the direction of our . . . my koppie. The koppie of the Darkcloud.'

Carnelian stood for a while unsure what the man wanted of him. 'You want me to see it?'

The man answered with a vigorous nod.

Carnelian and Krow covered themselves with their robes and the youth led them up out of the ditch. They surfaced into blinding incandescence. Beneath a flat, colourless sky, the land smouldered, wisped with dust. Carnelian concentrated on drawing scorched air slowly into his lungs. Sweat trickled down his neck, his back, his inner thighs. He realized the man was waiting for him, impatient. He pointed up at the Crag.

Carnelian measured the burning distance lying between him and the Newditch and began walking. Staggering, swooning, he cursed himself that he had not drunk for a while.

At last they crossed a bridge into the delicious shade under a magnolia. Running from one shadow to the next, Carnelian led them to the first cistern. Reluctantly, the man helped him wrestle its cover aside. Carnelian lowered a leather bucket to the water, swaying, ribboned with light. He drew the bucket up and let Krow drink first before he took a long, cool draught.

'Nectar,' Carnelian said and saw by the others' puzzled expressions that he must have spoken in Quya. The man refused a drink. He and Krow slid the cover back. A little more himself, Carnelian saw how desperate the man was that they should hurry. They jogged all the way to the Homeditch and were soon under the cedar canopy.

They took a route up the hill that was wholly in shadow. Other men, evidently all Darkcloud, were waiting anxiously by the Crag steps. As his guide ran up to them, he half turned. 'The stone will burn you if you touch it.'

Reaching the summit, Carnelian could feel heat radiating off the rock. They would shrivel up if they stayed too long.

'Show me,' Carnelian said.

The man led him across the summit and then pointed west over the simmering plain.

Carnelian peered and for a while could see nothing. Then he saw a dull haze smudging the horizon.

'That's in the direction of your koppie?' Carnelian asked.

The man nodded, staring.

'It really is fire,' said Krow.

'Let's talk down there,' Carnelian said moving back towards the steps.

In the clearing bathed in the deep shadow of the Crag Darkcloud men collected around Carnelian. He looked into their anxious faces. 'You're worried it might be your mother trees?'

'There's nothing else left to burn, Master,' said one.

'What do you want me to do?'

'Let us ride home,' said the man who had fetched him there.

Carnelian asked them to give him a little time to think. He leaned against the coolness of the Crag steps, wondering how Osidian might react to him letting them go. He imagined the Hold on its island several worlds away. He remembered how he had felt about his home. He had been unable to stop it being destroyed but the Darkcloud might still save theirs.

'I'll lead them, Master, if you want,' said Krow.

Carnelian looked round at the fretting Darkcloud.

'Gather every man you can find. We will all go together.'

While they filled waterskins and saddled aquar, Carnelian returned to the diggings. Locating some of the Bluedancing Elders, he told them he was leaving the Koppie in their care. While he was gone, they could rest from their labours. Though it had never been his intention, he realized that their children being in the hands of the Ochre would ensure their good behaviour.

He led the warriors out of the Koppie along the Southing and then turned west. He suppressed panic as he saw the green of the mother trees recede. They were adrift in a desert spined with a few charred acacias. The rest was dust and ashes. As the sun poured down its fire, Carnelian could not believe the earth would survive until the Rains. He drew his uba down over his eyes and rode blind, trusting to the Darkcloud to find their way home.

At last they came within sight of the dusty bed of a lagoon. At its narrowest point, a ring was incised into the earth.

'The Master's earthwork,' said Krow.

Curious to see one of Osidian's camps, Carnelian rode closer and was surprised how small it was.

'Rather cramped,' he said to Krow, then noticed the youth was staring off across the lagoon to where smoke was rising in two columns from a koppie on the horizon. As Carnelian's eyes met Krow's, understanding passed between them. The fires seemed man-made. But who? Carnelian watched Krow's face grow pale as his lips formed the word: Marula.

Others had seen the smoke. Several Darkcloud rode up to Carnelian clamouring. He explained what he and Krow suspected.

'We must go and kill them,' said one, his face dark with fury.

Glancing at Krow, fearing his reaction, imagining Poppy's, Carnelian shook his head. 'They're likely to outnumber us.'

Cries of protest rose from the Darkcloud. Carnelian regarded them, agonized. 'We must wait for the Master and then hit them with our combined forces.'

'They might escape us,' said Krow.

'We risk heavy casualties, perhaps annihilation.'

'You fear them because they massacred my tribe,' said Krow through gritted teeth. 'Even with surprise on their side, they still took a mauling. This time surprise is ours.'

Carnelian paused to watch the smoke again. It must be rising from among the Darkcloud's mother trees. He glanced round and saw their anguish. It was not hard to imagine their women's grief should they return to find their trees harmed in any way.

'I'll ask the others,' Carnelian said to Krow.

Krow's eyes flamed. 'Why ask when you can command?'

'I'll risk my blood but not that of others against their will.'

Krow rode his aquar in among the other men crying: 'Though we be of different tribes, we're all Plainsmen. Can we allow such defilement to go unpunished?'

Grimly, all there gave their assent.

'Very well,' said Carnelian. 'But if we are to approach unseen, we must wait for dusk.'

They found what shade they could within the earthwork and sheltered beneath blankets. Carnelian found if he sat very still, the heat rising from his body would lift his uba from his skin. As sweat trickled down his back, he carefully sipped sun-heated water from a waterskin. His slitted gaze lost hold of the white world. In a stupor he sat, tortured, imagining the disasters that might overcome their expedition.

The night was as cold as the day had been hot. Shadows in the starlight, they streamed across the lagoon bed and then began the long ride across the plain to the koppie of the Darkcloud.

A sliver moon rose as they neared the outer ditch. The Darkcloud led them across a bridge into a ferngarden. The ride to the next ditch was shorter than it would have been at the Koppie. Once across, Carnelian saw that the inner ferngardens were much wider than he was used to. To approach as silently as they could, they made their aquar walk. Carnelian had plenty of time to search the hill with its cedars and the irregular crags rising above them. All was in blackness and there was no sign of life except for the cedars shifting in a breeze that carried on it a hint of smoke.

At last they reached a bridge leading over the innermost ditch. Carnelian and Krow dismounted with the Darkcloud and watched them cross the bridge and disappear into shadow.

As he waited Carnelian listened to the sighing of their mother trees. Watching a canopy round to the north, he was sure that every so often it opened a chink through which he glimpsed what might have been a flicker of light on branches.

A single shape returning over the bridge made him jump. The Darkcloud came close enough for Carnelian to smell him.

'The huskman's still in his place, Master,' said the Darkcloud. 'Some of us have gone in to scout around.'

'You should've waited for instructions,' said Krow, his voice seeming loud after the man's whisper.

Carnelian reached out and gripped Krow's shoulder, wanting to calm him. 'We need to know where they are.'

They crept back to where the others were still mounted and waited, listening, watching.

At last the Darkcloud returned. Even though they were nothing but shadows, Carnelian could sense their rage. Their voices rose as they all began to speak at once.

'Choose one of you to speak,' Carnelian hissed.

One of them was pushed forward.

'The filthy bastards have cut down two mother trees.' They could hear that the man was close to tears.

'Marula?' asked Krow.

'A plague of them.'

'How many?' Carnelian asked.

'Hundreds.'

Carnelian grimaced. It was what he had most feared. 'Are they camped?'

The man's snort was echoed by the others. 'They're sprawled out over the rootearths of Magnolia, Erth, Ceda —'

'How many hearths? How densely?' Carnelian interrupted.

'Six.' He shrugged. 'Less than a hundred at each. All in a tight cluster in the north of the grove.'

Carnelian nodded. 'In the shade of the crags.' The Marula outnumbered his men at least four to one. 'There might be too many of them.'

The Darkcloud began protesting and Carnelian hissed them to silence.

'I'm with them,' said Krow, coldly.

Carnelian leaned close to the spokesman. 'Anything else?'

'The western edge of the grove where they came in is crowded with aquar.'

'They're covered in sores,' someone said from behind him.

The spokesman nodded. 'By the looks of them, the bastards haven't unhitched their drag-cradles or unsaddled them for days.'

'Probably don't know how to,' said Carnelian.

'Drag-cradles?' said Krow.

'Loaded with djada, water.'

Carnelian did not need to be able to see Krow's face to know they shared the same thought. Stolen from another massacred tribe.

That made Carnelian's mind up. 'Are they sleeping?'

The spokesman nodded. 'Fires dowsed, they lie around them.'

'Well, let's make sure most of them never wake again.'

They fell on them with mattocks as if they were beating undergrowth to drive game. A quarter of the Marula had their heads staved in as they slept. The rest woke to mayhem. Carnelian swung against another skull, memories of the Twostone massacre, of Poppy orphaned, driving away his instinct that this was dishonourable. Still, he was relieved when a number of the Marula found their spears. Butchery became battle and the Marula still outnumbered them. Carnelian cast away his bloodied mattock, took his spear in both hands and leapt to the attack, baying. Though dwarfed by the black men, the Darkcloud crashed into them and pushed them back. Some of the invaders fell, their ankles catching on the cedar roots. Others rolled, lost their spears, stumbled to their knees and were up trying to run down the slope. Their ranks were dissolving as Carnelian impaled one in the chest. The man fell clasping the spear haft, his teeth set in a grimace of surprise. Carnelian put his foot on the man and pulled. The spear came free, spurting hot blood on to his legs. He paused, reeling, watching the Marula fleeing, falling, rolling while Krow led the Plainsmen down the rootsteps after them, screaming with battle-lust.

Carnelian turned slowly, seeing the hillside in the light of the smouldering fires. He approached one, seeing the great bough in its midst from which the flames had taken a wide charcoal-edged bite. The soft bark showed it was cedar wood, the amputated limb of a mother tree. He wandered emotionless up towards the mutilated trees. He touched one, her proud head fallen into the earth, her branches broken, her waist splintered. He glanced down the hill and saw the Marula had fled out into the ferngardens where he had set Plainsmen to hunt them on aquar.

Something pale caught the corner of his eye. He whisked round and saw a house of bones nestling up among the crags. Smoke was leaking from it. He remembered the charred floor of the Twostone Ancestor House. Hefting his spear, he strode towards it. He found steps cut into the rock and climbed them. When he set his foot upon the porch the smoke was thick enough to sting his eyes. A leather door was set into the wall. He crept to it and listened and heard nothing. Tearing the door back, he entered.

Three Marula were lit by a blaze set into a pelvis in the floor. Two lay as if asleep. The third sat against a frieze of skulls, regarding him with disdain. Even under their powdery covering of ash, Carnelian could see this Maruli was much younger than the other two.

'Are you what you seem?' the Maruli asked in smooth Vulgate.

Carnelian stared. 'You speak . . . ?'

The man grinned his sharpened teeth and displayed a pale palm upon which there were some service glyphs. 'I served long in the service of the Masters.'

Carnelian saw that the man was identical to the Marula who had escorted him from the sea to Osrakum. When he indicated the other Marula, the man shook his head. 'They never served the Masters.' He raised his eyebrows.

'Yes, I *am* a Master,' Carnelian said in response to the man's earlier question. He put a finality in the tone that told the Maruli he would answer no more. The man showed his feral teeth again.

'And I am Morunasa,' he jabbed an arm in the direction of his older companions, 'with these others, Oracle and slave of the Darkness-under-the-Trees.'

'What are you doing here?'

Before the Maruli had a chance to answer, Carnelian was aware of someone coming in behind him. Turning, he saw it was Krow, staring in horror at the fire smouldering on the bony floor. His gaze jumped to the two Marula and settled on Morunasa. Carnelian moved to intercept him as the youth, teeth bared, raised his spear. He caught hold of Krow, who struggled.

'His filthy feet.'

Carnelian held him fast. 'Don't you want to know why your tribe was massacred?'

Krow searched Carnelian's eyes. As he felt the youth relax, he let him go. Krow threw his head back to indicate the world outside.

'The Darkcloud will be here any moment. Do you imagine you'll be able to stop them killing,' his lips curled in disgust as he looked at Morunasa, 'that ravening bastard!'

Carnelian addressed the Maruli. 'If the others find you here in their holy place, they'll kill you.' He pointed at the other two Marula. 'Wake them.'

Morunasa shook his head. 'They will not wake.'

'What's wrong with them?' cried Krow.

Morunasa regarded him with yellow eyes. 'They commune with our Lord.'

Carnelian could see Krow was unsettled by this. 'We can carry them.'

Too late. Men pushed into the room past Krow, Darkcloud, their bloodied faces becoming childlike in their dismay. One fell to his knees sobbing. Another advanced, a spear shaking in his hand, tears drawing channels through his mask of gore.

'Would you defile this place further with their stinking blood?' said Krow in Vulgate.

The Darkcloud hesitated, his brow creasing with agonied indecision. One of the others said something, swinging his arms and looking out, and the rest nodded grimly, their eyes fixing murderously on the Marula.

Morunasa stared at them, licking his lips. He fixed his eyes on Carnelian. 'Master, save our lives and I'll tell you everything you want to know and give you incomparable wealth besides.'

The Darkcloud erupted into a baying bloodlust but Carnelian dared to stand in their way. 'Hear me,' he bellowed.

They almost turned their spears on him, but he faced them down.

'You will have to give your tribe an account of this defilement of your home. And then there's the Master.'

He saw how that name put fear in them. Their leader began nodding. He half turned to the men behind him and spoke to them in their own tongue.

'What have you decided?' Carnelian demanded.

The Plainsman looked at him and leered. 'We shall keep them alive to give our people something on which to vent their vengeance.'

Carnelian crouched beside Morunasa. He could see from the man's swollen hands and feet how cruelly he had been bound. The Maruli leaned forward towards the embers Carnelian was carrying in a bowl.

'The night is cold.'

Carnelian set the bowl down, removed the blanket he had about his shoulders, and threw it over Morunasa, who smiled.

'You're not what I expected from a Master.'

'Tell me what you're doing here.'

Without taking his eyes off Carnelian, Morunasa shook his head slowly. Carnelian regarded the man through narrowed eyes.

Morunasa shrugged. 'In time I will speak, but only to the other Master.'

'Before that, you will die at the hands of the people you have wronged.'

Morunasa showed his sharpened teeth in a grin. 'I don't think so. I saw how much you all fear the other Master.'

'He is much more what you expect of a Master.'

That made Morunasa look uncertain but his lips remained firmly closed.

'I could have you tortured.'

Morunasa grinned grimly. 'I have been taught to withstand pain since I was a child. My secrets would die with me.'

It had been an empty threat. Carnelian did not have the stomach for torture. He could wait until Osidian returned. He allowed his gaze to wander away over the shadowy cedars which were here and there lit by the hearths. It was very like the Koppie. He thought of the destruction that lay on the other side of the hill. They had chosen to spend the night on its south side to be as far away as possible from the mutilated mother trees.

'Why did you cut down the cedars?'

'We needed their wood for fires.'

'You must have known these trees were sacred.'

'It is not the trees but what gathers under them that is sacred.'

'Your Darkness-under-the-Trees?'

'Our Lord curls around their trunks like a serpent.'

'But then –?'

'He is malignant when on earth. We coax him back into the sky.'

'How?'

'With man blood.'

Carnelian shuddered at his tone and the glint that came into his eye. Morunasa's teeth seemed ravener sharp. The Maruli gazed up at the starry sky. 'When his blackness hides the sun he returns to the earth as rain. We feed him and he whispers his secrets to us.'

Carnelian did not want to hear any more. He lifted the bowl, and considered taking back his blanket. He left it and walked away. It was indeed cold.

Carnelian came awake to find Krow wide-eyed, shouting something at him that made no sense. He sat up. 'What?'

'He's bitten their throats out.'

'Whose throats?'

'The Marula's.'

Anger made Carnelian come fully awake. 'The Darkcloud agreed not to harm them.'

'The Marula did it to each other.'

Carnelian rose. 'Show me.'

Krow led him to where a crowd of Plainsmen had gathered. Some of the Darkcloud came clamouring towards Carnelian.

'He's cheated us of our revenge.'

Carnelian did what he could to calm them. The crowd let him through to where Morunasa was sitting against a rock, one eye half-closed by a swelling from a blow he had taken to his head. His mouth, nose and chin were thick with gore. The other two Marula lay sprawled beside him. Carnelian crouched to look at them. Under their chins were ragged holes so deep their heads had rolled away at an unnatural angle. A movement under one of the old men's skins made him recoil.

'How can they already have maggots?'

'They were Oracles of the Darkness-under-the-Trees,' said Morunasa, as if that were an explanation.

Carnelian turned to look at the man, grimacing as he saw his teeth clotted with dried blood. 'Why?'

'We had a difference of opinion.'

The man's breath stank. 'What're you talking about, you savage?'

Morunasa's grin made Carnelian look for a spear. 'I should kill you now myself.'

The men around him shifted and murmured. Carnelian looked round at them and recognized many of them as Darkcloud. Morunasa grinned again.

'It seems I am precious to the Flatlanders, Master.'

'After what you did to their trees, their women will not be kind to you.'

'It seems I shall live at least until then.' He glanced towards the corpses. 'How does the Master intend to dispose of their bodies?'

'You would have us burn them, would you not, Maruli?'

Morunasa looked surprised. Carnelian asked the Plainsmen what they thought of this and saw how angry it made them. He turned back to Morunasa.

'Why do you burn your dead?'

'The smoke carries the soul up into the sky.'

'It seems to me, Maruli, you should have shown as much care for their bodies as now you appear to be doing for their souls.'

Morunasa shrugged. 'Once they are ashes, nothing is left behind but dross.' He displayed his arms with their dusty coating.

This revelation on top of the murders made Carnelian back off in disgust. He looked from the Maruli to the Plainsmen then back again.

'They will be exposed with all your other dead on the plain for scavengers to gnaw on,' he said, and received nods and smiles of approval from the Plainsmen. Carnelian did not like it that he took pleasure in Morunasa's scowl.

The Plainsmen divided themselves into groups, each with some aquar pulling drag-cradles, and moved across the ferngardens gathering the dead. Once they had fully loaded up, they took the corpses out and dumped them on the plain. After that, Carnelian ordered everyone to rest beneath the cedars, drowsing, squinting at the plain, waiting for the Darkcloud to do what they could to staunch the resin bleeding from their mother trees. In the later afternoon, the Plainsman dead were carried up to a summit of the crags where they were left bleaching on the funerary trestles waiting for the birds to return with the Rains.

At last, when the sun was descending the bronze sky, they set off back to the koppie of the Ochre. They had unhitched the Marula aquar the night before and applied what salves they could find to their wounds. The drag-cradles with the stolen djada and water they hitched to their own beasts, not wanting to burden the wounded. Morunasa, still bound, was lifted into a saddle-chair.

Though their shadows were long, the day still burned and it was with a desperate delight that they reached the first magnolia shade of the Ochre koppie.

Everything was as they had left it. Carnelian went to see the Bluedancing and found they were well enough and thankful for the days of rest his expedition had gifted them. Next he turned his attention to the captive. Morunasa's fingers and toes were swelling black, though he seemed to be indifferent to the pain. Nevertheless, Carnelian ignored the anger of the Darkcloud and had the bonds cut. He answered their fear that the Maruli might escape by exiling him to share the summit of the Crag with the dead on their trestles. The Darkcloud might guard him from the shaded comfort of the porch of the Ancestor House.

This done, Carnelian and Krow returned to Akaisha's hearth. They allowed themselves the luxury of a little water to wash with. To Krow's amusement, Carnelian prepared a meal. They spent the evening huddled round a fire reminiscing about their journey to the Earthsky. Krow asked what life was like in the Mountain and Carnelian was happy to indulge him. It seemed to them both an improbable fairytale.

It was days later that Osidian came out of the desert, swiftly, with the dawn, his men behind him in a column. News of his arrival was spread by shouts across the Koppie. Carnelian heard the commotion as he was walking wearily down through the Grove on his way to another day's toil among the Bluedancing. He could not make out any words, but knew what it must mean. He ran down the last few rootsteps to the Homing, but then slowed. He walked the rest of the way to the Lagoongate so as to have time to prepare himself. His heart was hammering. He yearned to see Fern alive, but feared him dead. There was Morunasa and the expedition to explain. He tried not to think about Osidian, for he knew he might soon have to kill him.

Standing at the gate waiting for him, Krow lit up. 'The Master has returned.'

Carnelian put on a smile and tried to appear pleased. Krow was too excited to see through the performance. Through the gate, the morning was hot but not yet unbearable. Carnelian saw his men in the ferngarden and a mass of riders riding towards them up the magnolia-shaded avenue. Osidian rode at their head. Carnelian searched the many dark shrouded shapes behind him. Osidian rode through the waiting men, across the bridge, and Carnelian and Krow had to jump out of the way as he brought his aquar right into the Grove. The creature knelt and he vaulted easily on to the ground.

'My Lord does not seem to have made as much progress as I expected.'

Carnelian stared, paralysed by the Quya and Osidian's presence.

'Is there something wrong with your voice, Carnelian?'

Krow had moved to the aquar and, making her rise, he led her away so more riders could come in. Carnelian's eyes were drawn to them searching. Ravan had dismounted and was coming towards them.

'The ditch, my Lord?'

Carnelian focused on Osidian, who was frowning. 'The conditions under which the Bluedancing have been working are almost unbearable.'

'I need no lectures about the conditions. I have been riding across that plain for ten days.'

'Then,' Carnelian said, stung to anger, 'you will understand it all.'

His heart leapt into his mouth when he saw a figure moving behind Ravan, whose height proclaimed it to be Fern. Carnelian became aware of Osidian turning to see what he was looking at.

'Ravan,' he said, trying to deflect Osidian.

'And Fern,' said Osidian, as Ravan gave Carnelian a curt bow.

Carnelian tried to appear calm. 'Is the Tribe well?'

For answer Ravan looked away. Carnelian thought the youth aged and worn. His eyes met Fern's and, feeling the intensity of that link, he broke it. A commotion was breaking out along the Homing, where Osidian's dusty men were meeting up with Carnelian's men. Osidian observed this with a furrowed brow and turned on Carnelian.

'Something has happened.'

Carnelian found it hard to return Osidian's piercing gaze. 'I took the men you left me to the koppie of the Darkcloud.'

Osidian's eyes flamed. 'I do not recall giving my Lord permission to indulge in expeditions.'

Carnelian felt trapped. 'I took it anyway. Do you imagine, Osidian, that seeing smoke rising from their home I could have stopped the Darkcloud from going to investigate? I bowed to the inevitable and went with them. Thank the Two I did or else they would most surely have been annihilated by the Marula.'

Osidian's eyes grew wide. 'Marula, you say?'

Carnelian explained and as he did so he watched Osidian's eyes. There was no doubt he was shocked. This was an element that had clearly not formed part of his calculations. Carnelian sensed something else. Momentarily having lost his Masterly composure, Osidian's emotions were open to scrutiny. Carnelian saw a wariness in the way Osidian was regarding him.

'You were victorious then?'

'We fell on them like raveners.'

'Did any Marula survive?'

'One. There were two others but he bit out their throats.'

Osidian raised an eyebrow.

'I have imprisoned him on the summit of the Crag awaiting your return.'

Osidian resumed his impassivity. 'What has he told you?'

'Once he learned of your existence, he would say nothing to me.'

'Indeed.'

Carnelian sensed that Osidian's apparent amusement was only a front. Osidian turned to Ravan.

'Go gather me a twenty of Darkcloud.'

Ravan bowed and went off. Fern was puzzled by the commotion among the Plainsmen. Carnelian watched them too, so as not to have to look at either Osidian or Fern.

When Ravan returned with the twenty, Krow was with him. Osidian motioned the two youths to stand on either side of him and the Darkcloud to surround them as they began to climb the root-stair. Carnelian was left with Fern. Desperately, he wished his friend were able to read handspeech. They gazed at each other but dared not speak.

Osidian paused on the stair. 'I would like both of you to come with me.'

Obediently, Carnelian and Fern began climbing. Osidian turned to Krow.

'When I am finished with our guest, I might give him to you. Tell me, what torments might you like to inflict on him?'

Looking apologetic, Krow glanced at Carnelian. 'The other Master has already promised the Maruli to the Darkcloud.'

The men around them nodded.

'Has he indeed,' said Osidian.

Though Morunasa stood his ground as they came up on to the summit, his yellow, slitted gaze flitted from one to the other, quickly settling on the towering figure of Osidian. Under the pressure of Osidian's regard, Morunasa eventually ducked a bow.

Fern and Ravan stared, startled at the black man.

As Osidian advanced on the Maruli, Krow cried out: 'Beware, Master, he's a ravener.'

Without turning, Osidian made a gesture of dismissal. Carnelian saw he did not overtop Morunasa by much. The two were facing each other near where the bones of the dead lay bleaching upon the funerary trestles. Carnelian strained to pick out words from the mutter of their talk.

'Carnie, where did this Maruli come from?'

Carnelian turned to see Fern and Ravan waiting for an answer and he launched into the story, every so often glancing off towards Osidian and Morunasa. Both winced and glanced at the Maruli when Carnelian described the two dead with their throats torn out.

'Were these the same Marula who massacred the Twostone?' asked Ravan.

'I found the same damage in the koppie of the Darkcloud.'

Krow, who had been gazing at the Master throughout, suddenly moved forward in response to his beckoning. The Maruli looked dejected. The Darkcloud were watching him as if he were a piece of meat they were salivating to consume. The black man exclaimed, pointing at Osidian's face. Osidian's affront softened as Morunasa said something. In response, Osidian pushed his uba from his forehead to expose his birthmark. As Morunasa rose on his toes to examine it, Carnelian felt a thrill of unease which only increased as the Maruli and Osidian began to talk together like conspirators. Watching them reinforced Carnelian's desire to overthrow Osidian.

He turned his attention back to Fern. His friend indicated Ravan with his eyes. They could not talk while he was there, but they could hardly move away without it being noticed.

'How is your mother?' Carnelian asked, hoping to find a way through innocent conversation to communicate with Fern.

'Well enough,' Fern said and proceeded to talk about their journey to the mountains. 'Everyone was miserable that we had to return here.'

Carnelian nodded. Fern continued, and from what he said, Carnelian became convinced there was unrest among the men; that many were growing uneasy with the new ways.

'The Master,' said Krow.

Osidian was coming towards them with Morunasa at his side. Carnelian saw immediately that the Maruli was possessed of a new confidence which dismayed Krow and the Darkcloud.

Osidian regarded them all as if from on high. 'Go, ready yourselves and the others. Each man should take enough djada for nine days; water for six. We march south at nightfall.'

THE VOICE OF GOD

Gods speak without words
Air mouthed by the branches of trees, by hills
Flame tongues whispering
Rain hiss and pattering rhythms
Water rumbling rolling against rock and shore
Gales screaming scouring, lifting precipices of sea
That roar as they consume

(Quyan fragment)

CARNELIAN FOLLOWED OSIDIAN DOWN TO THE PORCH OF THE ANCESTOR House.

'What has the Maruli told you? What is it that is in the south?'

Osidian smiled. 'The reason why the Marula have been launching attacks into the Earthsky.'

Carnelian waited for more, but still smiling, Osidian shook his head. Carnelian glanced up to the summit where they had left Morunasa. 'You cannot trust him.'

'Do you not find that ironic coming from you, Carnelian?'

Knowing it was true just made Carnelian angry. 'The men will not follow you.'

'There will be unrest, but they will follow me. Besides, it will be amusing to see my enemies reveal themselves.'

He turned away to look down into the clearing, which was filling up with Plainsmen. Carnelian's stomach clenched when he saw Fern was at their head. There was no way to warn him.

Fern looked up at them. 'Why do you want us to go south, Master?'

'Because that is where the lands of the Marula lie.'

Consternation rippled through the crowd.

'Why should we go there?'

'To win a battle.'

The crowd erupted. A single voice rose above the din. Carnelian saw it was Ravan. 'Who will escort our people back from the mountains?'

Osidian stood closer to the edge. 'We shall return victorious with time to spare.'

Many of the upturned faces showed doubt.

Fern leapt up the first few steps of the Crag and turned to face the crowd. He pointed up at Osidian. 'Can't you see the Master is possessed? What has he brought us but strife and bloodshed?'

Carnelian swallowed hard, seeing hope in the way the crowd was warming to Fern. His friend stabbed a finger at Osidian.

'Now he wants to lead us to die in the desert or in a foreign land. Do you want this?'

The crowd growled and many shook their heads.

'Let us return to the ways of our fathers and mothers.' Seeing them waver, Fern looked up at Carnelian. 'If we must follow someone, let us follow one who has spilled no Plainsman blood except in self-defence.'

The intensity of Fern's gaze made Carnelian eager to rise to his challenge.

'Are you certain, Carnelian, you could win a pitched battle?'

He turned to look at Osidian.

'If *you* were to lose, it is they,' he glanced down at the crowd, 'who would lose everything.'

Osidian's conviction stirred doubt in Carnelian. As Osidian's eyes fell on the Plainsmen, he seemed to grow larger.

'The Marula have already massacred two Plainsman tribes and would have done the same to the Darkcloud had they not been dealt with. This time, we were fortunate but which of you would risk being their next victims?'

Carnelian might have even then tried to wrest power from Osidian except that in his heart he feared the Marula danger.

Osidian's gaze moved over the Plainsmen. 'You can wait until they send another army or else you can march with me so that when your womenfolk return you can tell them you have destroyed this threat once and for all.'

As the Darkcloud shouted their agreement, Krow pushed to the front.

'Listen to the Master. You know my desire for revenge upon the

Marula, but more than that, I never again want them to do to any other tribe what they did to mine . . .'

The rest the crowd drowned out. Carnelian read Osidian's satisfaction from his posture. He had won again. Fern, among the riot, looked appalled.

Carnelian glanced at Osidian, fearful. 'Now you will punish those who opposed you.'

Osidian turned to regard him. 'On the contrary, Carnelian, by permitting them to continue living I will disarm the criticism that I have ambitions to be their master.'

In the dusk they rode down the Southing. Beyond the swathe of the Southgardens, Carnelian could see the Bluedancing fires as sparks in the gloomy Eastgarden. Craning round the back of his saddle-chair, he gazed with a deep yearning at the mother trees crowding round the Crag. Then he was riding out across the final earthbridge, following Osidian into the south-west where a livid wound in the edge of the sky was all that remained of the tyrant sun.

Night smothered them. Even mounted, Carnelian could feel the heat rising from the earth. He unwound the uba from his head to let the air from the aquar's movement cool the sweat on his skin. The ground muffled the drumming footfalls of the aquar. Sleepily, Carnelian watched the riders ahead moving through the moon-glossed tendrils of the dust they raised. In one place, the plain was stone-hard, fissured and cracked, its covering of dead ferns burned away by fire. Fire. They had already ridden far from any sheltering shade. It was growing cooler and soon it would be cold, but Carnelian was already fearing the dawn.

First light revealed the Mother's Backbone rising before them. As the dawn poured the shadows of the riders out to meet the ridge, Carnelian turned to face the sun, closing his eyes against the radiance, letting it dispel the chill of the night.

Reaching the Backbone, they dismounted and led their aquar up on to the shattered black rock. Krow and Morunasa at his side, Osidian chose a spot where there might be some shade from the coming onslaught of the sun.

Carnelian and Fern exchanged wary glances. They had not spoken since the gathering in the clearing. Brooding, Ravan was keeping his distance from the Master, making Carnelian wonder what had happened between them.

He busied himself angling his aquar so that it would receive as little sun as possible, and used it and its saddle-chair to make a shelter for himself as he saw others doing. Men were looking nervously into the east, where the sun was melting up from the earth. Carnelian lay behind his aquar, dreading when it should rise so high there would be no place left to hide.

The air was a fever that made it impossible to sleep. Even though he had kept his waterskin in his aquar's shadow, each gulp was as warm as blood. He sneaked out to give the creature a drink then lay trying to ignore the sweat dewing over his body. A saltstone was passed around which burned his tongue.

At last the furnace sun began to abate. Carnelian counted each moment as he watched it fall blind into the Plain. When darkness came the air sighed a breeze of relief. He rose, feeling the day's ague still vibrating the night. They resaddled their aquar and descended the Backbone back to the plain, where they remounted. Carnelian's headache was eased by the gentle rhythm of his creature's gait.

He must have fallen asleep, for suddenly he was aware he was hearing the sea. It took moments to work out that it was sand and not spume spitting in his face. Veils of it slid hissing towards them over the ground. His aquar had lowered her head and covered her eyes with the inner lids. Not caring that they should both be blind, Carnelian pulled his uba down over his eyes.

A brightening in the margin of the sky woke him. Heads were rising, seeing it, too tired to fear it yet. As Carnelian brought his aquar to a halt with the others, one continued to amble onwards. It was Morunasa's. He looked round to see if anyone else had noticed the Maruli moving away from them. Morunasa was sitting upright, searching for something.

'He runs away,' a voice shouted in Ochre.

Arguing broke out.

'Leave him be,' cried Krow. 'The Master has sent him scouting.'

Grumbling, the men made their aquar kneel and Carnelian followed their lead. Eyeing the dawn, he clambered out of his chair. Nearby, the Backbone rose as an unbroken wall they could not climb. He made his aquar rise and walked her round so that she was presenting her tail to the rising sun. He made her kneel again and began working at the rope girdles that secured her saddle-chair.

A gruff voice sounded from far away. Morunasa was hurtling back, waving his hands, shouting something in Vulgate. Everyone stopped to watch. His aquar overshot their position before the Maruli managed to bring her under control. As he rode towards them, Osidian went to meet him. Carnelian could hear the mutter of their talk but not what was being said.

Osidian strode back into their midst. 'Mount up,' he commanded, causing a tumult of protest.

Carnelian watched Osidian stooping to say something into Krow's ear. The youth shouted down the noise. 'We're close to our goal. There's a river nearby. Trees.'

That last word cast its cool shade over everyone.

'Trees,' the men echoed, hope widening their eyes.

'Yes, trees,' said Krow. 'If we ride now we can spend the rest of the day in shade, beside running water.' He grinned. 'Unless you lot would rather spend the day skulking here in the open?'

Everyone could already see the spindly stretch of their shadows. Though he feared the sun, Carnelian shared the general enthusiasm to go on.

Enduring the blinding starkness of the fully risen sun, he began to worry about what it was they were riding into.

Ahead, the scrubby, rusty land was columned by strange trees. Smooth trunks rose to a great height from which nests of branches splayed as leafless as roots. These were not the trees they had expected.

'Baobabs,' declared Morunasa, 'a sure sign we draw near to the Upper Reach.'

Carnelian saw the anxiety the Maruli was failing to conceal and wondered what kind of place this Upper Reach might be. These conjectures were forgotten as they came in among the baobabs. Soon, with the others, he was filing towards one along the shady road of the shadow that it cast. As they drew closer, Carnelian squinted up to see the tree looming vast, its branches startling black against the bronze sky. He became possessed by a feeling he was in the presence of a watching giant.

When they found a break in the Backbone, Morunasa led them clambering over it to the other side and, once they had reached flat ground again, Osidian and the Maruli drew them away into the south-west. Climbing the sky, the sun heated the world into trembling incandescence. Feeding on their own shadows, the baobabs grew ever more massive. Hunched against the migraine day, Carnelian was slow to become aware they were plodding down a gentle slope.

'The chasm?' croaked Osidian.

Lifting his head, Carnelian saw Morunasa give a heavy nod while his eyes were scouring the bleached, hazy forest to the east where

416

the Backbone ran along the horizon like a storm. Osidian said something to Krow and the youth turned his aquar and rode among them, rasping out: 'Unhitch your spears. Prepare to fight.'

At first the Plainsmen stared at him, stupefied, but then with tremulous hands they began loosing their weapons. Soon their march was bristling with bladed flint.

Carnelian saw Osidian beckoning him and rode forward.

'Take the right wing, I shall take the left,' he said.

'Battle then?'

Osidian terminated the interview by making his aquar swing away. Morunasa and Krow followed him, stretching the left flank of their march after them.

Fern rode up to Carnelian. They squinted at each other through the glare. 'Battle? In this heat?'

'I am to command the right.'

Fern gave a grim nod. 'I'll fight beside you?'

The offer revived him. 'Like we did against the Bluedancing.'

Their eyes met and Fern twitched a smile.

They were riding side by side when they saw the ground before them fall away.

'A cliff?' asked Fern, startled.

The gulf opening up before them caused their aquar to flare their eye-plumes in alarm. Carnelian gaped at the opposite green cliff and, far below, the shimmer of water.

'A river?' cried Fern, amazed.

'You didn't know it was here?'

Fern turned, his mouth still hanging open. 'We knew the lands of the Marula lay somewhere in the south.'

'But this is so close to the Koppie.'

'This land is waterless, shunned by saurians, besides, we have always feared the Marula.'

Fern looked down into the chasm. 'Do you think they live down there?'

Carnelian narrowed his eyes. The river traced a narrow ribbon down in the chasm floor, reminding him of the Cloaca that came out of the crater of Osrakum and ran in the Canyon of the Three Gates. The chasm was all barren sand and rock.

'Perhaps further downstream,' he muttered.

'We're holding the line back,' said Fern.

Carnelian turned from the chasm and saw the battleline was tearing apart as he and Fern anchored its end.

'Come on,' he said, and together they rode upstream along the chasm edge to pull the battleline taut.

Carnelian's head lolled. He felt sick from the long, churning anticipation of battle. The slow uneven judder of his aquar's stride betrayed how much she was suffering from the heat. The shadows of the baobabs had grown long as they rode along the chasm edge.

A whisper like the distant sea jerked his head up. The windings of his uba gave him a narrow window into the outer world. He was startled to see the wall of the Backbone rising before him. Its black rock ran unbroken to the chasm edge, dipped into it, then rose again upon the other side. Where it dipped, it formed the threshold to a wide and shallow valley that brought the river from the east in many channels. These braided into two feathery falls that had gouged into the Backbone, leaving a single buttress and island between them. This island tottering on the edge of the chasm was clothed by a dense grove of trees. Of an army of Marula, there was no sign.

The baobabs here were not as lofty as before. What they had lost in height they made up for in girth. Some particularly massive specimens squatted upon a knoll which lay beneath the frowning Backbone cliff.

At the edge of his vision, Carnelian registered the line of aquar buckling. Turning, he watched Osidian with Morunasa and Krow riding towards the knoll. He saw no further need to keep his station.

'No battle then,' said Fern expressing the general relief.

Carnelian looked to where Osidian was climbing the knoll.

'You follow him,' said Fern. 'I'd better stay with the men.'

Carnelian thanked him and coaxed his aquar towards the knoll. As they wound up its slope, the shade from the baobabs revived her a little. Breaching a ring of them that crowned the summit, Carnelian smelled charcoal and saw the trunks were fire-blackened. Round their roots the earth was littered with burnt wood. Morunasa was peering up at the baobabs and Carnelian saw openings high in the trunks.

'Where are the Marula we were meant to fight?' Carnelian asked.

Morunasa glanced at him, irritated. 'Marula? Pygmies.'

Carnelian was startled. Pygmies? He looked around uneasily, fearful of why Osidian had brought them there with a lie.

The Master was peering among the trees. 'Could they be hiding?'

The Maruli raised his head and his nostrils distended. He shook his head and frowned. 'I can smell nothing but the burning.'

'Perhaps they tried to set these trees alight before they fled.'

Morunasa shook his head. 'They worship baobabs, which is why we used these,' he indicated the charred trees, 'as fernroot granaries.'

Osidian let his aquar wander as he leaned over the edge of his saddle-chair examining the ground. Morunasa straightened in his chair and made his aquar turn slowly on the spot, searching for something.

'It seems your problem, Maruli, has solved itself,' said Osidian.

Morunasa continued to search as if he had not heard. Krow was watching the man through slitted eyes, perhaps considering that he was the only Marula left to kill.

'Come,' Osidian said with an edge in his voice, 'fulfil the oath you made to me.'

For a moment Morunasa regarded him with a look of barely suppressed rage, then, frowning, he led them down from the knoll. When they reached the edge of the chasm, the Maruli sat, motionless, gazing at the waterfalls. He waited until Osidian was at his side before he announced: 'Behold the Voice of God.'

Emotion snagged Morunasa's voice and Carnelian was close enough to see the light of reverence in his amber eyes.

'At the moment our Lord whispers,' Morunasa said without turning, 'but soon enough you'll hear Him roar.'

Something in his tone sent a shiver down Carnelian's spine.

Morunasa turned to Osidian with a fierce intensity. 'We must cross immediately to the Isle.'

'What isle?' asked Krow.

The Maruli looked at the youth in irritation. His ashy finger pointed to the tree-capped rock which Carnelian could now see stretched upstream above the level of the waterfalls to split the river and its many streams in two.

'Can't you see it there before your eyes?' Morunasa gave the youth a feral grin. 'Pray, boy, you never have cause to see it closer.'

Krow's failure to control his unease turned to anger. He looked to Osidian for support, but the Master, unaware, was gazing at the island. The youth ducked his head so that his uba fell over his face.

'First the other place, Maruli,' Osidian said and, for a moment, Carnelian thought Morunasa was about to erupt but again he brought his fury under control.

'As the Master wishes, so shall it be done.'

Carnelian recognized the traditional invocation of a legionary auxiliary but was more concerned by what Osidian might have meant by the 'other place'. He had not forgotten that Osidian had deceived them all.

Morunasa dismounted and the others copied him. He leaned over the edge.

'See, the pygmies cut the Ladder as I described.'

Perhaps a quarter of the way down the chasm wall Carnelian could see a mess of ropes.

'From here, the cables could be drawn up,' said Osidian.

'The land of the Marula lies down there, doesn't it?' asked Carnelian.

Osidian looked at him. 'They call it the Lower Reach.'

So that was it. 'This ladder was the only way up.'

Morunasa glowered at him. 'Long ago we had every foothold smoothed away.'

He turned to Osidian. 'New rope might need to be woven from baobab bark.'

Krow touched Carnelian's arm to get his attention. 'Why would the Master want to repair this ladder?' he mouthed.

Carnelian shook his head. He could not see how such a policy would do anything but increase the Marula threat.

Turning his back on the falls, Morunasa led them along the cliff to where two cables, coming up over the edge, wrapped themselves in a girdle around the trunk of a massive baobab. As the Maruli ducked under the nearest rope, Carnelian followed him with the others. Standing with the cables on either side, he peered over the edge and saw they plunged down the rock and, between them, strands were woven into netting.

'Down here?' Osidian asked Morunasa. When the Maruli gave a slow, ominous nod, Osidian turned to Carnelian and addressed him in Quya.

'Wait for me here, Carnelian. Keep the savages under your control.'

'Where are you going?'

Osidian's smile was enigmatic. 'For now, it is best you should not know.'

Annoyed, Carnelian said nothing more but watched Osidian and Morunasa lower themselves over the edge on to the netting and, slowly, begin to descend the chasm wall. He heard the rumble of approaching aquar and, turning, saw that it was Fern, Ravan and the other Plainsmen.

'What's going on?' Ravan called, sullen.

Carnelian shrugged.

Fern dismounted. 'The men are angry and confused.'

'So am I,' said Carnelian. He leaned over the edge and saw Osidian and Morunasa had disappeared.

'There must be caves down there,' Fern said.

*

They gave up waiting and were glad to retreat from the fearful drop into the shadow of the anchor tree. A quivering in the ladder ropes brought them back to the edge. Osidian and Morunasa were climbing the netting. As they came up, Carnelian saw a new light in Osidian's eyes. Not wishing to be denied an explanation, he did not ask, but probed Osidian's face seeking the answer for himself. Feeling Carnelian's gaze, Osidian looked at him and smiled with a warmth that took Carnelian by surprise.

'Was everything as the Maruli promised, my Lord?'

Osidian's grin was like the sun. 'Better than he promised.'

Morunasa's eyes had been looking from one to the other as they spoke, and perhaps it was the anger at not understanding that put the frown on his ashen face.

'Now we must go to the Isle of Flies,' he rumbled.

Osidian's eyes flashed. 'I've not forgotten the bargain we made, Maruli.'

He gazed across the chasm to where the island lay black between the shimmer of the falls.

Carnelian saw the light go out of Osidian's face. 'What lies there?'

'An ancient banyan.'

Carnelian regarded the island. 'Within that forest?'

'It *is* that forest.'

Carnelian was appalled. That so much earth should be captured by a single tree. He imagined how deep the shadows must be beneath its branches. 'A fearful place.'

'Indeed,' said Morunasa, grimly. He ducked under one of the cables and Osidian followed him. Krow had to run to keep up. Beside them, his stature made him seem a child. Carnelian followed on behind with everyone else.

Fern regarded the island. 'I don't like the look of it.'

'You don't need to come,' said Carnelian.

'Are you going?'

Carnelian was struggling with the same unease, but he nodded.

'Then I will go with you,' Fern said with a determination that made Carnelian smile.

They walked on, passing the knoll with its singed trees. Morunasa and Osidian were heading for where the Backbone butted on to the chasm. Morunasa bowed to something there before moving on to a ledge that ran along the chasm brink. He was quickly followed by Osidian and, more hesitantly, by Krow.

When Carnelian came closer he saw a carving of a head, thrown back as if it were pushing up out of the earth. Its mouth, hideously agape, was rimmed with splinter teeth; its tongue a spike upon which the skeleton of a man was impaled. The idol's face was crusted brown with old blood that had pooled in the mouth and empty eye-sockets, then overflowed on to the ears and stained the ground black.

Conquering dread, Carnelian peered past it and saw the path that squeezed between the sheer face of the Backbone and the shadowy gulf into which one of the waterfalls was tumbling. It was along this that Morunasa and the others were moving.

Carnelian edged round the idol and was about to follow Osidian when he noticed the Plainsmen had come to a halt. Carnelian saw their terror. His eyes met those of Fern, who mastered his fear and crossed the bloodstained ground averting his eyes from the impaler. When he reached Carnelian's side, Fern grabbed his arm and pulled him away on to the path. They were some way along this when they became aware Ravan was following them.

Gurgling, the river ran in many streams. Skeins of dark water parted by rock, reweaving together, tearing in rapids, churning in pools.

Morunasa's smile with its ravener teeth was unnerving. 'So you've been brave enough to come this far?' His amber eyes slid round so that he was looking across at the Isle of Flies from their corners. 'Are you now brave enough to cross with the Master and me?'

Ravan stood forward gazing at Osidian, his face sweaty, hopeful. 'I'll go with you, Master.'

'No,' said Fern.

Osidian ignored them and turned to Morunasa. 'Stop toying with them, Maruli.'

Morunasa looked down at Ravan. 'But this one offers himself and we need blood. The Darkness-under-the-Trees has been unfed for years.'

'In that case, Maruli, we shall give of our own blood.' It was Osidian's turn to smile. 'Unless you fear my fiery blood shall set your banyan alight.'

Morunasa regarded the island with nervous eyes. 'All I fear lives there.'

As the two men glanced at one another, Carnelian was dismayed to see how much they were alike. Morunasa might have been Osidian reflected murkily in a mirror of obsidian.

Osidian turned to them. 'Wait for me here.'

'Don't trust –'

Osidian choked Krow's protest with a flicker of his eyes and then he turned to follow Morunasa down towards the river.

*

422

They watched Osidian and Morunasa pick their way across the river. The route they took wound back and forth over the rocks so that it seemed they were finding their way through a maze. When at last they reached the island, they climbed up through its skirt of driftwood, walked along its shore beneath the towering banyan, before suddenly being swallowed between its trunks.

'How long do you think they'll be?' asked Fern.

'I hope the Maruli's god devours them both,' hissed Ravan through bared teeth.

Carnelian was shocked to see with what bitter eyes the youth was glaring at the island.

'The Master knows what he's doing.' The anxious way Krow resumed his vigil of the island belied his words.

Frowning, Fern watched as his brother went off to sulk on a rock. He leaned close to Carnelian. 'His behaviour has been steadily worsening. I can't understand, Carnie, why the Master tolerates it.'

Neither could Carnelian. 'Your brother has good reason to be aggrieved.'

Their eyes met and Fern nodded. Carnelian hoped for a return to their easy friendship.

It was nearing dusk when Krow sprang up and ran down the bank to the river. Carnelian could just make out Osidian and Morunasa emerging from the tangle of the banyan. He watched them winding back from rock to rock. He was dreading their return.

As they approached the shore, Krow went out to meet them. Carnelian saw the youth's dejection as the Master ignored him. Krow fell in behind him, snatching glances at his back as he picked his way among the boulders.

All three reached the shore together. As they approached, Morunasa seemed disturbed and Carnelian detected in Osidian's face the ghost of some horror he had witnessed.

'What was it you saw?' Carnelian asked in Quya.

'Cannibalism in the Labyrinth,' Osidian answered, in a tone that seemed to be one with the dismal gulping of the river.

Carnelian did not understand, did not want to understand. He noticed Osidian's left wrist was wrapped in a clot of leaves through which blood was soaking.

'Tomorrow I shall leave you, Carnelian. You will remain here. I would take you with me if I dared, but I need your Chosen face to instil terror and obedience into the Plainsmen that will be staying behind to garrison this Upper Reach.'

'What's he saying?' Ravan demanded.

'He's leaving us,' snapped Carnelian. His eyes met Fern's in a mutual glance of dismay.

Krow leapt in front of Osidian. 'Let me go with you, Master.'

Osidian looked right through the youth. 'The Oracle Morunasa shall be my only companion.'

Of the two of them, the Maruli seemed now the taller as he regarded them all with condescension. Krow regarded him with unconcealed hatred. Ravan skulked in the shadows.

'And where does my Lord intend to go?' asked Carnelian, already knowing the answer.

Lifting his chin, Osidian turned the emerald fire in his eyes on the brooding chasm below the falls. 'Down there, the Lower Reach, land of the Marula.'

RENDER

A man's desires are the best hook to catch him.
(a proverb of the Wise)

IN THE DUSK IT WAS HARD TO SEE THE MASTER ON THE KNOLL AGAINST the baobab that rose behind him like the night. Morunasa's presence was only betrayed by the blinking of his eyes.

The pale slit in the Master's uba scanned the Plainsmen he had gathered to hear him. 'Tomorrow, with your approval, I would go down to the land of the Marula.'

Among the crowd, Carnelian was deafened as they rose in uproar. Osidian's pale hands lifted to calm them.

'While I am away, the ladder down into the chasm must be repaired.'

The men erupted again, so that Carnelian was carried a few steps up the slope in their surge.

Fern pushed past him higher still. 'Why, Master, so that the murdering bastards can swarm up to destroy us?'

'If that had been their intention, do you not think they could have done so long ago?' Osidian's contempt withered them to silence. 'Their attacks on the Earthsky were incidental; merely a way in which they sought to regain access to their shrine,' he pointed, 'the Isle of Flies.

'The Ladder is the only link between the Lower and this Upper Reach. When it was cut by a revolt of their pygmy slaves, they were forced to send armies through swamp and jungle up on to the Earthsky. There they killed for the water and djada that they needed to get here.'

More men moved up to join Fern; among them, Ravan. The youth stabbed a finger at Morunasa.

'If we kill the Maruli, no news will reach his people of the destruction of their expedition. They have tried twice already and failed. What makes you believe, Master, they will dare to try again?'

A Darkcloud stood forward. 'Let's burn their Isle of Flies as they burned my tribe's mother trees.'

Morunasa bared his teeth. 'Any man who crosses to the Isle will be devoured by the Darkness-under-the-Trees. Understand this, Flatlanders, you may kill me, but my brethren in the land below will never forsake the dwelling of our Lord.'

'You see?' said Osidian. 'They will plague us until they have their Ladder back.'

Carnelian thought it time he said something. 'Why do you need to go down there with the Maruli?'

Osidian gazed at Carnelian for some moments. 'To make sure they believe that there is no need to send another force.'

Carnelian could not fault this. Osidian continued.

'Enough has been said. Now you must decide what is to be done.'

With that, he turned his back on them. Carnelian pushed his way to Fern's side. His friend recoiled.

'What if he sees us together?'

'We'll have to take the risk. Too much hangs on this decision.'

Fern saw the truth of it. 'Why is he doing this? Could it be as it seems that he does not want the Marula to interfere with his plans?'

Carnelian glanced over to the ladder Osidian and Morunasa had descended earlier. 'I cannot believe that is the only reason he brought us here.'

Fern spoke in his ear. 'We could kill him now.'

Carnelian considered that, then made sure before he spoke he was not doing so for emotional reasons. 'No. If we did, we'd not only have the problem of controlling the different tribes but there would be no way of reassuring them we knew how to deal with the Marula threat.'

Fern frowned. 'Combined, we could defeat anything they threw at us.'

'Combined, perhaps . . .'

Fern grimaced, knowing that such unity would be nigh impossible to achieve using any methods other than the Master's.

'And besides, we'd have to leave men behind in the koppies for the Sky knows how many Witherings.'

Fern nodded, wearily. He looked around him. 'As long as we control this Upper Reach the Marula are powerless against us.'

426

'So we go along with him?'

Fern glanced up to where the looming baobab had swallowed the Master and the Maruli. He leaned close to Carnelian. 'And kill him when he returns.'

Their eyes met in agreement. They parted, and Fern moved among the Plainsmen giving the Master's proposal support where it was needed. When Osidian asked what they had decided, grudgingly, the Plainsmen gave his plan their assent.

They camped upon the summit of the knoll. The Plainsmen huddled gratefully round the fires they had made with the dead wood they had found lying everywhere. Carnelian sat chewing djada with Fern, Krow, Ravan and others of Akaisha's hearth. Looking round at the familiar faces helped ease his anxiety about the decision he had made. Even through his brooding, Carnelian felt he and they, even Ravan, belonged to each other.

Two shadows forming out of the darkness made them all jump.

'We shall sit with you,' one of them said. Osidian's pale face came into the firelight followed by Morunasa's. Osidian chose to sit between Fern and Carnelian so that the Plainsman had to move away round the fire. The Maruli found a place on Osidian's left. Carnelian fixed his gaze deep into the flames and busied himself with chewing. A waterskin was passed around. When it was Carnelian's turn he put his lips to its spout, but had to tip it so much, that he did not feel he could take more than was essential to moisten the djada. He passed the skin to Osidian who drained it.

'We need water,' said Ravan, daring to glare at the Master.

'There is plenty in the river.'

His words produced a mutter of discontent in Ochre.

'What are they saying?' Osidian asked Carnelian.

Carnelian told him without taking his eyes from the fire.

'If they fear to fill their skins from the Blackwater,' Morunasa said through a sneer, 'they can drink from the caches the pygmies kept in these baobabs.' He lifted a chalky hand to indicate the giants looming round them in the dark.

'I saw no jars,' said Carnelian.

'Did I not say, *in* the baobabs?'

'They're hollow?'

Chewing, Morunasa gave a nod.

Carnelian remembered the openings he had seen in the charred trees. Osidian looked around the fire. 'All of you go and search these out.'

The Plainsmen were reluctant to leave their fire, but they obeyed.

Fern gave Carnelian a glance before disappearing into the night with them.

Carnelian felt a touch on his arm and turned to look at Osidian.

'We need to talk, you and I,' he said in Quya.

Carnelian was reluctant, but gave a nod.

'While I am gone it shall be your paramount task to rebuild the Ladder.'

Carnelian remembered the mess of the ropes he had seen so far down the chasm wall. 'It will be a great labour.'

'You can use aquar to lift it.'

Carnelian looked out over the camp. 'Still, men will have to be sent down somehow to attach ropes to the Ladder. It will be dangerous work.'

'I do not wish you to risk them.'

'Who else?'

'Sartlar,' said Osidian, a strange light showing again in his eyes.

Carnelian gawped.

Osidian patted the ground with his hand. 'Yes, they are here beneath our feet. They infest caves gouged into the wall of the chasm.'

'The other ladder,' Carnelian said. 'The one you descended with Morunasa?'

Osidian nodded. He leaned forward to capture Carnelian in his gaze. 'Listen to me and listen well, the Plainsmen must not descend that ladder. If you have need, go there alone. If you do, you will understand why it is I say this. You hear my words?'

Carnelian nodded, staring, confused. Something occurred to him. 'How shall I summon them?'

'Strike the cables of their ladder thrice and they will come.'

Carnelian returned to his fire-watching. The sartlar were there beneath his feet as they had been in the bowels of the ship as oarsmen on the voyage to the Three Lands. He wondered what they were doing in the Upper Reach and what it was Osidian was so determined to hide from the Plainsmen.

'When I return it will be with Marula Oracles and their pygmy slaves.'

'And then you shall give them back this place.'

Osidian glanced at Morunasa, who frowned. 'We shall see.'

Fern and the others appeared, looking frightened. 'The trees are all filled with children dried like huskmen.'

'What did he say?' asked Morunasa.

Carnelian translated.

Morunasa gave a snort. 'Not children, Flatlander, pygmies.'

'But they're dead,' Fern said.

Morunasa showed his pointed teeth. 'It would be strange if they were not; it's the tradition of the forest people to place their dead within the hollowed bellies of trees.'

Carnelian felt Osidian's hand grip his arm and turned to look into his eyes.

'Once, Carnelian, I knew in my heart you would give your life to save mine.'

They regarded each other with a sadness that made Fern and Krow both ask what was the matter. Osidian's gaze did not allow Carnelian to say anything to them and they stepped back, silent.

'Now it has become necessary for me to say to you that on my return, should the Ladder be not repaired, or should I receive any impediment to my ascent, then I shall offer myself to the Marula to lead their next attack on the Earthsky. If that should come to pass, be sure I will annihilate the Ochre.'

Hatred rose in Carnelian. Could Osidian manage nothing without threats or terror? He almost thanked him for making it easier to kill him.

Carnelian was trapped in the cabin of a ship riding a stormy sea. The smell of iron lingering in the air made him queasy. He leaned against a bulkhead. Under his touch its surface was dry and powdery. He lifted his hand and peered at where it had been resting. Hri-bread riddled with holes. The cabin was made of it; the ship. He could feel her hull soaking up the salty sea. Dark water welled up from the floor. The iron smell of blood. When he tried to pull his feet up he felt them tearing off at the ankles. It was disorientating that he felt no pain. His skin writhed and itched. He leaned over and saw his legs were bread. As he brought his hands close, they left a wake of fine powder in the air. His hands were porous, every hole itching from the writhe of weevils.

He awoke gasping. It was night in the garden of the Yden. The branches of the pomegranate trees were stark against the sky. Why were they leafless? He had believed autumn never came to Osrakum. He sat up. Hunched shapes were swarming in the darkness. His heart beat up into his mouth. They had come again for him and Osidian. Or was it his father they wished to wound? He closed his eyes and fought confusion. His mind cleared. He was in the Upper Reach. When he opened his eyes again, the night was as lifeless as the baobabs.

Carnelian woke still oppressed by his nightmare. He imagined the baobabs as corpses riddled with the maggots of pygmy cadavers and shuddered. He sought distraction in watching Osidian wander around their camp selecting those who were to remain behind. The rest seemed only too happy to saddle their aquar. Soon they had descended the knoll and were riding up the escarpment, while those who were left watched forlornly.

On the chasm edge, Carnelian busied himself helping to devise a way to lower Osidian and Morunasa down to the Ladder. It seemed impossibly far away but, Morunasa assured them, only the top fifth or so had come loose; the rest was still firmly held to the rock by wooden wedges.

Ropes were found and Osidian elected to go first.

'I shall announce my return with smoke,' he said in Quya.

Carnelian nodded and then they lowered him with the help of an aquar, using one of the Ladder anchor trees as a capstan. Morunasa was next. When the rope went slack, Carnelian joined the Plainsmen craning over the edge to watch the tiny figures descend the Ladder to the chasm floor.

'What now?' Ravan asked.

Carnelian eyed the youth. 'We repair the Ladder.'

'And if we choose not to help you?'

'I won't need your help.'

Fern's eyebrows rose.

Carnelian pushed his way past Ravan and walked along the chasm edge until he came to the tensioned cables of the sartlar ladder. Ravan, Fern and many of the other Plainsmen followed him.

'What're you doing, Carnie?' asked Fern.

'You'll see soon enough.' Carnelian hung himself on the nearest cable, then let it go. A satisfying quiver could be heard rattling down into the chasm.

'Where does this go?' Ravan asked, but Carnelian ignored him and pulled the cable down twice more. Then he waited. As time passed and nothing happened, he grew embarrassed. Carnelian pulled on the cable three times more in quick succession. He went to the edge and looked over. The rippling in the netting stilled, then nothing.

'What's going on?' Fern pleaded.

Carnelian confronted them. 'I'm trying to summon the sartlar the Master told me are lodged in caves beneath our feet.'

Ignoring their looks of disbelief, Carnelian turned his back on the fall, knelt on the chasm edge and, taking hold of the netting, lowered himself down.

The ladder was like rigging. Clambering down it, Carnelian snagged his foot often, so that each time he had to, precariously, disentangle his foot. He froze whenever he caught a glimpse of the rock face plunging away into the dizzying depths.

At last, reaching down and waving his foot around, Carnelian could find nothing but air. Peering down caused him to clutch the netting. There was nothing but space below him. Feeling a quivering in the netting, he looked up and saw Fern descending.

'What are you doing?' he called up.

Fern peered down. 'I'd have thought that was obvious. I'm coming with you.'

Carnelian sank his head with exasperation. 'The Master expressly forbade it.'

'He's not here though, is he?'

Carnelian could hear the smile in his friend's tone and, glancing up, saw him grinning. Carnelian was unable to stay angry and returned the grin.

'I suppose now that you're here already . . .'

'I thought you might see it my way,' said Fern, smugly.

'The others?'

'I'm the only one stupid enough to risk it.'

Both laughed. Carnelian felt a surge of emotion as he realized how much he had missed his friendship. The netting shook again as Fern resumed his descent.

'Wait,' Carnelian cried up, remembering the netting ran out below him. Looking to his left, he saw a ledge. Cold sweat sheathed his skin as he judged the swing to reach it.

Fern's voice drifted down from above. 'What's going on?'

'Hold on,' Carnelian cried. He reminded himself that Osidian and Morunasa had done it. He moved to the edge of the netting and leaned his body into the cable to which it was attached.

'Here goes,' he muttered. Clambering astride the cable, he let go and fell on to the ledge. He sidled along it and with a sigh of relief found the mouth of a cave. He spent moments peering into its gloom before Fern's thin voice brought him back to look up at the ladder.

Fern's face was twisted with anxiety. Carnelian explained what he had done and then retreated back into the safety of the cave. He heard the rasp of the ladder as its rope rubbed against the rock and then, after a few agonizing moments, Fern slipped round the rock and Carnelian grabbed him. They clung to each other laughing. Their eyes met and they fell silent. They drew apart. Fern blew out and shook his head. 'That was no fun at all.'

They squinted into the cave, listening.

'Can you hear anything?' Fern whispered.

Leaning into the cave mouth, Carnelian cried out in a clear ringing voice. 'Attend me.'

The gloom swallowed his words, then the echoes. Nothing stirred in the depths.

'We're going to have to go in,' said Carnelian.

Fern looked incredulous. 'In there?'

'You stay here.'

Fern shook his head. 'Where you go, I go.'

They gathered their courage and advanced into the cave mouth. When they had gone only a little way it became difficult to see. Carnelian put his mouth to Fern's ear.

'Sartlar are monstrous, but harmless.'

He felt Fern nodding.

They penetrated deeper, their hands sculling the damp air as they groped for the walls. On and on they crept. Carnelian thought of calling out, but did not dare. He was considering turning back when he saw some light dawning ahead.

'Torchlight?' Fern whispered.

Carnelian shrugged.

The light flickered brighter and they found they were coming into a region lit by a brazier.

Carnelian jumped when Fern lurched. 'What is it?' he hissed.

Fern pointed to the vague shapes ahead, both more alive than shadows. As they drew closer, these apparitions grew larger.

'Our reflections,' whispered Carnelian. He leaned close to the wall. Following a hunch he licked his finger, rubbed it down the wall, tasted it, then stood back amazed. 'Salt.'

Fern gaped. 'Salt?' He gingerly stretched out his hand to touch it.

'Taste it,' whispered Carnelian.

Fern did and his eyes grew enormous as he surveyed the cavern in which they stood. 'All salt,' he gasped.

'Who knows how much. Perhaps the whole cliff.' He let out a low whistle. 'No wonder he didn't want you Plainsmen to see this.'

Fern stared at him. 'The Master knows about this?'

'The Maruli brought him down here, remember.'

Fern gave a slow nod. 'There's enough here to make the Tribe rich.'

'There may well be enough here to buy the whole of the Earthsky,' said Carnelian, grimly.

Fern's look of wonder soured. 'This is why the Master brought us here.'

Carnelian nodded. 'I knew there was something else. No wonder the Marula are desperate to regain this place.'

Fern reached out to touch the salt wall. 'If the men found out . . .'

They looked grimly at each other.

'We can't let him have so much power,' said Carnelian voicing their common thought.

'The moment he returns, he dies.'

Carnelian was gripped by a rage against Osidian for driving them to murder. 'Come on.'

Deeper into the cavern, it narrowed into a cleft. Squeezing through, they came into a new cavern dimly lit in which an animal odour hung heavy in the air.

'This –' Carnelian began, but suddenly he tensed, sensing movement in the air, a rustling. Peering into the gloom, he saw the chamber before them was filling with shadows. Sartlar, menacing in their silence. Though their lank hair concealed their eyes, he could feel them watching him. Not for a long while had he felt so strongly the need for a mask. He straightened, and as he did the sartlar drew back moaning. He froze. When he lifted his hand a shudder moved through their mass.

'You terrify them,' whispered Fern.

Carnelian regarded the creatures with pity. He had good cause to know what cruel treatment they expected.

'I am a Master,' he said gently in Vulgate. They answered him with a muttering fear.

'We know . . . what you are,' a voice trembled from their midst.

The heads of the sartlar eddied as if a boat were cutting through them and a sartlar emerged. A creature the size of a child but with large, calloused hands and leathery feet like spades. As the creature shambled closer, Carnelian saw it was clothed in a matting of grey hair. It came close enough so he could smell its vinegar odour. He fought disgust. With a groan, it fell heavily to its knees. Pity, distaste, embarrassment even, all these emotions flowed through Carnelian as he looked down from his great height upon that pathetic bundle.

'Rise,' he said as kindly as he could manage.

The creature stumbled up on to its feet. It even dared to look up at him. The grey, greasy locks parted to show a gnarled leathery face, disfigured by the branding of the circular 'earth' glyph that proclaimed it a sartlar from the Guarded Land. He wondered what strange circumstances could have brought such a creature so far. He noticed the twin pockets of flesh sagging down the chest. Those dugs proved it was a female of its kind. Even though he could not see her eyes, he knew she was regarding him. Something about her manner made Carnelian recall the sartlar who had been kind to him when he himself had been a slave.

'She worships you,' hissed Fern.

Carnelian was wrenched free of his fascination. He spoke over his shoulder. 'How did we appear to you when you first looked upon us? To these creatures the Standing Dead must be like gods.'

'Our magic . . .' said the sartlar woman.

He looked down at her again and this time caught the glimmer of her dark eyes as they dared to search his face. Her scrutiny made him feel abused. From deep inside him rose a desire to have her taken away, disposed of.

'What?' he said, fighting the Masterly instinct.

'It can't work against you,' she said.

'I'm afraid I have no idea what you're talking about.'

'You want us to work . . . ?'

'Repairing the Ladder.' For some reason he found he was pointing vaguely back the way they had come, as if they could see the ladder of which he spoke.

The sartlar woman greeted his comment with silence. Her fellow creatures shifted like aquar behind her.

'I hoped the other Master might have made arrangements with you . . .' He bit his lip, not understanding his discomfiture.

The woman struck her forehead off the floor with a crack that made Carnelian wince.

'As the Master commands, so shall it be done.'

Carnelian stood for some moments more before, following Fern, they quit that place; almost running, so desperate were they to cleanse their lungs with bright, fresh air.

The disgust produced among the Plainsmen by the sartlar as they poured up from the netting avoided any questions about the caves. Seeing the creatures huddling in a herd, Carnelian began to wonder if they would be any use in repairing the Ladder. The sartlar he had spoken to before stood, head hanging, close enough he could smell her rank odour.

'Do you know what to do?' he asked her.

'What the Master commands,' she answered without lifting her head.

'Then I say that you and the rest of your kind must repair the Ladder.'

'As you command, Master.'

Her submissiveness irritated him: the Plainsmen looking on turned this feeling to anger.

'How am I supposed to . . . ?' His voice tailed off.

'You're the Master,' the sartlar muttered.

As he walked along the chasm edge, everyone followed him.

Peering over, he saw the broken Ladder. At that distance it was just a nest of rope.

'I'll have to go down there myself,' he said.

Krow stood forward. 'I'll go, Master.'

Carnelian smiled at the youth's eagerness. 'Thank you, Krow, but I need to see the damage for myself.'

As Krow's face fell, Fern spoke up. 'Carnie, you should let him go. He'll be able to tell you what he sees.'

Carnelian was warmed by what he saw in Fern's eyes. His friend fixed him with an intense look. 'If you should die?'

Carnelian understood Fern's fear. If anything should happen to him, how could the Master be thwarted?

'A Master can't die,' said a husky voice.

Carnelian saw the sartlar woman had crept up beside them. He gazed at her, wondering what she meant. He supposed that, to a sartlar, the Masters might well appear to be immortal.

'Let me go, Master,' said Krow.

Carnelian saw Fern's nod and gave way.

They tied Krow to the rope they had used to lower Osidian and Morunasa, then slowly, they lowered him down into the chasm.

After a while, Carnelian turned to Fern. 'Why were you so keen he should go?'

'He's taken the Master's rejection hard. He needs something to distract him.'

Krow had reached the Ladder. Carnelian watched him examine it. 'I fear he merely wishes to follow the Master.'

'If that's so, isn't it better he should do so with our help than without?'

Carnelian glanced at Fern and saw the truth of it.

Krow was waving. Carnelian gave the order to draw him back up. When the youth appeared over the edge, Carnelian grabbed hold of him. Krow looked pale but pleased with himself. Carnelian waited until he had calmed down a little before asking him to describe what he had seen. Carnelian pondered the problem.

'Have you worked out how to do it?' Fern asked at last.

'I think so,' said Carnelian. He put the back of a fist against the palm of his other hand. 'At the moment, the broken portion of the Ladder is sort of curled like my fist.' He looked at Krow, who confirmed it with a nod. Carnelian allowed his hand to uncurl. 'If we attach ropes from up here we can unroll the Ladder up the cliff high enough to secure it into the forked posts that Krow says have been left in the rock. Attaching ropes progressively higher each time' – his fist uncurled until the hand lay flat against the other – 'we should be able to bring it all the way up here.'

'And what do we do then?' asked Fern.

'We attach it to those anchor trees,' said Carnelian indicating the two baobabs with their rope girdles.

'How?'

Carnelian noticed the sartlar woman was watching his hands. 'We can sort that out once we get there.'

He turned to the sartlar and pushed his hands closer to her. 'You understand this?'

She gave a nod. 'Yes, Master.'

'We'll need lots of ropes, each long enough to reach the Ladder below.'

'We understand,' said the sartlar.

'We'll have to lower your people down there to attach the ropes . . .'

She turned her disfigured face up to look at him. 'People?'

He indicated the others of her kind with his hand. She looked round. 'Sartlar,' she said.

'We can use aquar to pull the ropes.'

The woman sunk her head.

'Is there anything the matter?' he asked her.

'Better we should do it, Master.'

He frowned. 'The Ladder will be immensely heavy.'

She struck the ground with her foot. 'We take our strength from the earth.'

Carnelian shrugged. 'I'll trust you . . . What are you called?'

The sartlar looked up, her eyes so narrowed the folds almost closed them altogether.

Carnelian grew uncomfortable under that scrutiny. 'You have a name?'

'Kor, Master.'

Carnelian was surprised. In Quya, that sound was the word for death.

'Well, Kor,' he said. 'You'll explain to the other . . . ?'

'People . . . ?' she suggested.

Carnelian felt off-balance. 'Yes . . .'

'As the Master commands,' said Kor and falling to her knees, made an abject prostration before him. He waited for her to get up but she lay there as if she were dead.

'You can go.'

The mess of rags came alive and was soon hobbling off towards the other sartlar.

'Disgusting creatures,' Fern said.

Carnelian turned on him. 'Her kind, even more than the Plainsmen, are the victims of the Standing Dead.'

Over the following days, the sartlar went at their task like ants. Krow assumed the role of overseer, but soon gave this up. The sartlar worked seemingly without instruction, though sometimes Carnelian saw Kor moving among them and concluded she must be directing them.

Sartlar were lowered to the Ladder. Heavy ropes were dropped down to them which, once attached to the left cable, were hoisted so that the dangling section of the Ladder ended up folded over the part still intact. Once the pulled-up corner was secured, the ropes were removed and sartlar clambered down the dangling portion to reattach them further down the loose section. Gangs of sartlar held on to each rope and, digging their heels into the soil, heaved the whole mass up. Once raised high enough, the Ladder was made secure and the whole procedure was repeated. The strength of the sartlar amazed Carnelian so that he could almost believe Kor's boast that they were drawing it from the earth.

Confident the sartlar could work without supervision, Carnelian let the Plainsmen linger up on the knoll and took to resting in the shadow of one of the anchor baobabs with Fern. Dozing, they talked about the Tribe, the Koppie, of the life they might have once they were free of the Master.

One such time they fell to discussing how they would kill him. Upset, Carnelian declared that he would do it; that it was his responsibility. Already unhappy about this, Fern was made worse when Carnelian suggested they bring Ravan into their plot.

'Why?'

'Have you seen the way he looked at the Master? He clearly hates him.'

Fern became miserable. 'The Master still possesses him.'

Carnelian decided he must trust Fern's instinct.

At that moment a commotion broke out. Leaping up, he ran round the tree and saw sartlar being dragged towards the chasm by their ropes. Some who had fallen were being flayed and were forced to let go. The others picked up speed, heading for the edge.

Carnelian ran towards them, shouting: 'Let go. Let go.'

Some did, but others seemed unable to release their grip and the ropes lashed them out into space. Carnelian reached the edge in time to watch them ride the ropes down, down into the chasm. The

Ladder hurtled earthwards, snapping free of the posts like cloth tearing buttons. He put his hands over his face as he watched sartlar spinning down through the air. Through his fingers, he saw far below the Ladder holding where it had held before. Its loose portion whipped into the cliff with a thud he could feel coming up through the ground.

'Great Father,' breathed Fern.

Carnelian let his hands fall and shook his head in disbelief, staring as if that might undo the disaster. He heard padding footfalls and turned to see Kor behind him.

'What happened?' he gasped.

She cowered. 'Shall I jump, Master?'

'What?' he cried.

'Punishment,' she whispered.

He understood and groaned. 'No. No, Kor. I'm sure it's not your fault.' He turned back, blaming himself. 'One of the forked posts must have given way. So much loss of life.'

'There're still enough of us, Master.'

He turned on her and the outrage in his face made her collapse. 'Do you feel nothing over the loss of your people?'

Kor peered up at him. He saw behind her other sartlar nursing limbs, knees and heels bloody where they had ripped furrows in the earth. He looked down at Kor.

'Send the unwounded down to see if there're any people that can be helped.'

Kor nodded slowly looking at him through her curtain hair.

'Shall we start all over again, Master?'

He looked off over her head. 'Perhaps . . . but not today and not until the wounded have had a chance to recover and, then, only if there remain enough of you.'

She stood up never taking her eyes off him. She seemed troubled.

'Is there anything more, Master?'

'Nothing,' he said.

She bowed. 'As the Master commands.'

Work resumed the following day. Laboriously, the sartlar pulled the Ladder straight again. If Carnelian had not shared their life as a slave upon the road, he might have been surprised they worked with so little fear, but he knew their lives were worthless.

In the gory sunset, Carnelian took one last look down the chasm wall and saw the Ladder had been brought so high it folded at no great distance below him. Kor had come to him saying they could finish it by night with torches, but fearing another disaster,

438

Carnelian told her they should finish the work the following day when they would all be rested. He watched them crawl down to the saltcaves before walking back towards the anchor trees. He strummed a note from one of the ropes he had insisted they leave attached to the fold in the Ladder as a precaution should one of the forked posts fail. Fern stood by one of the anchor trees running his hands over its cable girdle.

'What are you doing?' Carnelian called out.

Fern grimaced. 'I can't see how the cables are going to be long enough to reach these trees.' He showed Carnelian where the cable had been sawn through. 'They'll have lost all the length you can see wrapped around this trunk.'

Carnelian considered the problem. He walked round the tree, squinting at the girdle in the failing light. 'Is this made from one continuous piece?'

Fern said it was.

'Then we shall have to unwrap it and somehow or other attach it to its original cable.'

'How?'

Carnelian stood back and allowed his gaze to run up the trunk. He noticed a narrow opening in the bark high above. He pointed up at it. 'This one's hollow too.'

Fern looked at it. 'Then . . .' he said, his hands searching the bark. 'Aha,' he said and hung himself from a crevice. 'All the hollows have handholds up to them.'

'Another burial?'

Fern shrugged. 'Climb and see.'

Carnelian gazed up. 'Why not,' he said. 'I'm curious to see these husk pygmies.'

Fern guided Carnelian's hand to the crevice and he found another slightly higher to the right of the first. It took him a while to find some for his feet.

'You forget how small a man this was made for,' said Fern from behind him. 'You should take them two, maybe three at a time.'

Taking his advice, Carnelian began climbing the tree. As he neared the opening he became aware of an unpleasant smell. He screwed up his nose and looked down at Fern.

'I think the bodies in this one are more recent than the others.'

He reached up to the lip of the hole, then pulled himself up into the hollow. Crouching on its edge, he covered his nose and mouth with his hand. It was too dark to see anything. He leaned out.

'Fern, could you bring me some fire to see by?'

He heard his friend running off and waited, feeling the moist breath of whatever it was that lay within the tree. It seemed an age before he saw the shaking flicker of Fern returning.

'Shall I come up too?'

'What about the fire?'

Grinning, Fern wedged the brand between his teeth and began to climb. Soon the flames were blinding Carnelian.

'Here, take it,' said Fern.

Carnelian reached down and plucked the offered branch, carefully, drew its fire past his squinting eyes and pushed it into the hollow. What he saw made him start.

Fern cried out: 'What's the matter?'

Carnelian made space for his friend to squeeze in beside him. A dark pool filled the hollow, its surface broken by a face the size of a child's.

'Perhaps the rain got in,' Carnelian suggested.

'I don't think so,' said Fern. He took the branch from Carnelian's hand and waved it over the pool. 'See how thick the liquid is?'

'Like soup.'

'Render.'

Carnelian looked at his friend, whose face was luridly lit by the flames.

'Render: the stuff they fed us in the legions. It's given to men and aquar and, I heard, the dragons too. Jellied animal flesh, fat and bone. Didn't much care for it myself, though it was extravagantly laced with salt. A veteran told me I'd grow to like it.'

Carnelian looked with horror at the face floating in the pool. 'A different kind of animal this.'

'Only raveners eat human flesh.'

They shared their disgust.

'Look, it has no eyes,' said Fern.

Carnelian saw the sockets were pools of render. He turned away, speaking between retches. 'Come on . . . Let's leave . . .'

They clambered to the ground as quickly as they could. Sweaty, they both looked up at the opening and shuddered. Carnelian found himself remembering their first night in the Upper Reach when he had had the nightmare. Taking deep breaths, he began relating it to Fern.

'I thought I had dreamed the shapes I saw moving around here.'

They looked at each other. 'The sartlar,' said Fern.

Carnelian nodded. 'How many pygmies do you think that pool might hold?'

'Depends on how deep it is.'

The night was populated by huge, menacing baobabs. 'There might be other trees like this.'

Fern shook his head. 'Every tree nearby save these has been investigated for water.'

'It seems that Morunasa was right, the pygmies didn't flee after all.'

Fern's eyes widened. 'Then it was the sartlar who killed them, who cut the Ladder free.'

Fear was added to Carnelian's queasiness. 'Why?'

Fern looked sick. 'And we've been sleeping night after night without posting guards.'

Carnelian tried to work it out.

Fern spoke first. 'We must go and cut the ladder to their caves.'

Carnelian took Fern's arm and pulled him away towards the knoll. 'Better to face this in the morning. Tonight, you and I will stand watch.'

'Together?' Fern asked.

'No,' said Carnelian, 'one at a time. We'll each need some sleep.'

Fern stared at him aghast. 'You might manage to sleep, I know I won't.'

'Well, we should at least try and, Fern, it might be better if we weren't to mention any of this to the others until we know what's going on. There's no need to frighten them needlessly.'

'And then of course there's the Ladder to be finished,' said Fern.

'Yes, the Ladder,' said Carnelian glancing back. He shuddered, sure he could see shadows creeping around the anchor baobabs.

MUTINY

A war can turn on the decision of a moment.
(from a treatise on warfare composed by an unknown Quyan)

CARNELIAN TOOK THE FIRST WATCH. HE SAT WITH HIS BACK TO THE embers so that their light would not blind him to any movements in the night. Around him baobabs loomed, thrusting their skeletal arms into the starry sky. The waterfall grumbled. It was cold. He wrapped his blanket tighter round him and dug his nails into the palms of his hands to stave off sleep.

The moon rising full oozed its silver among the baobabs, betraying stark shadows gathered around the anchor trees. Frozen by the sight, wetting his lips, Carnelian readied a cry of alarm should they come creeping towards the knoll.

His eyes continued to see the sartlar even when he was certain they had returned to their caves. After that he tried not to imagine them under his feet feasting on the pygmy render.

Later, when Fern relieved him, Carnelian told him what he had seen and then, reluctantly, went to his blanket. At first he tried lying with his back to the chasm, his eyes closed, but his ears kept him awake, listening for the padding of sartlar feet. He rolled over to face his fear. That was worse. Every sound, real or imagined, forced his eyes open to search the darkness.

At last he gave up and moved to Fern's side.

'Can't sleep,' Carnelian whispered.

Fern smiled. 'During your watch, I was only pretending.'

Carnelian sat down close to his friend.

442

'It's cold,' he said.

Shyly, Fern opened his blanket to welcome him. Hesitating, Carnelian shuffled closer. They managed to wrap both blankets round them. Silent, they kept watch together.

Carnelian woke to find Fern lying against him asleep. For some moments he allowed his eyes to wander over the dark face so close to his. He smiled but then jerked round to look down towards the chasm.

'What . . . ?' his friend blurted, blinking, confused.

Carnelian could see the Plainsmen sleeping peacefully around their hearths. Some were stirring, perhaps woken by Fern's voice, among them Ravan. Ignoring the youth's stare, Carnelian turned to his friend.

'Sorry.'

Fern yawned and rubbed his eyes with the heels of his hands. 'We fell asleep then?'

'Thankfully there's no harm done.'

They stood up and stretched, groaning, their backs aching from the way they had been sleeping, propping each other up. Still wrapped in his blanket, Carnelian started walking down towards the chasm. Soon the sun would be scorching down but the morning was still cold and the ground glittered with dew.

Fern came to join him. 'Where are you going?'

Carnelian turned. 'To wait for our sartlar friends.'

'You were right. In the morning light, they seem less terrifying.'

When they reached the edge of the chasm, they saw it was clogged with mist. Carnelian was relieved to find the Ladder was where it had been the night before. He leaned over and looked along the wall of the chasm towards the sartlar ladder.

'No sign of them.'

'Everyone sleeps late after a night of feasting,' said Fern.

Carnelian turned and saw his friend's wry grin. Carnelian walked back towards one of the anchor baobabs. When he reached it he sat, leaning his back against its trunk.

'You're going to wait for them?' asked Fern.

'I want to make sure we finish the Ladder today.'

'Do you mean to confront them?'

Carnelian frowned. 'I'm not sure yet. Do we have enough food to share with them?'

Fern frowned and shook his head. 'I'll wait with you.'

He sat down beside Carnelian and, closing their eyes, they basked in the morning sun.

The sartlar came creeping over the chasm rim, bent as if they were carrying burdens on their backs. They fell still when Carnelian rose and gibbered as he approached.

'Kor,' he called, searching for her. Though he could not see the woman this did not mean she was not there. Sartlar were more alike than aquar.

One detached from the herd. He recognized Kor by her shambling gait. As she came closer she sank to her knees. Behind her came the rest, in sullen subservience. He tried to wave them away but they did not respond. Their heads were bowed down to their feet and he could not tell if any were even looking at him.

'Come, Kor, follow me,' he said and stooped. At his touch she jerked violently, causing him to pull his hand away. He watched her get slowly to her feet, groaning.

'Are you in pain?'

The sartlar looked up at him. 'For the living the world holds nothing but pain.'

He wondered that philosophy should come from such a creature.

'Follow me.' He turned his back and walked away but did not hear her following. Looking back, he saw she had remained where she was.

'Come on,' he said more insistently. His tone seemed to jerk her to life and she hobbled after him. They walked together towards the anchor baobab in which he had found the render.

'What's in this tree, Kor?'

'We have to labour on the Ladder, Master.'

'Tell me what this tree contains.'

The sartlar looked up at him through her hair. 'It's a tree, Master.'

'A hollow one.'

Her shoulders rose and fell.

'I've seen what lies in it.'

She lifted her face so that her chin emerged through her hair. He saw her raw lips opening. 'We have to eat.'

Carnelian's scrutiny lingered on her mouth with its rotting teeth. He tore his eyes away. 'Surely you could have found something else?'

'We could have eaten each other, Master.'

Carnelian failed to discern any emotion in her voice. 'You killed the pygmies.'

Again the shrug.

'Did you?' he insisted.

'They tried to starve us, Master.'

444

Carnelian's eyes were drawn to the Isle of Flies. 'What about their masters?'

'We didn't go there,' said Kor.

He looked down at her.

'The Darkness fed on the rainmen.'

'What?'

Her head fell.

'Do you mean Oracles?' Carnelian remembered something Osidian had said when he returned from the island. Cannibalism. Had a sartlar siege reduced the Oracles to that? Whatever had happened, Carnelian could guess what would befall this woman and her people should he tell Morunasa even the little she had confessed. Yet if he said nothing, who else might suffer? Osidian's death would not change the necessity to return the Upper Reach to the Oracles. If Morunasa was typical, they were merciless. Carnelian needed time to think.

'Go. Finish the Ladder.'

Kor stood like a boulder. 'Will the other Master return with rainmen?'

'I don't know.'

'Will you show them what's in the hollow tree?'

He shook his head. 'I'm not sure . . .'

'They would feed us alive to their Darkness.'

Her filthy mouth again drew his queasy fascination. He imagined what it had been eating. Suddenly he needed to be rid of her.

'You disgust me,' he spat and immediately felt his anger gone. Almost, he apologized.

'Yes, Master.' Kor made a painful prostration before him and then retreated towards the other sartlar. Carnelian looked on grimacing, feeling something of the desperation that had driven the creatures to eating human flesh. He had experienced their lot. What right had he to judge them?

As the sartlar toiled, raising the last section of the Ladder, Carnelian, Fern, Krow and some other Plainsmen struggled to remove the girdling cables from the anchor trees. They snapped several spear hafts in the knots before they managed to work them loose.

By this time, the sartlar were drawing the ends of the Ladder up on to level ground. As had been expected, these reached just to the anchor trees but no further. It was the turn of the Plainsmen. Using thin rope as a model, Carnelian had already shown them what he wanted to do. Using knots he had learned as a child on his island, they managed to join one of the Ladder cables to the fragment they had retied around the tree. The resulting knot was larger than a man's head. It was hard to believe it would hold. As Carnelian directed the sartlar to gradually release that side of the Ladder, everything began creaking, groaning, squeezing smaller. The whole system stuttered, then fell silent. Like everyone else, Carnelian was ready to run from the whiplash should it all come apart.

'It holds,' said Fern at last, his voice loud in the silence.

Carnelian and Krow whooped and the Plainsmen joined them.

It was already getting dark when the other side of the Ladder was similarly secured. The Plainsmen celebrated while the sartlar looked on, as animated as rocks. They shied away from Carnelian as he walked in among them. He found Kor.

'You've done well.' He gazed over the sartlar. 'You've all done well.'

He looked down at Kor. 'Now go and rest.'

'Rest is forbidden us,' the woman said.

'But I've nothing more for you to do.'

'The other Master commanded us to quarry salt.'

'Hush,' Carnelian said and looked round to see if any of the Plainsmen had heard her and was relieved when he saw them returning to the knoll.

He looked back at Kor. 'Then you must obey his commands.'

'And what shall we eat, Master?'

Carnelian grimaced. There was no spare djada. 'Eat what there is in the tree.'

'As the Master commands,' said the woman and limped off to join her fellow creatures, who were making their slow, melancholy way back to their caves.

When Carnelian returned to the knoll, the fires were already lit. Their crackle and the mutter of Plainsman voices were comforting. Fern made a space for him at his side. Carnelian sat down and took the djada offered.

'The men would like you to know that most of the water caches in the trees have been drained,' Fern said, in a voice all were meant to hear.

'Then we'll have to fetch water from the river.'

This was greeted with a murmur of discontent.

'We wish to return to our peoples in the mountains,' said Ravan.

'You know perfectly well the Master told us to wait here for him,' said Krow, his eyes flaming.

'And what if he doesn't return in time?'

'He will.'

Ravan stood up and looked around him. Loudly, he announced: 'Let's cut the Ladder and, in the morning, we'll leave this accursed place.'

Silence fell across the knoll, disturbed only by a few mutters of agreement. When Krow made to confront Ravan, Carnelian held up a hand to stay him. 'Let him speak.'

Ravan looked at Carnelian, surprised, then lifted his gaze over the camp.

'The Ochre who have lived with them will tell you the Standing Dead are nothing more than men. Yes, they have power, but it is not divine. We four tribes have now fought together. Why don't we go on? Which other tribe could stand against our joined might? Imagine what could flow from this alliance: the salt that would free us from service in the legions; the captured children we could send to the Mountain in place of our own. All this we could do once freed from the Master.'

As voices broke out supporting Ravan, Carnelian saw how much the youth had become Osidian's pupil. He saw also what the consequence of such upheaval would be. The Wise would not tolerate such a challenge to their systems. But how could he explain to the Plainsmen the complex realities that lay behind the face the Commonwealth presented to its subjects? Still, this had to be stopped before it went too far. He rose.

'Ravan is right, you could cut the Ladder and return to your peoples, but consider this: the Marula came up before and massacred two tribes; the next time they come up do you want them led by the Master?'

Ravan saw Carnelian's words had spread dread. 'What of it? Did the Darkcloud not defeat them?'

Several answered him.

'Prepared, we could do so again.' His eyes became possessed by firelight. 'Perhaps we might even become strong enough to defy the Gatherers.'

Fern leapt to his feet and began making appeals to those who had seen the dragons of the legions. 'Do you really believe we could defeat those?'

Ravan thrust his head towards his brother. 'The Master believes so. He told me that is his plan.'

Carnelian was shocked Osidian had confided so much in the youth. 'Then he has deceived you, as he has deceived himself. The methods he has used to overturn your lives are the same the Standing Dead use to rule the world. A legion is altogether another matter. The dragons cannot be defeated by riders however numer-

447

ous. As for defeating the Marula, up until now, when they have come up on to the Earthsky, they have wandered blind in a land they did not know. Even so, they destroyed two tribes. As for the Darkcloud's victory, I led the attack. We only won because we surprised them.' He located the Darkcloud around their fires. 'How many would have fallen in a pitched battle?'

Some of them shook their heads, but none spoke up.

'If the Master led the Marula, they would move with more certainty than even you in your own land. If you doubt this, ask Ravan and any of the rest of us whom he guided through the swamp and across the Earthsky when no Plainsman knew the way.'

Krow and Fern were nodding, as were many around other fires. Carnelian fixed Ravan with a glare.

'Do you really believe you could defeat the Master in battle? Would you have beaten the Bluedancing? You were there, Ravan, scared in the darkness with the rest of us before the Master came. Could you' – he looked out over the camp – 'or any of you have killed a ravener single-handed with a spear?'

His question echoed off the baobabs. Fern sat, then reached up and pulled his brother down. The youth scowled at the fire. Carnelian sank too and, ignoring Krow's stare, resumed the chewing of his djada. He was relieved when he heard chatter resume around the hearths.

At a sign from Carnelian, Fern and he slipped away from the drowsy camp to sit on the slope of the knoll from which they could keep a watch on the sartlar ladder.

'We got away with it this time,' said Fern.

Carnelian nodded. 'The next time might not be so easy.' He had hated threatening them with Osidian. It made him feel as if he was collaborating with him. He turned to his friend.

'Hasn't this made you feel it might well be safer if we were to bring Ravan into our circle?'

Fern shook his head vigorously. 'He's too erratic; too emotional. Besides, do you really believe he would support us in bringing back the old ways?'

'I suppose not. He will try this again.'

Fern hung his head, nodding. 'The problem is that the men are idle. I can't blame them for wanting to be back with their hearths.'

Light swelled in Carnelian's mind as he saw the valley in the mountains. He crushed the vision and peered into the night. 'And then there's the danger from the sartlar.'

'We could cut the ladder to their caves.'

Carnelian shook his head. 'I won't starve them.'

'We could keep watch every night.'

'We didn't even manage to stay awake.'

They hung their heads. Something occurred to Carnelian. He looked up. 'Perhaps we could knot our two problems into a solution. Let's fortify the camp.'

Fern considered this. 'What reason would we give them?'

'They fear the Marula, don't they?'

Fern nodded. 'And we Plainsmen feel exposed without our ditches. It might work.'

Carnelian slapped Fern on the back. 'We'll make it work.'

Fern's grin appeared in the starlight.

'Now, let's see if this time we can manage to stay awake.'

Grumbling, the Plainsmen set to fortifying their camp on the knoll. Carnelian joined them digging the dry earth in the cool of the morning. Fern and he had mapped where the ditch would run around the crown from baobab to baobab. They were using the trees as towers in the inner rampart. The impenetrable meshes of their roots forced them to sweep the ditch out in front of each monster.

For days they laboured, spending the hottest part of each in the shade. Weariness staunched the flow of complaints until they dried up altogether. The homely familiarity of the work made the men happier: the developing fortifications helped them feel secure. At night, exhausted, everyone slumped groaning around their fires and their talk was of their women, their little ones. Fern congratulated Carnelian on their stratagem with a smile.

'We've drunk the tree caches dry,' announced Fern.

Carnelian shrugged. 'We'll just have to make up a drag-cradle to take skins to the river.'

'You know how terrified the men are of going anywhere near the impaled man.'

A fearful superstition had grown up among the Plainsmen concerning the idol, the path it guarded and the island. Especially the island. Carnelian had seen how they refused even to look at it, as if whatever lived there might enter into a man through his eyes.

'Well, you and I will have to go.'

Carnelian saw Fern's fear. 'You too? I'll just have to go alone.'

Fern scowled. 'I never said I wouldn't go.'

They hitched a drag-cradle to the crossbeam of Carnelian's aquar, then loaded it with waterskins. Carnelian could not help laughing at the pile. 'Do we have to get all the water we'll ever need in one go?'

449

When enough waterskins had been removed, Carnelian moved up to the aquar's head and Fern moved round to the other side. Carnelian regarded the men. 'Anyone else want to come with us?'

Krow stood forward. 'I will.'

Carnelian nodded his approval and then the three of them led the aquar down the knoll towards the idol and the riverpath. When they reached level ground, Krow gazed up at the sky.

'The time is drawing near when we must return if we are to give the Tribe protection.'

Carnelian saw the sky was grey with heat. Turning he surveyed the escarpment, studded with baobabs all the way up towards the plain of the Earthsky. He turned back.

'Have faith. The Master will not forget the need of the Tribe. He'll return in time.'

Krow grimaced. 'Though I believe it, there are an increasing number who don't.'

Fern and Carnelian looked at each other, then thanked Krow for the warning.

The aquar shied away from the impaled man, but keeping a wary eye on the idol they managed to coax her on to the riverpath. Some distance along it, they found a track leading down to the river. Carnelian elected to fill the skins, passing them back to Fern, who passed them to Krow, who stowed them on the drag-cradle. As he worked, Carnelian was aware of the Isle of Flies brooding across the river. When he had filled the last skin, he stood for a moment gazing at the island, wondering if what had befallen the Oracles there was what gave it an aura of menace. Then he turned his back on it and climbed to join the others. He nestled the skin among the others and they returned to the knoll.

During one of their water-fetching expeditions, while filling a skin from the river, Carnelian was letting his eyes rove over the dark forbidding mass of the Isle of Flies.

'You're always looking at it,' Fern complained.

'Aren't you curious about it at all?'

Fern shrugged and Carnelian saw his friend's reluctance even to glimpse the black island.

'Shall we go there and see for ourselves what horror it hides?'

Fern looked at him aghast.

Carnelian lifted the skin from the water and sealed it. 'I don't believe in Morunasa's god. I think that banyan conceals a shrine, a wooden temple, but there's only one way to find out. We need only go close enough to peer through its outer trunks.'

Fern's pained expression irritated Carnelian.

'I'll go alone.' He leaned the waterskin against a boulder and clambered along the shore looking for a crossing. He turned when he heard the scrabbling of Fern following him. They regarded each other.

Fern frowned. 'I'm coming with you just to make sure you don't feel tempted to go further in than the edge.'

Carnelian was glad of Fern's company. Together they resumed the search for the route Morunasa and Osidian had taken across. Where the water swirled, the stream seemed spun from pure light; where it pooled, its mirrors cast the sun directly into their eyes.

When Carnelian was sure they had found the way, he glanced round. 'I'm glad you're coming with me, Fern.'

Squinting at the island a darkness of doubt descended, but before it could claim him, Carnelian clambered down the bank. He slipped into a slide that tore gritty dust into clouds. Half-choking, half-laughing, he managed to regain his balance only to be knocked forward as Fern careened into him. Carnelian spun, grabbed hold of him, and together they tumbled down the slope and crashed splashing into a pool.

Carnelian stood up, laughing as he pointed at Fern soaked, caked in dust. Fern scooped some water at him. Soon they were splashing around like boys, delighting in the cool flying diamond spray.

Dripping, they set off across the rocks. Through the dazzle, it took concentration. The footing became treacherous. Sometimes a route would end at a deep rush of water which they dared not ford for fear it should sweep them over the falls. They pushed on.

Closer, the banyan trunks rose scabrous black, taller than it had seemed possible from the other shore. Seeing its hall of columns, Carnelian recalled what Osidian had said.

'Labyrinth,' he said in Quya.

'What?' Fern demanded.

Carnelian turned and saw Fern's barbarian look of incomprehension. His hands rose to mask his face from the dark eyes. Fern's horror shocked Carnelian free of his mood.

'Why are you staring at me like that?'

Fern shook his head.

'What?' Carnelian demanded, knowing he was in the wrong.

Fern grew angry. 'You were looking at me the way the Master does.'

The Masterly pride that had woken in him would not allow him to apologize. 'We can go back now, I've seen enough.'

Fern bared his teeth. 'You were the one who wanted to see this accursed place and see it you will.'

He pushed past Carnelian who, cursing, followed him.

As they neared the shore of the island, they began to slip and fall because the banyan commanded their stares. Around its feet, what had appeared to be tangled driftwood was not that at all.

'Bones . . .' Fern said staring.

Yellowed white, immense spars snagged in a log jam that clung to the shore of the island. The black roots of the banyan snaked among them as if it were feeding on the dead. A vast carcass lay broken among the bones, grey-brown tatters of skin hanging on the skeleton. It seemed to Carnelian even more sinister than the slaughter of the heaveners. He peered upstream.

'This river in flood must bring corpses.'

Looking back to the other shore, the aquar and its drag-cradle looked tiny beneath the black cliff of the Backbone. Carnelian longed to return. Fern was peering into the cavernous darkness imprisoned by the trunks. Carnelian's eyes again became tangled in the banyan. Its breath was sweet decay.

'What are you staring at?' Fern demanded.

'I have . . .' He stopped, seeing Fern's incomprehension. He realized he had been speaking in Quya again. 'I've seen this place before.'

Fern looked incredulous. 'How could you have?'

Carnelian was unwilling to explain. Could this be the model for the Labyrinth? They were too far from Osrakum. No Masters save he and Osidian could ever have been here.

Fern, terrified, was framed by the banyan rising like night behind him. Neither of them could bear to be there a moment longer. As fast as they could, they made their way back to the safety of the other shore, arriving bloody and bruised from many falls.

Neither spoke as they coaxed the aquar with its fully loaded drag-cradle towards the camp. Carnelian had fallen back to put the bulk of the creature between him and Fern. He was embarrassed. After having all but forced his friend to go to the island, it was he who had most wanted to flee and that after having behaved abominably. Now they were past the impaled man and among the baobabs, it seemed as if it had been someone else who had panicked.

A commotion was echoing from the crown of the knoll. Fern made the aquar stop. Carnelian continued walking and they looked at each other. Fern began running. Carnelian looked around, decided the aquar could look after herself and took off after him. He felt the creature's footfalls through the earth and looking back saw she was loping after them, the drag-cradle rattling after her, shedding waterskins. They slid, and bounced and burst open, splashing water everywhere. Carnelian grimaced, but turned his back on the débâcle and raced on.

As he and Fern crossed the ditch into the camp, they saw the backs of Plainsmen who were focusing on something in their midst. Unable to make himself heard above their roar, Carnelian pushed his way through. Some responded violently, but sprang aside when they saw who it was. Silence spread through their ranks. A path opened to the centre of their crowd, where he saw a sartlar at bay, hair risen in a mane.

'Kor?' he said. 'What are you doing to her?' he bellowed, striding round the front row of men, shoving them aside. They drew back, awed by his rage. A growling made him turn. The animal sound was coming from the sartlar woman.

'Kor . . .' he said, gently, approaching her. The woman snarled at him and he pulled his hands up and stepped back to give her space.

'Have they hurt you?' he said, his voice slow, soothing.

Kor glared at him. Keeping a wary eye on her, he looked around. 'What's this about?'

'Salt,' one man cried, and many others took the word up in a chorus.

At first Carnelian did not understand, but then he noticed the snowy grains frosting the ground. Kor had more in her hands, more crumbled down her rags.

'She came with a great slab of it,' said Krow. 'She wouldn't give it to us, nor tell us where it came from.'

Avarice gleamed in every eye. Seeing Kor still looking hunted, Carnelian crouched beside her.

'It's all right now, little mother,' he said.

He continued talking until Kor relaxed, straightening up as much as she could.

'They tore it from me, Master,' she said and indicated the salt-strewn earth with her gnarled fists.

'It doesn't matter, Kor.'

He was trying to get close enough to lead her off before she said anything else but she backed away from him.

'I only came to ask the Master where he wants us to put the slabs we've cut.'

Carnelian groaned.

Ravan broke through into the circle. 'There's more . . . ?' he cried, staring at the sartlar.

'Caves of it,' said Fern. He stamped the ground. 'Here beneath our feet.'

The Plainsmen erupted. Carnelian glared at Fern, who grimaced. 'We have kept this from them too long.'

Carnelian gave a weary nod of acceptance.

Ravan's eyes burned with excitement as he looked out over the men. 'With so much wealth we could recruit a vast host.' He raised his arms. 'We would become invincible.'

He turned on Carnelian. 'Even against the Master and his Marula.'

'Do you imagine the Standing Dead would not notice the drying up of their recruits? How long do you think it would be before they came to punish your impudence?'

Ravan's lip curled up from his teeth. 'More threats, Master?' He stabbed a finger at Carnelian and looked round at the men. 'Does this one seem so terrifying that we must quake at the very mention of their retribution?' He circled Carnelian. 'Are these Standing Dead really so much mightier than us that we should obey them as if they were gods? What is the basis of their power except terror? I say that should we choose to be men and defy them, we will find their power is nothing more substantial than a mirage.'

Fern closed on his brother. 'The Master has possessed you as he has us all.' He surveyed the crowd. 'We have become murderers and thieves. He has made us forget our ancient ways, our humility, our honour and piety. He has made us give insult to the Mother.'

He looked at Ravan, shaking his head sadly. 'As for you, my brother, I do not hear wisdom but rather the bitterness of a lover spurned.'

Ravan clenched his fists and bared his teeth. 'You accuse me of that, you who are to him' – he pointed at Carnelian – 'in everything his wife.'

Fern swung and struck his brother a blow which made him reel but then return screaming. 'Do you want to hit me again? Come on, do you?'

Fern looked horrified. He seemed to become suddenly aware they had an audience. He threw himself bodily at the crowd, who made way for him.

Carnelian almost ran after him, but Ravan was staring, his face already bruising.

'Master, where shall we store the salt?' Kor asked.

Carnelian swung round and she cowered. 'Where do you normally put it?'

The sartlar angled her head towards the Isle of Flies.

'Store it in the caves.'

She fell into a prostration. As he looked at the white-flecked ground around her, he wondered if the creature could really have so little idea of how precious salt was that she innocently brought such a slab into the Plainsman camp.

454

He became aware of the men around him staring. 'Haven't you seen enough?' he bellowed. They ducked their heads and began dispersing. Carnelian asked Krow to look after Ravan and then he went to find Fern.

Carnelian found his friend standing at the chasm edge gazing across at the Isle of Flies. They stood side by side in silence.

'I couldn't bear to hear the Master's voice coming out of him,' said Fern at last.

'I know,' said Carnelian.

'It really is as if he is possessed.'

'In many ways he is.'

Water fell around the dark face of the Isle of Flies like hair. Carnelian felt the question forming on his lips as his heart pounded.

'Is that why you hit him?'

Sensing Fern turning towards him, Carnelian looked round and their eyes met with an intensity that snatched away his breath. Fern's irises were all black.

'He insulted us both.'

Carnelian controlled anger. 'Do men among the tribes never love each other?'

Fern looked pained. 'Boys do.'

'And when boys become men?'

Fern grimaced. 'Once we are married, such feelings are discouraged. A man should love his wife and his children above all others.'

Carnelian saw the desire burning in Fern, but knew now he must not let it ignite his own. 'Perhaps Ravan was acting from fear. We must assure him we will not tell the Master of the . . . arguments we've had with him.'

Fern was looking at him very seriously. Carnelian made light of his feelings and laughed. He slapped Fern on the back.

'Come on, let's go and see if any of the water survived our return.'

Days later, shouting brought everyone in the camp running down armed towards the Ladder. As he ran towards it with the others, Carnelian saw smoke wavering up from the chasm. His heart raced as he recognized Osidian's signal. He pushed his way through the Plainsmen to peer over the edge. Far below, from where the smoke was rising, a dark mass of men could be seen gathered at the base of the Ladder and others were already climbing it.

'Marula,' said Fern who was beside Carnelian.

They glanced at each other. Even at that distance, it was hard to believe these were all Oracles.

'The Master's not there,' said Ravan.

'He must be,' said Carnelian. 'He told me he would send up smoke to signal his return.'

'I can't see him.'

'He's there somewhere,' said Krow. 'I'm certain of it.' The anxious way he was searching suggested otherwise.

Ravan pulled back from the edge. 'We must cut the Ladder.'

Fern rounded on him.

Ravan ignored his brother's glare. 'Am I the only one who can see it is Marula warriors who are climbing towards us?'

Fern turned frowning to Carnelian. 'He's right.'

They both eyed the Plainsmen and saw how uneasy they were.

Carnelian knew it was true. If Osidian was there then it seemed he did not trust them and was sending up these warriors in advance of him. Warriors? There had been no talk of warriors.

Ravan had moved towards the anchor trees. 'Are we all just going to wait here to be slaughtered?'

As most of the Darkcloud moved to Ravan's side, Carnelian could see they meant to support the youth.

'We can't ignore the threat,' said Fern.

Carnelian nodded. 'Ravan is right, we must take precautions. You all have your spears. Let's form a hornwall.'

Ravan gaped, confused, as Carnelian formed the Plainsmen into a crescent surrounding the head of the Ladder. He interspersed their line with Ochre who had experience of the formation from the battle against the Bluedancing. Then they waited, hearing the approach of the Marula in the vibrations of the Ladder cables.

SCREAMING

Pleasure can stir a voice to song. At the extremes, pain will always exceed pleasure in intensity. How much more powerful, then, is the impetus pain can give a voice? Do the Wise not teach that the sounds of agony are the vocal mode the Dark God most prefers? If this is so, then it follows that the most sublime form such a performance might attain is that in which the vocalist is skilfully excruciated and held shimmering at the very brink of death.

(from 'Of This and That' by the Ruling Lord Kirinya Prase)

AT THE CENTRE OF THE HORNWALL, CARNELIAN WATCHED THE MARULA spill out from the chasm. Gleaming black, massive limbs banded with wood, bodies hidden beneath beaded corselets that rose up behind their heads like the backs of chairs. They bared their teeth and hissed as they saw the hedge of spears awaiting them.

Carnelian felt the hornwall losing cohesion and steadied it with a bellow. More and more of the Marula were coming up, until he began to fear that should he not act now, his men would be overwhelmed.

Then he saw a taller figure at their rear.

A murmur rose from the hornwall. 'The Master.'

Carnelian glanced round at Fern. They shared the same deadly intent. Carnelian faced the Marula and Osidian, ready to give the order to push them all back into the chasm.

Osidian's Quya carried clear across the tumult. 'There is something strange in the way you look at me, Carnelian.'

A hush settled as everyone listened to the beautiful voice.

'The reading of faces is an art practised in the House of the Masks. You, my dear, unlike many of the Great, have not acquired the skill to conceal your thoughts.'

Carnelian tried to blank his face, almost unmanned by its betrayal. More and more Marula were swelling the wall before Osidian. Ashen Oracles were gathering round him.

'You have perhaps become more Chosen than I expected, Carnelian.'

'Carnie?' cried Fern, shocking Carnelian free of Osidian's mesmerizing voice.

Glancing at him, Carnelian saw Fern's urgency to settle the matter. Before he could think, Osidian spoke again.

'These Marula have been told that should any harm befall me . . . or the Ladder, then their kin shall all be given to the Oracles for sacrifice. This, not to mention that they have their backs to the chasm, should ensure they put up a vigorous fight.'

Carnelian went cold. Not only had Osidian become aware of his intention to kill him, but worse, he now saw the enormity of his mistake: Osidian had returned with an army of his own.

'Excellent, you have understood the new balance of power.'

Carnelian sensed the men round him wavering. 'The Plainsmen are still more numerous than your Marula.'

Osidian inclined his head. 'Mounted, they might prevail. With me to lead them, however, I believe my Marula would have a decisive advantage.'

Carnelian felt sick. The time for rebellion had passed. Perhaps if he had charged when Osidian had first appeared . . .

'Come now, Carnelian, shall we two really do battle and cause such unnecessary bloodshed?'

Carnelian was crushed.

'Have your men put up their spears and retire.'

A desperate hope made Carnelian look towards their fortified camp. His glance took Osidian's gaze to the knoll.

'I would starve you out and then would take the most terrible reprisals.'

Carnelian hoped at least to save his men. 'This was all my doing.'

'Really?' The humour in Osidian's voice was chilling. 'You need have no fear for them.' He glanced at Fern. 'Not one of them will suffer as long as they serve me.'

Carnelian knew it was finished. He ordered the Plainsmen to stand down. As here and there along the wall spears fell, Fern spoke out, anguished.

'What's going on, Carnie?'

Fearing for him, Carnelian snarled: 'Retire with the rest.'

Scowling, Fern obeyed him and, as he did so, the hornwall dissolved.

With a gesture, Osidian sent the Marula swarming forward to take control of the anchor trees and the Ladder ropes. As they unblocked the top of the Ladder, a tide of tiny, honey-brown men was released, struggling under baskets densely packed with fernroot. Distracted by these pygmies, Carnelian started retreating but stopped when he saw Osidian beckoning. Carnelian hesitated, seeing Morunasa and other Oracles around Osidian like pale crows.

'What, my love, do you fear I will harm you?'

Carnelian marched towards him his spear still in his hand, a desire beating in his chest to plunge it into Osidian.

'Carnelian, cast aside your weapon.' Osidian sounded alarmed. 'The Marula are not fully under my control. They might kill you.'

Carnelian came to a halt, confused that after all that had happened, Osidian might still care for him.

Osidian spoke again. 'Even were you to slay me, the Marula would destroy your Plainsmen.'

Carnelian saw how merciless were the yellow eyes of the Marula. As he threw away the spear, their ranks responded by opening before him. He advanced into their midst. As he closed on Osidian, it felt strange to look into green eyes again.

'Since we are being open with each other,' Osidian said, 'did you enter the caves that lie beneath our feet?'

Carnelian nodded.

'I thought you might. Does anyone else know what they contain?'

Carnelian considered lying but knew it would soon be found out. 'Everyone.'

Osidian's eyes widened. 'It amazes me you could be so stupid.'

Carnelian almost blamed Kor, but he felt this unworthy and decided he could bear Osidian's contempt.

Osidian moved forward. 'Well, it seems then there is no reason why the Plainsmen should not help load the pygmies with salt.'

'What for?'

Osidian took in the Marula with an elegant sweep of his hand. 'I had to buy them with something.'

Carnelian feared the Plainsmen would resist such work. 'Can you not use the Marula?'

'They are warriors.'

'So are the Plainsmen,' said Carnelian.

'Nevertheless, it is my will that they should do it.'

Carnelian saw a harshness in Osidian's eyes and knew that not only was he wanting to make clear to the Plainsmen that he was now their master, but he also wanted to make Carnelian understand this was a punishment they would suffer on his behalf.

Carnelian looked for the Plainsmen and saw they had retreated towards the knoll. As he pushed into the flow of pygmies, they moved from his path as if his touch were poison. He broke into open ground. Approaching the Plainsmen, he saw how bewildered they looked and lost the courage to reveal his errand.

'Carnie?' said Fern.

Carnelian could see how desperate his friend was to talk to him. He tried to communicate that this was impossible with a shake of his head. Aware they were all looking at him, Carnelian had to tell them.

'You are to go down to the saltcaves.'

Their looks of unease exasperated him. 'We have to give the quarried salt to the Marula.'

They stared at him. Fern opened his mouth to protest but then he looked to where, looming above the pygmy tide, the Master was in conversation with Morunasa, and his mouth closed. Carnelian met Fern's despondent gaze. Both knew they had failed. Many of the Plainsmen cast looks of desire up at their fortress on the hill, then lowered their heads to hide the anger and betrayal in their eyes. Led by Ravan, they leaned their spears against a baobab and made their way towards the sartlar ladder. Carnelian was tortured by the thought that the youth had been right all along. It was better not to accompany them. To share such menial work would only serve to anger Osidian and it would be the Plainsmen who would suffer retribution.

Pygmies were moving past him, returning empty-handed from where they were piling their baskets of fernroot at the foot of the knoll. An odour was rising from their bodies. It was the same aura of fear which slaves gave off in the presence of a Master, and which had to be masked with perfume. At first Carnelian thought it was Osidian the pygmies feared, but their glances were for the Oracles.

When Morunasa and the rest approached the crowd of little men, they crumpled into a juddering, urinating mass from which the ash-smeared arms of the Oracles plucked and pulled them out one here, one there. Those selected tottered off to where they stood together in trembling misery. When the Oracles had finished, those that were left fled towards the Ladder, stumbling over each other in their desperation to escape.

460

The Oracles closed in on those they had chosen and herded them whimpering off towards the idol and the impaled man. Carnelian was still watching as the first Plainsmen began coming up from the caves. The tiny men were being driven across the stepping stones and meandering currents, to be swallowed up by the Isle of Flies.

Sick at heart, Carnelian went to watch the loading of the salt. The Plainsmen were helping the sartlar hoist slabs up and over the lip of the chasm. They were carefully wrapped in oily cloth then bound to the backs of the pygmies. Once burdened, each began his descent back into the chasm. Marula stood by, observing everything with an arrogant gaze. When the last slab had been strapped to a pygmy, they casually prodded him down the Ladder with their spears and followed.

The Plainsmen looked miserable, even Krow. Seeing Kor among the sartlar, Carnelian wished he could decide what to do with her. A Maruli appeared beside them. The black giant waited until he had their eyes and then stabbed his spear towards the grotesque idol and made some sounds that might have been speech. He strode away then stopped, turning to beckon them, until, sullenly, Carnelian and the Plainsmen began to follow him.

Osidian was waiting for them beneath the impaled man. On his left stood Morunasa with those Oracles who had not crossed to the island. Marula warriors formed a barbaric backdrop with their bead corselets and their ebony limbs. Shuffling, uncertain, the Plainsmen stood before the Master. Carnelian saw with what cruel eyes he was surveying them. His gaze fell on Carnelian.

'Come, my Lord,' he said, indicating a place at his right hand.

Carnelian felt he was betraying the Plainsmen, but dared not refuse. Under their eyes, he walked to where Osidian had pointed. It made him uncomfortable to be joining Osidian in standing judgement on them.

Osidian turned to him. 'Is there any matter that you might wish to convey to me?' he asked in Quya, as if the two of them were alone.

Carnelian brought his mind into focus. 'Matter . . . ?' He saw Fern's anxious face among the Plainsmen and found it hard not to glance at Ravan. He probed Osidian's eyes, wondering what he could possibly know or guess, and was terrified his face might betray him again.

At that moment a shriek tore the intolerably humid afternoon. An unhuman sound that set Carnelian's teeth to chattering. He turned just enough to catch a view of the Isle of Flies, whose brooding darkness seemed to be pulsing. He registered the terror of the Marula.

'My Lord?'

The elegant Quya wrenched Carnelian's eyes back.

'Did you not hear my –?'

Osidian was cut dead by another cry shrilling across the river. Carnelian felt something die in him.

'They're murdering . . .' he said, lapsing into Vulgate.

'An offering of blood to the Darkness-under-the-Trees,' said Morunasa.

Carnelian was caught in the Maruli's amber eyes.

'Our Lord's hunger must be sated.'

'I grow impatient, Carnelian, for your answer.'

Carnelian regarded Osidian and Morunasa as if he were seeing them for the first time. The indifference in their eyes made them brothers. Under no circumstances would he hand over any Plainsman or sartlar to their mercy.

'I have nothing to say to you.'

Carnelian had to withstand Osidian's emerald gaze for several moments before he turned it on the Plainsmen.

'Stand forward those among you who understand Vulgate.'

Fern, Ravan, Krow and others made it to the front. Many behind them were glancing towards the island in horror. Carnelian shared the agony of waiting for the next scream.

'No doubt you all wish to return to your tribes in the mountains.'

When all the interpreters save Fern nodded, Carnelian feared for him.

'You don't want to go, Fern?'

When his friend did not flinch, Carnelian was proud of him, but fearful.

'No, Master,' Fern answered.

'Have you then become so enamoured of this place?'

Another animal cry bruised the air.

Fern flinched with the other Plainsmen, then shook his head, slowly.

'Perhaps then, it's an attachment to myself that keeps you here? Or perhaps to another?' said Osidian and, as he spoke, he turned his head a little towards Carnelian, who pretended not to understand the implication, for Fern's sake.

'Well, savage?'

Carnelian could feel that his friend was struggling not to look at him.

'Since you will not speak, you shall leave with the others.'

462

As Fern let his gaze fall, Carnelian breathed his relief that it was not worse.

Krow took a step forward, anxious. 'Master, may I stay with you?'

As Osidian regarded him, the youth's face grew shiny with sweat. He ducked his thanks when the Master gave a nod.

Osidian surveyed the Plainsmen. 'You may return to the mountains to escort your tribes across the plain. Once they are safely in their koppies, I expect you back here. You understand me?'

The would-be interpreters all nodded.

Osidian made a loose gesture taking in the Plainsmen crowd. 'Make sure everyone understands. Any man who does not return here shall have me for an enemy.' He flung out a gesture of dismissal and was turning his back on them when a voice spoke out.

'Shall we return empty-handed to our people?' It was Ravan who had taken a pace forward.

Osidian turned back and regarded the youth, his head at an angle. They examined each other. Carnelian was shocked to see that, even now, Ravan was hungry for Osidian to show him some token of love.

'What did you have in mind?' Osidian asked, as if Ravan were a stranger.

Carnelian saw tears of cold anger in the youth's eyes and could not believe Osidian did not notice them.

'Salt,' said Ravan, as if he were hurling an insult.

Osidian rolled his hand in the air even as he turned away. 'Take as much as you want.'

That easy concession served only to deepen Ravan's misery. As the Plainsmen began to creep away, the youth lingered, glaring at Osidian's back as if the pressure of his gaze might make him turn back to see him. Fearing for the youth's life, Carnelian was on the verge of himself going to force him to leave when Fern reached out and, gently, turned his brother. Carnelian's eyes meshed with Fern's for a moment before he began guiding Ravan away, leaving Carnelian alone with Osidian and the Marula.

Accompanied by Marula warriors, Carnelian followed Osidian, Morunasa and the other Oracles along the riverpath. Soon a procession of them was winding its way across the rocks.

Osidian turned. 'Will you come to the Isle of Flies with me, Carnelian?'

'Why?' Carnelian asked in horror.

'To witness certain rituals.'

At that moment another shriek of agony came from the island. Carnelian controlled an instinct to retch. Osidian seemed amused, then began to turn away.

'What's to happen here?' Carnelian blurted out.

Osidian turned back, frowning slightly. Carnelian bore his examination until Morunasa came up.

'Master?' he said, indicating the way across the rocks.

'I shall follow on in a while,' Osidian said without taking his eyes off Carnelian.

Irritation distorted Morunasa's face. 'How will the Master find his way across?'

'Easily.'

Morunasa waited for more, and then he gave instructions to some of the warriors in their strange language before striding off after his fellows.

Osidian's gaze intensified. 'How did you hope to profit from my assassination?'

'By trying to rebuild what you have destroyed.'

'You would have set yourself up in my place?'

'I do not have your lust for power.'

Osidian inclined his head. 'I know who it was who conspired with you against me.'

Carnelian tried to turn his face to ice.

Osidian lifted a hand. 'Nothing will happen to them unless they move against me.' His eyes bored into Carnelian. 'Be sure you understand that should they do so, I will be merciless.'

Relief at this reprieve made Carnelian reckless. 'Put me to death, then, for I have betrayed you more than once already.'

Osidian's laughter drove Carnelian into angry confusion. 'If I had killed all those who betrayed me, there would have been few of the House of the Masks still living. This is a princely game we play, Carnelian, which we shall laugh about once we return to Osrakum.'

'The day when I laugh at the memory of so much suffering will never come,' said Carnelian, but this only served to make Osidian laugh again, so that Carnelian was left feeling foolish.

Osidian grew suddenly serious. 'I wish these plots against me to end. It is for this reason, my Lord, I shall deign to explain myself to you now.'

He crouched and drew something in the dust.

Carnelian stared at him, desiring to kill him there and then. The threat to his Plainsmen restrained him. Perhaps when they were safely away.

Osidian looked up. 'Shall I continue?'

Carnelian crouched, making an effort to be interested in the diagram in the dust. 'A serpent?'

'In a way; it is a serpent which I am holding by the tail.'

Carnelian looked at the loops writhing through the dust. Osidian pointed at it. 'This is their Lower Reach: a sluggish river meandering through a land of mud, hemmed in by jungle; choking, decaying . . .' Osidian looked into Carnelian's eyes. 'They fear its glooms above all else.' With his chin he indicated the Isle of Flies. 'They believe they have trapped their god in there. He is the Darkness-under-the-Trees which they appease by feeding the blood and souls of men.'

Carnelian knew enough to fear the malignant presence there.

'They push the jungle back a little way from the river and, there, cultivate fields which are the source of abundant sustenance.'

'They are farmers then?' Carnelian asked.

'Warriors.' And in response to Carnelian's look of incomprehension, 'They lure the pygmies out of the jungle, they bribe them, or buy them as slaves from their own kind.'

'With salt,' Carnelian said, understanding.

Osidian nodded. 'With salt.'

'Do they get this from the sea?' Carnelian asked, already guessing the answer.

'They know almost nothing of the sea.'

'Then it all comes from here.'

Osidian gave a nod.

'But they cannot have had any salt for two years.'

'More than three.'

Carnelian had a sickening realization. 'Then they must be in chaos.'

Osidian looked into space and his eyes narrowed. 'Plague, war and famine consume them. The pygmies have melted back into the jungle. The fields lie untilled.'

Carnelian half-covered his face with a hand. 'They couldn't send another expedition?'

Osidian nodded.

'Which is why Morunasa took the risk of bringing us here.'

'And slew his masters who opposed him.'

'So if I had not repaired the Ladder –'

Osidian smiled. 'I would most likely have died down there.'

The enormity of his mistake overwhelmed Carnelian.

'My life hung on your curiosity. I judged that seeing the saltcaves, you would imagine they were the whole purpose of my coming here.'

Carnelian looked round at the Marula. 'These were what you sought.'

'And many more like them. I need them to enforce my rule.' He opened a hand. 'Of course, given time, I could have welded the Plainsmen into the weapon I need, but I fear the Wise will not be so obliging.'

Carnelian saw in his mind the war Osidian was planning to bring down into the Earthsky. He shook his head free of it and looked around.

'So, whoever holds this Upper Reach is master of all the Marula.'

'Perhaps even their god.'

Carnelian was chilled by Osidian's smile. 'But by letting them come up the Ladder . . . Once the Plainsmen are gone . . . ?'

Osidian frowned. 'There is more you must learn before you can have full understanding. The Marula are not one people undivided.' He rolled his hand in the air. 'Morunasa says there are nine tribes, each ruled by a prince. These princes have for generations been vassals to the Oracles, who have ruled all the river from here with salt and the terror of their god. With Morunasa's aid, I have made an alliance with one of these princes. The warriors we brought with us and more that he shall send me I have bought from him with salt.'

'But surely, now that he allies himself with you he will be destroyed by the others?'

'So he himself said,' Osidian smiled. 'But consider the tesserae a moment and see if you do not see another mosaic emerging.'

Carnelian sunk his head and thought about it, but could see nothing but the fragments. 'I do not comprehend what is to stop the others attacking him.'

Osidian smiled indulgently. 'They will not do so because I have commanded them to refrain.'

Carnelian stared at him. 'Why should they obey . . .' The mosaic formed in his mind. 'Of course.' He looked at Osidian appalled, but with grudging admiration. 'You threaten to destroy the Ladder.'

Osidian rewarded him with a long slow nod.

'But if his warriors are here, what is to stop this prince usurping the position of power you now occupy?'

'There are many reasons. For one, if he did so, his peers would not believe he had the power to cut the Ladder.'

'Because he would be destroying himself?'

'That too, but to effect that, he would have to use his own people. Even if he had the desire to destroy his own world, do you think it likely his subjects would help him?'

466

Carnelian looked off towards the dark island, then brought his gaze back to Osidian. 'And what he gets from you is salt?'

'My position here ensures he can safely defy the power of the other princes. With the salt I shall send down to him, he will become saviour and overlord of the Lower Reach.'

'But surely then he would be free to turn on you.'

Osidian smiled again. 'I did say I had a serpent by the tail.'

Carnelian saw how it might all work. 'This is a desperate gamble.'

Osidian shrugged. 'I believe I can maintain the delicate balance of the forces.'

'And the Oracles?'

Brooding claimed Osidian. 'That is a darker matter. In some ways, they are very much like the Wise. For the moment, I have appeased them by giving them back their sacred grove, but they could yet become a foe more dangerous than the princes of the Lower Reach. It is always those who are accustomed to rule that one must fear the most.'

'And what of Morunasa?'

'That one has ambitions to return power to the Oracles and that only I can give him, which is why, you see, you must take care I should not die.'

Carnelian saw now why Osidian had bothered to explain it all to him.

Osidian raised an eyebrow. 'Do you imagine the Oracles could allow the knowledge of this place to become widespread across the Earthsky? If the Plainsmen did not take it from them, the Commonwealth would. They would destroy the whole Earthsky rather than let that happen.'

Carnelian lost hope, seeing how tightly woven was Osidian's net. 'And the Ochre?'

'As long as they remain obedient, they shall be safe.'

'Let me return to the Koppie to make sure.'

Osidian laughed. 'Oh no, Carnelian. You will stay here and rule in my place.'

'While you conquer the tribes?'

Osidian smiled. 'You see how we are in perfect understanding.'

'Will you sleep among the Plainsmen tonight?'

Osidian shook his head. 'Among my Marula.'

He rose and Carnelian followed him. Carnelian watched him walk away, the Marula warriors in his wake. As he began crossing the river, they remained behind. Carnelian watched him for a while and then, weary and demoralized, he turned his face towards the knoll and the Plainsmen.

Carnelian found Fern in the camp and drew him aside to talk to him.

'The Master knows we intended to kill him.'

Fern paled.

'You're safe unless you move against him.'

'Ravan too?' asked Fern.

'The Master seemed unaware of him, but we should keep them apart.'

Carnelian saw Fern was looking down to where the Marula had made a camp around the anchor baobabs. He turned to look at Carnelian. 'Are more of them coming up?'

Carnelian gave a nod.

'The Master intends to use them against the tribes, doesn't he?'

'They are more dependent on him than are the Plainsmen.'

Fern's gaze fell once more upon the Marula camp. 'We must attack them while we still can.'

Carnelian took hold of Fern's shoulder and pulled him round. 'Shall we do it now when they will see us coming or shall we wait until darkness when the Master will be with them and hope he does us the favour of not setting a watch?'

Fern backed away from Carnelian, upset. 'Why can't we surprise them at night as you did at the koppie of the Darkcloud?' And when Carnelian gave no response, 'Would you have us help him lead us all into ruin?'

Carnelian frowned. 'The best we can do now is pray that a chink opens in his armour that will allow us to strike.'

'And what if that never happens?'

Carnelian had no answer to that.

'My brother was right,' said Fern, bitterly. 'We should have destroyed the Ladder and taken our chances in the Earthsky when the Master came at us with Marula.'

Carnelian did not want to reveal how right Ravan had been. If Fern knew what chaos the Lower Reach was in, it might encourage him to go through with the ruinous attack on the Marula. The failure would be bad enough; far worse would be Osidian's reprisals.

Fern looked at Carnelian with pleading eyes. 'We must do something, Carnie.'

'We can stay alive. As long as we live, there is hope.'

Fern became suddenly weary. 'At least tomorrow we'll be leaving this accursed place.'

Something about Carnelian's silence made Fern regard him with narrowed eyes. 'You're staying behind.'

Carnelian had to nod. 'He wants me here.'

Fern's eyes grew fierce. 'Then I'll stay with you.'

'No. You must go. Together we are a danger to each other: apart we will still have a chance.'

The screaming from the Isle of Flies made it impossible to sleep. Intermittently, it would come trembling through the blackness. Each stuttering, tortured sound forced Carnelian to imagine what was being done on the island. The silence following was almost worse; a long suspense of waiting for the next scream. Pressing his hands to his ears made no difference. He rose and paced about. Others were suffering too, with moans, turning, sitting up. Someone stirred a fire to blazing life. Carnelian huddled round it with others seeking blind oblivion in the flames. Attempts were made to tell stories, but it was impossible to listen to anything other than the cries.

'Accursed,' groaned Fern.

Ravan turned on Krow. 'Do you still adore your precious Master?'

Krow drew his knees more tightly to his chest.

Ravan turned his rage on Carnelian and Fern. 'If you'd listened to me, none of this would have happened.'

Carnelian felt ashamed. There was a wild look in Fern's eyes he could not bear. He sank his head between his knees as he had done in the funeral urn, pressing them hard against his ears, trying not to hear his inner voice telling him that all this was his doing.

Eyes kept turning from the fire to peer past the utter blackness of the island, yearning for dawn. Ravan was the first to see the trail of light snaking across the river to the shore. Soon everyone was staring, possessed by the fear that the Oracles were coming for them.

'They're . . . they're on the riverpath,' said Ravan.

Men were rising all around him and Carnelian joined them.

'Let's go now,' someone pleaded. 'Let's not wait for morning.'

'We'd lose our way in the darkness,' said Fern.

'Our spears . . .' said a voice edging on hysteria.

Sparks began appearing at the corner of the baobab forest. As more and more torches came from the riverpath, their glow became bright enough to cast monstrous shadows from the trees towards the knoll.

'The impaled man,' groaned Ravan.

They watched tall shapes weave in among the torches and then the screaming began again, but this time it was nearby, coming from the heart of the torchlight. That close, the Plainsmen could hear every ragged note. Some began to whimper. Horror gripped

Carnelian's mind. The shrieking took on a panting, shrill, animal sound and they saw, lit from below, something twitching being hoisted up. Then one by one the torches snuffed out, leaving the animal noises to carry from the thing they had lifted aloft.

Men around Carnelian were crying. 'Make it stop,' someone prayed. 'Dear Father, make it stop.'

Carnelian snatched a spear and ran down the knoll towards the sounds. As he drew nearer, his legs weakened so that he had to slow to a walk. He felt each shriek like a cut. Coming nearer he fought for the courage to raise his eyes. Against the stars he saw a man impaled, his transfixed body shaking, his head beating against the tip of the idol's tongue erupting from his shoulder.

Quickly, Carnelian blinked his eyes clear, trembled the spear blade over the thin and quivering chest and, praying it should find the man's heart, he thrust. The blade caught and, snarling, he twisted it hard through the ribs. The impaled man let out a hacking sigh and then, silence.

Carnelian fell, adding his vomit into the filth. Blind and deaf, he was barely conscious when the Plainsmen came to carry him back up to their camp.

A black man with pits for eyes having his throat cut. The blade in Aurum's hand slowly slicing round. The Master's white face had the same bored expression it had had when he had burned the ant nest in the Naralan. Carnelian hated those misty blue eyes. A licking at his toes made him look down, then jump back in horror from the spreading blood. He reached out to touch Aurum, pleading that he stop the cutting lest they drown. The eyes that turned to look at him were the old Master's but they were peering from Kor's branded face.

Carnelian wrenched awake. Sweat congealed on his skin. A face swam into his vision. Fern. Carnelian grabbed him into an embrace and would not let him go. On the journey to Osrakum, he had tried to save a Maruli who had looked upon his face only to have the man make an attempt upon his life. Which was when Aurum had slit his throat.

Carnelian released Fern. His friend stared as Carnelian grasped his own throat and felt the scar of the rope. Was the dream a warning that he must not conceal Ravan's mutiny from Osidian?

'It's over now,' whispered Fern.

Carnelian could not understand.

'Thank you,' said Fern.

'For what?'

'For ending that poor bastard's suffering and ours.'

Carnelian remembered killing the impaled pygmy. Dawn was creeping from the east, its birth finding silver in the streams that fell around the island. The morning was still too thin to dispel the horror.

'Leave with me,' pleaded Fern.

Carnelian stared at him.

The sky blushed. The Plainsmen were rising, whispering as they got ready to leave.

Fern's face was filled with concern.

Wan-faced, the Plainsmen crept around as if there were people in the camp they were reluctant to wake. Carnelian saw with what bright hope and yearning they glanced up the escarpment towards the Earthsky.

He rose searching for Ravan and found him harnessing his aquar, fumbling with the girths and straps. The youth became aware of Carnelian and returned his gaze.

'What's the matter?' said Fern.

Carnelian broke the link with Ravan to look at his friend. 'Go without me. Take your brother with you.'

Fern frowned, upset, confused. Carnelian reached for his hand and squeezed it. 'Go now.'

A while later the Plainsmen were all mounted and, with a rush, they were coursing away down the knoll and up the escarpment. Fern gave Carnelian one last look and then his aquar ran to join the others who were fading into a great rising of red dust.

Carnelian stood watching until the cloud thinned enough for him to see they had gone. The nightmare lingered like an ache, bringing doubt. He dismissed it. He had made his decision.

WOUNDED EARTH

*One year sown, six years fallow
lest the earth should lose her fertility.*

(*Quyan fragment*)

TWO MARULA CAME TO SUMMON CARNELIAN. HIS HEART SANK WHEN HE saw where they were taking him. Still, he followed them. Krow came running to join him. Carnelian had forgotten Osidian had given the youth permission to remain behind. Neither was in the mood for conversation. Carnelian found distraction in counting the beads of bone and wood making up the corselet of the Maruli leading the way.

Carnelian's nose told him they were nearing the idol. It was impossible not to smell the rot rising from the blood-soaked earth upon which Osidian and Morunasa were standing waiting.

'Morunasa wishes to ask you something, my Lord,' Osidian said.

'Do we have to speak breathing this miasma?'

Marula showed Carnelian a spear.

'It's a spear,' Carnelian said, in Vulgate.

'A Flatlander spear,' Morunasa said, displaying it.

Carnelian was aware of nothing but the corpse of the man he had killed above him weighing the air with its fetor.

'Well?' demanded Morunasa.

'If you've something to say, Maruli, just say it!'

Morunasa regarded Carnelian with slitted eyes. 'We found this here, Master. It has blood on it.'

'Everything here has blood on it.'

Morunasa pointed up to the post where Carnelian did not want to look. 'See there.'

The Maruli pointed emphatically until Carnelian was forced to lift his eyes. At first he saw hanging above him only something like a scavenging bird utterly dark against the sepia sky. It resolved into the remains of the skewered man, his head pushed to one side by the idol's impaling tongue.

'There. The wound,' insisted Morunasa.

Carnelian saw the hole torn through the pygmy's chest.

'It was made by this spear,' the Maruli said.

'I know.'

Morunasa turned to Osidian. 'He confirms what I said. One of the Flatlanders took what belonged to our Lord. You, Master, know how important it is such sins should not go unpunished.'

Osidian sighed. 'When the Plainsmen return I shall find whoever it was and give him to you.'

Morunasa fixed Krow with an amber stare. 'Who did this, Flatlander?'

'It was me,' said Carnelian.

Morunasa turned on him, opening greedy jaws. Carnelian remembered how those teeth had been used to tear out throats, but he did not care: all he wanted was to get as far as he could from the impaled man.

Osidian regarded Carnelian with a frown. 'Why did you do this, Carnelian?'

'If you need to ask that, Osidian, then no answer I can give would make it any clearer to you.'

Osidian grew angry. 'You have nothing more to say, my Lord?'

Waves of nausea began surging through Carnelian. He clutched at the air for words. 'I could no longer bear the noise. I was trying to sleep.'

Osidian stared, then laughed.

Morunasa looked at him appalled. 'You must give him to me.'

Osidian turned on the Maruli, incomprehension on his face. 'Give him to *you*?'

Morunasa shrank away. 'He took what was the Lord's. His blood now belongs to Him.'

Osidian regarded the Maruli as if he were a stupid child. 'If you so much as touch him, I shall burn you and your precious banyan to ashes.'

Morunasa became a wooden man. He pointed at Carnelian. 'The Darkness-under-the-Trees must have his blood.'

Osidian slapped Morunasa's arm down. 'I'll feed your god enough blood to sate even his thirst.'

He put his arm around Carnelian's shoulders. 'Come, let us leave this place, it is beginning to turn my stomach.'

Letting himself be led away, Carnelian was feeling too sick to care about Morunasa's look of hatred.

Carnelian pulled himself free of Osidian as they walked deep into the baobab forest. He was glad Osidian was happy to walk in silence. The only sound was the footfalls of their Marula guards and Krow, who had followed them.

Carnelian became aware Osidian was measuring up the trees.

'We will have to cut them down all the way from the knoll to here. And from the edge of the chasm to perhaps up there.' Osidian pointed halfway up the escarpment.

'Why?' Carnelian asked.

'I need a training ground.'

Carnelian surveyed the whole wide sweep among the leafless giants. 'But these trees are sepulchres.'

'Then empty them of their dead.'

'And do what with them?'

Osidian shrugged. 'Did you not tell me they were desiccated?'

Carnelian nodded.

'Well, burn them.'

Carnelian grew uneasy. 'Perhaps you should oversee this yourself, my Lord.'

Osidian looked away towards the island. 'Would you then take my place negotiating with the Oracles?'

Carnelian glanced at Krow.

Osidian shook his head. 'I want that one with me.' He motioned more than half his escort to attend to Carnelian. 'I shall send you more.'

Accustomed as Carnelian had become to towering over everyone, the long-limbed Marula in their bead corselets were unnerving. They stood avoiding his gaze, several with axes hanging from their hands.

'Do any of you understand Vulgate?'

The Marula gave no answer but only stared at him with their yellow eyes. He pointed at the baobab under whose branches they stood. While they looked on, he made a pantomime of cutting it down. After he was done he saw they were regarding him with the same blank faces. He grew exasperated. When he moved into their ranks, they ebbed away from him. Lunging, he snatched an axe from one of them and returned with it to the tree. He gazed at the monster. Stark it was, menacing, but the Plainsmen had taught him to revere all trees. Besides, he was reluctant to desecrate any pygmy dead that it might hold. Such arguments were nothing to Osidian. The baobabs would die. Carnelian put aside his feelings and swung the axe. Its flint bit deeper than he had expected. He was pulling back for another stroke when he became aware of the murmuring. Looking round, he saw the Marula were all staring at the ground. It was clear he was getting nowhere and so he went in search of Osidian.

He found him with Morunasa and Krow upon the crown of the knoll now deserted by the Plainsmen. Osidian was crouching in an opening high in one of the trees. Morunasa and Krow were on the ground looking up at him.

'What do you want, Master?' the Maruli asked, malice in his eyes and teeth.

'I've come to speak to the Master.'

Carnelian called out in Quya: 'My Lord?'

Osidian looked down at him.

'The Marula –'

'Speak in Vulgate so that Morunasa might understand you.'

'The Marula,' he said, in Vulgate, resenting Morunasa even more, 'seem reluctant to cut down the trees.'

'Which trees?' Morunasa demanded.

Carnelian stretched his hand out indicating the forest lying below.

Morunasa smiled. 'But of course they'll not cut them down.'

'Because they're sacred?'

Morunasa raised his eyes to the sky. 'A childish belief of the pygmies, but the Lower Reachers are superstitious.'

'You must force them to comply, Morunasa,' Osidian called down.

Carnelian did not want to force anyone and besides, wanted to have nothing to do with Morunasa. 'It might be easier if I use the sartlar,' he called up.

'It would reduce salt production,' said Osidian.

'It should take only a few days to clear the area you wanted.'

Osidian considered it some moments and then gave a nod before turning back to Morunasa. 'This tree is as empty as the others.'

'So are all the granaries,' said the Maruli. 'The pygmies must have taken all the fernroot when they fled.'

What had really happened to the pygmies, Carnelian would maintain as his secret. He would not hand over more victims to the Oracles.

The sartlar swarmed the baobabs plucking the pygmy mummies from their tombs. Carnelian winced as he saw another fall to the ground, bones cracking like twigs. Other sartlar were gathering the mummies and heaping them in a mound.

When all the trees had been emptied, Carnelian walked around the pyramid of mummies. He gave the order and sartlar ambled in with torches. Carnelian heard the pyre ignite but the flames were invisible in the sunlight. Rustling like dry ferns, the dead folded tighter into foetus curls. Every so often one would pop, exploding into flakes that turned almost instantly to ash. The cadavers shrank, grew reddish brown, then began to singe black. Carnelian turned away when their skulls began to push grinning out through the charring leather of their flesh. He fled from the stench of their burning hair.

The next day he gathered the sartlar and told them they must cut down the trees they had emptied of the dead. Their reaction was to stand so still, he might have been standing in a ring of stones.

'What's the matter?' he said.

'Kor,' he called and was relieved when she emerged from among the sartlar and came to fall before him. He waited for her to look up at him.

'Master, the earth will rebel.'

'What do you mean?' he asked, but for an answer the woman only flattened herself to the ground. He stared, wanting to speak to her, to explain, but he had nothing in his heart but unease.

'It has to be done,' he said, at last.

Kor rose.

Her silence goaded Carnelian to anger. 'You will do it now.'

'As the Master commands, so shall it be done.'

With flint axes the sartlar chopped into the soft wood of the baobabs. There was something eerie in the way each blow set the naked branches far above to trembling. Carnelian became convinced the trees were feeling pain. The first one to topple gave out a stuttering cracking and then fell, gracefully, as if it were merely lying down, but when it struck the ground Carnelian was shaken by the impact and drew back from the slow mist of dust that rose and took so long to settle. The giant lay stretched out slain upon the earth. Another two were heeling over in the background. Watching this brought back a memory of the destruction of the Great Hall in the Hold; the first step on the path that had brought him so far. As the feelings of loss for his father, Ebeny, his brothers, his people, flooded into him, he had to turn his back on the felling and go away to stand upon the edge of the chasm. He stared blind into its depths, rethreading the whole improbable sequence of events that separated him from that time. He wondered, as he had not done for a shameful length of time, whether his people had made it safely up from the sea and were now with his father in Osrakum.

Carnelian, Osidian and Krow stood among a Marula guard surveying the clearing the sartlar had gouged from the baobab forest. For Carnelian the sight was punishment enough. With ropes, with levers cut from the branches of the fallen trees themselves, the sartlar had dragged and rolled the vast trunks towards the knoll so that they now enclosed it with a rampart of wood. This operation had ripped dark swathes through the meshing of dead ferns. All that was left of the baobabs in the clearing were the livid eruptions of their stumps.

Osidian pronounced himself satisfied. 'All that remains to be done is to excise those roots and then we shall burn the ferns and it will all be as smooth as a legionary parade ground.'

Carnelian could not believe Osidian was blind to the desecration. 'How do you propose we remove the stumps?'

'Dig them out, burn them.' Osidian shrugged. 'Do whatever works. I want them all removed.'

'Yes, my Lord,' said Carnelian, enough anger leaking into his voice to make Osidian raise an eyebrow.

'Then I shall return to my wood-walled citadel,' he said, and smiled as if he had made some great jest. Carnelian was glad his moroseness caused the smile to slip from Osidian's face. He watched him, Krow and the guards until they reached the dwarfing wall of trunks. Beyond, towering over the clearing, baobabs stood like Masters on the knoll.

Smoke from the burning stumps was choking the air when new arrivals clambered up out of the chasm in a dark and oily flood of flesh. Hundreds more Marula warriors and, in among them, a swarm of pygmies laden with baskets.

Carnelian had been supervising the gouging out of a stump. He had grown weary of the obstinate grip which the roots maintained upon the earth. Over the two days they had been working at it, he had grown to hate the stumps, oozing water as if they wept, each root having to be dug out, prised one by one like the fingers of a frantic hand until the mutilated tree was forced to release its grip on the earth.

Watching the Marula pour up on to the ravaged escarpment, Carnelian saw with what horror they surveyed his work. He did not like the looks they gave him and threw himself with redoubled fury into his work of destruction.

It was growing dark when the last stump was torn free. They rolled it so that its roots pointed up into the air in a grotesque mockery of the trees that had once stood there. Carnelian could not bear to wait until morning to order the burning.

As night fell, the stumps became infernal heads with fiery hair. Carnelian himself helped the sartlar spread fire across the ground they had cleared. Soon flames were crackling and popping on every side, lighting up the sartlar in an ungainly shadow dance. Eventually, the heat and the choking drifts of smoke drove them all to the safety of the knoll. From behind its wall of cut-down trees, Carnelian could see the whole escarpment luridly ablaze. Fire spread from the clearing to the ragged edge of the baobab forest and licked at the trunks, making Carnelian fear all the forest might be consumed.

Sickened, drained, Carnelian dragged his weary body up the knoll, seeking sleep. Groaning, he lay down, closing his eyes tight so that he would not see the shadows leaping on the trunks around him.

Carnelian must have been asleep for a while, because when he was woken the night was perfectly dark. Something terrible was happening. A low fearful moaning rose up from around him as if from the knoll itself. He lifted his head and saw shadow men all around him, pressing their hands to their ears. A scream came shrilling through the night, a sound he had prayed he would never hear again. On the Isle of Flies, the Oracles were feeding more pygmies to their god.

The screaming continued throughout the night. Weary beyond measure, distraught, Carnelian gave up any attempt at sleep. Rising, he found a fire to feed and hunched down with his hands crossed against his chest, pulling his blanket down hard around his head. He pressed his chin against his wrists, gritted his teeth and tried to find some vision of redemption in the fire. Living the misery of each silent wait, he could not tell how long it was since the Marula had begun to gather around his fire. The black men were shivering, huddling together, their bead corselets clinking against each other like the carapaces of turtles. In their wooden faces their eyes were crazed.

When another scream sounded, a shudder went through their ranks, and many cradled their heads in their arms. They drew comfort from seeing that Carnelian shared their fear.

First light made him rise to gaze at it with longing. As he stretched the stiffness from his limbs he saw everyone was gazing past the grim island, hungry to feel the cleansing sunlight upon their faces. Only when the sun rose did it became possible to believe the darkness could be banished from their minds.

'You do not look yourself.'

Shadowed by Krow, Osidian had just found Carnelian standing on the edge of the burned clearing. Carnelian searched his eyes for any hint of horror. 'Did my Lord sleep well?'

'Well enough,' Osidian said, his hand half forming a sign of dismissal.

'Did the screaming not disturb you at all?'

Osidian frowned, as if he had no idea what Carnelian might be talking about. Then he understood and looked towards the island.

'Yes, the screaming,' Carnelian spat in Vulgate, making Krow jump. 'Don't tell me you didn't hear it.'

The sign in Osidian's hand firmed up and with a flick of the wrist he threw the topic away. 'I have heard worse in the Labyrinth. Are you too fatigued to participate in the day's activities?'

The question took a while to reach Carnelian who was recalling his walk through the Labyrinth. Imagining unhuman cries winding among its pillar sepulchres, he shuddered. 'What?'

Osidian frowned. 'There are matters I would have you attend to.'

Carnelian raised his eyebrows.

'I would begin the training of my Marula.'

'Training?'

Osidian regarded him for a while silently. 'For war.'

That word pulled Carnelian's eyes fully into focus. 'Against the Plainsmen?'

'Only those who defy me will suffer.'

Carnelian shook his head.

Osidian looked upward exasperated. His eyes fell to catch Krow in their jade gaze. 'You will make spears and shields for the Marula.'

'Spears, Master . . . ? They have spears.'

Osidian frowned. 'I want them armed with blunt weapons.'

Krow wiped sweat from his face.

Osidian took hold of his shoulder and swung him round, pointing at the trunks of the baobabs. Krow tottered off towards them.

Carnelian was confused. 'Why blunt? Are you worried they might hurt each other?'

Osidian smiled sardonically. 'Rather that they might hurt what I intend to throw at them.'

479

Under Krow's guidance, the Marula set to splintering branches into crude spears. Shields were shaped from the soft heartwood of the fallen baobabs. At last, when everyone was armed, the youth led them out on to the burnt clearing, disappearing up to the knees in a slow rolling ashen mist.

As Carnelian watched them form up in the centre of the clearing, he was reminded of the burnt field in the Plain of Thrones where the tributaries gathered. A rumble alerted him to riders coming into the clearing. They churned up so much dust they looked as if they were splashing across a ford. Carnelian narrowed his eyes. Oracles, their skin sharing the pallor of the ashen ground, with Osidian riding in their midst. A muttering rippled through the Marula ranks. He could feel their anxiety and a yearning rose in him to be among them. The riders were walking their aquar slowly into a line. He realized they were preparing to charge.

'Form up,' he cried, 'or the Oracles will run you down.'

Krow glanced at him, terrified, doing the best he could. The ash clouds subsiding revealed the imposing solidity of the aquar. Carnelian swallowed hard as he saw them begin to move.

'A hornwall,' he cried.

Krow understood him, but only a handful of his Marula copied him. The approaching aquar were making the earth shake. Krow was screaming instructions but Carnelian could see the Marula were nothing more than a mob. Then the riders let out wailing cries and he had no eyes for anything other than their charge. Grim, Osidian rode at the apex of their wedge and careened into the Marula, scattering them. Within a blink, the Oracles were through and disappearing into a cloud of their own making.

Cursing Osidian, Carnelian ran towards the Marula. Soon he was in among them. There was a lot of blood, some limbs hanging useless, two dead. Cries of alarm from the men around him made him lift his head. Osidian was regrouping the Oracles for another charge. Bellowing, Carnelian ran through the Marula to the rear, which was now their front. He tore a makeshift shield from one man and used it to buffet them into line. Those that were nearest saw what he was doing and began bunching together. He heard Osidian's cry; felt again the rumble in the ground. Until the last moment he continued to marshal the Marula, but again when Osidian struck he pushed through easily, wounding more of the defenders.

Carnelian realized Osidian had seen him and had taken care to bring his attack into the line as far as he could from his position. Using rage as strength, Carnelian pushed back through to the other side of the Marula. He shouted instructions at Krow. Together they shoved the Marula into blocks. Beginning to understand what he wanted them to do, large swathes of them were coalescing into dense formation. Confusion spread as those at the back tried unsuccessfully to lower their spears between the heads of those in front.

Osidian's next charge broke them again, and several more in quick succession. The time after that, Carnelian held his breath as he saw the aquar confronted by a dishevelled hedge of spears. For a moment it seemed as if the creatures were going to veer away, but then the wall crumpled and they broke through as before.

All day long Carnelian and Krow struggled to make their men into a hornwall, but whenever any of them managed to form up in good order, Osidian would send his charge in somewhere else and smash through.

The sun was low when, gasping for breath, beyond weariness, they formed up again. Carnelian had found he could control them better if he took position a few lines from the front and made Krow do the same on the other flank. He watched as the more remote edges of his formation began to show something like serried ranks. He shoved harder in to the man beside him so that their shields interlocked. He heard the movement clash through the formation in imitation of him. Carefully he lowered his spear between the heads of the men in front. Osidian was hurtling towards them. Carnelian gritted his teeth. The aquar struck their wall like battering-rams. He felt as much as saw it buckle. The Oracles were pushing deeper, wailing the battle-cries they had learned in the legions. Carnelian felt the pressure as the front line was forced back. Shoving, he watched it reforming, putting pressure on the aquar. The creatures were becoming difficult for the Oracles to handle. Carnelian let out his triumph with a whoop. The sound caught in the throats around him and swelled into a roar. Plumes splaying with increasing panic, the aquar began backing away. The Oracles could not stop them retreating. As Osidian led them off towards the knoll camp, the roaring around Carnelian grew deafening and he was pulled into the embraces of his men.

'These Marula are nothing more than a rabble,' Osidian said.
'A rabble that beat you,' Carnelian barked back.
Osidian looked smug. 'I suspected you might want to help them.'
Looking at Carnelian, Krow was clearly glad he had.
Osidian gazed out over the camp. 'They beat a handful of riders and we weren't even using weapons.'

'We had nothing more than sticks,' said Carnelian. 'Besides, you could see the idea of fighting in formation was alien to them.'

'If I could scatter them so easily with a handful of aquar, how do you think they would fare against hundreds?'

'Tomorrow they will be better.'

Osidian gave him a warm smile, a real smile. 'You are sure of this?'

Carnelian glanced at Krow, igniting a smile. The youth's excitement started Carnelian's heart pounding. He spoke for both of them. 'Tomorrow we'll repulse anything you care to throw at us.'

Osidian nodded, growing serious. 'Tomorrow then.'

Watching him walk away with his guards, Carnelian's ardour faded. For a moment he and Osidian had become boys again, but now he remembered what these Marula were being trained for and felt he was betraying the Plainsmen. He let his gaze wander over the fires, where he could see Marula tending to their wounds as best they could. He grimaced; these were men too, and Osidian would continue to harry them until they became a weapon in his hand.

The next day did not go as Carnelian had hoped. The Marula failed to repulse Osidian's attacks. Several more of them died, crushed beneath the clawed feet of the aquar.

That night, tortured by the certainty he had let them down, Carnelian took Krow on a walk among them as they sat around their fires roasting fernroot. Mixing earth with water, he painted Quyan numbers upon their foreheads. With much gesture and pantomime, he eventually managed to make them understand that the men who sat around each hearth now constituted a fighting unit. From each unit he chose a lieutenant and, taking these men away, he brought them to a new hearth he had made. He made his lieutenants sit down in a ring facing the flames. He set himself to explaining what the numbers on their foreheads meant. He rubbed his fingertips with charcoal then, showing them his palm, he touched one finger to it leaving a black dot. He leaned to touch the shoulder of a man who had a single dot and held his finger up. He showed them his palm again and added a second dot, held up two fingers and identified the man who bore that cypher. He did this twice more. Then he rubbed his hand clean on the dusty ground. He coloured a finger of his other hand, held up five fingers, then slashed a charcoal line across his palm. Showing this to the Marula, he found the man whose forehead bore the line for five.

So he went on teaching them the Quyan numbers and showing

them how each of them and their units had been given a single number as their badge. Then he played a game with them. Lifting his hand he punched the air with his hand splayed three times and grinned when he saw them counting. He held aloft three fingers. He looked at them expectantly. He looked at the man who bore the number eighteen upon his forehead. He urged the man to stand up. Then it was the turn of man twelve. On and on he went until he was rewarded with the white crescents of their grins as they sprang up quickly as he indicated their number.

The next day was confused. With Krow's help, he tried to play his game with the whole force. Some of his lieutenants understood and tried to follow the commands he gave them using their numbers. Many others did not follow it at all. They put up a worse fight that day than they had the day before. Merciless, Osidian hurt many. This only made Carnelian more determined to defeat him.

After the fighting, Carnelian gathered his lieutenants on the edge of the ash clearing. Grimacing, they watched the other Marula file up to their camp. Carnelian drew their eyes to him with a bellow. He got the men to reapply their numbers themselves. Then he began to order them around. Identifying one of them by number and sending him to stand in a particular location. Soon he had them all arranged in a grid. Using their numbers, he began to make them manoeuvre. As they saw themselves advancing in lines, turning, marching and counter-marching, they began to laugh and soon were doing it with playful pleasure.

The next day, the Marula began to move together. Though they did not entirely manage to repulse Osidian's charges, they did manage to fight them off without panic and minimal wounding. In the days that followed, they became more and more an extension of Carnelian's will. Eventually, Osidian and the Oracles found that, from whichever direction they made their attack, they would always be confronted by an unbroken shieldwall bristling with the Marula's makeshift spears.

The western sky began to glower. Over days this darkness came rolling towards the Upper Reach. Sometimes Carnelian would discern a trembling along the horizon and become convinced he could hear a rhythm of distant drums.

At last the black clouds came, piling in angry towers on the rising wall of advancing night. Around the fires voices hardly seemed able to pierce the sultry air. Carnelian drifted in and out of sleep until he could no longer bear the weight of the night pressing on his chest. He rose and saw the skyfire playing across the inky west and almost touched his eyes to confirm they were open. His throat was parched and when he swallowed there was a popping in his ears.

Morning was nothing more than a faint glowing opalescence in the sky. The storm curled like tar smoke, slow, rumbling. Sweat clothed Carnelian though he stood almost naked; it oiled the ebony limbs of his Marula. All day the sky pressed down as if it were collapsing. Carnelian stood with his back to a baobab, surveying the clouds from under his brows, running his finger along his scar, recalling the first night of his slavery. A flash, then the first thunder-clap whiplashed him like an orgasm. The release was momentary, the air retightened its grip around his throat. He begged the sky to loose its water. Light was leaking through the heavens. Thunder hammered him to his knees. A torrid wind screamed through the encampment, whisking everything up into feverish flight. The baobabs groaned and shook their branches at the sky. Carnelian felt the first drop like an anointing. He turned his face up to catch another. More and more and more fell. Rain came hissing down, then roaring until he was sheathed in water, spluttering, blind and deaf, feeling the ground beneath him melt to mud, letting himself sink into it as the rain washed him clean of all thought, all feeling and of his sweating fear.

The sky rained down as if its angry darkness held the waters of the oceans just above their heads. Cool delight soon turned to misery. Osidian urged Carnelian to join him in the shelter of one of the granary baobabs overlooking the camp. The days of his captivity haunted Carnelian, driving him to hide from the rhythm of the rain upon his head. He chose a tree of his own. Brooding, he saw below him the Marula sitting like basalt boulders in a stream, sunk up to their haunches in the mud, their heads hanging, sometimes chewing at raw fernroot because it was impossible to kindle a fire.

From his eyrie Carnelian watched the level of the Blackwater rise. Three days after the downpour began, its waters had already risen high enough to swallow all its rocks and pools. The dark sliding water foamed in a rushing sheet which the Isle of Flies cut with its stony prow. The river became a flood. The murmur of the falls swelled to a roar that could be heard even above the tumult of the rain.

Day after day, with nothing to do but to watch the raging white cataracts, or the men miserable below, Carnelian began to feel that the rain that had washed away the days would soon wash away his mind and leave him only the emptiness he had known as a slave upon the road. He looked down upon the Marula and felt he had abandoned them. He descended from his tree. By the time he reached the mire between the roots, he was already drenched. He walked among the Marula, having to shout for them to notice he was there. Some lifted eyes that seemed dull against the varnished wood of their faces. The pressure of the downpour was making Carnelian stoop and, thinking he meant to sit down, some Marula made space for him. He could not deny their entreating eyes. He settled down into the mud holding a blanket over his head. Through the rain's grey veils the baobabs loomed like the sepulchres of the Labyrinth in faraway Osrakum.

Carnelian woke into the ending of the world. Beneath him, the earth was shaking apart. He fought to calm the gibbering bodies round him. Arms clung to him like chains. He could hear a rush and roaring rumble as if a herd of heaveners were stampeding around the knoll in the blackness. He squinted trying to see. The knoll and all its trees were turning slowly. No, it was the escarpment flowing past, a tide of earth pouring down into the chasm. He stared in horror. Moaning blew round him in a gale. The movement slowed. The earth settled, groaning. Some lonely voices broke raggedly, then fell silent. All he could hear was the gentle hiss of the rain and the dull percussive roar of the cataracts.

Carnelian had to wait until light began to filter through the curtain rain. He blinked away water and peered. The land around the knoll seemed gouged with immense wounds. He disengaged himself from the Marula waking all around him. He rose drunkenly, staggered over the ditch and began making his way down the slope. He had to look down at his feet so as not to get them snagged in the thickets of men's limbs.

When he reached the baobab wall he saw that under the pressure of the landslide, one of the trunks had hinged out like a door. Mud choked the gap. He clambered up the mound until he reached high enough to look out. What he saw made him gape. The ashy clearing was gone. Red sandstone showed raw through a film of mud and darkly foaming water. The earth that had once clothed it had been washed over the edge of the chasm. He remembered Kor's warning.

He became aware of the black bodies appearing around him, hunching, crossing their arms over their chests, their eyes wide with incomprehension.

He saw Krow among them, gaping.

'Keep them here.'

The youth looked alarmed. 'Where are you going, Master?'

Ignoring his cries, Carnelian slid down into the streams gushing over the exposed rock. Feeling he was treading on the earth's open wounds, he made his way carefully down towards the Ladder anchor trees. Amazingly, these had resisted the pouring mud which had piled against them. Carnelian climbed this mound. On its summit he saw what he had expected to see: the Ladder cables had snapped. Hugging the soaking hide of one of the baobabs, he inched around until his foot struck against a knot. Using the cable as a handrail, he edged towards the chasm one step at a time. Rivulets spluttered dark water out into space. Each time he slipped he would freeze, clinging to the cable. Each time he forced himself to go on, until, at last, he was close enough to be able to crane over the edge.

Far below, the Blackwater was swelling a lake behind the dam the landslide had dumped across the floor of the chasm. The Ladder had been ripped from the precipice and lay broken in the mud. The single anchor baobab for the ladder down to the saltcaves had deflected the mud. The sartlar were not marooned.

Back in the camp, Carnelian was overcome by a violent shaking as the full horror of what had happened soaked into him. In the faces of the Marula he saw fear that the downpour might wash away the rest of the world. A shout turned every eye to look up the scoured escarpment. Aquar were filing down, a march that wound away as far as Carnelian could see. He leapt to his feet.

'Plainsmen,' he cried, feeling a new rush of life. Marula jumped from his path as he ran down the knoll. He reached the baobab wall and clambered on to it. The riders were close enough for him to recognize Fern.

He slid down into the mud, then tore up the escarpment. The lead aquar knelt, allowing Fern to spring out of his saddle-chair and run towards him.

'It's you,' Carnelian gasped. They gazed at each other. Fern examined him with a look of concern.

'Are you all right?'

Carnelian nodded. 'How's your mother, Sil, Leaf, the others?'

'Well enough,' said Fern, nodding grimly. He looked out over the devastation. 'What happened?'

Carnelian saw Fern was hiding something, but knew this was not the time to probe for more. 'We felled the baobabs . . . the rain –'

'Carnie,' cried a girl's voice.

Carnelian saw Poppy flying towards him and opened his arms. When he caught her, he squeezed her, lifted her and spun her round and round. She shrieked with excitement and threw her arms around his neck.

'Fern told me you wouldn't want me here, but you're glad to see me, aren't you, Carnie? Tell me you're glad to see me.'

'Of course I am . . .' He sat her astride his hip, grinning at her through tears, then saw her face pale as she stared gaping over his shoulder. He spun round to confront the horror, but it was only some of his Marula spilling down the knoll. Marula. He pulled her head into his neck. How could he have forgotten she had witnessed the massacre of her people?

'Raveners. Raveners,' she said, against his skin.

He ran his fingers through her hair and rocked her. 'They're only men, Poppy, only men.'

REVOLT

A spark could set the world aflame.

(Plainsman proverb)

CARNELIAN STOOD WITH OSIDIAN AND MORUNASA LOOKING DOWN INTO the chasm.

'This is a disaster,' said Morunasa.

'A setback, certainly,' said Osidian.

Morunasa looked at him aghast. 'Without salt the Lower Reach . . .'

Though Osidian's face was showing concern, Carnelian sensed he was not wholly displeased with the turn of events.

'The Ladder can be remade,' said Osidian.

Morunasa gazed down at the remains. 'It took years to make and that was before we had the cliff face smoothed.'

Osidian put his hand on Carnelian's shoulder. 'I'm sure my friend here will have it done before that.'

Carnelian tried to imagine the work involved. 'If we can salvage the old structure . . . perhaps.'

Osidian turned to Morunasa. 'You see?'

'At least the ladder down to the saltcaves has survived,' said Carnelian.

Osidian ignored him. Morunasa looked grim.

'My brethren will be unable to come up with pygmies. It'll be perilous to leave the Darkness-under-the-Trees unfed.'

Morunasa lifted his head and Carnelian was horrified to see him gazing up towards the makeshift camp the Plainsmen were making on the escarpment above the knoll.

'I shall send enough captives to sate your god's appetite for blood,' said Osidian.

Morunasa fixed him with fevered eyes. 'And will the Master also provide the Upper Reach with fernroot?'

'That and meat.'

'Where will these captives come from?' Carnelian demanded.

'Do you believe, Carnelian, the Plainsmen will accept my yoke willingly?'

Carnelian grew morose imagining the war Osidian was preparing to launch against the Earthsky. 'When will you leave?'

'Tomorrow, at first light.'

Beyond the baobab wall, in the bleak encampment of the Plainsmen, Carnelian sat in the rain chewing djada with others of Akaisha's hearth. It was too dark to see but Carnelian could feel Poppy's hand in his and knew Fern was sitting near.

'Sweet Mother, what I wouldn't give for the shelter of a proper tree; a little fire,' groaned Hirane and was answered by a mutter of agreement.

'How's Mother Akaisha?' Carnelian asked.

'A little worse,' replied Fern.

Carnelian became concerned, suspecting Fern was hiding something. Later he would question Poppy, quietly. 'Sil and Leaf?'

'Both well.'

Carnelian could hear some grief behind the words. 'The Tribe?'

It was Poppy who answered. 'Everyone's miserable, Carnie.'

'The salt we brought back seemed to cheer them up quickly enough,' said Ravan.

Poppy's hand stirred in Carnelian's grip. 'We were happy to have our men back.'

Ravan spoke over her. 'If the people are unhappy it's because the old have been poisoning their contentment. The Tribe were happy enough with the power and wealth our victories brought them.'

'Power?' exploded Fern. 'Don't you mean slavery?'

Carnelian expected Ravan to fly into a rage, but instead, he fell silent. 'The main thing's that the Tribe's now safely back in the Koppie,' he said, longing for its homely comforts.

'Safe,' said Ravan with a snort. 'How can they be safe when all our strength is here save for a few feeble old men?'

'Who'd dare attack the Koppie?' said Hirane. 'We're the Ochre, first of all the Master's tribes.'

'And is he going to feed our people?'

'He did last year.'

'And who's going to fetch water? Who's going to protect our women from raveners when they work in the ditches?'

'You mean the Bluedancing?' said Carnelian.

'Shows how much you know.'

Carnelian was horrified. 'Did their water run out?'

Fern's hand gripped his arm. 'When we returned, we found them well enough, but the Master commanded that they should be sent off to the koppie of the Tallrunning.'

'Why?'

'He didn't say.'

No doubt Osidian intended they should dig a killing field in the home of the Tallrunning with which to slaughter another heavener herd.

As if that thought had summoned him, Carnelian felt his presence.

'How pleasing,' drawled Osidian in Quya, 'my Lord must find the company of savages.'

Carnelian could just make him out, an immense shadow in the night accompanied by his guards.

'I came to hear news of the Ochre,' Carnelian said.

'I could have provided you with all the news you seek, Carnelian.'

As the clear voice faded, Carnelian became aware that across the escarpment he could hear nothing but the pattering of rain.

'You shall be left to rule this place in my stead.'

'What about the Oracles?'

'They will keep to their island: the rest is yours.'

The rain began falling more heavily.

'The sartlar must continue to cut salt.'

'What of the Ladder?'

'Make sure you understand, my Lord, the production of salt must be your paramount concern.'

'But you still wish to have the Ladder repaired?'

'With whatever labour you have left. Besides, it is best to wait until the rain stops. Currently, the cables will be sodden and heavy.'

Carnelian considered his next question carefully. 'Who will be left here, my Lord, to oversee the sartlar?'

'I will leave you Plainsmen.'

'Ochre?'

'Oh no, my Lord . . .'

Carnelian could hear the smile in Osidian's voice.

'The Ochre will all be coming with me.'

Carnelian knew more harm than good was likely to come from

arguing. Clearly, Fern and the rest of the Ochre would be hostages to ensure his good behaviour.

'I trust we understand each other, my Lord?'

'I understand,' Carnelian said, resigned. Waiting for more, it was a while before he realized Osidian was gone.

'What did he say?' Poppy whispered.

'That tomorrow you all leave with him.'

'And you?' asked Fern, the resigned tone of his voice suggesting he already knew the answer.

'I am to remain behind again.'

'Then I'm staying with you,' said Poppy.

'No,' said Carnelian, outraged at the thought.

'Surely he intends to leave some of us here with you?' said Fern.

'No Ochre.'

Their talk was spreading murmurs across the encampment.

'Why are none of us to stay here?' said Hirane. 'Doesn't he trust us?'

'Have you forgotten the riches beneath our feet?' said Ravan. 'Did he mention Krow?'

'He mentioned no one by name.'

'Are we returning to the Koppie?' Ravan demanded, rancour loud in his voice.

'I have told you everything he said, Ravan.'

'I'm sure,' the youth said, bitterly.

Carnelian felt Poppy stroking his hand. 'Why can't I stay with you, Carnie? Please, let me stay. I've been so unhappy.'

He reached out for her, found her head wrapped in soaked cloth and leaned his cheek on her. 'You know I'd have you here if I could. It'll make things much easier for me if I know you're safely at home.'

Beneath a frowning sky, a vast tree caged a darkness Carnelian was terrified to enter. A yearning drew him in to search for his loved ones. It was only when he tried to cry out their names he realized he had forgotten them. Pulsing anguish, he could not even see their faces in his mind. He wandered, a blind betrayer, within the caverns of the tree that were hung with overripe fruit. Feeling a warm hand slip into his own, he saw Poppy looking up at him. Her eyes were an anchor in his despair. Hunted, they fled away across raw, red earth.

He awoke and saw her leaning over him, alarmed.

'Carnie, you're frightening me.'

He struggled to sit up against the sodden pull of the blanket.

Poppy's hair clung in feathers to her skull. He registered the look in her eyes.

'You were moaning in your sleep,' she said.

Carnelian frowned. 'A dream.'

He became aware of the commotion around them, men everywhere saddling their aquar, stowing away their dripping blankets, plodding through the mud, hanging their heads in the downpour, squinting against the water pouring down their faces.

A hand slipped into his. 'Please, please, let me stay, Carnie.'

Her pleading eyes made his heart resonate to the haunting rhythm of his dream. He gripped her hand, so small in his. His nod was rewarded by her dazzling delight.

Carnelian and Poppy watched the aquar churn their way up through the mud of the escarpment. Nearby, miserable and downcast, stood the Plainsmen who were staying behind. The colour of wet wood, Carnelian's Marula warriors loped up in a mass after the shrouded Oracles. Among them Osidian rode with Krow and Morunasa, the forbidding heart of the march.

Carnelian was remembering Fern's morose face when they had said goodbye. Everything seemed so hopeless. A movement at the edge of his vision made him glance round and see a sartlar creeping towards him. It was Kor, her spade feet bringing her steadily up the slope, her mane plastered over the angles of her ruined face. He felt Poppy edging round him and, glancing down, saw she was trying to hide.

'It's only Kor, Poppy. There's nothing to fear.'

The sartlar woman knelt in the mud.

'Get up, Kor,' Carnelian said, 'I'd like you to meet Poppy.'

The woman rose, reddened by the mud that smeared her rags and legs. Carnelian coaxed Poppy out in front of him and held her there by gripping her shoulders. Though she was of a height with the sartlar, Kor's bulk made Poppy appear as fragile as a leaf stalk. Woman and girl nodded at each other.

'The Ladder, Master?' asked Kor.

'Not until the rain stops,' Carnelian answered.

'Salt then?'

Carnelian nodded.

He sensed Kor was waiting for him to accompany her. Carnelian turned to look for the departing host, but they had already faded away into the rainy murk.

Later, Poppy told him how things had been in the mountains after the Master had taken their men away. How the Tribe had tried to carry on as normal without success. How when Harth and others had tried to give orders again, the people were too afraid to listen. Fading, Akaisha moved little, spoke less, so that Whin had become hearthmother in all but name. When the men had returned, the Tribe's joy was soured by news of what had happened in the koppie of the Darkcloud and the discovery of the Upper Reach. Carnelian saw how haunted Poppy still was and sensed how all this had reopened the horror of the massacre of her tribe. It was Fern who had taken the time to help her through those first few days, though Sil and he were constantly arguing. Carnelian wondered about this but he decided that to ask Poppy for details would be prying.

Day after dreary day, the rain fell unabated. High in the baobab they were sharing, Carnelian and Poppy tried to amuse themselves by telling each other stories; gossiping about the people they knew; sharing their hopes and dreams. Mostly, the monotonous hiss of the rain would wear their speech away to silence and then they would sit at the opening of the hollow and gaze out. The amount of earth left upon the escarpment showed the passage of time. Streams coursed down so filled with red earth they could have been blood. The knoll had become an island in the midst of a sea of stone. Streams gushed past on every side so that Carnelian feared that at any time the trees that rose from the knoll would lose their grip and the whole mass would slide down into the chasm.

Carnelian had divided what food there was among the Plainsmen and the sartlar. The sartlar had carried their portion down into their caves. The Plainsmen had followed his lead and carried theirs up into the dryness of other baobab hollows. Each day Carnelian had to force Poppy to chew gnarled fernroot. They were careful with it, but still, their store was running low.

Everyone dreaded the coming of night. In the darkness the roar of the falls seemed to become a deep and rumbling voice. Poppy became obsessed with the notion it was speaking to her, though she could not tell what it said. Carnelian could no more than her discern words, but the sound poured its malice into his dreams.

Sometimes a morning would bring with it a pause in the rain. The ceiling of clouds might even thin enough for the sun to peer in. In that light, the scoured and bony escarpment would not appear so bleak.

On one such morning, the lookout Carnelian had posted let out a cry that had them all scrambling down from their trees and searching in the direction he was pointing.

Poppy saw them first and cried out with excitement. A line of aquar and drag-cradles winding down towards them from the Earthsky.

She tugged on his arm. 'Let's go and meet them, Carnie.'

Carnelian shook his head, needing time to prepare himself. Desperate for, but dreading, the news the visitors might bring.

'You go,' he said, 'I'll wait here.'

For a few moments Poppy hesitated, wanting to be in both places at once, but then, whooping, she ran after the other Plainsmen. Carnelian watched her, smiling and then began to work out his questions.

They were all young; some in the first flowering of their manhood, many still boys. Everyone had his face painted white in imitation of the Master. One uncovered his drag-cradle with a flourish, pleased at the cries of delight greeting the sight of the bales of djada, the neatly stowed fernroot and some luxuries besides.

Carnelian had been watching from a distance. As he approached them, the visitors all at once fell on to one knee. Carnelian registered Poppy's surprise at this deference, unease even, before, angrily, he told them to get up.

'I'm not the Master.'

Their reverence just served to make him fear even more the news they brought.

'Which of you is the leader here?'

A youth stepped forward and Carnelian beckoned him to approach. The youth bowed his head and came to stand before Carnelian with his eyes downcast. He has made slaves of you, Carnelian thought.

'What's your name?'

'Woading Skaifether,' said the youth, his Vulgate thick with the accent of another koppie.

'Come, Skaifether, walk with me.'

Carnelian began climbing the knoll, shortening his stride so that the youth could keep up.

'The supplies you brought; where did they come from?'

'We took them, Master,' Skaifether said, in a rush of pride.

'From which tribe?'

'The Lagooning.'

'Didn't they resist you?'

'Oh yes, but the Master broke them in a great battle.'

'Was there much slaughter?'

The youth shrugged. 'Not much. The Master is the father of battles.'

Carnelian nodded grimly. 'And what did he do to the Lagooning once he conquered them?'

'He took their men into his army . . .'

Carnelian waited, knowing there would be more.

'And their children that were marked for the tithe.'

'Took them where?'

'Back to the koppie of the Ochre. They'll be kept there until it's time for my tribe . . . the allied tribes' – the youth looked proud – 'until it's time for us to send our tribute to the Mountain –'

'He's promised you Lagooning children to send instead of your own?'

The youth smiled. 'Or those from the other tribes that will be conquered.'

Carnelian could see how this policy might strengthen support among the 'ally' tribes but only at the expense of making the conquered tribes hate the Ochre.

'Is there more?'

'If the men from the conquered tribes fight well for us, then they'll be given salt and their children will be returned to them.'

'To be replaced by those from the newly conquered?'

The youth grinned and nodded.

Carnelian turned away to hide his disgust.

'Have I offended you?' the youth asked, in a fearful tone.

Carnelian reassured him. 'Did the Master send any message for me?'

The youth was clearly still frightened. 'None came from him.'

'Came from . . . ? Did you not come from him?'

'No, Master, our commander is Ochre Fern.'

Carnelian regarded the youth with disbelief. 'He commands you?'

The youth gave a slow, fearful nod.

'Are there other commanders?'

'Twostone.'

'Twostone Krow?'

Skaifether nodded.

'And Ochre Ravan?'

The youth frowned, shaking his head as if he had never heard the name before.

'What did Ochre Fern bid you do?'

'To bring the supplies here and to return with all the salt you have collected for us.'

'Nothing else?'

'Nothing, Master.'

Two days of brooding later, a cry brought Carnelian to the opening to his hollow. One of his Plainsmen, Cloudy, was shouting something up at him that was lost in the gusting rain. The man pointed east. There beneath the frowning wall of the Backbone, Carnelian saw shrouded Oracles riding down the escarpment, dragging behind their aquar a stumbling string of captives alongside which jogged Marula spearmen. Even through the rain, Carnelian could see the captives were Plainsmen and that the Marula were driving them towards the riverpath. When he saw many of his own men streaming down the knoll to intercept the party, he threw a blanket about his shoulders.

'I'll come with you,' said Poppy.

'No. Stay here. Wait for me.'

At first, startled by his tone, the girl was soon protesting, but he did not have the time to argue with her. He abandoned the dryness of their hollow and swung out to descend to the ground. Once there, Cloudy confronted him, soaked, looking sick.

'What shall we do, Master?'

'Whatever we can,' cried Carnelian and bounded down the slope, quickly leaving the man behind.

As he reached the open ground beyond the wooden wall, he saw the Marula had levelled their spears at the approaching Plainsmen. He coursed towards them bellowing, desperate to avoid bloodshed. Hearing him, his men turned, backing away from the Marula as they waited for him. Out of breath, he saw in their eyes their confidence that he would do something to save the captives. Carnelian moved in among them, glancing up at the Oracles sitting haughty in their saddle-chairs. Bound naked one to the other, the captives were mostly men past their prime. He saw how their ribcages were pumping for breath, how they hung their heads. Strangely, what shocked him most was their bloody feet. They had been forced against their most deeply held belief to run barefoot across the Earthsky.

His own Plainsmen began crying out to him. They made many pleas, demands. Though he could make none out clearly, he did not need to. He could see and feel their pity and their outrage that men should be treated thus. Many of the captives had lifted their heads and, as their eyes fell on Carnelian, they ignited with a hatred that struck him hard. He knew who it was they thought they saw or, as likely, they did not care. He was as much of the Standing Dead as the conqueror who had delivered them into misery.

Carnelian looked to either side of him and saw how numerous were his men: how few Marula the Oracles commanded. He was desperate to free the captives.

A voice carried through the hissing rain as one of the Oracles addressed him. Even had there been silence, Carnelian would have not understood a word. He considered approaching them, negotiating in Vulgate. The realization sank in that even if he could make himself understood to the Oracles there would be no pity in their hearts. One of them lifted an arm swathed in indigo cloth and pointed. Carnelian did not turn his head to look, always aware in which direction lay the malign presence of the Isle of Flies.

He turned to his own people. With the accent of the Ochre, he told them the captives had been condemned by the Master himself and that his commands none could gainsay without bringing his wrath down upon themselves and their kin. His speech was hardly finished before they erupted into rage. He caught their feeling and threw it back at them. He told them that if he could, he would set the captives free. He could see they did not believe him and had to resort to commanding them back to the knoll. They railed against him, they even dared to threaten him, but then their resolve cracked and, unable to look the captives in the face, they turned like punished children and began the slog back to the camp.

Carnelian remained behind to watch the Oracles resume their march. He threw away the sodden weight of the blanket and turned his face up towards the glowering sky and prayed the rain would wash him clean. When absolution did not come, he forced himself to stand there long enough to watch the captives being ferried across the swollen river in narrow boats.

When night fell, the screaming began. Carnelian had prayed the storm would drown it out. His first thought was to reassure Poppy, to comfort her, but the look of accusation in her eyes was a wall of thorns between them. He cursed the weakness that had made him keep her in the Upper Reach. He tried to hide away in sleep. The rain lessened. Exposed by the silence, the sounds of agony formed an infernal harmony with the roaring Thunderfalls. Poppy joined her whimpering to the nightmare until Carnelian could bear it no longer and crushed her in his arms. Rocking together, they tried as best they could to survive sane until the dawn.

For many nights, the horror was repeated. Then it stopped. The rainfall began to ease. Carnelian descended with Poppy and they found a salve for their nightmares in lighting fires upon the crown of the knoll. Huddling round them with Plainsmen, they exchanged stories of their peoples, yearning to return home.

Often, Carnelian would find Poppy staring at the Isle of Flies. He would try to draw her away, but the girl always returned as if she had some need to keep a watch upon that awful place. She was the first to observe the shapes slipping from the Isle of Flies into the flood. As he watched them tumble amidst white fury down into the chasm, Carnelian tried to pretend they were logs, but Poppy turned to him and bleakly said, 'No, Carnie, they're the corpses of our tortured dead.'

The sky cleared to an infinite blue. Rain, when it fell, was diamond bright from clouds as pale as wood smoke. As the Thunderfalls lost their fury, they became sheathed in rainbows. The days sank into a pregnant murmuring in which, stealthily, the world came back to life. Even the ridges of earth that were all that was left upon the scoured rock of the clearing began to uncurl ferns. With his back to the Isle of Flies, in the clean sunlight, Carnelian found it hard to deny hope and a fragile joy. He summoned Kor and had her bring the sartlar blinking up from their caves and begin the vast labour of lifting the Ladder from the chasm floor. He and Kor together supervised the lowering of the first sartlar down into the chasm. Soon they were drawing the Ladder up from where it had fallen, unrolling it up the cliff face, pegging it with new posts they carved from the fallen baobabs.

The busy rhythm of their lives allowed them momentarily to forget the Isle of Flies. It was an illusory reprieve. Every twenty days or so, convoys of Plainsmen would appear with supplies. Carnelian's men would welcome them up on to the knoll and there the visitors would tell of the battles they had fought; of the tribes they had conquered. Carnelian would sit among them concealed, his back to the sun so as to hide his alien green eyes. The visitors would speak of the Master as if he were a god. The following day, they would leave with the slabs of salt the sartlar brought up from the caves. Sickly anticipation would come as a fever in the succeeding days. When the next batch of captives were spotted coming down from the Earthsky, people became busy with the tasks they had reserved for the occasion. None would look up in case they saw the new victims being ferried across to the Isle of Flies. Carnelian might have shared their cowardice, except that Poppy seemed compelled to witness the whole sickening business and he could not bear that she should do so alone. In the nights that would follow, unable to sleep, it became their habit to join the men around the fire trying to drown out the screaming with their talk.

Marula poured down the escarpment following a host of riders. The rumble, their slipping movement, recalled for Carnelian the night of the landslide. In their midst, any of the shrouded Oracles might have been the Master.

Carnelian turned to Poppy somewhere in the darkness behind him. 'Our people have returned.'

She gave no reply, though he knew she was there. He looked down again from their tree at where the massed aquar were sinking into their own dust. He would have to go and meet the host, however reluctant he might be to see Osidian.

'I'll return as soon as I can,' he said over his shoulder and then descended to the ground.

His appearance among his Plainsmen produced a clamour as they asked him what they should do. He shook his head, watching over their heads the black tide breaking against the baobab wall. One of the shrouded figures broke through, pulling behind him a ragged entourage. Carnelian recognized it was Osidian by his rangy stride, and had to move sideways to keep him in sight as he wove up through the trees.

'My Lord,' Carnelian said when Osidian was almost upon him.

'Carnelian,' said Osidian, his face wholly concealed in the shadow of his uba.

Carnelian noticed for the first time the tall man coming up behind him. The curled hair told him it was Fern, though it was difficult to see him in the man looking at him with a white face. As their eyes met, Carnelian became almost distraught enough to ask Fern if that covering of ash meant that he had become a disciple of the Master.

'I would speak to you, my Lord,' Osidian said.

Confronted with the menace of his voice, his great height, the Master drove thoughts of Fern from Carnelian's mind.

'Here?'

'Anywhere else but here.'

Carnelian looked up at his tree and remembered Poppy. He feared the consequences for her if she and Osidian should meet.

Osidian cut through Carnelian's indecision. 'We'll walk together in the baobab forest.'

He turned to Fern. 'Make sure no one follows us.'

Carnelian sensed that Fern was making an effort not to look at him. His friend bowed his head.

'As you command, Master.'

Carnelian and Osidian stood among the baobabs alone. Carnelian looked back the way they had come. Across the bare rock of the clearing, the knoll appeared to be a many-masted ship, becalmed.

'Come,' said Osidian.

His gentle tone made Carnelian feel more uneasy than if Osidian had used his customary, imperious manner.

'Are you not afraid to be with me alone?'

'I have made the Ochre the hated masters of more than thirty tribes. I do not believe you would threaten their only protector.'

Osidian's sadness produced in Carnelian something like shame. They walked on, Osidian looking blindly before him, Carnelian reluctantly crushing the reborn green spirals of the ferns beneath his feet. As they penetrated deeper into the forest, brooding baobabs rose ever more massive on either hand. Glancing up, Carnelian expected to see a face in the wood, but the trunk was smooth right up to the branches that held a bowl of blue sky.

Carnelian spoke to dispel the smothering silence. 'Why have you returned?'

Osidian sighed. 'My host is grown weary of conquests.'

'And bloodshed?'

Osidian glanced at him but made no answer, instead leading them into the cool shadow of a baobab.

'Their edge is blunted, I will resharpen it by letting them return to their homes.'

'I see,' said Carnelian, unable to grasp the nature of Osidian's mood.

Unwinding his uba, Osidian revealed a face thinner than Carnelian remembered. The green eyes were seeing him but there was something distracting them, a haunting presence of pain.

'You are changed, my Lord.'

Osidian smiled bleakly. 'All the world is changed.'

Carnelian registered Osidian's vulnerability with disbelief. 'I had thought everything was progressing as you would wish.'

'All moves according to my will, but . . .'

Carnelian waited, searching Osidian's face. In some ways it was a stranger's but in the eyes there stirred something of the boy in the Yden.

Osidian looked deep into Carnelian. 'I've lost faith in my destiny and without it I am empty.'

Carnelian's body began responding to the plea in Osidian's voice and eyes, but when Osidian made to embrace him, he recoiled. He expected rage but Osidian merely dropped his arms and sank to the ground. When he looked up his face was lined with misery.

'Will you at least stay beside me tonight?'
In spite of everything, Carnelian's heart could not refuse him.

They lay on their backs in a hollow between the roots of a baobab, watching clouds flow westwards. Osidian began to speak in Vulgate.

'My faith has grown weaker than Morunasa's, though I'm certain he worships the same god as I. Without faith there's no certainty: without certainty, one is enslaved by doubt.'

Carnelian propped himself up on his elbow. 'What is it that you doubt?'

Osidian frowned. 'That I can defeat the legions with a rabble of savages.'

Carnelian denied himself the hope of reprieve there was in that. 'Is that all?'

Osidian's frown deepened. 'I have been too long in the company of barbarians. My blood no longer burns.' He grew sad. 'Sometimes, I feel pity.'

Shame made Osidian beautiful. Carnelian ached for him, but he would rather cut off his arm than reach out to him.

Osidian pierced Carnelian with his eyes. 'Have you felt how much the Maruli is with his god?'

Carnelian was struggling for an answer when he saw Osidian's eyes had gone opaque. Pain suffused into his face.

'I need that certainty. I must know what he knows. I must feel what he has felt. I must hear the Darkness-under-the-Trees speak.'

'What are you talking about?'

'I intend to submit myself to the ritual of initiation of an Oracle.'

Carnelian jerked to his feet. He paced away, then came back to glare down at Osidian.

'Have you lost your mind?'

'Haven't you been listening?'

Carnelian dropped his head, exasperated. 'You came to tell me this?'

'I came to prepare you.'

'For what?'

'My possible death.'

Carnelian slumped to the earth. He had spent so much time desiring Osidian dead and now the thought filled him with nothing but dread. 'What does this initiation involve?'

Carnelian saw how pale Osidian had become. His head was shaking as if he were seeing something too horrible to describe. His eyes closed.

Carnelian could not help fearing for him. 'What is it you're going to allow them to do to you?'

Osidian's eyes widened like a child's. 'All you need know is that I may die.'

Carnelian resisted an urge to violence.

'If on the twelfth day, I've not returned, you must go back to Osrakum. It won't be safe for you here.'

'Oh, it's as simple as that, is it? You die and then I'll just saunter back to Osrakum.'

Osidian's shoulders slumped. He raised his eyebrows and gazed at the ground. 'I don't know why I'm surprised. If you insist on not returning, then you must survive here.'

He looked around with distaste. 'It might be possible for you to undo what I have done. When I'm gone, the Plainsmen will obey you. With care and skill, you might be able to coax them back into their old ways. Listen carefully. The hostage children the Ochre hold, you must send back to their tribes. Some might try to continue the great hunts as I have taught them but these will quickly show themselves to be unsustainable. The heaveners near enough to the killing fields will soon be exhausted. The lesser saurians would have to be herded in such numbers that the procedure will be uncontrollable with a single tribe's resources. Hunger would soon make the barbarians revert to their traditional hunts. With the readoption of their ancient ways, the old would regain their ascendancy.'

'And the Commonwealth?'

'Give my body to the Wise. They'll not care about you once they have proof that I am dead.' Osidian shrugged. 'No doubt they'll make reprisals throughout the Earthsky but these will be measured; the Wise will not wish to damage the Plainsmen's breeding populations.'

'What about the saltcaves? The Plainsmen will not forget them and having here this source of salt, they're unlikely to want to serve in the legions.'

'Cut down the anchor baobabs. There are no other suitable replacement trees and the landslide has ensured that other anchor points cannot be built with the primitive skills the Plainsmen or the Marula have at their disposal.'

Carnelian frowned. 'This will destroy the Oracles and the Lower Reach Marula.'

'You are free to dream up another way to save your precious Plainsmen.'

Carnelian would search for other possibilities but was not confident he would find any. He was sure the sartlar would cut down the anchor baobabs at his command. He wondered what would happen to Kor and her people. A thought occurred to him.

'Neither the Oracles nor the Marula will allow this to be done.'

'Show the Marula the Ladder intact and they'll flee back to their lands below. I've made sure their commanders fell in battle. Without me, they are a rabble in a foreign land; a land they fear.' He smiled coldly. 'As for the Oracles, without me, they will be too weak to oppose you.'

'And if you do not die?'

Osidian looked away to where a copper sun hung molten in the sky. 'You had better hope I do. If I do not it will be because I shall be possessed by the God and then I will finish what I have begun.'

Carnelian saw how weary, how fragile Osidian appeared, but he was not feeling tender. 'I could kill you now.'

Osidian chuckled opening his arms wide. 'Do it. I would welcome the release from the canker of doubt that eats at me.'

Seeing in Osidian that which he had once loved, Carnelian turned away, melancholic as he watched the sun layering the sky with crimson.

Carnelian awoke in a red dawn and saw Osidian was already up. They made their way back to the knoll in silence. Before they reached it, Osidian veered towards the Marula camp around the Ladder baobabs. The black men rose, staring as the two Masters walked among them. Looking over the edge, Carnelian and Osidian saw that the Ladder had been brought more than half of the way up from the chasm floor. Osidian announced himself satisfied and they turned to face the Thunderfalls. The Isle of Flies lay sombre in the morning light. As they walked along the chasm edge towards it, Carnelian saw Morunasa and some other Oracles were waiting beneath the impaling post. He had no wish to go any further and took his leave of Osidian.

'Remember: the twelfth day,' Osidian said, in Quya.

Carnelian nodded. Osidian gazed at Morunasa and the Oracles as if they were his executioners. As Carnelian watched him walk towards them, he wondered if he would ever see him alive again.

Carnelian found Fern in the camp. As he had climbed the knoll, his heart had told him that his friend could not possibly have gone over to Osidian, but seeing him there before him, all Carnelian could see was his painted face.

'How did he force you to do that?' he said.

503

Fern frowned. 'All the commanders wear ash as a symbol of the Master to show they act in his name.'

'So he pressured you to lead one of his armies?'

'It was I who asked for a command.'

Carnelian shook his head, feeling bleak, empty. 'I would never have believed . . .'

Fern narrowed his eyes. 'What, Master, what would you never have believed?'

There was still a part of Carnelian that refused to accept that Fern would betray the Plainsmen; betray their friendship. 'You are collaborating with him.'

Fern's eyes flamed. 'Is that what you think?'

Seeing Fern's anger, Carnelian became confused.

Fern leaned forward baring his teeth. 'Did it never occur to you that I became a commander to protect my people? What has our resistance to the Master achieved? By joining him, I have at least some chance of softening the effects of his conquests.'

Carnelian saw the truth of it and was ashamed.

Fern's lip curled. 'Who are you to accuse me when, after everything he has done, you chose to spend the night with him?'

Carnelian was outraged. His pride spoke: 'What business is that of yours?'

They glared at each other. Carnelian could not find a way out of his anger. Fearing what he might say next, Carnelian desired only to end their meeting. 'The Master has gone to the Isle of Flies. While he is gone, I am to rule in his place.'

'What then are your commands, Master?'

Carnelian cast around for some instruction. 'Just make sure that you keep order here in the camp.'

Fern's curt nod and his 'You shall be obeyed, Master' made Carnelian wince. Turning, he walked away.

That night, Carnelian took Poppy with him when he went to look for Fern's fire to apologize. When they found Fern, his cold greeting left Carnelian unwilling to speak. At least Fern had washed his face. A growl made them both turn to see Poppy scowling, her hands on her hips.

'You're both behaving like children.'

Carnelian and Fern stared at her, startled. They looked at each other. Carnelian tried a smile. 'I should have trusted you.'

Fern looked pained. 'And I had no right to –'

'We just talked,' Carnelian said, quickly.

'Hug each other,' Poppy commanded.

Awkwardly, grinning, they obeyed her. As they released each other, Carnelian felt embarrassed by the look in Fern's eyes. 'Aren't you going to offer us some food?'

Fern became flustered and Carnelian and Poppy exchanged a secret smile. She threw herself at the Plainsman so that he was forced to catch her. She buried her face in his neck.

A scent of roasting fernroot rose from the fire.

'Where's Ravan?' Poppy asked.

Carnelian had forgotten about him. 'He's not here?'

Fern looked grim. 'He remained in the Koppie.'

Carnelian raised his eyebrows. 'Have things grown worse between him and the Master?'

Fern grew angry. 'It's not my brother's fault. At every opportunity, the Master humiliates him. Time and time again he has passed him over to give others a command. When I dared to intervene, the Master told me, curtly, that he needed my brother as an interpreter. I offered myself in that capacity but he turned me down, not that he needs one, so many of the army speak Vulgate. It's as if he is deliberately trying to grind him down.'

Carnelian gave Fern a suggestive look. Fern shook his head. 'I'd swear they've not been lovers for a long time.'

'You can tell?'

Fern looked Carnelian deep in the eyes, nodding. 'I can tell.'

Carnelian looked away. Another motive occurred to Carnelian that made him go cold. 'Was it Ravan himself who chose to return to the Koppie?'

'Can you blame him?'

'But the Master let him go?'

Fern's nod confirmed Carnelian's fear. He tried to conceal what he was feeling but saw how worried both of them had become.

'What is it?' Poppy asked, her eyes very round.

Carnelian shook his head. 'Nothing,' he said, then busied himself with fishing a cooked root from the flames.

As the days passed no news came across the water from the Isle of Flies. Carnelian's dreams were haunted by his imaginings of what was being done to Osidian there. The conviction grew in him that Osidian was already dead. He became increasingly desperate to complete work on the Ladder and drove the sartlar harder than he had ever done before. He had told Fern everything and, in the time they spent together, they planned what they would do once Carnelian stood in Osidian's place.

505

One day, a pygmy appeared in the camp. It was Fern who brought him to Carnelian. The little man cowered then fell prostrate at his feet. Fern stooped to lift him but stayed his hand. The pygmy's back was smeared with blood. Crouching, then leaning closer, Carnelian saw disfiguring scars. He called for some water and, himself, carefully washed the brown skin as the little man shook with pain and fear. Carnelian sat back.

'What are you seeing?' Fern asked, his face screwed up in horror.

'This man is a messenger sent to tell us the Master still lives.'

Fern frowned. 'But the pygmy has said nothing.'

Carnelian pointed. 'It is these marks that speak.'

Quyan glyphs cut into the little man's back read: 'My Father speaks to me.'

The next day, Fern found Carnelian with the sartlar. The Ladder cables had finally reached the edge of the chasm and Carnelian was overseeing their attachment to the anchor trees.

'I must speak to you,' Fern said.

'Not now.'

'A messenger's come from the Earthsky with news.'

Carnelian turned, exasperated, but his heart almost stopped when he saw how pale Fern looked. He told Kor to take over and led Fern away from the trees.

'What's happened?' Carnelian demanded.

'The Tribe have risen against the Master.'

Carnelian grabbed Fern. 'Has this news been sent across to the Isle of Flies?'

'Who would dare?'

Carnelian clasped his head in despair.

'You knew, didn't you?' said Fern.

'I feared it.'

'How . . . ?' Fern's face drained of blood. 'Ravan,' he breathed.

Carnelian's hands dropped to his side and he nodded heavily.

Fern's eyes widened with realization. 'The Master did it on purpose. The bastard did it on purpose. But why?'

'The Ochre have witnessed his humiliation.' Carnelian massaged his forehead, thinking furiously.

'You can do what you want, Carnie, but I'm going home immediately.'

Carnelian stared at him in fear. 'And do what?'

Fern swung his head as if in pain. 'I don't know: stop it; perhaps raise the other tribes to join the revolt.'

'How hated have we become among the other tribes?'

'We killed their men; we took their children.'

Carnelian saw how hopeless it was. 'The Tribe has fallen into the Master's trap. Having removed themselves from his protection, there is nothing to stop the other tribes taking their revenge. Only the Master can save them now.'

'And if he chooses not to?'

'Then I will fight with you against him.'

They looked at each other grimly.

'Will you wait for me, Fern?'

'Where are you going?'

For answer, Carnelian looked off towards the Isle of Flies.

THE DARKNESS UNDER THE TREES

The sacrifice our Lord likes best is the flesh of living men.

(Marula precept)

'THIS IS MADNESS,' SAID FERN AS HE WATCHED CARNELIAN PACE BACK and forth along the riverpath. 'Once the Oracles have you both on their island, what's to stop them killing you?'

Carnelian stopped and glared at his friend. 'Only the Master could have carved that obscene message into the pygmy's back and he wouldn't have sent it if he were a prisoner of the Oracles.'

'So you've said, but is that enough to risk your life on?'

A movement drew their eyes across the angry river to where a boat, appearing from the Isle of Flies, was snatched then carried swiftly in the flow. In the stern the hunched figure of an Oracle was working an oar that projected behind the boat.

'The river's going to take him over the falls,' said Fern, staring.

Carnelian shook his head. 'I don't believe an Oracle would make such a mistake.'

Though he had been losing hope of finding a way across, now that he saw a boat coming for him Carnelian gazed with dread at the brooding mass of the banyan. He could feel the pressure of blood in his ears as he faced the real consequences of his choice. He fought a desire to flee.

Nearing the bank, the boat was being carried rapidly downstream. Carnelian and Fern strode back along the riverpath keeping parallel with it. Wrapped in his indigo robes, the Oracle was rowing the oar back and forth with furious speed. Carnelian wondered at the man's strength. As the boat knifed into the bank, the current snatched at its stern and swung it round. Carnelian scrambled down to help, hearing Fern cursing behind him, and was relieved when he sensed him following. The Oracle slipped over the stern into the water, spread his arms and grasped the gunwale, then began to drag the boat up out of the river. Gripping the prow, Carnelian helped. The Oracle looked up and Carnelian was able to see his face.

'Morunasa,' he gasped, letting go of the boat so that it lurched into the Maruli, making him stagger and almost fall into the river. Morunasa glowered at Carnelian, who took hold of the prow again and heaved.

'Why are you here, Master?' asked Morunasa, leaning on the boat now safe from the rush of the river.

'I have news for the Master.'

Morunasa's amber eyes did not blink.

'I can tell it to no one but the Master,' Carnelian said, at last.

'He lies in the heart of the Isle of Flies dreaming.'

'Will you take me to him?'

Though Morunasa's face registered no surprise, Carnelian sensed it. The man looked away, thinking. Several times Carnelian saw Morunasa turn back just enough to catch him in the corner of his eye. When he turned fully back, he showed his ravener teeth.

'It might cost you more than a little blood.'

Carnelian knew that he was putting himself into Morunasa's power, but he had made his choice and would not give in to fear.

'I'll pay the price.'

Morunasa regarded Carnelian as if he were some choice morsel. 'Very well. Help me with the boat. We must pull it upstream.'

Carnelian looked round to find Fern regarding him with undisguised misery. They nodded at each other in confirmation of the bargain Carnelian had made Fern agree to. If he were not to return from the island, Fern would destroy the anchor baobabs before taking Poppy and the other Ochre back to the Koppie.

Carnelian and Fern helped Morunasa drag the boat upstream. When the Maruli judged they had gone far enough, they pushed the boat back into the water and Morunasa held it while Carnelian climbed in. His weight made the boat pull into the stream. He saw Morunasa's hands loose their grip. Carnelian looked into the man's eyes and, for a moment, believed he was considering letting the boat go, perhaps calculating that, by the time Carnelian should reach the oar, it would be too late to stop the boat flying over the falls. If those were truly Morunasa's thoughts, he dismissed them, clambered aboard, then took hold of the oar.

Free of the bank, the boat swung into the deeper, faster flow. Morunasa hung his weight upon the oar and they carved a bucking course through twisting, leaping water. Carnelian held on desperately as they were rocked violently, all the while watching the frantic weave of the river tearing towards them. Inclining his head to the right, he saw the shore of the island looming. Craning further round, he saw, terrifyingly close, the livid thresh where the river poured into the chasm. Snapping his head round, he fixed his gaze upon Morunasa, whose lower jaw was pulled to one side by the meshing of his sharpened teeth.

With a grinding shudder, the boat impaled the shore's nest of bones. Small hands appeared along the gunwale and Carnelian saw that pygmies were pulling the boat up in among the great black roots of the banyan. Carnelian vaulted out into the shallows and helped the little men pull the boat out of the water. Letting go, he turned to gaze upon the tree. Its trunks lifted their pillars into a high canopy. Tendrils falling from this had been woven into screens of tortuous complexity through which he could just make out the gloomy cavernous spaces beyond.

Morunasa appeared beside him and beckoned him to follow. The Oracle took him along the shore towards where the roar of the falls was emanating from floating clouds of vapour. Entering these, they were instantly drenched. It was hard to see. Carnelian could feel the endless detonation of the falls through the rocks upon which he walked. The roar was becoming unbearable when it began to soften and the mist to thin. A brightening vision of the world drew him until he was gazing down into the chasm in whose depths the river ran glinting away into blue distance.

Carnelian became aware Morunasa was standing near him. Looking round, he saw the Maruli open his mouth to speak and so leaned closer.

'From here since ancient times we've ruled the Blackwater almost to the sea.'

Morunasa gazed out as if he beheld it all. His face bore an expression Carnelian recognized.

'You have a Master's heart,' he cried.

Morunasa turned to pierce Carnelian with his eyes. 'My heart is the Darkness-under-the-Trees.' He extended his arm and curled his fingers into a fist. 'That darkness has taken possession of your friend.'

Carnelian felt the gesture lacked conviction. Examining Morunasa more acutely, he saw how thin was his arrogance.

'What's happened?' Carnelian demanded.

Morunasa narrowed his eyes. He considered saying something but then his breath exploded. 'Taaagh!' He flung his hand up as if he were tearing off a mask and his face was revealed twisted with anger and fear.

'Do you dare set eyes upon the Darkness-under-the-Trees?'

'If the Master is there.'

'Oh, he is there.'

Without another word, Morunasa walked towards the grove and was swallowed into its gloom. Cursing under his breath, Carnelian followed him.

As Carnelian crept in under the first branches, they snuffed out the sunlight. His hackles rose as he became aware of the gloom not just as an absence of light but a thing in itself.

'You must give of your blood,' said Morunasa.

Carnelian remembered how the first time Osidian had returned he had a wound on his wrist.

Morunasa pointed back towards the light. 'Shall we return?'

Carnelian knew he had no choice. 'Have you a knife?'

Morunasa grinned, then, quick as thought, grabbed Carnelian's arm and sank his teeth into the wrist. Carnelian jerked his arm back. It was too dark to see the wound clearly. Morunasa urged him to sprinkle blood on to the ground and, resentfully, Carnelian did so, then plucked some leaves to staunch the flow.

The Maruli led him through a series of caverns separated by pillars, between which hung webs of infernal design woven from the roots hanging from every branch. High above, the sky was a scattering of stars peeping through a leafy firmament. The glooms reverberated with the thunder of the falls. A sweet, decaying smell clogged Carnelian's nostrils. The ground beneath his feet squelched and sucked with each step. Disgusted, he stooped to peer and saw he was walking on a carpet of rotting red figs. Morunasa had turned to wait for him, his face transformed by an expression of ecstasy. The air around him hazed as if with smoke. As Carnelian walked to meet him, he became aware of another sound which, masked by the rumble of the falls, was almost an itch in his ear. A thousand snagging tears, as if the fabric of space around him was being sliced apart. The air was thick with flies. His steps faltered and at that moment a stench wafted over him. His heart gave way and he almost cried out, except he feared to open his mouth lest he choke on flies. Close to retching, he became aware of Morunasa looming close, grinning his ravener teeth, his eyes glowing.

'The God can taste your fear, he drinks it like a draught of still-warm blood.'

Carnelian glanced round and saw against the loopholes of distant daylight how dense was the swirling of the flies.

'You wish to return,' sneered Morunasa.

Carnelian shook his head, not daring to close his eyes for fear he might never be brave enough to reopen them. He waved Morunasa on.

Deeper into the banyan they went and, with each step, the stench grew. The flies became so numerous he could feel their hail against his skin. To survive the nightmare, Carnelian withdrew inside, tried to dull his senses.

They came into a region where the root tapestries had something at their centres. Squinting, Carnelian saw these were the bodies of Plainsmen, their sallow flesh striped with lacerations. He doubled up and his hands fell into the mush of figs as his body convulsed and pumped out vomit. He stumbled away in horror as he saw the matter turning black with flies.

He rose, trying to rub his hands clean down his robe, staggering as he turned, seeing men hanging everywhere.

Morunasa loomed close.

'Why do you hang up the dead?' Carnelian gasped.

The Maruli seemed amused. 'What makes you think they are dead? Our Lord prefers to sup on living flesh.'

Morunasa's head fell back and he closed his eyes, in ecstasy and pain. 'Even now he feeds.'

Carnelian would not allow himself to understand.

Morunasa lowered his chin and gazed at Carnelian. 'Where do you imagine these flies come from?'

The Maruli's lips curled with disgust. 'Does your pathetic weakness stop you feeling the glory here? The majesty?' He pointed up at one of the men. 'From death comes life. It is the deepest sacrament.'

Carnelian felt the bile rise again. His eyes welled tears and as fast as he could brush the flies away, they settled on to his sweaty skin, itching his mouth and eyes, trying to find a crevice to lay their eggs.

'Is he here?' he hissed through his teeth.

'Very close, Master. Very close.' Morunasa pulled Carnelian upright and forced him to take several steps, before, enraged, Carnelian threw him off.

'Move, Maruli, take me to the heart of this filthy place.'

Morunasa smiled again. 'You'll find the Master does not share your sacrilegious opinion of our sacred tree.'

'Move on.'

Morunasa began to move away. Carnelian followed, desperately trying to inure himself against the assaults of touch and smell. However much he squinted, he was aware of the hanging men twitching as maggots feasted on their flesh.

The density of flies deepened the murk. Each step mulched the figs up to his ankles. The trunks grew in girth, their roots narrowing the way with their arches. At last they reached a trunk so immense it might have been the night sky. As Carnelian followed Morunasa round this, he saw that it rose from the swamp of figs upon innumerable roots. Along these lay Oracles, their nakedness revealing the swirling mandalas of their tattoos; their chins jerked back as if they were in the process of being impaled.

A white body came in sight around which Oracles were kneeling.

'He has the pallor of the maggots and like them even bears upon his forehead the seal of our Lord,' whispered Morunasa.

Carnelian crept over the bole of a root to reach Osidian. He came close enough to see the rise and fall of his chest. Wounds cut into the pale, clammy flesh mimicked his mouth, which gaped in a silent scream. Trembling, Carnelian reached over one of the kneeling Oracles to touch an unblemished portion of skin. His hand recoiled as Osidian came awake with a madman's stare. The red eyes found him, but showed no recognition.

'This is the Isle of the Dead, of which the Labyrinth is only an imitation. I have fed myself to the God alive and now he speaks to me.'

Carnelian's eyes were drawn to the inflamed, weeping lips of Osidian's wounds. Osidian's gaze wandered as he twitched a frown. He released a sigh of words: 'Can you not hear him?'

Carnelian listened with dread. He could hear nothing but the buzzing of flies and, as if from some subterranean world, the deep pulsating thunder of the falls.

Osidian chuckled showing yellowed teeth. 'I feel him in me. He does not give without taking.'

Carnelian leaned close, horrified. 'You have allowed them to put maggots into you?'

Osidian caught Carnelian's hand in a gouging grip. 'The pain is not unbearable.' The veined orbs of his eyes swivelled to take in the other dreamers. 'They bear it. They carry him always in their bodies so that they can hear the Lord when he speaks.'

As Carnelian tore free, Osidian settled back closing his eyes, his lips pulled into a pale, rictus grin. 'His voice is *so . . . beautiful . . .*'

There was furtive movement beneath Osidian's skin. He seemed so much a corpse, it was a shock to see sight in the dulled green eyes.

'Why are you here?' Osidian said.

Carnelian stared, nauseous, desperate to flee. He was in a world of death far from the living. He shrank away from Osidian's fingers.

'Why?'

Carnelian remembered why he had come. 'The Ochre are in revolt.'

Osidian smiled. 'So soon.'

That smile made Carnelian terrified for Fern, Poppy and the Tribe. He drew strength from his love for them. 'It is part of your design?'

'I am merely the instrument of the Lord's will.'

'Don't hide behind that!' he said using anger as a shield. 'It is your lust for vengeance that drives you.'

Osidian was still smiling. 'How could you hope to understand?'

Carnelian felt his face twisting in disgust. 'What understanding have you gained by giving in to this obscenity?'

'Even now, I can hear the Lord speaking more easily than I can hear you.' He frowned. 'Perhaps you could try –'

'No!'

As Carnelian lurched forward murderously, the kneeling Oracles rose as a fence around Osidian. Flaccid expressions of pleasure alternated with pain on their faces as they sank back.

'I shall not let them do it to you against your will,' said Osidian.

'Not let them? What power is it you believe you have in this filthy place?'

'I am become an Oracle of the Darkness-under-the-Trees. More, he has spoken secrets to me which prove I am his Son. He has whispered to me proofs which the Oracles cannot deny.'

Carnelian brought his hands up to cover his mouth and nose. 'Morunasa accepts these proofs?'

Osidian smiled and closed his eyes.

'What do you intend to do?'

'I shall walk the black road my father has made for me,' Osidian said without opening his eyes.

'And the Ochre?'

'They have laid their eyes and hands upon me.'

Carnelian's head was pounding. His vision swimming. 'I will not allow you to harm them.'

The eyes Osidian opened to look at him, welled concern. 'Those who stand in my way the Lord will crush.'

'So be it,' Carnelian said, backing away. Morunasa was watching him with a knowing smile. Carnelian could feel his wrist pulsing where it had been bitten. 'Show me the way we came.'

The Maruli shook his head slowly and his black face opened into a ravener grin. Carnelian became convinced those teeth had poisoned him. He shoved Morunasa from his path. He staggered past more roots bearing Oracles, infested, dreaming. Peering, he searched for even a glimpse of the living world, but everywhere he looked his vision was blocked by root weavings hung with victims. He cast around but every way seemed the same. Choosing one, he fled. Through the caverns of the banyan he lurched, seeking a chink of daylight he might use as a beacon to guide him out. He was desperate to breathe air free of flies. The fig mulch were sucking at his feet. He broke into a run, dazed, refusing to yield to madness.

Carnelian awoke in the gloom. Flickers of indigo sky showing through the canopy above, signalled that it was late. He could not remember falling asleep. The ache from his wrist reached up into his chest. His skin itched. He sprang to his feet gasping in horror, swatting at the flies clothing him. He ran his hands over his body, searching for wounds that might have allowed maggots into his flesh. He was as sticky as if he had been lying in blood. Praying, he peered for a way out, but only shadow showed in any direction. It was a blessing it was so cool the flies were not misting the air, though the ground was alive with them. He wondered with a shudder if he was doomed to perish there, his body food for maggots. The banyan's red figs lay all about him but he would rather have eaten poison. Their smell was on his skin. He had slept in their ooze. Thoughts of the Tribe pierced his desolation. If not for himself, he must live for them. In the distance he could hear the percussive thunder of the falls.

'Of course,' he breathed.

Grimacing, he began striding, with each step sinking into the mouldering, noisome floor, guided by the voice of the falling water.

At last he saw daylight peering in at the edge of the grove. He broke into a jog. Soon he could feel the percussion of the falls through his feet. Coming out on to a cliff edge, he fell to his knees, sucking in air shimmering with the diamond veils the falls were throwing off. The sun was a glorious mass of light made vague by the mist. The Blackwater was all the rest of the world slipping by. With a jolt, he realized the sun was in the east. It was morning. Fighting panic, he rose and ran round the cliff, reaching the prow the island thrust out over the chasm. From there, he gazed over the drop to where the knoll stood crowned with tiny trees amidst the clearing red as a wound. The anchor baobabs seemed flimsy. The Ladder fell as

515

a mere skein into the depths. He searched for signs of life, but saw none. Dread spurred him on. He followed the path he and Morunasa had used the previous day. As he ran past the margins of the banyan he refused to look into its glooms. He pushed on through soaking clouds then alongside the river until, at last, hidden among the roots, he found a boat. Trusting it had been left there ready for a crossing, he pushed it into the rush and vaulted aboard. The violence of the river swept him along and it took him a while to catch the steering oar. Then he leaned against it, feeling the power of the river come shuddering up through the wood so that he lessened the thrust from fear the oar might snap. Gritting his teeth, he gazed out past the prow as the boat veered slowly across the river.

Where the boat struck the bank was not much further than perhaps ten lengths from the maelstrom. Carnelian flung himself out on to the bank and clung to a rock as he saw the boat swing out and begin spinning in the torrent. Shivering with cold, he watched it fold into the white water and disappear.

He hauled himself up on to the riverpath, then stumbled along it, past the impaled man and through the baobabs towards the knoll. As he ran he looked for people. He found a way through the wooden wall and sprinted up the slope. In his bones he knew the place would be deserted. He reached the camp panting. The Marula, the Plainsmen had all disappeared. There was only one place they could have gone.

Carnelian slumped morose near a hearth which was still warm. It had not taken long to determine that all the aquar had been taken too. On foot, he could not hope to reach the Koppie in time. If his bleak self-disgust had allowed it, he would have wept.

A faraway voice crying out his name made him jump to his feet. It called again. 'Carnie.' It was unmistakably Poppy's voice. He strode over the ditch and, seeing her stumbling up towards him, leapt shouting down the slope to meet her. When they met, he snatched her up into his arms.

'The Mother be praised,' he cried.

Poppy buried her head against his neck. 'Fern said you were dead, but I just knew you weren't.'

He crouched to put her down. Her grubby face was all smeared with tears.

'Fern?' he asked.

She half-turned in his arms.

Carnelian's fierce delight released tears. 'He's here?'

'He hid me when the Master came last night.'

He stared at her. 'He came himself?'

She nodded.

'Where's Fern?'

'Tying up our aquar. Come on.'

Carnelian put her down, then allowed her to tug him down the slope. Fern appeared around a trunk. His relief at seeing Carnelian made him halt staring. Carnelian picked Poppy up again so that they would get to him more quickly. Fern rushed to meet them.

'I thought you dead,' he said.

'I know,' said Carnelian. 'How many aquar do we have?'

Fern grimaced. 'I only managed to hide one.'

Carnelian clasped his shoulder. 'You did better than I deserve.'

'When the Master appeared unexpectedly in the camp –'

'Morunasa and the other Oracles?'

'They came carrying him on a litter.'

'He took everyone with him,' said Poppy.

Fern stared distraught. 'He's gone to the Koppie, hasn't he?'

Carnelian's bleak look was answer enough.

'Can we stop him?' Fern's voice, his face, his body even, were all a plea.

Carnelian felt empty, exhausted, weighed down. He hoped Poppy did not guess the holocaust that was threatening. 'We must.'

For a moment, his fierceness gave Fern hope and vigour, but then he drooped. 'We've only one aquar.'

'Will she carry three?'

Fern bit his lip. 'Not the whole way.'

'Well, then, we two will have to take turns running alongside.'

Fern thought about it then nodded grimly. 'We'll need food and water.'

'Have they left any?'

'I'm sure I can find something.'

'Good,' said Carnelian. 'Keep Poppy with you.'

'Where are you going?' Fern asked.

'To release the sartlar.'

Carnelian summoned Kor in the usual way. When she appeared over the edge of the chasm, he was there waiting for her. He crouched to look her in the face. She regarded him as if he had her in a cage. He had grown accustomed to her fearful ugliness.

'Little mother,' he said. 'I'm going away.'

'Everyone is going away, Master.'

'Can you count up to ten?'

Kor showed him her gnarled fingers.

'If I don't return or send a message within ten days' – he flared his hands and her eyes flickered as if she were being blinded – 'then you must cut down the ladder trees.'

Her face crumpled in a frown. She pointed carefully at first one and then the other of the baobabs anchoring the Ladder.

'Those two, but also that one.' He pointed at the saltcaves tree.

She revealed her peg teeth in what might have been a grin or a grimace. 'The Master wishes to leave the sartlar starving in the caves below?'

Recoiling from the foulness of her breath, he waved his hand in front of him. 'No. No. You must take all your people and flee.'

'Flee where, Master?'

Carnelian visualized the Three Lands laid out before him. 'The Leper Valleys.'

Her face collapsed into sad impassivity.

'You know where those lie?'

'Far away, Master.'

He had to agree with her. 'I'm sorry, I know of no other place.'

Her chin dug deeper into her chest so that her hair fell to hide her face. 'As the Master commands, so shall it be done.'

Carnelian rose and looked down at the poor creature. She seemed more like an outcrop of the red stone upon which she stood than a living thing. He could think of nothing more to say. Feeling sad, he walked away.

Midday found Carnelian, Fern and Poppy moving through a dry shadowless land thralled by immense baobabs. Fern was riding the aquar with Poppy on his lap, swaddled against the merciless sun. Carnelian jogged along beside them, trying to match the saurian's easy stride, his robe, his uba, plastered to his skin.

When it was his turn to ride and Fern's to run, Carnelian had to stop the aquar often to wait for him. For all his height, Fern did not have a Master's stride.

The baobabs ended abruptly, as if they were defending a border, and they moved into a region which might have been a becalmed sea. It was Poppy who pointed out the thread of smoke wavering in the east. They stopped to squint at it.

'It's definitely a koppie beacon,' said Fern.

As they rode further they saw more beacons rising in the west and several more even as the sun was dropping to earth. Carnelian had asked what it was that could alarm all these tribes together, but Fern could only shake his head.

'Perhaps all have joined the Ochre in revolt,' said Carnelian.

'If so, to what purpose would they send out such signals of alarm? The Master couldn't possibly be attacking them all at once.'

Filled with foreboding, they pushed on. They made better progress as the sun lost its fire and would have continued on except Fern pointed out that it was getting late. Over Poppy's head, he mouthed the word 'ravener' and, nodding, Carnelian agreed they should camp for the night.

Hastily they gathered enough fernwood to make a fire and were thankful they managed to light it before the sun had vanished from the world. Ravener cries seemed to carry further in the blackness. The stars seemed painfully bright. They ate djada and had several licks of Fern's saltstone. When Poppy asked Carnelian about what he had seen on the Isle of Flies he would only shake his head. They settled down and slept sharing the warmth of their bodies.

When Carnelian awoke he realized he had only dreamed escaping the Isle of Flies. In the darkness he could feel them spitting through the air. Squinting up confused, he saw the stars obscured as if by drifts of smoke. He moaned, desolate. Something clutched him and, crying out, he threw it off.

'Carnie. What's the matter?' Fern shouted over the hissing in the air.

'I told you not to come here,' said Carnelian.

Poppy was crying with fear.

Carnelian curled up, not understanding, wanting to scream. 'The flies,' he said, shakily. 'The devouring flies.'

Strong hands grabbed hold of him. He was drawn towards a body and could feel a mouth speaking in his ear.

'Sporewind, Carnie. It's just the sporewind. Now lie down and I'll cover you and Poppy. Then I'll go and see to the aquar.'

Carnelian felt around for Poppy and drew her close, and Fern threw a blanket over them.

'It's not flies then, Carnie?' Poppy asked through her tears.

He stroked her hair. The sporewind striking the blanket was like someone throwing sand.

'Not flies,' he muttered. 'Not flies.'

Next morning, the dawn twilight never brightened to day. Wrapped up in blankets, they harnessed the aquar by touch.

'Will she be able to go on?' Carnelian cried.

'We'll go slowly and all ride her,' said Fern.

Being the heaviest, Carnelian sat in the saddle-chair. Fern rigged some ropes between the front and back crossbeams and lay across them on one side, after they had placed Poppy along the other. To make sure she did not slip out, but also to help counter Fern's weight, Carnelian leaned over to hold Poppy in place. When he asked the aquar to rise, she did so. The distribution of weight made her rock a little but with some adjustments, they managed to make it possible for her to walk.

They set off. The air swirled black all around them. It hissed and rattled constantly as it struck them. Mostly it drove like sleet from the east, in which the sun showed the dark ridge of the Backbone. Carnelian guided them towards it and, for the rest of the day, in its lee, they made what headway they could through the sporestorm.

Three more days they struggled on while the sporewind blew relentlessly. It was at night they suffered most. Their backs and limbs ached. Poppy's tears had run dry. Carnelian was plagued by nightmares of the Isle of Flies.

On the morning of the fourth day, the storm began to abate. The sun rose hazy but distinct. Some of the sky's blue shone through and gave them hope. It became possible again for one of them to run while the other rode. It eased their ache of worry to pick up the pace.

As the day wore on, it became possible again to see into the far distance. Four separate columns of smoke were eddying in the breeze.

'I know where we are,' Fern said grimly. 'That smoke is rising from the Tallgreen, the Darkcloud, the Smallochre and the Woading.'

'Not from the Koppie?' asked Poppy.

Fern's eyes when they locked to Carnelian's, were like wounds. 'No, not from the Koppie.'

They crossed the Backbone a little to the south so as to avoid having to pass anywhere near the Darkcloud. Fern's route brought them within sight of the koppie of the Bluedancing. Even from a distance, they could all see the damage Osidian's fire had wrought there. They veered away from that desolate sight, northwards, towards the glistening run of lagoons beyond which lay their home.

Riding while Carnelian ran, Fern guided them through the gap between two lagoons. Bellowers roosted on islands. Earthers were strewn like boulders across the land. When they stopped to make a changeover, Carnelian searched for heaveners but could find none. Once he was settled with Poppy into the saddle-chair, they pushed on.

Carnelian's heart jumped up into his throat and Poppy let out a squeal of delight when they saw the beloved shape of the Koppie rising up out of the plain. Both he and Fern allowed her chatter to pour over them as they scrutinized their home, nervously.

Carnelian pulled the aquar up. 'Shouldn't they have seen us by now?'

Grimacing, hands on knees as he leaned over panting, Fern nodded, never once taking his eyes off the silhouette.

Carnelian made the aquar kneel and dismounted. 'We might as well both walk.'

They marched on. Sensing their anxiety, Poppy asked: 'What's the matter?'

Carnelian glanced up at her. 'Nothing.'

When they came close enough to see the individual mother trees, Fern steered them towards the Horngate. As they drew nearer they began to smell the rot of blood. The ruins of vast creatures still partially walled with flesh spoke of a recent hunt. It seemed to Carnelian an evil omen.

'Couldn't we use another gate?'

Fern shook his head slowly, unable to free his gaze from the sight.

The fernland before the Newditch was scorched and black. They stopped when they reached the earthbridge and looked over it to the Killing Field. The carcasses were verminous with ravens and sky-saurians. Carnelian looked across at the Eastgarden and saw the drying racks like an abandoned military camp.

'Come on,' said Fern. Carnelian hoisted Poppy up with one arm and followed him.

Even though they pushed their ubas hard against their mouths and noses they could not shut out the overwhelming fetor of the Killing Field. Flies shimmered and rippled in mats over walls of brown mucused flesh that sagged rotting from the struts of bones. The ground was a churn of blood and mud and lumps of fat. They wound their way through towards the fallen Bloodwood Tree lying like a corpse amongst the carnage, its roots hung with entrails.

They found the bridge and won their way over to the Blooding, where they rubbed the filth off their shoes and opened their ubas to suck in the perfume of the easterly breeze. Ahead, the Grove looked as it always did and yet, it lacked something intangible. They could feel something was wrong as they marched up the Blooding.

Over the bridge, the gate had been torn down. They stopped to gaze through under the arching cedars, desperate to see a friendly Ochre face.

'Maybe everyone's gathered below the Ancestor House,' whispered Poppy.

'Maybe,' said Carnelian, exchanging a look of despair with Fern.

Carnelian put Poppy down. 'Will you stay here, Poppy?'

The girl shook her head slowly. Anger welled up in Carnelian but he controlled it. He offered Poppy his hand and, when she took it, he led her across the bridge.

Beneath the canopy of the mother trees rather than the usual sensuous coolness, the air felt cold. Even before Carnelian's eyes had adapted enough for him to see in the gloom, he recognized the smell and snatched Poppy up, crushing her against his chest, forcing her head back over his shoulder. As his sight returned, the branches of the mother trees were revealed hung with horrifying fruit.

Keening, Fern careered, stumbling, up the rootstair, leaving Carnelian panting, gaping, staring round, nauseous as he saw how many people were hanging from the trees.

'Carnie, you're hurting me,' Poppy whined in a tearful panic, but Carnelian could not release his hold on her and could only stare transfixed with horror. Osidian had done this. Carnelian could sense his presence as if he smelled him on the fetid air.

Carnelian became aware of Poppy shrieking, frantic in his arms. He slid her down his body and crushed her face to his chest, then fled back over the bridge into the ferngarden, into the bright clean day. When he had run far enough for the sun to burn the blackness from his eyes, he crouched to let Poppy go. She flew at him, screaming, beating him with her little fists and he gave himself over to her fury, which was nothing compared to the utter dread and desolation that now filled him.

He hardly noticed the blizzard of her blows cease, but he did see the terrified look she gave him and tried to find his voice, tried to comfort her.

'Is it the Master?' she asked, tears and mucus glistening on her cheeks and upper lip.

Carnelian could find no words, nor even thought.

'Where's Fern?' she screamed at him.

Carnelian's mind coalesced around that name. He glanced back at the gape of the gate across the bridge. He coughed his voice back into being. 'Stay, stay.'

Poppy licked her lips and stared at him, unblinking.

'Stay here. Please, stay here,' he begged.

She was shaking her head. 'No. I'm not leaving you.'

Carnelian kneaded his forehead, seeing her twisting in his tears.

He rose and glared down at her and his anguish poured out into his voice.

'You'll not move from here until I return.'

His wrath flattened her to the ground among the fresh green ferns. He stooped to lift her.

'Please stay here, Poppy, for me?'

She gave him a tiny nod and he leaned close to kiss her. Soon he was loping back towards the earthbridge. He glanced back once to make sure she had not moved and then, hesitating at the gate, he re-entered the darkness beneath the mother trees.

Carnelian crawled up the rootstair towards Akaisha's hearth, his eyes fixed on his feet, clawing at the roots, desperate not to look to either side, too aware of the shapes hanging everywhere, so close to the ground they appeared to be standing.

He moved away from the stair towards Akaisha's hearth. His fingers touched the beloved roots of her mother tree. The stench was too thick to breathe. He felt them round him but dared not look; instead he crept searching with narrowed eyes for Fern. He felt the movement and was drawn to it. Glancing up he saw too much. Faces he knew, melting in death, and Fern moving among them with an expression of wonder as he gazed from one to another. Carnelian saw Akaisha strung up by her uba, her toes brushing the earth. Nausea and grief convulsed him into a spasm of vomiting. He wiped his mouth and scrambled to Fern's side. He took hold of him and was thrown off with a snarl. Fern fixed him with a look of such pure hatred Carnelian was turned to stone. The Plainsman resumed his wandering among the dead. When Carnelian glimpsed Sil's distorted face he fled, mindless.

The scream pouring from his mouth felt as if it was emptying him of flesh. His lungs drank air. He heard the delicate rasping of flies. Three Marula were standing by the Crag. Their fear of him made him ravenous for their blood. They fled and he pursued them. Round the Crag he hunted them and came to where a number of them had gathered their oily, sweating flesh. He advanced and they drew away, chattering their fear. Something pale hung above them like the moon. He discerned its symmetries of bone. A waft of carnage air reminded him of death, of the Isle of Death, of Osidian maggot-pale among the roots of the black banyan. He looked up and saw the Ancestor House: a casket of the slain, its walls as pale as Osidian's face.

Hatred threatened to overwhelm Carnelian. His gaze fell upon one of the Marula, paler than the others in his Oracle's ash, and saw it was Morunasa offering him a spear. Carnelian took it. A way opened to the steps. They seemed steeped in blood. The whole world was red with murder. He was climbing the steps. He reached the porch and moved to stand before the leather curtain. He drew it back with the spear and looked in.

Osidian's pale body made the bone floor upon which it lay look yellow. Carnelian entered, hefting the spear. It bucked in his fist as the curtain slid off it and then the room went black.

'I have come to kill you, Osidian.'

'You cannot,' said Osidian in a sepulchral voice.

Carnelian could see him laid out as if he were a corpse. 'I am going to kill you for this atrocity.'

'The barbarians were executed because they sinned against the Law-that-must-be-obeyed not once but countless times.'

'That is a filthy lie! You murdered them because of your pride and for that I *will* kill you.'

'You will not.'

The certainty in Osidian's voice cheated Carnelian of strength. He fell to his knees but managed to keep the spearhead questing for Osidian's throat.

'I *must* kill you,' he whispered.

'If you do, the whole Earthsky will die with me.'

'You have already destroyed the best of it,' said Carnelian, desperate to thrust the spear into the heart of that voice.

'Did you not see the columns of smoke?' Osidian said.

Carnelian groaned, the spear tangling in the words.

'They rise from every koppie from here to the very edge of the Guarded Land.'

Sweat ran into Carnelian's eyes, slicking his face so that he could taste salt on his lips, but still, he held the spearpoint to Osidian's throat.

It moved again. 'I saw them as I came north and did not know what they might mean. The old told me, before I hung them from their trees.'

Carnelian clenched and reclenched the spear, fighting cramp in his arm.

'It is a signal a thousand years old. It warns the Plainsmen that the Masters have come down from the upper land with dragons. They are coming here burning everything in their path. I alone can stop them.'

'I shall give them your body and they will leave.'

'That would not save the Earthsky.'

'You yourself told me it would,' cried Carnelian.

'I told you how you might appease the Wise. It is not they but one of the Great who comes.'

Carnelian laughed mirthlessly. 'Your foul God no doubt has told you this.'

'Three days ago I sent scouts into the north. When they returned, they brought with them a rumour. A name. An ancient name that is a terror to the Plainsmen. Hookfork.'

'What are you talking about?' Carnelian hissed through his grinding teeth, drawing back the spear for the strike.

Osidian lifted his hands and shaped a sign like a long stalked lily.

The spear trembled in Carnelian's hand as he spoke the name to whom such heraldry belonged.

'Aurum.'

The name cleared his mind like the pealing of a bell. How could Aurum be coming with a legion when it was forbidden for any of the Great to have such a command? Only the Wise could have given him such terrible power. Contemplating cruel Aurum having at his whim the terror of the dragons and their flame, Carnelian threw back his head and let forth a cry of anguish that made the bone walls tremble.